# CIVIL RIGHTS CHRONICLE

*The African-American Struggle for Freedom*

**PRIMARY CONSULTANT**
Clayborne Carson, Ph.D.,
Director, Martin Luther King, Jr. Papers Project

**CONSULTANTS**
Charles R. Branham, Ph.D.
Ralph David Fertig, J.D.

**WRITERS**
Mark Bauerlein, Ph.D.
Charles R. Branham, Ph.D.
Todd Steven Burroughs, Ph.D.
Clayborne Carson, Ph.D.
Ella Forbes, Ph.D.
Jim Haskins
Paul Lee
Howard Lindsey, Ph.D.
Jerald E. Podair, Ph.D.
Jo Ellen Warner

**FOREWORD**
Myrlie Evers-Williams

**INTRODUCTION**
Clayborne Carson, Ph.D.

LEGACY

**Publisher & CEO**
Louis Weber

**Editor-in-Chief**
David J. Hogan

**Editor**
David Aretha

**Art Director**
James Slate

**Creative Director**
Marissa Conner

**Acquisitions Editor**
Jacque E. Day

**Director of Acquisitions & Visual Resources**
Doug Brooks

**Associate Director of Acquisitions**
Susan Barbee

**Production Editor**
Valerie A. Iglar–Mobley

**Production Director**
Steven Grundt

**Electronic Publishing Specialist**
Michael A. Anderson

**Visual Resources Specialist**
Matthew Schwarz

**Legacy Logo Designer**
James Schlottman

**Assistant to the Publisher**
Renee G. Haring

**Editorial Assistants**
Shavahn Dorris
Kathline Jones

**Publications Coordinator**
Julie Greene

**Director, Pre-Press**
David Darian

**Assistant Director, Pre-Press**
Laura Schmidt

**Imaging Development Manager**
Paul Fromberg

**Imaging Specialists**
Sara Allen
Keith Browne
Melissa Hamilton
Harry Kapsalis

**Vice-President, Purchasing & Manufacturing**
Rocky Wu

**Manufacturing Manager**
Kent Keutzer

**Legal Adviser**
Dorothy Weber

Legacy Publishing is a division of Publications International, Ltd.

Copyright © 2003 Publications International, Ltd. All rights reserved. This book may not be reproduced or quoted in whole or in part by any means whatsoever without written permission from:

Louis Weber, CEO
Publications International, Ltd.
7373 North Cicero Avenue
Lincolnwood, Illinois 60712

Manufactured in China.

8 7 6 5 4 3 2 1

ISBN: 0-7853-4924-3

Library of Congress Control Number: 2003107317

## Contributors

### Foreword

**Myrlie Evers–Williams's** life was forever changed on June 12, 1963, when, in front of their home, a sniper's bullet struck down her husband, civil rights leader Medgar Evers. In the decades following her husband's death, she emerged as one of America's most influential civil rights leaders. In 1994, after 30 years of perseverance and two mistrials, she found justice for Medgar's assassination in the conviction of Byron de la Beckwith. In 1995 she again made history by becoming the first woman to chair the NAACP on a full-time basis. An accomplished lecturer, and author of such books as *For Us, the Living,* and *Watch Me Fly,* Myrlie Evers–Williams founded the Medgar Evers Institute, based in Jackson, Mississippi.

### Consultants

**Clayborne Carson, Ph.D.** (primary consultant and essayist), was an active participant in the Civil Rights Movement. He went on to become the founder and director of the Martin Luther King, Jr. Papers Project at Stanford University, where he is also a professor of history. Initiated by the Martin Luther King, Jr. Center for Nonviolent Social Change in Atlanta, the project is being conducted in association with Stanford University and the Martin Luther King, Jr. Estate. Under Dr. Carson's direction, the King Papers Project has produced four volumes of a projected 14-volume comprehensive edition of King's speeches, sermons, correspondence, publications, and unpublished writings. In addition to his books *In Struggle: SNCC and the Black Awakening of the 1960s* and *Malcolm X: The FBI File,* Dr. Carson has coedited many works based on the King papers, including *A Knock at Midnight: Inspiration from the Great Sermons of Reverend Martin Luther King, Jr.; The Autobiography of Martin Luther King, Jr.,* compiled from King's autobiographical writings; and *A Call to Conscience: The Landmark Speeches of Dr. Martin Luther King, Jr.*

**Charles R. Branham, Ph.D.** (consultant and essayist), is senior historian for the DuSable Museum of African-American History. He was the writer, coproducer, and host of *The Black Experience,* a series of 60 half-hour programs for Chicago's WTTW–TV, the first nationally televised series on African-American history. He is the author of *The Transformation of Black Political Leadership* and *Black Chicago Accommodationist Politics Before the Great Migration.* A recipient of the Silver Circle Excellence in Teaching Award from the University of Illinois, Dr. Branham was a consultant for the books *Profiles of Great African Americans* and *Great African Americans.*

**Ralph David Fertig, J.D.** (eyewitness accounts consultant), is a lifelong human rights activist. As a teen in the 1940s he joined the Congress of Racial Equality (CORE), and as a Freedom Rider in 1961 he endured severe beatings in a Selma, Alabama, jail. For his work in the national capital area, *The Washington Post* dubbed him "the conscience of Washington." Fertig has fought for social justice as a sociologist, social worker, civil rights lawyer, federal administrative judge, and currently as a professor at the University of Southern California's Graduate School of Social Work. He is president of the Humanitarian Law Project and vice-president of Americans for Democratic Action. His historical novel *Love and Liberation* was a *Los Angeles Times* bestseller.

## Primary Authors

**Mark Bauerlein, Ph.D.** (sidebars author), has written several scholarly books and articles, including the book *Negrophobia: A Race Riot in Atlanta, 1906*. A professor of English at Emory University, he is currently leading a project for the Bush Administration, drafting federal policy for arts education.

**Todd Steven Burroughs, Ph.D.** (captions author), is an independent researcher, scholar, and journalist who has written for *The Source* and *The Crisis* magazines, *Africana.com*, and *The New York Amsterdam News.* He served as an editor, contributing columnist, and national correspondent for the National Newspaper Publishers Association, also known as the Black Press of America, a leading national news service for black print media. A lifelong student of the history of black media, Burroughs is writing a biography of death row journalist Mumia Abu-Jamal.

**Ella Forbes, Ph.D.** (essayist for the chapter "The Early Struggle"), is an associate professor and director of graduate studies in the Department of African American Studies at Temple University. Her areas of specialty include African-American history, women, mass media, and public policy. She is the author of *But We Have No Country: The 1851 Christiana, Pennsylvania Resistance* and *African American Women During the Civil War,* and is the coauthor of *American Democracy in Africa in the Twenty-First Century?*.

**Jim Haskins** (essayist and sidebars author) is professor of English at the University of Florida. Author of more than 100 books for adults, young adults, and children, he has won awards for his work for all three audiences, including the *Washington Post*-Children's Book Guild Nonfiction Award for body of work in nonfiction for young readers. Several of his books on Civil Rights Movement topics have been honored by the Coretta Scott King and Carter G. Woodson award committees, among them *Bayard Rustin: Behind the Scenes of the Civil Rights Movement; I Am Rosa Parks,* written with Rosa Parks; and *The March on Washington.*

## Additional Writers

**Paul Lee** (captions contributor) is an historian, filmmaker, and widely published writer, and the director of Best Efforts, Inc. (BEI), a professional research and consulting service that specializes in the recovery, preservation, and

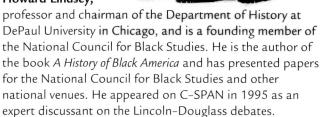

dissemination of [...] served as the histo[...] motion picture bi[...]

**Howard Lindsey,** professor and chairman of the Department of History at DePaul University in Chicago, and is a founding member of the National Council for Black Studies. He is the author of the book *A History of Black America* and has presented papers for the National Council for Black Studies and other national venues. He appeared on C-SPAN in 1995 as an expert discussant on the Lincoln-Douglass debates.

**Jerald Podair, Ph.D.** (captions contributor), is an associate professor of history at Lawrence University. He won the Allen Nevins Prize, awarded by the Society of American Historians for "literary distinction in the writing of history." He earned an award for his book *The Strike That Changed New York: Blacks, Whites, and the Ocean Hill-Brownsville Crisis.*

**Jo Ellen Warner** (captions contributor) is the former policy director for the Seattle Office for Civil Rights. As a freelance writer, she has contributed to *The Seattle Medium* (a weekly African-American newspaper) and *The Seattle Post-Intelligencer* on antidiscrimination policy.

## Other Contributors

We wish to acknowledge the following members of the **Martin Luther King, Jr. Papers Project** for their contributions: **Tenisha Armstrong** (essay contributor), associate editor for the King Papers Project; **Beth Brummel** (essay contributor), research assistant for the King Papers Project; **Erin Cook** (essay contributor), associate director of the Liberation Curriculum of the King Papers Project; **Susan Englander, Ph.D.** (essay contributor), assistant editor for the King Papers Project; and **Damani Rivers** (essay contributor and researcher), research assistant for the King Papers Project. Additional chronology research by **Mary Anne Morgan,** former research assistant for the King Papers Project.

Additional writing contributions by **Jan Harris Temple** and **Christy M. Nadalin**.

Additional consulting by **Jean Currie Church**, chief of the library division of the Moorland-Spingarn Research Center at Howard University in Washington, D.C.

Factual verification by **Evelyn Bender, Ed.D.**; **Barbara Cross**; **Regina J. Montgomery**; **Christy M. Nadalin**; **Kathleen Paparchontis**; and **Jennifer E. Rosenberg**. Index by **Ina Gravitz**. Photo research by **Alice Adamczyk** and **Jane A. Martin, Folio/The Photo Editor**.

*Acknowledgments can be found on page 447.*

# Contents

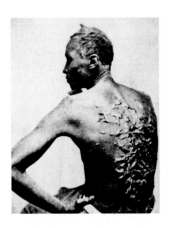

Beginning in the 1400s, Europeans sailing to and from West Africa initiated a trade in human slaves that eventually took root on American shores. Slavery's subsequent importance to the economy of the southern United States led to friction that sparked an impassioned abolitionist movement and, finally, civil war. Postwar Reconstruction held out some promise for black rights, but the federal government, despite passing a variety of "civil rights" acts, soon turned its back on former slaves and their American-born sons and daughters. At the dawn of the 20th century, institutionalized discrimination still thrived.

Slavery had been abolished in 1863, but economic peonage continued. Southern blacks were illegally prevented from owning land, from voting, even from traveling freely. Lynchings were not uncommon in the South, and blacks were railroaded into jails and prisons in the North. Booker T. Washington, a black leader who stressed economic rather than political activism, clashed with more politically oriented leaders, including W.E.B. Du Bois, who cofounded the integrationist NAACP in 1909. Blacks were determined to enter the American mainstream.

America's economic Depression hit African-Americans especially hard. When jobs opened up, they went to whites first. Further, education of black children was clearly inferior to white education. African-American attorney and educator Charles Houston created the legal framework that challenged discrimination and became the foundation of the modern Civil Rights Movement. The political allegiance of many black Americans shifted to the Democratic Party, whose leaders did not completely ignore black concerns.

During World War II, many African-Americans in the South migrated north for defense jobs. Others served in the Armed Forces. An activist black organization, CORE, was founded early in the decade. A. Philip Randolph's Brotherhood of Sleeping Car Porters was America's first successful black American trade union. By war's end in 1945, African-Americans who had contributed to victory insisted on their fair share of the American Dream. One great symbolic victory came in 1947, when ballplayer Jackie Robinson became the first black man to play in the major leagues. A year later, President Truman desegregated the U.S. Armed Forces.

The *Brown v. Board of Education* decision in 1954 and other court rulings mandated African-Americans' rights to equal public education. But Jim Crow lived on in the South, where Little Rock's Central High was the center of an ugly battle over desegregation. In southern states, many blacks still could not vote; could neither eat, swim, nor go to the bathroom in the same facilities as whites; and were threatened and sometimes murdered by the Ku Klux Klan. Great black leaders emerged, among them Reverend Martin Luther King, Jr., who, with NAACP activist Rosa Parks, successfully forced desegregation of the Montgomery, Alabama, bus system; Medgar Evers, a determined NAACP organizer in Mississippi; and attorney Thurgood Marshall, who successfully argued the *Brown* case. These bold figures were just a few of the many who inspired millions.

Some 200 years of oppression and discrimination came to a head in this particularly eventful American decade, when African-Americans perfected the art of the sit-in, Freedom Rides, and other nonviolent protests encouraged by Martin Luther King and his organization, the SCLC. This nonviolence was met with terrible, criminal force by the Klan, white citizens' councils, and police. Civil rights activists and even children were assaulted and sometimes killed. Aggressive and prideful black leaders, such as Malcolm X, Black Panthers cofounders Bobby Seale and Huey Newton, and SNCC leader Stokely Carmichael, urged African-Americans to seize the initiative, and force change. The assassinations of NAACP organizer Medgar Evers and Malcolm were terrible blows. With Dr. King's 1968 assassination by a white racist, urban streets across America exploded in frustration and rage.

Civil rights activity carried on in the 1970s, but often with unhappy results: two black students killed by police at Jackson State in Mississippi; a bloody prison uprising at Attica, New York, where inmates and hostages alike were shot down by guards and soldiers; black academic-activist Angela Davis hunted by the FBI; violently racist reactions from whites in Boston over court-ordered school busing plans designed to achieve racial desegregation. Too many Movement leaders of the '60s were dead or locked in dissension with each other. And a protracted period of runaway inflation and stagnant wages only made the economic and social outlooks for African-Americans look worse.

American political life in the 1980s was dominated by Republican President Ronald Reagan and his political heir, George H. Bush. Affirmative action mandates were rolled back during these years, inhibiting black opportunities for higher education. Social welfare programs that benefited the urban poor, particularly children, were neglected. The black middle class grew under the Reagan philosophy of limited government and "trickle-down" economics, but the numbers of African-American poor also increased. Two grace notes were Jesse Jackson's exciting runs for the Democratic presidential nomination in 1984 and 1988, and the official recognition of Martin Luther King's birthday as a federal holiday.

If white Americans assumed racial tension was a thing of the past by the 1990s, their illusions were shattered by the Los Angeles riot of 1992. The disturbance was precipitated by the acquittals of four white L.A. policemen whose severe beating of a black motorist was captured on eyewitness video. Democrat Bill Clinton, a pragmatic president with genuine interest in black rights, helped to create a better climate after 1992. He gave positive emphasis to affirmative action, public education, and other issues important to African-Americans. The 1995 Million Man March on Washington by black men was a moment of solidarity and promise. By the 2000s, as America became understandably preoccupied with foreign affairs, African-Americans and progressive whites understood that commitments to public education, youth intervention, and family life remained issues of profound domestic importance.

# Foreword

WHEN MY FIRST GRANDCHILD, Danny, was four days old, I walked into his parents' bedroom, picked him up, held him, and began to sob, because Medgar missed seeing his first grandchild—the child who would bear his name.

And then I wondered what my grandchild would have to face—a male African-American in this country, in this time. What challenges would he confront, and would he understand that his grandfather did not die in vain?

How would he understand the meaning behind the African-American struggle for freedom, in a country in which he would grow up to sing about "the land of the free and the home of the brave"?

As my grandson grew up, we kept his grandfather's memory alive by relating stories about what life was like when we were young, and the things for which Medgar, I, and others fought. We'd recount the stories about our inability to vote or run for public office; how we were barred from municipal pools, parks, libraries, and even dressing rooms in stores; how in movie theaters we had to sit in the balcony, the "buzzard's roost" as it was called then.

My grandson would listen as we would tell these stories, and then he would shake his head and say, "I don't see how you lived with that. I'd never put up with it. I'd never tolerate it." And I don't think his generation would, not in the manner that we did.

When I think about how young we were during that period—some of the most tumultuous times in this country's history—I realize that we were not much older than my grandson is today. And yet there is still struggle. Perhaps there's not so much of the obvious kind, which pitted a human being against killer dogs, torrents from fire hoses, and tear gas. But when we read today about the subtle attempts to undermine the laws of the Constitution, to twist civil rights into civil wrongs, to continue to dismantle basic civil liberties, it is evident that the struggle continues.

The African-American struggle for freedom is underscored by anniversaries that occurred in 2003. The year marked 40 years of history since the famed March on Washington, 40 years since the death of my husband, Medgar Evers. The year 2004 commemorates 50 years since *Brown v. Board of Education*—the Supreme Court decision that changed the face of this country. And yet there is still much to be done, as proponents of anti-affirmative action and segregationists continue to spew the venom that cripples a progressive nation and paralyzes a forward-thinking people.

Why another book on the Civil Rights Movement in America? Why another narrative—rewriting the same horrid stories of human oppression and, for some of us, reliving forever-painful memories?

U.S. census figures show that the American population is projected to increase by 50 percent by the year 2040 from 263 million in 1995. As the United States continues to become increasingly diverse, it is expected that the minority population will account for nearly 90 percent of this increase. This is the picture of the nation our children will inherit.

It is impossible to develop future leaders of tomorrow without providing them with a solid historical foundation.

When it is time to pass the torch, our youth must be ready. They must be armed with the tools that will help them to forge the elements of tolerance and forgiveness into a universal shield of peace. It is imperative that they be equipped to ward off new attacks of hatred and discrimination.

We provide those tools through education.

*Civil Rights Chronicle* offers a comprehensive rendering of the historical facts of the struggle of African-Americans in their quest for freedom. And yet, it is not just an African-American struggle, because America cannot truly be free if one segment of her people is oppressed.

This book helps readers understand the emotional, mental, and physical strains of blacks and whites who gave blood, sweat, and tears to the struggle. Its detailed account acknowledges the reality of the times for those who lived it, and offers a point of reference for those who need to learn from it.

One of my favorite authors, and a neighbor, Margaret Walker Alexander, wrote: "Let a new earth rise. Let another world be born. Let a bloody peace be written in the sky. Let a second generation full of courage issue forth; let a people loving freedom come to growth."

We are a people loving freedom. It is time to grow.

The torch passes to the next generation.

*Myrlie Evers-Williams*

Myrlie Evers-Williams

*Myrlie Evers–Williams served as chairwoman of the NAACP from 1995 to 1998. Her husband, Medgar Evers, the NAACP field secretary for Mississippi, was assassinated on June 12, 1963.*

Beneath a portrait of Medgar Evers, Myrlie sits with her children, Rena, Van, and Darrell (*left to right*).

# Introduction

IN JULY OF 1900, African-American scholar William E. B. Du Bois spoke at the first Pan-African Congress in London and offered a bold prediction: "The problem of the 20th century is the problem of the color line." Questioning whether race differences should be "the basis of denying to over half the world the right of sharing to their utmost ability the opportunities and privileges of modern civilization," Du Bois anticipated and inspired a worldwide movement to achieve basic rights for most of the world's people.

At the time Du Bois made his prediction, he had already witnessed a gradual deterioration of the political status of African-Americans in the United States: the end of Reconstruction in the southern states, Supreme Court rulings culminating in *Plessy v. Ferguson* (1896) that eviscerated the civil rights protections of the 14th Amendment, numerous lynchings and other forms of racial violence, and passage of "Jim Crow" segregation laws at the end of the 19th century. These changes, when combined with the European colonial "Scramble for Africa," seemed to offer scant hope that much could be done about the problem of the color line.

Yet, during his long subsequent career as a social scientist, journalist, and civil rights proponent, Du Bois would witness and often write about a sustained and ultimately successful freedom struggle that is recounted in *Civil Rights Chronicle*. In 1905 he became one of the founders of the Niagara Movement, seeking "full manhood suffrage." In 1909 he became a founding member of the interracial National Association for the Advancement of Colored People (NAACP), and soon afterward began editing the NAACP's influential journal, *The Crisis: A Record of the Darker Races*. As black soldiers returned from World War I to encounter the racist violence of the "Red Summer" of 1919, Du Bois epitomized New Negro militancy. "Make way for Democracy!" he declared. He insisted that if the United States could fight for freedom in foreign countries, it should do so on its own soil.

Du Bois was a powerful voice demanding civil rights, but he was just one of many influential black leaders of his time. Having challenged Booker T. Washington's accommodationist strategy for racial advancement, Du Bois's own views would face challenges from succeeding generations of black activists, including the black nationalists of Marcus Garvey's Universal Negro Improvement Association as well as black socialists, such as labor leader A. Philip Randolph and invet-

W.E.B. Du Bois approached black self-determinism from the perspective of a globalist. Brilliant and highly educated, he helped define the modern Civil Rights Movement.

erate protester Bayard Rustin. Within the NAACP were many other contending voices: administrators Walter White and Roy Wilkins, Legal Defense and Education Fund lawyers Charles Houston and Thurgood Marshall, and Director of Branches Ella Baker.

Du Bois's evolving attitudes reflected the larger political currents of his times. During the Great Depression, he sparked controversy when he argued that African-Americans should not fear voluntary segregation, but to cooperate with fellow oppressed people. In the aftermath of World War II, he insisted that the destiny of African-Americans was inextricably linked with that of colonized Africans and Asians. He warned that Cold War anticommunism would weaken the civil rights struggle at home and strengthen colonialism abroad. His increasingly leftist political stance led NAACP leaders to force him out of the organizations he had founded.

Jim Crow—segregation of black Americans that was enforced by the rule of racist laws on the books across the American South—undercut black self-regard, and allowed African-Americans no voice in their destinies.

By the early 1950s, black leftists such as Du Bois and singer-actor Paul Robeson were becoming increasingly supplanted by other figures who would guide the African-American civil rights struggle through a period of tumultuous changes. In 1954 Marshall and his staff of NAACP lawyers won a major victory when the Supreme Court unanimously ruled in *Brown v. Board of Education* that public school segregation violated the 14th Amendment. The chronicle of the next decade and a half was a dense procession of litigation and lobbying, increasingly massive protests, occasional outbursts of racial violence, and continued debates over strategies of black advancement. As dozens of African nations gained their independence, African-Americans staged their own struggle for inclusion as full citizens in a transformed United States.

Reverend Martin Luther King, Jr., committed his life to justice, and left a peerless legacy that inspires oppressed peoples around the world.

The new era of massive and sustained civil rights protests began with a simple act of refusal: Rosa Parks's decision to remain in her seat on a Montgomery, Alabama, bus. The resulting boycott movement, which lasted 381 days, gave the civil rights struggle a major victory and a major new leader. Martin Luther King, Jr., would quickly become the nation's best-known civil rights leader and proponent of Gandhian-style nonviolence. Like Du Bois (who died on the eve of King's "I Have a Dream" speech given at the 1963 March on Washington), King saw the African-American struggle as part of a worldwide struggle of oppressed people.

Although King would remain the most prominent figure of the civil rights revolution of the 1950s and 1960s, many less-known activists made crucial contributions: the resourceful members of the Montgomery Women's Political Council, the nine brave students who desegregated Little Rock's Central High School, the college students who spearheaded the 1960 sit-in campaign and who sustained the 1961 Freedom Rides despite racist violence in Alabama, the field secretaries of the Student Nonviolent Coordinating Committee, and many others. *Civil Rights Chronicle* recounts their stories.

The blast of fire hoses turned against black demonstrators in Birmingham, Alabama, was a last spasm of a racist culture. Images such as this shocked America, and the world.

This volume makes clear that the Civil Rights Movement was comprised of strong, self-reliant, grassroots leaders who did not wait for instructions from King. Fred Shuttlesworth's determined campaign against racist violence in "Bombingham" prepared the way for King's involvement in the Birmingham campaign of 1963. Mississippi NAACP leader Medgar Evers was one of a number of civil rights organizers who kept hope alive in Deep South segregationist strongholds until white volunteers arrived in the mid-1960s. Other organizers who emerged from the Mississippi movement included Robert Moses, Fannie Lou Hamer, and Stokely Carmichael.

By the mid-1960s the civil rights struggle had achieved its most significant goals—the Civil Rights Act of 1964 and the Voting Rights Act of 1965—but years of militancy had produced new aspirations and new frustrations. As Du Bois and King realized, the Civil Rights Movement had always been part of a broader freedom struggle, and this became evident when the Selma voting rights campaign stimulated debates about the future direction of African-American politics.

Unlike other civil rights narratives, *Civil Rights Chronicle* covers the period after 1965, when King and other black activists turned their attention to the problems that had not been addressed by civil rights legislation. By illuminating the recent decades of American history, *Civil Rights Chronicle* contributes to our understanding of the Poor People's Campaign of 1968 and the Black Power revolt of the late 1960s. The "long, hot summers" of racial violence and the law-and-order response gave rise to the new efforts to protect previous civil rights gains. Modern activists also have attempted to deal with the growing gulf between affluent Americans of all races and those trapped in cycles of poverty. The contentious issues of busing to achieve school integration and affirmative action programs to combat racial discrimination profoundly affected American politics of the post-1960s era.

Although some veterans of earlier civil rights battles remained prominent in this era—notably Andrew Young, John Lewis, and presidential candidate Jesse Jackson—new leaders emerged on the scene. As the pages of *Civil Rights Chronicle* approach the 21st century, the text increasingly focuses on female leaders and gender issues. Among the black feminist—or womanist—leaders who illuminated the special concerns and problems of black women were Angela Davis, Maya Angelou, Shirley Chisholm, Alice Walker, and Anita Hill.

By the 1990s, gender issues included the concerns of black men, a group that was disproportionately affected by a new set of civil rights issues—especially patterns of police misconduct in predominantly black neighborhoods and racial biases in the criminal justice system. Gansta rap, the Los Angeles riot of 1992, and the Million Man March of 1995 defined a decade that demonstrated the growing importance of gender issues as well as the continued significance of race and civil rights. At the beginning of the 21st century, important civil rights issues such as affirmative action remained unresolved and a source of major divisions in American politics.

The color line that Du Bois predicted would be the problem of the 20th century has continued to be a problem in the next century. But the past century of civil rights struggles has been a story of interracial cooperation as well as conflict, of heroic idealism as well as vicious racism. The American civil rights struggle drew inspiration from other freedom struggles, and it inspired many of the world's freedom struggles of the past four decades. *Civil Rights Chronicle* allows us to learn from and progress beyond the past.

CLAYBORNE CARSON, PH.D.
DIRECTOR, MARTIN LUTHER KING, JR. PAPERS PROJECT
STANFORD UNIVERSITY

Marxist-feminist Angela Davis was a fiery and purposely provocative activist who burst upon the national stage in the late 1960s. Her concerns helped broaden the Movement's focus.

Hopefulness was in the air during the Million Man March of 1995. The Movement had entered a new, and critical, phase.

# THE Early Struggle

This 1882 illustration depicts the lynching of a black man by a terrorist hate group called the Regulators. Southern blacks, who seemingly had won their freedom with the passage of the 13th Amendment in 1865, lost most of their rights by 1877, when federal troops left the South.

On July 4, 1776, in Philadelphia, 56 representatives of the new 13 colonies signed the Declaration of Independence, drafted by Thomas Jefferson. The second sentence of the historic document reads: "We hold these truths to be self-evident, that all men are created equal, that they are endowed by their Creator with certain unalienable Rights, that among these are Life, Liberty and the pursuit of Happiness."

Unsaid in these ennobling lines is the shameful truth that the Founding Fathers of the United States regarded the new nation's African and African-American residents as less than human. In the United States Constitution that was framed 11 years later, in 1787, each slave was designated as *three-fifths* of a human being, unable to vote and completely powerless to shape his or her personal destiny. In the southern states, those of African descent were mere chattel, with no more rights than a plow horse.

Of course, the plow horses suffered less. Countless black men, women, and children in the United States endured horrifying abuses that did not begin to be addressed in a meaningful way until the midpoint of the 20th century, during what we now know as the Civil Rights Movement.

The term "civil rights" is perhaps a misnomer, because it speaks to man-made laws, statutes, and practices. What people of African descent have struggled for in the United States and elsewhere have been basic human rights. In the United States, civil rights depend upon people who, through law or public policy, grant certain civil liberties as the basis of citizenship. White public opinion has always determined, through *de jure* and *de facto* public policy, the extent and degree of American citizenship that Africans have or have not enjoyed.

# Early Struggle

## 1441–1776

**1441:** Portuguese men kidnap 12 black Africans from Cabo Blanco and transport them to Portugal.

**1490s–1685:** The following countries enter the African slave trade: Spain (beginning in the 1490s), England (1562), Holland (1597), France (1640), Sweden (1649), Denmark (1651), and Germany (1685).

**1526:** In what are now the Carolinas, Spaniards put kidnapped Africans to work as slaves.

**August 1619:** Africans arrive in Jamestown, Virginia, to work as indentured servants and/or slaves.

**1641:** Massachusetts becomes the first colony to declare slavery legal.

**1660s:** Colonies begin to define and regulate the practice of slavery.

**1688:** Quakers and Mennonites in the colony of Pennsylvania protest against slavery.

**September 9, 1739:** In the Stono Rebellion, scores of slaves revolt near Charleston, South Carolina, killing masters and burning plantations. Sixty people, including 35 slaves, are killed.

**1775:** Numerous black soldiers fight in the Revolutionary War until the Continental Army—pressured by George Washington—rules to exclude blacks from service.

**April 14, 1775:** The Pennsylvania Society for the Abolition of Slavery is founded. It's the first abolitionist organization in the United States.

**July 4, 1776:** The Declaration of Independence is signed. The second sentence reads: "We hold these Truths to be self-evident, that all Men are created equal, that they are endowed by their Creator with certain unalienable Rights, that among these are Life, Liberty and the Pursuit of Happiness." The framers, however, skirt the slavery issue. ➤

**LADIES' DEPARTMENT.**

'Am I not a Woman and a Sister?'

White Lady, happy, proud and free,
Lend awhile thine ear to me ;
Let the Negro Mother's wail
Turn thy pale cheek still more pale.
Can the Negro Mother joy
Over this her captive boy,
Which in bondage and in tears,
For a life of wo she rears ?
Though she bears a Mother's name,
A Mother's rights she may not claim ;
For the white man's will can part,
Her darling from her bursting heart.

*From the Genius of Universal Emancipation.*
**LETTERS ON SLAVERY.—No. III.**

A black mother appeals to the collective conscience of America's white mothers. Such pleas for empathy fell on deaf ears in the South for more than 300 years.

In fact, the greatest obstacle to black civil rights has been white public opinion.

The civil rights struggle is a part of the continuum of resistance that runs through all of black history. For centuries, Africans have reacted to and resisted enslavement and oppression. Their struggle in America has been a moral endeavor, as they have sought to make their country live up to its professed democratic ideals of life, liberty, and the pursuit of happiness for all its citizens.

The development of white public opinion, which allowed the legal and extralegal enslavement, oppression, and disenfranchisement (prevention of voting) of Africans in the United States, began long before the country was established. It began with the creation of the European Slave Trade and its underlying economic root. Eric Williams asserts in the book *Capitalism and Slavery*: "A racial twist has…been given to what is basically an economic phenomenon. Slavery was not born of racism; rather, racism was the consequence of slavery."

In order to justify their enslavement of Africans for economic profit, Europeans dehumanized Africans, corrupted their universal rights through flawed manmade laws, created a distorted reality, refashioned religious beliefs, and warped historical truth. This complex process allowed whites to

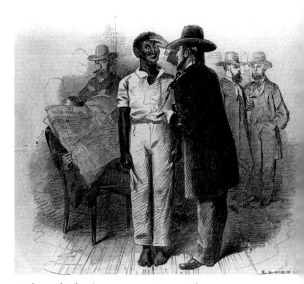

A slave dealer inspects a prospective slave in this deceptively cheerful interpretation of slave purchasing. To those in the slave-trading business, Africans were nothing more than human chattel.

For economic reasons, some African leaders agreed to facilitate the European Slave Trade. Here, men, women, and children are rounded up by slave hunters in Zanzibar.

engage in the barbarous actions necessary to enslave human beings by overlooking murder, suffering, degradation, and moral and ethical considerations. At the same time, Africans developed a tradition of resistance to oppression, thereby guaranteeing, at least for themselves, their own humanity.

From the outset of the European Slave Trade, Europeans used the notion of black inferiority as a rationale for enslaving Africans. This reasoning was preached from the pulpit, stated in front of legislative bodies and courts, espoused in philosophical and historical treatises, spread through newspapers and magazines, seen in popular culture, taught in classrooms, and inculcated into children by parents. In 1748 Scottish philosopher David Hume stated in his essay "Of National Characters," without fear of challenge: "I am apt to suspect the Negroes and in general all the other species of men to be naturally inferior to the whites. There never was a civilized nation of any other complexion than white." This pretext has been used for centuries to deny human rights to Africans—even in America in the mid-20th century.

## The Roots of Slavery

Europeans were by no means the first to enslave African people. North Africans, or, more specifically, Arab traders from the north of Africa, had been involved in the buying and selling of Asians, Indians, Africans, and Europeans for markets in Persia, India, and Arabia for many years before Europeans entered the trade. Europeans simply capitalized on the already existing lucrative Arab trading empire in Africa.

Slavery actually dates back thousands of years. Records are replete with references to the custom among Hebrews, Greeks, Romans, Babylonians, Vikings, and others. Like the European Slave Trade and the United States' brand of slavery, ancient slavery was motivated by social, political, and economic concerns. Most often, people were enslaved because they were prisoners of war or were captured through acts of piracy. Sometimes they were enslaved because they committed infractions against their society's social code, such as unpaid debt, witchcraft, adultery, and theft.

Slave traders capture African villagers, who will be sold into slavery in America. Anywhere from 11 million to 100 million Africans were enslaved during the European Slave Trade.

# Early Struggle

Records left in ancient Egyptian tombs and pyramids show that slavery existed in Africa as early as 3000 BCE (Before the Common Era) and was usually the result of ethnic warfare in which the victor enslaved the loser. Africans, therefore, were familiar with slavery before the imposition of the Arab and European slave trades. Europeans justified their declarations of African inferiority by contending that since Africans sold each other, they had a unique racial flaw.

It is important to remember that, as a continent, Africa has thousands of ethnic groups with diverse languages, cultures, and traditions. The concept of "Africa" did not exist until the intrusion of Europeans into the continent. Africans, like Europeans, saw themselves as a part of their ethnic group, not as a part of the continent. In other words, *Africans* were not out to enslave *fellow Africans*. Instead, Ibo enslaved Hausa, Yoruba enslaved Fulani, and Moors enslaved Bambara. In a similar way, Romans sold Britons, Greeks enslaved Spartans, Vikings captured and sold Irish, and so on.

Moreover, it is clear that traditional African slavery was vastly different from the chattel slavery instituted by Europeans. Olaudah Equiano, who was kidnapped from his home in Nigeria, was enslaved and sold in Virginia and then England, and eventually bought his freedom, explains the nature of

*The Life of Olaudah Equiano* offers compelling and valuable insights into the practice of slavery in the 18th century. A native of Nigeria, Equiano was enslaved and sold in Virginia.

African slavery in his 1789 narrative *The Life of Olaudah Equiano:* "Sometimes indeed we sold slaves...but they were only prisoners of war, or such among us as had been convicted of kidnapping, or adultery, and some other crimes, which we esteemed heinous.... With us they do no more work than other members of the community, even their master; their food, clothing, and lodging were nearly the same as theirs (except they were not permitted to eat with those who were free born), and there was scarce any other difference between them.... Some of these slaves have even slaves under them as their own property and for their own use." Africans enslaved by other Africans, as Equiano discussed, could at least hope to be absorbed into the existing social structure on a status

resembling that of their enslavers. That was not to be true for Africans who were enslaved by Europeans or Americans.

As the European Slave Trade progressed, the nature of African slavery and society changed. John Barbot, a European slaver, explains in *A Description of the Coasts of North and South Guinea* (1732) how Europeans controlled the trade by fomenting conflicts between ethnic groups: "I remember...that in the year 1681, an English interloper at Commendo [West Africa] got three hundred good slaves, almost for nothing...as the Commendo men brought them from the field of battle, having obtained a victory over a neighboring nation, and taken a great many prisoners."

Like Europeans, Africans got involved in the European Slave Trade for economic reasons, and this had disastrous consequences for many African ethnic groups. Nzinga Mbemba, a Congolese leader who took the Christian name Affonso, participated in the European Slave Trade in order to receive technical aid from Portugal for his nation. The Portuguese were responsible for helping Affonso maintain his leadership by putting down rebellions in his kingdom. Eventually, however, Affonso saw the damage that the European Slave Trade was doing to his kingdom. He wrote John III in 1526, asking for a cessation of trade in the Congo: "Sir...[you] should know how our Kingdom is being lost in so many ways.... [O]fficials to the men and merchants...daily seize our subjects, sons of the land and sons of our noblemen and vassals and our relatives.... They grab them and cause them to be sold: and so great, Sir, is their corruption and licentiousness that our country is being utterly depopulated...."

Affonso's plea to John III was not successful; Portugal's stake in the European Slave Trade was great, and the Congo was one of the most lucrative areas for providing human goods.

Europeans' enslavement of Africans began as early as 1441, when Portuguese navigator Antonio Gonzales brought 12 Africans back to Portugal for his king, Prince Henry the Navigator, who gave them as a gift to Pope Euge-

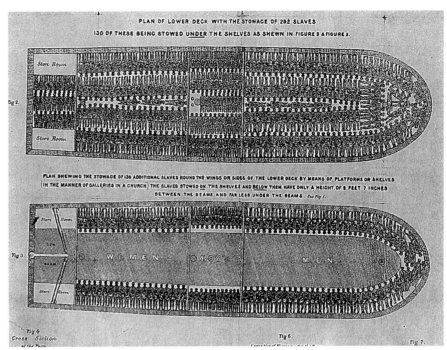

During the Middle Passage, slavers chained Africans together and packed them into the hot, tight quarters of slave ships. Men, women, and children lay on wooden planks for weeks, sometimes months, wallowing in human waste.

Some Africans jumped off slave ships, preferring suicide to a life of suffering. Many diseased slaves were thrown overboard so that the other slaves wouldn't become infected.

nius IV. From then on, Africans were regularly captured and forcibly taken to Portugal, where they usually were enslaved in the royal courts. By 1447, 900 Africans were enslaved in Portugal.

As implied by the term "trade," the primary motivation for Europe's incursion into Africa was economic. At first it was the goods—gold, spices, ivory—that Europeans sought from Africans. Later, as the Americas (the "New World") were colonized, "triangular trade" evolved. It worked like this: Europeans exported cheap goods, including guns, to African merchants; Europeans captured or purchased Africans in Africa and transported them on ships via the "Middle Passage" to the New World, where they were sold for

profit; and they purchased the raw materials (sugar, tobacco, coffee) produced in the New World and took them back to Europe to be manufactured into cheap goods.

The Middle Passage is one of the more horrendous aspects of the European Slave Trade. Each journey took approximately one month, but often Africans were held on slave ships or in slave dungeons for multiple months before they sailed. Disease and unsanitary conditions, as well as acts of resistance (including suicide, revolt, and infanticide), were responsible for most of the deaths attributed to this perilous journey. It is clear that European enslavers expected resistance. They fashioned all the equipment necessary to forestall, battle, and punish resisters. They used

# Early Struggle

## 1777–1830

**1777–1804:** Massachusetts, New York, Pennsylvania, Connecticut, New Jersey, Vermont, New Hampshire, and Rhode Island all adopt plans for the emancipation of slaves.

**1784:** By this year, all Quaker leaders have prohibited followers of their faith from owning slaves.

**Summer 1787:** At the Constitutional Convention, Northerners and Southerners debate whether slaves should be counted as part of a state's population. They finally determine that a slave should count as three-fifths of a person.

**July 13, 1787:** The Northwest Ordinance is passed, outlawing slavery in the Northwest Territory. However, fugitive slaves found in the Northwest Territory can be returned to their owners.

**1793:** Eli Whitney invents the cotton gin, which will encourage the use of slavery in southern states.

**February 12, 1793:** Congress passes the Fugitive Slave Act, which requires the return of escaped slaves to their owners even if they have fled their state.

**January 1, 1808:** The United States outlaws the importation of slaves, although the practice will continue illegally.

**March 1820:** Congress passes the Missouri Compromise. Missouri will be admitted to the Union as a slave state while Maine will join as a free state. Moreover, no territories north of Missouri would be slave states.

**1827:** *Freedom's Journal*, the first African-American newspaper, is published.

**September 1830:** The National Negro Convention is held in Philadelphia. Members strive to improve employment and education opportunities and to resist oppression. ➤

whips, chains, guns, restraints, and torture devices.

The logs, diaries, and journals of slave ship captains as well as narratives of enslaved Africans detail the horrors of the Middle Passage and African resistance. Olaudah Equiano's narrative describes the Middle Passage, a voyage he knew firsthand as a captive: "The stench of the hold while we were on the coast was so intolerably loathsome.... The closeness of the place, and the heat of the climate, added to the number in the ship, which was so crowded that each had scarcely room to turn himself, almost suffocated us. This produced copious perspirations, so that the air soon became unfit for respiration, from a variety of loathsome smells, and brought on a sickness among the slaves, of which many died.... This wretched situation was again aggravated by the galling of the chains, now became unsupportable, and the filth of the necessary tubs, into which the children often fell...." It is no wonder that Equiano tried to starve himself to death to escape the conditions of the Middle Passage. He was whipped and forcibly fed, however. Because he survived to write his narrative, we know what the journey was like for the Africans who endured it.

Estimates vary regarding the total number of Africans enslaved during the European Slave Trade, from a high of 100 million (with 50 million perishing in the process) to a low of 11 million. Theodore Canot, a slave trader, records in his *Adventures of an African Slaver* (1854) that during one voyage he lost nearly 40 percent of his human cargo to disease: "The eight hundred beings we had shipped in high health [from Africa] had dwindled to four hundred and ninety-seven skeletons."

The European Slave Trade helped build the economies of the New World and Europe. The New World colonies were able to produce sugar (a rare item in Europe) and tobacco. The manufacture of these products was labor-intensive, requiring a large number of manual laborers to work in the fields. As the European demand for these and other products—such as rum, molasses, coffee, and cotton—increased, the need for labor (that is, enslaved Africans) to supply the demand rose as well.

In 1746 Malachy Postlethwayt justified Great Britain's participation in the slave trade by showing just how essential it was to his country's economy: "The Negroe-trade...and the natural consequences resulting from it, may be justly esteemed an inexhaustible fund of wealth and naval power to this nation.... What renders the Negroe-trade still more estimable and important, is, that near nine-tenths of those Negroes are paid for in Africa with British produce and manufacturers only.... We send no

# The "Peculiar Institution"

IN THE LONG PANORAMA of U.S. history, slavery casts the darkest shadow. It began with the colonists in 17th century Virginia, was sanctioned by the Constitution, and burgeoned into a massive social enterprise that defined antebellum southern life. An estimated half-million Africans were seized and shipped to America for sale. By 1860 the population had reached four million, and it took the bloodiest conflict in American history to free them.

Legally, slavery was a matter of property rights: One person owned another, both his person and his labor. Racially, it focused on ancestry: Whereas most previous forms of slavery were class-based, American slavery targeted people of African descent. Economically, it was a question of profit: Were slaves more productive and less costly than employees?

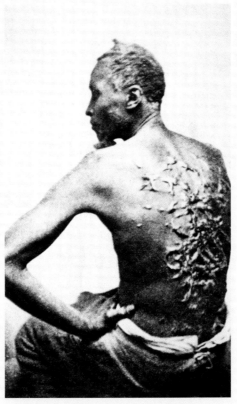

A slave scarred by lashes from a whip

and exploitative. If money was short, masters sold slaves at auction, separating husbands from wives, children from mothers. Women endured the sexual advances of white men, infants suffered malnutrition, and the elderly were neglected. Most male slaves were field hands; their days began before dawn and ended after sunset. Women often worked longer hours. They, too, worked the fields, but they also washed and sewed, cooked and cleaned, and raised children. Those serving in the "Big House" were at the beck and call of the plantaion mistress, and seldom escaped her watchful eyes. Violations of the master's will were answered with the whip.

It was a "peculiar institution," placing whites and blacks in intimate, but drastically hierarchical relations. The carnage of Shiloh, Antietam, and Gettysburg helped end it, but its legacy would affect social policy and racial thinking in the 19th, 20th, and even 21st centuries.

Apologists for slavery interpreted the practice as paternalism—care-taking and discipline exercised by a civilized race upon a primitive race. But actual practices were cruel

---

specie or bullion [money] to pay for the products of Africa [human beings], but tis certain, we bring from thence very large quantities of gold; and not only that but wax and ivory...." Britain's gunsmithing, sailmaking, shipbuilding, and textile industries particularly prospered.

Most European countries profited from the European Slave Trade, but it was Britain's participation in the practice that has had the greatest impact on Africans in the United States. Of all the slaves

that arrived on the shores of the colonies and United States, the vast majority were brought by the British. Moreover, the British not only settled the United States, but their law and social mores became the basis for American society. Consequently, the British provided much of the racist social, political, and economic justification for the European Slave Trade that would be used to rationalize American slavery and, later, the denial of civil rights for Africans in the United States.

### Slavery in America: Oppression and Resistance

Jamestown, Virginia, was the first North American British colony to receive Africans as forced laborers. In August 1619, 20 Africans arrived in Jamestown on a Dutch ship. Scholars have proved that these laborers were not enslaved but rather indentured servants who became "free" people at the conclusion of their contracts. One reason for their being considered indentured servants was that Virginia, like the other colonies, had no laws

# Early Struggle

## Sojourner Truth

IN 1851 SOJOURNER TRUTH addressed a convention in Akron, Ohio. "I have as much muscle as any man, and can do as much work as any man," she said. "I have plowed and reaped and husked and chopped and mowed, and can any man do more than that?"

Tall, dignified, and devout, Truth was the leading black female champion of abolition and women's rights in the antebellum period. Born Isabella Baumfree in Ulster County, New York, she experienced the customary sufferings of northern slavery—a dark, humid cellar for a home and siblings sold for profit. Leaving her master a year before a state law would have freed her, Truth lived in New York City until a religious vision sent her across New England preaching the word of God and the dignity of slaves and women.

Once, when warned that if she spoke, proslavery gangs would burn the hall, Truth replied, "Then I will speak upon the ashes." Though she was illiterate, her speeches and *Narrative* electrified audiences and advanced antislavery causes. Truth, who met with President Lincoln during the Civil War, also staged several "ride-ins" on streetcars. When one driver forced her off his streetcar, she sued him and won. In the 19th century, no other leader so skillfully combined issues of race, class, and gender into a seamless crusade against oppression.

ated solely with race. Law, through slave and black codes, regulated that condition. While initially no laws existed that allowed the colonists to enslave Africans, American colonists expanded on a racist psyche—nurtured and promoted by participants in the European Slave Trade—constructing in the process a uniquely "American" worldview. This racist mentality developed slowly until it became an unquestioned, accepted part of the white colonists' collective psyche.

This racist psyche needed to incorporate a belief system that denied the humanity of the people being enslaved. Moreover, since race was the determining factor in the enslavement process, all

This illustration is captioned "The introduction of slavery." In 1619, 20 Africans climbed off Dutch ships in Jamestown, Virginia, and became the first slaves (actually indentured servants) in the colonies.

allowing slavery, while indentureship was widely practiced.

Virginia was not the first British colony to mandate, by law, the enslavement of Africans; that honor belongs to Massachusetts, which recognized the enslavement of Africans as not only legal but moral in 1641. This was not a momentous step for the Puritans, since they had already legally sanctioned the enslavement of Native Americans. All the other colonies followed suit, each creating laws that progressively gave rise to the opinion that the enslavement of Africans was legitimately a part of the natural order. The custom of enslaving Africans, as well as their offspring, for life was accomplished through deceit and dishonesty. People who held Africans in indentureships found ways to extend their service; eventually, laws were passed that made Africans servants for life. Laws simply made legal what was often already done in practice.

In the United States, the condition of enslavement became associ-

A woman is sold at a slave auction in Richmond, Virginia. Often called "Negro wenches," female slaves were assigned domestic and field work. Many were beaten and/or raped.

Africans needed to be branded inferior; one couldn't justify enslaving some Africans and not others. White religious leaders supplied the fuel for racist belief systems when they, just as the British had, refashioned religious beliefs to rationalize the enslavement of Africans. In his 1706 treatise *The Negro Christianized*, Cotton Mather, a leading Puritan minister, uses the story of Ham to contend that the enslavement of Africans and Native Americans ("heathens," he says) is divinely ordained. It is interesting that Mather was also one of the principal figures in the Salem, Massachusetts, Witch Trials, which resulted in the hanging of 19 people.

Slave and black codes institutionalized racism by regulating every aspect of life for enslaved and free Africans. For example, an African was automatically presumed to be enslaved, placing the burden on the African to prove that he or she was not enslaved. Laws were passed in most colonies mandating that free Africans carry passes or documents attesting to their free status or risk being enslaved. Other laws regulated black speech, employment, activities, marriage, living standards, and practically every other aspect of black life.

The laws expose white colonists' fear of African insurrection. They also reveal the extent of African resistance to enslavement because they were usually enacted as a response to acts of African rebellion. Virginia passed an Act for Preventing Negroes Insurrections in 1680 that prohibited blacks from carrying clubs, sticks, or arms of any kind. A black person who raised his or her hand in opposition to a Christian could be punished with 30 lashes. The penalty for running away and resisting capture was death.

Early advertisements for runaways reveal that flight was one of the first acts of resistance. An issue of *Pennsylvania Gazette* carries an announcement for a runaway named Caesar, who had "both his Legs cut off, and walks on his knees" when he fled enslavement in Queen Anne County, Maryland.

## Murder of the Helpless

ONE OF THE COWS had dragged the rope away from the stake to which Hetty had fastened it, and got loose. My master flew into a terrible passion, and ordered the poor creature to be stripped quite naked, notwithstanding her pregnancy, and to be tied up to a tree in the yard. He then flogged her as hard as he could lick, both with the whip and cow-skin, till she was all over streaming with blood. He rested, and then beat her again and again. Her shrieks were terrible. The consequence was that poor Hetty was brought to bed before her time, and was delivered after severe labour of a dead child.... Ere long her body and limbs swelled to a great size; and she lay on a mat in the kitchen, till the water burst out of her body and she died. All the slaves said that death was a good thing for poor Hetty; but I cried very much for her death. The manner of it filled me with horror.

—*Mary Prince,* The History of Mary Prince, a West Indian Slave, Related by Herself

# Early Struggle

## 1831–1850

**January 1, 1831:** William Lloyd Garrison and Isaac Knapp publish the first issue of *Liberator*, a prominent abolitionist newspaper.

**August 1831:** Nat Turner leads the largest slave insurrection ever in the United States, as his band murders 57 whites in Virginia. More than 100 blacks are killed.

**January 6, 1832:** William Lloyd Garrison founds the New England Anti-Slavery Society.

**December 4, 1833:** The American Anti-Slavery Society is founded in Philadelphia.

**1834:** Slavery is abolished in the British Empire.

**1839:** American abolitionists form the Liberty Party and name James Birney their presidential candidate.

**1841:** Africans who revolted on *Amistad*, a ship carrying slaves, are tried for murder and piracy. Former President John Adams defends them in front of the U.S. Supreme Court, which rules justifiable homicide.

**1842:** In *Prigg v. Pennsylvania*, the U.S. Supreme Court rules that if a master's slave flees to another state, that state cannot hinder the master's right to retrieve the slave.

**1843:** Abolition activist Sojourner Truth begins to speak out publicly against slavery.

**August 9, 1848:** The Free-Soil Party is formed. It opposes the extension of slavery into the territories newly acquired by the U.S. from Mexico.

**September 1850:** In the Compromise of 1850, California joins the Union as a free state while the slavery issue in New Mexico and Utah will be determined by the populous.

▶

Many ads refer to the scars from whippings that both men and women wore, testifying to massive individual African resistance and to the enslavers' inhumanity.

The federal Fugitive Slave Law of 1793 attempted to address the problem of self-liberating Africans. The law permitted slave-holders to enter another state to recapture escapees. The lawmakers' motivation was purely economic. It is significant that 1793 was the year that Eli Whitney invented the cotton gin, which gave an even stronger economic rationale for enslaving Africans.

Another means of resistance, and one that has been a hallmark of African-American history, was through protest and agitation. During the colonial era, Africans, both enslaved and free, sent thou-

Leeds Anti-slavery Series   No. 23.

**SLAVE-BRANDING.**

Slaves who disobeyed the rules of the plantation often faced severe consequences. Punishments included branding, whipping, chaining, and mutilation.

sands of petitions to colonial governors and legislatures demanding and begging for their freedom, for basic rights, or to be sent back to Africa. The Declaration of Inde-

Sometimes, the punishment of a slave was a public spectacle. Here, white bystanders smile as a slave endures "cold water treatment."

pendence and the activities surrounding the colonies' break with Great Britain increased African demands for rights and freedom in the colonies. Africans used the same language of freedom, equality, and the rights of man in their petitions to press for rights for African-Americans as the white colonists had used in their struggle to free themselves from the yoke of British tyranny.

In 1779 a group of 20 blacks in New Hampshire—including Prince Whipple, who had crossed the Delaware in 1776 in the same boat as George Washington—requested that the state restore their freedom. They called themselves "natives of

As slave dealers conducted business inside this building in Alexandria, Virginia, slaves were kept in the backyard, which was surrounded by a high, whitewashed brick wall.

# National Negro Convention

IN 1830, 300,000 free blacks lived in the United States. As their numbers increased, so did social tensions. Whites and blacks vied for jobs, schooling, and property. As local authorities contrived statutes that favored whites, blacks realized the need to organize, frame protests, and push for reform. In an era of slow communication and scattered constituents, the prime venue for black policymaking became the national convention.

The first convention was held in Philadelphia in 1830, partly as a response to the emigration threat posed by the American Colonization Society. Although sparsely attended, the delegates drafted strong resolutions supporting emigration to Canada and opposing it to Liberia. The second convention transpired the following year, when white attendees, including William Lloyd Garrison, proposed that a Negro college be created in New Haven, Connecticut. White residents of New Haven would prevent that dream from becoming reality.

Another nine national conventions were held before war broke out in 1861, with dozens of local conventions funneling delegates and recommendations. In a nation whose southern half lived on Negro bondage and whose northern half maintained white supremacy, the national convention gave blacks a forum to articulate their grievances, collaborate, and demonstrate to white society the political and intellectual potential of African-Americans.

Africa" who had been "born free." They asked for their freedom "for the sake of justice, humanity, and the rights of mankind."

Such petitions were rarely successful because the colonial governors and legislatures refused to consider petitions from people who were not citizens. In other words, Africans, as noncitizens, were appealing to a system to which they had no access. Nevertheless, some Africans attempted to use the legal system to petition for justice because they felt they were entitled, as human beings, to basic civil rights. Because the petitions tried to appeal to the consciences of the white immigrants, they were the forerunners of the moral suasion

technique that abolitionists would later use. Martin Luther King, Jr., would perfect the same technique in the 1950s and '60s.

Ironically, the first American to fall in the conflict that started the American Revolution, the 1770 Boston Massacre, was Crispus Attucks, an African who had escaped enslavement 20 years earlier. Despite Attucks's action, Africans were more concerned with the principles of freedom associated with the American Revolution than they were with freeing the colonies from English rule. In order to secure their own "life, liberty, and the pursuit of happiness," Africans fought on whichever side they felt would supply freedom.

# Early Struggle

## 1850–1861

**September 1850:** Congress passes the Fugitive Slave Act of 1850, in which government officials are encouraged to return runaway slaves.

**March 20, 1852:** Harriet Beecher Stowe's antislavery novel *Uncle Tom's Cabin*, which will become the biggest-selling novel of the century, is published.

**1855:** Massachusetts abolishes segregation in its schools.

**March 1857:** In *Dred Scott v. Sandford*, the U.S. Supreme Court declares that the U.S. territories cannot prohibit slavery and that blacks—even free blacks—do not have constitutional rights.

**October 16, 1859:** White abolitionist John Brown leads a raid of the federal arsenal at Harper's Ferry, Virginia, hoping to obtain enough resources to start a large-scale slave uprising. Brown will be executed but hailed as a martyr.

**1860:** Five northern states—Massachusetts, Rhode Island, New Hampshire, Vermont, and Maine—allow African-Americans to vote without restrictions in the 1860 presidential election.

**1860:** Slavery is the No. 1 issue in the presidential election. Republican Abraham Lincoln, who opposes slavery, prevails.

**December 1860–February 1861:** South Carolina, Mississippi, Florida, Alabama, Georgia, Louisiana, and Texas secede from the Union.

**April 1861–June 1861:** Virginia, Arkansas, North Carolina, and Tennessee secede.

**April 12, 1861:** Confederate forces attack Union troops at Fort Sumter in South Carolina, commencing the start of the Civil War. ➤

An enslaved mother lived with the fear that she could someday be separated from her child and never see him or her again.

Estimates place the number of Africans who served on the side of the colonists at 5,000 for the seven years of the war. However, it is estimated that thousands of Africans fought on the British side, especially those in South Carolina and Georgia. During and after the war, several thousand Africans who had fought for England were evacuated by the British, primarily to Nova Scotia.

Instead of living up to their own creed of freedom, the new Americans strengthened the institution of slavery. The United States Constitution overtly dehumanized slaves, determining each slave's representative value as three-fifths of a white person's. Southerners had wanted slaves to be counted as whole people in the census so that their states would have greater political representation in Congress; others had argued that slaves weren't citizens and shouldn't be counted at all. Eventually, the "three-fifths" compromise was struck. Thus, slaves received no benefits of citizenship yet, tragically, their mere existence gave more political clout to their owners—political clout that allowed the southern politicians to maintain and perpetuate slavery.

Africans repeatedly chastised white Americans for their hypocrisy in creating, for themselves, "a near perfect union" while enslaving and oppressing Africans. Benjamin Banneker, an African-American astronomer, clockmaker, almanac writer,

The abolitionist movement gained energy in the 1830s with the creation of antislavery societies and periodicals, including this one published by Isaac Knapp.

farmer, and surveyor, challenged Thomas Jefferson, drafter of the Declaration of Independence, in a well-publicized 1791 letter: "...sir, how pitiable it is to reflect, that although you were so fully convinced of the benevolence of the Father of mankind, and of his equal and impartial distribution of these rights and privileges which he hath conferred upon them, that you should at the same time counteract his mercies, in detaining by fraud and violence so numerous a part of my brethren under groaning captivity and cruel oppression; that you should at the same time be found guilty of that most criminal act which you professedly detested in others with respect to yourselves."

Like Banneker, Africans continued to resist. The National Negro Conventions, which began in 1830, were held in major cities and attended by the most prominent African-Americans. At these meetings, Africans articulated their thoughts about defiance, calling for the violent overthrow of the slave system, rebellion against oppression, self-reliance, and, sometimes, voluntary emigration from the United States.

The slaveholder-led American Colonization Society (ACS) also wanted free blacks to leave the country. The ACS was founded in 1816 by 50 leading white, primarily southern, slave-holders and sympathizers. Among them were promi-

From 1831 to 1865, William Lloyd Garrison wrote eloquently and passionately about the evils of slavery in his weekly abolitionist newspaper, *Liberator*.

nent clergymen and politicians, such as John Randolph, a descendant of Pocahontas and John Wolfe; Judge Bushrod Washington, nephew of George Washington; Francis Scott Key, writer of the "Star Spangled Banner"; Henry Clay, speaker of the House of Representatives; and General Andrew Jackson, future president of the United States. Such well-known people as Abraham Lincoln, Thomas Jefferson, Stephen A. Douglas, Millard Fillmore, and Daniel Webster were ACS members or sympathizers.

In P. J. Staudenraus's book *The African Colonization Movement 1816–1865*, ACS member John Randolph stated that colonization of African-Americans—which would mean moving them to a settlement in West Africa—would help secure

slavery by eliminating the free black population, which was "one of the greatest sources of insecurity" to slave labor. He saw freedmen as "promoters of mischief" who excited "a feeling of discontent among slaves" and "served as couriers in insurrection plots." The ACS was very aware of the power of black activism and resistance, especially by free African-Americans.

One of the most vocal and visible opponents to colonization was fiery orator and black abolitionist Frederick Douglass. He objected to colonization, whether proposed by whites or blacks. In 1859 Douglass stated in his newspaper *The Douglass Monthly*: "...upon no consideration do we intend that our paper shall favor any schemes of colonization, or any measures the natural tendency of which will be to draw off the attention of free colored people from the means of improvement and elevation here...we are Americans;...America is our native land...this is our home;...we are American citizens...." Douglass would change this position later as he became disillusioned about the possibility of black equality in America. He reported in his paper in 1861 that he was making plans to visit Haiti to investigate its suitability for African-American emigration. The Civil War broke out before he could make his trip.

Other African-Americans counseled emigration. H. Ford Douglas asserted: "When I remember that

# Early Struggle

## 1862–1865

**1862–1865:** Approximately 180,000 black men serve in the Union Army.

**January 1, 1863:** President Lincoln issues the Emancipation Proclamation, declaring "that all persons held as slaves" within the rebellious states "are, and henceforward shall be free."

**March 3, 1863:** President Lincoln signs the Conscription Act into law.

**July 13–16, 1863:** Thousands of working-class whites in New York City, angry over the implementation of the draft and having to "fight a war for the niggers," unleash their wrath on the city's black population. At least 11 black people are killed and hundreds are injured.

**January 31, 1865:** Congress passes the 13th Amendment to the Constitution, which abolishes slavery. *See* December 1865.

**March 3, 1865:** Congress establishes the Freedmen's Bureau to aid former slaves.

**March 13, 1865:** Jefferson Davis, president of the crumbling Confederacy, authorizes the use of slaves as Confederate soldiers.

**April 9, 1865:** The Confederacy surrenders, ending the Civil War.

**April 14, 1865:** President Lincoln is assassinated in a Washington, D.C., theater by John Wilkes Booth.

**April 15, 1865:** Vice-president Andrew Johnson succeeds Abraham Lincoln as president.

**May 1865:** Massachusetts enacts the country's first public accommodations law. Black citizens are guaranteed the right to vote and to frequent all licensed public establishments.

**December 1865:** Ratified by the states, the 13th Amendment goes into effect. ➤

from Maine to Georgia, from the Atlantic waves to the Pacific shore, I am an alien and an outcast, unprotected by law, proscribed and persecuted by cruel prejudice, I am willing to forget the endearing name of home and country, and as an unwilling exile seek on other shores the freedom which has been denied me in the land of my birth."

## Pushed to the Breaking Point

The sense of isolation and alienation that H. Ford Douglas speaks of permeated African-American life. Therefore, public policy as embodied in discriminatory laws became one of the major issues addressed at the National Negro Conventions. The Fugitive Slave Law of 1850 is one of the best examples. It was perhaps the most significant event to happen in the antebellum period (the decades leading up to the Civil War) because it became a test of the country's ability to house two opposing and radically different viewpoints in a nation attempting to present some semblance of unity.

The Fugitive Slave Law of 1850 was aimed at keeping the country together by making certain concessions to southern slave-holding states. Frederick Douglass argued

The Fugitive Slave Law of 1850 stripped fugitives of their rights and made it easier for slave catchers to find and return escaped slaves.

in his 1881 autobiography *Life and Times of Frederick Douglass* that the Fugitive Slave Law was "designed to involve the North in complicity with slavery and deaden its moral sentiment [more] than to procure the return of fugitives to their so-called owners." The statute pitted states' laws against federal laws.

As a portion of the Compromise of 1850, the Fugitive Slave Law was an attempt to deal with the issues dividing the nation into pro- and antislavery factions. The bill was intended to amend and supplement the Fugitive Slave Law of 1793. The new law stiffened the penalties for aiding and abetting fugitives, eliminated the possibility of due process for those accused of

A SLAVE-HUNT.

> " 'What shall we do with the Negro?' I have had but one answer from the beginning. Do nothing with him. Your doing with us has already played the mischief with us. . . . If you see him on his way to school, let him alone, don't disturb him. If you see him at the dinner table at a hotel, let him go. If you see him going into the ballot box, let him alone, don't disturb him!"

—FREDERICK DOUGLASS, AT THE ANNUAL MEETING OF THE MASSACHUSETTS ANTI-SLAVERY SOCIETY AT BOSTON, APRIL 1865

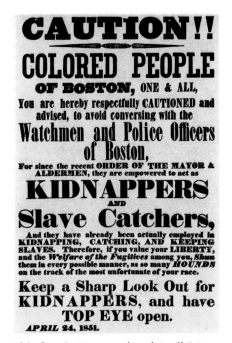

This flyer in Boston, dated April 24, 1861 (12 days after the start of the Civil War), warns the city's free blacks that they could be captured and sold into slavery.

# Frederick Douglass

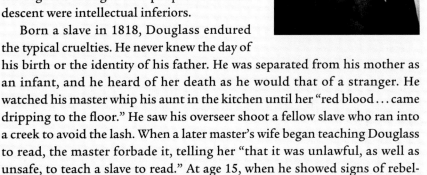

WHEN FREDERICK DOUGLASS climbed the podium to lecture on the evils of slavery, many couldn't believe that he himself had been reared in the "peculiar institution." He spoke of the slaves' ignorance and debasement, yet he appeared to be an intelligent man, dignified in bearing and wise in argument. His eloquent book *Narrative of the Life of Frederick Douglass* (1845) repudiated the bigoted thought that people of African descent were intellectual inferiors.

Born a slave in 1818, Douglass endured the typical cruelties. He never knew the day of his birth or the identity of his father. He was separated from his mother as an infant, and he heard of her death as he would that of a stranger. He watched his master whip his aunt in the kitchen until her "red blood . . . came dripping to the floor." He saw his overseer shoot a fellow slave who ran into a creek to avoid the lash. When a later master's wife began teaching Douglass to read, the master forbade it, telling her "that it was unlawful, as well as unsafe, to teach a slave to read." At age 15, when he showed signs of rebelliousness, his master sent him to a farm to be "broken."

Despite the ravages, Douglass did learn to read and write, and he escaped in 1838. His talents led him to the abolitionist movement. He pressed the antislavery cause and backed Abraham Lincoln's presidency. With General Lee's surrender, Douglass entered federal politics, working first as U.S. marshal for the District of Columbia and then in the diplomatic service—all the while protesting the failings of Reconstruction and the rise of Jim Crow. When Douglass died in 1895, he was hailed as one of the great moral voices of the 19th century.

being fugitives, and forbade the testimony of any African claimed as a fugitive in his or her own defense. The law also made it a federal crime for any citizen to refuse to aid in the recapture of a fugitive slave, gave broad police powers to marshals and fugitive slave commissioners, and made the return of fugitives a lucrative business. The law allowed any claimant of a fugitive to place him or her in custody without a warrant, jury trial, or hearing.

Naturally, attempts by slaveholders to recapture fugitives increased. Because no safeguards existed, many free blacks were kidnapped and sold into slavery. Just as naturally, the African community reacted with outrage. They saw it as an effort to cement the institution of slavery, and they knew that the federal government had abandoned them. African leaders spoke out furiously and forcefully.

# Early Struggle

## 1865–1870

**Mid- to late 1865:** Legislatures in former Confederate states enact "black codes." Examples: freedmen cannot rent land, serve on juries, bear arms, assemble except for religious purposes, drink alcohol, travel, or learn to read.

**1866:** The Ku Klux Klan is formed in Pulaski, Tennessee. Members will unleash violence on African-Americans and those involved in or sympathetic to Reconstruction.

**April 9, 1866:** Congress overrides President Andrew Johnson's veto and passes the Civil Rights Act. It grants full citizenship and equal rights to all people born in the United States, excluding Native Americans.

**May 1, 1866:** Resentful of the recent influx of freedmen in the city, white policemen in Memphis instigate a race riot that leaves more than 40 people dead.

**March 2, 1867:** Congress passes the Reconstruction Act over President Johnson's veto. It calls for new constitutions in each state, with freed male slaves being allowed to vote.

**July 9, 1868:** The 14th Amendment to the Constitution is ratified. It grants full citizenship to all people born or naturalized in the United States, except Native Americans. *See* April 14, 1873.

**September 18, 1868:** During a Republican march through Camilla, Georgia, heavily armed whites fire on black marchers, killing at least 12 and wounding more than 40.

**February 3, 1870:** The 15th Amendment to the Constitution is ratified, guaranteeing voting rights to all adult male citizens. The rights cannot be "denied or abridged . . . on account of race, color, or previous condition of servitude." *See* 1876. ➤

On August 22–23, 1831, Nat Turner and a band of at least 60 slaves murdered 57 white people. The rebellion, the largest in the South's history, frightened white Southerners and led to stricter slave laws.

Organizations, such as vigilance committees, were founded or expanded—in Canada as well as the United States.

The October 1850 issue of *The Impartial Citizen*, an African-American paper based in Boston, stated: "Now, this bill strips us of all manner of protection. . . . But while it does this, it throws us back upon the natural and inalienable right of self-defence—self-protection. It solemnly refers to each of us, individually, the question, whether we will submit to being enslaved by the hyenas which this law creates and encourages, or whether we will protect ourselves, even if, in so doing, we have to peril our lives, and more than peril the useless and devilish carcasses of Negro-catchers. It gives us the alternative of dying freemen, or living slaves. Let the men who would execute this bill beware. . . . Let them know that to enlist in that warfare is present, certain, inevitable death and damnation."

The Fugitive Slave Law did not stop Africans from fleeing bondage or contesting efforts to disenfranchise and enslave them. The law, in fact, increased resistance. For some blacks, it was the final straw. Many Africans fled the United States for Canada and the Caribbean. They fled even from "free" states, because Africans, in bondage and free, recognized that the Fugitive Slave Law made their situation in the United States very precarious.

Another ruling that excited much protest and agitation was the landmark 1857 *Dred Scott* decision. The U.S. Supreme Court ruled that Africans in the United States were not citizens because—the court interpreted—the Founding Fathers had not thought of Africans in the colonies as citizens when they drafted the Constitution. Therefore, stated Chief Supreme Court Justice Roger B. Taney, Africans "had no rights which the white man was bound to respect."

Frederick Douglass was among those who challenged the *Dred Scott* decision, making it clear that he and other Africans were close to the point of discarding passive resistance. Speaking a few months after the decision, he stated to the American Abolition Society: "The limits of tyrants are prescribed by the endurance of those whom they oppress.... If we ever get free from the oppressions and wrongs heaped upon us, we must pay for their removal. We must do this by labor, by suffering, by sacrifice, and if needs be, by our lives and the lives of others."

# Dred Scott v. Sandford

BEFORE THE CIVIL WAR, few events inflamed the antislavery movement more than the *Dred Scott* case. Scott was born a slave in Virginia around 1800. When his master took him to Illinois and Minnesota, Scott filed a lawsuit claiming that residence in free jurisdictions effectively freed him and his family. Many slaves had filed similar suits and won, but with the slavery question becoming a national strain, the Missouri Supreme Court denied Scott's claim. The *Dred Scott v. Sandford* case reached the U.S. Supreme Court in 1856 and was decided the following year.

Chief Justice Roger B. Taney's opinion boiled down to one question: Are persons of African descent counted as citizens under the Constitution? "We think they are not," he answered, for when the Constitution was adopted, neither slaves nor their dependents, "whether they had become free or not, were then acknowledged as a part of the people." The Founding Fathers, Taney said, considered African-Americans "beings of an inferior order...so far inferior, that they had no rights which the white man was bound to respect."

The court ruled against Scott 7–2, and the nation edged closer to civil war. Many historians consider it the worst decision ever handed down by the Supreme Court.

In July 1839 captive Africans took over the Spanish slave ship *Amistad*. Waylaid by the U.S. Navy, the "mutineers" were granted their freedom by the U.S. Supreme Court in 1841.

# Early Struggle

**1870:** Tennessee passes the first "Jim Crow" (segregation) law. It mandates the separation of black and white riders on trains.

**February 21, 1870:** Hiram R. Revels becomes the first African-American to join the U.S. Senate, as he's selected by the Mississippi legislature to replace Jefferson Davis.

**December 12, 1870:** Joseph H. Rainey of South Carolina becomes the first African-American member of the U.S. House of Representatives.

**1870–71:** Congress enacts the Enforcement Acts, which are intended to help black Americans achieve the rights granted them in the 14th and 15th amendments. It gives the president the authorization to use military force against those who attempt to deny black citizens their rights. *See* January 22, 1883.

**May 1872:** Congress passes the Amnesty Act, which allows former Confederates to resume political activity.

**June 10, 1872:** The Freedman's Bureau is closed by the federal government.

**December 9, 1872:** In Louisiana, Governor Henry Clay Warmouth is impeached and replaced by Lieutenant Governor P.B.S. Pinchback, who thus becomes the first black governor in the U.S.

**April 1873:** White supremacists murder dozens of black citizens in Colfax, Louisiana.

**April 14, 1873:** The U.S. Supreme Court rules that the 14th Amendment covers only those rights received under federal—not state—citizenship.

**March 1, 1875:** Congress passes the Civil Rights Act of 1875. It prohibits discrimination in such public accommodations as restaurants, hotels, and theaters. *See* October 15, 1883.➤

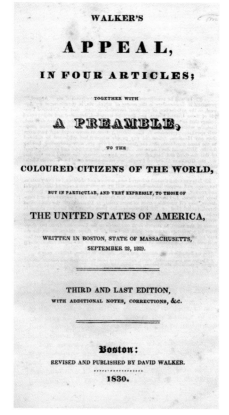

WALKER'S

# APPEAL,

IN FOUR ARTICLES;

TOGETHER WITH

## A PREAMBLE,

TO THE

### COLOURED CITIZENS OF THE WORLD,

BUT IN PARTICULAR, AND VERY EXPRESSLY, TO THOSE OF

### THE UNITED STATES OF AMERICA,

WRITTEN IN BOSTON, STATE OF MASSACHUSETTS,
SEPTEMBER 28, 1829.

THIRD AND LAST EDITION,
WITH ADDITIONAL NOTES, CORRECTIONS, &c.

**Boston:**
REVISED AND PUBLISHED BY DAVID WALKER.
**1830.**

David Walker, a free black in Boston, urged slaves to revolt in his 1829 *Appeal,* which circulated throughout the South. Walker was found dead, likely murdered, the following year.

Protest, agitation, and the National Negro Conventions gave rise to the African-American press. The proceedings of the conventions and messages of protest and resistance were widely disseminated through black and abolitionist newspapers. John Russwurm and Samuel Cornish started the first black newspaper, *Freedom's Journal,* in 1827. It was owned and operated by African-Americans and was directed to black readers. The purpose of the newspaper, and for all African-American newspapers that followed, was stated in the first issue: "We wish to plead our own cause. Too long have others spoken for us. Too long has the public been deceived by misrepresentations."

The black press was accustomed to disputing white allegations of black inferiority. In refutation, black writers and speakers pointed to the primacy of ancient Africa. In 1850 Samuel Ringgold Ward, at an annual meeting of the American and Foreign Anti-Slavery Society in New York, alleged that whites engaged in the "falsification of history" for the purpose of concealing the merits of blacks. C. V. Caples, an educator, had enumerated those merits in 1836 at a New England Anti-Slavery Convention in Boston. "What built up Athens?" Caples aksed. "What extended Rome? The learning and arts which came from colored men. Who built the pyramids? Colored men. Who humbled Rome itself? Hannibal, a colored man."

David Walker used his pen to produce one of the most inflammatory antislavery documents ever written. Walker, a black shopkeeper from Boston, published a pamphlet, *Appeal to the Coloured Citizens of the World,* in 1829 that exhorted enslaved Africans to armed resistance. "Kill, or be killed," he told them. "The man who would not fight…in the glorious and heavenly cause of freedom…to be delivered from the most wretched, abject and servile slavery…ought to be kept with all his children or family, in slavery, or in chains, to be

Harriet Tubman, an escaped slave, became the most prolific "conductor" of the Underground Railroad, leading more than 200 slaves to freedom.

butchered by his cruel enemies." Walker attacked the hypocrisy of America, "this Republican Land of Liberty" that, he pointed out, benefited from the enslavement of Africans. Walker characterized whites as "unjust, jealous, unmerciful, avaricious and blood-thirsty . . . always seeking after power and authority."

Walker's *Appeal* was widely distributed, even in the South. Many historians speculate that the pamphlet incited Nat Turner's uprising in 1831. White reaction to the pamphlet was as negative and as brutal as expected, given white fear of revolts. Georgia offered a reward for Walker's capture of $10,000 alive and $1,000 dead. Walker was

found dead on the street near his home in 1830. Cause of death was undetermined, although poison was suspected.

Africans banded together in self-help organizations designed to make themselves secure in a hostile nation. In 1787, the year that the U.S. Constitution was written, several African groups were formed, including the Philadelphia Free African Society and the African Masonic Lodge. The organizations strove to attain rights for African-Americans, foster race pride, and provide moral and financial support for each other. Other organizations were established to carry on self-help activities, among them: the African Association for Mutual Relief, the Sons of Africa Society, the Daughters of Africa, and the African Education and Benevolent Society. Schools, churches, and

lodges were established. Forming separate organizations allowed Africans to band together to speak with one voice, collectively, in the struggle for the abolition of slavery, for constitutional enfranchisement, and for inclusion into the American social order. The organized efforts of African-Americans helped them succeed in attaining civil rights, however limited.

During the antebellum period, Africans were also active in the Underground Railroad (a secret network that led runaway slaves in the South to freedom in the North) and other antislavery activities. They often used established organizations to press for the abolition of slavery. Many Africans were on the speaker's circuit for white abolitionist associations, including Frederick Douglass, Sojourner Truth, Robert Purvis, Frances Ellen

The Underground Railroad was a secret network of people, routes, and modes of transportation that led thousands of slaves to freedom in the North and Canada.

Harriet Beecher Stowe's *Uncle Tom's Cabin* (1852), the top-selling novel of the 19th century, elicited worldwide sympathy for the plight of American slaves.

In 1859 abolitionist John Brown led a 22-man raid of a federal armory in Harper's Ferry, Virginia, hoping to incite a large-scale slave rebellion. He failed, but died a martyr.

Watkins Harper, William Wells Brown, and Harriet Tubman. A number of the African speakers were refugees who had self-liberated and could speak directly to the reality of black resistance. Often they had to wage a crusade against discrimination even within those organizations.

Frederick Douglass carried on one of the most visible battles, criticizing antislavery whites for their paternalism. After some whites in William Lloyd Garrison's organization complained that Douglass was too independent and caused problems, he declared that he was not going to allow himself to be led by whites. He was firmly out of the Garrison camp when he declared in the summer of 1857: "Your humble speaker has been branded as an ingrate, because he has ventured to stand up on his own right, and to plead our common cause as a colored man, rather than as a Garrisonian. I hold it to be no part of gratitude to allow our white friends to do all the work, while we merely hold their coats."

Revolts and rebellions were other means Africans used to resist oppression in the era before the Civil War. Major insurrections were led by Gabriel Prosser in 1800 in Virginia, Charles Deslandes in 1811 in Louisiana, Denmark Vesey in 1822 in South Carolina, Cinque in 1839 aboard the slave ship *Amistad*, Nat Turner in 1831 in Virginia, William Parker in 1851 in Pennsylvania, and John Brown in 1859 on the federal arsenal in Harper's Ferry, Virginia. Whites consistently feared armed revolt. Despite the depiction throughout white culture of a docile, passive "Sambo" who was happy in enslavement, defiance was always assumed and anticipated. Thomas Jefferson asserted that this resistance was to be expected because of "the insurrectionary spirit of the slaves." He envisioned a huge conflagration that would be "easily quelled in its first efforts; but from being local it will become general, and whenever it does it will rise more formidable after every defeat, until we shall be forced, after dreadful scenes & sufferings to release them [enslaved Africans] in their own way."

### Brief Glimpse of Freedom

The Civil War became the next great testing ground for African-Americans. Frederick Douglass, like so many other African-Americans, saw the war and black participation as a means of ending slavery and of ensuring full citizenship for African-Americans. He wrote in a March 1863 broadside entitled *Men of Color, To Arms!*: "I urge you to fly to arms, and smite with death the

Many northern blacks volunteered to serve in the Union Army and Navy to help win freedom for their southern brothers and sisters. In all, more than 200,000 African-Americans fought for the Union.

power that would bury the government and your liberty in the same hopeless grave.... [F]our millions of our brothers and sisters shall march out into liberty. The chance is now given you to end in a day the bondage of centuries, and to rise in one bound from social degradation to the plane of common equality with all other varieties of men."

During the Civil War, approximately 186,000 Africans served in the Union Army and 18,000 served in the Union Navy. Despite their valuable and valorous service, African-American troops suffered discrimination. The poor treatment of black soldiers reflected the widespread racist attitudes about black people. They were at first considered laborers instead of soldiers

# Emancipation Proclamation

ON MONDAY, SEPTEMBER 22, 1862, President Abraham Lincoln summoned his Cabinet to the Executive Mansion. The Battle of Antietam was over, General Lee's army had retreated across the Potomac, and wounded soldiers filled the halls of the Capitol. "I have, as you are aware, thought a great deal about the relation of this war to slavery," Lincoln told his Cabinet members. Since the war started, he had believed that the Union cause eventually would be linked to emancipation. "I think the time has come now," he said.

Lincoln read a draft of what he called "A Proclamation." Some Cabinet members suggested revisions, while others warned of political fallout in the upcoming election. Lincoln adopted the changes but rejected the politics. The next day newspapers across the country printed the statement in full. It stated: "I do order and declare that all persons held as slaves within said designated States, and parts of States, are, and henceforward shall be free."

The areas "designated" were only those still in rebellion. Elsewhere, slavery would remain, although everybody seemed to understand that the Proclamation would signal the end to slavery everywhere should the Union triumph. The seventh paragraph asked freed slaves "to abstain from all violence," advising that they labor "faithfully for reasonable wages." Moreover, they "will be received into the armed service of the United States."

As the new year approached, runaway slaves poured into General Grant's headquarters in Vicksburg. Meanwhile, Midwesterners feared a mass exodus of blacks northward, and Southerners anticipated a slave rebellion at home. Whatever the objections, however, the Emancipation Proclamation gave the Union a moral sanction and signaled the end of legal bondage in the United States. Months later, Lincoln donated his manuscript copy of the Proclamation to a delegation of women raising funds for wounded veterans. The paper disappeared in the Chicago Fire of 1871.

# Early Struggle

**1876:** In *United States v. Reese*, the U.S. Supreme Court rules that the 15th Amendment does not guarantee citizens the right to vote. It lists the grounds impermissible for denying the vote, which indirectly gives southern states ways to disfranchise black voters.

**March 2, 1877:** Presidential candidate Rutherford B. Hayes wins the election after promising southern leaders that he'll withdraw federal troops in the South. *See* April 24, 1877.

**March 18, 1877:** Frederick Douglass is confirmed as United States marshal for the District of Columbia.

**April 24, 1877:** The last federal troops leave the South, ending the Reconstruction Era. Southern black citizens are now at the mercy of local and state governments and law enforcement.

**1878:** In *Hall v. Decuir*, the U.S. Supreme Court rules that states cannot prohibit segregation on interstate public transportation.

**October 1879:** In *Strauder v. West Virginia*, the U.S. Supreme Court holds that a state cannot exclude black citizens from jury service or deny them any right of citizenship simply because of their race.

**1881:** Tennessee passes a law requiring railroad companies to furnish separate cars for black passengers. Other southern states will pass similar segregation laws throughout the decade.

**July 4, 1881:** In Tuskegee, Alabama, Booker T. Washington opens the Normal School for Colored Teachers, which will become the top vocational school for black Americans. ➤

"Whenever I hear anyone arguing for slavery, I feel a strong impulse to see it tried on him personally."

—Abraham Lincoln

and thus were assigned to the most menial, backbreaking work, such as digging ditches and collecting dead bodies. Until late in 1864, Africans received inferior equipment, guns, food, clothing, and medical care—and less money.

Some African-American soldiers protested against their unequal treatment. In 1864 Sergeant William Walker, formerly enslaved, of the Third South Carolina Volunteers led his company in a protest against the inequities in the Union Army. He was court-martialed and executed. Other black soldiers who protested their treatment were shot or jailed.

This state of affairs could only exist because of the white Union's ambivalent attitude about African-Americans. Abraham Lincoln had expressed this ambivalence during his 1858 presidential campaign against Stephen Douglas when he contended: "I have no purpose directly or indirectly, to interfere with the institution of slavery in the states where it exists.... I have no disposition to introduce political and social equality between the white and black races. There is a physical difference between the two, which in my judgment will probably forever forbid their living together on terms of respect, social and political equality, and inasmuch as it becomes a necessity that there must be a superiority somewhere, I... am in favor of the race to which I belong having the superior position." Although he became known as the Great Emancipator, Lincoln never reconciled his racial ambivalence. He had supported the American Colonization Society,

The Reconstruction Act (1867) and 15th Amendment (1870) guaranteed the right to vote to male African-Americans. However, an 1876 U.S. Supreme Court ruling opened the door for disenfranchisement.

and after the Civil War he urged the expatriation of Africans out of the United States.

The Union's victory in the Civil War caused great rejoicing in the black community. The passage of the 13th, 14th, and 15th amendments to the Constitution—which abolished slavery and entitled African-Americans to citizenship and the right to vote—bolstered hopes among blacks that they would be treated as full citizens. They also were encouraged by Reconstruction, in which the Union helped rebuild the South while safeguarding the rights of and creating opportunities for southern blacks. African-Americans were allowed to vote, and they even replaced many former Confederates in public office. It was through African-American legislative efforts during Reconstruction that free public school education became available for all children, black and white, in the South. The Civil Rights Act of 1875, which prohibited discrimination in public facilities, further encouraged African-American optimism.

Reconstruction was not without its problems, however. Many whites who held racist views staffed the Freedmen's Bureau, whose mission was to ease formerly enslaved Africans into citizenship. Many of the policies put in place actually foiled black attempts at economic, social, and political independence. Discriminatory practices and sub-

# Legislating Freedom

MANY PEOPLE BELIEVE that legalized inequality in the United States ended with the Emancipation Proclamation in 1863. In fact, it took seven subsequent years of federal legislation before full rights of citizenship were enacted. However, "guarantees" of citizenship lasted only a few more years, as several U.S. Supreme Court rulings chipped away at black Americans' rights.

The Proclamation was a war measure applicable only to states in rebellion against the Union. Not until the 13th Amendment (1865) was slavery ruled illegal everywhere. The amendment stated: "Neither slavery nor involuntary servitude, except as punishment for crime...shall exist within the United States, or any place subject to their jurisdiction."

Congress then passed the Civil Rights Act of 1866, decreeing that citizens "of every race and color" enjoyed "full and equal benefit of all laws and proceedings for the security of person and property, as is enjoyed by white persons." In support came the Reconstruction Act of 1867 and the 14th Amendment in 1868. With the former, freedmen assumed the right of full participation in the political life of the South, with the protection of federal troops.

The 14th Amendment was a correction of the *Dred Scott* case (1857), in which the U.S. Supreme Court held that no persons of African descent could ever claim citizenship. It countered: "All persons born or naturalized in the United States, and subject to the jurisdiction thereof, are citizens of the United States and of the State wherein they reside." To keep the states from enacting local legislation against the Civil Rights Act, the 14th Amendment insisted on "due process of law" and "equal protection of the laws."

The 15th Amendment was passed in 1870. It stated: "The right of citizens of the United States to vote shall not be denied...on account of race, color, or previous condition of servitude."

The U.S. Supreme Court, however, was not as eager to guarantee full citizenship. In 1876 it listed the grounds impermissible for denying the vote (indirectly offering ways to deny it), and in 1890 it determined that presidential elections fell under the jurisdiction of states. Moreover, it ruled in 1883 that while states could not discriminate against blacks, individuals were not under the same obligation. The doors of discrimination were now open.

sequent laws effectively placed freedpeople into a pseudoslavery.

## The Bottom Falls Out

One of the most destructive measures that the Freedmen's Bureau introduced was the practice of forced labor. The bureau passed a regulation stating that if a black man refused to sign a contract and accept a job, he would be forced to work for no pay. White employers immediately seized upon this regulation to abuse African-Americans who just had been emancipated from enslavement. The sharecropping and the convict labor systems were used to exploit the labor of African-Americans. The convict labor system allowed white planters

# Early Struggle

## 1883–1890

**January 22, 1883:** The U.S. Supreme Court rules that aspects of the Enforcement Acts of 1870–71 are unconstitutional. The court holds that while *states* are constitutionally bound to respect the rights of black Americans, *individuals* are not under such obligation.

**October 15, 1883:** The U.S. Supreme Court declares the Civil Rights Act of 1875, which prohibited discrimination in public accommodations, unconstitutional. It rules that while states cannot discriminate based on race, individual business owners can choose who they serve.

**1888:** Mississippi passes a law that requires segregation in railway coaches.

**1890:** In *Louisville, New Orleans and Texas Railway Company v. Mississippi*, the U.S. Supreme Court permits states to segregate public transportation facilities.

**March 24, 1890:** In *Fitzgerald v. Green*, the U.S. Supreme Court determines that the federal government has very limited jurisdiction over presidential elections, thus leaving nearly all election decisions up to the states.

**June 1890:** Congressman Henry Cabot Lodge of Massachusetts submits the "Force Bill," which would allow federal government officials to oversee elections in the South. The bill will pass through the House of Representatives but die in the Senate.

**November 1, 1890:** The new Mississippi Constitution (the Second Mississippi Plan) requires the state's citizens to pass literacy and "understanding" tests in order to vote. It is created to keep black citizens off the voting rolls. Similar statutes will be passed in other southern states from 1895 to 1910. ➤

In 1866 in Pulaski, Tennessee, Confederate veterans formed a terrorist group called the Ku Klux Klan. They were determined to fight the policies of Reconstruction and maintain "white supremacy."

to rent the labor of prisoners from the state. The laborers were not paid. Sharecroppers who protested their treatment by white landowners were charged with contract violations and jailed; the landowner could then rent his labor from the convict labor system. James Orr, the Reconstruction governor of South Carolina from 1865 to 1868, wrote President Andrew Johnson in 1865, explaining the need for forced labor laws: "The vagrant Laws are stringent but necessary…many of them will not work without the compulsion of law."

Southern whites refused to accept all of the new amendments to the Constitution. The South Carolina Democratic Party issued a plan in 1876 to prevent African-American men from exercising their right to vote. It stated: "Every Democrat must feel honor-bound to control the vote of at least one Negro, by intimidation, purchase, keeping him away or as each individual may determine, how he may best accomplish it." This racist document went on to say: "Never threaten a man individually. If he deserves to be threatened, the necessities of the times require that he should die." It is clear that these policies would not have succeeded without the cooperation of white authorities, because they were blatantly illegal and criminal.

Most of the rights that blacks gained during Reconstruction were quickly lost by 1877, when the federal government pulled troops out

## A Humble Plea for a New School

L AST SPRING we built a schoolhouse and hired a white lady to teach. Friday night, February 5, our schoolhouse was burned up. We have a deed of one and a half acres but there is no timber on it and the owners of the land around have put up a paper forbidding us to cut a stick on theirs. See how tight they have got us. We want the Government or somebody to help us build. We could burn their churches and schoolhouses but we don't want to break the law or harm anybody. All we want is to live under the law.

*—Richard Reese, in a letter to the Freedmen's Bureau, 1870*

In 1873 in Colfax, Louisiana, the paramilitary group White League—which was intent on securing white rule in Louisiana—murdered about a hundred black state militiamen. Many were killed after surrendering.

of the South and abandoned African-Americans, effectively ending the Reconstruction Era. Southern whites, secure in the knowledge that the federal government would not interfere, began a systematic abridgement of African-American rights. Enacted on the basis of states' rights, "Jim Crow" laws legislated segregation and other discriminatory practices, such as poll taxes, grandfather clauses, literacy tests, vagrancy laws, property requirements, voting fraud, intimidation at polling places, and whites-only primaries. Education was separate, unequal, and, sometimes nonexistent for African-Americans.

The U.S. Supreme Court ruled in 1883 that the public accommodation portion of the 1875 Civil Rights Act, which had guaranteed nondiscrimination in public facilities, was unconstitutional, thereby allowing individual states to institute segregated facilities. In 1890 Mississippi revised its constitution with the publicly expressed goal of completely disenfranchising black Americans in their state: "The policy of crushing out the manhood of the Negro citizens is to be carried on to success." It was a policy they and other southern states carried out assiduously.

Like the *Dred Scott* decision, the 1896 *Plessy v. Ferguson* decision equated white public opinion with public policy. The United States Supreme Court ruled, eight to one, the legality of "separate but equal" facilities—everything from schools (one for whites, one for blacks) to streetcars (white section, black section). Segregation would be the law of the land, especially in the South, for decades to come.

Naturally, African-Americans protested the imposition of Jim Crow laws. They attempted to use the legal system by bringing civil rights cases before the courts. They agitated in the press and from the pulpit, they revolted, and they called for emigration. One of the major migrations away from the South occurred from 1879 to 1881, as more than 25,000 African-Americans migrated to and purchased

This illustration's original caption reads: "Of course he wants to vote the Democratic ticket!" "You're as free as air, ain't you! Say you are, or I'll blow your black head off!"

# Early Struggle

## 1895–1899

**1895:** Ida B. Wells–Barnett, a crusader against Jim Crow laws and lynching, publishes *A Red Record*, a statistical report on lynching.

**September 18, 1895:** Booker T. Washington emerges as a national black leader after his "Atlanta Compromise" speech, in which he urges African-Americans to accept segregation and strive for economic improvement.

**1896:** The National Association of Colored Women is formed, with Mary Eliza Church Terrell as president.

**May 18, 1896:** In *Plessy v. Ferguson*, the U.S. Supreme Court rules that it is constitutional for governments to maintain separate facilities for black and white citizens as long as the facilities are "equal."

**May 12, 1898:** Louisiana becomes the first of several southern states to adopt a "grandfather clause." This makes male citizens exempt from paying a poll tax and passing a literacy test in order to vote if their fathers or grandfathers were eligible to vote before January 1, 1867. The clause is meant to keep blacks off the voting rolls. *See* June 21, 1915.

**November 1898:** White citizens of Wilmington, North Carolina, incensed over the political power of local black citizens, incite a riot. Between seven and 30 African-Americans are killed.

**April 1899:** Sam Hose, a black Georgian who allegedly killed a white farmer, is burned alive. Local whites struggle for chunks of his flesh to take home as souvenirs.

**December 18, 1899:** The U.S. Supreme Court rules in *Cumming v. School Board of Richmond County, Georgia* that a city can provide a high school for white students even if it does not provide one for black students.

land in Kansas. Calling themselves Exodusters, they were led by Benjamin "Pap" Singleton, a former slave who had fled to Canada before the Civil War. Like the Jews leaving Egypt in biblical times, the Exodusters considered themselves to be making an exodus out of bondage.

African-Americans established several all-black towns in the West during this period, including Boley and Langston, Oklahoma, and Nicodemus, Kansas. Sojourner Truth, the passionate abolitionist and suffragette, campaigned for land to be given in the West to freedpeople. She pleaded in 1871: "I am urging the people to sign petitions to Congress to have a grant of land set apart for the freed people to earn their living on.... Instead of sending these people to Liberia, why can't they have a colony in the West?" Truth was alluding to the colonization plans that were being proposed by many white leaders and to the land grants in the West that were being handed out by the government to white settlers and railroads.

After serving as a chaplain to black troops during the Civil War, Bishop Henry McNeal Turner was elected to the Georgia House of Representatives in 1868. The white congressmen refused to seat him or the other 20-plus African-American representatives and two black senators. Bishop Turner addressed the men who had refused him a seat:

Southern states began passing segregation laws in the 1880s. African-Americans were confined to the "colored" sections of railway coaches (*pictured*) and numerous other public facilities, marking the beginning of the "Jim Crow" era.

"Whose Legislature is this?... They question my right to a seat in this body, to represent the people whose legal votes elected me.... This... is an unheard of monopoly of power.... I dare to be the exponent of the views of those who sent me here.... We are told if black men want to speak, they must speak through white trumpets; if black men want their sentiments expressed, they must be adulterated and sent through white messengers, who will quibble, and equivocate, and evade.... The great question is this: Am I a man? I am such, I claim the rights of a man."

Bishop Henry McNeal Turner, who delivered a scathing address to the Georgia House of Representatives, later demanded slave reparations from the federal government.

Bishop Turner and his expelled colleagues were seated in 1869. By 1895 Turner had taken the position that African-Americans should leave the United States: "I believe that the Negroid race has been free long enough now to begin to think for himself and plan for better conditions than he can lay claim to in this country or ever will. There is no manhood future in the United States for the Negro. He may eke out an existence for generations to come, but he can never be a man—full, symmetrical and undwarfed." Turner demanded reparations for African-Americans from the U.S. government for the years of enslavement. The money was to be used to transport black Americans to Africa.

# Plessy v. Ferguson

ON JUNE 7, 1892, Homer Plessy entered a New Orleans railroad station and boarded a whites-only coach. But although he looked white, Plessy was an "octaroon" (one-eighth black) and, therefore, in violation of state law. When the conductor ordered him out, Plessy refused and was arrested.

The incident was planned. Plessy wanted to test the segregation law in the courts, claiming the law infringed upon his civil rights. When the case went to the U.S. Supreme Court, Louisiana's attorneys argued that the law required that facilities be equal—hence, no discrimination. But Plessy's lawyer, Albion Tourgee, asked the justices to imagine themselves as black men enduring such policies, then wondered: Why not require all colored people to walk on one side of the street and whites on the other?

On May 18, 1896, the Court ruled against Plessy 7–1. Segregation laws "do not necessarily imply the inferiority of either race," the majority maintained, and "community sentiment" favored separation. Justice John Harlan, the lone dissenter, offered a simple rebuttal: "Our Constitution is color-blind and neither knows nor tolerates classes among citizens." Harlan likened it to the *Dred Scott* decision (1857), predicting it would "arouse race hate" for generations. For nearly 60 years, until *Brown v. Board of Education* (1954), the separate-but-equal decision would license segregation in schools, hospitals, parks, and other public places.

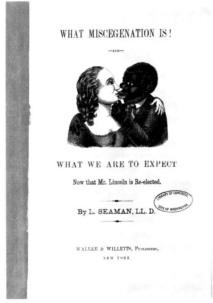

Southern whites feared miscegenation (the marriage or sexual relationship between members of different races) and inevitable "mongrel" offspring. The fear fueled the drive for strong segregation laws.

In order to maintain white supremacy in the South, whites resorted to violent means and acts of atrocity to strip African-Americans of rights. They formed such racist and terrorist hate groups as the Ku Klux Klan, Knights of the White Camellia, Knights of the White Rose, Pale Faces, White Brotherhood, and Constitutional Union Guards. Thousands of African-Americans were killed during and after Reconstruction, as lynching and mob rule became the means to control African-American resistance to oppression.

From 1882 to 1900, 1,677 African-Americans were documented as lynching victims. Lynch-

# Early Struggle

According to a Tuskegee Institute study, 3,386 African-Americans were lynched from 1882 through 1930, including 1,111 in the 1890s.

ing took many forms: castration, hanging, shooting, beating—even roasting over slow fires. Lynching was often a festive occasion for whites. Whole families came to see and rejoice at the lynching. Pictures were taken, people picnicked, and souvenirs from the lynch victim's body were prized: fingers, toes, genital organs. Newspapers announced when lynchings were going to take place, then printed articles and pictures afterward.

Ida B. Wells-Barnett, a black journalist, led the antilynching crusade. A militant activist, she stated in 1892 that a Winchester rifle should have a place of honor in every African-American home. She contended in her book *On Lynchings*: "When the white man ... knows that he runs as great a risk of biting the dust every time his Afro-American victim does, he will have greater respect for Afro-American life."

The extensive research that Wells conducted showed that alleged rape of a white woman was not the reason that most of the lynchings occurred (as whites had alleged). Rather, black men, women, and children were lynched for "misdemeanors, while others have suffered death for no offense known to the law, the causes assigned being 'mistaken identity,' 'insult,' 'bad reputation,' 'unpopularity,' 'violating contract,' 'running quarantine,' 'giving evidence,' 'frightening children by shooting at rabbits,' etc."

Wells knew firsthand that rape was rarely the reason for lynching. In 1892 three of her friends—Thomas Moss, Henry Stewart, and Calvin McDowell—were lynched in Memphis, Tennessee. The three were prosperous grocers who were viewed with jealousy by white store owners. A group of armed whites came to their store to destroy it, but the men fought back, shooting three whites. Moss, McDowell, and Stewart were arrested and jailed. A white mob hauled them out of jail, then murdered them.

Whites also engaged in campaigns to besmirch and impugn African-American intelligence, suitability for citizenship, and moral character. Blacks were stereotyped and demeaned on stage, as white actors appeared in blackface in vaudeville or minstrel shows purporting to be depicting "authentic" African-American culture. Such scholarly magazines as *Harper's* and *Scribner's* routinely referred to African-Americans as "niggers" and "darkies." Bigoted historians deliberately distorted the experience of enslavement. Stephen Foster, the famous white songmaker, blackened his face and caricatured African-Americans as he appropriated black culture in his songs: "Camptown Races," "My Old Kentucky Home," "Beautiful Dreamer," "Old Black Joe," and others. Racist social scientists used Charles Darwin's theory of evolution to allege that African-Americans were genet-

In the South, "Jim Crow" meant segregation. Originally, Jim Crow was a bumbling black character who was popular in minstrel shows in the 1800s.

A black family stands in front of a makeshift cabin near Guthrie, Oklahoma. Many southern blacks, fed up with Jim Crow, migrated to western towns.

ically inferior. White politicians called for the disenfranchisement of black citizens. Newspapers misrepresented the African-American experience. Manufacturers fashioned products with racist motifs. Advertisements showed Africans in servile and demeaning positions. Even white ministers asserted that God made Africans inferior to whites.

Into this hostile arena stepped Booker T. Washington, the founder and first president of Tuskegee Institute in Alabama, with an accommodationist doctrine. Washington said African-Americans should compromise with white supremacists by forgoing political and social rights for economic self-sufficiency. Presuming to speak for all African-Americans, he said in his 1895 "Atlanta Compromise" speech: "The wisest among my race understand that the agitation of questions of social equality is the extremest folly…." Washington used the word "privileges" instead of "rights" to describe the constitutional guarantee of civil liberties, implying that African-Americans were not ready for true citizenship. Less than 20 years after the destruction of Reconstruction, white Southerners had been successful in almost completely disenfranchising African-Americans in the South. The *Plessy v. Ferguson* decision, one year after Washington's speech, instituted legal segregation and reinforced white racist attitudes and practices.

Ironically, Washington's acquiescence to disenfranchisement did not shield him from white attack. When President Theodore Roosevelt invited him to the White House, many whites were infuriated. U.S. Senator Ben Tillman of South Carolina raged that "entertaining that nigger [would] necessitate our killing a thousand niggers in the South before they will learn their place again." A southern newspaper editor asserted, "No Southern woman with proper respect would now accept an invitation to the White House."

Washington's accommodationist philosophy, needless to say, did not sit well with many African-American leaders. W.E.B. Du Bois, William Monroe Trotter, Ida B. Wells-Barnett, and others felt that the right of African-Americans to equality in all areas was a right of citizenship. They recognized that Washington's program of self-sufficiency at the expense of civil rights depended upon the goodwill and philanthropy of whites, something that, historically, African-Americans could not count on.

Booker T. Washington's negative and debilitating legacy propelled many African-Americans to fight harder for full citizenship. As the 20th century dawned, white racist attitudes remained deeply entrenched and the color line solidified. African-Americans felt a great sense of isolation and alienation from the nation's social, economic, and political structure. White Americans continued to violently deny African-Americans their rights, and these black Americans continued to struggle for those rights. This struggle would culminate in the modern Civil Rights Movement.

# 1900-29

"Nowhere in the civilized world save the United States of America do men, possessing all civil and political power, go out in a band of 50 to 5,000 to hunt down, shoot, hang or burn to death a single individual unarmed and absolutely powerless...."

—IDA B. WELLS-BARNETT

AT THE DAWN OF THE 20TH CENTURY, most African-Americans were farmers without land. By 1900, the vast majority of black farmers were sharecroppers, bound to the soil in a downward spiral of debt and dependency. Two generations after the death of slavery, they were as securely shackled to the land as they had been before the Emancipation Proclamation.

Notable successes had occurred, to be sure. Illiteracy had declined at a dramatic rate, and a new black *bourgeoisie* emerged that would transform African-American leadership in the 20th century. But participation in skilled artisanship by blacks had abruptly declined. Civil rights had eroded. The right to vote had all but disappeared for African-Americans in the South. And segregation rigidly hemmed in individuals and institutions more than it had before the Civil War. Southern states had laws that criminalized the pettiest of behaviors and swelled jails with black Americans.

Most frightening of all was the ever-present prospect of racial violence. The southern landscape became darkened with black blood, as lynching became an effective means of white social control. Bodies bobbed up in the Bayou Teche after elections—a reminder that a "whites only" sign had been hung on the American franchise.

Many African-Americans responded by leaving the South in search of "better." While much attention has been focused on the Great Migration of the First World War (Southerners moving to northern cities), at least a dozen distinct migrations occurred from 1879 to 1920. Blacks migrated to Kansas, to Boley, Oklahoma, to the southwestern frontier. Some looked longingly at Africa.

The century began with a restlessness that would not abate. Leaders would emerge who would harness the anger, devise strategies to challenge the injustices, and create organizations. They would file lawsuits, lead marches, give voice to the voiceless, and dare to dream of a day when racial injustice would perish from the earth.

As sharecroppers, black farmers in the South worked long hours for white owners while mired in perpetual debt. Moreover, Jim Crow laws and customs denied them their rights as U.S. citizens.

But activists would have to begin at the margins, braving a constant threat of violence. The years 1900 and 1901 were scarred by several urban riots, as blacks began the century as a pariah race. One by one, the North, the Republican Party, and the Supreme Court all turned their backs. Booker T. Washington, considered the most powerful African-American leader of his time, gave aid and comfort to southern segregationists in his famed "Atlanta Address" by offering to exchange civil rights and constitutional protections for economic advancement and white paternalism.

But Washington's leadership did not go unchallenged. William Monroe Trotter, now largely forgotten, was one of the great early leaders of the Civil Rights Movement. When he launched the *Guardian* in Boston in 1901, it was the opening salvo in the war against Washington's accommodationist approach. With W.E.B. Du Bois's publication of *The Souls of Black Folk* (1903) and its blistering essay "Of Mr. Booker T. Washington and Others," the stage became set for new leadership, a second-generation abolitionism that would take up Frederick Douglass's fallen mantle of protest.

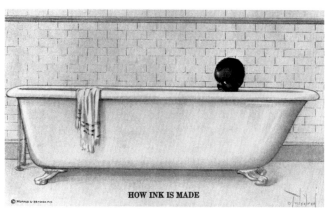

HOW INK IS MADE

This artwork was among multiple racist illustrations that adorned a calendar in the early 20th century. The image rings with the hostility that many whites had toward African-Americans during the time period, even though whites were confident that most blacks "knew their place."

Du Bois was helped, and Washington hurt, by several events that neither man could control. Blacks were put to the fire by a series of riots, including a pogrom-like attack in Atlanta (1906) and a riot in Abraham Lincoln's hometown of Springfield, Illinois (1908).

African-Americans also felt betrayed by President Theodore Roosevelt's highhanded treatment of black soldiers in Brownsville, Texas, in 1906. Roosevelt discharged the first battalion—an all-black unit—of the 25th Infantry "without honor" based merely on hearsay that the soldiers had been involved in a murder. In general, black soldiers held an iconographic place in the hearts of African-Americans. Their hopes for racial justice were wrapped up in their claim to Americanism; they often reminded white America of the contributions blacks had made by shedding their blood in defense of their country. Roosevelt's treatment of the soldiers was thus a slap in the face to all African-Americans. Moreover, Washington's reluctance to criticize Roosevelt further confirmed the suspicion of many that he no longer spoke for, nor to, the black middle-class.

Washington was correct to view the multiracial National Association for the Advancement of Colored People (NAACP), formed in 1909, as a rival and a threat. And while he had no hand in the formation of the National Urban League (NUL) two years later, he welcomed this organization, whose approach and goals were more compatible with his own. He needn't have worried about the NAACP, as that organization grew slowly. It was principally a northern organization, and 90 percent of blacks lived in the South. Its initial board of directors was all white except for Du Bois, editor of the organization's magazine, *The Crisis*. In the aftermath of the Great Migration, the NAACP could not hope to rival the mass-based, black nationalist Universal Negro Improvement Association (UNIA), led by the charismatic Marcus Garvey.

Three women sort peanuts in a factory in Chicago in 1928. During the 1920s, a million southern blacks migrated to other regions. Most traded the menial jobs and oppressive segregation of the South for factory work and small homes in congested northern cities.

The Great Migration continued through the 1920s. African-Americans swelled the contours of northern urban centers, creating northern black politics and ultimately sending to the United States House of Representatives the first black congressman from the North, Chicago's Oscar DePriest. In one sense, this was Washington's dream come true—blacks taking advantage of their disadvantage, profiting from imposed residential segregation, and creating their own political, economic, and cultural institutions within their Harlems and Bronzevilles, their Smoketowns and Nigger Hills. On the other hand, it foreshadowed the dark side of modernization: *de facto* rather than *de jure* segregation; the emergence of large, crowded, and dangerous black ghettos; overpriced housing; exploitative landlords; and the practice of "last hired, first fired." The Great Migration would changed the course of black history and transform northern American cities.

No longer the passive victims of racial violence, blacks began to fight back—especially during the Red Summer of 1919, when riots erupted in numerous cities. This "retaliatory violence," as historian August Meier called it, sent a clear signal that many black men were both emboldened and disillusioned by the Great War, in which they had risked their lives for America in Europe but were treated as second-class citizens again when they returned. Garvey's UNIA fed on this resentment, as did hundreds of smaller, local black nationalist organizations that sprang up in northern cities. However, as evidenced by the white-on-black pogroms in Elaine, Arkansas (1919), Tulsa, Oklahoma (1921), and Rosewood, Florida (1923), their anger and resolve was no match for the concerted violence of those committed to keeping blacks in their place.

When a white woman alleged in 1923 that a black man from Rosewood, Florida, had raped her, a white mob converged on the predominantly black town. The mob killed African-Americans, set fire to homes, and drove all black residents out of town.

## 1900–1906

**1900:** The U.S. Supreme Court OKs the segregation of railcars in interstate travel even if the trains pass through states in which segregation is illegal.

**July 1900:** After a black man allegedly shoots and wounds two policemen in New Orleans, a white mob instigates a bloody riot.

**March 4, 1901:** U.S. Congressman (and former slave) George H. White of North Carolina gives up his seat. No African-American will serve in Congress for the next 28 years.

**October 16, 1901:** President Theodore Roosevelt invites black leader Booker T. Washington to dine at the White House, stirring controversy throughout the South.

**November 1901:** William Monroe Trotter and George Washington Forbes found the newspaper *Guardian*, which aggressively challenges Booker T. Washington's philosophy of accommodation.

**1903:** *The Souls of Black Folk*, by W.E.B. Du Bois, is published.

**1905:** In Nashville, black citizens boycott the city's newly segregated streetcars.

**May 6, 1905:** Robert Sengstacke Abbott establishes *The Chicago Defender*, a seminal urban black newspaper.

**July 11–14, 1905:** William Monroe Trotter, W.E.B. Du Bois, and 27 others create the Niagara Movement, which will agitate for black civil rights.

**1906:** Frances A. Kellor founds the National League for the Protection of Colored Women to aid black women emigrating from the South.

**September 22–26, 1906:** Atlanta police allow white mobs to rampage in and around the city. The mobs murder 25 black citizens. ➤

The central idea behind Jim Crow—that African-Americans should be separated from whites because they were genetically inferior—was perpetuated by racist books. This one, Charles Carroll's *The Negro a Beast; or In the Image of God*, was published by the American Book and Bible House of St. Louis in 1900. Carroll wrote that people of African descent were inhuman and didn't have souls. The book used both biblical text and "forbidden" sexual imagery to support its statements.

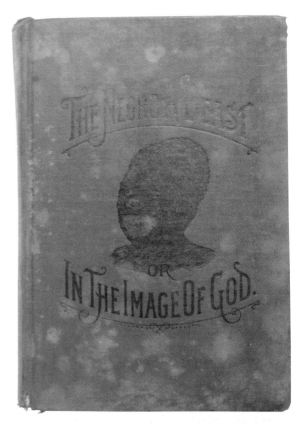

DINNER GIVEN AT THE WHITE HOUSE BY PRESIDENT ROOSEVELT TO BOOKER T. WASHINGTON, OCTOBER 16TH, 1901

Booker T. Washington, the educator who taught self-sufficiency to African-Americans in the post-Reconstruction era, was an unofficial adviser on black affairs to several presidents, including Theodore Roosevelt. Roosevelt invited Washington to dinner in 1901, an act that infuriated many whites. *The Memphis Scimitar* called the event "the most damnable outrage that has ever been perpetrated by any citizen of the United States." Roosevelt, who had spoken out against lynching and appointed African-Americans to government posts, never invited Washington back to the White House.

# Booker T. Washington

FOR 25 YEARS, Booker T. Washington was the focal point of African-American issues in the United States. An educator of black youth, a presidential advisor, and a backroom politician, Washington (born in 1856) towered over the age. His network of devotees and operatives—the so-called "Tuskegee Machine"—spread the gospel of hard work and economic advancement.

Washington's philosophy was simple. At a time when civil rights were disappearing, lynchings rising, and fiscal crises constant, he felt that blacks should strive for economic independence and forsake political agitation. Washington urged blacks to learn a skill, buy property, let segregation be, and not worry about the franchise. If the race is to gain respect, he reasoned, it must first achieve economic power.

The message propelled Washington to fame, and his orations drew thousands. Reporters tracked his movements and quoted him, and politicians solicited his advice and support. He testified before Congress and dined at the White House. President Theodore Roosevelt consulted him on federal appointments, and Harvard granted him an honorary degree.

White philanthropists such as Andrew Carnegie regarded Tuskegee Institute, founded by Washington in 1881, as a noble experiment in African-American uplift. White racists thought Washington's vision raised dangerous ambitions in the minds of ordinary blacks, but white businessmen believed that his Protestant work ethic ensured a class of industrious laborers and consumers from whom they could profit. Black citizens regarded him as the race's best hope.

As the years passed, however, black leaders began to think Washington was too conciliatory, too quick to rationalize injustice. W.E.B. Du Bois, William Monroe Trotter, and others demanded immediate political action—voting drives, militant publications, and higher education (not Washington's vocational training). They attacked Washington in the press, and he employed spies to undermine them.

Whether his accommodationist outlook was a strategy to strengthen black power for future action, a strategy for self-aggrandizement, or an expression of timidity, Washington gradually lost influence. By the time of his death in 1915, the "radicals" were in the ascent.

You can plainly see how miserable I am.

In the early decades of the 20th century, racist images adorned a wide variety of products, including postcards, as many whites indulged in the ridicule of African-Americans. This postcard, printed in 1908, portrays a black man as a layabout who lacks drive and ambition. The character chomps on a watermelon, the classic symbol of black indolence. In some minstrel shows, blacks would steal watermelons, since thievery also was considered an African-American characteristic.

# 1900-29

"We want full manhood suffrage and we want it now. . . . We want discrimination in public accommodation to cease. . . . We want the Constitution of the country enforced. . . . We are men! We will be treated as men. And we shall win!"

—W.E.B. Du Bois, on the goals of the Niagara Movement, 1906

In 1905 W.E.B. Du Bois (*middle row, second from right*) invited "race men" of different professions to Niagara Falls in Canada to create the Niagara Movement, of which many prominent members would later form the National Association for the Advancement of Colored People (NAACP). To Du Bois's right is J. Max Barber, who used his *Voice of the Negro* periodical as the unofficial newspaper for the Niagara Movement. Alonzo Herndon (*top row, second from left*) was a successful businessman who brought his young son, Norris (*pictured*). For activists such as lawyer Frederick McGhee (*middle row, far left*), an alternative to Booker T. Washington's accommodationist policies needed to be found. These were the people who would do just that.

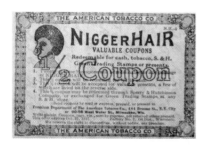

Stereotypical images of African-Americans could be found on many products in the early 20th century. The American Tobacco Company's Premium Department distributed this "Nigger Hair" coupon. Many marketers encouraged the use of black stereotypes, feeling that the provocative images would draw attention to the products. Of course, the images often offended people. The American Tobacco Company eventually changed "Nigger Hair" to "Bigger Hair."

The NAACP, as a whole, was not overly enthusiastic about the idea. But W.E.B. Du Bois understood that a magazine—a journal of news, opinion, and analysis—would serve the cause of African-Americans by introducing black people to the world as well as to themselves. Du Bois, the NAACP's director of publicity and research, scrabbled together a budget and a staff and began publishing *The Crisis* in 1910, only a year after the NAACP was organized. Under his 24-year tenure as editor-in-chief, the monthly magazine was the leading journal of African-American thought and a national forum for Du Bois and the NAACP.

# The NAACP

O N FEBRUARY 12, 1909, the 100th anniversary of President Abraham Lincoln's birth, the National Negro Conference issued a call for a national meeting to discuss racial justice. The initial stimulus for this action had been a race riot in Springfield, Illinois, in 1908, in which eight African-Americans had died and the black section of Springfield was destroyed. The National Association for the Advancement of Colored People (NAACP) grew out of that 1909 meeting. Its purpose was to "secure for all people the rights guaranteed in the 13th, 14th, and 15th amendments to the United States Constitution, which promised an end to slavery, the equal protection of the law, and universal adult male suffrage."

The NAACP was a membership organization that depended on dues and largely white philanthropy for its operating expenses. With its funds, NAACP members fought discrimination on all fronts. One of its earliest campaigns, in 1910, was an unsuccessful legal effort in support of a black farmhand named Pink Franklin, who inadvertently killed a police officer in self-defense when the officer broke into his home at 3 A.M. to arrest him on a civil charge. In 1915 the NAACP led the nationwide protest campaign against D. W. Griffith's silent film *The Birth of a Nation*, which glorified the Ku Klux Klan. For years, the organization waged a concerted battle against lynching, armed with statistics gathered by the intrepid Ida B. Wells-Barnett, a founder and board member of the NAACP. By the late 1920s, the antilynching campaign had been largely successful.

In the 1930s the NAACP decided to devote its major resources to overturning *Plessy v. Ferguson*, starting with school segregation. It established a separate legal arm, the NAACP Legal Defense Fund. In a well-executed drive, the NAACP fought in the courts for access to state colleges for black students, equal pay for black teachers, equal financial support of black schools, and finally the elimination of "separate but equal" education.

W.E.B. Du Bois was among the towering personalities of the Civil Rights Movement associated with the NAACP. Du Bois was the intellectual force in the organization's early years and the founder and editor of its journal, *The Crisis*. Many of the NAACP's executive directors became household names, including James Weldon Johnson, Walter White, and Roy Wilkins. Medgar Evers, one of the Civil Rights Movement's most beloved martyrs, was an NAACP field secretary in Mississippi. Attorneys Charles Houston and Thurgood Marshall were the leaders of the NAACP Legal Defense Fund. Marshall was the lead counsel in the landmark *Brown v. Board of Education* case in 1954, which ruled that "separate but equal" school systems were unconstitutional.

The NAACP's membership grew from about 9,000 in 1917 to 90,000 by 1919.

In the post-*Brown* era, the NAACP yielded influence to such activist grassroots organizations as the Southern Christian Leadership Conference (SCLC) and the Student Nonviolent Coordinating Committee (SNCC), which spearheaded the direct-action Civil Rights Movement in the South. Nevertheless, the NAACP actively participated in Movement activities. In later years, the organization survived the militant post-Movement era as well as its own internal political struggles. The NAACP reemerged in the late 20th and early 21st centuries with a platform devoted to voting rights and economic issues. Today, the NAACP is revered as the longest-lasting and most successful civil rights organization in American history.

## 1908–1914

**August 14–16, 1908:** In Springfield, Illinois, a rampaging white mob kills eight local black citizens, injures 70, and forces 2,000 blacks to flee the city. Appalled by the violence, writer William English Walling calls for citizens to come together and fight for racial equality. *See* February 12, 1909.

**November 9, 1908:** The U.S. Supreme Court rules against Berea College, a privately chartered institution, which teaches students of both races despite a Kentucky law that mandates segregation.

**February 12, 1909:** A multiracial group of activists forms the National Negro Committee, which will be renamed the National Association for the Advancement of Colored People (NAACP). Founders include W.E.B. Du Bois, Mary White Ovington, Henry Moscowitz, Oswald Garrison Villiard, William English Walling, and Ida B. Wells-Barnett.

**1910:** The NAACP fights its first legal case. It represents Pink Franklin, who claims his shooting of a white policeman—who broke into his home at 3 A.M.—was in self-defense.

**November 1910:** The NAACP publishes the first issue of the journal *The Crisis*.

**October 1911:** The National Urban League is founded. Through research, lobbying, and direct social services, the organization will try to help black citizens obtain full participation in American society.

**April 11, 1913:** President Woodrow Wilson segregates federal government departments.

**August 1, 1914:** In Jamaica, Marcus Garvey founds the Universal Negro Improvement Association. ➤

In the first decade of the 20th century, the General Education Board designed the educational system for African-Americans. Board officials decided that blacks would be educated to be laborers, so they designed a curriculum for that purpose. The GEB supported educational leaders such as Booker T. Washington, whose Tuskegee Institute produced literate men and women skilled in vocational training. The GEB's goal was to both sustain the South's agricultural economy and to discourage education that might lead to political and social agitation.

Director D. W. Griffith's *The Birth of a Nation,* based on Thomas Dixon's 1905 novel *The Clansman,* premiered in 1915. Hollywood's first epic film portrays the post-Civil War era South as a region of lawlessness, filled with lazy black elected officials, rampaging black men, and victimized whites. In one scene, a virginal white woman commits suicide to prevent herself from being raped by a black male predator. The Ku Klux Klan comes to the rescue of the southern whites in the film, reestablishing "civilization" by ferociously subjugating blacks and establishing Jim Crow. President Woodrow Wilson marveled that the film was like "history written with lightning," adding that it was "all so terribly true."

D.W. GRIFFITH'S
-AMERICAN INSTITUTION-
**THE BIRTH OF A NATION**
"THE SUPREME PICTURE OF ALL TIME"
NEW YORK MAIL

In the early 1900s, African-Americans frequently were ridiculed as ignorant savages. This 1916 calendar image shows a typical drawing: a black child drinking ink as "nigger milk." African-Americans sought to combat these images by fighting to maintain their dignity, regardless of class or education level.

## BIG MASS MEETING

### A CALL TO THE
### COLORED CITIZENS
#### OF
#### ATLANTA, GEORGIA
#### To Hear the Great West Indian Negro Leader
### HON. MARCUS GARVEY
#### President of the Universal Negro Improvement Association of Jamaica, West Indies.

### Big Bethel A. M. E. Church
#### Corner Auburn Avenue and Butler Street

### SUNDAY AFTERNOON, AT 3 O'CLOCK
### MARCH 25, 1917

He brings a message of inspiration to the 12,000,000 of our people in this country.
#### SUBJECT:

### "The Negroes of the West Indies, after 78 years of Emancipation." With a general talk on the world position of the race.

An orator of exceptional force, Professor Garvey has spoken to packed audiences in England, New York, Boston, Washington, Philadelphia, Chicago, Milwaukee, St. Louis, Detroit, Cleveland, Cincinatti, Indianapolis, Louisville, Nashville and other cities. He has travelled to the principal countries of Europe, and was the first Negro to speak to the Veterans' Club of London, England.

This is the only chance to hear a great man who has taken his message before the world. **COME OUT EARLY TO SECURE SEATS.** It is worth travelling 1,000 miles to hear.

### All Invited. Rev. R. H. Singleton, D.D., Pastor.

Marcus Garvey's movement combined the best of the black nationalist tradition and Booker T. Washington's self-sufficiency model. Garvey wanted black people all around the world to not only think of themselves as one people, but to work together to build factories, corporations, and kingdoms. In the beginning of the movement, which would spawn his Universal Negro Improvement Association, Garvey spread his word via meetings, handbills, and word of mouth. His written and spoken words reached around the world, inspiring generations of black people.

# Economic Slavery

SLAVERY MAY HAVE ENDED, officially, in 1865. For decades afterward, however, southern whites devised economic practices that sustained blacks as unskilled, indebted workers.

The most common ploy was sharecropping, a scheme whereby blacks rented land, borrowed farming equipment, and bought food on credit until they harvested and sold their crops, then paid off their landowner and creditor. Abuses were rampant. Illiterate freedmen signed contracts they could never fulfill, ensuring their debt at year's end. They agreed to purchase supplies from specified merchants, who tagged prices at twice the market rate. No provision was made for fluctuating crop prices.

Sharecroppers who fell too far into debt or fled their farms often slid into peonage and convict-lease systems. Under peonage, if a person was arrested and fined, or owed a debt, a citizen could pay it off and earn the debtor's servitude for a stated term. In the convict-lease system, private businesses "rented" prisoners from the county jail, who then labored for the firms in exchange for a fee paid to the government. Both systems, while exploitative, were an integral part of southern economies. Citizens and companies regarded them as sources of cheap labor. The states saw the practices as a way to ease prison overcrowding and boost revenue.

Whites in general believed the systems controlled itinerant black workers. Whenever a shopkeeper needed help, he paid a debt and secured a "peon" for six months. At harvest time, farmers contacted sheriffs, who would increase their arrests for loitering and drunkenness. When the prisoners appeared in court, farmers were there waiting to "purchase" the accused. When reform efforts arose—annual mortality rates for convicts often exceeded 10 percent—counties protested that without the revenue of peonage and leasing, they would go bankrupt. In 1911 the U.S. Supreme Court declared peonage unconstitutional, although prosecutions for peonage were filed by the U.S. Justice Department as late as the 1950s.

# 1900-29

## 1915–1919

**1915:** The NAACP pickets D. W. Griffith's hit film *The Birth of a Nation*, which portrays black men as predators while glorifying the Ku Klux Klan.

**June 21, 1915:** In *Guinn v. United States*, the U.S. Supreme Court declares grandfather clauses unconstitutional. *See* May 12, 1898.

**September 9, 1915:** Black historian Carter G. Woodson founds the Association for the Study of Negro Life and History to help eliminate white misconceptions about blacks. Woodson will soon launch *The Journal of Negro History*.

**1917:** The NAACP wins its battle to allow African-Americans to be commissioned as officers in World War I.

**July 1–2, 1917:** Racial tension in East St. Louis, Illinois, erupts into rioting. Dozens of people are killed, most of them African-Americans.

**July 28, 1917:** In New York, the NAACP stages a silent protest parade, about 10,000 strong, in reaction to the East St. Louis riot.

**1917–1918:** More than 370,000 black Americans serve in the Army during World War I, with 42,000 of them in combat units.

**1917–1920:** In what is dubbed the Great Migration, hundreds of thousands of black Southerners move to the North.

**May–October 1919:** During "Red Summer," riots rage in numerous American cities, including Chicago (38 people killed), Washington, Charleston, Knoxville, Omaha, and Elaine, Arkansas.

**September 1919:** Cyril V. Briggs forms the African Blood Brotherhood, a militant black nationalist organization, in New York City. ➤

Before and during World War I, southern blacks flocked to northern cities to work in factories, which created resentment from whites in those cities. Whites in East St. Louis, Illinois, angered by rising unemployment levels in the city, unleashed their wrath on African-Americans in July 1917. They murdered at least 40 black citizens, beat black women and children, and burned black homes. While some of the National Guardsmen called in to restore order attempted to do so, as pictured above, others marauded with the white crowds. The riot was the first of many war-related racial disturbances in northern cities.

After the race riot in East St. Louis, Illinois, in July 1917, NAACP leaders organized a "Silent March" on Fifth Avenue in New York City. They wanted to send a message to President Woodrow Wilson, who had refused again and again to speak out against lynching, that blacks found American democracy to be a lie. "Mr. PRESIDENT, WHY NOT MAKE AMERICA SAFE FOR DEMOCRACY?" declared one of the banners. Most of all, the march was to show the dignity and humanity of black Americans. W.E.B. Du Bois was one of the 8,000 to 10,000 immaculately dressed protesters.

Black soldiers in World War I, as warriors for a country that refused to recognize their rights, fought to "make the world safe for democracy" and to prove themselves in another war. For the most part, the military relegated black soldiers to menial jobs whenever it could, but many did fight in Europe. They introduced themselves—and their music, jazz—to France. A black regiment there, the 369th Infantry, fought along with the French after American brass refused to lead it, then earned medals and acclaim. After fighting in a segregated military, black soldiers came home to racist violence. Many white racists, incensed by the sight of African-Americans in uniform, attacked black soldiers.

Tensions were high between blacks and whites in post-World War I America. Racial incidents became cause for riots, and in such skirmishes whites had both numbers and the police on their side. In what became known as "Red Summer," bloody race riots flared in numerous American cities in 1919. In Chicago, a black boy's drowning due to a stone-throwing scuffle between blacks and whites led to insurrection. Whites, such as those pictured here in Chicago, were not afraid to form mobs to kill blacks because they knew they would not be punished. The original caption for this photo read: "White children cheering outside negro residence which had just been fired [set afire] by them."

## Always Separate, Always Unequal

IT WAS NEVER THE HARDSHIP which hurt so much as the *contrast* between what we had and what the white children had. We got the greasy, torn, dog-eared books; they got the new ones. They had field day in the city park; we had it on a furrowed stubbly hill-side. They got wide mention in the newspaper; we got a paragraph at the bottom. The entire city officialdom from the mayor down turned out to review their pageantry; we got a solitary official.

Our seedy run-down school told us that if we had any place at all in the scheme of things it was a separate place, marked off, proscribed and unwanted by the white people. We were bottled up and labeled and set aside—sent to the Jim Crow car, the back of the bus, the side door of the theater, the side window of a restaurant. We came to understand that whatever we had was always inferior.

—*Pauli Murray, who grew up in Durham, North Carolina;*
Proud Shoes: The Story of an American Family

The red in "Red Summer" referred to blood, not Communism. Washington, D.C., Chicago, and Elaine, Arkansas, witnessed the bloodiest of the 1919 confrontations. Twenty-three African-Americans, including the man in this photo, were killed in the Chicago riot. Fifteen whites also died, with hundreds wounded. Chicagoans rioted for four days. When the smoke subsided, hundreds of black families were left homeless.

# World of Jim Crow

THE TERM "JIM CROW" DERIVES from a song performed by Daddy Rice, a white minstrel entertainer who was popular in the 1830s. Rice blackened his face and mimicked a bumbling black man with his song-and-dance routine. For many years, the Jim Crow character was popular in minstrel shows throughout the southern states. In the late 1800s, as southern legislatures and communities systematically deprived African-Americans of equal rights, "Jim Crow" became for southern whites a euphemism for segregation in the South. Jim Crow laws and customs would permeate southern life until the 1960s.

What state legislatures did not think of, local officials did. The existence of separate railway cars, drinking fountains, and theater seats is well known, as is, perhaps, the segregation of laundries for "colored" and "white." Not so commonly known are the minutiae of Jim Crow. South Carolina laws, for example, forbade blacks and whites from playing checkers together in public or looking out the same factory window together. In Atlanta, an African-American could not "swear to tell the truth" with the same Bible that white witnesses used. A Louisiana law required all circuses, shows, and tent exhibitions to maintain two ticket windows, spaced not less than 25 feet apart, with separate ticket sellers for black and white patrons.

Accompanying such statutes were the practices that became traditions of southern racial life. Whites called a black man "boy," and blacks called a white man "Mister." Black children couldn't begin their new school year until after Columbus Day, as they were needed to harvest white people's crops. A black person had to step off the sidewalk when encountering a white person, place money on a store counter to avoid touching a white salesperson's hand, and buy clothing from a white-owned store without first trying it on to avoid "contaminating" the merchandise. Indeed, Jim Crow practices might have been even more emotionally devastating than Jim Crow laws.

Beginning in 1890, when Mississippi led southern states in amending their constitutions to exclude most blacks from voting, any chance of changing the segregation laws through the vote ended. As a result of the disenfranchisement of black Southerners, jury pools—drawn from voter registration records—were exclusively white. Other requirements, such as poll taxes, "literacy" tests, and property requirements, effectively kept African-Americans and many poor whites from exercising their constitutional right to vote.

With the ascendancy of the Democrats after 1870, the growing number of southern sympathizers and Southerners on the United States Supreme Court made it their business to legitimize segregation. Over the course of two

A man drinks from a segregated water cooler in Oklahoma City.

This facility in Louisville, Kentucky, served as both an outhouse for whites and a "dining room" for blacks.

decades, the Court deliberately eroded the legal protections and freedoms African-Americans had gained in the aftermath of the Civil War: *United States v. Cruikshank* (1876) weakened the 14th Amendment, and the Civil Rights Cases (1883) voided the Civil Rights Act of 1875. The Court's ruling in *Plessy v. Ferguson* (1896) finished the job by upholding as constitutional the "separate but equal" doctrine. Thus, even in the early 1900s, the highest court in the land recognized Jim Crow as acceptable.

"Don't challenge white people." That was the necessary wisdom imparted by generations of black parents to their children because of the rigid caste system that allowed only a relatively few African-Americans to break free. Southern laws and customs combined to create an almost insurmountable barrier to education, to self-esteem, to other than menial jobs, to living even part of the American Dream. Blacks had little recourse but to avoid confrontation.

Many African-Americans left the South, traveling west after the end of Reconstruction and north in the first half of the 20th century. Those who stayed faced not just legal but extralegal consequences for challenging the system.

The Ku Klux Klan, White Citizens' Councils, and other groups, which were formed as private efforts to keep blacks in their place, established close ties to and did the dirty work for local law enforcement officials. Lynching became one of the most common ways of maintaining the system. According to the Tuskegee Institute, 886 lynchings took place in the United States from 1900 through 1909; 791 of the victims (nearly 90 percent) were African-Americans.

Jim Crow wasn't restricted to the southern states. African-Americans who migrated to large northern cities in the early 1900s had little choice but to congregate in black neighborhoods. The dividing lines were clear: Whites wouldn't allow blacks to buy or rent in their sections of the cities. Even in Harlem, the "cultural capital of black America," black patrons were barred from the Cotton Club and other famous nightclubs that featured black entertainment.

In New York City in 1919, Bessie Delany enrolled in Columbia University's dental school. In a class of 170 students, she was the only African-American woman. After she received a failing grade for her work in a course, a white female classmate submitted the same work and passed. On another occasion, Delany was falsely accused of stealing equipment but fortunately saw the real culprit and reported her. On graduation day, June 6, 1923, Delany's class selected her as marshal. She thought it was an honor until she heard some of her classmates talking. She recalled the real reason in *Having Our Say: The Delany Sisters' First 100 Years*: ". . . it was because no one wanted to march beside me in front of their parents. It was a way to get rid of me."

In light of Jim Crow, it is no wonder that many African-Americans were deeply religious. Faith gave them the moral principles and inner strength they needed to carry on with daily life and—for many—to resist their oppressors.

Fittingly, it was southern black ministers who emerged as key figures in the Civil Rights Movement. They drew on their congregations as a significant power base and appealed to the deep religiosity of many white Southerners to end the Jim Crow era. Jim Crow was "officially" put to death with the Civil Rights Act of 1964 and the Voting Rights Act of 1965. However, the ghost of Jim Crow lingered for years afterward in many American communities.

## 1919–1929

**September 30, 1919:** In Elaine, Arkansas, a church meeting of unionized black sharecroppers is stormed by a group of white officials, igniting a riot. Several hundred armed whites roam the countryside, hunting blacks. Approximately 200 black people are killed.

**1920:** James Weldon Johnson is appointed executive secretary of the NAACP.

**August 18, 1920:** The 19th Amendment is ratified, giving women the right to vote.

**October 1920:** Black and white women exchange views on lynching at a conference sponsored by the Commission on Interracial Cooperation in Memphis.

**May 31–June 1, 1921:** In Tulsa, Oklahoma, racially motivated shootings leave at least 36, and perhaps as many as 300, people dead, the vast majority of whom are black.

**1922:** An antilynching bill passes the House but is filibustered in the Senate.

**January 1923:** One day after hearing that a black man had sexually assaulted a white woman, whites storm through predominantly black Rosewood, Florida, razing the town. State officials list the black death toll as six, though subsequent survivor testimonies suggest that scores were killed.

**August 8, 1925:** The Ku Klux Klan, 40,000 strong, marches through Washington, D.C.

**November 6, 1928:** Oscar DePriest of Illinois becomes the first black person elected to the U.S. House of Representatives in the 20th century and the first black from a northern state ever elected to Congress.

**January 15, 1929:** Martin Luther King, Jr., is born in Atlanta.

Almost two million African-Americans attempted to escape Jim Crow by traveling "Up South" from 1916 through 1930. "If you can freeze to death in the North and be free," editorialized *The Chicago Defender,* "why freeze to death in the South and be a slave . . . ?" Some southern states got nervous about the exodus. In Jacksonville, Florida, city officials passed legislation requiring a $1,000 fee to operate as a migration agent. Nevertheless, a new generation of black urbanites was born, filling factories, jazz clubs, and storefront churches.

William Brown, a black man, was accused of robbing a white, handicapped man and raping his fiancée in Nebraska in 1919. Such accusations—particularly the latter—were enough to get a lynch mob together. An angry mob grabbed Brown inside the Douglas County Courthouse. He was stripped, beaten unconscious, shot, dragged by an automobile, and hung from a downtown light pole. His remains were set on fire (*pictured*). The incident was a forceful reminder that lynching was not just a phenomenon of the Deep South.

The Committee on Urban Conditions Among Negroes, founded in 1910, grew into the National Urban League, a civil rights organization dedicated to providing economic opportunities for African-Americans and ending discrimination. Eugene Kinckle Jones, an NUL staff member, lauded NUL President L. Hollingsworth Wood (*front row, far left*) for his great leadership and hard work. Jones also praised Wood for sharing the members' "mental anguish" and lifting their spirits when things looked bleak. The National Urban League and the NAACP would become the most powerful and effective black organizations in America.

Like other African-Americans of achievement in the early part of the 20th century, James Weldon Johnson took on many roles—songwriter, poet, educator, newspaper publisher, and editorial writer. He became well known in the literary community for his anonymous writing of *An Autobiography of an Ex-Colored Man,* a novel that caused a sensation when it was released in 1912. Johnson wrote popular poetry, but it was the lyrics "Lift Every Voice and Sing" that became a black national anthem. Johnson also became the first black executive secretary of the NAACP, a post he held from 1920 to 1930.

# Marcus Garvey

"FOR THE NEGRO TO DEPEND on the ballot and his industrial progress alone, will be hopeless as it does not help him when he is lynched, burned, jim-crowed and segregated. The future of the Negro therefore, outside of Africa, spells ruin and disaster." So wrote Marcus Garvey, black nationalist, entrepreneur, and visionary.

Born in Jamaica in 1887, Garvey started his political career as a 20-year-old printer in Kingston, leading fellow workers in a strike for better wages. Employers broke the strike and blacklisted Garvey, but soon after he led a protest movement against the treatment of banana farm workers. Visiting the Panama Canal construction site, Garvey witnessed the lowly status given to black laborers. These events convinced him that only independent action by blacks would improve their condition.

In 1916 Garvey moved to Harlem. He founded the Universal Negro Improvement Association, a group that flourished after World War I and advocated a single solution for antiblack racism: emigration to Africa. Garvey argued that only in Africa—once that continent was free of European colonialism—could blacks create the one guarantee of rights, namely a national government of their own.

Garvey made the UNIA the wealthiest and largest black organization in the country. In 1919 he formed the Black Star Line, a steamship company dedicated in part to transporting African-Americans to Africa. Next came the Negro Factories Corporation, an enterprise to support black-owned factories across the U.S. and Caribbean.

At the height of Garvey's fame, however, the projects collapsed. Financial mismanagement bankrupted the Black Star Line and brought charges of fraud. The Republic of Liberia rejected his colonization plan, and other black organizations termed Garvey a con man. He served two years in prison and never recovered his former glory. Today, however, he stands as a pioneering champion of black nationalism.

# 1900-29

The Greenwood section of Tulsa, Oklahoma, had such a strong black business district that it was nicknamed "Black Wall Street." What took years to build took only days to burn down in 1921. Dick Rowland (*not pictured*), a black man accused of accosting a white woman in an elevator, was at the riot's center. An erroneous newspaper article said Rowland attempted to rape her. Again and again in America, the charge of a black man raping a white woman created a white mob that gathered to take justice into its own hands. In Greenwood, blacks were shot like prey. Whites set fires. More than 1,400 buildings and businesses were destroyed, and dozens of people, most of them black, were killed.

## Ida B. Wells-Barnett

SOUTH OF ATLANTA IN 1899, a white mob seized Sam Hose, accused him of raping a white woman and murdering her husband, then tortured, burned, and mutilated him. Soon after, a private detective's report on the incident, entitled *Lynch Law in Georgia*, was printed. The detective was hired by Ida B. Wells-Barnett, the leading antilynching crusader of the day.

Born in Mississippi in 1862, Wells combined articulate intelligence with hatred of injustice. Jim Crow, lynch law, lily-white courts—she condemned them all without compromise. Wells taught briefly in Memphis until she was dismissed for criticizing those who ran that city's schools. She turned to journalism, editing the newspaper *Free Speech* until her article on a multiple lynching nearby led mobs to ransack her office and drive her northward. From that point, she dedicated her life to ending the lynching craze.

Apologists for lynching claimed it was just punishment for black men who raped white women, but Wells showed that only one-quarter of lynchings followed allegations of rape. When Southerners called lynching a form of community justice, she offered gruesome descriptions of torture to prove the bloodlust at its root. Her talent and bravery spotlighted a national shame.

Some of the most popular American food brands have featured racist images of African-Americans. Uncle Ben's rice is one. Aunt Jemima's pancake mix is another. A third is Cream of Wheat. Rastus was the name of the first "Uncle Tom" on the box of hot cereal. The character was created in 1890 and used until the 1920s, when another portrait of a black chef—actually, the image of a Chicago waiter who was paid five dollars to pose as a chef—took his place, without the Uncle Tom-like name. The images were overtly offensive because they showed blacks as happy "darkies" who were grateful to be of service to white America. These two images of Rastus are especially cruel. The top advertisement portrays him as ignorant, while the other ad shows him as nothing more than a mule.

One of the NAACP's greatest frustrations was its inability to get any American president to commit to signing an antilynching bill. At least 3,000 lynchings of blacks took place from the end of Reconstruction until the end of World War II. On June 24, 1922, 3,000 black Americans staged an antilynching protest in Washington, D.C. (*pictured*). The march was in support of the Dyer bill, legislation that would have made lynching a federal offense. The bill was defeated when southern senators filibustered it. However, public discussion of the issue caused the number of lynchings to fall.

Rosewood, Florida, a predominately black town, was set afire in January 1923. The charge of rape, made by a white woman against a black man, sparked the violence. The woman's name was Fannie Taylor. The suspect was Jesse Hunter. Whites, many of whom lived in nearby Sumner, quickly formed a lynch mob. The mob found three men whom they believed to be associated with Hunter—Sam Carter, Aaron Carrier, and Aaron's cousin Sylvester. Aaron was jailed and Carter was lynched. Whites shot Sylvester's mother, and Sylvester killed two men and wounded four. The area's white citizens considered those shots a declaration of war. A larger white mob came back and began burning and killing. Hundreds of Rosewood's black residents fled, but many were killed.

Levy County Sheriff Robert Elias Walker, shown here with Sylvester Carrier's gun, led the mob that jailed Aaron Carrier in Rosewood, Florida, in January 1923. The posse included bloodhounds. Some accounts of the massacre explain that Walker was torn between mob justice and American justice, trying to keep order in chaos. But during the insurrection, he refused an offer by the Florida governor to bring in the National Guard.

# Brotherhood of Sleeping Car Porters

I N 1925 SOME PULLMAN railroad porters asked A. Philip Randolph to organize them into a union. Many educated, ambitious black men were porters, for the post was one of the few careers open to them that didn't require backbreaking, grubby labor. But the average work week lasted 100 hours at a meager salary of $15. They paid for their own meals and uniforms, and sometimes they were stranded in stations far from home with no help from the company. Those suspected of union activity were fired.

Randolph, born in Florida in 1889, was a well-known labor and civil rights activist in Harlem, a former Socialist Party member, and editor of militant periodicals. Wherever he found a job, he rallied his fellows to strike for better wages and conditions (usually losing his position in the process). After studying railroad policies, Randolph inaugurated the Brotherhood of Sleeping Car Porters and toured the country signing up members. Bosses threat-

A. Philip Randolph

ened sympathizers, but "when Randolph stood there and talked that day," a porter remembered, "it made a different man out of me."

In 1926 Congress passed a labor act protecting the right of workers to organize, and by 1928 about 7,000 porters had joined Randolph's union. With the Depression, however, funds and membership lagged, and Pullman set up its own "union," a group of porters willing to do the company's bidding to keep their jobs. But when the government forced an election to see which was the "true" union, the Brotherhood received 80 percent of the tally.

In 1937 Randolph marched into Pullman headquarters to negotiate a new contract, winning cuts in hours and increased salaries. For the first time, a black union had brought a white corporation to the bargaining table. Randolph's lesson was clear: Only collective action led by blacks themselves could overturn racism in the workplace.

Postcard topics often reflect the popular culture of a time period. This 1924 postcard shows a "whipping post," a public place where lawbreakers were punished. The scene is in Dover, Delaware. The person who sent the card wrote, "This is what they do to black people in Delaware." The whipping post was one of four types of public punishment used in the antebellum era (before the Civil War); the other three were the halter, the hot iron, and the pillory. The image here, reproduced for popular consumption, showed that such times were not forgotten.

Blacks would test the laws of the land again and again throughout the 20th century. One of those who won an important victory was Ossian Sweet, a doctor who had moved to an all-white section of Detroit in 1925. When his white neighbors surrounded the house and attempted to intimidate him with bottles and rocks, someone from the house fired shots, killing one of the white protesters. Sweet and his wife, Gladys, were charged with murder. The NAACP hired Clarence Darrow, one of America's most famous lawyers, to defend them, saying the constitutional right to defend one's home applied to African-Americans, too. They won.

Membership in the Ku Klux Klan, originally a Reconstruction organization, was on the rise in the 1920s. Its combination of post-World War I patriotism, fundamentalist Christianity, and promotion of white superiority made a new generation seriously consider the Klan as a viable organization that promoted the values of the United States. This "modern" Klan's membership totaled four million by the time of this parade in Washington, D.C., on August 8, 1925. An estimated 40,000 marched on Pennsylvania Avenue while nearly a million persons watched. The Klan's allies included scores of local government officials, including state officeholders in Maine, Indiana, Texas, Oklahoma, and Oregon.

Most film historians consider Al Jolson's 1927 film *The Jazz Singer* the first motion picture with sound—the first "talking" American film. But the content of the film was not as groundbreaking. The story of a young man's growth into manhood—he's torn between following his parents' wishes to become a cantor and following his heart into show business—is marked by Jolson's use of "blackface." Darkening one's skin (called "blackening up") to perform comical impersonations of African-Americans had enjoyed a long tradition in American show business. Ironically, blackface in the context of *The Jazz Singer* represented not racial oppression but freedom—the ability to express one's innermost emotions without inhibition. The poster seen here was created for audiences in Germany, a nation with a thriving and sophisticated film industry, and a place that was beginning to refine its own brand of racial thought and blatant discrimination.

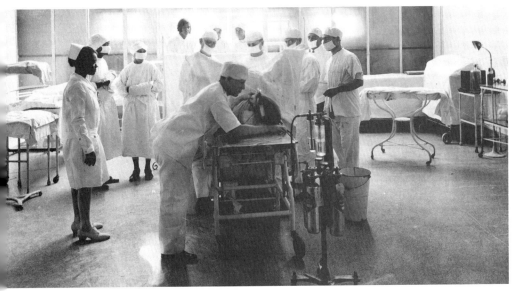

Despite the limitations placed on African-Americans, some still persevered into professions. Meharry Medical College in Nashville and Howard University in Washington, D.C., established medical schools in the 1800s. The two schools would produce the vast majority of the nation's black doctors until the Civil Rights Movement. By 1930 black doctors were pushing into major hospitals, such as Harlem Hospital (*pictured*). These doctors would be the primary caretakers of black people during *de jure* and *de facto* segregation.

# THE 1930s

"We didn't have the best food to eat anymore, [just] peas. My daddy was a big hunter, too. In the fall of the year, he'd get his gun and go kill rabbits, kill squirrel. So he might kill five or six squirrel. My mother cooked them, put them on the pot there and, man, we had a big eating."

—Leroy Boyd, recalling Depression life in the Mississippi Delta

In the early 1930s, members of the NAACP campaigned on behalf of an antilynching bill, only to see it killed by southern congressmen. Moreover, the NAACP could do little to stop the most urgent problems facing African-Americans in the 1930s: unemployment and poverty.

AFTER THE STOCK MARKET CRASH OF 1929, America plunged into the cold waters of the Great Depression. African-Americans were particularly devastated, with their unemployment rate in major cities often approaching 50 percent. Children ate out of garbage cans, young men slept in parks. College-educated black women, dressed in their best Sunday-go-to-meeting clothes, lined up on street corners hoping to be hired for pennies a day as domestic workers. Some kindhearted hoteliers had a standing rule: If you could keep your feet tapping while you sat in the lobby, they would not roust you. For at least one night, you could have a roof over your head.

Throughout this decade of crisis, black activists differed dramatically in their approaches to battle racism and oppression. The mainstream approach was best characterized by the civil rights tactics of lobbying, litigation, and propaganda offered by the NAACP. In 1930 the NAACP and organized labor, seldom allied in the past, scored a surprising victory. They were able to defeat President Herbert Hoover's nominee to the U.S. Supreme Court, Judge John J. Parker. The organization also would make strides in desegregating graduate schools during the decade. However, their support for the Wagner–Costigan bill, which would have made it a crime to participate in a lynch mob, was unsuccessful, as southern Democrats filibustered it to death.

For most African-Americans, the NAACP's campaigns were largely irrelevant. The organization offered no strategy that would help black Americans battle unemployment and starvation. Dissension swelled within its ranks. NAACP cofounder W.E.B. Du Bois called for voluntary segregation to achieve racial advancement. This stance rankled the NAACP's ardently integrationist leadership and was one of the factors that precipitated Du Bois's exit from the organization.

Meanwhile, such leading activists as A. Philip Randolph, Ralph Bunche, and John P. Davis questioned the NAACP's agenda in such dire times. Many of them gravitated to the National Negro Congress,

# 1930s

an umbrella organization for civic, civil rights, and religious organizations. Randolph tried to address the unaddressed and challenge a capitalist economic system that seemed to have failed.

The Depression only compounded the dire poverty of many southern rural blacks, such as this girl in Gee's Bend, Alabama.

As some younger blacks drifted leftward, they fell into the open arms of the Communist Party USA (CPUSA). At one point, CPUSA members helped fill Chicago's Washington Park with protestors after three black men were shot by Chicago police. The party gained international attention when it supplanted the NAACP as chief defender of the Scottsboro Boys, a group of young, southern black transients railroaded into prison and death sentences without a fair trial.

Along with the Southern Tenant Farmers Union, the CPUSA appeared to be doing what centrists seemed unable or unwilling to do: confront racism, preach and practice worker solidarity, and offer an alternative to the boom and bust cycle of 20th century capitalism. So why weren't more blacks attracted to their banner? Perhaps a people so steeped in Old Testament fundamentalism were repulsed by Marxist atheism. Yet there is no reason that blacks could not have adopted the analysis and ignored the ideology. More likely, they felt that they were already marginalized enough. Why join forces with a group so actively despised?

Another strategic error of the Left was the Communist Party's adoption of a "Black Belt" strategy—the creation of an all-black state in the South—which came direct from Moscow. The idea that African-Americans would actively embrace a strategy that would further segregate the races was a serious miscalculation.

While activists challenged discrimination in some northern cities in the 1930s (such as through the "Don't Buy Where You Can't Work" campaign), segregation remained firmly entrenched in the South. African-Americans in Leland, Mississippi, could view films only at the Rex Theatre.

However, some African-Americans didn't fear an all-black society. In 1930 in Detroit's Paradise Valley, Wallace D. Fard founded the Nation of Islam, advocating black separatism. At first the NOI was merely one of hundreds of urban nationalist cults springing up in the aftermath of Marcus Garvey's deportation. But under the leadership of the Honorable Elijah Muhammad, the Nation of Islam eventually would command a large following. It spoke to blacks who felt ignored and excluded from mainstream churches and civil rights organizations. The Nation of Islam reached out to the black urban underclass with a message and a discipline that its conventional rivals could not match.

For the first time, the voice of the black dispossessed was being heard. The sense of urgency, and the dissolution of deference to a seemingly impotent black bourgeois leadership, meant new stratagems would be employed and a new leadership would challenge for black allegiance. In the mid-1930s, the "Don't Buy Where You Can't Work" campaign spread across the country, from the Midwest to the East Coast. Grassroots black leaders called on African-Americans to boycott white-owned stores in black neighborhoods that did not offer black employment.

On the left, the National Negro Congress degenerated into a Communist front organization. A. Philip Randolph, leader of the Brotherhood of Sleeping Car Porters—the nation's first successful black union—resigned as president of the Congress. Throughout the 1930s and 1940s, no single civil rights advocate commanded center stage like Randolph. His organizational skills brought the black working class and black laborer closer to the American middle-class. The direct-action strategies he employed as a labor organizer, and his legacy of self-directed and self-financed protest, paved the way for the direct-action campaigns of the Civil Rights Movement.

Civil rights groups were outraged by the "Scottsboro Boys" case involving nine youths who had been convicted of rape without fair trials. The Communist Party USA provided legal defense for the young men.

Most blacks, however, moved neither right nor left. Most sought inclusion and demanded only simple justice and basic decency. One avenue for justice was practical politics. Blacks had been Republican since the Civil War, but they moved gradually (and begrudgingly in some cities) into the liberal-labor coalition of the Democratic Party. Black leaders such as Mary McLeod Bethune, Robert Weaver, and *Pittsburgh Courier* editor Robert Vann formed an informal group, the "Black Cabinet," that advised President Franklin D. Roosevelt's administration. Roosevelt attempted to pull all of Americans out of the Depression with his New Deal—social programs that put millions of Americans to work (including blacks, albeit at lower wages).

Despite the hard times and turmoil, something fundamental had changed during the 1930s. New African-American leadership had emerged. A black Republican (Chicago's Oscar DePriest) sat in Congress, a black federal judge (William H. Hastie) upon the bench. A black boxer (Joe Louis) was heavyweight champion of the world. As the storm clouds of war gathered, a new generation of black leaders was poised to mount its own offensive against the American color line.

# 1930s

## 1930–1933

**1930:** The NAACP successfully lobbies the U.S. Supreme Court against the nomination of Judge John J. Parker, who had spoken against black suffrage.

**1930:** Wallace D. Fard founds the Nation of Islam in Detroit. Fard advocates black separatism and rails against "blue-eyed devils."

**1930:** The Communist Party establishes the League of Struggle for Negro Rights, which will campaign against lynching and for civil rights.

**November 1930:** White women in the Commission on Interracial Cooperation found the Association of Southern Women for the Prevention of Lynching.

**April 9, 1931:** In Scottsboro, Alabama, eight of nine black males accused of raping two white women are sentenced to death despite their innocence. The trial of the ninth defendant ends in a mistrial. After two cases in the U.S. Supreme Court and seven years of trials in lower courts, the Scottsboro defendants will be slowly released. *See* April 1, 1935.

**1932–1972:** To study the effects of syphilis, the U.S. Public Health Service entices black male volunteers with a promise of free basic medical treatment and burial insurance to participate in the study. However, the subjects are not told the true nature of the experiments and are not given medicine to treat the disease. More than 100 of these men will die from untreated syphilis.

**1933:** President Franklin Roosevelt appoints several African-Americans as advisors. They'll be dubbed the "Black Cabinet."

**March 15, 1933:** In its effort to attack discrimination in public schools, the NAACP files a lawsuit, its first, against the University of North Carolina. ➤

A large, enthusiastic crowd happily gathers at a lynching in Marion, Indiana, on August 7, 1930. Watching black men "strung up" and hung until they choked from lack of oxygen was seen as an exciting public event—a spectacle, like a parade or a circus show. Victim Abram Smith (*left*) was 19. Thomas Shipp (*right*) was 18. They were accused of murdering 24-year-old Claude Deeter and assaulting his girlfriend, Mary Ball. With lynchings, the sentence took the place of the trial.

This 1930 postcard is an example of the "pickaninny" stereotype. Pickaninnies were supposedly comical images of black children as little naked subhumans. These lifelike characters often were pictured with wild animals, including alligators. Such postcards were common from the early years of the century up until the Civil Rights Movement.

The Micheaux Book and Film Company scored another triumph in 1931. The black-owned company, which created and produced films for black audiences, released *The Exile*, its first full-length sound picture. It was one of at least 30 movies made in at least as many years by Oscar Micheaux, a black entrepreneur who wrote, directed,

produced, and distributed his own films. Micheaux's movies dramatized black Americans' struggles against prejudice.

## "No jobs for niggers until every white man has a job."

—SLOGAN IN THE SOUTH DURING THE DEPRESSION

The Great Depression hit black America like a tornado. More than half of the black workers in New York, Philadelphia, Chicago, and Detroit were unemployed in 1932. One in every three black families was on "the dole" (public assistance). Blacks found it seemingly impossible to find work because the low-skilled jobs they came North for—jobs in factories and plants—were decimated by the Depression. That, coupled with racial discrimination in hiring practices, created long public assistance lines in black communities.

# The Black Depression

IN 1931 A. PHILIP RANDOLPH wrote, "We are in the grip of an intensive and economic crisis." Referring to the Depression that hit in 1929, Randolph noted that it struck people around the world regardless of race and social status. But on the scale of misery in the United States, African-Americans suffered the most.

In good times and bad, the saying went, blacks were "the last hired and the first fired." During the Depression, whites who once had avoided menial labor took jobs traditionally held by black men and women—maids, janitors, busboys, messengers—putting more blacks on the welfare rolls. Black men in higher positions, such as firemen on the railroads, were harassed and sometimes murdered. Though unemployment rates for whites were extremely high during the Depression, the rates for blacks were roughly twice as high. In some cities at the peak of the Depression, the black unemployment rate exceeded 50 percent.

After Franklin D. Roosevelt won the presidency in 1932, the federal government began to address black America's unique problem. Roosevelt's New Deal plan was applauded by labor, liberals, and African-Americans. Such legislation as the National Labor Relations Act banned discrimination in unions and federal agencies. A black economic advisor, Robert Weaver, joined the Roosevelt Administration, and Executive Order No. 8802 outlawed discrimination in defense industries and throughout the federal government. Despite the suffering, economic reform proceeded and a new collective labor consciousness spread through African-American society.

# 1930s

Richard B. Moore was a dedicated Pan-Africanist based in Harlem, which was known as black America's "capital" in the 1930s. Moore was one of many black intellectuals who, after a brief involvement with the Communist Party, became a leading cultural figure in that section of Manhattan. He owned a bookstore and was chairman of the "Committee to Present the Truth About the Name Negro." (The truth was that the word *Negro* was a misnomer; blacks were Africans in America, he argued.) He also wrote articles for the journal *Freedomways*.

As a peddler in Detroit in the early 1930s, Wallace Fard taught his black customers about black history, the problems of Christianity, and the "blue-eyed white devil." Fard developed his Lost-Found Nation of Islam, and established a school and temple in Detroit before disappearing mysteriously in 1934. His disciple, Elijah Poole, would rename himself Elijah Muhammad and claim that Fard had been the embodiment of Allah. The FBI, which kept detailed files on Fard, and said he had many aliases, asserts that the man pictured here is indeed Fard. Many NOI adherents disagree.

In November 1933 in San Jose, California, a mob used a battering ram to break into jail for the confessed slayers of Brooke L. Hart. Thomas Thurmond and Jack Holmes were dragged out, beaten, and strung up while the authorities stood by, watching. The mob members knew that no charges would be brought against them—not as they "avenged" the crime of blacks attacking whites.

The NAACP, which had lobbied hard to get the Dyer bill passed throughout the 1920s, tried again with the Wagner–Costigan bill in 1931. These bills would have made lynching a federal crime. But southern congressional representatives filibustered each time. Upset but unbowed, the NAACP kept up the public pressure with rallies and demonstrations, such as this one at a crime conference in Washington, D.C., in December 1934. During the previous decade, NAACP field secretaries such as James Weldon Johnson and Walter White risked their lives while documenting lynchings. (White, who was very fair-skinned, passed for white as he ventured into the Deep South.) The NAACP's *The Crisis* ran numerous exposés on the terrible crimes.

# The Antilynching Movement

IN FEBRUARY 1918, just days after Walter White joined the staff of the NAACP, he learned of "an incredibly horrible lynching" in Tennessee. A black sharecropper, Jim McIlherron, "had been slowly burned to death by a mob for defending himself from a beating by his employer." The following year, the NAACP's report, *Thirty Years of Lynching in the United States, 1889–1918*, counted 2,522 black men and women who had been violently executed by mobs who took the law into their own hands.

The excuse for many of these lynchings was that white males needed to protect white women, but the murders served a broader purpose: to maintain the system of white supremacy that had replaced slavery. The corpses often were left in public view as a warning

Rubin Stacy, 32, was lynched in Florida in 1935.

for blacks to remain subservient. Activists such as Ida B. Wells conducted antilynching campaigns beginning in the 1890s, and White would devote the rest of his NAACP career seeking federal legislation against the practice. His efforts were unsuccessful, and lynching persisted.

Beginning in the early 1920s, women in the South carried out a different strategy. African-American women and then white women took up an educational campaign, mainly based in church organizations and women's clubs, to end lynching through public condemnation and state and local law enforcement. Speaking at a conference on interracial cooperation in 1920, black educator and club woman Charlotte Hawkins Brown maintained, "We feel that so far as lynching is concerned that, if the white woman would take hold of the situation, lynching would be stopped, mob violence [would be] stamped out and yet the guilty would have justice meted out by due course of law and would be punished accordingly."

Encouraged by the positive response to the speech, the Southeastern Federation of Colored Women's Clubs adopted a 1921 statement proclaiming lynching as "the greatest menace to good will between the races, and a constant factor in undermining respect for all law and order." The women appealed to their white sisters to protest potential acts of lynching, promote bringing lynchers to justice, and support the condemnation of lynching from the pulpit and in the press.

It took almost another decade for southern white women to take up this challenge. In November 1930 Jessie Daniel Ames organized a meeting of white club and church women that led to the formation of the Association of Southern Women for the Prevention of Lynching (ASWPL). A pamphlet published in 1936 by the organization condemned "the claim that lynchings are necessary to the protection of southern white women." The ASWPL pledged to carry out an educational campaign "day by day in the home, in the school, in the press, and in the church" that would transform public opinion and "end lynching by public demand."

By 1936 the ASWPL claimed that 35,000 women from 65 national and state organizations worked to further the goals of the organization. Those member groups included the Young Women's Christian Association and the Women's Christian Missionary Society. First Lady Eleanor Roosevelt became a supporter of the antilynching movement, but she failed to persuade her husband, Franklin Delano Roosevelt, to publicly endorse the NAACP-backed antilynching legislation.

By the 1940s the frequency of lynchings in the country had dropped significantly, largely due to the campaign against the practice. Nevertheless, even as late as the 1960s, white segregationists in some areas of the South could murder black civil rights proponents with little fear of prosecution.

# 1930s

## 1934–1935

**1934:** Elijah Muhammad succeeds Wallace D. Fard as the leader of the Nation of Islam.

**1934:** After writing a controversial article calling for voluntary segregation to achieve racial advancement, W.E.B. Du Bois is forced out of his job as editor of the NAACP's *The Crisis*.

**1934:** Arthur Mitchell of Chicago becomes the first black Democrat in Congress.

**1935:** The NAACP convinces attorney Charles Houston to head the organization's legal challenge to educational segregation.

**1935:** The National Conference on the Economic Status of the Negro is held at Howard University.

**March 19, 1935:** Rumors spread throughout Harlem that a Latino boy was beaten and/or killed by a white store owner. Black residents riot, destroying mainly white-owned businesses.

**April 1, 1935:** In *Norris v. Alabama*, the U.S. Supreme Court overturns the conviction of a Scottsboro defendant, stating that black jurors had been systematically excluded. *See July 24, 1937.*

**Fall 1935:** The interracial Southern Tenant Farmers' Union organizes a multistate strike of cotton pickers, who seek better wages.

**December 5, 1935:** Mary McLeod Bethune founds the National Council of Negro Women.

**Mid-1930s:** Through picketing and boycotts, black protestors stage a "Don't Buy Where You Can't Work" campaign, pushing white employers to hire black workers. The campaign starts in Chicago and quickly spreads to other northern cities. ➤

As it grew more established within black communities, the NAACP responded to more and more of the needs of its growing constituency. Although its priorities still would be to obtain full rights for all Americans and halt violence against blacks, the NAACP broadened its agenda in the 1930s. Two major initiatives were the examination of economic rights, including charges of discrimination made by blacks who unsuccessfully tried to participate in New Deal programs, and the development of NAACP Youth Councils. One reason the NAACP formed youth groups was to provide an alternative to the Communist Party, which had become effective at recruiting young African-Americans to its ranks.

Often when an African-American broke through another popular-culture barrier, a tremendous price was paid. In Hollywood, Stepin Fetchit became a true star—one of the most familiar movie actors of the 1930s. However, he always portrayed a lazy, good-for-nothing, slow-spoken dullard, reinforcing the worst stereotypes about African-Americans. Fetchit appeared in about 40 films from 1927 to 1976.

Daisy Lampkin was one of those hard workers who made sure movements moved. She raised funds and traveled the country to assist branches as a national field organizer for the NAACP. She rallied people with her speeches, and she lobbied for NAACP causes. In fact, she was a major reason why the NAACP was able to block the nomination of segregationist Judge John J. Parker to the U.S. Supreme Court in 1930. The *Pittsburgh Courier*, in tribute to Lampkin when she died in 1965, called her an "institution" and "Mrs. NAACP."

The rumor spread quickly through Harlem. On March 19, 1935, a Puerto Rican teenager who had stolen a knife from a department store on 135th Street allegedly had been beaten by whites. The police-beating part of the story, spread by Communist Party leaflets, wasn't true, but it was all the jobless and underprivileged needed to hear. Harlem erupted, and more than 5,000 police officers, firefighters, and soldiers responded. Three African-Americans were killed, about 200 were injured, and at least 125 were arrested.

U.S. Senator Edward P. Costigan (*right*) (R–CO), and Walter White (*left*), executive secretary of the NAACP, were determined to get a bill sponsored by Costigan signed into law. The Wagner–Costigan bill would have made it a federal crime for authorities to stand by while someone was being lynched. It also would have made it a federal crime to be part of a lynch mob. President Franklin Roosevelt, a Democrat who feared he would lose support from southern Democrats, refused to support the bill. Southern senators filibustered it to death.

# W.E.B. Du Bois

IN THE LONG HISTORY of African-American militance, nobody combined social activism, literary skill, and intellectual brilliance better than W.E.B. Du Bois. In a sweeping, contentious life that began as the 14th Amendment was passed and ended with the civil rights march on Washington, Du Bois led protest movements, edited magazines, composed renowned works of American thought, challenged white supremacists, and debated rival black figures.

Today Du Bois is known for his political involvement—head of the Niagara Movement and the NAACP, polemicist decrying lynching and colonialism, apologist for the Soviet Union, indicted as a foreign agent (the case was thrown out by the judge). His contemporaries, however, were more impressed by his erudite leanings and high-culture tastes. Du Bois had attended Fisk University and then Harvard, where he earned a B.A. in philosophy. He spent a year in Berlin studying social science before becoming the first African-American to earn a Ph.D. from Harvard.

In 1897 Du Bois became president of the American Negro Academy, a society devoted to scholarship and education. He later accepted a professorship in economics and history at Atlanta University, where he hosted annual conferences on social and political themes. His third book, *The Souls of Black Folk* (1903), is a profound and moving expression of African-American spiritual consciousness that awed even the most hostile readers. White supremacist Thomas Dixon termed it "the naked soul of a Negro beating itself to death against the bars in which Aryan society has caged him!"

After the 1906 Atlanta riot, Du Bois moved north, and in 1909 he became one of the founders of the NAACP. In his new role, Du Bois argued for better treatment of black soldiers, greater respect among blacks for higher education, and a new "race consciousness." In the 1930s Du Bois's writings moved away from the integrationist thrust of the NAACP, which cost him his job in 1934 as editor of the NAACP's *The Crisis*. In 1961 Du Bois emigrated to Africa and became a citizen of Ghana, where he died two years later at age 95.

# Charles Houston

IN 1935 ONE OF THE SHARPEST legal minds of the time became the first special counsel of the NAACP. He was Charles Houston, a Washington, D.C., native, graduate of Harvard Law School, the first black member of the *Harvard Law Review*, World War I veteran, and dean of Howard University Law School.

While other black leaders were forming labor unions and editing militant periodicals, Houston believed that attacking existing case law was the surest way to racial progress. Serving on the D.C. Board of Education, he noticed grievous disparities in black and white schools. He thought the best way to eliminate them was not by protest but by lawsuit.

"All we need is about $10.00, then we can file a case in court," he stated. "Five dollars more, and we can bring the whole state education department into court with all its records, put each official on the stand under oath and wring him dry of information."

In actuality, the strategy was incremental, a slow chipping away at the statutes and policies that sanctioned segregation. From 1945 to 1948, Houston urged President Harry Truman to integrate the military, demanded the expulsion of Mississippi Senator Theodore Bilbo (a blatant racist), advocated independence for African nations, and, most important of all, masterminded dozens of legal challenges. His efforts made him the most influential civil rights attorney in the land. Thurgood Marshall, Houston's top pupil, later recalled that of the more than two dozen attorneys representing the plaintiffs in *Brown v. Board of Education* (1954), there were "only two who hadn't been touched by Charlie Houston."

The pace took its toll. Heart disease sent Houston to the hospital in 1949, and he died of acute coronary thrombosis in 1950 at the age of 54.

The mission the NAACP gave Thurgood Marshall (*left*), pictured with his mentor, Charles H. Houston (*right*), was simple yet profound: find the legal button that would shut down Jim Crow. Houston, Marshall, and other attorneys had to try to destroy segregation, legalized by *Plessy v. Ferguson* in 1896, case by case. One of Marshall and Houston's first cases was close to Marshall's heart: to desegregate the University of Maryland. Marshall, a Baltimore native, had wanted to attend the university's law school, but could not because it didn't accept African-Americans. So it was a significant victory in more ways than one for Marshall (who attended Howard's law school) when, in the mid-1930s, he successfully sued the University of Maryland to admit Donald Gaines Murray (*center*) to its law school.

A former president of the National Association of Colored Women, Mary McLeod Bethune founded the National Council of Negro Women in 1935 to take an active stance on behalf of black Americans. Bethune was a member of President Franklin Roosevelt's unofficial "Black Cabinet," advising him on race relations. Her newspaper column was nationally syndicated in black newspapers. She also was the founder of what by the 1930s was Bethune–Cookman College, an institute of higher education for black women. Bethune's commitment to racial uplift through education earned her everlasting praise.

Lloyd L. Gaines, a graduate of historically black Lincoln University, took on Jim Crow for the sake of higher education. In 1936 he sued the University of Missouri to admit him as a law student. Since its 1839 founding, the university had banned blacks. Gaines, with the help of the NAACP's legal division, believed that the admission ban abridged his "equality of rights" under the 14th Amendment to the Constitution. Attorney Charles H. Houston of the NAACP argued that the state was required to either admit Gaines or create an equal graduate school for blacks. When the Supreme Court agreed with Houston, the state responded by creating a law school for Lincoln University. Taxpayers were discovering that segregation was becoming more and more expensive.

The 1936 Olympics were held in Berlin, in Adolf Hitler's Germany. It was an opportunity for the dictator to showcase the accomplishments of his Third Reich government and its followers—the "master race." But Jesse Owens, an African-American, angered and humiliated Hitler. Owens won four gold medals—in the long jump, 400-meter relay, 200-meter sprint, and 100-meter sprint. In the long jump competition, Owens beat Lutz Long (right), the athletic pride of the Nazi Party. However, his historic triumphs in Berlin did not shield Owens from Jim Crow when he returned home. Said Owens: "I wasn't invited up to shake hands with Hitler, but I wasn't invited to the White House to shake hands with the President, either."

In the 1930s even the world of fantasy was Jim Crowed. Some Hollywood filmmakers, both African-American and white, mimicked traditional film genres but used all-black casts. Thus, black moviegoers, who were banned from white theaters, were able to watch black crime dramas, black love stories, and even black westerns. Sam Newfield, a white man, directed *Harlem on the Prairie* in 1937.

## 1936–1937

**1936:** NAACP chief counsel Charles Houston wins a significant case before the Maryland Supreme Court. The court orders the University of Maryland to admit African-American student Donald Murray to its law school rather than send him out of state.

**1936:** President Franklin Roosevelt appoints Mary McLeod Bethune as director of the National Youth Administration's Division of Negro Affairs.

**February 1936:** The National Negro Congress is formed during a conference in Chicago. Labor leader A. Philip Randolph is named president.

**August 1936:** Track and field star Jesse Owens, an African-American, wins four gold medals at the Berlin Olympics, humiliating racist Nazi leader Adolf Hitler.

**1937:** In Washington, D.C., Mary McLeod Bethune convenes the National Conference on the Problems of the Negro and Negro Youth.

**1937:** The Brotherhood of Sleeping Car Porters, led by A. Philip Randolph, is recognized as a union by the Pullman Company.

**February 1937:** The Southern Negro Youth Congress is formed. It will fight for political, social, and economic justice for African-Americans.

**March 19, 1937:** William H. Hastie is confirmed as a federal district judge, becoming the first African-American to hold such a position.

**July 24, 1937:** Rape charges are dropped against four of the Scottsboro defendants. *See* June 9, 1950. ▶

It was a long wait for Olen Montgomery (*wearing overalls*) and Eugene Williams (*wearing suspenders*). They were among the nine Scottsboro Boys who originally were arrested in 1931, when Montgomery and Williams were just teenagers. For six years, the young men sat in jail while the trials and appeals went on and on. They were defended by the NAACP as well as the International Labor Defense (a group made up of members of the Communist Party). Five of the Scottsboro Boys, including Williams and Montgomery, were released in 1937.

# The Lowdown on Scottsboro

I WAS NEVER GUILTY of anything except stealing a ride on a freight train during the Depression, just as the poor whites were doing. Mean, prejudiced crackers, thinking they were better than me, decided to throw me off that train along with the other blacks. I imagine they thought it would be easy enough. They would tell us to unload and we'd go peacefully. When we didn't do their bidding, they threw rocks at us and we just didn't go for it. We threw their asses off the train in a fair fight and they went running to the nearest sheriff to report a pack of uppity niggers.

Victoria Price and Ruby Bates were riding on a different part of that train and I never saw either of them until they accused me of rape in Scottsboro....I think the women were intimidated by the mob, and some of those crackers probably asked them what they were doing on that train with "all these niggers." They put the finger on us to win sympathy for themselves.

—*Clarence Norris*, The Last of the Scottsboro Boys

# The Scottsboro Boys

THE FIRST OF THE RAPE TRIALS in Scottsboro, Alabama, began in early April 1931, just 12 days after nine black males were arrested and charged with sexually assaulting two white females. The defendants were soon called the "Scottsboro Boys," although the oldest, Charles Weems, was 20. Eugene Williams and Roy Wright were only 13. Roy's brother Andrew was 19, as was Haywood Patterson. Willie Roberson was 15, while Olen Montgomery, Ozie Powell, and Clarence Norris were 17. A white defense attorney was the only lawyer in the area who would accept the case. He had little time to prepare and was reluctant to challenge the rape charges.

However, the stories of the accusers—alleged prostitutes Victoria Price and Ruby Bates—included many inconsistencies and improbabilities. They claimed they had been viciously assaulted by armed black men. While a medical examination discovered evidence of semen, the women's bodies carried no bruises or evidence of assault, and no weapons were found on the defendants. But such considerations did not deter prosecutors. Within four days, all-white juries convicted eight of the defendants, who were sentenced to death. Jurors deadlocked in the case of Roy Wright. When prosecutors sought life imprisonment for him, 11 of the jurors voted for the death penalty, resulting in a mistrial.

A few days after the guilty verdicts, the Communist Party of the United States sent representatives to offer support. The chief counsel of the Communist-backed International Labor Defense (ILD) convinced the defendants and their families to ignore warnings against accepting Communist help. "These were the first people to call on us," Patterson recalled, "to show any feelings for our lives, and we were glad."

After the Alabama Supreme Court upheld the convictions, the ILD appealed, and Communist activists throughout the nation organized rallies to free the Scottsboro Boys. In the political climate of the Great Depression, there was a receptive audience for Communist calls for workers to mobilize on behalf of the defendants. Extensive press coverage exposed the flimsiness of the evidence against them. In *Powell v. Alabama* (1932), the U.S. Supreme Court ruled that Alabama's failure to provide the defendants with adequate, timely legal counsel violated the 14th Amendment's due process clause.

Attorney Samuel Leibowitz represented the nine Scottsboro Boys.

The Scottsboro Boys remained in jail, however. At the retrials, defense lawyers exposed weaknesses in the prosecution's case and argued that qualified black Alabama residents were systematically excluded from juries. Stunningly, Ruby Bates repudiated her rape charges and testified for the defense. The retrials nonetheless ended in convictions. Once again, the U.S. Supreme Court reversed the convictions, ruling in *Norris v. Alabama* (1935) that black residents had been systematically excluded from the jury pool—an historically significant decision. Nevertheless, the defendants remained imprisoned.

After *Norris*, the defense of the Scottsboro Boys was taken up by the Scottsboro Defense Committee, which included representatives from the ILD, the NAACP, the ACLU, and the Methodist Federation of Social Service. In 1937 the committee convinced Alabama officials to drop charges against four of the defendants—Eugene Williams, Roy Wright, Olen Montgomery, and Willie Roberson. The state dropped rape charges against Ozie Powell, but sentenced him to 20 years for attacking a deputy sheriff.

In a new trial, Clarence Norris was sentenced to death, but he was paroled in 1944. Three of the defendants were sentenced to 75 to 99 years in prison: Charles Weems, Andrew Wright, and Haywood Patterson. Weems and Wright were paroled in 1938 and 1944, respectively, and Patterson escaped jail in 1948. In 1976 Alabama Governor George Wallace pardoned all of the Scottsboro Boys, but by that time only Norris was still alive.

# 1930s

**1938:** First Lady Eleanor Roosevelt attends the first meeting of the Southern Conference for Human Welfare. Over the next decade, the organization will push for voting rights for disenfranchised citizens and help organize opposition to segregation.

**June 22, 1938:** Black heavyweight boxer Joe Louis knocks out Nazi Germany icon Max Schmeling in a politically charged boxing match. Millions of Americans, especially black Americans, celebrate the triumph.

**December 12, 1938:** In *Missouri ex rel. Gaines v. Canada*, the U.S. Supreme Court rules that the University of Missouri created an unfair privilege for white students when it refused law school admission to a black student and sent him out of the state for law school.

**1939:** Jazz singer Billie Holiday popularizes Abel Meeropol's "Strange Fruit," a potent antilynching song.

**April 1939:** Senator Theodore Bilbo (D–MS), a white racist, submits the "Greater Liberia" bill, which would encourage black Americans to move to Africa.

**April 9, 1939:** After being denied the opportunity to sing at Constitution Hall in Washington, D.C., African-American singer Marian Anderson performs in front of 75,000 people at the Lincoln Memorial.

The USSR welcomed African-Americans with open arms. Marxists theorized that all of the oppressed—the proletariat—would lead the revolt against the ruling class. African-Americans, especially artists and members of the media, were invited to visit the Soviet Union. (Writer Langston Hughes was one of many who did, in 1932.) Blacks who settled in to the USSR were publicly—and demonstratively—given all of the freedoms of "democracy," including the ostensible right to vote. Tayland Rudd, one of those expatriates, is shown casting a ballot, something most African-Americans in the South could not do without peril. The USSR utilized images of this sort as priceless pro-Soviet, anti-American propaganda.

Reverend Major Jealous Divine (*next to railing*), known better as "Father Divine," was the mysterious minister of the International Peace Mission Movement. He was also one of the most powerful black evangelists of his day. In 1931 Father Divine drew between 5,000 and 10,000 people at a single New York City rally. In Harlem during the 1930s, he provided jobs for his flock while his restaurants fed the hungry. Father Divine also taught that all races were equal. He became a messiah to his followers, who considered him the Second Coming of Christ.

The radio show *Amos 'n' Andy* delighted white America while embarrassing black Americans nationwide. Two white men, Freeman Gosden as Amos (*left*) and Charles Correll as Andy (*right*), acted as black characters in the most popular sitcom of radio's early years. The show's popularity reached a peak in the 1930s, when movie theaters postponed screenings until *Amos 'n' Andy*, piped through the theaters' speaker systems, was over. The NBC program was considered racist because the main characters were more stupid, lazy, and crafty than their white counterparts on other shows. The show moved to CBS television in 1951, with black actors, and ran for two years. It flourished in syndication until an NAACP boycott in 1966.

Heavyweight boxer Joe Louis became an American hero in 1938 when he beat German challenger Max Schmeling, whom Adolf Hitler touted as his country's "Aryan superman." On June 22, Louis knocked Schmeling down three times in Yankee Stadium in New York, scoring a technical knockout. Louis's resounding victory avenged his 1936 loss to Schmeling. During World War II, Louis served in the U.S. Army, fighting exhibition matches for American soldiers.

Lakeland, Florida, which included a tight-knit black community, drew the interest of the Ku Klux Klan. After two African-Americans were slain in August 1938, Klansmen and blacks met head-to-head in a tense showdown on Florida Avenue (*pictured*). A year earlier, Klansmen from Lakeland had traveled to St. Petersburg, Florida, where KKK leaders approached black onlookers and told them to stay away from the election polls.

African-Americans considered U.S. Senator Theodore G. Bilbo (D–MS) one of the most vile racists of his era. Bilbo was the champion of the "Dixiecrats" who filibustered civil rights and voting rights bills into oblivion. While governor of Mississippi, Bilbo called for the deportation of black Americans. He also praised Hitler for his racial policies during an address to the Senate in 1938. His death in 1947, the same year that his book *Take Your Choice: Separation or Mongrelization* hit the bookstores, was all but celebrated in black communities.

A group of schoolchildren prepares for a minstrel show at the May Day–Health Day festivities in South Carolina in 1939. Whites putting on "blackface" to perform, a tradition that dates back to the minstrel shows of the 1700s, was an acceptable practice through the early decades of the 20th century. The minstrel shows were collections of comical song-and-dance routines that originally ridiculed enslaved African-Americans. In the early 20th century, white actors donned blackface (using burnt cork or greasepaint makeup) for stage productions as well as for the silver screen. The practice was popluar not only in the United States but in Great Britain and other countries in Europe.

In the 1930s Adam Clayton Powell, Jr., reigned as a flamboyantly aggressive political champion of Harlem. As an activist pastor, Powell led demonstrations to get more black doctors hired at Harlem Hospital and to push business owners to hire blacks at stores where they shopped. He wrote opinion pieces, first for *The New York Post,* on the causes of the Harlem riots. He later penned a regular column, "Soap Box," for the *New York Amsterdam News.* His political career took off in 1941, when he became the first African-American elected to the New York City Council.

The decade of the 1930s witnessed great strides in the labor movement. Across America, groups of urban dwellers fought for improved conditions in the factories in which they worked. In some cases, blacks and whites struggled together for better wages and other changes. Thousands of black industrial workers were organized in desegregated unions by the United Auto Workers, the United Steel Workers, and the AFL-CIO (American Federation of Labor and Congress of Industrial Organizations).

Marian Anderson had paid her dues to sing anywhere by the late 1930s. She had finished a decade of study and touring in Europe, and was becoming well known in American concert circles. She could sing in several languages. But all of that was not enough for the Daughters of the American Revolution (DAR), a national patriotic women's group. They denied Anderson, an African-American, the opportunity to sing in Constitution Hall in the nation's capital in 1939. First Lady Eleanor Roosevelt, angered by the DAR's action, resigned her membership. The Roosevelt Administration set up a special Easter Sunday concert for Anderson at the Lincoln Memorial, which was attended by 75,000 people.

In the South and in rural areas in other regions, blacks worked as sharecroppers—tenants on land owned by whites. They picked fruit and cotton from morning to night, from "can't see to can't see." The back-breaking work was so financially unrewarding that it seemed only a short step up from slavery. A sharecropper worked hard but was caught in a cycle of debt to the landlord. During bad harvests, many sharecropping families were evicted. Members of this Missouri family, pictured in December 1939, said they were evicted because their white landlords didn't want to share the profits of their harvest with them. The NAACP would collect and investigate the complaints of black sharecroppers—and compete with the Communist Party to organize them.

# "Strange Fruit"

ONE NIGHT IN 1939, in the Manhattan nightclub Cafe Society, Billie Holiday stepped to the microphone and sang a mournful, bluesy song. Some of the verses offered pastoral images of poplar trees and the "scent of magnolia sweet and fresh." But the "strange fruit" of the title wasn't citrus. It was a "black body swinging in the Southern breeze." The crowd fell into a solemn stillness, then some clapped hesitantly. In moments people shouted, "You did it, girl! Great, great!"

"Strange Fruit" became the anthem of antilynching sentiment. Although lynching had become a rarity (three took place in 1939), many white Southerners still believed it was justified in cases of black-on-white violence. The writer of the song, Abel Meeropol, a white Jewish schoolteacher from New York City, composed it after seeing a grisly magazine photo of a lynching. When Holiday recorded the song and its fame spread, Meeropol, a leftist, was brought before a state inquiry to answer whether the Communist Party paid him for it. *Time* called the song "a prime piece of musical propaganda for the NAACP."

### Strange Fruit
*Southern trees bear a strange fruit,*
*Blood on the leaves and blood at the root,*
*Black body swinging in the Southern breeze,*
*Strange fruit hanging from the poplar trees.*

*Pastoral scene of the gallant South,*
*The bulging eyes and the twisted mouth,*
*Scent of magnolia sweet and fresh,*
*And the sudden smell of burning flesh.*

*Here is a fruit for the crows to pluck,*
*For the rain to gather, for the wind to suck,*
*For the sun to rot, for the trees to drop,*
*Here is a strange and bitter crop.*

# THE 1940s

WITHIN THE REALM OF CIVIL RIGHTS, the 1940s began with a murmur and a scream. In the same year that the battle for an antilynching bill went down in defeat, in 1940, the *brrring!* of Richard Wright's alarm clock told white America what time it was. Wright's widely read novel, *Native Son*, conveyed the oppression and anguish felt by blacks. As a nation approached war, a new sense of militancy, a new confidence emboldened African-Americans.

Epitomizing the new "race man"—proud, confident, demanding respect—was A. Philip Randolph. The bold labor leader and civil rights activist saw the approaching war as an opportunity to challenge the racial status quo. In 1941 he threatened to organize a large demonstration in Washington unless President Franklin Roosevelt banned racial discrimination in defense industries. Randolph rallied his followers, soliciting support from civic organizations, the black press, and black churches, sororities, and fraternities. Randolph declared that the only way the administration would address black America's concerns was if tens of thousands of black protesters marched to the White House.

A March on Washington Committee was created, supported by both the National Urban League and the NAACP. Randolph, though, was wary of alliances. He had seen their limitations. He stated that he did not want even white supporters to march with the black activists, saying that African-Americans should supply the money and make the sacrifices to achieve their citizenship rights in America.

When the White House got wind of Randolph's plan to flood the White House grounds with tens of thousands of African-Americans, First Lady Eleanor Roosevelt and New York Mayor Fiorello La Guardia persuaded Randolph and the NAACP's Walter White to meet with President Roosevelt. Roosevelt responded by establishing the Fair Employment Practices Committee, which forbade racial discrimination in the defense industry. For the first time, the threat of direct

Many African-Americans took pride in defending democracy abroad, and expected a just democratic system in their own country, as well. This man picketed on behalf of the Negro Labor Relations League in Chicago in 1941.

action had moved the White House to act on its commitment to equal opportunity. For the first time, blacks viewed the federal government as an agent of social as well as economic change.

A year after Randolph's threat, a small group of Chicago religious students and pacifists organized the Committee (later changed to Congress) of Racial Equality (CORE). Led by James Farmer, CORE launched a series of demonstrations against segregated theaters, lunch counters, and stores throughout northern and border states. Using sit-ins, wade-ins, and later Freedom Rides to integrate public facilities, CORE exposed and confronted racial exclusion.

In the courts, the 1940s was a decade of repeated triumphs for the NAACP. In 1940 its attorneys won a case that ended the racially exclusionary practices of real estate agents in Chicago's Washington Park rowhouse development. And in 1944 the U.S. Supreme Court ruled that black citizens could not be denied their right to vote in state primary elections. New Deal liberalism was slowly transforming the nation's courts as the NAACP gradually chipped away at racial discrimination.

The NAACP's membership grew tremendously during the decade, largely because of the emergence of a relatively stable black working class in major American cities. A second wave of the Great Migration, spurred by the availability of defense jobs in urban factories, brought 4.5 million African-Americans north and west during the decade. With the emergence of the Congress of Industrial Organizations, black citizens found job security and the prospect of promotion. Working men and women could save their money, perhaps get a mortgage, and even dare to dream that their children might go to college.

Most African-American soldiers were assigned support duties during World War II, such as these men in France who emplaced a howitzer that white soldiers would operate. Military leaders didn't believe that blacks were competent enough for combat, a notion soundly disproved by the grand success of the Tuskegee Airmen, black tank corps, and other ground units.

The NAACP was also part of a broader coalition of groups that promoted the "Double V" campaign, which originated with Robert Lee Vann's black newspaper, *The Pittsburgh Courier*. They called for both victory abroad against fascism and victory at home against racial injustice. Meanwhile, millions of white Americans, sobered by war and the Jewish Holocaust in Europe, became more sensitive to racism. They were more aware that racism could kill, that "polite" antisemitism or the occasional "darky" joke were germs that could grow monstrously into genocide.

Black participation and heroism during the war also helped to break down racial barriers. Many white Americans respected the heroics of the all-black Tuskegee Airmen (who never lost a plane) and the sacrifice of countless African-Americans on the domestic front. White support of progressive thought spurred President Harry Truman's decision to establish a civil rights committee and, in 1948, to order the desegregation of the Armed Forces.

Truman also may have been responding to a new political reality. As thousands of blacks swelled the contours of the black ghettos in the nation's largest cities, black voters became the "balance of power" in several tight races. In 1948, seeking a full term, Truman became the first presidential candidate to campaign before a black audience in Harlem. Earlier, U.S. Senate candidate Hubert Humphrey's crusade for a strongly worded civil rights plank had spurred the Alabama and Mississippi delegations to walk out of the Democratic National Convention. But Truman won, and a few months later Congressman William L. Dawson became the first African-American to chair a congressional committee.

The 1940s was not a decade of unmitigated triumph, however. Oppressive conditions for blacks sparked racial violence in Detroit and Harlem in 1943, and three years later Alabama imposed a literacy test—a thinly veiled conceit to prevent African-Americans from registering to vote. When Charles H. Houston, Thurgood Marshall, and other NAACP attorneys persuaded the U.S. Supreme Court to ensure that the University of Oklahoma Law School admit Ada Sipuel, they never could have imagined that the university would create a special law school for a lone black woman in two weeks. The legal battle against segregation still had a long way to go.

However, those who held firm to segregation were on the losing side of history. From 1940 to 1946, the NAACP's membership grew from 50,000 to 450,000. In 1947 Jackie Robinson smashed Major League Baseball's color line in heroic fashion, winning over white fans with his class, courage, and dynamic play. At the beginning of the decade, Hattie McDaniel won an Academy Award for best supporting actress for her role as a maid in *Gone With the Wind*. McDaniel read a speech, written for her by a white studio flack, saying she hoped she would always be a "credit to her race." By the end of the decade, African-Americans were writing a new script. And this time they were speaking for themselves.

During the war years, southern blacks migrated en masse to northern cities, where many found work in war-production factories. Chicago's black population swelled from 233,000 in 1930 to 492,000 by 1950. Most of these newcomers settled on the city's South Side, where overcrowding and education became serious issues.

Two black men vote in the 1946 Democratic primary in Jackson, Mississippi—a rare occurence in that state. In 1947, 0.9 percent of voting-age blacks in Mississippi were registered to vote. To cast their ballots, southern blacks had to pay a poll tax, pass a literacy test, and/or risk their jobs.

# 1940s

## 1940–1941

**1940:** The NAACP forms the Legal Defense and Educational Fund, a group that will use the legal system to make civil rights advances.

**1940:** Richard Wright's novel *Native Son*, about a Chicago man trapped by racism and poverty, is published.

**February 12, 1940:** In *Chambers v. Florida*, the U.S. Supreme Court rules that forced confessions cannot be introduced as evidence in criminal trials.

**October 9, 1940:** President Franklin Roosevelt announces that African-Americans will have equal opportunities in the Armed Forces but will not serve in integrated regiments.

**1941:** Adam Clayton Powell, Jr., leads a successful four-week bus boycott in Harlem. The bus company agrees to hire black drivers and mechanics.

**May 1, 1941:** Black labor organizer A. Philip Randolph calls for a March on Washington to protest discriminatory hiring practices in U.S. defense industries.

**June 25, 1941:** In response to A. Philip Randolph's threat of a March on Washington, President Roosevelt establishes the Fair Employment Practices Committee to prevent racial discrimination in defense plants.

**1941–1945:** Black soldiers comprise about 9 percent of the U.S. Army during World War II, although segregation remains the general policy.

**1941–1945:** The Tuskegee Airmen, a segregated group of black fighter pilots in the U.S. Army Air Force, prove amazingly effective during World War II, destroying or damaging more than 400 enemy planes without losing one of their own aircraft. ➤

In the 1940s, America began to read and listen to the words of Richard Wright, whose literature educated whites about black anger and frustration. His *Native Son,* the classic 1940 novel about embattled black man Bigger Thomas, was such a strong bestseller that Orson Welles adapted it to the stage. Wright's autobiography, *Black Boy,* published five years later, was hailed for its brutal honesty.

To prepare for war in the early 1940s, the northern factories needed laborers. African-Americans who had grown weary of the segregated South saw their opportunity, and the second wave of the Great Migration began. By 1960 almost half of America's black population—which totaled at least 10 million—would live in the West and North. This made black Americans more urbanized, with greater access to education, entrepreneurship, and the arts. However, this second wave of migration inflamed racial tensions in numerous northern cities, resulting in violence in the 1940s and, to a greater extent, in the late 1960s.

Racist caricatures were not confined to the United States. This image is a "Golliwog," an immensely popular children's book character in Great Britain. Like America's "Little Black Sambo," the Golliwog character was held to ridicule. In Europe, Golliwog became a "nigger"-like slur against dark-skinned people.

Black students attend a one-room school in Georgia in 1941. In the segregated South, black and white facilities were supposed to be "separate but equal," according to the U.S. Supreme Court. Of course, that was rarely the case. In the late 1930s, the American Council on Education found that most southern black students didn't attend school for more than 20 weeks per year. They were taught by poorly trained teachers with old textbooks in inferior facilities. In 1930 Alabama spent more than five times more money per student to educate white children. The study showed that the maximum percentage of blacks who attended high school in the South was 20 percent, and that was only in North Carolina. The report also stated that nearly 90 percent of the secondary schools for blacks in the South were "essentially elementary schools."

# National Council of Negro Women

IN 1935 MARY MCLEOD BETHUNE, special adviser to President Franklin Roosevelt on Negro Affairs, founded the National Council of Negro Women. An experienced educator, businesswoman, and organization leader, Bethune envisioned the NCNW as coordinating other African-American women's groups and working with the federal government on domestic policy affecting women and children. When she retired in 1949, the Council boasted 21 affiliates and 90 local chapters reaching 850,000 women.

The council's activities reached national and international levels. In 1940 it conducted a study in Havana documenting the Negro's role in Cuban history and culture. After World War II, the NCNW gained permanent National Government Organization status to the United Nations. In the 1950s representatives campaigned to end apartheid in South Africa and held international conferences on women's rights. At the height of the Civil Rights Era, the council started a school breakfast plan in Mississippi, opened day care centers, and established home ownership programs in Louisiana, Missouri, and North Carolina.

Since then, the NCNW has continued its progressive work. It has served the United Nations, the Centers for Disease Control and Prevention, and other organizations as a partner in improving the quality of life for women and children in the U.S., Africa, and Latin America.

African-Americans picket in front of the Mid-City Realty Company in Chicago in July 1941. Many real estate companies in the North maintained exclusively white areas by a collective, if unwritten, agreement that they would never sell or rent any housing to black citizens in certain areas. Some real estate title documents included "restrictive convenants," which restricted the sale of homes to whites. The places they did allow blacks to live were rundown and overcrowded. Blacks lived in the worst parts of the cities and sometimes paid higher rents than whites in better sections.

Under Jim Crow, every facet of public life was segregated. This sign in Roma, Georgia, led black passengers into the "colored" seating area of a Greyhound bus terminal. While waiting in segregated seating sections, African-Americans could use the "colored" restrooms and drink from the "colored" drinking fountains before boarding the segregated buses.

By 1941 the NAACP had grown from an idea by white and black progressives into a national organization with a stated agenda, legal and political strategies, chapters, and a national magazine. It was becoming a major public force in America and the unofficial headquarters of black America's fight for equality. Illustrations such as this, which appeared in the *Louisville Defender,* helped inspire African-Americans to contribute needed funds to the NAACP.

Like other southern governors of his time, Georgia Governor Eugene Talmadge (*left*) was well known for his opposition to civil rights. When a board of regents rejected his attempts to fire two school officials who supposedly had advocated school desegregation, he replaced three of the regents. Here, Talmadge takes heat from Assistant Solicitor Dan Duke of Fulton Superior Court in November 1941. Talmadge had granted clemency to six convicted floggers—all Ku Klux Klan members—in East Point, Georgia, infuriating Duke. Talmadge was quite familiar with the Klan. On Election Eve in 1946, the KKK helped keep blacks away from the voting booths by placing miniature coffins on their doorsteps and tacking threatening notes on their churches—all done with the governor's blessing.

Even in death, whites separated themselves from blacks. Communities created "white" cemeteries and "colored" cemeteries. Some white cemeteries included "colored" sections. Usually, the white cemeteries were well kept while the black cemeteries were unkempt, often with homemade tombstones. Many grave sites, such as the one for Zora Neale Hurston, the great writer and anthropologist of the Harlem Renaissance, were unmarked. It was the final indignity of lives lived under Jim Crow.

Around 1940, a federal investigator described the "Negro quarter" of rural Belle Glade, Florida, as having "no regular streets, just a jumble of alleyways, hodgepodge streets and footpaths, [with] two- and three-story buildings, most of which are shed-like, barn-like, ramshackle." But strictly segregated Belle Glade, located on the fertile southern shore of Lake Okeechobee, was a magnet for migrant workers who were paid $4 a week to pick string beans, tomatoes, and other labor-intensive crops. Harlem Renaissance writer Zora Neale Hurston, who settled in Belle Glade in 1950, wrote about the town in her 1937 book, *Their Eyes Were Watching God*. One of the book's more naive characters enthuses, "Folks don't do nothin' down dere but make money and fun and foolishness." The modest, black-owned store seen here illustrates the reality that Hurston knew well.

# 1940s

**1942:** The "Double V" symbol—victory abroad and at home—becomes popular in the black community.

**1942:** The U.S. Justice Department threatens the editors of 20 black newspapers with sedition because they have run articles denouncing segregation in the U.S. military.

**May 1942:** James Farmer and the recently formed Congress of Racial Equality (CORE), an interracial civil rights group based on Gandhi's nonviolent protest strategies, stage their first sit-in, at Jack Spratt coffeehouse in Chicago.

**June 20–21, 1943:** After a population explosion in Detroit causes a severe housing crisis, a riot erupts when blacks and whites start fighting at Belle Isle amusement park. Nine whites and 25 blacks are killed.

**August 1–2, 1943:** Fed up with police brutality, black citizens riot in Harlem. Six African-Americans are killed and 185 injured. New York Mayor Fiorello La Guardia will respond with efforts to improve conditions for blacks in Harlem.

**1944:** Secretary of the Navy James V. Forrestal orders the integration of 25 fleet auxiliaries.

**April 3, 1944:** In *Smith v. Allwright*, the U.S. Supreme Court rules that black citizens cannot be denied their right to vote in state primary elections, bringing an end to white primaries.

**April 25, 1944:** The United Negro College Fund is founded to offer financial aid to students attending black colleges and universities.

**July 1944:** At the Democratic National Convention, Houston entrepreneur Hobart Taylor, Sr., becomes the first African-American to serve as a delegate from a southern state since Reconstruction. ➤

During segregation, readers could find three "national" newspapers for news about black America: the *Pittsburgh Courier, Chicago Defender,* and *Baltimore Afro-American*. These newspapers, whose national editions were available in virtually every black section of America's major cities, mixed sensational crime reporting with investigative stories about lynchings and incidents of discrimination. They also included powerful commentary by leading African-Americans. The newspapers' circulations peaked during World War II, with each paper boasting a six-figure readership. The *Defender* seen here dates from 1942.

On October 12, 1942, Charles Lang and Ernest Green were lynched in Quitman, Mississippi (*pictured*). Each was 14 years old. By the 1940s lynchings in the South had decreased significantly. On an incomplete list of 237 lynch victims in Mississippi history, six were murdered during the 1940s, including Reverend Isaac Simmons in Liberty in March 1944.

In the early 1940s black social psychologist Kenneth Clark conducted a study of black and white children in which they were shown black and white dolls and asked which they preferred. He found that a majority of the children—even most of the black kids—chose the white doll. Clark's study was used by the NAACP Legal Defense Fund to bolster its argument that segregated public schooling made black students feel inferior. This argument became the basis of the U.S. Supreme Court's landmark *Brown v. Board of Education* decision in 1954.

# James Farmer and CORE

I N APRIL 1942 A GROUP of men gathered in a house in Chicago with a single objective. As leader James Farmer put it, they would "form an organization that would seek to impale racism and segregation on the sword of nonviolent techniques"—much like Mahatma Gandhi had done in India. The group called itself the Committee (later Congress) of Racial Equality, or CORE.

One month later, while mingling with white friends, the group filed into Chicago's Jack Spratt coffeehouse, which had refused to serve African-Americans. Casual and quiet, the CORE members sat down in mixed parties of three and four. Waitresses hesitated, patrons gawked. The manager offered to move the black customers to the basement, but they declined. Whites were given food, but they wouldn't eat until all were served. Police officers arrived (Farmer had telephoned them beforehand) and told the manager they had no grounds for removing peaceful customers. The manager relented, and within weeks black patrons were seen in the restaurant all the time.

This was the first planned civil rights sit-in in U.S. history. Word of CORE's tactics and success spread, and chapters sprung up across the country. Farmer, a thoughtful man who grew up in Mississippi and Texas, traveled from city to city collecting funds. He secured endorsements from Eleanor Roosevelt, the ACLU, and A. Philip Randolph.

By the 1950s, with the rise of Martin Luther King, Jr., and the success of the Montgomery bus boycott, CORE-

style nonviolence had become a national story. Farmer led union drives in Virginia, and CORE members integrated lunch counters in North Carolina, prompting black students to repeat the strategy across the South. The height of CORE's activism came in the early 1960s with the famed Freedom Rides, when CORE leaders and followers braved death threats, FBI harassment, imprisonment, and beatings to end Jim Crow in buses and waiting rooms. The organization dropped its nonviolent philosophy and became militant in the mid-1960s.

African-Americans did not passively accept discrimination during wartime. Here, blacks and others picket the Capitol Transit Company in Washington, D.C., on May 7, 1943, for its failure to hire black workers. A year earlier, the Congress of Racial Equality (CORE), an interracial civil rights group that believed in using nonviolent direct action, was formed. Initially, it had some success in desegregating recreation areas and restaurants.

The Great Migration and white racism converged on Detroit in the early 1940s. As the factory city received an influx of African-Americans from the South, white workers protested against the desegregation of their ranks. Another controversy began when the city decided to build two new housing sites—one for blacks and one for whites. The federal government wanted to put the black housing project, named after 19th century activist Sojourner Truth, in a white neighborhood. This led to threats from the white community and increased racial tension, as indicated by this sign.

Detroit was ready to explode in 1943. Tensions surrounding the Sojourner Truth housing project controversy hadn't gone away. African-Americans, emboldened by their increasing population and angered by their treatment, reportedly began bumping into whites on the sidewalk as a protest. Whites, feeling threatened by an integrated workforce and possibly integrated neighborhoods, were ready to rumble. On June 20, 1943, scuffles between black and white teens broke out on Belle Isle, an integrated amusement park. At the Belle Isle Bridge, several thousand white Detroiters attempted to physically block blacks from crossing. Add to this two rumors (that whites had thrown a black woman and her baby off the bridge and that blacks had raped and murdered a white woman), and a riot began. Thirty-four people were killed over two days.

How do riots begin? Heat, poverty, and discrimination usually are the catalysts. In Harlem in August 1943, black soldiers returned home to their old enemy, Jim Crow. The spark was easily set aflame when a black soldier was shot by a police officer in the Braddock Hotel in Harlem as he tried to intervene between authorities and a woman who wouldn't pay her hotel bill. The story crackled through Harlem like electricity. Windows were broken, six people were killed, and 185 were reported injured.

Relatively few black soldiers who served with the U.S. armed forces during World War II were assigned to combat units; most toiled in maintenance or service roles. Exceptions, when they occurred, proved that black troops possessed as much bravery and motivation as their white counterparts. This mortar company of the 92nd Division was photographed in November 1944 in Italy, where it effectively pounded German machine gun nests.

A billboard in Birmingham, Alabama, featuring three white servicemen, reads: "One nation indivisible with liberty and justice for all." For African-Americans, the new war provided as much contradiction as opportunity. Black servicemen and servicewomen were seen primarily as last-ditch laborers instead of capable soldiers. Those blacks who fought did so to "maintain their freedom," which to a large extent they didn't have.

## "I'd rather see Hitler and Hirohito win than work beside a nigger on the assembly line."

—DETROIT FACTORY WORKER, JUNE 1943

Lena Horne was seemingly every black GI's favorite pinup girl during World War II. Hollywood refused to give her any starring roles in "white" films, other than the 1943 classic "race" musical *Stormy Weather*. Instead, studios cast her in singing roles (for example, as a saloon songstress) that easily could be cut out of southern screenings. Horne, a gifted singer and actress, was outspoken about the conditions of black America. She wrote articles on her struggles in the entertainment industry for black newspapers.

The Tuskegee Airmen were the pride of black America during World War II. The 99th Squadron trained at the segregated Tuskegee Army Air Field in Tuskegee, Alabama. The training of the airmen was considered an "experiment"; the U.S. military was convinced blacks lacked the intelligence and skill needed to become fighter pilots. The airmen proved everyone wrong. The all-black fighter squadron, known by its red tail wings, was used to escort Allied bombers. The segregated unit, given more than 200 missions as the 99th and as part of the 332nd Fighter Group, never lost a single plane. Almost a thousand men graduated from Tuskegee's flying school by the end of the war.

## 1945–1946

**1945:** Richard Wright's autobiography, *Black Boy*, is published.

**1945:** Alabama passes an amendment stating that citizens can vote only if they can read, write, or interpret the U.S. Constitution to the registrars' satisfaction.

**January 20, 1945:** The U.S. Army Nurse Corps agrees to accept black recruits.

**September 18, 1945:** Hundreds of white students in Gary, Indiana, walk out of classes to protest integration.

**November 1945:** John H. Johnson publishes the first issue of *Ebony* magazine, which focuses on black achievements.

**1946:** WWII veteran Maceo Snipes becomes the first black person since Reconstruction to vote in Taylor County, Georgia. As retribution, he is shot dead and then denied burial. His body is buried in a hole behind the mortician's place of business.

**January 1946:** The Women's Political Council is founded by Mary Fair Burks to encourage black women to vote and participate in politics.

**June 3, 1946:** In *Morgan v. Commonwealth of Virginia*, the U.S. Supreme Court rules that segregation in interstate bus travel is unconstitutional. *See* April 1947.

**July 25, 1946:** Two young black couples, Roger and Dorothy Malcom and George and Mae Murray Dorsey, are massacred at a bridge in Monroe, Georgia. A mob of unmasked white men ties them up and then shoots them hundreds of times. Despite an FBI investigation, no one will be brought to trial.

**December 5, 1946:** President Harry Truman establishes the President's Committee on Civil Rights, whose mission is to investigate racial injustice and recommend solutions. *See* October 29, 1947. ➤

Black America slowly changed during the 1940s. It became more northern, more urban. The success of the Tuskegee Airmen and other black soldiers gave African-Americans a new sense of pride. Blacks knew that they would be free one day of Jim Crow, and in 1944 they celebrated his "death" while they fought to kill it. The death of Jim Crow, they felt, was only a matter of time and continued hard work.

## Marching on the White Highway

ON MANEUVERS WE were in a wooded area. We had rifles but no ammunition, not even bayonets. Our officers had their 45s and that was all the protection we had in an area that was getting more hostile every minute....As we marched along counting cadence,...a group of mounted farmers came out of nowhere.... Their spokesman told our lieutenant to "Get those god-damned niggers off of the white highway and march 'em in the ditch." The ditch he spoke of had several inches of water in it; water moccasins' playground. Our lieutenant objected and told them if they weren't careful the area would be placed under martial law.... The rednecks rode him down with their horses, then pistol-whipped him—one of their own color! The lieutenant was later given a medical discharge because of this beating; they damned near killed him.

While this was happening a truckload of white MPs, who were armed, sat in their truck and offered no assistance to this white officer. More horse-riding dirt farmers...burn[ed] our one truck with our supplies.

—*Sergeant Lester Duance Simons,* The Invisible Soldier: The Experience of the Black Soldier, World War II

The opening of the integrated Sydenham Hospital in New York City in 1944 thrilled Eleanor Roosevelt. The First Lady, pictured with trustees of the hospital, had become a champion of civil rights. She pushed for better treatment of African-Americans in the New Deal programs, and threw her support behind the doomed Costigan–Wagner antilynching bill. Roosevelt wrote the article "If I Was a Negro" for *Negro Digest,* and she became close friends with Mary McLeod Bethune, the great black educator. Black civil rights activists wished the First Lady's husband could have been half the champion of their cause.

Reverend Adam Clayton Powell, Jr., a U.S. congressman representing Harlem, was on the move in 1945, the year *Marching Blacks,* his first book, was published. Powell wrote that southern blacks should respect themselves enough to leave Jim Crow behind and come north. He wrote: "The South evidently does not want blacks, even though it needs them, or it would not treat them so cruelly. Some blacks in the South are happy with their lot as slaves. Let them remain. There are others who, though blacks, have reaped great profits from the misery of their fellow blacks. Let them stay and starve. But to the vast millions who have been suckled with the milk of freedom from the depths of black bosoms—let them leave!" Powell's book confirmed that a "new" Negro, a more militant one, had arrived in postwar America.

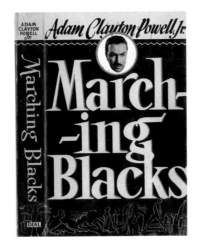

# Irene Morgan

A DECADE BEFORE Rosa Parks refused to give up her bus seat in Montgomery, Alabama, Irene Morgan displayed similar defiance in Virginia. In 1944 Morgan, a 27-year-old mother, boarded a Greyhound bus on her way to consult a doctor in Baltimore. She sat in the fourth row from the rear, in the designated "colored" section. But when more white passengers boarded, the driver ordered her to move farther back. Morgan said no. At that point a sheriff was called, but when he served Morgan with an arrest warrant, she tore it up. The sheriff dragged her kicking and screaming off the bus and took her to jail.

Morgan was fined $100 for resisting arrest and $10 for violating Virginia's segregation law. She pleaded guilty to the first crime but appealed the second, and the case went to the U.S. Supreme Court. One of Morgan's attorneys, Thurgood Marshall of the NAACP, argued that segregation on interstate travel was an improper burden on commerce. The court agreed by vote of 7 to 1, and the case became the statutory basis for subsequent actions to integrate public services, such as the Freedom Rides.

In 2001 President Bill Clinton awarded Irene Morgan the Presidential Citizens Medal.

Washington, D.C., a post-Civil War destination for many former slaves, was still a racially segregated city in the 1940s. A substantial middle-class black community existed, but the lives of the black poor were especially difficult. A few blocks east of the Capitol lay one of the worst slums in the country. Despite the Alley Dwelling Act of 1934, designed to regulate substandard housing, many continued to live in squalor within sight of the symbol of American equality and opportunity.

# 1940s

Friends and relatives of two married couples who were lynched, George and Mae Murray Dorsey and Roger and Dorothy Malcom, pay their respects to the four deceased in Monroe, Georgia. On July 25, 1946, the Dorseys and Malcoms were pulled from a car by a mob of 20 white men, who lined them up and shot them dead. John L. LeFlore, an NAACP activist who investigated the case, called the murder the end result of a sharecropping dispute between Roger Malcom and the white man for whom he worked. Said LeFlore: "The lynching of those four people shocked the nation.... This lynching was one of the ghastly and tragic happenings of the mid-20th century."

Pigmeat Markham was a veteran of the "chitlin' circuit"—the national tour of segregated theaters, juke joints, and outdoor festivals of Jim Crow black America. Shown here is a poster for the 1946 movie *House-Rent Party*. A "rent party" was a social gathering given at a home whose occupants needed rent money; guests offered donations. The rent party, which was a standard social event in Harlem and other northern black neighborhoods, allowed recent migrants to get to know each other. Markham's brand of boisterous, language-based humor was perfect for this kind of "race" movie.

I see the F.B.I. cleared up another big postage stamp robbery."

The caption for this Bill Mauldin cartoon, published on October 29, 1946, reads, "I see the F.B.I. cleared up another big postage stamp robbery." Mauldin implied that whites and the FBI were indifferent to the lynchings of the Malcoms and Dorseys in Georgia in July. A month earlier, entertainer and activist Paul Robeson led the Crusade Against Lynching, a coalition of 50 organizations, asking President Harry Truman to establish a "definite legislative and educational program to end the disgrace of mob violence." Truman responded that the time wasn't right for such action.

*Democracy*—THE CHALLENGE OF VICTORY

AN INVITATION
TO THE
*Sixth All-Southern Negro Youth Conference*
ATLANTA, GA.—NOV. 30, DEC. 1-2-3, 1944

THE SOUTHERN NEGRO YOUTH CONGRESS
*Summons you to—*
The **Southern Youth Legislature**
COLUMBIA        SOUTH CAROLINA
OCTOBER        18, 19, 20        1946

The Southern Negro Youth Congress was founded in 1937 to improve the conditions of and opportunities for young African-Americans. SNYC's literature during the war years (*far left photo*) was nonconfrontational, urging prospective members to "join with fellow Americans in common allegiance to democracy." The postwar literature took on a more militant tone, as conveyed by the image on the right.

Due to northern migration and GIs returning from service, many cities in the North experienced a housing shortage after World War II. In racially mixed areas, that often led to friction between blacks and whites. Here, white men overturn a car driven by Kenneth Kennedy, a black man, in Chicago on December 5, 1946. The men were angry that black families had been assigned apartments in their South Side neighborhood by the Chicago Housing Authority.

# 1940s

## 1947

**April:** The Congress of Racial Equality (CORE) sends eight African-Americans and eight whites on a Journey of Reconciliation, a bus trip through the South, to test the 1946 U.S. Supreme Court ruling that banned segregation in interstate bus travel. The travelers are met with heavy resistance. Some members, after being arrested in North Carolina, will serve time on a chain gang.

**April 15:** Jackie Robinson debuts with the Brooklyn Dodgers, becoming the first African-American to play in the major leagues since 1885.

**October 24:** W.E.B. Du Bois, addressing the United Nations on behalf of the NAACP, makes an appeal against racism in the United States.

**October 29:** The President's Committee on Civil Rights issues the report *To Secure These Rights*, which condemns discrimination and makes specific recommendations as to how the government could further civil rights.

**December 31:** A Tuskegee Institute report on lynching states that 3,432 African-Americans have been lynched since 1882. ➤

The response from these young Brooklyn Dodgers fans indicates that New Yorkers were more than ready to accept a black Major League ballplayer. They asked Jackie Robinson for his autograph prior to an exhibition game on April 10, 1947, five days before Opening Day. Most Major Leaguers welcomed Robinson, but some opposing players abused him with insults, hard slides, and pounding tags. In late August, some St. Louis Cardinals players called for a strike against Robinson and the Dodgers. Responded Major League Baseball Commissioner Ford Frick: "I don't care if half the league strikes. This is the United States of America, and one citizen has as much right to play as another." The strike never materialized.

While a boy in Jacksonville, Florida, in the early 1920s, Stetson Kennedy witnessed a white bus driver physically assault the Kennedy family maid, a young black woman who was visited soon after by the Ku Klux Klan, beaten some more, and raped. Although Kennedy's uncle was prominent in the Jacksonville Klan, Stetson grew to hate the organization. His 1942 book, *Palmetto County*, revealed much of the Klan's rotten history, and earned the enmity of many in the South. Following World War II, Kennedy assumed a false name and joined the Atlanta Klan, risking his life to discover the organization's secret rites and activities. He revealed himself at a January 1947 press conference (*above*) at the Manhattan headquarters of the Anti-Defamation League. When Kennedy's book about his undercover experiences, *I Rode with the Ku Klux Klan*, was published in 1954, KKK Grand Dragon Samuel Green said, "Kennedy's ass is worth $1,000 per pound, FOB Atlanta!"

# Jackie Robinson

ON OPENING DAY IN 1947, when the Brooklyn Dodgers took the field, Jackie Robinson trotted out to second base as the first black Major Leaguer in the 20th century. He had been signed two years earlier by Dodgers President Branch Rickey, who felt that the time had come to break down the color line in America's national pastime.

Robinson was a star athlete at UCLA. Though humble and upstanding, he said he "never tolerated affronts to his dignity." When Rickey asked Robinson if he wanted to end segregation in baseball, he warned the ballplayer about what would follow: teammates who resented him, pitchers throwing beanballs, hotels forcing him to sleep separately, crowds chanting, "Nigger! Nigger! Nigger!" Nevertheless, Robinson accepted the challenge.

After a year with a farm team in Montreal, Robinson joined the Dodgers, his every move monitored by sportwriters, skeptical team owners, Rickey himself, and millions of black fans. Death threats came every week, and opposing players taunted him: "They're waiting for you in the jungles, black boy!" Other teams plotted to strike, and baserunners aimed their spikes at his ankles.

Robinson suffered the insults and threats in silence, choking down the rage. Fighting back, he knew, would provoke more race-baiting and hurt the integrationist cause. Besides, the Dodgers were winning. At season's end, they were in the World Series and Robinson was named Rookie of the Year. His competitive drive had won over teammates and fans, and his personal composure abashed the racists. Other black players soon debuted in the Majors, including Larry Doby with Cleveland just three months after Robinson's breakthrough.

After he retired from baseball in 1956, Robinson worked for the Chock Full O'Nuts Corporation and contributed to the Civil Rights Movement. He chaired the NAACP's Freedom Fund Drive, argued for equal housing before the Federal Civil Rights Commission, and strove to keep civil rights issues on the Republican Party's agenda. Robinson is the only player ever to have his uniform number (42) retired by Major League Baseball.

W.E.B. Du Bois wanted the newly established United Nations to deal with the plight of black Americans as an international human rights problem. In 1947 Du Bois's "An Appeal to the World: A Statement on the Denial of Human Rights to Minorities in the Case of Citizens of Negro Descent in the United States of America," was presented to the U.N. The Soviet Union proposed that the petition be received by a United Nations human rights subcommission, which the United States and its friends rejected.

# 1940s

## 1948

**1948:** "Dixiecrats," southern Democrats who oppose integration, form the States' Rights Democratic Party. South Carolina Governor Strom Thurmond is their nominee for president.

**1948:** The Atlanta Police Department hires its first black officers.

**1948:** William Gardner Smith's novel *Last of the Conquerors*, about a black soldier involved in the U.S. Army's occupation of Germany, is published.

**January 12:** In *Sipuel v. Board of Regents of the University of Oklahoma*, the U.S. Supreme Court rules that states cannot racially discriminate against law school applicants.

**May 3:** The U.S. Supreme Court rules in *Shelley v. Kraemer* that states cannot enforce racially restrictive housing covenants.

**June 26:** A. Philip Randolph establishes the League for Non-Violent Civil Disobedience Against Military Segregation.

**July 14:** Objecting to the Democratic Party's civil rights platform, Alabama and Mississippi delegates walk out of the Democratic National Convention.

**July 23:** In Philadelphia, the Progressive Party opens its convention. As part of its platform, it demands an end to segregation in interstate travel.

**July 26:** President Harry Truman signs Executive Order 9981, which officially ends segregation of the U.S. Armed Forces. *See* October 30, 1954.

**November:** NAACP President D. V. Carter is beaten by whites in Montgomery, Alabama, for escorting black citizens to the polls. ➤

Atlanta often strived to prove it was "The City Too Busy to Hate." In 1947 the City Council did something that shocked many southern whites: It passed a resolution allowing African-Americans to become police officers. But although a few blacks joined law enforcement, white supremacy was still the larger law. Black officers were assigned only to black districts, and they were not permitted to arrest white citizens.

In October 1947 President Harry Truman formed the President's Committee on Civil Rights to study the problems of racial discrimination in the United States. The chairman of the commission was Charles E. Wilson (*addressing Truman*). The commission wrote the report *To Secure These Rights*, which recommended the immediate "elimination of segregation based on race, color, creed, or national origin, from American life." Ever the pragmatist, Truman moved one step at a time. Using the power of an executive order, he desegregated the military in 1948. The committee was a forerunner of the U.S. Commission on Civil Rights, which would be established 10 years later.

# President Truman and Civil Rights

WHEN HARRY TRUMAN became president in 1945, a million black men served in the armed forces, all in segregated units. No blacks stood as federal judges, and only a small percentage voted. Republicans, who controlled the Senate, invariably joined southern Democrats to kill civil rights legislation.

Against the will of Congress and despite his lagging poll numbers, Truman in 1946 created the President's Committee on Civil Rights, mandating that federal employees provide it with any documents and information it required. In June 1947 Truman climbed the steps of the Lincoln Memorial to become the first president to address the NAACP, his speech broadcast nationwide. "It is my deep conviction that we have reached a turning point in the long history of our country's efforts to guarantee freedom and equality to all our citizens," he declared. "When I say all Americans, I mean all Americans."

Four months later the Committee on Civil Rights issued a 178-page report on civil rights in America. It revealed violence, discrimination, and exploitation against blacks, not as exceptions to the workings of U.S. democracy but as pervasive forms of social, political, and economic policy. Blacks were denied education, jobs, the right to vote, and many basic services. The chain gang, the whip, and the rope awaited those who fought back.

The Committee made 35 recommendations for reform, and Truman responded. He lectured Congress on equal protection for all people under the law, then demanded that the Democratic Party adopt a civil rights plank in the 1948 election. Truman knew that legislation wouldn't pass, but on July 26, 1948, he issued an executive order ending discrimination in the armed services and in federal employment. In his last presidential address, he claimed, "There has been a great awakening of the American conscience on the issues of civil rights."

The dramatic changes in American society during and after World War II hurt the Invisible Empire. The Ku Klux Klan's membership dwindled dramatically in the 1940s from the four to five million it had in the 1920s, as did lynching. Nevertheless, many in the KKK attempted to keep the faith. On July 23, 1948, some 700 Klansmen gathered on Stone Mountain, Georgia, the site where Nathan Bedford Forrest and other Confederate Army veterans founded the KKK in 1866. The Klan would rise again when the Civil Rights Movement gained steam.

# 1940s

White southern Democrats began to feel betrayed by their own party in 1948. President Harry Truman's push to make civil rights part of the Democratic Party platform stirred open revolt in the South, with many wanting to form their own party. This Birmingham, Alabama, meeting of the "Dixie Democrats" was one of many held in the South. White Southerners decided to be either loyal supporters of the Dixie Democrats or spoilers who would allow Republican Thomas E. Dewey to win the presidency in 1948. Many southern Democrats actually voted for Dewey, since maintaining segregation was far more important to them than party loyalty.

South Carolina Governor Strom Thurmond, a staunch segregationist, felt completely abandoned by the Democratic Party—a party that originally had stood up to Abraham Lincoln and his Radical Republicans; that had defended states' rights; and that understood the (segregated) southern way of life. The estrangement was caused by President Harry Truman's endorsement of civil rights. Thurmond and other Southerners were looking for alternatives, and the governor decided to run for president in 1948 on the States' Rights ticket. He traveled the country, garnering support from offended white southern Democrats. On election night, Thurmond won four states: Louisiana, Mississippi, Alabama, and South Carolina, his home state.

First, President Harry Truman made statements in support of civil rights. Then Richard Russell, a segregationist U.S. senator from Georgia, failed in his attempt to win the Democratic nomination. Finally, at the 1948 Democratic National Convention, the party endorsed moderate civil rights policies. On the losing end of race issues, southern Democrats were ready to abandon their party. Said South Carolina Governor Strom Thurmond, "We have been betrayed, and the guilty should not go unpunished." At the July convention in Philadelphia, the Mississippi delegation and some Alabama delegates decided to walk out of the convention hall. Emmett S. Cunningham and William Booker of Detroit (*pictured*) were among those who booed the delegates' actions.

The Democratic Party was torn at both ends in 1948. The segregationist Dixie Democrats wanted to bolt. Meanwhile, progressives, including black American leftists such as Paul Robeson (*seated, third from left*), threw their hopes and votes to Henry Wallace (*seated, second from left*). Wallace's third-party effort, the Progressive Party, attracted such mainstream Democrats as U.S. Senator Glen Taylor (*seated, far left*) of Idaho, Wallace's vice presidential candidate. The party's platform included the support of nations struggling against colonialism, a more peaceful relationship with the Soviet Union, and the destruction of Jim Crow. On election night, the Progressive Party received less than 3 percent of the popular vote. President Harry Truman survived the onslaughts within his party, but the fissures would reverberate for decades.

# 1940s

"Thirteen million Negroes, representing a vast reservoir of possible war material, are being ignored and in some instances openly humiliated. It is therefore not surprising that Negro citizens are without enthusiasm for national defense. They can have no faith in the leadership of an army or a navy that denies them the right to serve their country on an equal footing with other citizens."

—*Chicago Defender* editor Metz T. P. Lochard, 1941

The life of the desegregation pioneer was hard, lonely, and often humiliating. G. W. McLaurin, a black man, won a U.S. Supreme Court battle to attend graduate school at the University of Oklahoma. But when he arrived for classes in fall 1948, McLaurin, 54, was forced to sit in the "Negro row." He also was assigned a segregated section in the library and the cafeteria. In 1950 the U.S. Supreme Court ruled that McLaurin had the right to not only attend a white graduate school but to receive full academic benefits from the school.

The NAACP's primary legal tactic was to force the U.S. Supreme Court to overrule state school segregation laws by successfully arguing that black schools did not provide "equal" education. The strategy was paying off, case by case. Ada Sipuel (*pictured*) wanted to attend law school in her home state, but she was barred from the University of Oklahoma School of Law because of her race. Thurgood Marshall (*center*) and the NAACP took on the case, using the now standard argument. Sipuel won in January 1948, and the law school had to admit her—although they did so in unconventional fashion. They created a law school on campus just for her.

# Desegregating the Military

IN WORLD WAR II, as in previous wars, black soldiers served in segregated units. The Navy used black sailors mostly in menial roles, and there were few black Marines. As one black soldier complained to a newspaper, the *Pittsburgh Courier*, "Why can't we eat, live and be respected as the whites? We're constantly being cursed at and mocked. But yet we too have to die as well as them, and even perhaps beside them."

In 1941 African-Americans demanded new policies in the military, as the United States prepared for a possible entry into World War II. A. Philip Randolph, president of the Brotherhood of Sleeping Car Porters, threatened President Franklin Delano Roosevelt with a march on Washington by African-Americans if Roosevelt did not meet two demands: 1) access to defense jobs for blacks and 2) an end to racial segregation in the Armed Forces. Concerned that such a march would slow the momentum of public support for involvement in the war, Roosevelt gave in. In June 1941 he signed Executive Order 8802, which prohibited racial discrimination in the employment of workers in defense industries.

Roosevelt ignored Randolph's call for a desegregated army. By that time, all branches of the military separated black soldiers into their own units, deployed them on segregated trains, and housed them in old, dilapidated barracks. Most black soldiers served as stewards and cooks or performed menial labor such as maintaining latrines. As late as 1940, the U.S. armed services included only five black commissioned officers, including Benjamin O. Davis, Sr., the first African-American to reach the rank of general, and Benjamin O. Davis, Jr., the 20th century's first black graduate of West Point. Military leaders routinely denied black soldiers entry into many training classes that would have enabled them to advance in rank.

At the war's end, Randolph once again took up the cause of integration of the military, this time with President Harry Truman. Truman's 1947 Committee on Civil Rights recommended that segregated units and facilities be eliminated from the military in its report, *To Secure These Rights*.

On March 31, 1948, Randolph testified before the Senate Armed Services Committee. He threatened a campaign of draft resistance unless racial segregation and discrimination were eliminated from the military. Randolph announced, "I personally pledge myself to openly counsel, aid, and abet youth, both white and Negro, to quarantine any Jim Crow conscription system."

Together with A. J. Muste of the Fellowship for Reconciliation, a pacifist organization, Randolph in June 1948 formed the League for Non-Violent Civil Disobedience Against Military Segregation to encourage resistance to draft registration and induction. That summer he picketed the Democratic and Republican national conventions. Both conventions passed planks to their platforms that denounced segregation in the military.

Pressured by this strategy, and eager to attract the black vote for his troubled run for reelection as president, Truman signed Executive Order 9981 on July 26, 1948. The order mandated equality of treatment and opportunity for all persons in the armed services. Satisfied with the directive, Randolph called off the campaign for draft resistance and disbanded the league he had formed.

Despite the executive order, it was not until the Korean War of 1950–53 that efforts to integrate black and white units and facilities began in earnest. The NAACP's chief legal counsel, Thurgood Marshall, investigated charges of continuing segregation and poor treatment by soldiers on the front lines during the Korean War. The NAACP's efforts, as well as the pressing need for combat troops, encouraged the elimination of segregation. On October 30, 1954, the Department of Defense announced that all branches of the U.S. military were officially integrated.

Sergeant Curtis Pugh is honored for his heroism during the Korean War.

## 1949

**January 18:** Congressman William Dawson (D–IL) becomes the first African-American elected to chair a regular congressional committee as he's appointed the head of the House Committee on Expenditures in Executive Departments.

**January 28:** Senator Richard Russell (D–GA) introduces a bill proposing that southern black citizens be dispersed throughout the United States with the help of a relocation bureau.

**April 6:** The U.S. Armed Forces creates a policy of equal treatment and opportunity.

**June 3:** Wesley A. Brown becomes the first African-American to graduate from the United States Naval Academy.

**October 3:** WERD-AM, the first black-owned radio station in the United States, begins broadcasting from Atlanta.

On June 21, 1949, 200 white teenage boys made their opinion clear about the desegregation of the Fairground Park Pool in St. Louis. The whites responded to St. Louis Mayor Joseph M. Darst's order that the city-owned pool be open to African-Americans. Some of the 50 black citizens who decided to test the new order were badly beaten by whites. Darst subsequently changed his mind, although a court order eventually led to the pool's desegregation.

As the 1940s ended, Hollywood began to gingerly tackle the topic of race in America—but only from a perspective with which whites could feel comfortable. *Pinky,* a 1949 film, is about a black woman who "passes" for white. She falls in love with a white man but is terrified he will discover her true racial identity. This kind of mixed-race film character became known as "the tragic mulatto." At the end of the film, the lovers go their separate ways. Since African-Americans were not yet allowed to take on major film roles, the star of *Pinky* was Jeanne Crain, a white woman.

*De facto* Jim Crow flared up again and again in the North, particularly with issues of housing. In New York City in 1949, Hardine Hendricks (*center*) and her family sublet an apartment in Stuyvesant Town, the Metropolitan Life Insurance housing project, from whites. The projects' owners attempted to evict the Hendrickses. The New York State Supreme Court ruled that a private development could evict whom they wished on their own criteria, including racial.

Public housing in the North had a way of reinforcing a national Jim Crow agenda. As the second wave of the Great Migration spread, blacks moved into public housing complexes in northern cities. But as the cities formed, the construction of highways and freeways (including one pictured here in New York City) wound up creating "inner cities"—black sections of cities cut off by those roadways and by lack of economic opportunity. Highways and freeways provided easy access from white suburbs to downtowns, the centers for big business and entertainment. The poor, including poor blacks, were left out of the urban economic equation. The beginning of modern-day black "ghettos" had begun.

William Levi Dawson fought inside the corridors of power for the rights of black Americans. A member of the U.S. House of Representatives beginning in 1942, Dawson developed a reputation as "Mr. Inside" while his colleague, Adam Clayton Powell, Jr., was "Mr. Outside." Dawson, representing Chicago, helped secure the desegregation of the armed forces and spoke out against voting barriers. In 1949 he became the first African-American to chair a standard congressional committee when he became chair of the House Committee on Expenditures in Executive Departments.

Howard University, an historically black college in Washington, D.C., became known as the "Negro Harvard." Funded by a congressional appropriation, the university was the first—and remains today the only—historically black college classified as a research institution. Its law and medical schools graduated the majority of black professionals in those fields. Its other courses provided the best in "classic" liberal arts, including theater. Here, Marilyn Berry and Robert Brown of Howard's drama school rehearse Ibsen's *The Wild Duck*.

# THE 1950s

"Human blood may stain southern soil in many places because of this decision, but the dark red stains of that blood will be on the marble of the United States Supreme Court Building."

—EDITORIAL, ON THE *BROWN V. BOARD OF EDUCATION* DESEGREGATION RULING, *JACKSON* (MISSISSIPPI) *DAILY NEWS*, MAY 18, 1954

Nettie Hunt hugs her daughter, Nickie, on the steps of the U.S. Supreme Court in May 1954. The court ruled in *Brown v. Board of Education* that segregation in public schools was unconstitutional, a decision that sent shock waves through the South.

THE PROSPEROUS 1950s brought new opportunities for Americans—if they were of European descent. Job and housing discrimination was still commonplace in the North, while segregation remained firmly entrenched in Dixie. The NAACP, determined to weaken or defeat Jim Crow, tried to do so in the courtroom.

Before it fought for integration, the NAACP in the late 1930s and 1940s strove for educational "equalization." With this legal strategy, the organization hoped to force southern states to establish equal facilities and pay equal salaries at all levels of instruction, from elementary to graduate school. The NAACP hoped that by making segregation prohibitively expensive, it could force the South into integrating its schools.

The NAACP had reason to be optimistic. For years, the organization's greatest triumphs had been not on the picket lines or in legislative chambers, but in the courtroom. In case after case, despite some reversals, the NAACP successfully had challenged racial discrimination in housing, interstate transportation, employment, and public accommodations. In 1915 it had succeeded in getting the notorious grandfather clause (in which descendents of slaves had to pay a poll tax and pass a literacy test in order to vote) outlawed in *Guinn v. United States*. Two years later, municipal ordinances mandating residential segregation were outlawed in *Buchanan v. Warley*. A decade later, in *Nixon v. Herndon*, the U.S. Supreme Court declared null and void a Texas statute that excluded blacks from voting in the state Democratic primary.

Although it failed to secure passage of antilynching legislation in the 1930s and 1940s, the NAACP was the vanguard civil rights organization. The NAACP's legal team was led by Charles H. Houston, the vice-dean of the Howard University Law School. Houston, who died in April 1950, made contributions to the modern Civil Rights Movement that often have been overlooked. No one was more responsible

In the fall of 1954, Washington, D.C., (*pictured*) and Baltimore were the only major cities to desegregate their public schools in accordance with the *Brown* decision. In both cities, white parents picketed against integration.

While many white southern children took integration in stride, others were encouraged to be belligerent in their treatment of African-Americans new to their schools. Some white youths ridiculed, demeaned, spat upon, and/or physically abused black students.

for the organization's most impressive legal victories, and no one better reflected its persistent commitment to changing the laws. It was Houston who personally recruited a young Thurgood Marshall to his staff.

Southern schools that lost race-related court cases demonstrated remarkable inventiveness. When the University of Oklahoma was ordered to admit a qualified black woman, Ada Sipuel, to its law school, the university regents quickly arranged for the creation of a separate law school for African-Americans. By 1950 it had become apparent to the NAACP that its "equalization" strategy wasn't working. Thus, the organization decided to directly attack the constitutionality of school segregation laws.

In early 1954 the NAACP's concerted assault on segregation in public education culminated in *Brown v. Board of Education of Topeka*, a U.S. Supreme Court case. The NAACP challenged the doctrine of "separate but equal" schools for whites and African-Americans, as legitimized in the 1896 *Plessy v. Ferguson* decision. A nation anxiously awaited the court's decision.

Historians continue to debate the exact origins of the modern Civil Rights Movement. Many point to the Montgomery bus boycott in 1955–56 and the emergence of Martin Luther King, Jr. Others point to Harry Truman's order to integrate the U.S. Armed Forces in 1948 or Jackie Robinson's inclusion in America's pastime in 1947. A few note the demographic shift and startling economic advancements accompanying the Second Great Migration and World War II. For most historians, however, no event in the 20th century was as pivotal to the civil rights cause as the *Brown* decision.

Thurgood Marshall served as the NAACP's lead counsel for the *Brown* case. Marshall literally had risked his life to gather documentation and secure witnesses to testify. Marshall's court case hinged on his contention that the *Plessy v. Ferguson* decision violated the 14th Amendment, which granted full citizenship to all people born or naturalized in the United States. As it turned out, the justices were not so concerned with the 19th century decisions. Chief Justice Earl Warren explained:

> In approaching this problem, we cannot turn the clock back to 1868 when the Amendment was adopted, or even to 1896 when *Plessy v. Ferguson* was written. We must consider public education in the light of its full development and its present place in American life throughout the Nation. We come then to the question presented: Does segregation of chil-

dren in public schools solely on the basis of race, even though the physical facilities and other tangible factors may be equal, deprive the children of the minority group of equal educational opportunities? We believe that it does.

Shortly after winning his case, Marshall stood on the courthouse steps, expressing both exuberance and optimism about the future rate of social change. How long did he think it would take to get rid of segregated schools? "Up to five years," he said. As events soon would demonstrate, he was overly optimistic. Still, Marshall had reason to celebrate. Here was an unexpected triumph of momentous proportion.

Why did the Supreme Court throw precedent aside and repeal *Plessy v. Ferguson*? Historians have proposed several theories. One is that the court, loaded with justices nominated by former President Franklin D. Roosevelt (a Democrat), had been trending left since the 1930s. Another is that black contributions during World War II and the Korean War had spawned racial goodwill. African-American troops of the U.S. Army's 24th Infantry Regiment had helped capture Yechon in Korea, the first U.S. victory in the war.

Mamie Bradley grieves for her son, Emmett Till, who was murdered in Mississippi in August 1955. The crime, and the killers' acquittal by an all-white jury, inspired many African-Americans to join the fight for civil rights.

Moreover, American political and business elites were aware that the Soviet Union was feeding anti-American propaganda to nonaligned nations in Africa and Asia. The powers in Washington didn't want to be viewed as two-faced when it came to democracy. A dark-skinned man who was refused service at a Howard Johnson's restaurant in Dover, Maryland, turned out to be the finance minister of Ghana; President Dwight Eisenhower invited the minister to breakfast at the White House to make amends. When Eisenhower went on national television in 1957 to explain why he sent troops to Little Rock, Arkansas, to enforce court-ordered integration of Central High School, he laid heavy stress on the foreign impact of the incident. Arkansas Governor Orval Faubus's resistance to the integration was, in Eisenhower's words, a "tremendous disservice to the nation in the eyes of the world."

Nevertheless, were these exertions necessary? Was *Brown* even necessary? Was *Brown* good law or even good public policy? For at least the last quarter century, some historians have questioned whether *Brown* was needed or desirable. They point to evidence of substantial educational advancement and economic progress throughout the

# 1950s

The arrest of Rosa Parks, who refused to give up her seat to a white man on a Montgomery city bus, triggered a citywide bus boycott by blacks on December 5, 1955. Some local black leaders urged a one-day boycott, but Reverend E. D. Nixon (*left*) pushed to extend the boycott until the city changed its public transportation laws.

On April 23, 1956, the U.S. Supreme Court ruled that segregation on public transportation was unconstitutional. Here, on April 25, a bus rider in Dallas points to a sign that mandates segregation. Local authorities took down such signs that very same day.

1950s, and they argue that black progress would have continued without *Brown* or the Civil Rights Movement.

However, the case of Emmett Till illustrates that Jim Crow remained firmly entrenched in the American South. Till was a 14-year-old Chicago boy who was brutally lynched—apparently beaten, tortured, and shot—in Mississippi in August 1955 because he had said "Hey, baby" to a white woman. The Till case made national headlines, in part because of the drama surrounding the decision of Emmett's mother to publicly display his deformed and mangled corpse. Also, since the number of lynchings had dropped significantly by the 1950s, a real flesh-and-blood lynching was now hot news.

The trial of the two white men accused of murdering Till was a sham. It seemed apparent that Roy Bryant and J. W. Milam were guilty, but the all-male, all-white jury set the men free anyway, as they weren't about to convict whites for killing a black man. After exoneration, the murderers even sold their confession to a magazine and made a tidy profit. Such casual brutality brings to mind Tom Sawyer running to tell Aunt Sally about a riverboat fire on the Mississippi. "Anybody hurt?," she asks. "No, ma'am," Tom replies. "Just killed a nigger."

Just three months after Till's murder, Rosa Parks, a seamstress who also happened to be the secretary of the local branch of the NAACP, refused to give up her bus seat to a white man in Montgomery, Alabama. Her arrest sparked the Montgomery bus boycott and the meteoric career of the young and charismatic Dr. Martin Luther King, Jr., who had been named pastor of the Dexter Avenue Baptist Church in 1954.

The Montgomery boycott of 1955–56 played a major role in ushering in what was then referred to as the "Negro Revolt." Parks was not the first African-American to refuse to give up a seat on public transportation. She was not even the first black woman to refuse to move to the back of a Montgomery bus. But she was the right woman, educated and dignified, a role model of character and resolve. For 381 days, African-Americans in Montgomery boycotted the city's buses. Their persistence signaled to the nation that the promise of *Brown* would deliver, that the dream would not be deferred.

Despite his public support of civil rights, Eisenhower was a reluctant warrior. Before the momentous *Brown* decision in 1954, Ike had arranged a meeting between Supreme Court Chief Justice Earl Warren and States' Rights Party lawyer John W. Davis in a clumsy attempt to sway Warren's vote. "These are not bad people," Warren quotes Eisenhower as saying about Southerners. "All they are concerned about is to see that their sweet little girls are not required to sit in school alongside some big overgrown Negroes." Whatever his personal opinions, the *Brown* decision forced Eisenhower to defend the Constitution and send federal troops to ensure that nine black children would be admitted to Little Rock's Central High, even if their path had to be cleared by fixed bayonets.

Throughout the South, white resistance to desegregation was fierce and, at times, fanatical. White Citizens' Councils sprang up. Virginia adopted a policy of "massive resistance," and private schools materialized to provide "safe havens" for white children. Some southern legislators tried to make NAACP activity illegal in their states. Others sought to force the organization to make its membership rosters public so that white employers could harass and intimidate members. Racial violence increased in the South, but so did black resolve.

In Little Rock, Arkansas, nine black students needed the backing of President Dwight Eisenhower and the National Guard to attend Central High School in September 1957. Even by October 16 (*pictured*), the "Little Rock Nine" faced a gauntlet of abuse from the school's white students.

Besides the dramatics in Little Rock, other encouraging events occurred in 1957. Marian Anderson, who had been denied permission to sing at Constitution Hall by the Daughters of the American Revolution in 1939, sang at the inauguration of President Eisenhower. Months later, Eisenhower signed the Civil Rights Bill of 1957. Although relatively weak, it was the first major piece of civil rights legislation passed by Congress in the 20th century.

In 1959 the most popular speaker on college campuses was Arizona Senator Barry Goldwater, an ultraconservative Republican. The runner-up: Malcolm X. That same year Lorraine Hansberry's play *A Raisin in the Sun* won the New York Drama Critics Circle Award. The title was taken from the Langston Hughes poem "Montage of a Dream Deferred":

*What happens to a dream deferred?*

*Does it dry up*

*like a raisin in the sun?...*

*Or does it explode?*

In the 1950s, Southerners tried desperately to defer African-Americans' dream of equal rights. Would the dream dry up, or would it explode into something glorious...or something violent...or both?

# 1950s

## 1950

**1950:** The U.S. State Department strips Paul Robeson of his passport after he criticizes American foreign policy and racism in the U.S.

**1950:** Black Congressman Adam Clayton Powell, Jr., (D–NY) introduces what will become known as the "Powell Amendment." The amendment states that federal funds will be denied to any project in which racial discrimination is discovered.

**January:** A. Philip Randolph, Arnold Aronson, and Roy Wilkins form the Leadership Conference on Civil Rights.

**January 15:** Delegates from a hundred national organizations meet in Washington, D.C., at the National Emergency Civil Rights Conference, organized by the NAACP.

**May 1:** Gwendolyn Brooks becomes the first African-American to win a Pulitzer Prize, awarded for her book of poetry, *Annie Allen*.

**May 16:** In *Briggs v. Elliot*, NAACP attorney Thurgood Marshall challenges school segregation in Clarendon County, South Carolina. *See* June 1951.

**June 5:** The U.S. Supreme Court issues decisions on *Sweatt v. Painter* and *McLaurin v. Oklahoma State Regents*. The court rules that blacks have the right to attend white graduate schools and receive full academic benefits from those schools.

**June 5:** In *Henderson v. United States*, the U.S. Supreme Court strikes down an Interstate Commerce Commission ruling that required black rail passengers to eat behind a partition that separated them from whites on dining cars. *See* February 19, 1952.

**June 9:** Andrew Wright, the last imprisoned Scottsboro defendant, is released—19 years after his arrest.

**July 17:** A federal court rules that municipal swimming pools in St. Louis must be opened to blacks. ➤

In May 1950 the NAACP Legal Defense Fund went after school segregation in Clarendon County, South Carolina. The county spent $179 for each white child in school and only $43 per African-American child. Without public school buses, black children walked up to eight miles to sit at cracked tables on broken chairs and be taught by deplorably underpaid teachers. Black schools included no lunchrooms, gymnasiums, or toilets (indoor or outdoor). Harold Boulware (*second from right*) was the chief attorney in the case, titled *Briggs v. Elliot*. Twenty African-American parents seeking better schools for their children were the plaintiffs, and they and their supporters suffered retaliation for their courage. Two parents, Harry Briggs and Anne Gibson, were fired from their jobs, and the home of Reverend J. A. DeLaine, a local teacher, was burned.

On the 50th anniversary of the Nobel Prizes, Dr. Ralph J. Bunche became the first person of color to be awarded the Nobel Peace Prize. A United Nations diplomat and scholar, he accepted the award on December 10, 1950, for daringly negotiating four armistice agreements that ended the first Arab–Israeli war in 1949. Bunche attributed his history-making accomplishment to his grandmother, who taught his sister and him patience, tolerance, and "to stand up for our rights, to suffer no indignity, but to harbor no bitterness toward anyone. . . ."

Most high-rise public housing projects had cold, isolating designs that virtually ensured social and economic disaster. But "planned" high-rise urban housing can succeed when it is created with a sensitivity to human needs, and when the motive is profit. The Park LaBrea Project (*above*), a rental community in the predominantly white Fairfax District of mid-Los Angeles, was developed by Met Life, and anticipated L.A.'s wartime and postwar population boom. The first phase (two-story garden apartments) opened in 1944. By 1950, 18 radial-style towers of 13 floors each had been completed. The 4,200-unit complex had considerable green space and was attractively landscaped. It was surrounded by major boulevards that gave Park LaBrea residents easy access to jobs and services, things too often denied black residents of low-income public housing.

Supporters of Willie McGee, who would be executed on May 8, 1951, rally at the Lincoln Memorial in Washington, D.C., on May 6. Prior to his death, McGee wrote in a letter to his wife that the reason he was being executed was to "keep the Negro down." McGee had been convicted of raping a married white woman even though evidence suggested that the woman had seduced McGee into a relationship he later tried to sever. McGee was condemned by Harvey McGehee, chief justice of the Mississippi Supreme Court, who said, "If you believe . . . any white woman in the South, who was not completely down and out, degenerate, degraded and corrupted, could have anything to do with a Negro man, you not only do not know what you are talking about, you are insulting us, the whole South."

# Two Legal Milestones

A MAIL CARRIER IN TEXAS and a 68-year-old educator in Oklahoma were the lead plaintiffs in two landmark cases decided by the U.S. Supreme Court on June 5, 1950. Both plaintiffs, Herman Marion Sweatt and George W. McLaurin, had been denied admission to state graduate schools because they were black. Both had been offered inadequate redress by the states—a one-student law school in the *Sweatt v. Painter* case and individualized segregation at the state university in *McLaurin v. Oklahoma State Regents*.

Both the *Sweatt* and *McLaurin* cases established the right of African-Americans to equal opportunity in graduate education. Ruling for *Sweatt*, the Supreme Court ordered his admission to the University of Texas Law School. In *McLaurin*, the Court ordered an end to the restrictions placed upon McLaurin by the University of Oklahoma. The Court did not directly challenge the 1896 *Plessy v. Ferguson* "separate but equal" decision in either ruling. However, its decisions opened the way for such a challenge. Three weeks after the *Sweatt* and *McLaurin* decisions were handed down, NAACP counsel Thurgood Marshall convened a conference of lawyers with the specific purpose of planning an all-out attack on school segregation.

Herman Marion Sweatt

# 1950s

**October 16, 1950:** After the Florida Supreme Court supported a Miami Springs Golf Course rule that said black golfers could play only on Mondays, the U.S. Supreme Court rules that the Florida court must reconsider its decision.

**December 11, 1950:** Ralph Bunche, a successful mediator of the 1948 Arab–Israeli War, is awarded the Nobel Peace Prize. He becomes the first African-American to receive a Nobel Prize.

**1951:** Congress defeats William Arthur Winstead's proposed amendment, which would have allowed military personnel to choose between all-white and integrated units.

**February 16, 1951:** New York City bans racial discrimination in public housing.

**February 28, 1951:** *Brown v. Board of Education of Topeka*, which challenges school segregation, is filed in the U.S. District Court of Kansas. *See* August 3, 1951.

**March 14, 1951:** South Carolina passes a tough antilynching bill.

**April 24, 1951:** The University of North Carolina at Chapel Hill admits its first black student.

**May 23, 1951:** *Davis v. County School Board of Prince Edward County*, another school segregation suit, is filed in federal court in Richmond, Virginia. *See* March 7, 1952.

**June 1951:** In *Briggs v. Elliot*, a U.S. district court denies the petitioners' claim that black schoolchildren are psychologically harmed by segregation. However, it does ask that schools in Clarendon County, South Carolina, rectify educational inequalities. This case will find its ultimate resolution with the U.S. Supreme Court. *See* December 9, 1952. ➤

Believing in the American promise of equality, Harvey E. Clark, Jr., moved his family—his wife, Johnetta, and their two children—across the color line to Cicero, Illinois, an all-white suburb. In July 1951 a white mob ransacked the Clark family's apartment and burned their furniture and belongings on the lawn of the building, forcing the Clarks to leave their home. The NAACP stepped in to support the Clarks and inform the nation of their story. Cicero, notorious for its racial intolerance, would make more national headlines in the mid-1960s.

William Patterson, leader of the Civil Rights Congress, autographs copies of the 1951 petition to the United Nations entitled *We Charge Genocide,* which he edited. It carefully documented hundreds of cases of murder, bombing, and torture of African-Americans, and called upon the U.N. to declare the U.S. government "guilty of the crime of Genocide against the Negro people." The petition was neither the first nor last effort by African-Americans to appeal to the U.N. In 1946 the National Negro Congress submitted a petition, and in 1947 W.E.B. Du Bois presented "An Appeal to the World" on behalf of the NAACP.

# Fighting School Segregation

UNDER JIM CROW, public education for African-Americans in the South was blatantly inferior. The separate elementary schools for blacks were woefully understaffed, poorly equipped, and closed during planting and harvesting seasons. Only large cities had high schools for blacks, who had even fewer opportunities for higher education.

From September 1926 through July 1928, *The Crisis*, the official publication of the NAACP, ran a series of articles based on studies it had conducted on school financing in several southern states. Those studies revealed a huge disparity in state expenditures for white and black students. Georgia, for example, spent an average of eight times more per white student than per black student. Average teacher salaries were $97.88 per month for whites and $49.41 for blacks. The class size for black students in South Carolina was, on average, twice that of white students.

In an editorial written after the series of articles ended, W.E.B. Du Bois, editor of *The Crisis*, wrote that the NAACP should inititiate a movement that would "secure justice" for black students throughout America. He urged that school desegregation cases be brought before both state and federal courts.

In the 1930s Du Bois's proposed movement began. Charles Hamilton Houston, hired by Howard University in 1929 to create a first-class law school, groomed black attorneys to utilize the legal system to end school segregation. Houston trained his students in both theoretical and practical law, with a strong emphasis on civil rights law. One of his best students was Thurgood Marshall. In 1935 Houston left Howard University to become the NAACP's chief legal counsel.

In 1938 Houston successfully argued before the United States Supreme Court in the case of *Missouri ex rel. Gaines v. Canada* that the state of Missouri either had to build a separate law school for blacks or desegregate the white law school. Houston retired soon after the case, and Marshall took his place as chief counsel. In 1940 the NAACP set up a separate legal branch, the NAACP Legal Defense Fund, with Marshall as its director.

In 1948, after President Harry Truman had banned segregation in the armed services, Marshall and the NAACP began the concerted drive to overturn the "separate but equal" doctrine in education for which Du Bois had called 20 years earlier. Focusing on graduate-school cases, NAACP attorneys piled up victory after victory in the courts.

In 1950, with success in two landmark cases, *Sweatt v. Painter* and *McLaurin v. Oklahoma State Regents*, Marshall convened a conference of lawyers with the specific purpose of planning an all-out legal attack on school segregation. By that time, several key cases were in the works in which the aim was to dismantle the separate-but-equal doctrine. In 1954 they would coalesce into one: *Brown v. Board of Education*.

Black students in New Orleans attended this segregated school.

# 1950s

**July 12, 1951:** More than 3,000 white protesters riot in Cicero, Illinois, after a black family moves into town.

**August 3, 1951:** In *Brown v. Board of Education*, the U.S. District Court of Kansas rules that no significant discrimination exists in Topeka's school system. However, it states that segregation is detrimental to black children. The decision is a ray of hope for the NAACP, which will appeal this case to the U.S. Supreme Court. *See* December 9, 1952.

**October 1951:** Coleman Young helps establish the National Negro Labor Council to combat unfair hiring and employment practices.

**November 1, 1951:** The Johnson Publishing Company publishes its first issue of *Jet,* which offers weekly news coverage of black America.

**December 3, 1951:** President Harry Truman creates the Committee on Government Contract Compliance. Its purpose is to enforce nondiscriminatory practices within agencies that have government contracts.

**December 25, 1951:** NAACP activist Harry Tyson Moore and his wife, Harriet, are killed by a bomb in their home in Mims, Florida.

**January 27, 1952:** Ralph Ellison's novel, *Invisible Man*, about a young black man who feels disenfranchised, lost, and invisible in a prejudiced white America, is published.

**February 19, 1952:** The Interstate Commerce Commission upholds segregation on Southern Railway dining cars. *See* November 10, 1952.

**March 7, 1952:** In *Davis v. County School Board of Prince Edward County*, a U.S. district court in Virginia upholds the doctrine of "separate but equal." The NAACP Legal Defense and Educational Fund will appeal the decision to the U.S. Supreme Court. *See* December 9, 1952. ➤

In the 1950s, tensions on southern buses were often high, for several reasons: frequently hot weather, stop-and-go traffic, tight quarters, general animosity between blacks and whites, and—most significantly—segregated seating policies. In most southern communities, African-Americans were required to enter public buses from the rear; only whites were allowed to use the front door. Moreover, the first several rows of seats were reserved for white passengers only. Black riders were forced to stand even if "white seats" were vacant. Tensions eventually led to bus boycotts in multiple cities, including Baton Rouge, Louisiana; Montgomery and Birmingham, Alabama; Tallahassee, Florida; and others.

Nelson Mandela stands in the law office he opened in 1952 with fellow anti-apartheid activist Oliver Tambo—the first black legal practice in Johannesburg, South Africa. At the time, Mandela was serving a suspended prison sentence (he was confined to Johannesburg for six months) for leading the African National Congress Campaign for the Defiance of Unjust Laws, a mass civil disobedience campaign against apartheid. Apartheid laws, legally enacted in South Africa in 1948, required blacks to carry "pass books" with identification, restricted their access to white-populated areas, denied them certain jobs, and subjected them to state-sanctioned police brutality and violence. Mandela continued to challenge South Africa's atrocities against blacks, even following his eventual imprisonment in 1962. He was released on February 11, 1990, and was inaugurated as the first democratically elected state president of South Africa on May 10, 1994. Mandela's willingness to suffer for his cause inspired two generations of American civil rights activists.

"I am an invisible man. . . . I am a man of substance, of flesh and bone, fiber and liquids—and I might even be said to possess a mind. I am invisible, understand, simply because people refuse to see me."

—NOVELIST RALPH ELLISON, *INVISIBLE MAN*, 1952

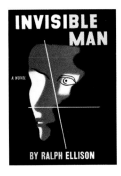

The naive and nameless narrator of Ralph Ellison's novel, *Invisible Man,* journeys from a black college in the South to Harlem, where cynical Communists recruit him as an organizer. His eventual dismay with all of society suggests that he's invisible to *everybody,* including other blacks. African-Americans of the far left felt betrayed by Ellison, and objected to the book's bawdy, often satiric portraits of black street hustlers and other undesirables. Those objections are largely forgotten: *Invisible Man* is acknowledged as a lively, thoughtful classic.

Charlotta Spears Bass, Progressive Party vice presidential candidate, tells reporters on October 16, 1952, that she sees "no hope" for progress toward civil rights in either the Democratic or Republican parties. Bass was the longtime editor of *The California Eagle,* the oldest and largest black newspaper on the West Coast. In 1948 she helped found the Progressive Party, and in 1952 she became America's first black, female vice presidential candidate. On election day, the Progressives were buried in Dwight Eisenhower's landslide victory, mustering about a fifth of their tiny 1948 count. They never fielded a national ticket again.

# Adam Clayton Powell, Jr.

AN OUTSPOKEN, FLAMBOYANT U.S. congressmen, Adam Clayton Powell, Jr., was also the strongest and most effective defender of civil rights that body had ever seen.

Born in 1908, Powell was raised in New York City and ordained in his father's church, Abyssinian Baptist Church in Harlem, at the onset of the Great Depression. He organized the Greater New York Coordinating Committee for Employment, and he railed against discrimination and police brutality in his newspaper column. Powell participated in the "Don't Buy Where You Can't Work" campaign, and he led Harlemites in protests against employment discrimination. After he assumed the pastorship of his father's church in 1937, Powell used that power base to win election as New York City's first black City Council member in 1941.

Three years later Powell won election to the U.S. House of Representatives, becoming the fourth African-American to serve in that body since 1901. He won election to 10 more consecutive terms. As chair of the powerful House Committee on Education and Labor from 1960 to 1969, Powell shepherded to passage in Congress a number of important bills that benefited not just black people but poor people, workers, children, and the disabled of all races.

Often, Powell did not behave with the decorum expected of a congressman. He was married three times and charged twice with income tax evasion by the IRS. In 1963, after a Harlem woman won a judgment against him for slander (he had accused her of collecting payoffs for the police) and he refused to pay the damages assessed, a New York Court issued an arrest warrant.

Thereafter, Powell could not return to his district except to preach on Sundays. His congressional colleagues accused him of unbecoming conduct and misusing public funds, and in January 1967 they refused to seat him in the new Congressional term. Although the U.S. Supreme Court ruled two years later that the House had acted unconstitutionally, Powell's constituents were tired of his excesses. In 1970 Charles Rangel was elected to Harlem's Congressional seat. Powell died two years later.

## 1952–1953

**April 1, 1952:** The Delaware Court of Chancery issues opinions in *Belton v. Gebhart* and *Bulah v. Gebhart*. The court determines that the white high school in Claymont and the black high school in Wilmington are not equal and that Claymont High School must admit the black student plaintiffs. *See* August 28, 1952.

**June 27, 1952:** Congress passes the Immigration and Naturalization Act, which removes racial barriers to naturalization.

**August 28, 1952:** The Supreme Court of Delaware upholds the *Belton v. Gebhart* and *Bulah v. Gebhart* decisions, stating that separate schools must be equal.

**November 10, 1952:** The U.S. Supreme Court upholds the ban on segregation on the Atlantic Coast Line Railroad. *See* November 25, 1955.

**December 9, 1952:** The U.S. Supreme Court begins hearing combined arguments for five related school segregation cases: *Brown v. Board of Education*; *Briggs v. Elliot*; *Davis v. County School Board of Prince Edward County*; *Belton v. Gebhart*; and *Bolling v. Sharpe*. The cases will be consolidated under the name of *Oliver Brown et al. v. Board of Education of Topeka*. *See* May 17, 1954.

**June 8, 1953:** The U.S. Supreme Court upholds an 1873 law that bans segregation in D.C. eating places.

**June 19, 1953:** In Baton Rouge, Louisiana, Reverend T. J. Jemison initiates the first successful bus boycott by southern blacks. After five days, the city agrees to an open seating policy, excluding the first two seats (which will be reserved for whites) and the two rear seats (for blacks).

**December 31, 1953:** Hulan E. Jack is elected as the first black borough president of Manhattan. ➤

Black churches, such as this one in Harlem, were the wombs of the black freedom movement. Each Sunday, churches offered a haven for all-black congregations to gather and transform their woes into songs of despair, longing, and hope. Often, prayer and sermons galvanized their faith into political action. Ministers, many of whom were local civil rights leaders, sometimes organized boycotts or protests from their pulpits.

In June 1953 African-Americans in Baton Rouge, Louisiana, waged war against segregation in public transportation. After white bus drivers refused to obey a local ordinance providing for "first-come, first-served" seating, with whites proceeding from the front and blacks from the rear, the city's black community, led by Reverend T. J. Jemison, conducted a seven-day boycott. It included free car service for protesters (*pictured*). The boycott ended successfully when city officials reaffirmed the ordinance.

# Failure of Public Housing

FOLLOWING WORLD WAR II, the federal government helped fund construction of public housing in many northern cities. The new no-frills apartment buildings were intended not only to house low-income people but to provide them with a stepping-stone to a better life elsewhere. Most whites in public housing indeed moved on to other neighborhoods. However, African-Americans—with old black neighborhoods demolished and unwelcome in white areas—remained in the housing projects. Public housing effectively warehoused African-Americans and other minorities.

After the war, New York Construction Coordinator Robert Moses championed the bulldozing of black neighborhoods to construct federally funded buildings, saying one had "to swing the meat axe." Many of the "projects" were physically isolated by highways and other barriers. In the burgeoning Puerto Rican neighborhood of East Harlem, a so-called "project wall" literally blocked the upper portions of the neighborhood from the white "silk stocking" district of the Upper East Side.

Because of the projects' isolation, residents couldn't easily get to supermarkets, drugstores, or other stores and businesses—and very few corporations wanted to construct new stores in the projects. Moreover, black-owned businesses that had thrived in black neighborhoods died out due to the reconfiguration. Over the years, residents despaired. Largely cut off from society, most residents struggled to find decent work. Companies moved to the suburbs, and inner-city blacks lacked adequate transportation to get to these new sites. Local schools were poor, college education too expensive.

Public housing complexes became overcrowded breeding grounds for crime, vandalism, and drug use. One of the most notorious examples was the Pruitt-Igoe complex in St. Louis. Constructed in the mid–1950s, the complex declined dramatically and was demolished by the early 1970s.

Recent public housing projects have been built on a more human scale—but not without controversy. In Chicago in the 1990s, projects were torn down and replaced with scattered-site housing: low-rise buildings constructed in largely white neighborhoods. Armed with Chicago Housing Authority vouchers, former tenants scoured the city's neighborhoods pock-marked with abandoned and boarded-up buildings and a dwindling housing stock. Many were forced to leave the city for its southern suburbs.

Racist images still adorned mainstream products as late as the 1950s and 1960s. This image on "Black Jacks Bar-B-Q-Sauce" was patterned after the black porter of the Coon Chicken Inn restaurant chain, which operated in northwest states as late as the 1950s. Patrons entered the Coon Chicken Inn by walking through the mouth (the doorway) of a giant "coon."

Scores of people line up outside the U.S. Supreme Court on December 8, 1953, hoping to hear the second day of arguments regarding the constitutionality of school segregation. In *Brown v. Board of Education of Topeka,* the NAACP sought to end segregation in public education. Although the case first reached the Supreme Court in fall 1952, the Court would not render its opinion until May 1954.

# Brown v. Board of Education

IN 1951 IN TOPEKA, KANSAS, a third-grade black girl named Linda Brown and her kindergarten-age sister, Terry, were prohibited by local authorities from attending the exclusively white public school that was located close to their home. Instead, they had to walk a long distance through a dangerous railroad switchyard to reach a bus that would take them to an all-black public school.

The girls' father, Reverend Oliver Brown, was infuriated by the institutionalized injustice of school segregation. Brown was sympathetic with the goals of the Kansas NAACP, a group anxious to test the legality of antisegregation suits recently brought in other states. Brown agreed to join with the NAACP and file suit.

The Brown case was one of four school desegregation cases that wended their way to the highest court in the land by the fall of 1952. There was also a fifth case in Washington, D.C., which was eventually separated from the other four. The Court heard each case separately, but it grouped them together as *Oliver Brown et al. v. Board of Education of Topeka* in delivering its opinion.

In his presentation to the court, NAACP lead counsel Thurgood Marshall discussed the work of psychologist Kenneth Clark, who had studied the psychological consequences of segregation on black children. Clark and his wife, psychologist Mamie Phipps Clark, had devised "the doll test" to assess children's responses to race. As Kenneth Clark testified in the separate cases in the lower courts, black children, when shown brown and pink dolls, had correctly identified themselves as looking like the brown dolls. Three out of four of the children had shown a marked preference for the white dolls and, when asked to "show me the doll that looks bad," had chosen a brown doll. It was clear to Clark that growing up in a segregated society had made the black children feel inferior.

In preparing for arguments before the Supreme Court, Marshall had asked Clark to prepare a summary of his findings in the dolls test, then sent those findings to dozens of social scientists, asking them to sign it to signify their support. They received 35 signatures.

On December 13, 1952, the Court convened to deliberate the cases. All of the nine justices, each appointed by Democratic presidents Franklin D. Roosevelt and Harry

Linda and Terry Brown walk to school in Topeka, Kansas.

Truman, sided with the NAACP's clients. However, they were concerned about issuing a ruling that might need to be implemented by force. By May 1953, they still had not made a decision. On June 8 the Court restored all four cases to the Court's docket for reargument in the fall.

That September, Chief Justice Fred Vinson died of a heart attack at age 63. Although no one will ever know for sure how he would have voted in *Brown*, at the time of his death he was leaning toward upholding the *Plessy v. Ferguson* decision of 1896, which legitimized "separate but equal" facilities for blacks and whites. Republican President Dwight Eisenhower now had his first opportunity to nominate a Supreme Court justice. He chose Earl Warren, the Republican governor of California who was moderately progressive in his social philosophy. The appointment, which was confirmed by Congress, would prove to be Eisenhower's main contribution to civil rights.

The Court heard rearguments in the Brown case in December 1953, then met to discuss the case. In the opinion of new Chief Justice Earl Warren, it was a simple case: The doctrine of "separate but equal" rested on the premise that African-Americans were inferior to whites, and thus was unconstitutional. He was very clear in his discussion with the other justices about how he wanted the decision to come out, and he believed he had the majority of five that he needed. But Warren understood that on such a momentous issue the Court could not hand down a divided decision. It had to be unanimous. Some time between late February and late March, the Court reached its decision on the school desegregation cases. There exists no record of the vote.

On Monday, May 17, 1954, Chief Justice Warren delivered the Court's opinion in *Brown v. Board of Education*. He stated that the only purpose of segregation was to subjugate African-Americans. He said it was impossible to "turn the clock back to 1868 when the [14th] Amendment was adopted, or even to 1896 when *Plessy v. Ferguson* was written. We must consider public education in the light of its full development and its present place in American life throughout the Nation...."

Warren made reference to the psychological effects of segregation, stating that the damage caused by segregation was amply supported by modern authority. Noting that in the *Plessy* opinion, the Court had essentially said that inferiority was only in the mind of the Negro, the Warren opinion rejected any language in *Plessy* contrary to the modern finding.

"We conclude," the chief justice read, "unanimously," he added, although that word was not in the written opinion, "that in the field of public education the doctrine of 'separate but equal' has no place. Separate educational facilities are inherently unequal." Warren then announced that the Court would schedule further argument in the fall on how to best implement the ruling.

There were two basic arguments on how to apply the ruling. One, favored by Thurgood Marshall, was that desegregation should proceed at once, by direct court order. The Court adopted the more cautious choice, remanding the matter to district courts, which should "take such proceedings and enter such orders and decrees consistent with this opinion as are necessary and proper to admit to public schools on a racially nondiscriminatory basis with all deliberate speed the parties to these cases."

The oxymoronic phrase "with all deliberate speed" proved to be the salvation of segregationists and the

Victorious attorneys George E. C. Hayes, Thurgood Marshall, and James Nabrit

stumbling block for integrationists for years to come. Marshall realized that he faced many more years in court, but as he said, "You can say all you want but those white crackers are going to get tired of having Negro lawyers beating 'em every day in court." For most southern localities, "all deliberate speed" meant never, as attested to by the 1957–60 Little Rock crisis and other violent episodes in school desegregation after *Brown*—as well as by the various programs that paid lip service to integration while maintaining the status quo.

By the late 1960s, the Supreme Court's patience was wearing thin. In its 1968 ruling in *Green v. County School Board of New Kent County, Virginia*, the Warren Court during its last term ruled that the "freedom of choice" plans operating in many school districts were just new versions of segregation.

Warren's successor as chief justice, Warren E. Burger, also supported desegregation without further delay. He wrote in the unanimous opinion in *Alexander v. Holmes County* (Mississippi) *Board of Education* in 1969: "Under explicit holdings of this Court, the obligation of every school district is to terminate dual school systems at once and to operate now and hereafter only unitary schools."

Slowly, the southern school districts complied. By the 1972–73 school year, nearly half of the black children in 11 southern states were attending schools that had been predominantly white.

# 1950s

## 1954

**1954:** White America, Inc., a racist, segregationist group, is formed in response to *Brown v. Board of Education*.

**1954:** William Gardner Smith's *South Street*, a novel about lynching, is published.

**January 12:** Secretary of Defense Charles E. Wilson orders the integration of military post schools.

**May 17:** In *Brown v. Board of Education*, the U.S. Supreme Court unanimously declares school segregation unconstitutional, overturning the decades-old "separate but equal" doctrine.

**June 10:** At a meeting in Richmond, Virginia, southern governors vow to defy the Supreme Court's *Brown v. Board of Education* ruling.

**July 7:** The Louisiana state legislature votes to maintain its segregated public school system.

**July 10:** The Alabama Board of Education votes to maintain segregation in public schools.

**July 11:** Upset by the *Brown v. Board of Education* decision, segregationists in Indianola, Mississippi, form the first of many White Citizens' Councils. The councils will oppose integration, often by economically attacking black people active in voters' rights.

**August 7:** Charles H. Mahoney is confirmed as a permanent delegate to the United Nations, becoming the first black American to hold the position.

**September 7:** Massive school desegregation begins in Baltimore and Washington, D.C.

**October 30:** Six years after President Harry Truman banned segregation in the U.S. Armed Forces, the last of the Army's segregated units are finally integrated.

**December 21:** Citizens in Jackson, Mississippi, vote to continue school segregation. ➤

Recently appointed as the U.S. Supreme Court's chief justice, Earl Warren posed for this photo in December 1953, when the case of *Brown v. Board of Education* was before the Court. On May 17, 1954, the Court, in an opinion by Warren, broke with long tradition and unanimously overruled the "separate but equal" doctrine of *Plessy v. Ferguson*. Warren stated that the segregation of black school children "from others of similar age and qualifications solely because of their race generates a feeling of inferiority as to their status in the community that may affect their hearts and minds in a way unlikely ever to be undone."

In what is likely a posed photograph, students in Atlanta listen to the *Brown v. Board of Education* decision. Given that the Supreme Court's 1954 desegregation decision was an unprecedented crisis for most Southerners, it is unlikely that the ruling evoked a temperate response from these students. The *Jackson* (Mississippi) *Clarion–Ledger* referred to May 17 as "a black day of tragedy for the South." Reacting to the ruling, South Carolina Governor James F. Byrnes said that ending segregation would "mark the beginning of the end of civilization in the South as we have known it."

# Thurgood Marshall

**D**URING ARGUMENTS IN *Brown v. Board of Education of Topeka* before the U.S. Supreme Court, Justice Felix Frankfurter asked NAACP attorney Thurgood Marshall to define the term *equal*. Marshall responded simply, "Equal means getting the *same* thing, at the *same* time, and in the *same* place." The plain-talking Marshall spent much of his legendary career proving the simple fact that African-Americans did not enjoy equal anything.

Born in 1908 and raised in segregated Baltimore, Marshall wanted to devote himself to black civil rights. By happy coincidence, attorney Charles H. Houston was starting to train a cadre of black civil rights lawyers at Howard University. Marshall enrolled at Howard Law, graduated first in his class in 1933, and three years later followed Houston to NAACP national headquarters in New York City. In 1938, on Houston's retirement, Marshall assumed the position of chief counsel and head of the newly created NAACP Legal Defense and Education Fund.

At great risk to his health, and sometimes to his life, Marshall tried to be everywhere at once, pursuing a school desegregation case here, an unequal pay case there, a lynching case somewhere else. Eventually, he and the NAACP decided to focus on school desegregation. It took about a decade of intense legal battles for Marshall and his associates to achieve the landmark victory in *Brown v. Board of Education* in 1954.

Marshall served on the U.S. Court of Appeals (1961–1965) and as solicitor general of the United States (1965–1967) before President Lyndon Johnson appointed him to the U.S. Supreme Court. As the Court became increasingly conservative under President Richard Nixon, Marshall was often a lonely dissenting voice in decisions affecting personal and civil liberties. He was famous for his angry, emotional departures from majority opinions.

Marshall retired from the Court in 1991 and died of heart failure in 1993 at the age of 84. No single person has done more to advance the legal and civil rights of African-Americans.

Spottswood T. Bolling, Jr., 12 years old, and his mother, Sarah, a bookbinder in Washington, D.C., rejoice over newspaper coverage of the U.S. Supreme Court decision in *Brown v. Board of Education* on May 17, 1954. Spottswood and his mother had put themselves on the front lines in the fight for equal educational opportunity. In 1951 Spottswood, along with other African-American youth, requested admittance to Washington, D.C.'s modern new high school for white students. All were denied admission based solely on their race. The Bollings and 10 other families filed *Bolling v. Sharpe* in a U.S. District Court. Although initially unsuccessful, the Bolling case later met with success as one of the cases combined under *Brown*.

# 1950s

Emboldened by the Supreme Court decision in *Brown v. Board of Education,* a group of black parents and their children gather outside Linfield Elementary School on September 7, 1954, in Hutchins, Texas, demanding that the children be admitted to the white school. Texas was hostile to federal intervention. In 1956 Texas voters approved one referendum that opposed integrated schools and another that prohibited interracial marriage. In 1957 the state legislature urged school districts to resist integration.

On September 7, 1954, in a classroom in Fort Myer, Virginia, black and white children finally stand together to recite the Pledge of Allegiance. After the *Brown v. Board of Education* decision, the U.S. Defense Department ordered schools on military bases—such as the one pictured—to open their doors to black students for the first time in history.

## *Brown* Decision Sparks Movement

I THINK THE BEGINNING of this period from 1954 has its roots in the returning soldiers after 1945. There was a great feeling on the part of many of these youngsters that they had been away, that they had fought in the war—that they were not getting what they should have. Already, black and white soldiers coming home from the war were sitting anywhere they wanted in the buses and they were being thrown in jail. There was a great feeling that the A. Philip Randolph movement to stop discrimination in the armed forces had been helpful but it was not enough. There was a building up of militancy, not so much by going into the streets as by a feeling of "We are not going to put up with this anymore."…But when the Supreme Court came out with the *Brown* decision in '54, things began rapidly to move….What made '54 so unusual was that the Supreme Court…established black people as being citizens with all the rights of all other citizens.

—*CORE cofounder Bayard Rustin*

Just eight days after Chief Justice Earl Warren issued the Supreme Court's *Brown* decision, Washington D.C.'s Board of Education adopted a desegregation plan. On September 13, 1954, schools across the city opened with integrated faculties and student bodies. Here, Marjorie Beach teaches the first integrated kindergarten class ever held in her classroom. However, undercurrents of racial tension ran throughout Washington's schools, especially among older students. Groups of white students led strikes, and—after years of attending poor, substandard schools—many black students fell behind their white peers academically.

School integration was met with angry resistance from white students at Anacostia High School in Washington, D.C., in the fall of 1954. On October 8, as a protest to integration, hundreds of white students refused to enter the building when the morning bell sounded. For the next several days, boycotting students taunted classmates who attended classes. The confrontations and protests grew so intense that police were called in to avert rioting.

On October 18, 1954, students at New Rochelle High School in Baltimore reached out to students from Souther High, a Baltimore school rocked by anti-integration protests. Robert Forbes (*standing, third from right*) was a human relations and history teacher who originated the idea. New Rochelle Principal Willis Thompson said he hoped Souther kids would see that integration could work and that they would carry a message of harmony back to their school.

In October 1954 a group of Baltimore mothers took the fight against segregation to school superintendent John Fischer. Only a few groups of white citizens protested Baltimore's school desegregation efforts in 1954, as the process went relatively smoothly. (The city's Polytechnic High School actually had become desegrated in 1952.) However, school desegregation in Baltimore was not a total success. Thousands of white families, not willing to let their kids go to school with "coloreds," moved to the suburbs, lowering the city's tax base.

## 1955

**1955:** Whites attack the church (arson) and home (gunfire) of Reverend J. A. DeLaine, who had spearheaded the *Briggs v. Elliot* segregation suit in Clarendon County, South Carolina, in the early 1950s.

**January 23:** In a vote of 42–0, the Georgia Senate approves a bill that bars state funds to integrated schools.

**January 31:** Integration of St. Louis high schools begins.

**February:** Dorothy Dandridge, star of *Carmen Jones*, becomes the first black woman nominated for an Academy Award for Best Actress.

**March 2:** Claudette Colvin, a 15-year-old black girl, is arrested after refusing to move to the back of a city bus in Montgomery, Alabama. *See December 1, 1955.*

**May 31:** In *Brown II*, the U.S. Supreme Court establishes guidelines for undoing segregated public education, although it fails to establish a timetable.

**July 9:** President Dwight Eisenhower appoints E. Frederick Morrow as administrative officer for the Special Projects group, making him the first black White House staff member.

**August 1:** The State of Georgia demands that black teachers leave the NAACP or forfeit their teaching licenses.

**August 24:** Emmett Louis Till, a 14-year-old African-American from Chicago, makes a flirtatious remark to Carolyn Bryant, a white woman, in Bryant's grocery and meat market in Money, Mississippi.

**August 28:** Roy Bryant, husband of Carolyn Bryant, and his half brother, J. W. Milam, kidnap and murder Emmett Till, then dump his body in the Tallahatchie River. ➤

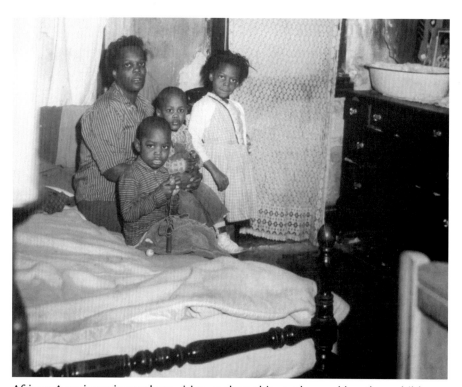

African-Americans in northern cities, such as this mother and her three children in Pittsburgh, commonly lived in substandard housing with leaky roofs, cracked walls, and major disrepair. Blacks in the ghettos were cut off from good-paying jobs because of historically substandard schooling, discriminatory hiring practices, and city planning that left them physically isolated from potential employers. Even when black families could afford to leave the ghetto, whites often reverted to violence to keep them in. Moreover, real estate agents commonly wouldn't sell homes in white neighborhoods to black families. The federal government eventually built low-income housing, but it would not be the "stepping stone" out of the ghetto that it was intended to be.

Alfred S. James of the NAACP carries a picket sign in front of San Antonio's Texas Theater in April 1955. James protested the theater's policy of restricting paying black customers to the mezzanine and balcony to see the film *Carmen Jones,* an all-black version of Bizet's *Carmen. Carmen Jones* starred Dorothy Dandridge, the first black woman to receive an Academy Award nomination for Best Actress, as well as Harry Belafonte and Pearl Bailey. As pressure to integrate increased in the South, some movie theaters shut their doors rather than admit African-Americans.

In the mid-1950s an unwritten law banned African-Americans from the Las Vegas Strip, except for black domestic help and entertainers who helped make casino owners rich. However, the Moulin Rouge Hotel, which opened in May 1955, billed itself as "the nation's first major interracial hotel." It served black patrons who were denied access to other hotels, dining areas, and casinos. Moulin Rouge quickly became a magnet for such entertainers as Frank Sinatra and Harry Belafonte. After midnight, crowds left the Strip and headed to this hot spot. The casino, however, closed before 1955 was over.

Septima Clark (*left*), a black educator and Movement activist, greatly influenced Rosa Parks (*right*). The woman who would be called the "Mother of the Movement" met Clark in summer 1955 at the Highlander Folk School in Tennessee, where Clark taught civil rights workshops. At the time, Parks was troubled about segregation and racial strife in Montgomery. Clark, however, inspired her. Despite the dangers of operating the workshops, Clark remained calm and dedicated. Years later, Parks stated that she had hoped to catch some of Clark's spirit and muster some of her courage. Parks returned to Alabama and made history before the year was over.

On May 31, 1955, NAACP chief counsel Thurgood Marshall discussed the U.S. Supreme Court's decision in *Brown II,* which ordered school desegregation to proceed "with all deliberate speed." The Court's ruling in *Brown v. Board of Education* the previous May had outraged whites in the South, and some schools tried to derail the decision by defying the new law or even closing schools. *The Atlanta Constitution* stated that the court's decision did not mean that black and white children would go to school together in the fall, and that the court provided for a "cooling off" period. Marshall petitioned the Supreme Court to require states to aggressively push for integration.

# 1950s

## The Crime Against Emmett Till

FOURTEEN-YEAR-OLD EMMETT TILL grew up on the South Side of Chicago. An only child, he was a smart dresser, brash, and a practical jokester. In August 1955 he and his cousin, Curtis Jones, were staying with Curtis's grandfather, Mose Wright, near Money, Mississippi, whose motto was "A Great Place to Raise a Boy." One evening while hanging out at a local general store, Emmett took a dare to speak to a white woman, Carolyn Bryant. He went into the store, bought some candy, and as he was leaving said, "Bye, baby."

Three days later the woman's husband, Roy Bryant, and his half-brother, J. W. Milam, drove to Mose Wright's cabin and dragged Emmett into Bryant's car. Three days after that, Emmett's body was found in the Tallahatchie River. One of his eyes was gouged out, his forehead was crushed on one side, and a bullet was lodged in his skull.

Emmett's mother, Mamie Bradley, demanded that her son's body be sent home to Chicago immediately. When she saw the brutalized corpse, she ordered an open-casket funeral. *Jet* magazine published a photograph of the body, and the shocking case made headlines around the country.

The two accused murderers were tried in a segregated courtroom before an all-white, all-male jury. Mose Wright testified. Asked to point out the man who kidnapped Till, Wright stood up, pointed to Bryant, and—in spite of death threats against himself and his family—said, "Thar he." Other witnesses came forward after Wright testified, but the two men were found not guilty.

The brutal murder, the photograph, and the gross injustice of the trial infuriated many northern whites as well as African-Americans nationwide. Some consider Emmett Till a martyr, since his murder inspired many to join the fight for civil rights.

Carolyn Bryant's sexually suggestive and racially incendiary claims, which were wholly unsubstantiated, led to the lynching of young Emmett Till in Tallahatchie County, Mississippi, on August 28, 1955. The mother of two sons, she worked in Bryant's Grocery & Meat Market, owned by her husband, Roy, in nearby Money. Described by white southern newspapers as "pretty" and a "slim brunette," Bryant testified at a Tallahatchie County grand jury that Till verbally and physically accosted her in the grocery on August 24. Four days later, his corpse was found in the Tallahatchie River. Roy Bryant and his half-brother, John W. Milam, were accused of abducting and murdering Till.

A grief-stricken Mamie E. Bradley (later Mobley) collapses before the crated body of her slain son, Emmett Till, upon its arrival at a Chicago train station on September 2, 1955. Bradley's decision, made against the advice of the undertakers, to display her son's horribly disfigured corpse for public viewing galvanized world opinion against the crime of lynching. Bradley said that it looked as though all the hatred and scorn that white racists ever had for African-Americans was taken out on her child.

"Have you ever sent a loved son on a vacation and had him returned to you in a pine box, so horribly battered and waterlogged that someone needs to tell you that this sickening sight is your son—lynched?"

—MAMIE BRADLEY, MOTHER OF EMMETT TILL, SEPTEMBER 1955

Mourners, reporters, and curiosity-seekers swarm the entrance of Roberts Temple in Chicago to view the body of Emmett Till on September 3, 1955. An estimated 50,000 people filed past Till's open casket during the public viewing. Outrage over the killing reached beyond the United States. According to an extensive survey of newspapers in six European and North African countries by the American Jewish Committee, the Till lynching seriously damaged U.S. prestige abroad. Condemnation in Belgium, France, Germany, Italy, Switzerland, and Tunisia was "swift, violent and universal," the committee reported.

Mose Wright, great-uncle of Emmett Till, points at defendants Roy Bryant and J. W. Milam when asked on September 21, 1955, to identify the men who abducted Till from his cabin in the predawn hours of August 28. "Thar he," the sharecropper and minister declared as he pointed to each defendant. The testimony of "Uncle Mose" was courageous in light of threats made upon his life. The day before Till's body was discovered on August 31, Wright's wife, Elizabeth, wrote him from hiding, telling him to join her. After the trial, he moved to Chicago.

An all-white, 12-man jury awaits testimony at the Tallahatchie County Courthouse on September 20, 1955, in the case of Roy Bryant and J. W. Milam, charged with murdering Emmett Till. They are from left, front row: Gus Ramsey, James Toole, E. L. Price, J. A. Shaw, Ray Tribble, and Ed Devaney; back row: Travis Thomas, George Holland, Jim Pennington, Davis Newton, Howard Armstrong, and Bishop Matthews. The jury deliberated for only one hour and five minutes before reaching a "not guilty" verdict, claiming the state failed to prove that the swollen body pulled from the Tallahatchie River was Till's. One juror said they would have delivered their verdict sooner if they hadn't taken a soda pop break.

# 1950s

## 1955

**September 3–6:** In Chicago, thousands view the mutilated body of Emmett Till in an open casket at A. A. Raynor Funeral Home and Roberts Temple Church of God in Christ. These visitors, as well as African-American citizens who see pictures of the body in *Jet* magazine, are outraged.

**September 23:** In Sumner, Mississippi, an all-white, all-male jury acquits Roy Bryant and J. W. Milam of the murder of Emmett Till even though the two defendants admit to abducting Till. In response, black citizens will hold large rallies in Chicago, New York, and other major northern cities.

**October:** African-Americans stage an economic boycott in Selma, Alabama.

**November 7:** The U.S. Supreme Court rules that segregation in public recreational facilities is unconstitutional.

**November 25:** The Interstate Commerce Commission bans segregation in interstate bus and rail travel.

**December 1:** In defiance of the bus segregation law in Montgomery, Alabama, Rosa Parks refuses to yield her seat to a white man. She is thus arrested. *See* December 5, 1955.

**December 2:** Though the Georgia Tech football team is invited to play in the Sugar Bowl against Pittsburgh, Georgia Governor Marvin Griffin objects to Tech participating because Pitt has a black player on its team. The two teams will play anyway. ➤

The Till murder trial came to a quick and dramatic close on September 23, 1955, when Roy Bryant and John W. Milam were acquitted by what *The New York Times* called "a jury of twelve white neighbors." Pictured are (*from left*) "Big" John and Juanita Milam and Carolyn and Roy Bryant. After being acquitted in a subsequent kidnapping trial, Bryant and Milam accepted money from *Look* magazine for an exclusive interview, in which they admitted they had killed Till. Before shooting him, Milam claimed to have told Till: "God damn you, I'm going to make an example of you—just so everybody can know how me and my folks stand."

Alert Washington, D.C., police officers observe a demonstration by black Chicago religious leaders in front of the White House on October 24, 1955. Led by Reverend C. W. Harding of the Afro-American Congress of Christian Organizations, the demonstrators protested the poll tax, the unpunished killings of two African-Americans in Mississippi, and the Emmett Till lynching. The Till murder was a major spur to the growing Civil Rights Movement.

Four teammates of Bobby Grier (*center*), a running back for the University of Pittsburgh, give an amused thumbs-down to segregationist Georgia Governor Marvin Griffin's attempt to block the participation of Georgia Tech's football squad in the Sugar Bowl, scheduled for January 2, 1956. Governor Griffin had requested that no state college athletic team in Georgia be "permitted to engage in contests with other teams where the races are mixed" or where spectators were not segregated. Grier is holding a newspaper account of the violent reaction of Georgia Tech students to Griffin's comments.

Georgia Tech students burn Governor Marvin Griffin in effigy at the state capitol in Atlanta during a violent demonstration on December 2, 1955. About 2,500 students—some angry about Griffin's proposed boycott of the Sugar Bowl, others upset by his racism—marched through downtown Atlanta, where they pushed past police and stormed the capitol building, smashing through the doors and overturning furniture. They then rushed the governor's mansion and tore down historic markers. One of the students' signs taunts Griffin: "WE HOPE ALL THE GOV'S CHILDREN ARE BLACK." Three days later, Georgia Tech's Board of Regents denied the governor's request that the school boycott the Sugar Bowl. Pittsburgh's black player, Bobby Grier, committed a costly penalty in the game, eliciting pronounced jubilation from Tech fans.

Prominent Oklahoman Dr. Charles Atkins, his wife, Hannah, and their sons, Edmond (*left*) and Charles, stand under a "Negro waiting room" sign at the Santa Fe Depot in Oklahoma City on November 25, 1955. That day, the Interstate Commerce Commission outlawed racial segregation in train and bus transportation as well as in waiting rooms in interstate travel. In general, the white South resented the new ruling and would refuse to obey it for years. African-Americans could at least hope for better days. Since the 1800s, railroad companies often made black passengers sit in a half-car next to the engine. The *Call*, a black newspaper, described the half-cars as hot, dirty, crowded, and smoke-filled.

# 1950s

## 1955–1956

**December 5, 1955:** Black citizens in Montgomery begin a one-day bus boycott of the city's segregated bus system to protest Rosa Parks's trial. Black community leaders, impressed with the boycott's initial success, decide to lengthen the boycott and press for changes in the segregated bus system. The Montgomery Improvement Association (MIA) is formed to coordinate the boycott, and Reverend Martin Luther King, Jr., the 26-year-old pastor of Dexter Avenue Baptist Church, is elected president. Meanwhile, Parks loses her case and is fined $14 for violating Montgomery's bus segregation law.

**December 5, 1955:** In support of the Montgomery bus boycott, Martin Luther King delivers his first civil rights speech, at the Holt Street Baptist Church in Montgomery.

**December 8, 1955:** Montgomery's city commissioners and representatives from the bus company reject the bus desegregation demands of the Montgomery Improvement Association. *See* January 26, 1956.

**January 25, 1956:** The Mississippi legislature passes a bill designed to counteract the desegregation activities of the NAACP and other organizations.

**January 26, 1956:** Martin Luther King, leader of the Montgomery bus boycott, is arrested for driving 30 mph in a 25-mph zone.

**January 30, 1956:** Martin Luther King's home is bombed.

**February 1, 1956:** Challenging the bus segregation law in Montgomery, attorney Fred Gray files a lawsuit, *Browder v. Gayle*, in a U.S. district court. *See* February 21, 1956. ➤

George Meany (*far left*), president of the AFL–CIO, and Walter Reuther, president of the United Auto Workers, show solidarity with black labor leaders Willard S. Townsend (*second from right*) and A. Phillip Randolph in December 1955. Meany called the civil rights struggle "a moral issue" and argued for full union privileges for black union members. By 1962, however, Meany was at odds with the NAACP when that organization took a stand against the union's longtime seniority standard for promotion. Critics claimed that the labor unions wanted to admit African-Americans only to swell their ranks (the bigger the union, the greater the political clout) and were not interested in improving the social standing of African-Americans.

Medgar Evers (*right*), the NAACP field secretary for Mississippi, was constantly on the move, risking his life every day just by doing his job. One of the situations Evers confronted was the suffering of the Melton family. Clinton Melton, a black gas station attendant, was fatally shot in December 1955 after a dispute with a white customer. His widow, shown here with their four children, was afraid that justice would remain blind if the NAACP became involved. So the family told Evers to stay out of the case. He did, and the accused—Elmer Kimbell, an associate of the men who killed Emmett Till—was found innocent by an all-white jury, even though Melton was highly thought of by the whites in his community. Over and over again, white racism created African-American widows who had to raise families alone. It was a fate from which even the Evers family would not escape.

Following a U.S. Supreme Court decision against segregation on public golf courses, African-Americans hit the links for the first time at one of Atlanta's formerly all-white golf courses, North Fulton, on December 24, 1955. Pictured are (*from left*) C. T. Bell, Alfred "Tup" Holmes, and Reverend Oliver Holmes. The Holmes brothers and their father, Dr. H. M. Holmes, had brought suit against Atlanta for excluding them from a different segregated course two years earlier. In implementing the order, Mayor William B. Hartsfield said to his segregationist constituents: "This is but a foretaste of what the people can expect in those communities where the white people are divided at the ballot box and where the NAACP element holds the balance of power on election day."

After the U.S. Supreme Court mandated desegregation in the nation's public schools, Virginia legislators tried to skirt the ruling. In January 1956—despite the probable nay votes from this African-American couple—Virginia voters overwhelmingly approved amending the state constitution to allow state funding of whites-only private schools. Some Virginia public schools—namely those in Front Royal, Charlottesville, and Norfolk—closed their doors rather than admit black students. The federal court stepped in, however, ruling that closing the schools violated the 14th Amendment, which guarantees equal protection.

In his inaugural address on January 17, 1956, newly elected Mississippi Governor James P. Coleman vowed that the "color line" would neither bend nor break during his administration. Coleman promised that the federal government "will never be able to force racial integration in Mississippi." A week later, Coleman met in Richmond, Virginia, with South Carolina Governor George Bell Timmerman and Virginia Governor Thomas Stanley to discuss state "interposition" against the federal order to desegregate public schools. Interposition was a long-abandoned constitutional interpretation that compelled states to "interpose" their own authority in order to protect their citizens from unjust actions of the federal government.

# 1950s

## 1956

**February 6:** Students at the University of Alabama riot against the admission of Autherine Lucy, the school's first black student. Lucy is suspended during the evening for "her own safety." The NAACP will pressure the university to drop the suspension, which will prompt the school to expel Lucy.

**February 18:** Thomas H. Brewer, a founder of the local NAACP in Columbus, Georgia, is shot to death outside his office by a local white politician.

**February 21:** In Montgomery, Martin Luther King and 88 fellow African-Americans are indicted by a grand jury for violating a law that prohibits boycotts in the city. *See* March 22, 1956.

**March:** In an effort to sidestep school integration, Virginia amends the state constitution to allow state funding for private schools. *See* September 1959.

**March 1:** The Alabama state legislature votes to ask Congress for funds to relocate African-Americans from Alabama to cities in the North and Midwest.

**March 5:** The U.S. Supreme Court affirms its ban on segregation in public schools.

**March 12:** One hundred and one southern members of Congress sign the *Southern Manifesto* to reject and resist the 1954 U.S. Supreme Court ruling against segregation.

**March 22:** Martin Luther King is found guilty of conspiring to conduct an illegal boycott in Montgomery. Initially sentenced to a prison term, King instead receives a $500 fine. *See* June 5, 1956.

**April 11:** While performing before a segregated, all-white audience, singer Nat "King" Cole is attacked by white concertgoers in Birmingham. ▶

Martin Luther King raises his hand to silence a crowd of several hundred angry African-Americans, some of them armed, who had gathered outside his home on January 30, 1956, after learning that it had been firebombed. After King confirmed that his wife and 10-week-old daughter were unharmed by the bomb that blew out the front windows, King advised the people to put away their weapons and peacefully disperse. "Remember," he added, "if I am stopped, this movement will not stop, because God is with the movement."

Dr. Thomas H. Brewer, a 72-year-old civil rights leader and high-ranking member of the Republican Party in Georgia, was killed on February 18, 1956. He was shot while arguing with a flower shop owner over an alleged police brutality case involving an African-American. No assailant ever was charged or brought to justice. In the North that year, the Detroit NAACP held its first Fight for Freedom Fund Dinner to memorialize Dr. Brewer. Thurgood Marshall, who delivered the keynote address, hailed the doctor as an ardent NAACP volunteer.

In spring 1952 Autherine Lucy graduated from all-black Miles College in Fairfield, Alabama, and applied for and was denied admission to the University of Alabama. After exhausting appeals through the university's hierarchy, NAACP attorneys filed suit against the school in federal court on July 3, 1953. On July 1, 1955, Judge Harlan Hobart Grooms ruled in favor of Lucy's admittance for the 1955 fall term; appeals delayed enrollment until February 1956. That month, Lucy became the first African-American ever to attend the 126-year-old university.

University of Alabama students burn desegregation literature to protest the enrollment of Autherine Lucy, the school's first black student. Just days after Lucy was admitted on February 3, she was accosted by angry whites who hurled rocks, eggs, and tomatoes at her as she was leaving a classroom building. She was forced to leave the campus facedown in the back of a state police car on February 6. The university suspended Lucy the next day "for her own safety."

Autherine Lucy talks with Ruby Hurley, southeast regional secretary of the NAACP, and attorney Arthur Shores on February 7, 1956, after Lucy's suspension from the University of Alabama. When Lucy decided to fight the suspension by taking the university to court, U of A responded by expelling her, claiming that her legal action was maligning the school. Lucy's attorneys attempted to have her reinstated, and filed a conspiracy charge against the university for failing to protect her. The university responded by charging Lucy with libel. Eventually, Lucy and the NAACP decided to drop the case— but the saga wasn't over. In 1988 the University of Alabama sent Autherine Lucy Foster a letter stating that she was being readmitted. In 1992 Lucy Foster and her daughter graduated together—Lucy Foster with a master's degree in elementary education, and Grazia Foster with a bachelor's degree in corporate finance.

# 1950s

# Montgomery Bus Boycott

"WHY DO YOU ALL push us around?" Rosa Parks asked the Montgomery, Alabama, policeman who arrested her for refusing to give up her bus seat to a white man. "I don't know," the policeman replied, "but the law is the law and you're under arrest."

Parks's arrest on December 1, 1955, sparked the Montgomery bus boycott, a year-long mass protest that ended with a U.S. Supreme Court ruling declaring public bus segregation unconstitutional. The boycott inspired other civil rights campaigns by demonstrating the potential effectiveness of nonviolent protest tactics against Jim Crow segregation laws.

The Montgomery movement had deep roots in the earlier activism of black residents. Although news accounts described Parks as a middle-aged seamstress, she had served as the secretary for the NAACP's Montgomery branch since 1943. Twelve years before her arrest, Parks had refused an order from the same driver. He had told her to board from the back of the bus. She refused and, defiantly, sat on one of the front seats. He grabbed her sleeve and told her to get off the bus, which she did. A few months before her 1955 arrest, Parks attended a workshop on civil rights organizing at the Highlander Folk School in Monteagle, Tennessee.

Moreover, the Women's Political Council (WPC), a group of black professionals, had protested against Jim Crow practices on the Montgomery city buses since 1952. When a 1954 meeting with Montgomery's mayor produced few tangible gains, WPC President Jo Ann Robinson reiterated the council's requests in written form. Her letter also insinuated that a boycott of Montgomery's buses was in the planning stages.

After Parks's arrest, Robinson's WPC and local NAACP leader E. D. Nixon, after obtaining Parks's approval, responded by calling for a one-day protest of the city's buses on Monday, December 5. WPC members prepared more than 50,000 leaflets and organized groups to distribute them throughout the black community. Many black ministers mentioned the boycott during their Sunday services, and the following morning black residents gave overwhelming support to the boycott by staying off the buses. Following the initial success of the campaign, black leaders voted to form the Montgomery Improvement Association (MIA). Dr. Martin Luther King, Jr., a 26-year-old minister new to Montgomery, was selected to be its president.

King, who had lived in Montgomery for only 15 months, had already demonstrated a commitment to civil rights reform, and exceptional abilities as an orator. King had studied the nonviolent teachings of Mahatma Gandhi and identified himself as an advocate of the "social gospel." Parks recalled that King's selection came largely because he was so new to the city that he hadn't been there long enough to make any strong friends or enemies. Montgomery residents learned of King's unique talents as an orator when he noted the boycott's larger significance during his first address at an MIA rally. "If we are wrong, the Constitution of the United States is wrong," King told an audience at Montgomery's Holt Street Baptist Church. "If we are wrong, God Almighty is wrong."

MIA members initially issued a modest list of demands: courteous treatment by the bus operator; first-come, first-serve seating for all, with blacks seating from

Martin Luther King emerged as the leader of the boycott.

During the yearlong boycott in Montgomery, many black residents carpooled to work, leaving the buses nearly empty.

the rear and whites from the front; and black bus operators on predominately black routes. As they became more confident in their ability to sustain the boycott, however, King and other MIA leaders agreed to support a legal suit against Montgomery's bus segregation law.

Black residents stayed off the buses throughout 1956, as city officials and white citizens tried various strategies to defeat the boycott. Taxi drivers supporting the boycott were penalized when they began charging black customers 10 cents—the regular bus fare. Car pool drivers were ticketed for driving too slowly. King's home was bombed, and the membership of the local White Citizens' Council increased dramatically. City officials obtained injunctions against the boycott in February 1956 and arrested scores of protesters under a 1921 state boycott law. King was tried and convicted on the charge and ordered to pay $1,000 or serve 386 days in jail, but the intimidation effort stirred even greater determination by the boycotters. "Freedom doesn't come on a silver platter," King remarked at a rally following his conviction. "You don't get to the promised land without going through the wilderness."

Under pressure to address the conflict in Montgomery, a federal district court ruled bus segregation unconstitutional on June 4, 1956. In late fall, while MIA leaders were in a Montgomery courtroom seeking to prevent local officials from obtaining an injunction against MIA car pool operations, the U.S. Supreme Court affirmed the district court ruling in *Browder v. Gayle*. The court order arrived in Montgomery on December 20. That evening, in a series of spirited mass meetings, King called upon supporters to end the boycott. The next morning King, Nixon, and local Baptist minister Ralph Abernathy became the first black bus riders to sit legally in the front section of a Montgomery bus.

Although King had not initiated the boycott, he emerged as a major civil rights leader because of his central role in sustaining it and communicating its goals to a national and international audience. The MIA's tactics of combining mass nonviolent protest within a Christian framework became the model for challenging segregation in the South. African-Americans had shown that a nonviolent movement could succeed if they remained undivided and courageous.

# Rosa Parks

ORN IN 1913, ROSA McCauley grew up in Pine Level, Alabama, the daughter of a carpenter and a teacher. After elementary school, Rosa was sent to Montgomery for further education, and there she met Raymond Parks, a barber 10 years her senior. She was 19 years old when she married Parks, the first activist she had ever known.

Rosa Parks became an activist, too. In 1943 she joined the Montgomery branch of the NAACP and served as its unpaid secretary, keeping records on cases of discrimination, unfair treatment, and violence against blacks. She also advised the NAACP Youth Council. When she refused to give up her seat to a white passenger on a Montgomery city bus on December 1, 1955, she was not tired from working all day as a department store seamstress. As she said in her 1992 autobiography, "No, the only tired I was, was tired of giving in."

Plagued by death threats to herself and her family, and unable to find a job, Parks left Montgomery soon after the boycott ended and moved with her husband and mother to Detroit. For several years afterward, she traveled around the country giving speeches and accepting honors for her part in sparking the Civil Rights Movement. However, she played no official role. "Nowadays," Parks said in her autobiography, "women wouldn't stand for being kept so much in the background, but back then women's rights hadn't become a popular cause yet."

Reverend Thomas Kilgore, Jr., and Rosa Parks

Parks lived quietly in Detroit, employed in her later working years in the office of Michigan Congressman John Conyers and caring for her mother, brother, and husband, all of whom died in the late 1970s. In 1987 she formed the Rosa and Raymond Parks Institute for Self-Development, which helps youth continue their education and have hope for the future. And in 1999 she was awarded the Congressional Gold Medal, personally presented by President Bill Clinton.

Rosa Parks goes through the process of being booked, fingerprinted, photographed, and released by Deputy Sheriff D. H. Lackey at the Montgomery County Courthouse on February 22, 1956. Parks cheerfully surrendered herself after being indicted for violating an obscure state statute prohibiting illegal boycotts, thus converting a traditionally humiliating experience into a badge of honor that attracted national attention. "Those who had previously trembled before the law were now proud to be arrested for the cause of freedom," wrote Martin Luther King, the boycott's young leader.

> "The driver of the bus saw me still sitting there, and he asked was I going to stand up. I said, 'No.' He said, 'I'm going to have you arrested.' Then I said, 'You may do that.' These were the only words we said to each other."
>
> —ROSA PARKS

Whites in Montgomery threaten a black man during the bus boycott. The city's white citizens did what they could to end this "crisis." Police arrested black car pool drivers for the slightest moving violations, and they pressured taxi drivers who gave rides to African-Americans. Some whites took more severe action, bombing Martin Luther King's house on January 30, 1956, and E. D. Nixon's home two days later. Nevertheless, Montgomery's black citizens would not be intimidated. The boycott continued.

## Parks: Tired of Giving In

PEOPLE ALWAYS SAY that I didn't give up my seat because I was tired, but that isn't true. I was not tired physically, or no more tired than I usually was at the end of a working day. I was not old, although some people have an image of me as being old then. I was forty-two. No, the only tired I was, was tired of giving in.

The driver of the bus saw me still sitting there, and he asked was I going to stand up. I said, "No." He said, "Well, I'm going to have you arrested." Then I said, "You may do that." These were the only words we said to each other. I didn't even know his name, which was James Blake, until we were in court together. He got out of the bus and stayed outside for a few minutes, waiting for the police.

As I sat there, I tried not to think about what might happen. I knew that anything was possible. I could be manhandled or beaten. I could be arrested. People have asked me if it occurred to me then that I could be the test case the NAACP had been looking for. I did not think about that at all. In fact if I had let myself think too deeply about what might happen to me, I might have gotten off the bus. But I chose to remain.

—*Rosa Parks,* Rosa Parks: My Story

Coretta Scott King (the wife of Martin Luther King) and well-wishers welcome King on the Montgomery County Courthouse steps on March 22, 1956, after he was found guilty of organizing the bus boycott in violation of Alabama's anti-boycott law. "Long live the king!" and "No more buses!" supporters shouted. The arrest was a blunder by local authorities, as it attracted international attention and strengthened the resolve of African-Americans to continue the boycott. "I knew that I was a convicted criminal," King wrote, "but I was proud of my crime . . . the crime of joining my people in a nonviolent protest against injustice."

## 1956

**April 14:** Leaders of the Presbyterian Church of the United States urge moderation in handling segregation, stating that Christians may follow preferences in personal interracial associations.

**April 19:** In an effort to diminish the effectiveness of the NAACP, the South Carolina state legislature bans state employees from affiliating with civil rights organizations.

**April 23:** In *South Carolina Electric and Gas Company v. Flemming*, the U.S. Supreme Court rules that segregation on public transportation is unconstitutional.

**Late May:** In Tallahassee, Florida, black college students Wilhelmina Jakes and Carrie Patterson are arrested for refusing to sit in the back of the bus. The incident sparks a citywide bus boycott by black citizens, which will continue until December 1956.

**June 1:** Alabama outlaws the NAACP throughout the state.

**June 5:** In response to Alabama's ban on the NAACP, Reverend Fred Shuttlesworth helps found the Alabama Christian Movement for Human Rights in Birmingham to continue the fight for civil rights.

**June 5:** The U.S. District Court in Montgomery rules that bus segregation is unconstitutional. The city appeals to the U.S. Supreme Court. *See* November 13, 1956.

**August 30–31:** The enrollment of black high school students in Mansfield, Texas, triggers rioting. The governor calls in the Texas Rangers to uphold segregation, preventing integration.

**September:** Violence erupts in Clinton, Tennessee, over the admission of 12 black high school students. *See* October 5, 1958. ➤

Four southern senators who helped draft the Southern Manifesto pose in Washington, D.C., on March 12, 1956, after the formal statement was presented to the U.S. Senate. Left to right are John Stennis (D–MS), Richard Russell (D–GA), Walter George (D–GA), and Sam Ervin (D–NC). Signed by 19 senators and 81 representatives from the South, the Southern Manifesto sought to repeal the Supreme Court's decision outlawing segregation in public schools. The manifesto presented the argument that because the "Constitution does not mention education," no legal basis existed for banning segregation. The signers alleged that the Supreme Court justices "exercised their naked judicial power and substituted their personal, political and social ideas for the established law of the land . . . destroying the amicable relations between the white and Negro races. . . ."

School districts around the country chose to follow their own interpretation of the U.S. Supreme Court's "all deliberate speed" mandate when it came to desegregating their schools. Here, black children and parents carry signs demanding school desegregation in Hillsboro, Oregon, in April 1956, two years after the *Brown v. Board of Education* ruling. The children marched to Hillsboro's white public school, Webster School, where they were turned away. Throughout the country, many states and communities would avoid integrating their schools until they were absolutely forced to by the federal government.

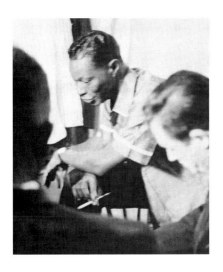

No black person was immune to racial violence, not even such beloved entertainers as Nat "King" Cole. Here, the legendary singer talks to reporters in Raleigh, North Carolina, about the six white supremacists who attacked him in Birmingham on April 11, 1956.

Cole had returned to his home state of Alabama to perform with an integrated band, a progressive action that some whites took offense to. Three white men jumped up on stage and assaulted Cole. The attack, which some historical accounts say was an attempted kidnapping of Cole, was masterminded by Kenneth Adams, a member of the board of directors of the local White Citizens' Council. A consummate professional, Cole performed his second show that night after being treated for his injuries.

In 1956 the U.S. Supreme Court ruled that racial segregation on public transportation was unconstitutional. But although this sign came down in Dallas in April 1956, other signs stayed up throughout the South until protests created the necessary social friction to bring them down. As with the *Brown v. Board of Education* decision, local municipalities would use their own timetables. In Montgomery, for example, the bus company's announcement that it would desegregate was immediately countered by Mayor W. A. Gayle, who said the policy would stay the same. Again and again, the Movement would continue to press the South to live up to the edicts of the Supreme Court and federal courts.

On May 31, 1956, three black women alight from a station wagon owned by the Bell Street Baptist Church. Support from the local black community and donations from around the world allowed the Montgomery Improvement Association to purchase and operate a fleet of 15 new station wagons that replaced the black-owned cabs and police-harassed volunteer drivers originally used in the bus boycott. Ironically, whites who employed African-Americans as domestics were among the first to provide transportation. They didn't want to lose their workers.

# Martin Luther King, Jr.

**W**HEN HE FOUND HIMSELF unexpectedly thrust into the leadership of the Montgomery bus boycott, Dr. Martin Luther King, Jr., often reminded his audiences that he had not initiated the movement. Even if he had never been born, he remarked at a meeting of the Montgomery Improvement Association, the boycott would have transpired.

Despite his recognition that the African-American freedom struggle was beyond the control of one individual, King saw himself as a divinely inspired leader determined to use his skills on behalf of social justice. His grandfather and father had also been civil rights leaders as well as Baptist ministers. From the time of his birth in 1929 in Atlanta, he had absorbed the ideals of social gospel Christianity. While an undergraduate at Atlanta's Morehouse College, he had decided to enter the ministry after responding to a strong urge to serve God and humanity. At Crozer Theological Seminary and Boston University, he continued to develop his distinctive form of Christianity based in social justice.

King earned the Nobel Peace Prize in 1964.

King emerged from the Montgomery boycott as a nationally prominent civil rights leader, becoming the founding president of the Southern Christian Leadership Conference (SCLC) in 1957. A trip to India in 1959 strengthened his commitment to Gandhian precepts of nonviolent struggle. Yet, following the successful conclusion of the Montgomery bus boycott, King wavered between caution and aggressive action. He remained on the sidelines of the sit-in movement of 1960 until prodded by activists of the Student Nonviolent Coordinating Committee (SNCC). In October 1960 King's arrest in Atlanta at a student-led sit-in became an issue in the presidential campaign when Democratic candidate John F. Kennedy called Coretta Scott King to express his concern.

Kennedy supporters' successful efforts to secure King's release contributed to the Democratic candidate's narrow victory.

After emerging from an unsuccessful effort during 1962 to wrest concessions from Albany, Georgia's white leaders, King reestablished his preeminence within the Civil Rights Movement through his leadership of the Birmingham campaign of 1963. With the help of Reverend Fred Shuttlesworth, SCLC organizers were able to orchestrate a series of clashes during April and May between black demonstrators and police with dogs that attracted enormous press attention. The Birmingham protests eventually forced the Kennedy Administration to intervene and in June to introduce major new civil rights legislation. King's "Letter From Birmingham Jail"—an extended justification of civil disobedience—became his most widely quoted written work.

King's "I Have a Dream" speech at the 1963 March on Washington for Jobs and Freedom—particularly his extemporaneous closing remarks—confirmed his position as the Civil Rights Movement's foremost spokesperson. At the end of the year, *Time* magazine named him Man of the Year. A year later he became, at the time, the youngest recipient of the Nobel Peace Prize. As King's fame grew, however, so too did the pressures placed upon him. Other black leaders, such as Malcolm X and SNCC's Stokely Carmichael, questioned his philosophy of nonviolence and interracialism. King's fame also prompted FBI Director J. Edgar Hoover to intensify his effort to damage King's reputation through phone taps and bugs.

In the mid-1960s the African-American struggle expanded from desegregation protests to mass movements seeking economic and political gains in the North as well as the South. King's active involvement was limited to a few highly publicized civil rights campaigns, particularly the series of voting rights protests that began in Selma, Alabama, early in 1965, which secured popular support for the passage of the Voting Rights Act of 1965.

After the successful campaign in Selma, King was unable to drum up similar support in his effort to confront the problems of northern urban blacks. In 1966 he launched a major campaign against poverty and other urban problems, moving into an apartment in a black ghetto of Chicago. As King shifted the focus of his activities to the North, however, he discovered that the successful tactics used in the South were not as effective there. He encountered a formidable opponent in Mayor Richard Daley and was unable to mobilize Chicago's large and diverse black community. King was stoned by irate whites in Chicago's Marquette Park when he led a march against racial discrimination in housing. Despite multiple mass protests, the Chicago campaign did not achieve any significant gains and tarnished King's reputation as an effective civil rights leader.

In the mid- to late 1960s, King was not among the black militants who trumpeted "Black Power."

King was arrested 20 times in his life.

However, he acknowledged that they responded to a psychological need among African-Americans that he had not previously addressed. "Psychological freedom, a firm sense of self-esteem, is the most powerful weapon against the long night of physical slavery," King stated. "The Negro will only be truly free when he reaches down to the inner depths of his own being and signs with the pen and ink of assertive selfhood his own emancipation proclamation."

While rejecting calls for black retaliatory violence, King also spoke out strongly against American involvement in the Vietnam War. He made his position public in an address on April 4, 1967, at New York's Riverside Church. This stand made him a target of further FBI investigations, but he became even more insistent that his version of Gandhian nonviolence and social gospel Chris-

tianity was the most appropriate response to the problems of black Americans.

In November 1967 King announced the formation of the Poor People's Campaign, which he hoped would spur the federal government to strengthen its antipoverty efforts. King and other SCLC workers began to persuade poor people and antipoverty activists to go to Washington, D.C., to lobby for improved antipoverty programs. This effort was in its early stages when King became involved in a sanitation workers' strike in Memphis, Tennessee, in March 1968.

An outbreak of violence during a King-led march in Memphis led him to return to that city on April 3. Speaking to an audience at Bishop Charles H. Mason Temple that evening, King affirmed his optimism despite the "difficult days" that lay ahead. "But it doesn't matter with me now," he declared, "because I've been to the mountaintop . . . and I've seen the promised land." He continued, "I may not get there with you. But I want you to know tonight, that we, as a people, will get to the promised land." The following evening King was assassinated as he stood on a balcony of the Lorraine Motel in Memphis. The Poor People's Campaign continued after his death but did not achieve its objectives.

Until his death, King remained steadfast in his commitment to the radical transformation of American society through nonviolent activism. In his posthumously published essay "A Testament of Hope" (1986), he urged African-Americans to refrain from violence but also noted that black citizens couldn't achieve full justice until the structure of American society was dramatically changed. The black revolution was more than a civil rights movement, he insisted. It was forcing America to face up to its problems, which he listed as racism, poverty, militarism, and materialism.

After her husband's death, Coretta Scott King led the successful effort to honor King with a federal holiday on the anniversary of his birthday, which was first celebrated in 1986.

# 1950s

## Tallahassee Bus Boycott

On May 27, 1956, a Tallahassee, Florida, bus driver ordered two young black women to vacate their places because a white woman was sitting at the end of the seat they occupied. The two black women, students at Florida A&M University, demanded a refund of their fare. The driver called the police, who promptly arrested the women.

The entire student body of Florida A&M stayed off the buses in protest, joined within days by the rest of Tallahassee's black citizens. Without the 15,000 black riders on which it depended, the bus company ceased operation indefinitely on July 1.

Efforts to quell the protest ranged from Ku Klux Klan meetings and cross burnings to an appeal by city authorities to the religious nature of its black citizens (by saying it was sinful to deprive a state's capital city of its transportation system). Despite the protests, the City Commission announced on January 7, 1957, the repeal of the bus company's segregation clause because of its "doubtful legality." In its place, the commission adopted a face-saving and unenforceable bus seating assignment plan. The new plan made drivers responsible for assigning seats to provide "maximum health and safety" for passengers.

Florida A&M student Eugene Lincoln serves as a dispatcher for a car pool system during the Tallahassee bus boycott. Tallahassee's police chief and City Commission took strides to crack down on the car pools. On August 22 and 27, seven car pool drivers were arrested for violating the state's "for hire" laws regulating commercial transportation. It was clear that Tallahassee's establishment was not on the side of the boycotters. When the boycott leaders wrote at one point that they wanted total integration of the buses—to sit anywhere they want—the *Tallahassee Democrat* editorialized that they were being unreasonable.

The bus boycott in Tallahassee, Florida, was led by Reverend C. K. Steele. Along with other ministers and activists, Steele took out a full-page newspaper advertisement entitled "An Appeal to the People of Tallahassee for Moral Justice." Steele wrote that since appeals to the bus company had fallen on deaf ears, the city's African-Americans were taking action. "Sometimes the answer to a problem is so simple that we make it hard by trying to look for a complicated answer," he wrote. "This is the situation here. The issue is simply one of granting all American citizens who ride the public bus, regardless of race, the right to sit wherever they choose. This is the only morally just solution."

Albert Boutwell was serving his third term in the Alabama State Senate when he saw his opportunity to strike a blow for the segregated South. In defiance of *Brown v. Board of Education,* Boutwell sponsored a "Freedom of Choice School Amendment" that aimed to preserve school segregation. The amendment was approved overwhelmingly. For his efforts, he was elected lieutenant governor of Alabama in 1958. In 1963 he became mayor of Birmingham, the South's most segregated city.

Roy Lee Howlett, 14, stands determined on the Mansfield High School grounds as student registration begins in August 1956. Howlett was one of the hundreds of whites in Mansfield, Texas, who opposed school desegregation enough to block black students from registering for classes. The high school had been ordered by a federal court to desegregate after an NAACP lawsuit proved successful, but Mansfield's white residents responded by forming mobs outside the school. The sheriff was threatened, and black students were burned in effigy. Texas Governor Allan Shivers, a supporter of the Mansfield whites, sent in Texas Rangers to help keep Jim Crow alive at Mansfield High. Meanwhile, the black students were transferred to Fort Worth. The Mansfield school district wouldn't desegregate until 1965, and only after being threatened with the loss of federal funds.

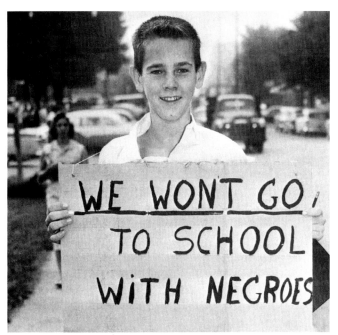

The sign held by John Carter, 17, in Clinton, Tennessee, expressed the view of a vocal and violent faction of whites who did not want to see Clinton's schools desegregated. The town's school system had been ordered to desegregate after an NAACP legal victory. White citizens were enraged and threatened African-Americans. Alfred Williams, one of the black students who desegregated the school in 1956, remembered the fear. "You couldn't possibly get anything learned or done," he said, "because you were constantly afraid that the white kid next to you was planning to kill you."

In late summer 1956, Clinton, Tennessee, erupted in violence in response to the desegregation of Clinton High School. The National Guard and state troopers were called in when it was rumored that white segregationists would stage a cross burning at a football game. Although it didn't happen, whites rioted at the courthouse the following night. Here, a white Clinton youth uses his shoe to smash a window of an out-of-state car driven by an African-American. The mob, fired up by segregationist speeches, stoned and bounced at least six vehicles driven by blacks.

# 1950s

## 1956–1957

**September 6, 1956:** In Sturgis, Kentucky, 500 white citizens try to block the admission of eight black students to the local high school. More than 200 National Guardsmen contain the crowd.

**November 13, 1956:** The U.S. Supreme Court rules that segregation on intrastate buses is unconstitutional, invalidating Montgomery's law.

**Early December 1956:** The first annual Institute on Nonviolence and Social Change is held in Montgomery, marking the first anniversary of the Montgomery bus boycott.

**December 20, 1956:** With black citizens now free to sit where they please on Montgomery's city buses, the Montgomery Improvement Association calls off its 381-day boycott.

**December 25–26, 1956:** In Birmingham, the home of Reverend Fred Shuttlesworth, a civil rights leader, is bombed, stirring unrest in the city. African-Americans defy segregation regulations on the city's buses, leading to arrests.

**1957:** The NAACP pushes Monroe, North Carolina, to desegregate its public swimming pool after several African-American boys had drowned in unsupervised swimming holes. City officials refuse the request.

**1957:** Edward Frazier's book *Black Bourgeoisie*, which criticizes a complacent black middle class, is published.

**1957:** The U.S. Army tells black servicemen stationed in West Germany and married to German women that they must transfer out of their division (2nd Armored) or leave their wives behind when the division moves on to Fort Hood, Texas.

**January 9, 1957:** In Atlanta, black demonstrators are arrested for picketing segregated public trolley facilities. ➤

In Fort Worth, Texas, on September 2, 1956, local whites hit the streets in protest of a black family that had moved into a previously all-white neighborhood. The head of that family, Lloyd Austin, held off a mob of demonstrators with a rifle. Five years earlier in Fort Worth, Essie B. Sturgess was arrested for violating the segregated seating rules on a city bus. When she asked one city official what rule she had violated, he replied, "You're a nigger and not in California."

Whites were not averse to using massive intimidation—direct and physical—to prevent the desegregation of their schools. In Sturgis, Kentucky, in September 1956, five black students waiting for their black schoolmates were engulfed by local whites. Some whites burned a cross in an evening demonstration. The Sturgis schools eventually were desegregated after Kentucky Governor A. B. Chandler sent in the National Guard and the state police.

By the time this photo was snapped on November 24, 1956, the Montgomery bus boycott was a certified success. Almost an entire year had passed in which whites watched black people openly defy white authority. This angered the Ku Klux Klan to no end. Circulars advertising a Klan meeting said, "We believe in white supremacy; we need you—you need us." Klan members knew that whites had to stop a visible and viable black victory or it would be the beginning of the end of black accommodation to blatant white racism.

Two black men ride in the front of a Montgomery city bus on December 21, 1956. A day earlier, deputy U.S. marshals served notice on the city that the U.S. Supreme Court had affirmed a lower court decision declaring Alabama's state and local bus segregation laws unconstitutional. Though actually handed down on November 13, the order was not enforceable until the city exhausted its petitions. In the meantime, local authorities managed to ban the Montgomery Improvement Association's car pool system, forcing Montgomery's blacks to walk during the final five weeks of their campaign.

African-Americans gather in front of the damaged Bethel Baptist Church and the destroyed home of its pastor, Reverend Fred Shuttlesworth, in Birmingham on December 26, 1956. Both buildings had been bombed on Christmas. Inspired by the successful Montgomery bus boycott, Shuttlesworth and a deacon had sat up on Christmas night planning a challenge to bus segregation in their city. The explosion of six sticks of dynamite, planted by a local Klansman, collapsed the home's roof and shattered the floor, plunging Shuttlesworth into the basement. Miraculously, he was not harmed. The next day he led 200 followers into the "white" sections of Birmingham's buses. Over 25 of them were arrested and convicted of violating the city's segregation laws. In June 1958 a second bomb damaged the church.

## 1957

**January 10:** Four black churches, as well as the homes of Reverends Ralph Abernathy and Robert Graetz, are bombed in Montgomery.

**January 11:** The Southern Christian Leadership Conference (SCLC) is founded to coordinate the activities of nonviolent protest groups. Martin Luther King will be named its first president.

**January 21:** Marian Anderson, a black woman, sings the national anthem at the inauguration of President Dwight Eisenhower.

**February 14:** The Georgia Senate outlaws interracial athletics.

**March 6:** Ghana achieves its independence from British rule. Martin Luther King, Ralph Bunche, A. Philip Randolph, and Adam Clayton Powell, Jr., attend ceremonies.

**April 29:** The U.S. Supreme Court rules against Girard College, an elementary and secondary school for orphans in Philadelphia. Because the school is run by the city, the court states that the school can no longer deny admission to black orphans because of their race.

**May 17:** In the Prayer Pilgrimage for Freedom, 30,000 people assemble at the Lincoln Memorial in Washington, D.C., to demonstrate for voters' rights and desegregation.

**June 25:** In Tuskegee, Alabama, black citizens decide to boycott white businesses in response to a discriminatory plan by local leaders, who reconfigure the city limits so that all but a few black citizens would live outside the city. *See* November 14, 1960.

**August:** Black citizens in Rock Hill, South Carolina, begin a successful boycott of the city's segregated bus system. ➤

Police officers and reporters inspect the damage to Montgomery's Bell Street Baptist Church on January 10, 1957, the day after it almost was completely destroyed by a dynamite blast. The attack was part of a fresh wave of bombings by white racists that followed the integration of the city's buses. Three other black churches and two residences also were bombed that evening, including the church and parsonage of Reverend Ralph Abernathy and the home of Reverend Robert Graetz, a white minister of the black Trinity Lutheran Church. Three weeks later, a gas station and taxi stand were bombed and 12 sticks of unexploded dynamite were found on Martin Luther King's porch. Though seven white men were arrested for the bombings, none were convicted.

After the successful bus boycotts in Montgomery and Tallahassee, the Miami NAACP decided to use the judicial system to attack segregated transportation in that city. In federal court in 1956, the NAACP claimed that local ordinances that mandated segregated busing were unconstitutional. In January 1957 a federal judge agreed. However, Miami's city commission gave bus drivers the authority to tell riders where to sit. That could be why teenagers Joseph Sand (*left*) and Vernon Clark were ordered to move to the rear of the bus. They refused, then left the bus after being confronted by police.

# Ralph Abernathy

LARGELY OVERSHADOWED by his friend Martin Luther King, Reverend Ralph David Abernathy was himself a monumental figure in the Civil Rights Movement. Born in 1926 in Linden, Alabama, the 10th of 12 children, Abernathy served in the military during World War II before attending Alabama State College in Montgomery. In 1951 he assumed the pastorship of the First Baptist Church in Montgomery. He also joined the NAACP.

In December 1955 Abernathy worked with King to form the Montgomery Improvement Association to sustain the famous Montgomery bus boycott. On January 10, 1957, Abernathy got word that both his home and his church had been bombed.

Abernathy helped King establish the Southern Christian Leadership Conference (SCLC) and became its secretary/treasurer in 1961. Over the next four years, he went to jail 19 times with King as the SCLC undertook desegregation campaigns in Selma, Birmingham, and elsewhere. Abernathy reacted defiantly after Alabama police attacked marchers in Selma in March 1965. "Bring on your tear gas, bring on your grenades, your new supplies of Mace, your state troopers, and even your national guards," he said. "But let the record show we ain't going to be turned around!"

Abernathy later assisted King in civil rights campaigns in northern cities. After King's assassination in April 1968, Abernathy assumed leadership of the SCLC and led the Poor People's Campaign that built Resurrection City on the Mall in Washington, D.C. In 1977 he resigned as president of the SCLC. He said he wanted to campaign for the Alabama congressional seat vacated by Andrew Young, who was appointed U.S. ambassador to the United Nations. Abernathy lost the election and did not return to the SCLC.

As pastor of West Hunter Street Baptist Church in Atlanta, Abernathy concentrated on making life better for the people of his community. His autobiography, *And the Walls Came Tumbling Down*, was published in 1989, and he died a year later.

Netta Fields (*left*), age nine, and Marie Gianisella, age eight, eat a desegregated lunch in St. Anne Parochial School in Rock Hill, South Carolina, in February 1957. The only integrated school in the state made headlines in both the black and white press. Outside of St. Anne, racial tension raged throughout South Carolina. State legislators were so at odds with the NAACP that in 1956 they banned state employees from affiliating with civil rights organizations.

The Prayer Pilgrimage, the first national event organized by the leaders of the modern Civil Rights Movement, was designed to support the Civil Rights Bill of 1957 and to push for stronger measures. The demonstration in Washington, D.C., was held on May 17, 1957, the third anniversary of the U.S. Supreme Court's *Brown v. Board of Education* decision. It was the largest crowd that Martin Luther King had yet addressed, with estimates ranging from 15,000 to 37,000. "Give us the ballot," King declared, "and we will transform the salient misdeeds of bloodthirsty mobs into the abiding good deeds of orderly citizens." The crowd roared, chanting the words "give us the ballot."

## Southern Christian Leadership Conference

FRESH FROM THE SUCCESS of the Montgomery bus boycott, Martin Luther King hoped to build on its momentum. In January 1957 he invited southern black preachers to the Negro Leaders Conference on Nonviolent Integration to establish a plan for coordinating civil rights work in the South. Sixty ministers responded, and at a meeting at Ebenezer Baptist Church in Atlanta they formed the Southern Christian Leadership Conference (SCLC).

The SCLC's first initiative was a Crusade for Citizenship. Launched with a Prayer Pilgrimage to Washington, D.C., on the third anniversary of the *Brown* decision on May 17, 1957, the crusade included leadership training programs and citizen education projects. SCLC leaders also nurtured the formation of the Student Nonviolent Coordinating Committee (SNCC) in 1960.

With King at its helm, the SCLC played a major role in the March on Washington for Jobs and Freedom in August 1963. It also led antidiscrimination and voter reg-istration drives, notably in the early 1960s in Birmingham; Albany, Georgia; and Selma, Alabama. After passage of major federal civil rights and voting rights legislation in the mid-1960s, King tried to establish the SCLC's presence in the North, but with limited success.

After King's assassination in April 1968, the SCLC lost even more momentum. Led by Reverend Ralph Abernathy, the organization focused on economic rights, notably the Poor People's Campaign and Operation Breadbasket. The SCLC was further weakened by several schisms, including the departure in 1972 of Reverend Jesse Jackson, who had led Operation Breadbasket.

The SCLC, headquartered in Atlanta, remains active in community development projects and programs that address problems such as crime and drug abuse. The SCLC is financed by contributions from individuals and groups and by grants from foundations. In 1997 Martin Luther King III was elected to the post that his father once held with the hope of reenergizing the organization.

Richard Wayne Penniman, known by his stage name Little Richard, was called the wild man of rock 'n' roll. His flamboyant performance style was amusingly complemented by the suggestive lyrics of some of his hits. Young whites went crazy for the so-called "new" sound. Many white parents, who were accustomed to Bing Crosby and Frank Sinatra, were outraged. It was bad enough for Elvis Presley to appropriate black sensuality on stage, but to get it directly, they felt, was beyond toleration.

Gloria Parker, shown protesting outside the RCA building in New York City, believed rock 'n' roll would ruin a generation of young white Americans. "We must put an end to the obscenity that is inundating American music," she was quoted as saying in this photo's original caption. "We must exile the grunters and the groaners, the twitches and twitchers, the gyrations and the animal posturings from the airwaves." By "animal," she was referring to the appropriated sounds and moves of black performers, which formed the cultural base of rock 'n' roll.

Movements for liberation cannot shy away from sacrificing children. The students who desegregated schools in the South were young people, not seasoned adult activists. Most were under the age of 18. In the photo on the left, Russell Herring, one of the first black students to attend Gillespie Elementary School in Greensboro, North Carolina, endures heckles from Ku Klux Klansman Clyde Webster (*left*) in August 1957. In the photo at right, Herring sits in the back row (*third from left*) during a Gillespie school assembly. The black students not only knew they weren't wanted, but they were reminded every day in subtle and not-so-subtle ways that many white people considered them inferior and unworthy of association.

On August 20, 1957, William and Daisy Myers (*left photo*) became the first African-Americans to move into the formerly all-white planned community of Levittown, Pennsylvania. They were met by hostile whites (*right photo*). Whites claimed that the presence of blacks would lead to crime, falling property values, and "white flight." An anonymous resident wrote the governor, "If you had ever lived near those savages, then you would know why people object to their moving into Levittown." The state police were called in after the Myers's home was stoned and three crosses were burned on their lawn.

# Civil Rights Act of 1957

PASSAGE OF THE FIRST civil rights bill since 1875 followed closely on the heels of the Little Rock school desegregation events. Introduced by the Eisenhower Administration, the bill was aimed primarily at securing voting rights for black Southerners. In the Senate, diehard southern segregationists were determined to kill the bill by staging a filibuster that lasted nearly 122 hours. South Carolina's Strom Thurmond alone accounted for a record-breaking 24 of those hours.

Senate Majority Leader Lyndon Johnson of Texas worked equally hard to pass the bill, paring it down to what he considered the essentials. He told pro-civil rights legislators that it was as strong as it could be and segregationists that it was as weak as possible.

Eventually, negotiations on the bill came down to a single sticking point: an amendment guaranteeing the right of a jury trial to state officials accused of violating court orders on voting rights. Civil Rights leaders argued vehemently against the amendment, saying that it would effectively nullify the bill's voting rights provision. They claimed that a state official accused of obstructing someone's right to register rarely would be found guilty by an all-white southern jury. Despite those arguments, the bill passed easily in August 1957.

The bill created a Commission on Civil Rights in the executive branch and established a new civil rights division in the Justice Department. It also set forth procedures for securing the right to vote for all citizens, and provided for the jury trials in civil rights cases. Though the bill had few provisions for enforcement, it was at least a good starting point, a base on which to anchor future, stronger legislation.

In late August 1957 U.S. Senator Strom Thurmond of South Carolina attempted to filibuster the Civil Rights Bill—to stall its vote—by speaking for a record-breaking 24 hours and 18 minutes on the Senate floor. His wife, Jean, who kept a sometimes lonely vigil in the Senate gallery, is at Strom's side. Such conduct was not surprising for a segregationist who said in 1948 "that there's not enough troops in the Army to force the southern people to break down segregation and admit the nigger race into our theaters, into our swimming pools, into our homes, and into our churches." Thurmond had assured his fellow segregationist senators that he would *not* filibuster; they agreed that to do so could result in a civil rights bill that the South would like even less. But Thurmond made his 24-hour gesture anyway, causing his comrades to look like do-nothings to the folks back home. Not long after Thurmond relinquished the floor, the bill was passed.

Dorothy Counts, 15, and Dr. Edwin Thompkins, a family friend, convey bravery, resolve, and disgust as Counts desegregates Harding High School in Charlotte, North Carolina, in September 1957. Harding students hurled more than just insults. When Counts's brother picked her up from school, someone threw an object at his car, cracking a window. After Dorothy had attended Harding for two weeks, her family—concerned for her safety—pulled her out of the school. Although Charlotte "voluntarily" desegregated its schools in 1957, only an infinitesimal percentage of black students actually enrolled in white schools that fall.

Daisy Gatson Bates (*left*) made her mark on civil rights history as a mentor to the nine black students who ultimately desegregated Central High School in Little Rock in 1957. Bates counseled and comforted the teens while simultaneously fearing for her own life. As tensions escalated, whites drove to her home, taunted her, and—in a note attached to a rock that smashed through her window—threatened to kill her. Born and raised in Arkansas, Bates served as president of the Arkansas conference of the NAACP. With her husband, L. C. Bates (whom she married in 1941), she also campaigned against segregation in the pages of their newspaper, the *Arkansas State Press*.

After being denied admission to Central High School on September 4, the Little Rock Nine studied together while the U.S. Justice Department, a federal court, Arkansas's governor, and the President of the United States battled over their fate. Pictured in the front row, left to right, are Thelma Mothershed, Elizabeth Eckford, and Melba Patillo. In the back row are Jefferson Thomas, Ernest Green, Minnijean Brown, Carlotta Walls, Terrence Roberts, and Gloria Ray.

# Crisis in Little Rock

IN 1955, IN ITS SECOND ruling in *Brown v. Board of Education*, the United States Supreme Court ordered that desegregation of public schools should be implemented "with all deliberate speed," establishing yet another battlefield for the NAACP Legal Defense Fund. As in the cases leading up to the historic *Brown* decision, the soldiers in the trenches on that new battlefield had to be special. Courageous young people, whose reputations were beyond reproach, would be needed to challenge entrenched school segregation in the South.

Little Rock, Arkansas, had the soldiers with the necessary mettle for this new battlefield. Daisy Gatson Bates, president of the Arkansas NAACP, had long attacked segregation in the pages of the *Arkansas State Press*, the newspaper she published with her husband, L. C. Bates. As she wrote in her memoir, *The Long Shadow of Little Rock*, the Supreme Court's *Brown* ruling meant that "the time for delay, evasion, or procrastination was over."

In a carefully planned and well-executed campaign, Bates and others in the Arkansas NAACP recruited nine students to enroll at Little Rock's Central High School. Minnijean Brown, Elizabeth Eckford, Ernest Green, Thelma Mothershed, Melba Patillo, Gloria Ray, Terrence Roberts, Jefferson Thomas, and Carlotta Walls were from respected, religious families and were deemed by Bates and NAACP attorney Wiley Branton to have the faith and strength to be "firsts." In the weeks before the start of school in September 1957, the "Little Rock Nine" underwent intensive counseling sessions on what to expect and how to respond in various hypothetical but anticipated situations.

Just before the first day of classes, on September 3, Governor Orval Faubus announced that he would call in the Arkansas National Guard to prevent the students from entering Central High. Faubus had been raised as a racially tolerant socialist. Elected governor in 1954 on a liberal platform that promised increased spending on schools and roads, he had already desegregated state buses and public transportation by 1957 and had begun to investigate ways to integrate the public schools. In the face of attacks by the right wing of his party, however, the threat to his own political survival took precedence.

On September 4, after walking a virtual gauntlet of hysterical whites to reach the front door of Central High, the Little Rock Nine were turned back by Arkansas National Guardsmen. The white crowd hooted and cheered, shouted, stomped, and whistled. The segregationist whites of Little Rock did not see the vulnerability or the bravery of the students. Instead, they saw symbols of the South's defeat in the War Between the States, its perceived degradation during the Reconstruction that followed, and the threats to the southern way of life they had been taught to believe was sacrosanct.

President Dwight Eisenhower was no great liberal, but he could not allow blatant disregard of the law of the land as established by its highest court. Moreover, like many others during this Red Scare period, he knew that racial problems in the United States, the "home of the free," provided propaganda fodder for Communists. He tried for nearly three weeks to persuade Governor Faubus to back down.

Finally, on September 24, Eisenhower went on national television to address the American people: "At a time when we face grave situations abroad because of the hatred that communism bears towards a system of gov-

A mob surrounds Central High student Elizabeth Eckford.

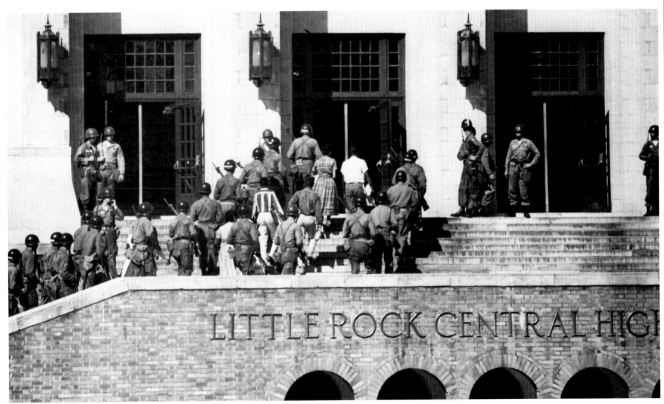

President Eisenhower had to federalize the Arkansas National Guard to enable the Little Rock Nine to attend classes.

ernment based on human rights, it would be difficult to exaggerate the harm that is being done to the prestige and influence and indeed to the safety of our nation and the world. Our enemies are gloating over this incident and using it everywhere to misrepresent our whole nation." With great reluctance, Eisenhower sent federal troops to Little Rock and put the Arkansas National Guard under federal command in order to ensure the integration of the school.

U.S. Army and Arkansas National Guard troops remained at Central High throughout the school year, but the nine students continued to suffer psychological, verbal, and even physical abuse. In her book, *Warriors Don't Cry*, Melba Patillo told of dynamite sticks being thrown at her. She recalled white students following closely behind her as she walked through the school halls and stepping on her heels until they were sore and bleeding. She wrote that a group of football players cornered her and promised: "We're gonna make your life hell, nigger. Y'all are gonna go screaming out of here, taking those nigger-loving soldiers with you." The one senior among the nine, Ernest Green, attended graduation ceremonies under heavy guard.

The following September, the students, represented by the NAACP, won the right to return to Central High. Rather than allow them admittance, Governor Faubus closed all of Little Rock's high schools, which remained shut for an entire school year. During that year, two of the nine students and their families moved away. The remaining seven students went elsewhere to finish high school. Not until September 1960 did legal victories won by the NAACP force the reopening of Little Rock's high schools. Only two black students were allowed to enroll that year.

Orval Faubus won reelection as governor of Arkansas five times and served in the post for 12 years. After the 1965 Voting Rights Act made it easier for African-Americans to vote, black ballots ensured that Faubus would never win again. He lost in the elections of 1970, 1974, and 1986, the last time to Bill Clinton.

In the fall of 1987, the nine students reunited on the 30th anniversary of their entry into Central High School. Greeted warmly by Governor Clinton on the steps of the school, they were further impressed when a young black man emerged from the front door dressed in a jacket and bow tie. "Good morning," he said. "I am Derrick Noble, president of the student body. Welcome to Central High."

## 1957

**September 3:** Federal District Judge Ronald N. Davies rules that Central High School in Little Rock, Arkansas, be integrated the following day.

**September 4:** Under orders from Governor Orval Faubus, the Arkansas National Guard prevents nine black students from entering Little Rock's Central High School on the second day of classes. *See* September 10, 1957.

**September 9:** President Eisenhower signs the Civil Rights Act of 1957. The act establishes a civil rights division within the Justice Department and calls for the creation of the U.S. Commission on Civil Rights. The act also allows the federal government to bring suit against anyone interfering with another person's right to vote.

**September 9:** A bomb explodes at Hattie Cotton Elementary School in Nashville during a week in which white citizens protest the admission of a black student.

**September 10:** The U.S. Justice Department files a petition for an injunction against Arkansas Governor Orval Faubus, as it attempts to force Faubus to comply with a federal court's order to desegregate Central High School. The injunction hearing is set for September 20. In the meantime, Faubus will continue to employ the National Guard at Little Rock.

**September 20:** Federal District Judge Ronald N. Davies orders Arkansas Governor Orval Faubus to remove the Arkansas National Guard from Central High School. Faubus announces he soon will comply with the order but asks black students to stay away from the school in the meantime.

**September 23:** The "Little Rock Nine" are admitted to Central High School, but they soon are sent home when the police fear they won't be able to maintain control of the mob waiting outside the school. ➤

"They've gone in," a man roared. "Oh, God, the niggers are in the school."... "Oh, my God," the woman screamed. She burst into tears and tore at her hair. Hysteria swept the crowd.

—ASSOCIATED PRESS REPORTER RELMAN MORIN, DESCRIBING THE SCENE OUTSIDE CENTRAL HIGH SCHOOL ON SEPTEMBER 23, 1957

On September 4, 1957, Elizabeth Eckford walked to Little Rock's Central High School. She had not received the message from Daisy Bates, the black students' adviser, to meet Bates and the other students elsewhere. As Eckford approached the school, a mob cried out for her lynching. Under the orders of Governor Orval Faubus, the National Guard did nothing but turn her away in front of the school, leaving her to the mercy of the hostile whites, some of whom spat at her and tore her clothing. None of the black students entered school that day.

## Threatened by a Hostile Mob

THE CROWD WAS QUIET. I guess they were waiting to see what was going to happen. When I was able to steady my knees, I walked up to the guard who had let the white students in. He too didn't move. When I tried to squeeze past him, he raised his bayonet and then the other guards closed in and they raised their bayonets.

They glared at me with a mean look and I was very frightened and didn't know what to do. I turned around and the crowd came toward me.

They moved closer and closer. Somebody started yelling, "Lynch her! Lynch her!"

I tried to see a friendly face somewhere in the mob—someone who maybe would help. I looked into the face of an old woman and it seemed a kind face, but when I looked at her again, she spat on me.

They came closer, shouting, "No nigger bitch is going to get in our school. Get out of here!"

—*Elizabeth Eckford*, The Long Shadow of Little Rock

What kind of black mother would allow her child to endure mob violence to attend an all-white high school in the segregated South? Mrs. A. L. Mothershed (*right*), mother of Little Rock Nine member Thelma Mothershed (*left*), was one of those parents. Arkansas NAACP President Daisy Bates not only needed the kind of black students who could withstand overt racism, but also the kind of parents who would allow their children to withstand such abuse. Parents of desegregation pioneers experienced fear, guilt, and eventually pride. Courage also was essential, as multiple parents lost their jobs for their defiance of Jim Crow.

Arkansas Governor Orval Faubus considered President Eisenhower's intrusion in his state to be nothing less than an invasion. On September 26 the segregationist said the federal government had sent in troops to "occupy" Little Rock. Faubus would fight hard to maintain segregated schools. It was he who ordered the Arkansas National Guard to keep the Little Rock Nine out of Central High. It was he who shut down the city's public high schools for a year to try to hold off the inevitable. "If [Arkansas NAACP President] Daisy Bates would find an honest job and go to work," he cracked, "and if the U.S. Supreme Court would keep its cotton-picking hands off the Little Rock School Board's affairs, we could open the Little Rock [public] schools!" But the Supreme Court successfully countered Faubus every time. Jim Crow would not win the day in Arkansas.

Federal troops were not afraid to shed blood to protect the U.S. Constitution. Here, members of the 101st Airborne Division prod three men down the street and away from Little Rock's Central High School on September 25, 1957, the day the Little Rock Nine finally were allowed admittance. The nine attended classes behind the bayonets of paratroopers, who bashed one white man in the head, stabbed another in the arm, and hustled dozens off to jail.

# 1950s

## 1957–1958

**September 24, 1957:** On national television, President Dwight Eisenhower announces he's sending U.S. Army troops from the 101st Airborne Division to Little Rock to enforce the court-ordered desegregation of Central High School. He also federalizes the Arkansas National Guard.

**September 25, 1957:** Federal troops escort the Little Rock Nine to their classes at Central High School. *See* November 27, 1957.

**November 1957:** The citizens of Pleasanton, Texas, vote overwhelmingly in favor of integrating the local public schools. Thirty-five black students begin studies. The process is carried out peacefully.

**November 27, 1957:** U.S. Army troops withdraw from Little Rock's Central High School. The federalized Arkansas National Guard remains.

**December 17, 1957:** Minnijean Brown, one of the nine black students at Little Rock's Central High School, dumps a bowl of chili on the head of a white boy who had been taunting her. She's given a six-day suspension. *See* February 6, 1958.

**February 6, 1958:** Minnijean Brown, one of the Little Rock Nine, calls a white girl who was provoking her "white trash." Brown will be expelled for her action. *See* May 27, 1958.

**February 12, 1958:** The SCLC begins its Crusade for Citizenship with meetings in 22 southern cities. Its goal is to double the number of black voters by 1960. ➤

Tensions did not lessen after the Little Rock Nine were enrolled. In early October, several dozen Central High School students hoped that their walkout would start a general walkout by the school's white student body. When the exodus didn't materialize, the protesters let off steam by hanging a black person in effigy. Sometimes the threat was more direct. Melba Patillo got acid thrown in her eyes. She said she had to become a warrior, to learn how to get from one end of the hall to the other "without dying."

White students yelled insults at the Little Rock Nine, including Jefferson Thomas (*left*) and Elizabeth Eckford (*right*). They hit them, stepped on their heels, destroyed their lockers, and threw flaming paper wads and lighted sticks of dynamite toward them. Yet in addition to all this abuse, some of the Little Rock Nine had to endure criticism even from African-Americans. Melba Patillo recalled an incident she experienced in church one Sunday during that first year. An African-American woman whom she didn't know well approached her. The woman was fuming, and Patillo thought the lady was going to hit her. Practically shouting, the woman told Patillo that she was being too "fancy for [her] britches" and that other people in Little Rock would pay for Patillo's "uppity need" to be with white people. Alone, but not lonely, the Little Rock Nine would stand for what they believed in until the opposition broke.

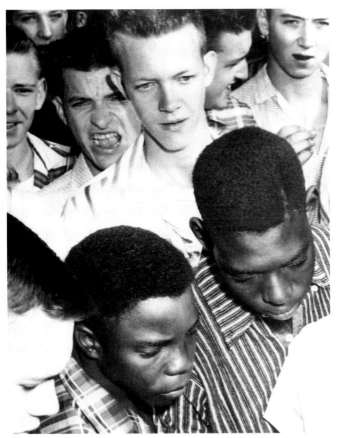

Ernest Green recalled an incident between fellow Little Rock Nine member Minnijean Brown (*pictured*) and a white student in Central High School's cafeteria in late 1957: "Minni was about five-foot-ten, and this fellow couldn't have been more than five-five, five-four. And he reminded me of a small dog, yelping at somebody's leg. Minni had just picked up her chili, and before I could even say, 'Minni, why don't you tell him to shut up?' Minni had taken this chili and dumped it on this dude's head. There was absolute silence in the place, and then the help, all black, broke into applause. And the white kids, the other white kids, didn't know what to do. It was the first time that anybody, I'm sure, had seen somebody black retaliate in that sense." Brown continued to defend herself against white attacks until she was expelled in February 1958. Some Central High whites celebrated by making up cards that said, "One down, eight to go!" Brown transferred to a private, desegregated school in New York City.

In September 1957 seven black teens tried to desegregate North Little Rock High School. However, due to the crisis at Little Rock's Central High, the school board on September 3 postponed plans to integrate North Little Rock High. When six of the black teens, including Richard Richardson (*left*) and Harold Smith (*right*), showed up at North Little Rock anyway, they were herded away by white parents and students (*pictured*). The hate and arrogance many whites felt is easily seen on the faces of these white teens.

A firefighter examines the debris in a junior high school in Osage, West Virginia, in May 1958. The school, which had been desegregated five years earlier, was heavily damaged by dynamite. Switching to white schools was frightening for African-American students in West Virginia. Intense racism existed at many schools, while white teachers were known to paddle black students.

Ernest Green, one of the Little Rock Nine, recounted his graduation day: "At the graduate ceremony, one of the guests was Martin Luther King. . . . He came up to sit with my mother and Mrs. [Daisy] Bates and a couple of other friends in the audience. I figured all I had to do was to walk across that big huge stage, which looked the length of a football field. . . . When they called my name there was nothing, just the name, and there was this eerie silence. Nobody clapped. But I figured they didn't have to. Because after I got that diploma, that was it. I had accomplished what I had come there for."

## 1958

**May 27:** Ernest Green, the only senior among the Little Rock Nine, graduates from Central High School.

**June 21:** Federal District Judge Harry Lemley allows Little Rock schools to postpone integration for two and a half years. *See* September 12, 1958.

**June 23:** President Dwight Eisenhower discusses civil rights issues at the White House with Martin Luther King, Roy Wilkins, A. Philip Randolph, and Lester Granger.

**June 29:** In Birmingham, a bomb explodes at the church of Reverend Fred Shuttlesworth—one of numerous bombings throughout the South during the year.

**June 30:** In *NAACP v. Alabama*, the U.S. Supreme Court validates the right of the NAACP to conceal its lists of members.

**July 19:** Using a "sit-in" technique, members of the NAACP Youth Council begin the successful desegregation of dozens of lunch counters in Wichita and Oklahoma City.

**September 12:** In *Cooper v. Aaron*, the U.S. Supreme Court overturns a U.S. district court's decision to suspend further integration of Little Rock schools for two and a half years. It also rules that public money cannot be used to fund private schools that sidestep federal desegregation orders. *See* September 27, 1958.

**September 20:** In a Harlem department store, Martin Luther King is stabbed by Izola Curry, a black woman, as he autographs copies of his first book, *Stride Toward Freedom*.

**September 27:** Little Rock citizens vote against integration of their city's public schools, 19,470 to 7,561.

**September 30:** Arkansas Governor Orval Faubus rules that public high schools in Little Rock will be closed for the rest of the school year. *See* June 18, 1959.

➤

David Isom (*pictured*), 19, took a swim in a St. Petersburg, Florida, public swimming pool on June 8, 1958. In response, city officials closed the pool. It was the second time in three days that a public pool was closed in St. Petersburg for this reason. In the 1950s it was not uncommon to see whites climb out of pools and head home after a black person had jumped into their swimming water. In their minds, the water had become "polluted."

Black leaders pose with President Dwight Eisenhower at a White House meeting on June 23, 1958. Left to right are Lester Granger, executive director of the National Urban League; Martin Luther King; presidential assistant E. Frederick Morrow; Eisenhower; A. Philip Randolph, president of the Brotherhood of Sleeping Car Porters; Attorney General William Rogers; presidential assistant Rocco Siciliano; and Roy Wilkins, executive secretary of the NAACP. Wilkins later wrote that the President was polite but not at ease among black leaders. In 1958 Eisenhower retreated from the activism he had mustered during the Little Rock school integration battle the previous year.

# Roy Wilkins

AT THE DAWN OF THE 20TH CENTURY, Roy Wilkins's father fled St. Louis after fearing for his life for standing up to racists. The Wilkinses, including Roy (born in 1901), moved to St. Paul, Minnesota. The young Wilkins, who described himself as a loner, studied sociology and journalism at the University of Minnesota. He also joined the local branch of the NAACP.

After receiving his bachelor of arts degree in 1923, Wilkins worked for the *Call*, a leading black weekly in Kansas City. Increasingly active in the NAACP, he left the *Call* in 1931 to become assistant executive secretary of the national organization under Walter White. In 1934 he succeeded W.E.B. Du Bois as editor of the NAACP journal *The Crisis*, a post he would hold for some 15 years.

Wilkins served as an advisor to the War Department during World War II and as an observer to the United States delegation at the United Nations conference in San Francisco. Having shown great understanding of the mechanics of power in Washington, D.C., Wilkins in 1949 became chair of the National Emergency Civil Rights Mobilization, a lobbying group for civil rights and fair employment legislation.

Wilkins succeeded to the leadership of the NAACP after Walter White died in 1955. He was a key player among

civil rights leaders and chaired the Leadership Conference on Civil Rights, a coalition of several dozen national civic, labor, fraternal, and religious organizations.

As more militant black spokesmen claimed the spotlight in the 1970s, Wilkins took criticism for his courtly manner and thoughtful, deliberate pace. He did not waver, however, in his determination to work through the system to achieve full equality for African-Americans. "Muffle your rage," he advised young militants. "Get smart instead of muscular." Wilkins died in New York City in 1981.

In August 1958 members of the NAACP Youth Council began a series of sit-ins at segregated restaurants in Oklahoma City, Oklahoma. Though sit-ins wouldn't become widespread until 1960, the Oklahoma City attempts were successful, resulting in the desegregation of dozens of lunch counters. In these two photos, African-Americans attempt to eat at Brown's Basement Luncheonette in Oklahoma in 1958. Their mere presence led to raised eyebrows, snickers, the waving of the Confederate flag, and even the removal of one of their tables.

**Late September 1958:** Alabama Governor James Folsom commutes the death sentence of Jimmy Wilson, a black man, to life imprisonment. Wilson was convicted of stealing $1.95 from an elderly white woman.

**October 5, 1958:** In Clinton, Tennessee, a bomb destroys 16 classrooms at the local high school.

**October 14, 1958:** The District of Columbia Bar Association votes to accept black lawyers as members.

**October 20, 1958:** Reverend Fred Shuttlesworth heads the organization of a bus boycott in Birmingham. A federal court ruling on December 14, 1959, will mandate that the city's buses be desegregated.

**October 25, 1958:** About 10,000 students participate in the Youth March for Integrated Schools in Washington, D.C. They're led by A. Philip Randolph, Harry Belafonte, and Jackie Robinson. *See* April 18, 1959.

**February 2, 1959:** Public schools in Arlington and Norfolk, Virginia, are peacefully desegregated.

**February 3, 1959:** Martin Luther King travels to India, where he studies Gandhi's principles of nonviolent resistance.

**March 11, 1959:** *A Raisin in the Sun*, written by black playwright Lorraine Hansberry, debuts on Broadway. The play dramatizes a black family's attempt to realize its dream while faced with racial prejudice.

**April 1959:** Hazel Payne, a black woman, nearly dies in Little Rock because state law prohibits the transfusion of "white blood" into black people.

**April 18, 1959:** More than 25,000 students partake in the second Youth March for Integrated Schools in Washington, D.C. Thousands sign a petition for school integration. ➤

John Kasper (*center*) was the leader of the National Association for the Advancement of White People. During the late 1950s, Kasper traveled the South attempting to inflame white racism as a weapon against the desegregation of schools. Here he's shown in Tallahassee, Florida, in 1958 after recently serving time for inciting a riot in Clinton, Tennessee. With him in front of the Florida state capitol is Bill Hendrix (*left*), a veteran Ku Klux Klan leader in Florida, and Reverend John Cole, a Klan leader in the Carolinas.

President Dwight Eisenhower was not a part of the Movement, but he made sure that neither the Constitution was contradicted nor the Supreme Court ignored. So with Little Rock in turmoil, he took tentative steps toward calling for full civil rights for black Americans. He called Little Rock's white leaders "extremists" and said that mob rule "cannot be allowed to override the decisions of our courts."

Johnny Gray, 15, points a warning finger at one of two white boys who had tried to force him and his sister, Mary, from the sidewalk as they walked to school in Little Rock on September 16, 1958. The argument led to a fistfight and ended with Johnny chasing the white boys down the block. The stand taken by the Little Rock Nine inspired pride in black communities around the nation. African-Americans discovered that they could stand up to white intimidation without automatically being murdered or burned out of their homes.

After World War II, many of the 8,000 servicemen from the British West Indies who had been based in England wished to remain. A subsequent wave of immigration from Jamaica and elsewhere in the Indies began in 1948. Although the then-new British Nationality Act said that any resident of a U.K. colony was a British subject entitled to settle in England, many Britons reacted badly to the arrival of blacks. Class consciousness had a lot to do with this, but so did simple resentment: The postwar British economy was in tatters, and jobs were scarce. Many immigrants, such as this West Indian photographed in 1958, discovered that "NO COLOURED MEN" were welcome by landlords and employers.

Dr. Emil Naclerio stands beside a sedated Martin Luther King in Harlem Hospital after a deranged black woman stabbed him in the chest with a letter opener on September 20, 1958. King had been signing copies of his new book, *Stride Toward Freedom,* at Blumstein's department store. According to Dr. Aubré Maynard, the head of the interracial surgical team, King would have died if he had sneezed because the tip of the knife had reached his aorta. Two ribs and a portion of King's breastbone had to be removed to free the blade.

# 1950s

The "peace" that Clinton High School had achieved after it became Ground Zero for Tennessee's battle over desegregated schools was violently interrupted on October 5, 1958. Only the school's top section and the gym remained after about 75 to 100 dynamite sticks did their work. Since the blast occurred on a Sunday, no one was killed or injured. Another school made space for the students of Clinton High, which eventually was rebuilt. However, a sense of social and physical disruption continued to weigh on Clinton residents for years.

In January 1959 Georgia Governor Ernest Vandiver spoke to the state legislature about resisting desegregation. The audience was receptive, as the state's constitution required that a district's funds be cut if the district included any desegregated schools. Vandiver tried to use the power of his office to resist desegregation. In 1961 he cut off funds to the University of Georgia after it was ordered by a federal judge in Macon to admit black students. The university immediately suspended the students. However, federal judge W. A. Bootle had had enough: He ordered the students reinstated and required the state—meaning Vandiver—to protect them. The governor saw the proverbial writing on the wall. He addressed the legislature later in 1961, asking that all Jim Crow education laws be repealed. Suddenly, all could see that segregation would not last forever, regardless of who declared what in a statehouse.

Martin and Coretta Scott King are welcomed to New Delhi, India, on February 10, 1959, by Prime Minister Jawaharlal Nehru, who had helped Mahatma Gandhi lead India's nonviolent struggle against British colonialism. King and Nehru talked for four hours during a sumptuous formal dinner, comparing the application of nonviolence to their respective struggles. Later, the Kings embarked on a month-long tour of India, meeting other prominent Gandhians and government officials.

# Citizenship Schools

CITIZENSHIP SCHOOLS WERE a mass literacy program—the largest and most effective such program ever undertaken in the United States—designed to teach blacks to read and write so they could register to vote. Organized between 1953 and 1961 by Highlander Folk School in Monteagle, Tennessee, they represented grassroots activism as opposed to the legalism advocated by the NAACP.

Myles Horton established Highlander in 1932 to teach poor and disenfranchised Americans the leadership skills necessary to challenge the social, economic, and political structures that kept them impoverished and powerless. First serving oppressed white workers in the Appalachian Mountains, the school turned its attention to civil rights for black Southerners by the early 1950s.

In 1951 Highlander inaugurated its citizenship schools program under the leadership of Septima Poinsette Clark. John Lewis, James Bevel, and many other future Civil Rights Movement leaders studied at Highlander. Rosa Parks spent time there in the summer of 1955, just months before she took her courageous stand on a Montgomery bus. It was her first experience in an integrated setting.

Among the best known of the citizenship schools outside of Highlander was Dorchester, a missionary school near Savannah, Georgia, which served the people of the Sea Islands. In his autobiography, *The Long Haul*, Horton explained that the people "learned that you couldn't read

Highlander Folk School

and write yourself into freedom. You had to fight for that and you had to do it as part of a group, not as an individual."

Highlander's blatant disregard of Tennessee's segregation laws did not sit well with people in the surrounding community, who set fire to the school while Horton was away and Clark was in charge. In 1960 the state padlocked the school. But as Horton put it, "You can't padlock an idea." The school reopened as the Highlander Research and Education Center. It operates today under that name in New Market, Tennessee.

As a response to *Brown v. Board of Education,* the state of Virginia shut down its public schools in 1958. When some of the schools reopened because of federal court orders, white students stayed away. For example, the formerly all-white Warren High School (*pictured*) reopened on February 18, 1959, but only 21 students showed up—all African-Americans. Whites raised money and created their own private academies. One of the private schools, the Prince Edward Academy, hired all of the white school district's 66 teachers at their old salaries. The city of Prince Edward closed its public schools for five years.

## 1959

**April 29:** CORE organizes nonviolent sit-ins in Miami.

**May 11:** The Florida state legislature authorizes the closing of any park or beach threatened by a desegregation order.

**May 19:** Public access to the Atlanta Public Library becomes integrated.

**June 1:** The Florida legislature approves a bill to pay for ads in northern periodicals that promote the southern stance on segregation.

**June 18:** A federal court rules that Arkansas's law to close its public schools is unconstitutional. The school board will not appeal the ruling and will reopen Little Rock's schools in the fall. *See* August 12, 1959.

**July 13–17:** ABC–TV airs *The Hate That Hate Produced*, a five-part documentary about Malcolm X and the Nation of Islam.

**July 31:** The Civil Rights Commission reports that when blacks and whites make the same mistakes on voting registration tests, blacks are not allowed to register while whites can.

**August 12:** Little Rock's public high schools reopen a month early and are now integrated. *See* February 9, 1960.

**September:** In Prince Edward County, Virginia, public schools are closed to avoid integration. White students are placed in private schools, and black students are left with no schools at all. *See* September 8, 1964.

**October 23:** Juanita Kidd Stout is elected judge of the Common Pleas Court in Philadelphia, becoming the first black female judge in the United States.

**November:** The Nashville Christian Leadership Conference begins sit-ins in downtown department stores.

Despite the negative publicity surrounding the murder of Emmett Till in 1955, his was not the last case of lynching in Mississippi. On May 4, 1959, the body of Mack Parker was recovered from Pearl River near Poplarville, Mississippi. Here, a fisherman points to the spot where the body was found. Accused of raping a white woman, Parker had been abducted from jail and killed. Members of the local White Citizens' Council were suspected of participating in the murder, but no indictments were returned.

Ernest Green's graduation from Central High School in 1959 did little to change some minds in Little Rock, Arkansas. In August a small group of sign-carrying segregationists assembled in front of the state's capitol building, protesting the desegregation of Little Rock's high schools. (The two pictured here are the children of Arkansas State Representative Dale Alford.) Politicians within Arkansas warred among themselves. For example, segregationists on the Little Rock school board, who attempted to purge suspected desegregationists, got purged themselves. On June 18, 1959, a federal court declared that the state could not close its public schools.

# Race and Sex

IN THE SOUTH prior to the 1960s, African-American males were afraid to make any contact with white women—including eye contact. York Garrett, who grew up in North Carolina in the early 1900s, said that if a black man looked at a white woman the wrong way, "he could be lynched."

At one point or another, 42 states passed laws prohibiting miscegenation—the marriage or sexual relationship between a white person and a person of another race. Some of these laws remained on the books until the 1960s.

Many white southern men dreaded miscegenation for two reasons. First, they considered a black person to be subhuman while viewing the southern white woman as the epitome of virtue. Second, they feared that black-white unions would lead to mixed-race children—the beginning of the genetic devolution of the white race. (The fact that white men had raped black women for gen-erations, producing children, was not a public part of the miscegenation hysteria.) In 1954 the *Jackson* (Mississippi) *Daily News* editorialized: "White and Negro children in the same schools will lead to miscegenation. Miscegenation leads to mixed marriages and mixed marriages lead to mongrelization of the human race."

The fear of black-white unions was the fuel that made lynching common in the South. The thought of a black man raping a white woman pushed white men to cut off the penises of black lynching victims and stuff them into the dead victims' mouths. The specter drove white men to kill Emmett Till, a 14-year-old, and dump his body into a river in Mississippi, all for saying "Bye, baby" to a white woman. The terror made white parents quickly pull their daughters out of desegregated schools and Ku Klux Klansmen shout with animal rage under burning crosses. Even a U.S. Senator, Theodore Bilbo of Mississippi, con-doned violence to protect southern white women.

The 1959–60 school year was going to be a desegregated one in Little Rock, Arkansas, and everyone knew it. But that still didn't mean it had to happen peacefully. Two of the Little Rock Nine, Jefferson Thomas (*pictured*) and Carlotta Walls, began their senior years at Central High, but 250 segregationists didn't want to see them graduate. On August 12 the segregationists marched to the school carrying American flags. However, no one in power wanted to repeat what had happened two years earlier. Twenty-one protesters were arrested that day, and fire hoses cooled down the rest.

# Restrictive Covenants and Block-Busting

IN THE MID-20TH CENTURY, residential segregation outside the South was often more rigid than in the heart of Dixie. In the North and West, segregation was buttressed by restrictive covenants and block-busting.

Restrictive covenants were clauses in real estate title documents that prevented future sales of the property based on race or ethnicity. Singer Nat "King" Cole and other well-known African-Americans in Hollywood faced such clauses in the 1940s when they moved to the film capital after World War II. In *Shelley v. Kramer* in 1948, the U.S. Supreme Court declared that state and federal courts could not enforce such racial restrictions. Cole and his family moved into a home in previously all-white Hancock Park in August of that year.

Block-busting was a money-grubbing scheme employed by real estate agents. If a black family moved into a white neighborhood, agents quickly warned the white homeowners that their property values would fall. The agents urged them to move out before that happened (and, of course, offered to represent them). Through block-busting, entire neighborhoods changed from white to black in a short time, giving rise to the joke: "What is racial integration? It's the time elapsed between when the first black family moves in and the last white family moves out."

Segregation was as blatant as it was dehumanizing. This designation of restrooms—"Ladies," "Men," and "Colored"—was humiliating to African-Americans on at least two levels. The first level: Black men and women had to share one bathroom, as if gender privacy and modesty didn't matter to them; to whites, they were just "black," not human beings of different genders. The second: Whites wanted to make it clear to everyone that their former slaves were not now, nor would they ever be, "Ladies" and "Men."

Although black Americans were making significant progress in gaining first-class citizenship rights, they still received painful reminders that retaliatory violence could claim them at any time. Roy Wilkins, executive secretary of the NAACP, displays such a reminder. The noose was shipped anonymously from Florida to the association's national headquarters in New York City.

Lorraine Hansberry was the first black woman to write a play that would make it to Broadway. *A Raisin in the Sun,* her powerful story about a black family and its struggle to overcome its class circumstances—accentuated by a move into an all-white neighborhood—was a triumph for the 28-year-old in 1959. Although Hansberry was pleased with the play's success, she worried that whites regarded the play's conclusion as a "happy ending" that illustrated the power of faith. That was not Hansberry's intent. For her, the ending was only slightly hopeful; the family's future as racial pioneers promises to be one of grinding difficulty.

The flyers at this segregationists meeting in Houston declared, "There'll be no Little Rock episode in Clarendon County." They were right, but perhaps not in the way they thought. Houston led southern states in quiet desegregation, as black leaders pushed the city's leaders to dispose of Jim Crow. In some southern regions, the potential social friction caused by white racists on one side and the NAACP on the other wasn't worth the headache of keeping segregation alive.

# THE 1960s

**"I have a dream that one day on the red hills of Georgia the sons of former slaves and the sons of former slave owners will be able to sit down together at a table of brotherhood. . . . I have a dream that my four children will one day live in a nation where they will not be judged by the color of their skin but by the content of their character. I have a dream today."**

—Martin Luther King, during his March on Washington speech, August 28, 1963

On August 28, 1963, an integrated crowd of more than 200,000 attended the March on Washington for Jobs and Freedom. Martin Luther King's "I Have a Dream" speech inspired the nation and helped ease the passage of the Civil Rights Act of 1964.

Maybe they should have just served them that cup of coffee. . . . On February 1, 1960, a group of four black students from North Carolina A&T College sat down at a "white" lunch counter in a Woolworth store in Greensboro. They were refused service. Keeping their seats, the students opened up their textbooks and began to read their lessons. The counter was closed down.

The next day the four students—Ezell Blair, Jr., David Richmond, Joseph McNeil, and Franklin McCain—came back. They recruited reinforcements from the student body, and they returned again and again. At the same time, they formed an organization: the Student Executive Committee for Justice. The struggle broadened and deepened. Woolworth ultimately capitulated, but more importantly the struggle became national in scope, with many sit-ins including both black and white protesters. Arrests at these "sit-ins," which took place throughout the South as well as in certain northern cities, numbered in the thousands, but the youths fired the imagination of the entire country.

The sit-in, as a tactic, was not new. Since Reconstruction days, African-Americans had protested against segregation. The Congress of Racial Equality (CORE) staged sit-ins in the 1940s, and the NAACP pulled off successful sit-ins in Kansas and Oklahoma in 1958. Then, as well as in 1960, the tactic had the virtue of simplicity: A customer took a seat, requested service, and, if refused, remained seated. If struck or manhandled by hoodlums, he or she refused to retaliate. If ordered to leave by the police, he or she politely declined. The code of conduct drawn up by Nashville college students in 1960 was:

Don't strike back or curse if abused.
Don't laugh out loud.
Don't hold conversations with floor workers.
Don't block entrances to the store or aisles.
Show yourself courteous and friendly at all times.
Sit straight and always face the counter.

# 1960s

Remember love and nonviolence.
May God bless each of you.

The Civil Rights Movement would never be the same. The student sit-ins shook the Movement's power structure; direct action became the preeminent tactic. NAACP hegemony in the civil rights struggle ended. Attention now turned to the masses of African-Americans, their social and economic struggles.

Both the NAACP and Martin Luther King's SCLC sought to identify themselves with the new "freedom fighters" of the Movement. King attended the organizing meeting of the Student Nonviolent Coordinating Committee (SNCC) in Raleigh, North Carolina, in April 1960. The NAACP took advantage of the young protesters, organizing youth chapters in the southern and border states. A dual dependency emerged: The young depended on the legal and financial aid that the adults supplied, but they spurred the initiative.

Meanwhile, James Farmer was installed as the national director of CORE in January 1961, and the organization moved into Alabama and Mississippi with the famous Freedom Rides that spring. The Freedom Riders attempted to dramatize the failure of southern states to integrate their interstate transportation facilities. Black and white riders purchased tickets to ride buses from northern to southern destinations. They pointedly sat black and white, side by side, in defiance of racial etiquette and southern laws. The results were incendiary. Black and white demonstrators were dragged from the buses and beaten savagely. Some never recovered from the brutality, spending the rest of their lives in wheelchairs. The price of social change was high.

Almost two decades later, the American Civil Liberties Union released nearly 3,000 pages of government documents. The papers revealed that in 1961 the FBI gave a detailed itinerary for two busloads of Freedom Riders to Thomas Cook of the Birmingham Police Department's intelligence branch. Cook, in turn, passed the information directly to the Ku Klux Klan's top leadership. The buses were met by gangs of Klansmen, who beat riders with pipes, chains, and baseball bats. An FBI informer said that Cook and Birmingham Commissioner of Public Safety Eugene "Bull" Connor conspired with the Klan. According to the report, the Birmingham police agreed to show up at the bus terminal 15 to 20 minutes late in order to give the Klan time to attack demonstrators.

After the Greensboro, North Carolina, sit-in on February 1, 1960, sit-ins spread like wildfire throughout the South. In Portsmouth, Virginia, on February 16, an integrated group of protesters (*pictured*) demanded sodas at a restaurant's lunch counter, but only the whites received drinks.

With white backlash becoming more violent, the strain on civil rights organizations increased. Moreover, rivalries among these groups emerged, as each agency sought publicity and proper credit in order to compete for limited financial contributions. Nevertheless, the rivalries had a positive effect, accelerating the dialectic and speeding up the pace of social change.

The NAACP had the most diverse program: litigation, lobbies on the local and national level, and some direct-action campaigns. Roy Wilkins, who succeeded Walter White as NAACP executive secretary in 1955, was a competent if colorless administrator who lacked oratorical skills. On the local level, NAACP branches often acted quite independently. In Philadelphia, for example, the organization was headed by attorney Cecil Moore, who had a flair for blustery rhetoric and relished the politics of confrontation.

After the Supreme Court ruled that segregation in interstate bus terminals was unconstitutional, "Freedom Riders" traveled to the South in 1961 to test the ruling. On May 20 in Anniston, Alabama, irate locals firebombed this bus and then beat the riders as they exited.

Meanwhile, in urban centers across the nation, younger blacks were responding to an even more forceful call for racial pride—the Nation of Islam, headed by the Honorable Elijah Muhammad. Despite the collapse of the Marcus Garvey movement in the 1920s, a number of smaller, more insular black nationalist groups still dotted the landscape, many inspired by Haile Selasse's heroic battle against fascist Italy in the 1935–36 Italo-Ethiopian War. With such names as "Abyssinians" and "Ethiopian World Federation Council," they understandably attracted little attention. That would change, rather suddenly, with the emergence of the Nation of Islam's charismatic spokesman, Malcolm X.

By the early 1960s Malcolm had put America on notice. The Nation of Islam now spoke for the dispossessed. Even their severest critics admitted that the Nation had been remarkably successful in rescuing and rehabilitating some of society's most alienated rejects: drug addicts, criminals, and ex-convicts. They focused their attention on those forgotten by the middle class, on those left largely untouched and decidedly unaffected by the triumphalism of the early years of the Civil Rights Movement. They offered hope, pride, and a sense of community. Malcolm knew such redemptive power first-hand. As "Detroit Red," a pimp and narcotics pusher, Malcolm was sent to prison, where he first heard the words of the Messenger.

Malcolm brought urgency to the civil rights struggle. "The worst crime the white man has committed," he said, "has been to teach us to hate ourselves." While civil rights leaders pushed assimilation, Mal-

James Zwerg, the first off the Freedom Ride bus in Montgomery, Alabama, on May 20, 1961, was bloodied by a mob.

colm spoke of the need for what Elijah Muhammad called "knowledge of self." While major black leaders spoke of love and compassion, Malcolm spoke of justice and redemption. If Martin Luther King was the spirit of charity found in the New Testament, Malcolm was the fire and "awful swift sword" of the Old.

"Is white America really sorry for her crimes against the black people?" Malcolm wrote. "Does white America have the capacity to repent and to atone? . . . What atonement would the God of Justice demand

Malcolm X viewed American society in stark black and white. Until his last year of life, he considered whites his enemies and railed for the establishment of a separate black society.

for the robbery of the black people's labor, their lives, their true identities, their culture, their history—and even their human dignity?"

The Nation enforced a strict moral code that forbade alcohol, tobacco, and gambling, and stressed cleanliness, thrift, and self-reliance. Muslim men and women dressed conservatively. Many owned their own businesses. Malcolm not only offered a plausible alternative, he spoke common-sense truths that were difficult to ignore. "Revolutions are never based upon that which is begging a corrupt society or a corrupt system to accept us into it," he preached. "Revolutions overturn systems."

Malcolm spoke quickly, bluntly, without ambivalence or ambiguity. His charisma and message earned him millions of admirers—as well as several powerful enemies within the Nation. They were jealous of his celebrity and the implicit threat that celebrity posed to the Nation's leadership. When Malcolm blithely characterized President John F. Kennedy's assassination in 1963 as the "chickens coming home to roost," it provided the Nation's leaders with a pretext to silence their most popular spokesman.

In 1964 Malcolm formed the rival Organization of Afro-American Unity, and he returned from Mecca with a transformed vision of race relations. Whites, he now felt, could be brothers. The "changed" Malcolm lived only a few more months. On February 21, 1965, he was assassinated by members of the Nation. However, his autobiography, released later that year, would influence black Americans for decades.

The student movement, as exemplified by SNCC, also began to move beyond integration. SNCC members were the first generation of

To register at the University of Mississippi, African-American James Meredith had to overcome several court battles, defiance by Governor Ross Barnett, and a campus-wide riot. Only after the arrival of 23,000 soldiers was Meredith able to register, on October 1, 1962.

black college students whom Julian Bond dubbed "the striving lower class." Their revolt was as much against traditional black leadership as white injustice. Social historian Lerone Bennett observed that the rebelious students were making America realize that peace could not exist between the oppressors and the oppressed.

John Lewis, an American Baptist Seminary student and later national chairman of SNCC, pronounced an appropriate epitaph. When sitting in a Nashville jail with scores of other sit-in students in May 1961, he opened his Bible, peered through the bars at the guards and his fellow students, and announced the text from Matthew 10:34: "Think not that I am come to send peace on earth: I came not to send peace, but a sword."

No decade in the 20th century witnessed greater social change than the 1960s. It began with the presidential election of John F. Kennedy, who actually lost the white vote to his opponent, Richard Nixon, and yet, with overwhelming black support, secured a razor-thin victory. Kennedy was immediately confronted with crises in the streets: sit-ins, ride-ins, and James Meredith's application for admission to the University of Mississippi, "Ole Miss."

During the 1960 campaign, Kennedy had courted white Southerners by vaguely hinting that he would not have sent troops to Little Rock, Arkansas, in 1957 as President Dwight Eisenhower had done. Now he was forced to confront racial segregation and Mississippi Governor Ross Barnett. Despite Barnett's repeated defiance as well as violent hostility at the University of Mississippi, Kennedy made sure that Meredith attended the school. He sent 500 U.S. marshals to the campus and federalized the Mississippi National Guard to get the job done.

An even more formidable opponent for President Kennedy, and successor Lyndon B. Johnson, was Alabama Governor George Wallace. A rabid segregationist, Wallace stood in the schoolhouse door at the University of Alabama in 1963, protesting the federally mandated admission of two black students. Wallace also allowed local police and firefighters to abuse demonstrators in Birmingham in spring 1963, and he green-lighted the beatings of marchers by state troopers in Selma in March 1965.

However Neanderthal their politics and heavy-handed their approaches, the Barnetts and Wallaces and Bull Connors of America were critical actors in the civil rights drama. Without them, Martin Luther King could not have dramatized the violence and fear that attended the everyday lives of black Americans. Without them, King

In Birmingham, Alabama, in spring 1963, African-Americans staged multiple demonstrations in protest of segregation. On May 3 and May 7, local firefighters blasted demonstrators—including many children— with water from their fire hoses, which roared from the nozzles with enough force to break human ribs.

FREEDOM'S UNHOLY LIGHT.

The beatings of Freedom Riders in Alabama in 1961 tarnished the state's image nationwide. Other ugly incidents in Alabama, such as the abuse of demonstrators in Birmingham in 1963 and Bloody Sunday in Selma in 1965, further sullied the state's reputation.

In support of voting rights, demonstrators in Alabama attempted a 54-mile march from Selma to Montgomery. The march was aborted by state troopers on March 7, 1963, (Bloody Sunday) as was another on March 9, but federal troops protected the third attempt *(pictured)*, which began on March 21 and ended four days later.

couldn't have fed complacent Americans a diet of fire hoses, angry mobs, and police dogs as they ate their dinners in front of the nightly news. Without the segregationist politicians and officials, King's "I Have a Dream" speech—in front of a quarter million people during the March on Washington in August 1963—might never have been delivered.

Now, in the afterglow of his martyrdom, it is easy to forget just how controversial a figure Martin Luther King really was. By mid-decade, many Northerners already were questioning the relevancy of his campaign against *de facto* segregation in the North. Yet King remained the one man best equipped to pull together the tattered shards of an increasingly fragmented movement. He alone melded the personal authenticity of a southern preacher with the vocabulary and sensibility that appealed to an increasingly secular and urban black middle-class. He brilliantly articulated the dreams and aspirations of millions of Americans of conscience, black and white.

King also emerged as the master tactician of the Movement. A man of faith, he also was a man of this world. "I'm not concerned with the New Jerusalem," he said. "I'm concerned with the New Atlanta, the New Birmingham, the New Montgomery, the New South." And yet he never lost sight of the spiritual dimension of the struggle. "One day we shall win freedom, but not only for ourselves," he wrote in *Strength to Love*. "We shall so appeal to your heart and conscience that we shall win you in the process."

Each major battle called for a refined strategy. In Albany, Georgia, in 1961–62, King moved beyond desegregation to demand the recognition of the black community itself—the hiring of more black police officers, the creation of a biracial committee on jobs and public services. In Chicago in 1966, he confronted *de facto* segregation.

To many, King seemed too cautious, too willing to listen to the pleas of the President or his representatives. Many of the students were never as emotionally committed to nonviolence as King himself was. For them it was a tactic. As one student put it, "When one side has all the guns, then the other side is nonviolent."

Moreover, many of the younger activists were becoming increasingly critical of King personally. His harshest critics felt that he swallowed up all of the oxygen in the room, that intentionally or not, he was so famous, so revered, and so important that his very celebrity monopolized the funds and publicity of the Movement.

In December 1961, after an SNCC-led campaign packed the jails in Albany, King arrived in town. He was arrested, made the headlines, and indirectly deflected attention from SNCC. In SNCC's view, the Movement's total dependence on King's charisma ultimately weakened the Movement, for it discouraged the development of black leadership at the grassroots level.

For SNCC, the danger posed by local racists was compounded by the infuriating timidity of the U.S. Justice Department. SNCC believed that in 1961 the Kennedy Administration promised them federal protection for voter registration workers. But in Mississippi in 1961 and 1963, their only contact with federal agents was with Justice Department officials who placidly took notes as white racists beat them. Sometimes, FBI agents were openly complicit with hostile local authorities. By 1963 SNCC leaders doubted the sincerity of the federal government and were convinced that John Kennedy and his brother, Attorney General Robert Kennedy, had broken their promise for political reasons. SNCC already was becoming estranged from established authority and suspicious of liberal politicians.

Nor should one forget that other civil rights leaders had visions that differed from King's. It was Robert Moses who launched Freedom Summer in 1964, helped create the umbrella voting-registration organization COFO (Council of Federated Organizations), and shifted the direction of the Deep South movement from protest to political empowerment. It was Fannie Lou Hamer and other Mississippi delegates to the 1964 Democratic National Convention who refused to be quieted or compromised as they challenged the political machine that had, for decades, kept southern politics in exclusively white hands.

Younger blacks, such as Stokely Carmichael, called for "Black Power" beginning in 1966, and SNCC and CORE, once avowedly integrationist, were moving to exclude whites from membership. Leaders of the Black Panther Party, formed in 1966, posed with guns held high while advocating revolution. The more that young blacks learned about racial injustice in America, the angrier and more militant they became. Protests evolved into riots in dozens of major cities.

Though he opposed violent methods, King's strategic vision began to synchronize with more radical viewpoints. He came out against the Vietnam War, and in 1968 he planned the Poor People's Campaign in Washington, D.C.—this time without paternal approval of the President. When King was assassinated in Memphis on April 4, 1968, still so far from the mountaintop, more than a single life was ended. An era of energy and optimism and purpose took a bullet to the heart.

For Bobby Seale *(left)* and Huey Newton *(right),* nonviolent protest wasn't sufficiently effective to eradicate the urgent problems facing African-Americans. In October 1966 Seale and Newton cofounded the Black Panther Party to address black issues more aggressively.

A police officer fires at a sniper in a black neighborhood in Indianapolis on June 7, 1969. By the late 1960s, many black youths—angry and emboldened—took to the streets and picked up the gun. White America's response was to assert law and order.

# 1960s

## 1960

**1960:** Throughout the South, black activists stage "wade-ins" to desegregate public beaches and "kneel-ins" in whites-only churches.

**January 11:** Georgia Governor S. Ernest Vandiver, Jr., threatens to withhold state funding from any school that attempts to integrate.

**February:** A drugstore sit-in in Chattanooga, Tennessee, sparks a riot.

**February 1:** North Carolina A&T students Ezell Blair, Jr., Joseph McNeil, David Richmond, and Franklin McCain stage a sit-in at a whites-only lunch counter at Woolworth in Greensboro, North Carolina. The publicity given to the demonstration will spark sit-ins in more than 50 cities over the next two months. *See* July 25, 1960.

**February 9:** A bomb explodes at the home of Carlotta Walls, youngest of the Little Rock Nine.

**February 17:** In Atlanta, Martin Luther King is arrested and jailed for falsifying Alabama state income tax returns. He eventually will be acquitted by an all-white jury.

**February 27:** In Nashville, 82 protesters are arrested for disorderly conduct in a nonviolent demonstration against segregated stores. *See* March 2, 1960.

**March:** The NAACP and CORE call for a national boycott of Woolworth, which operates segregated lunch counters. *See* October 17, 1960.

**March:** Officials in Orangeburg, South Carolina, assault hundreds of black demonstrators with tear gas and water hoses. Police arrest more than 300. ➤

Franklin McCain (*left*) and David Richmond (*right*) were two of the four North Carolina A&T freshmen who staged the famous sit-ins at a segregated Woolworth lunch counter in Greensboro in February 1960. During one of the sit-ins, an older white woman said to McCain, "I'm disappointed in you boys." "Ma'am?" he replied. "I'm disappointed in you boys," she said, "because it took so long for you to do this." Though most southern whites resisted integration in the early 1960s, some felt it was just.

Despite black and white resistance, more and more students joined the initial four sit-in protesters. Not all white youths, however, took such nonviolent resistance passively. Here, young whites take up counter space at the Greensboro Woolworth in an attempt to block the sit-in protesters. Some of the resistance to the Woolworth sit-in protest came from unexpected sources. "You are stupid, ignorant!" said a black woman working behind a counter. "You are dumb! That's why we can't get anywhere today. You are supposed to eat at the other end!"

# Sitting at the White Counter

I WAS FROM NORTH CAROLINA but I had lived in New York and when I went back down there to school I realized the transition, the difference in public accommodations.... It seemed to me that people in Alabama, where they had the Montgomery bus boycott, were at least trying to do something about it. The people in Little Rock, with the trouble at Central High School, were trying to do something. And we weren't.

I had heard people talk about demanding service but no one had ever done it. You either ate in Negro areas or you took a sandwich out. So I decided to see if we could do it.

*—Joseph McNeil, North Carolina AT&T student who helped launch the first sit-in in Greensboro on February 1, 1960*

On February 29, 1960, Alabama Governor John Patterson warned Alabama State students at their state capitol protest that "someone is likely to get killed" if demonstrations in Montgomery continued. The students ignored him, showing up a thousand strong the next day. Some of the students were expelled for protesting at the capitol and at a local lunch counter. They were reinstated the following year, however, after Fred Gray, a black lawyer, took the case to court.

In Somerville, Tennessee, on March 2, 1960, about 170 blacks and an estimated 106 whites braved icy roads to register to vote (*pictured*). Blacks stood in one line, whites another. By the time the office closed, 76 of the whites (about 70 percent) and 70 of the blacks (about 40 percent) had been registered. Southern whites used all kinds of tricks to keep African-Americans from registering to vote. In one town, blacks needed to guess how many jellybeans were in a jar as a "test" to see if they were qualified voters.

# Sit-in Movement

ON FEBRUARY 1, 1960, four black college students sat down at Woolworth's lunch counter in downtown Greensboro, North Carolina. The four students—Joseph McNeil, Ezell Blair, Jr., Franklin McCain, and David Richmond—were in their first year at North Carolina A&T College. After purchasing several items, the four students sat at the lunch counter reserved for white customers. When a waitress asked them to leave, they politely explained that they had purchased items in the store and that they should be allowed to take a seat, rather than stand. To their surprise, they were not arrested. The four students remained seated for close to an hour, until the store closed.

Returning to campus, the four immediately began recruiting more students. The following morning about two dozen students returned to the store and sat at the lunch counter. While no confrontations occurred, the second sit-in attracted the local media. A national news service covered the story of the "well-dressed" black college students who ended their sit-in with a prayer. By day three of the sit-ins, the students had formed the Student Executive Committee for Justice. Five months later, after bomb threats, clashes between protesters and segregationists, and an effective boycott of stores with segregated lunch counters, local white officials agreed to negotiate changes in store policies if demonstrations and boycotts ended.

The Greensboro protesters eventually agreed to terminate their sit-ins, but black students in other communities launched lunch counter protests of their own. By the end of February's second week, the sit-in movement had spread from North Carolina to Virginia. In the campaign's first major arrests, police in Raleigh, North Carolina, jailed more than 40 students. The same week, on February 13, 124 students in Nashville, Tennessee, occupied seats at several lunch counters in the city. By the end of the month, sit-ins had taken place at more than 30 locations in seven states.

The sustained student protests in Nashville were especially well organized. Vanderbilt Divinity School student James Lawson led workshops on Gandhian nonviolence that attracted a number of students from Nashville's black colleges. Many of them would become leaders of the southern civil rights struggle, including John Lewis and Diane Nash. Lawson also enlisted Marion Barry, a Fisk University graduate student who years later would become mayor of Washington, D.C. Barry realized that his participation in the sit-ins might cost him his scholarship, but he decided that if he "was not a free man," he "was not a man at all." The Nashville movement proved successful, as store owners desegregated their lunch counters.

Although the initial Greensboro protesters had been peaceful and polite, participants in the sit-in movement gradually became more assertive. As they achieved concessions from white leaders, black student activists transformed their self-conceptions. They felt a new sense of racial pride, and they were excited that their ideas were taken seriously. Moreover, the students grew ever more confident in their ability to direct campaigns without adult leadership.

Even outside the South, blacks were moved by news accounts of the student protest movement. "Before, the

Students stage a sit-in at Greensboro's Woolworth on February 2, 1960.

Negro in the South had always looked on the defensive, cringing," 25-year-old Robert Moses, a teacher in New York, recalled after seeing newspaper photographs of the sit-in protesters. "I knew this had something to do with my own life. It made me realize that for a long time I had been troubled by the problem of being a Negro and at the same time being an American. This was the answer."

The student sit-ins of 1960 inspired the creation of the Student Nonviolent Coordinating Committee (SNCC) in April of that year. Ella Baker,

A worker at a Nashville restaurant refuses to let sit-in demonstrators through the door.

administrator for the Southern Christian Leadership Conference, invited student sit-in leaders to Shaw University in Raleigh, North Carolina, to address nonviolent resistance and ways to sustain their movement. About 200 southern black students showed up, as did a dozen southern white students, people from 13 student and social reform organizations, and representatives from northern and border state colleges. Although other SCLC officials at the meeting wanted the students to affiliate with the SCLC, Baker had become disenchanted with SCLC's top-down leadership style and encouraged the students to maintain their autonomy. Baker, who left the SCLC in the summer of 1960, remained an advisor for SNCC, encouraging its group-centered decision-making process.

Marion Barry became SNCC's first chairman, and other Nashville activists, including Lewis and Nash, would play important roles in SNCC during its early years. James Lawson drafted SNCC's "Statement of Purpose," which expressed the Gandhian ideals that pervaded the group during the early 1960s: "We affirm the philosophical or religious ideal of nonviolence as the foundation of our purpose, the presupposition of our faith, and the manner of our action."

Although many of the student sit-in protesters were affiliated with NAACP youth groups, the new student movement offered an implicit challenge to the litigation strategy of the nation's oldest civil rights group. NAACP

leaders, for their part, gave public support to the sit-ins, although some privately questioned the usefulness of student-led civil disobedience.

Martin Luther King's response to the sit-ins was more complex. He spoke at SNCC's founding conference and expressed pride that the new movement was launched and sustained by students. He applauded the fact that American students had come of age and were joining in the fight for freedom. Nevertheless, King found himself the target of criticisms from SNCC activists who saw him as too cautious.

The lunch counter sit-ins had demonstrated the potential strength of grass-roots militancy and enabled a new generation of young people to gain confidence in their leadership. By fall 1960 there were signs that the southern Civil Rights Movement had been profoundly transformed by the fiercely independent student protest movement. Those who attended SNCC's second conference in October were determined to continue the direct-action tactics that were seizing the initiative from older, more cautious organizations. Lawson's address to the gathering sounded a tone of militancy that would characterize subsequent SNCC campaigns: "Instead of letting the adults scurry around getting bail, we should have insisted that they scurry about to end the system which had put us in jail. If history offers us such an opportunity again, let us be prepared to seize it."

# 1960s

## 1960

**March 1:** Hundreds of black students stage a peaceful protest against segregation in front of the former Confederate capitol building in Montgomery. Nine Alabama State students connected with the protest will be expelled. *See* March 6, 1960.

**March 2:** More than 60 students are arrested during a bus station protest in Nashville. *See* April 19, 1960.

**March 6:** Eight hundred African-Americans march toward the Alabama state capitol building in Montgomery, only to be turned away by 500 police officers.

**March 15:** Julian Bond and the newly formed Committee on Appeal for Human Rights, based in Atlanta, holds its first sit-in.

**March 16:** San Antonio, Texas, becomes the first major southern city to integrate its lunch counters.

**March 30:** In Marshall, Texas, police use fire hoses to break up a lunch counter sit-in.

**April 15:** In Raleigh, North Carolina, college students establish the Student Nonviolent Coordinating Committee (SNCC), which will take an active role in student sit-ins, Freedom Rides, marches, and voter registration.

**April 15:** William Levitt, a home builder known for his creation of large suburbs, decides to desegregate the new Levittown under construction in New Jersey. Levitt was under pressure from New Jersey courts and fearful of negative publicity.

**April 19:** The home of African-American lawyer and city councilman Z. Alexander Looby is bombed in Nashville. *See* May 10, 1960.

**April 24:** A riot develops in Biloxi, Mississippi, after black citizens attempt to desegregate the whites-only beach. Two white men and eight black men are shot. ➤

"They said, 'Everybody's under arrest.' So all the students got up and marched to the wagon. Then they turned and looked around at the lunch counter again, and the second wave of students had all taken seats . . . then a third wave. No matter what they did and how many they arrested, there was still a lunch counter full of students there."

—DIANE NASH, RECALLING A SIT-IN IN NASHVILLE ON FEBRUARY 27, 1960

A native of Chicago, Diane Nash (*second from right*) attended Fisk University in Nashville, where she first encountered "white" and "colored" restrooms. Outraged by segregation, Nash hooked up with civil rights activists. Though at first she was afraid to go to jail for justice (she offered to type and answer phones instead), she eventually became the leader of the Nashville Student Movement. In 1960 she led the campaign to desegregate lunch counters in Nashville. For participating in sit-ins and other protests, she was arrested multiple times.

Reverend James Lawson, the teacher of the students who attempted to desegregate Nashville's public accommodations in 1960, had trained himself in Gandhian resistance. Lawson had served jail time as a conscientious objector to the Korean War, and he knew it was only a matter of time before Nashville's city fathers would detain him. They waited until after he was expelled from Vanderbilt University's divinity school, arresting him on March 5, 1960. The police handled Lawson roughly, escorting him out of First Baptist Church in manacles while his wife angrily and loudly criticized the officers' abuse. During all this, the First Baptist Church's sign detailed the week's sermon: "Father, Forgive Them."

Representing a Movement participant in court often resulted in being treated like a Movement participant by the enemies. The house of Nashville City Councilman Alexander Looby, a black man who happily served as the head counsel for the student sit-in demonstrators, was bombed on April 19, 1960. In response, some 2,500 people marched to the City Hall in a silent protest.

Nashville Mayor Ben West did not fit the stereotype of the segregationist city official. He was angry about the bombing of black City Councilman Alexander Looby's house on April 19, 1960. Later that day, when student protester Diane Nash asked him in front of TV cameras whether it was wrong to racially discriminate, he nodded and said yes without skipping a beat. He stated years later that it was a moral question "that a *man* had to answer," not a politician. Nashville's store and restaurant owners, who had lost business because of the protests, soon desegregated.

# Nashville Movement

JAMES LAWSON, A DIVINITY student at Vanderbilt University in Nashville, Tennessee, had traveled to India to study the movement led by Gandhi. Encouraged by the success of Gandhian tactics in Montgomery, Lawson in 1958 began offering workshops in nonviolence to students at the several colleges in Nashville, the "Athens of the South." Lawson sent the students in teams to test lunch counter segregation in preparation for a full-scale campaign to abolish segregation in Nashville.

They were still in the testing phase on February 1, 1960, when the Greensboro, North Carolina, student sit-in began independently. By February 18 the Nashville students, feeling the power of an idea whose time had come, had mobilized 200 people for sit-ins at the city's major stores. When they were arrested, other students took their places. The movement soon spread to interstate bus ter-

minals. In mid-March four students were finally served at the Greyhound food counter in Nashville—the first sit-in victory in the nation.

A month later, on April 19, the home of local black councilman Alexander Looby was destroyed by dynamite. The students staged a march on City Hall, the Nashville movement's first major protest of that kind. In a televised confrontation, Nashville movement leader Diane Nash asked Mayor Ben West if segregation was wrong. West did not hesitate. Yes, he said, he believed that it was wrong.

A major shift had taken place in the Civil Rights Movement. The students had wrested the desegregation cause from the Movement's older leaders, who preferred to fight in the courtroom, and brought the cause to the places where the insults of segregation actually occurred. It had become, as Nash explained, a people's movement.

# SNCC

THE STUDENT NONVIOLENT Coordinating Committee (SNCC) was founded in spring 1960 as an outgrowth of the student sit-in movement. SNCC (commonly called "snick") was a decentralized organization of young people, open to all, that stressed direct-action tactics and leadership roles by youth, women, and the poor. SNCC brought new energy to the Civil Rights Movement, organizing voter registration drives and providing front-line troops in major efforts such as the Freedom Rides.

During a voter registration drive in Mississippi in summer 1964, SNCC workers were arrested, beaten, and murdered. In the most infamous case, three young SNCC workers—James Chaney, Michael Schwerner, and Andrew Goodman—were brutally murdered by racist whites near Philadelphia, Mississippi. The conviction of seven men by an all-white jury was a first for civil rights slayings in Mississippi.

In the mid-1960s SNCC broke into factions due to "battle fatigue," the frustration of "turn-the-other-cheek" nonviolence, and resentment against whites on the part of some SNCC members. By 1966 John Lewis, a low-key theology student from Alabama, was replaced as chairman of SNCC by charismatic Trinidad native Stokely Carmichael.

Under Carmichael, SNCC became more militant. It was the first major civil rights organization to denounce U.S. involvement in Vietnam and the first to proclaim the concept of "Black Power," a slogan that Carmichael first used at a voting rights march in June 1966. After being replaced as SNCC chairman by H. Rap Brown in 1967, Carmichael spearheaded a short-lived alliance between SNCC and the Black Panther Party.

In 1968 the organization shed the concept of nonviolence altogether by changing its name to the Student National Coordinating Committee. By this time, however, it was disorganized and divided, and had lost most of its influence.

Black college students read their textbooks in a jail in Atlanta on March 15, 1960. They had participated in one of scores of student-spurred sit-ins in the South in early 1960. They not only occupied segregated public facilities, but they decided to accept whatever punishment local authorities meted out. This meant, for example, serving full jail sentences as model prisoners. This "jail, no bail" technique, popularized by Mahatma Gandhi during his decades-long fight for India's independence from England, would catch on as one of the regular tactics of the growing Civil Rights Movement.

The Woolworth protest in North Carolina set off a national boycott of the store chain. The Congress of Racial Equality issued an appeal for nationwide picketing. Shown here are student protesters from the City College of New York at a Woolworth on Herald Square on April 2, 1960. The protest was sponsored by the New York Youth Committee for Integration. Similar protests were held at Woolworth in such cities as Minneapolis and Boston. The NAACP was directly involved in the Minneapolis protest.

Many African-American adults were stirred by the courage shown by the young sit-in protesters. One inspired individual was popular entertainer Harry Belafonte. By 1960 Belafonte had recorded an enormously popular album, *Calypso,* and starred in a major Hollywood film, *Carmen Jones.* But success did not spoil Belafonte; instead, it freed him to participate in the Movement. Here, he leads a student protest against Woolworth in Cambridge, Massachusetts, on April 21, 1960. Already a friend of Martin Luther King at this time, Belafonte would become one of King's closest allies, putting his reputation on the line again and again for the Movement.

"PRAY KEEP MOVING, BROTHER"

Editorial cartoonist Herbert Block (Herblock), a three-time Pulitzer Prize winner, sketched the "First Segregationist Church" in 1960. Martin Luther King, Malcolm X, and James Baldwin all agreed on one thing: America's most segregated hour fell on Sunday morning. White Christians believed in universal brotherhood, but many also believed that God created some of the earth's people closer to His own image than others.

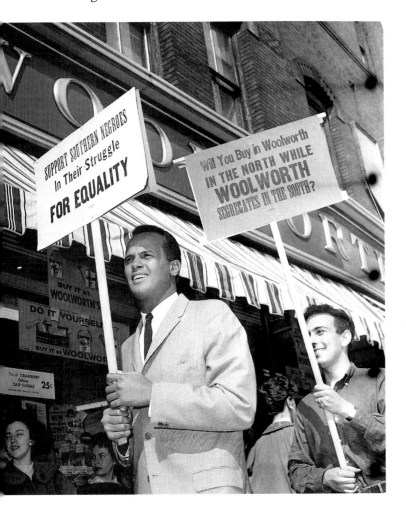

The 15th Amendment to the Constitution, ratified in 1870, prohibited the denial of suffrage on the basis of race. Southern states, however, developed a number of schemes to effectively disenfranchise African-Americans for almost a century. One of the most effective was the "literacy test," in which white registrars routinely denied the vote to black applicants who could not answer questions such as those pictured. White applicants, regardless of literacy level, were given rudimentary tests and then registered. The Voting Rights Act of 1965 finally ended this practice by permitting federal officials to supervise election practices at the state and local levels.

(41)
"B"

1. Can the president of the United States be removed from office for conviction of bribery?  Yes

2. Check the applicable definition for "treaty":

   X   agreement between nations

   _____ a tax

   _____ a written oration

3. Name the man who is nationally known for heading the Federal Bureau of Investigation for many years.  Hoover

4. What officer is designated by the Constitution to be president of the Senate of the United States?  Vice President

-----------------------------------------------------------------------

"C"

1. Can the state coin money with the consent of Congress?   No

2. Name one area of authority over state militia reserved exclusively to the states.  The appointment of officers

3. The power of granting patents, that is, of securing to inventors the exclusive right to their discoveries, is given to the Congress for the purpose of  promoting progress.

4. The only legal tender which may be authorized by states for payment of debts is  U. S. Currency      .

# 1960s

## 1960

**April 25:** A federal court ends restrictions against black voting in Fayette County, Tennessee.

**May:** African-American labor leader A. Philip Randolph helps establish the Negro American Labor Council to challenge discrimination in hiring and promotion.

**May 6:** President Dwight Eisenhower signs the Civil Rights Act of 1960, which is intended to remove the barriers for southern black citizens who try to vote.

**May 10:** Several stores in Nashville decide to desegregate their lunch counters.

**July 10:** One day before the Democratic National Convention begins in Los Angeles, Martin Luther King and A. Philip Randolph lead a march in the city, protesting the party's weak stance on civil rights.

**July 25:** Lunch counters in Greensboro, North Carolina, are desegregated.

**July 31:** Nation of Islam leader Elijah Muhammad calls for the establishment of an all-black state within the United States.

**August:** A longstanding sit-in demonstration in Jacksonville, Florida, turns violent, resulting in numerous injuries.

**October 17:** Woolworth, Grant, Kress, and McCrory–McClellan announce they will integrate their lunch counters in 112 cities.

**October 19–25:** Martin Luther King is arrested in Atlanta for participating in a sit-in at a store lunch counter. After King spends several days in jail, the charge is dropped. He is then held for violating an earlier probation by driving in Georgia with an Alabama license. After being convicted and sentenced to four months hard labor, he is transferred to Reidsville State Prison. ➤

Every bold step by the Movement's young people inspired more to take action—which, in turn, inspired equally bold opposition. In Biloxi, Mississippi, eight blacks and two whites were injured by gunfire during a riot on the beach on April 25, 1960. The melee started when a group of African-Americans decided to start a "wade-in," moving to the "whites only" section of the beach. The whites went to get their guns. This man, Dr. Gilbert Mason, was arrested for obstructing traffic and disturbing the peace. He had stopped his car to give medical attention to a black youngster who was being beaten by a mob of white men. Authorities said Mason had swum in the white-beach section a week prior to the riot.

The success of the sit-ins inspired all sorts of people to try the tactic. Here, Reverend Theodore Roosevelt Thompson, 66 years old, stages a one-man sit-in at a Dallas lunch counter on April 26, 1960. Texans knew change was coming, so they slowly, carefully, yielded to the inevitable. In San Antonio, business owners integrated all of their lunch counters that year. Thompson's waitress, perhaps sensing that times were changing, served Thompson.

By 1960 Martin Luther King had become accustomed to threats against his life. Here, he and his two-year-old son, Martin III, stand near a burnt cross in front of his Atlanta home on April 27, 1960. The spiritual strength and courage he had found by leading the Montgomery bus boycott five years earlier had not left him. Still a follower of Mahatma Gandhi's example of detachment from material possessions, King chose to rent instead of own his home. Often on the road for long stretches, King tried to cherish his family time when he was home, regardless of distractions from the media, the Movement, and local racists.

White racists often showed up to torment lunch counter sit-in protesters. On June 9, 1960, members of the American Nazi Party picketed next to drugstore lunch counter demonstrators in Arlington, Virginia. The state was a hot spot for sit-ins. In February and March 1960, sit-ins occurred in both Hampton and Richmond, Virginia.

# Ella Baker

ORN IN 1903 IN NORFOLK, Virginia, Ella Baker grew up hearing her grandmother's stories about slavery and resistance. It was only fitting, then, that Baker would become known as *"Fundi,"* a Swahili word for a person who passes skills from one generation to the next. Baker fought for civil rights throughout her life and was a driving force behind the formation of the Student Nonviolent Coordinating Committee (SNCC).

After graduating from Shaw University as class valedictorian in 1927, Baker moved to New York City. She worked for the Works Progress Administration during the Great Depression and was active in several groups that organized blacks at the grassroots level. Baker became a field secretary for the NAACP in 1940 and was employed by the organization for six years, working unsuccessfully to shift the NAACP's focus away from legal battles and toward community-based activism. She resigned her position in 1946 but remained an active volunteer.

In 1957, following the Montgomery bus boycott, Baker moved to Atlanta to help Martin Luther King form the SCLC. She disagreed with the SCLC's philosophy of strong central leadership, however, and left the organization after the student sit-ins in Greensboro, North Carolina. Baker felt that strong, focused people could function effectively even in the absence of strong leadership. At a meeting of student activists she hosted at Shaw University, SNCC was born. Baker returned to New York in 1964 and continued her grassroots efforts on behalf of civil rights until her death in 1986.

# 1960s

As the 1960s began, Hollywood carefully attempted to deal with racial themes, although the "tragic mulatto" character was still the star of too many such films. The 1960 film *I Passed for White*, starring Sonya Wilde, appealed to viewers' prurient interests more than anything else. Light-skinned black actress Ellen Holly had applied for the lead role, but the producers chose the white Wilde instead. Holly lamented that whenever there was a part for a black character who looked white, it always was given to a white actor.

Martin Luther King was sentenced to 12 months probation in October 1960 for driving with expired license plates and failure to get a Georgia driver's license. The next month King was among many protesters arrested for a sit-in demonstration at the restaurant inside Rich's—Atlanta's largest department store. Because he violated probation, King was sentenced to prison and four months hard labor. Coretta Scott King feared her husband would be badly abused or even killed in Reidsville State Prison. U.S. Senator John F. Kennedy, the Democratic presidential candidate in 1960, called Mrs. King to reassure her. Robert Kennedy, the candidate's brother and one of his top aides, called the DeKalb County Courthouse with his concerns. On October 27, King was released on bond.

Ruby Bridges, a six-year-old resident of New Orleans, put on her new dress on the morning of November 14, 1960. She was getting ready to attend her new school. Her mother told her to behave and not to be scared. Later that day, Ruby was escorted to and from the William Frantz Elementary School by U.S. deputy marshals. Looking back as an adult, Ruby remembered seeing a large crowd of people in front of the school and thinking it had something to do with Mardi Gras. Due to a court-ordered integration law, the first-grader became the first (and only) black child enrolled in the school.

At a pro-segregation rally in New Orleans on November 15, 1960, (*above photo*), jeering spectators waved Confederate flags and placards. White opposition to school integration was so intense in New Orleans that all the parents of William Frantz Elementary School students pulled their children out of school when black first-grader Ruby Bridges was admitted on November 4. The white boycott of the school lasted five months. In the bottom photo, the mother of a William Frantz student kicks a supporter of desegregation.

## 1960

**October 27:** At the urging of Robert F. Kennedy, authorities in Georgia release Martin Luther King from Reidsville State Prison on a $2,000 bond.

**November 8:** Democrat John F. Kennedy defeats Republican Richard Nixon in a close race for the U.S. presidency. The black population's support of Kennedy helps him win the election.

**November 14:** A national television audience watches six-year-old Ruby Nell Bridges become the first African-American child to attend William Frantz Elementary School after a federal court ordered the New Orleans school system to desegregate.

**November 14:** In *Gomillion v. Lightfoot*, the U.S. Supreme Court rules that an Alabama law that had altered the city of Tuskegee's boundaries is unconstitutional because the law attempts to deprive blacks of the right to vote.

**November 16:** Hundreds of demonstrators in New Orleans protest against integrated schools.

**December 5:** In *Boynton v. Virginia*, the U.S. Supreme Court rules that segregation in interstate bus terminal restaurants is unconstitutional.

**December 13:** The English Avenue Elementary School in Atlanta is bombed.

**December 31:** By the end of 1960, thousands of students have been arrested and/or expelled from colleges and universities for participating in sit-ins during the year.

Integration ran counter to not just social but religious beliefs held by many white Christians, particularly in the South. One of the main interpretations of the faith by many white Southerners was a clear separation of the races. They believed that a consequence of integration was what they called the "mongrelization" of the races—and the consequence of that was literally hell: "A bastard shall not enter into the Congregation of the Lord: even to his tenth generation none of his decendants shall he not enter into the Congregation of the Lord" (Deuteronomy 23:2). Based on the white Southerners' fears, it was easy to understand why protests over integration, such as this one in New Orleans, often turned violent.

In slavery times, white Christians taught enslaved Africans that God ordained segregation. Scriptures, they said, supported their claim, such as the second half of Exodus 33:16 ("So shall we be separated, I and Thy people, from all the people that are upon the face of the earth") and the second half of Leviticus 20:24 ("I am the Lord thy God, which have separated you from other people"). The fact that black Christians rebelled against these teachings—rebelled against *the word of God*—produced righteous anger from white racist Christians, including this woman protesting in New Orleans.

Atlanta's black college students were tired of waiting for the Civil Rights Movement's older leaders. In 1960 it was time to strike in Atlanta, and Rich's, the city's largest department store, was the perfect target. The owner, Richard H. Rich, was not a friend of the Movement. Atlanta's "old guard" black leaders tried to quell picketers in the "City Too Busy to Hate," but the students and other activists wouldn't relent. After months of protests, Rich, who wanted to save face, and Fulton County officials eventually negotiated how his store would be desegregated: It would take place at the same time as Atlanta's school desegregation (which would begin in September 1961). The deal included the halt of all protests.

African-American Jacob Lawrence was one of many artists who captured Movement themes in his works. Lawrence, who dedicated himself to the black experience, created this painting, "Four Students," as a representation of the student sit-ins that occurred throughout the southern states. Lawrence also painted works related to the Great Migration and the "Red Summer" of 1919.

"THAT'S THE FREE WORLD DECIDING HOW FREE TO BE."

The system of segregation did more than just keep separate whites and blacks. Jim Crow was designed to show that whites were at the top of the social order and blacks were at the bottom. This Louisiana restaurant permitted African-Americans only if they were maids wearing proper attire.

During the Cold War, few U.S. failings gave the USSR as much propaganda ammunition as America's highly visible, often violent resistance to its black citizens' struggles for political and social equality. This 1960 cartoon by Bill Mauldin captures Soviet glee over American hypocrisy.

# 1960s

## 1961

**1961:** At the Highlander Folk School in Monteagle, Tennessee, Septima Clark and Bernice Robinson lead the training of teachers who will run Citizenship Schools in southern communities. The schools help African-Americans improve their literacy, a necessity for voter registration.

**1961:** James Baldwin's *Nobody Knows My Name*, a collection of essays, is published.

**January 3:** Congressman Adam Clayton Powell, Jr., an African-American, becomes chairman of the influential House Education and Labor Committee.

**January 9:** Black students Charlayne Hunter and Hamilton Holmes integrate the University of Georgia. Two days later, more than 1,000 whites will gather outside Hunter's dorm building and throw rocks and bottles at her window.

**January 12:** In his final State of the Union Address, President Eisenhower says that discrimination is morally wrong.

**January 28:** On instructions from Elijah Muhammad, Nation of Islam minister Malcolm X meets with Ku Klux Klan officials, who, like Malcolm, support racial segregation. Malcolm solicits the Klan's help in obtaining land to create a separate nation for black Muslims.

**February 6:** Demonstrators in Rock Hill, South Carolina, are arrested and decide to remain in jail to show their militancy, beginning a "jail, no bail" policy. The strategy will be picked up in other cities, leading a flood of activists into jails throughout the South.

**February 11:** Robert Clifton Weaver is sworn in as the director of the U.S. Housing and Home Finance Agency. It's the highest federal position held by an African-American up to this time. *See* January 18, 1966. ➤

In 1960 recent high school graduates Hamilton Holmes (*pictured*) and Charlayne Hunter attempted to desegregate the University of Georgia. Holmes was from a family of civil rights activists, while Hunter was the daughter of an Army chaplain. Both teenagers were outgoing, independent, and ready for the university. The school, however, wasn't ready for them. (During the admission interview, Holmes was asked if he ever had been to a house of prostitution or known any "beatnik places.") School officials claimed the university was overcrowded, so Holmes and Hunter's admissions were held up for a year. It took a court order to finally allow them to register at Georgia in early 1961.

Angered by the admission of two black students to the University of Georgia, white students planned an anti-integration rally, with some even getting dates for the occasion. It would happen right after the men's basketball game on January 11, 1961. After the game, a group of students gathered in front of Charlayne Hunter's dormitory, hurling bricks, stones, and pop bottles through her window. Outside they unfurled a sign that read, "Nigger, Go Home." Hunter was spirited from her dormitory after police used tear gas to stop rioting students. Instead of members of the mob being suspended, Hunter and Hamilton Holmes, the university's other black student, were suspended—for their own safety, school officials said.

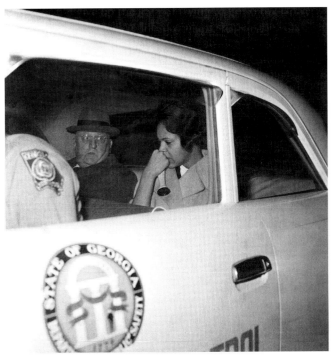

Charylane Hunter, holding a Madonna statue to her lips on January 12, 1961, cried because she felt she had failed herself and her people by being suspended from the University of Georgia. The driver took Hunter and fellow black student Hamilton Holmes to their parents' homes. "Before I knew it," Hunter said, "we were in Atlanta, turning into my block and pulling up in front of a porch where a local black man had stood so many months before telling me that I should give up the idea of trying to go to the University of Georgia." The Wednesday night suspension was reversed when a judge ruled that the students were free to go back to class on Monday morning. Holmes and Hunter both would graduate from Georgia and go on to highly successful careers—Holmes as a doctor and Hunter as a reporter for PBS and CNN.

In the early years of cinema, blacks and whites watched films in separate movie houses, although there were 20 times more white theaters in America than black theaters. After World War II, more and more southern white theaters allowed African-Americans, but they had to sit in the balcony. On March 11, 1961, 18 well-dressed African-Americans picketed a movie theater in Fayetteville, North Carolina, protesting its policy of segregation.

On March 28, 1961, nine black students were arrested because of their sit-in efforts at the white city library in Jackson, Mississippi. The next day, as the nine activists stood trial, African-Americans protested in front of the courthouse, which prompted the arrival of police armed with nightsticks and dogs. "Move 'em out! Get 'em!" officers shouted as they broke up the crowd. The nine protesters each were slapped with $100 fines, which they would appeal. The quickly held trial and the employment of police dogs signified the fear that black protests, no matter how nonviolent, stirred in the hearts of whites—especially law enforcement officers.

# Freedom Rides

THE CONGRESS OF RACIAL EQUALITY (CORE) made clear the dangers that participants in the organization's planned "Freedom Ride" in 1961 would face. CORE, in fact, asked volunteers to sign a waiver with frightening language: "I understand that I shall be participating in a nonviolent protest against racial discrimination, that arrest or personal injury to me might result, and that, by signing this application, I waive all rights to damages against CORE." Yet, even though volunteers had to be willing to sacrifice their lives to confront the injustice of segregated interstate transportation facilities, many activists completed applications.

The Freedom Rides were modeled after CORE's 1947 Journey of Reconciliation, when an interracial group of 16 men traveled through the upper South testing the Supreme Court's mandate of desegregating interstate bus transportation in *Morgan v. Virginia* (1946). The 1961 ride tested the enforcement of another Supreme Court decision, *Boynton v. Virginia* (1960), which extended the desegregation mandate to all interstate transportation facilities, including terminals.

One week before the first bus of Freedom Riders was scheduled to leave Washington, D.C., James Farmer, CORE's newly appointed national director, alerted the Kennedy Administration of the organization's plans to test compliance of the *Boynton* decision. In an April letter addressed to President John F. Kennedy, Farmer enumerated the goals of the campaigners, stating that they felt it was their duty to assert their rights as U.S. citizens. The administration did not respond to Farmer's letter, and as planned the Freedom Ride began on May 4.

CORE officials selected a group of 13 Freedom Riders, seven black (including Farmer) and six white. On May 4 the group boarded a Greyhound bus in Washington, D.C., and headed toward New Orleans, where they hoped to arrive on May 17 to celebrate the seventh anniversary of the *Brown v. Board of Education* decision. For several days the group traveled through Virginia and North Carolina without incident and with little media attention. In Rock Hill, South Carolina, they encountered violence. John Lewis, a student at American Baptist Theological Seminary in Nashville, and another rider were viciously attacked as they attempted to enter the "whites only" waiting room. The violence was just what the Freedom Riders needed to give their cause momentum.

After arriving in Atlanta on May 13, the Freedom Riders divided into two groups. The following day, as the first bus approached the terminal in Anniston, Alabama, they were ambushed by a mob of about 200 whites. Brandishing weapons and throwing stones, the mob caused considerable damage to the bus's exterior. In an effort to avoid a bloody confrontation, the driver continued past the Anniston station—until the

Angry whites firebombed this Freedom Ride bus in Anniston, Alabama.

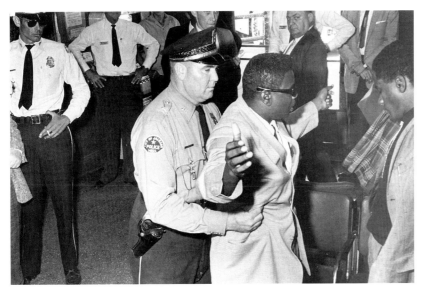
Freedom Riders are arrested as they arrive in Jackson on May 29, 1961.

tires on the bus blew out. The mob, which followed closely behind in automobiles, once again surrounded the bus. A bomb was hurled into the bus's broken window, sending a cloud of smoke wafting through the air. The bus burst into flames as the Freedom Riders fled into the arms of the angry whites, who savagely beat them. When the second Freedom Ride bus arrived in Birmingham, the riders were greeted by segregationists wielding metal pipes. Many of them were seriously beaten.

On May 15 a picture of the burning Greyhound bus and the severely injured riders appeared on the front pages of newspapers throughout the country and around the world. The Freedom Rides had achieved international attention, and they forced the Kennedy Administration to respond.

Following the violence in Anniston and Birmingham, the demonstrators were unable to find a bus driver to continue the rest of trip. With violence looming, CORE officials decided to discontinue the Freedom Rides. However, SNCC activist Diane Nash quickly organized a group of 10 Nashville students to resume the rides. Nash stated later that some of the students made out wills before they left on the rides, while others gave her sealed letters for her to mail if they were killed. She said that some riders admitted they were afraid but were willing to die for their cause.

Once the Kennedy Administration realized that the students intended to continue the rides, Attorney General Robert F. Kennedy ordered the FBI to investigate the two

mob attacks. Kennedy also attempted to persuade Alabama Governor John Patterson to provide state protection for the Freedom Riders. Patterson, a staunch segregationist, maintained that his state would not "escort busloads or carloads of rabble-rousers." After extensive negotiations involving students, state and federal officials, and the bus companies, the new Freedom Rides commenced, with a police escort, on the morning of May 20.

Just before the Freedom Riders' bus arrived at the Montgomery bus terminal, the escorting police left the scene. The riders were promptly greeted by a white mob, which attacked the riders with baseball bats and clubs as they disembarked the bus. Robert Kennedy sent 600 federal marshals to Montgomery to try to quell the violence.

The following night, more than a thousand black supporters gathered at Ralph Abernathy's First Baptist Church in Montgomery to hear Martin Luther King. As King addressed the mass meeting, a rioting crowd of angry whites surrounded the church. King told those in the church to maintain their fath and stay calm. Yet, fearing for their safety, he telephoned Robert Kennedy and pleaded for protection. Again, Kennedy summoned federal marshals, who used tear gas to break up the mob outside the church. Patterson, meanwhile, declared martial law in Montgomery and sent National Guardsmen to restore order in the city.

On May 24 Freedom Riders boarded a bus headed for Jackson, Mississippi. As they attempted to use the "whites only" facilities, they were arrested. By the end of the day, 27 protestors had been jailed, and they would go on to serve sentences in Parchman Prison. As more participants descended upon Mississippi, they vowed to continue the rides until interstate travel was desegregated. During the next four months, several hundred protesters tested the Supreme Court's *Boynton* decision. In September 1961, under pressure from the Kennedy Administration, the Interstate Commerce Commission issued regulations prohibiting segregation in bus and train terminals, which would go into effect on November 1. The Freedom Rides ended, although segregationists continued to defy the ruling in many southern cities.

# 1960s

## 1961

**March 6:** President John F. Kennedy establishes the President's Committee on Equal Employment Opportunity.

**March 7:** A boycott of stores in Atlanta ends as city officials agree to integrate lunch counters. *See* September 1961.

**March 28:** In Jackson, Mississippi, police use clubs and dogs to clear out a hundred black demonstrators from the courthouse.

**May 4:** Seven black and six white CORE volunteers board two buses in Washington, D.C., bound for New Orleans. These "Freedom Riders" are out to test the Supreme Court decision that outlawed segregation in interstate buses and facilities.

**May 14:** A mob of about 200 attacks one of the two Freedom Ride buses in Anniston, Alabama, slashing tires and destroying the bus with a fire-bomb. The riders escape with only minor injuries. Riders in the other bus are badly beaten in Birmingham, as a mob boards the bus and pummels them with lead pipes and clubs.

**May 17:** A new group of 10 Freedom Riders from Nashville, sponsored by SNCC, is arrested while waiting for buses in Birmingham. The police will drive them to the state border and drop them off on the side of the road early the next morning. The Freedom Riders will make their way back to Alabama.

**May 20:** The SNCC Freedom Riders board a bus and travel with a police escort to Montgomery. As they enter the city, police flee the scene, leaving the riders to the mercies of a mob. Several riders and U.S. Justice Department representative John Seigenthaler are beaten. Six hundred federal marshals arrive in Montgomery later in the day. ➤

The Congress of Racial Equality (CORE) not only pioneered the modern sit-in movement (in the 1940s), but it also initiated the Freedom Rides. On May 4, 1961, CORE members, led by James Farmer (*second from left*), planned what would be an historic Freedom Ride from Washington, D.C., through the Deep South. The interracial group planned to use the restrooms and eat at the restaurants of southern bus terminals. Segregation at such facilities had been banned by the Interstate Commerce Commission and ruled unconstitutional by the U.S. Supreme Court.

On May 14, 1961, two buses of Freedom Riders left Atlanta for Birmingham. One bus never made it, as whites destroyed it outside Anniston. The other bus pulled into the Birmingham bus station, where a mob of whites beat the Freedom Riders. Here, the Birmingham mob unloads on white rider James Peck, who would need 50 stitches to close his gashes. Another rider, William Barbee, was seriously injured. Public Safety Commissioner Bull Connor had known that the Freedom Riders were coming and that hostile whites would greet them. However, he posted no officers at the station because, he said, it was Mother's Day.

Freedom Rider James Peck recalled what happened to the riders in Anniston, Alabama, on May 14, 1961: "When the Greyhound bus pulled into Anniston, it was immediately surrounded by an angry mob armed with iron bars. They set about the vehicle, denting the sides, breaking windows, and slashing tires. Finally, the police arrived and the bus managed to depart. But the mob pursued in cars. Within minutes, the pursuing mob was hitting the bus with iron bars. The rear window was broken and a bomb was hurled inside. All the passengers managed to escape before the bus burst into flames and was totally destroyed. Policemen, who had been standing by, belatedly came on the scene. A couple of them fired into the air. The mob dispersed and the injured were taken to a local hospital."

After the violence in Birmingham and Anniston, the Freedom Riders couldn't find an interstate bus company that would accept them, so they instead flew to New Orleans. However, a different group of Freedom Riders, Nashville-based students led by Diane Nash, traveled by bus to Birmingham. On May 19 police drove them to the Tennessee state line and dropped them off. With help from their contacts in Nashville, the students drove right back to Birmingham that day. Meanwhile, U.S. Attorney General Robert Kennedy (*pictured*) demanded from Alabama Governor John Patterson that the new Freedom Riders be given police protection for their planned bus ride from Birmingham to Montgomery. RFK aide John Seigenthaler told Patterson that the federal government would "positively move in whatever force is necessary to get these people through." Though furious with the riders and Kennedy, Patterson agreed to the demand.

On May 20, as Governor John Patterson promised, the Freedom Riders were given a state-police escort from Birmingham to Montgomery. However, as the Greyhound bus pulled into Montgomery, the police drove away, leaving the 21 riders to the mercies of another hostile white mob. "They carried every makeshift weapon imaginable," recalled Freedom Rider John Lewis (*left*). The mob, including women, vented their wrath on the Freedom Riders, including James Zwerg (*right*). "Nigger lover!" they shouted as they brutally beat him. "It was madness," said Lewis, who was beaten until he blacked out. John Siegenthaler, an aide to Robert Kennedy, also was knocked unconscious. The attorney general responded by sending more than 600 federal marshals to Maxwell Air Force Base outside Montgomery.

# 1960s

On May 21 Martin Luther King flew to Montgomery to support the Freedom Riders. While speaking at the First Baptist Church (*right*) that evening, several thousand whites surrounded the church even though it was heavily guarded by federal marshals (*below*). The hostile whites threatened blacks inside, injured some of the marshals, and set fire to automobiles. To control the mob, the marshals employed tear gas—which wafted into the church. Those inside feared for their lives, including King, who phoned Robert Kennedy from a church phone. Kennedy then called Governor John Patterson, who ordered the police and Alabama National Guard to disperse the crowd.

**"I was hit over the head with a club. Even now my chest hurts and I almost conk out every time I climb a few steps. But I'm ready to volunteer for another ride. Sure. Any time."**
—BLACK FREEDOM RIDER HENRY THOMAS, AFTER BEING ATTACKED OUTSIDE ANNISTON, ALABAMA, MAY 1961

After the hostilities in Montgomery, Robert Kennedy called for a cooling-off period. The Freedom Riders, however, were anxious to continue their journey. On May 24, 27 Freedom Riders planned to take two Greyhound buses from Montgomery to New Orleans, with a scheduled stop in Jackson, Mississippi. National Guard patrols were stationed in all three cities to protect the riders.

When the Alabama National Guard escorted the Freedom Riders out of Montgomery on May 24, it was a national news event. The two buses were escorted by 16 highway patrol cars each containing three National Guardsmen and two highway patrolmen. The Freedom Rides were making their mark. The American people were now aware of CORE, and Northerners were reminded of the dark side of the southern "custom" of segregation.

The Freedom Riders arrived in Jackson peacefully on May 24, with no rabid white mobs awaiting them. However, as the riders entered the whites-only waiting room, they immediately were steered by police into a paddy wagon, which drove them to jail. The next day, the Freedom Riders were tried and convicted for violating state law. At the trial, the prosecution accused the riders of trespassing. As defense attorney Jack Young spoke in defense of the riders, the judge turned his back and looked at the wall. After Young finished, the judge immediately sentenced the activists to 60 days in the state penitentiary. The riders, with NAACP support, eventually would have their convictions overturned. Mean-while, more Freedom Riders—an estimated 300—journeyed through southern states in 1961.

# No Freedom in Selma's Jail

ON A GREYHOUND BUS from Montgomery to Jackson, I had yielded my seat to a black lady, placing her alongside an angry white woman and enraging other white passengers. As we pulled into Selma, Alabama, Sheriff Jim Clark came on board, grabbed me by my collar, and threw me in jail.

Klansmen came by to visit me: "He's a gah-damned, nigger-loving Freedom Rider, boys, wants to put black bucks upside yer wives!"

"We've got a necktie party waitin' fer him outside. If he don't leave here feet first, he ain't leavin' town no other way."

The white prisoners whipped, beat, and crushed my every rib until only the proud awareness that I would die for my most passionately held ideals kept me from crying out. They stopped beating me only while Dave, a black porter, mopped the floors. Understanding this, Dave kept on mopping. Never had that prison been so thoroughly swabbed.

For 36 hours I murmured freedom songs and mouthed phrases of brotherly love. Finally, Fred Gray, Solomon Seay, and Charles Connolley, lawyers for the Movement, led me out into the sunlight. We walked between two mobs—one white, ready to carry me off, and one black, whose quiet witness saved my life.

Between tears, I blurted out, "How do you keep from hating white folks?"

—*Ralph D. Fertig, recalling his experiences on June 2–3, 1961*

# 1960s

## 1961

**May 21:** While Martin Luther King speaks at the First Baptist Church in Montgomery, more than 1,000 white citizens surround the building and smash windows. Federal marshals disperse the mob with tear gas.

**May 24:** Twenty-seven Freedom Riders leave Montgomery for Jackson, Mississippi. They arrive safely in Jackson, but all 27 are promptly arrested for attempting to use whites-only facilities.

**May 26:** The 27 Freedom Riders are convicted and sent to Parchman State Penitentiary.

**May–June:** Freedom Riders continue to arrive in Jackson but are promptly arrested. *See* September 22, 1961.

**June 16:** Civil rights organizers meet with U.S. Attorney General Robert Kennedy regarding voters' rights.

**August:** SNCC leader Robert Moses begins a voter registration campaign in McComb, Mississippi. *See* August 29, 1961.

**August 9:** President Kennedy appoints James B. Parsons as judge of the District Court of Northern Illinois, making him the first black federal judge in the continental U.S.

**August 29:** Robert Moses is beaten by three white men while he tries to register two voters in Liberty, Mississippi. *See* September 25, 1961.

**August 30:** Integration begins in Atlanta's high schools.

**September:** Business leaders in Atlanta agree to desegregate the city's eating establishments.

**September 22:** In response to the Freedom Rides, the Interstate Commerce Commission bans segregation at interstate travel facilities. The order will go into effect on November 1, 1961. ➤

George Lincoln Rockwell, leader of the American Nazi Party, epitomized radical white backlash against the Civil Rights Movement. The son of a vaudeville comedian, Rockwell discovered neo-Nazi thought while serving as a Navy reservist during the Korean War. He founded the American Nazi Party in 1958, and although the group never gained a large following, it generated national media coverage that made Rockwell a minor celebrity. He said that the harder black people pushed for "race mixing," the madder white people would get. Rockwell, who trumpeted the phrase "White Power," died broke outside a laundromat in 1967, murdered by a disenchanted party member.

The American Nazi Party numbered only a few hundred, but its publicity stunts made up for its small size. Here, members of the party stand in front of the group's "hate bus" as they stop for gas in Montgomery, Alabama, on May 23, 1961. The back of the bus stated, "WE DO HATE RACE MIXING"; the side read, "WE HATE JEW COMMUNISM."

Members of the Nation of Islam did not believe in protesting for either desegregation or integration. They believed that white people were devils who were beyond salvation. Thus, they taught, it made no sense for African-Americans to sacrifice their bodies fighting to enter a system controlled by corrupt people. The Nation believed that the black man's primary fight was to maintain the dignity and respect of himself and his family. The Nation argued that self-sufficiency, not dependency, was the key to *real* black liberation. Although this philosophy kept the Nation of Islam out of the Movement, many blacks admired how the Nation did not need the assistance of whites to exist and to grow.

Even airports were not exempt from Jim Crow. They, like other public places south of the Mason–Dixon line, segregated bathrooms into "black" and "white." In Jackson, Mississippi, Police Captain J. L. Ray (*right*) ordered the arrest of Gwendolyn Jenkins of St. Louis after she and two other African-Americans attempted to desegregate facilities at a local airport. Jenkins had tried to enter the women's restroom but was blocked by a male officer.

# John Lewis

BORN TO POOR SHARECROPPERS in Troy, Alabama, in 1940, John Lewis overcame the odds to attend American Baptist Theological Seminary in Nashville. When the local student movement arose in 1960, Lewis eagerly contributed. From there, he became one of the most committed and bravest civil rights activists.

Lewis rose to leadership in the Nashville movement, and he was instrumental in forming the Student Nonviolent Coordinating Committee (SNCC). In 1961 he volunteered for the first Freedom Rides coordinated by SNCC and CORE. Lewis suffered a severe beating during the rides—one of several attacks he endured in his life. He also was arrested on 40 occasions.

Elected chairman of SNCC in 1963, Lewis was one of the "Big Six" civil rights leaders who participated in the historic March on Washington. Just 23, he was a keynote speaker at the event, delivering the most aggressive speech of the day. The following year Lewis coordinated SNCC efforts to organize voter registration drives and community action programs during Mississippi Freedom Summer. On March 7, 1965, thereafter known as "Bloody Sunday," he was in the lead as hundreds of people marched across the Edmund Pettus Bridge in Selma, Alabama, and were beaten by Alabama state troopers.

After SNCC took its radical turn in 1966, Lewis lost his position and later left the organization. He worked in community organizing and voter registration before winning election to Atlanta's City Council in 1981. In 1986 he was elected to the U.S. Congress from Georgia's Fifth Congressional District, and he remained in the post well into the 21st century. In 2002 Lewis was influential in redistricting Georgia, which resulted in more black representation in Congress than for any other state.

The leaders of the Prince Edward County public school system in Virginia went to extreme measures to prevent desegregation, shutting down their schools from 1959 to 1964. They could do so because the state, in defiance of *Brown v. Board of Education,* passed a series of laws allowing school systems to close rather than to desegregate by court order. Whites in the county built a private academy for their 1,550 students. Meanwhile, only a small percentage of the area's 1,800 black students attended the makeshift "freedom schools" that were set up by the NAACP and black ministers. The rest stayed home, missing out on their educations. In 1964 the U.S. Supreme Court addressed the Prince Edward situation, ruling that it was unconstitutional to close public schools to circumvent desegregation.

Atlanta's business and government leaders took desegregation one step at a time. First, it was public facilities. Then, in 1961, the city allowed nine black students to attend four white high schools—including Northside High School (*pictured*). The city's board of education planned it carefully, making sure everyone involved was prepared. The experiment went relatively smoothly, with none of the white rioting that had greeted black students desegregating schools in other southern cities. Atlanta was determined to have neither civil rights-style protests nor white reactionary violence.

A year after sit-ins swept the South in 1960, activists still employed the tactic in various public establishments. On June 9, 1961, demonstrators tried to desegregate the lunch counter of this downtown department store in Memphis. Blacks in Memphis battled racial injustice throughout the 1960s. Protests by black sanitaion workers drew Martin Luther King to the city in 1968, when he was assassinated at a Memphis motel.

The United States had difficulty preaching freedom and democracy to other nations when the world saw how America was treating its black citizens. The Soviet Union often trumpeted how its few blacks—those expatriated from America—were treated as first-class citizens who had equal access to education, health care, and other human rights. Here, in September 1961, 14-year-old Huldah Clark, a former resident of Newark, New Jersey, is greeted by her new classmates in Moscow. Her father moved her to Moscow because, he said, the Newark schools were inadequate.

Sidney Poitier portrayed Walter Lee in the 1961 film version of *A Raisin in the Sun,* Lorraine Hansberry's story about a black family integrating a white neighborhood. Walter struggles against racism and lack of economic opportunity to build a better life for his family. He has several decisions to make in the film, including whether or not to compromise with the whites who don't want his family in their community. The story hit home with the actor. Growing up dirt-poor in the Bahamas, Poitier moved in with his brother in Miami at age 15—until a warning visit from the Ku Klux Klan prompted him to flee to New York City.

# Robert F. Williams

IN 1955 ROBERT F. WILLIAMS, an ex-Marine who had lived and worked in Detroit, returned to his hometown of Monroe, North Carolina, to fight "Jim Crow." Williams was president of the NAACP's Monroe chapter, which was unique in that both its leadership and its membership were working-class. Monroe was also the southeastern regional headquarters of the Ku Klux Klan. Those in Williams's chapter, eschewing the legal and nonviolent tactics favored by other civil rights leaders, armed themselves with machine guns, dynamite, and Molotov cocktails.

Suspended from the NAACP for six months because of his proclaimed intention to meet violence with violence, Williams wrote *Negroes with Guns,* originally published in 1962 and recently republished. The book had a powerful influence on Huey P. Newton, cofounder of the Black Panther Party, which also advocated "picking up the gun" in self-defense.

By the time the book was published, Williams was in exile. Falsely accused of kidnapping and facing an FBI dragnet, he and his wife fled to Cuba, where they lived for five years and where Williams established *Radio Free Dixie* to broadcast to the American South. He later spent time in China and Vietnam.

Returning to the United States in 1969 after eight years in exile, Williams served briefly as president of the Republic of New Afrika, a Detroit-based black separatist group. He spent the rest of his life fighting against police brutality and discrimination in education. He died in 1996.

# 1960s

## 1961

**September 25:** In Liberty, Mississippi, Herbert Lee, a local black farmer who had become active in voter registration efforts, is murdered by his white neighbor. *See* January 31, 1964.

**November 17:** Several civil rights groups launch the Albany Movement in Albany, Georgia. *See* December 12–13, 1961.

**December 10:** Freedom Riders (several of whom are white) are arrested in Albany, Georgia, for entering a railway station's waiting room, even though the Interstate Commerce Commission had mandated the integration of such rooms.

**December 11:** The U.S. Supreme Court overturns the convictions of 16 sit-in demonstrators who were accused of "breaching the peace."

**December 12:** In Montgomery, police arrest 737 civil rights demonstrators.

**December 12–13:** More than 400 black protesters are arrested in Albany for marching without a permit. *See* December 16, 1961.

**December 15:** Attack dogs and tear gas are used to control civil rights demonstrators in Baton Rouge, Louisiana.

**December 16:** Martin Luther King and 264 fellow demonstrators are arrested in Albany, Georgia, as they pray for the release of jailed protesters.

**December 18:** Albany city representatives negotiate a deal with Albany movement leaders. The city agrees to release all jailed demonstrators, desegregate Albany's bus and train facilities, and arrange a meeting to listen to the grievances of local black citizens. The city will renege on the deal. *See* July 10, 1962.

White segregationists hated "nigger lovers"—sympathetic whites who protested with blacks against Jim Crow—as much as they hated "uppity niggers." So the whites got the same violent treatment, as shown here in McComb, Mississippi, in 1961. Tom Hayden (*on ground*), who would become a prominent leader of the New Left organization Students for a Democratic Society, was beaten by Carl Hayes (*standing*). Hayden and fellow activist/journalist Paul Potter were dragged from their car while talking with black marchers, who had walked out of Burgland High School. The students were protesting the refusal of the school board to readmit two students who had participated in a bus station sit-in.

U.S. Attorney General Robert Kennedy, a genuine supporter of civil rights, asked the Interstate Commerce Commission to ban segregation. It did, effective November 1, 1961. Martin Luther King was pleased enough with Kennedy's action to steer his focus away from the Freedom Rides. Meanwhile, southern states continued to cling to Jim Crow for as long as they could, as shown here in McComb, Mississippi. Some municipalities continued to ignore the ICC altogether.

President John F. Kennedy, shown here with eight white members of the Commission on Civil Rights in November 1961, was far from a civil rights crusader. Although sympathetic to the plight of black Americans, the young president viewed civil rights activism as a bothersome problem that often flared up with awkward political ramifications. He also knew that by supporting the black cause, he was losing white support throughout the South. Time and again, President Kennedy had to be prodded by Movement actions to make statements and to push for legislation.

> **"Don't stop now. Keep moving. Don't get weary. We will wear them down with our capacity to suffer."**
>
> —MARTIN LUTHER KING, AT A RALLY AT SHILOH BAPTIST CHURCH IN ALBANY, GEORGIA, DECEMBER 15, 1961

Fed up with segregation, harassment, and white reprisals for attempting to vote, blacks in Albany, Georgia, took action in late 1961. On December 12, 267 black students—prompted by SNCC—marched to Albany's segregated Union Railway Terminal. They were arrested. The next day 200 protesters knelt at the steps of the courthouse (*pictured*), praying for the students' release from jail. They, too, were arrested. Police Chief Laurie Pritchett said that Albany would not tolerate mass demonstrations by any "nigger organization."

## 1962

**1962:** African-American psychologist Kenneth Clark helps establish Harlem Youth Opportunities Unlimited, which will influence President Lyndon Johnson's War on Poverty.

**1962:** James Baldwin's novel *Another Country*, which delves into bisexuality and interracial relations, is published.

**January 19:** Protesters at Southern University in Baton Rouge, Louisiana, force the school to temporarily shut down. Demonstrators object to the expulsion of several antisegregation activists.

**February:** To prevent divisiveness, the NAACP, SNCC, and CORE join together and form an umbrella organization, Council of Federated Organizations (COFO), to address civil rights issues in Mississippi.

**Spring:** Segregationists in New Orleans offer black citizens free one-way bus tickets to northern cities. Some accept the offer.

**March 26:** The U.S. Supreme Court rules that Tennessee must abide by the U.S. Constitution when apportioning the state legislature, thus prohibiting discrimination.

**April:** President Kennedy withdraws from the private Cosmos Club of Washington, D.C., in protest of the club's rejection of African-American Carl T. Rowan, the deputy assistant secretary of state.

**April 3:** The Department of Defense orders that military reserve units, excluding the National Guard, be fully integrated.

**April 21:** Days of boycotting and violence threaten The Masters golf tournament in Augusta, Georgia, prompting an agreement to end discriminatory hiring practices in the city's supermarkets.

**May:** The NAACP sues the Rochester, New York, school system for *de facto* segregation. ➤

Whitney Young (*center*) was hesitant at first about taking over the reins of the National Urban League because of its conservative leanings. However, the position put the former social worker in the room with President John F. Kennedy. It also gave him a seat at the table of activists who organized the March on Washington, and it made him a nationally recognized leader of black America. During Young's 10-year reign, he made the National Urban League a household name and secured tens of thousands of jobs for African-Americans. President Lyndon Johnson's "War on Poverty" was rooted in the NUL's "Domestic Marshall Plan."

The "mammy" caricature of black women—the desexualized and dedicated black servant of white America—still lived in the 1960s. This cleaning product was produced by the Bauer Manufacturing Company in Wooster, Ohio. The mammy image was popularized in every medium from the Civil War up through the 1960s. Wrote Ferris State sociology professor David Pilgrim: "The caricature portrayed an obese, coarse, maternal figure. She had great love for her white 'family,' but often treated her own family with disdain.... She had no black friends; the white family was her entire world."

Although Atlanta's city leaders pushed for gradual desegregation, it was not always a smooth transition. Here, Police Captain J. L. Mosley talks with two young women, Elizabeth Hirshfield (*left*) of Franklin, Michigan, and Bertha Gober of Atlanta on February 5, 1962. Hirshfield and Gober refused to leave when asked to do so by restaurant employees. Ironically, the sign on the wall reads, "If you like our food and service . . . tell others. If not . . . tell us."

Two years of sit-ins across the country emboldened the Movement's students. On March 16, 1962, four college students staged a sit-in in the outer office of U.S. Attorney General Robert Kennedy. Two of the four activists, Howard University students Courtland Cox and Stokely Carmichael, would become major leaders within SNCC. The quartet wanted to discuss with Kennedy the case of Dion Diamond, an African-American held in a Baton Rouge, Louisiana, jail on criminal anarchy charges.

In spring 1962 the White Citizens' Council of New Orleans offered African-Americans one-way bus tickets out of their city, to New York. These black men, shown here at the Port Authority bus terminal on May 2, 1962, accepted the one-way rides. Nevertheless, the days of the New Orleans WCC being a major factor in the city were coming to an end. Desegregation had begun in New Orleans.

As a lawyer and an NAACP field director in Georgia, Vernon Jordan escorted Charlayne Hunter through a howling white gauntlet to register at the University of Georgia in 1961. In his role with the NAACP, Jordan tried "to build the membership of local chapters, help them organize events, respond whenever there were allegations of discrimination, and—in an era of protests and demonstrations—to decide when and if those activities were warranted." Jordan would succeed Whitney Young as head of the National Urban League when Young died in 1971.

Initially, Martin Luther King—the son and grandson of Baptist preachers—resisted "calls" to the ministry because he had lost faith in the black church's ability to be much more than a weekly release of emotion. But Benjamin E. Mays (*pictured*), president of Morehouse College, changed King's mind. Mays denounced the black church's "socially irrelevant patterns of escape," and instead advocated building the black community. King, inspired by Mays while a student at Morehouse, adopted his proactive philosophy. Mays, in fact, often is hailed as King's most important mentor.

# Ku Klux Klan

IN 1866 CONFEDERATE VETERANS of the Civil War in Pulaski, Tennessee, founded the Ku Klux Klan under the leadership of Nathan Bedford-Forrest. Their mission: to fight the Reconstruction policies of the Radical Republican Congress and to maintain "white supremacy." Their strange disguises (white robes and hooded masks were a representation of the ghosts of the Confederate dead), secret language, silent parades, and midnight rides captured the imagination of friend and foe alike. In time, the KKK absorbed many other informal vigilante associations or armed patrols throughout the South.

A "grand wizard" headed the KKK empire, assisted by 10 "genii." Each state constituted a "realm," which was led by a "grand dragon" and a staff of eight "hydra." Officially disbanded in 1869 by its first grand dragon, who did not approve of the recklessness of some of its members, the Klan nonetheless became the target of congressional legislation in 1870 and 1871.

A second Ku Klux Klan was established in 1915 in Stone Mountain, Georgia, with a wider program of intense nationalism and anti-Catholicism (it was also antisemitic). The Klan's religious fundamentalism and militant patriotism played well during World War I and after, and at its peak in the 1920s Klan membership was estimated at more than four million. Corruption at the KKK's highest levels and the Great Depression caused a steep decline in membership, and its influence was minimal by the mid-1930s.

The Civil Rights Movement of the 1950s and 1960s gave the Klan new impetus and led to revivals of scattered

Klan organizations, most notably in Mississippi under Robert Shelton. Violent attacks against civil rights workers in cities throughout the South again brought the Klan to national attention. The killings of three SNCC workers in Mississippi during the summer of 1964 prompted the most aggressive FBI investigation of the KKK in its history. The postwar Klan's numbers were never large, and its power and membership declined by the end of the 1960s.

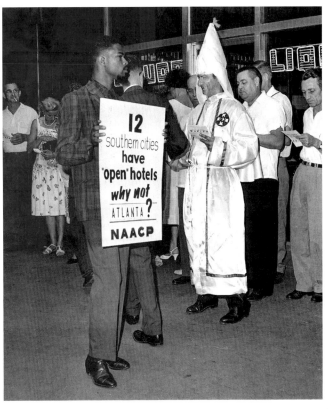

The Ku Klux Klan occasionally would mount counter-protests as a way to stall the Civil Rights Movement. Here, members of the KKK stand in front of an Atlanta hotel passing out pamphlets to their supporters on July 4, 1962. The Klan took action after NAACP members began picketing hotels, motels, and eating establishments in protest of segregation policies. Standing up to the Klan, and demanding desegregation of Atlanta's hotels, is civil rights activist Glenn Gurley, a University of Michigan student.

Many southern white women shared the same views as their men: that white liberals in the North were trying to destroy their way of life. They considered the forces for integration—the NAACP, the U.S. Supreme Court, the Kennedys, and Martin Luther King—as the South's greatest enemies. According to these women, President John F. Kennedy was a tyrant and a treasonist who was worthy of impeachment.

The library was a main target of sit-ins across the country. The "whites only" library was inevitably superior to the ones blacks used, if they indeed had a "colored" library at all. On July 31, 1962, a black youth in Albany, Georgia, risked arrest and abuse by white police officers in order to use the main library.

# The Albany Movement

WHEN EXPERIENCED civil rights activists Charles Sherrod and Cordell Reagon went to Albany, Georgia, in October 1961, black residents at first avoided them. "They were just extremely afraid of us, because we represented something that had never been done," Reagon recalled. As field secretaries for the Student Nonviolent Coordinating Committee (SNCC), the two young activists were looking to stir Albany's 20,000-plus African-Americans toward direct-action protests against institutionalized segregation.

Albany (pronounced "All-BENNY" by local folks) had experienced little protest activity prior to SNCC's arrival. However, black residents were growing increasingly dissatisfied with the city commission's refusal to address the community's grievances. Anticipating strong resistance from Albany police, Sherrod and Reagon led nonviolent workshops in local churches, attracting young people from all walks of life.

On November 1, 1961, the Interstate Commerce Commission's ban of racial segregation in interstate bus terminals went into effect. That same day, nine students, armed with nonviolent training, conducted a sit-in at the Albany bus station to test compliance of the ruling. Local black citizens came to watch the students. No arrests were made, but this protest prompted the city's black leaders to found the Albany movement, an organization comprised of members from the local Ministerial Alliance, the NAACP, SNCC, the Federation of Women's Clubs, and other black organizations. Dr. William Anderson, a local osteopath, was chosen as the organization's president, and longtime Albany leader Slater King was elected vice-president.

Over the next several weeks, the Albany movement orchestrated a frontal attack on segregated city facilities.

Albany activists kneel in prayer prior to their arrest on July 21, 1962.

Scores of activists participated in mass demonstrations, marches, boycotts of white stores, sit-ins, jail-ins, and Freedom Rides. Unlike other campaigns in southern cities, the demonstrators were not met with violent opposition. Aware that violence would elicit negative publicity, Albany Chief of Police Laurie Pritchett responded to the demonstrations with massive arrests but without brutality. According to local news reports, nearly 500 protesters were arrested in the first two weeks of demonstrations.

Albany movement leaders said they would end demonstrations if the city met three requirements: the release of those jailed in recent demonstrations, desegregation of local bus and train terminals, and formation of a biracial committee dedicated to eradicating racial barriers in the city. In an article published in *The Albany Herald*, the local newspaper, Albany Mayor Asa Kelley vehemently rejected the organization's demands, asserting that the leaders were "acting in bad faith."

Dr. Anderson sent a telegram to Martin Luther King, urging him to come to Albany. King arrived in the city on December 15 and immediately attracted media attention. Speaking at a mass meeting held at Shiloh Baptist Church that evening, King told those in attendance to put on their walking shoes and march together. Immediately following King's address, Anderson prepared the audience for the following day's confrontation with Chief Pritchett and his officials. He told them to gather at 7:00 A.M., eat a good breakfast, and wear warm clothes. The mass meeting ended with sustained applause and a refrain from "We Shall Overcome."

On December 16 King, Anderson, and Ralph Abernathy joined about 250 protesters in a march toward City Hall. Singing hymns, which had become a trademark of the Albany campaign, the demonstrators were confronted by Chief Pritchett. All of the demonstrators were arrested for parading without a permit, bringing the number of people jailed to more than 700. King, Anderson, and Abernathy were carted off to the Sumter County jail in Americus, Georgia, 35 miles away from Albany. Hoping to spur concessions from Albany officials, King vowed to spend Christmas in jail. Privately, black leaders and city officials met and reached a compromise: The demonstrators agreed to a moratorium on demonstrations, and Pritchett agreed to release the jailed protesters. Immediately, however, city officials reneged on the agreement.

King left Albany in despair as news reports across the county portrayed the Albany protest as a "devastating loss of face." Behind the scenes, reports of organizational conflicts between the SCLC and SNCC may have marred the campaign. SNCC members, who had been in Albany prior to King's arrival, felt slighted due to the assertion of leadership that some SCLC leaders exhibited. Despite the organizational conflicts, King refused to publicly criticize the student leaders and tried to downplay the seriousness of his differences with SNCC.

On Tuesday, July 10, 1962, King returned to Albany to face sentencing for his involvement in the December demonstration. King and Abernathy were found guilty and ordered to pay $178 or serve 45 days in jail. Choosing the latter, they were remanded to jail. On Thursday morning, however, bail for King and Abernathy supposedly was posted by a mysterious black man, a tactic many believe was orchestrated by either Chief Pritchett or Mayor Kelley to avoid a media frenzy. "I've been thrown out of lots of places in my day," Abernathy later remarked, "but never before have I been thrown out of jail."

Through July, boycotts of white businesses and buses, sit-ins, and other protests continued in Albany. King and other leaders were arrested a third time on July 27 at City Hall after attempting to meet with city commissioners despite repeated warnings from Pritchett to vacate the premises. After two weeks in jail, the defendants were found guilty of disturbing the peace and parading without a permit, but their sentences were suspended.

In August King decided to leave Albany. While the majority of the black community had participated in the demonstrations, King later admitted that tactical blunders led to the movement's failure. He said that his biggest mistake in Albany had been to protest against segregation generally instead of against a distinct aspect of it. Nevertheless, the lessons learned during the nine months of protest in Albany would later be applied in desegregation campaigns throughout the South, most notably in Birmingham.

Martin Luther King confronts Albany Police Chief Laurie Pritchett.

## 1962

**Summer:** Eight hooded men chase black construction workers from a school-construction site in Heflin, Alabama. Under threat, the white contractor fires the black workers the following day.

**July 10:** Martin Luther King and Ralph Abernathy, convicted in February of marching in Albany, Georgia, without a permit, are sentenced. They choose 45 days in jail rather than pay a fine.

**Mid-July:** Albany Police Chief Laurie Pritchett makes an arrangement with an anonymous person to pay the fines for the release from jail of Martin Luther King and Ralph Abernathy. *See* July 24, 1962.

**July 23:** Jackie Robinson becomes the first black man inducted into the Baseball Hall of Fame.

**July 24:** Blacks march in Albany in protest of a recent beating of a pregnant woman by a sheriff's deputy in a nearby town. When those protesters are arrested, black onlookers throw rocks and bottles at police.

**July 25:** Martin Luther King enjoins Albany residents in a Day of Penance for their violence.

**July 27:** Martin Luther King and others are arrested for holding a prayer vigil in front of Albany's city hall.

**August 15:** Martin Luther King is released from jail and agrees to end demonstrations in Albany, effectively ending the movement in that city.

**August 29:** Mal Goode becomes the first black news correspondent for a television network, ABC.

**September:** The SCLC creates Operation Breadbasket, whose mission is to create jobs for African-Americans and to encourage the growth of black-owned businesses. ➤

The protests in Albany, Georgia, were not the most organized of the Civil Rights Movement. The demonstrators, though, were passionately committed to their cause, as hundreds bravely tried to force the city to desegregate. At this evening meeting on July 25, 1962, African-Americans wave the papers they've signed—promises to go to jail when they stage another march on City Hall. Georgia Governor Ernest Vandiver made a promise, too: He threatened to call out the National Guard if the peace was disturbed. A rock-throwing incident by demonstrators the night before had raised alarm.

At times during the civil rights struggle, the Movement's leaders had to take risks. Martin Luther King knew that the Albany movement wasn't working. The jails were filled with protesters, but the tactic didn't cause the city fathers—nor Albany Police Chief Laurie Pritchett (*right*)—to yield. Moreover, SNCC members began to criticize King and the SCLC for their handling of the Albany campaign. In order to stir public support for their side, King, Ralph Abernathy, Dr. William G. Anderson, and others went to City Hall on July 27, 1962, to lead a protest demonstration (*pictured*). They hoped to be arrested, and were.

Dr. William G. Anderson (*right*), an osteopath and president of the Albany Movement, knew he needed help. The Albany Movement was a hodge-podge of local civil rights groups that wanted to desegregate the city. To do that, Anderson had to find a way to unite and focus his constituency. In December 1961 he asked Martin Luther King, a former schoolmate, to become involved, which he did. Though inexperienced in civil rights activism before the Albany Movement, Anderson became a national figure. Here he speaks on *Meet the Press* on July 29, 1962.

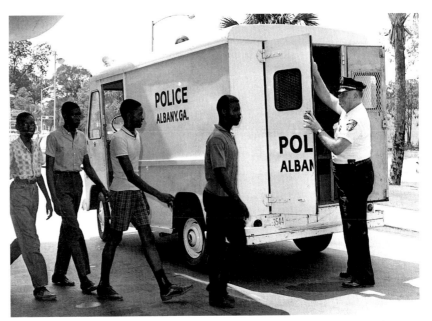

King thought that the Albany movement would be a perfect opportunity to fill the jails with protesters—the key to creating the social tension needed to transform Albany from a segregated city into an integrated one. But Albany police filled the jails easily and nonviolently, as they did with these African-Americans on August 1, 1962. The youths had tried to integrate four city lunch counters. Eventually, Albany's protesting citizens got tired of going to prison for a campaign that was not yielding significant results.

Albany Police Chief Laurie Pritchett refused to play the role assigned to him by the Civil Rights Movement's scriptwriters. He had done his homework on Martin Luther King. He knew that King's direct-action campaign depended on Movement forces running into a blatantly racist, and violent, police force and government. So Pritchett was determined not to give King the satisfaction of playing victim in the eyes of the American public. He ordered his police force to be courteous and nonviolent toward the protesters, arresting them without incident. Pritchett placed King under police protection for 24 hours a day, which disrupted King's actions. At the end of King's unsuccessful campaign, Pritchett gloated that Albany "is as segregated as ever."

Reverend Ralph Abernathy (*left*) and Reverend Wyatt Tee Walker overlook what's left of the Shady Grove Baptist Church in Leesburg, Georgia (near Albany), which was bombed on the night of August 14–15, 1962. The destruction of the church was another blow to the Albany movement. The protests also were ineffective, and in response to the campaign, Albany shut down its parks rather than desegregate. Filling the jails without racist violence provoked praise, not condemnation, for city officials by the press and the Kennedy Administration. All this troubled King and the SCLC. They realized they would have to choose their next target with more care.

# 1960s

## 1962

**September 10:** In his attempt to enroll at the University of Mississippi, African-American James Meredith wins a drawn-out court battle that's finally decided in the U.S. Supreme Court.

**September 20:** Mississippi Governor Ross R. Barnett denies James Meredith admission to the University of Mississippi even after a U.S. Court of Appeals ruled that Barnett would be held in contempt for doing so.

**September 26:** State police prevent James Meredith and the federal marshals escorting him from entering the University of Mississippi.

**September 28:** Mississippi Governor Ross R. Barnett is found guilty of contempt of the federal court. He is given four days to admit James Meredith to Ole Miss or else face arrest. *See September 30, 1962.*

**September 28:** Martin Luther King is attacked in Birmingham by American Nazi Party member Roy James during an annual gathering of the SCLC.

**September 30:** After getting the go-ahead from Governor Ross R. Barnett, 300 U.S. marshals escort James Meredith to the University of Mississippi. Meanwhile, 3,000 whites begin to riot on campus. President John F. Kennedy federalizes the Mississippi National Guard and addresses the nation on television.

**October 1:** More than 23,000 soldiers are needed to end the rioting at Ole Miss. Two men have been killed and 160 injured. James Meredith enrolls at 8:30 A.M. *See August 18, 1963.*

**November:** Leroy R. Johnson becomes the first black man since Reconstruction to be named to a southern legislature, Georgia's Senate.

**November 20:** President Kennedy signs an executive order that bans discrimination in government-sponsored housing. ➤

On August 19, 1962, civil rights advocates staged demonstrations at two Howard Johnson's restaurants and motor lodges in North Carolina. In Raleigh (*pictured*), about 300 black protesters sang hymns and marched around a Ho Jo's. Meanwhile in Stateville, 21 demonstrators were arrested for trying to eat at a Howard Johnson's. The two demonstrations were part of a statewide effort to desegregate public eating places. The Ho Jo's were chosen because of their prominence in American life. Until the rise of fast-food chains, Howard Johnson's was the nation's premier national restaurant, with franchises found on highways throughout America.

Larraine Clark, the child of sharecroppers who migrated from South Carolina to Englewood, New Jersey, believed that the *Brown v. Board of Education* decision applied to her children, too. Thus, she testified in the New Jersey Supreme Court in a case that called for the desegregation of Englewood's all-white public schools. Black children in the township attended the all-black Lincoln School. In 1962 Clark joined another school desegregation lawsuit. When it failed, she and other activists called for a boycott of Lincoln School. This photo of Lincoln, taken on September 5, 1962, indicates that most families adhered to the boycott.

# James Meredith

Born in Kosciusko, Mississippi, in 1933, James Meredith graduated from high school in St. Petersburg, Florida, and enlisted in the Air Force, serving as a staff sergeant from 1951 to 1960, including a tour of duty in Japan. After his discharge, he returned to his home state and enrolled at Jackson State on the GI Bill. After two years, he sought the help of the NAACP to transfer to the University of Mississippi, an all-white institution. Meredith considered himself in a war with school and government officials. He said his goal was to force the federal government into a position in which it would have to use the military to enforce his rights as a U.S. citizen.

On September 13, 1962, a federal district court ordered the university to admit Meredith. Mississippi Governor Ross Barnett, an ardent segregationist, took a determined stand against the order. When Meredith arrived on campus to enroll, for the third time, on September 26, state police—following orders from Barnett—turned away both Meredith and the federal marshals who escorted him.

Meredith displays the *New Orleans States–Item.*

Only after Barnett was found guilty of contempt of the federal court was Meredith allowed to register at the university. But when he did go to register on September 30—while supported by more than 100 federal marshals, 300 U.S. border guards, and 100 prison guards—mayhem broke out on campus. Rioting raged throughout the night, resulting in the death of two men and injuries to approximately 160 others. About 23,000 U.S. troops were sent to quell the violence. Meredith finally registered on the morning of October 1. Federal marshals remained on campus to guard Meredith, who graduated from the University of Mississippi in June 1963 with a bachelor's degree in political science.

During the unrest over Meredith's arrival at Ole Miss, a black-faced effigy was hung from a window facing his dormitory and set ablaze. A sign on the effigy read, "Go back to Africa where you belong." Perhaps not coincidentally, Meredith went to Africa, visiting more than 20 countries and attending classes for a time at a university in Nigeria. In 1966 he published a memoir of his experiences, *Three Years in Mississippi*.

In the summer of 1966, Meredith began his one-man "Walk Against Fear," a march from Memphis, Tennessee, to Jackson, Mississippi, as a personal repudiation of the violence to which blacks were being subjected in their campaign for voting rights. While on the march, Meredith was shot in the back by a sniper, whereupon Martin Luther King and other prominent civil rights leaders rallied to his cause. When Meredith was well enough to resume the march, legions of other marchers joined him.

Meredith received a law degree from Columbia University in 1968. Four years later, he ran unsuccessfully for a seat in Congress from Mississippi. In a controversial move, he joined the staff of conservative South Carolina Senator Jesse Helms in 1989. Six years later, he published *Mississippi: A Volume of Eleven Books*, dedicated to the state where he made his home.

In the summer of 1998, Meredith embarked on a "March for Education," visiting 42 towns and counties throughout Mississippi to introduce his literacy program (reading, writing, and speaking proper English). The march ended on September 20, 1998, in Oxford. On October 1, 2002, the Mississippi legislature declared a James H. Meredith Day to mark the 40th anniversary of the desegregation of the University of Mississippi.

# 1960s

"During the first few weeks almost all of the focus was on the possibility of my being killed by the 'White Supremacists.' People have asked me if I was not terribly afraid the night we went to Oxford and thereafter. My apprehensions had been faced a long time before that. The hardest thing in human nature is to decide to act.... Once I had made that decision, things just had to happen the way they did."

—JAMES MEREDITH

Flanked by a horde of Mississippi highway patrolmen on September 25, 1962, James Meredith (*center*) is escorted away from the offices of the Board of Trustees, where his bid to enroll in the University of Mississippi was rejected personally by Mississippi Governor Ross Barnett. Even though the U.S. Supreme Court had confirmed Meredith's right to register, the Kennedy Administration chose to bargain with Barnett in order for Meredith to join the university. Meredith would be escorted secretly to the campus on September 30 to register for classes. But word got out, and a riot began.

Mississippi Governor Ross Barnett, a staunch segregationist, loved to play to the crowd. He appointed himself registrar at the University of Mississippi to make sure he could deny James Meredith's admission—and he did, several times, in person or through intermediaries. But quietly, behind the scenes, Barnett negotiated with the Kennedy Administration to allow Meredith's registration. At one point, Barnett appeared at one of the university's football games and yelled, "I love Mississippi! I love her people, her customs! And I love and respect her heritage!" The fans roared in approval.

On September 30 federal marshals arrived in Oxford, Mississippi, with nightsticks and tear gas, which they would need. The white students were determined to defend the "heritage" of the University of Mississippi. The marshals, who would be abandoned by state troopers as the campus began to explode that evening, needed emergency assistance from the Mississippi National Guard, which arrived on campus during the night.

Mississippi state troopers stand by as a student shouts insults at U.S. marshals on September 30. The marshals had gathered outside the University of Mississippi to await the arrival of James Meredith. The protesters taunted the marshals, then threw things at them. The violence prompted President John F. Kennedy to address the nation on television that evening.

## Meredith Gets Cold Shoulder at Ole Miss

THROUGH IT ALL, the most intolerable thing was the campaign of ostracizing me. It did not harm me directly. If anyone does not want to associate with me, I am sure that the feeling is at least mutual. I don't think anyone should be forced to enter into association with anyone else unless they choose to do so. However, the ostracizers also assumed the right to see that no one else associated with me. If a white student sat down and drank a cup of coffee with me or walked with me across the campus, he was subjected to unhampered intimidation and harassment. I had been denied my privileges all along, but these whites had not been. Now they had lost a simple freedom. This was a setback for the Negro, because any time there is a move backward, the person already down suffers more. This campaign, which apparently had been permitted by the university officials, really resulted in a reduction of everybody's rights.

—*James Meredith,*
*Three Years in Mississippi*

The protest over James Meredith's admission to Ole Miss was not confined to the campus. Students gathered around the courthouse in downtown Oxford, throwing bottles, rocks, and everything they could find at federal marshals. Troops used tear gas and rifle bayonets to disperse the crowd.

James Meredith was harassed every day on campus. He was jeered on the way to class, and firecrackers were set off in his dormitory. This effigy, hung outside a dorm window on October 3, 1962, includes the words, "Go back to Africa where you belong." But Meredith, a former U.S. Air Force staff sergeant, was determined that white racists were not going to scare him away from Ole Miss. He stuck to the books and graduated from the university on August 18, 1963.

Tear gas and the Mississippi National Guard were not enough to stop the Ole Miss rioters from burning cars. By the time rioting ended on October 1, 1962, two people had been killed and 160 injured. The riot, and the circumstances surrounding it, damaged the university's and the state's reputation in other parts of the nation— and America's reputation abroad. Meanwhile, James Meredith did indeed register at the school, at 8:30 A.M. on October 1.

African-Americans knew that to allow any physical barrier between black and white communities was, in effect, acceptance of a residential caste system, with whites on top and blacks at the bottom. Nearly 100 years of Jim Crow had taught them that lesson all too well. So, on Christmas Eve, 1962, protesters in Atlanta gathered around a "freedom torch" in front of a city-erected barricade. The city had erected the barricade to help maintain a "buffer zone" between the black and white residential areas and to prevent further integration of a white neighborhood.

# James Baldwin

JAMES BALDWIN, BORN IN Harlem in 1924, was strongly influenced by his stepfather, a storefront preacher. Baldwin became a true writer of his time, fusing auto-biographical material with analysis of social injustice and prejudice. He also provided an intellectual underpinning for the major African-American movements of the 1950s and '60s.

Although Baldwin spent much of his career abroad, living mainly in Paris and Istanbul, most of his writings concerned life in the United States. His novels explored racial, national, and sexual identity, including uncommonly matter-of-fact depictions of gay relationships. His nonfiction work focused on American culture and its tangled web of race relations. In his book *The Fire Next Time* (1963), Baldwin wrote: "And if the word *integration* means anything, this is what it means: that we, with love, shall force our brothers to see themselves as they are, to cease fleeing from reality, and begin to change it."

A shrewd and profound commentator, Baldwin gave voice to the Civil Rights Movement in such volumes of essays as *Notes of a Native Son* (1955) and *Nobody Knows My Name* (1961). In *The Fire Next Time* (1962), Baldwin predicted the militant turn that the African-American social

movements would take, earning a reputation as a prophet. The assassination of Martin Luther King in 1968 caused Baldwin to acknowledge bitterly that violence may be the only route to racial justice. Still, he never lost his faith completely in possible reconciliation between the races.

# 1960s

## 1963

**1963:** Michael Harrington's *The Other America: Poverty in the United States* is published.

**January 1:** This date marks the 100th anniversary of the Emancipation Proclamation.

**January 14:** In his inaugural address as Alabama governor, George Wallace declares, "Segregation now! Segregation tomorrow! Segregation forever!"

**January 14–17:** A coalition of Protestant, Catholic, and Jewish delegates meets in Chicago for the National Conference on Religion and Race. The group aims to end race discrimination.

**January 28:** Harvey Gantt becomes the first black student at Clemson University in South Carolina. His admission is uneventful and publicly unopposed.

**January 31:** *The Fire Next Time*, James Baldwin's collection of predictive essays, is published.

**February:** Four hundred protesters are arrested at a whites-only movie theater in Baltimore. They will force the theater's management to change its policy.

**February 25:** In *Edwards v. South Carolina*, the U.S. Supreme Court upholds the right of all Americans to hold public demonstrations to redress their grievances.

**February 28:** President Kennedy delivers a special message to Congress proposing civil rights reforms, including empowering federal referees to register black voters, while litigation is pending.

**March:** Tensions run high in Greenwood, Mississippi, as groups of African-Americans, led by SNCC, attempt to register to vote. ➤

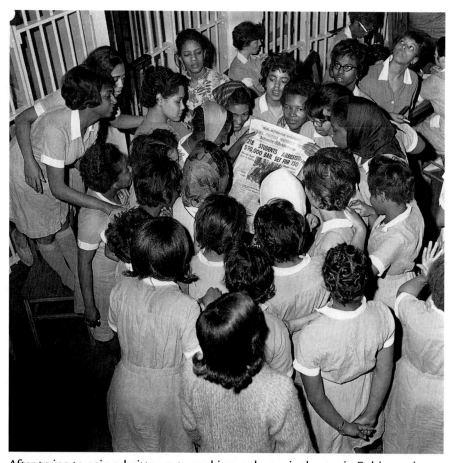

After trying to gain admittance to a whites-only movie theater in Baltimore in February 1963, these Morgan College students were arrested on trespassing charges and tossed into jail. The next day (*pictured*), they read about their efforts in the local newspaper. A municipal court judge released the women on their own recognizance on February 22—the same day that the theater's management announced it was desegregating. Victories such as these gave black students a sense of collective power.

After slipping out of death's arms again and again, Hosea Williams became a fearless warrior. At age 13, Williams ran away from home after he was almost lynched for being too close to a white girl. During World War II, he survived the bombing of his platoon and was the only one to survive after the ambulance was bombed. After he returned to Georgia, a white mob beat him nearly to death after he dared to use a bus station's only water fountain. That mob beat Williams into the Movement—first to the NAACP, then to the SCLC. He was named to Martin Luther King's executive staff by 1964. Williams, who would be jailed more than 100 times, developed a reputation for being brash, loud, and loyal.

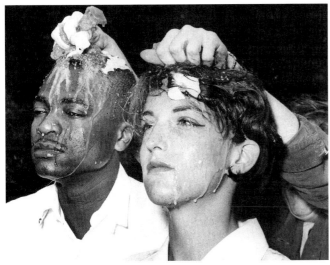

CORE's San Francisco chapter was one of many chapters across the country that conducted workshops on nonviolent resistance. Here, in 1963, Richard Siller and Lois Bonzell practice their stoicism while undergoing an "egg shower." Movement participants had to withstand harsh training to prepare themselves for the trials ahead. Many times they were told that the Movement was a life-and-death struggle and that they might not return from a campaign.

CORE workers demonstrate the posture a protester needs to assume while being abused. To guard against rabbit punches, a young man protects his face while locking his hands behind his head. The workshop was held at CORE's School of Nonviolence in Jackson, Mississippi, in 1963.

In Chicago in 1942, 27-year-old John H. Johnson founded *Negro Digest*, a periodical that was similar to *Reader's Digest*, with a bankroll of $500. Half a century later, his Johnson Publishing Company had become one of the largest black-owned businesses in America, with more than 2,300 employees and $275 million in annual sales. Johnson's *Ebony* magazine, modeled after *Life*, appealed to the black middle class. *Jet* magazine, which focused on politics, entertainment, and sports, went on to surpass a million in weekly circulation.

# The Birmingham Campaign

WYATT WALKER, executive director of the SCLC, said he wasn't sure whether the Birmingham movement would be successful. But he and the SCLC knew that as Birmingham went, so would go the South.

Some black residents called Alabama's largest city "Bombingham" because of the frequent dynamite attacks by Ku Klux Klan terrorists. Reverend Fred L. Shuttlesworth, who had founded the Alabama Christian Movement for Human Rights (ACMHR) in 1956 after the state outlawed the NAACP, had braved brutal beatings and the bombing of his house. After the SCLC's unsuccessful effort to wrest major concessions from white leaders in Albany, Georgia, Shuttlesworth convinced the group to launch a protest campaign in Birmingham.

Walker dubbed the campaign "Project C"—for confrontation—and planned a series of confrontations with Birmingham's most famous segregationist, Public Safety Commissioner Eugene "Bull" Connor. Concerned, however, that demonstrations would boost Connor's campaign to become mayor, the SCLC and the ACMHR postponed the scheduled start of the campaign until April 3, 1963, one day after the more moderate Albert Boutwell defeated Connor.

At least 20 demonstrators were arrested on the campaign's first day, and Shuttlesworth led the first march of the movement three days later. The campaign, however, attracted little national attention, as Connor uncharacteristically treated the demonstrators with a modicum of respect, arresting them without being abusive. On Palm Sunday, April 7, A. D. King, the pastor of a Birmingham church and Martin Luther King's brother, joined with other ministers to lead a march to City Hall. This time, the police brought dogs and wielded nightsticks.

On April 11 police served Martin Luther King and Shuttlesworth an injunction that barred civil rights leaders from leading or participating in any sort of demonstrations. Two days later, on Good Friday, Abernathy and King attempted to jumpstart the movement by disobeying the injunction and leading a march toward downtown Birmingham. They marched for several blocks before being arrested and taken to city jail.

While locked in solitary confinement, King composed a response to a letter published in a Birmingham newspaper by eight white clergymen denouncing the demonstrations as "unwise and untimely." King's response, written on newspaper margins and other scraps of paper, would later gain fame as his "Letter From Birmingham Jail." "There comes a time when the cup of endurance runs over," he wrote, "and men are no longer willing to be plunged into an abyss of injustice where they experience the bleakness of corroding despair."

King and Abernathy were bailed out of jail on April 20 to find the movement all but silenced. Fewer and fewer people were accepting the call to demonstrate. SCLC staff member James Bevel offered a solution: allow children to march. After a great deal of trepidation, SCLC and ACMHR leaders agreed; children would march on Thursday, May 2. Bevel, Dorothy Cotton, and Andrew Young canvassed local schools for volunteers.

By noon on May 2, hundreds of students were ready to demonstrate. The first group of youths, with the youngest just six years old, emerged from the Sixteenth Street Baptist Church toting signs and singing freedom songs. Onlookers cheered as the children marched toward police lines. An amazed policeman asked Shuttlesworth how many more child protesters he had. Shuttlesworth said at least a thousand, eliciting a "God Ah'mighty" from the

Firefighters turn their hoses on black youths in Birmingham.

Emboldened youths in Birmingham jeer at police on May 7, 1963.

policeman. The students were arrested en masse. When police ran out of paddy wagons, school buses were used to haul children to jail.

Children marched again on May 3, but they saw a vastly different face of Bull Connor's forces. Deciding he would rather dissuade the demonstrators from marching than put them in his already overflowing jails, Connor ordered policemen to use police dogs and billy clubs, and fireman to use their hoses. The hoses blasted demonstrators with force enough to tear bricks from their mortar. Angered onlookers began hurling bottles and bricks as well as insults at police officers until they, too, were smacked with high-pressure water and confronted with vicious dogs.

Photographers captured the melee on film, and the next day they shared Birmingham's atrocities with the world. President Kennedy, who had previously resisted calls for strong action on civil rights, remarked at a press conference, "I can understand why the Negroes of Birmingham are tired of being patient." Demonstrations continued through May 7.

Fearing widespread racial violence, Burke Marshall, head of the Justice Department's Civil Rights Division, arrived to broker talks involving civil rights leaders, business leaders, and members of the Senior Citizens Committee. White leaders resisted making concessions until the particularly tumultuous demonstrations of May 7.

Amid chaotic, increasingly violent clashes involving police, firefighters, hundreds of demonstrators, and thousands of onlookers, water from a fire hose slammed Shuttlesworth against a wall.

The following day King called for a one-day truce in demonstrations to show good faith for the negotiations. Although Shuttlesworth was enraged that the decision was made while he was hospitalized, he finally acquiesced to pleas from Attorney General Robert F. Kennedy to give the settlement a chance to work.

By May 10 negotiators reached a truce that outlined five major points to move toward an integrated Birmingham. At a press conference that afternoon, King described the terms of the truce. They included desegregating the city's lunch counters and fitting rooms, removing physical signs of segregation from bathrooms and drinking fountains, upgrading black employment, and forming a biracial committee to continue discussion of desegregation in the city.

At the Sixteenth Street Baptist Church, King congratulated the congregation. He praised them for standing up to hostile mobs, violent dogs, and fire hoses, adding that segregation in Birmingham would collapse due to their efforts.

King returned home to Atlanta on May 11. That same evening the Ku Klux Klan held a meeting on the outskirts of Birmingham. Not long after their meeting, bombs exploded at A. D. King's home and directly underneath Room 30 at the Gaston Motel, where SCLC strategy meetings had been held. Although the room was vacant at the time, the bombings sparked riots in Birmingham. The violence threatened to undermine the settlement until President Kennedy moved federal troops to the area to restore order.

The Birmingham campaign was the largest of several mass protest movements during the spring and summer of 1963, which culminated in the March on Washington for Jobs and Freedom on August 28. Widespread news coverage of the campaign helped prompt President Kennedy to propose major legislation, which became the Civil Rights Act of 1964.

## 1963

**April 3:** Martin Luther King and the SCLC launch "Project C" (for "Confrontation"), a well-planned protest movement in Birmingham. Their "Birmingham Manifesto" details the SCLC's goals for Birmingham, including the desegregation of all businesses and fair hiring practices in the city. The movement begins on this day with sit-ins in downtown stores.

**April 6–7:** Dozens of marchers are arrested in Birmingham. TV cameras record the arrests as well as the police dogs that are used to intimidate the protesters.

**April 12:** Despite a state-court injunction against further demonstrations, Martin Luther King and Ralph Abernathy lead a march in Birmingham on Good Friday. They are arrested, and King is placed in solitary confinement.

**April 14:** A. D. King, brother of Martin Luther King, and two other Birmingham ministers are arrested after leading hundreds of marchers to city jail.

**April 15:** President Kennedy makes a sympathy telephone call to Coretta Scott King, wife of the jailed civil rights leader.

**April 16:** In his "Letter From Birmingham Jail," Martin Luther King explains why black citizens cannot wait patiently for justice to be served. *See* May 2, 1963.

**April 29:** In *Johnson v. Virginia*, the U.S. Supreme Court rules that racial segregation in courtrooms is unconstitutional.

**April–June:** Gloria Richardson and the Cambridge Nonviolent Action Committee stage protests and sit-ins in Cambridge, Maryland. With the aid of U.S. Attorney General Robert Kennedy, the city desegregates its schools and hospital, and initiates several changes to aid African-Americans. ➤

In March 1963 Martin Luther King made numerous speeches throughout the country in an attempt to raise bail money that inevitably would be needed for the upcoming Birmingham campaign. King and his SCLC colleagues arrived in Birmingham on April 2, 1963, ready to desegregate the South's most segregated major city. As in other cities, the Birmingham campaign started with small steps. Here, on April 4, college student Dorothy Bell stages a one-woman sit-in at a downtown lunch counter. She would not be served.

Segregation wasn't the only injustice that activists fought against during the Birmingham campaign. The Birmingham Police Department, with ties to the Ku Klux Klan, treated perpetrators far more severely if they were black than white. Here, protesters remind the nation how brutal the BPD had been—and likely would be in the upcoming weeks, as Movement leaders anticipated.

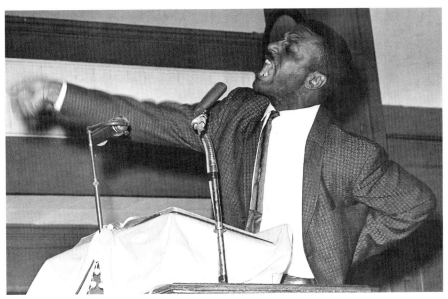

His home was bombed twice, and he was beaten by whites multiple times. But Reverend Fred Shuttlesworth of Bethel Baptist Church was not afraid of white people, whether in Birmingham or anywhere else. His long crusade against segregation in that city prepared local blacks for Martin Luther King and the SCLC, whom he called in to help defeat Jim Crow. In this speech on April 3, 1963, Shuttlesworth stated that African-Americans would not back down, that instead "we are just getting started."

The Movement's emphasis on economics, not morals, was key to its most successful victories. By the time Martin Luther King arrived in Birmingham, Movement activists understood the goal: break the back of the city's business community, which discriminated against blacks both as patrons and as possible employees. Economic and political stability stood hand in hand; if the business community crumbled under Movement pressure, so would the city fathers. Here, civil rights activists gather to discuss strategy in Birmingham's Lucky Star Employment Agency.

Demonstrators kneel to pray on April 6, 1963, after police halted a march to Birmingham's City Hall. The protesters said they were praying for segregationist Public Safety Commissioner Bull Connor and those who arrested black sit-in protesters. One reason civil rights activists staged prayer protests was to shame their adversaries, but their opponents in Birmingham, virtually all Christian, never seemed shamed or moved. The racist belief that blacks were subhuman was stronger than any appeals to common civility or faith. One white police officer stated that African-Americans' prayers never rose above their heads.

# 1960s

In Birmingham, Martin Luther King promised Movement activists that he would go to jail with them. But to do so he had to both defy a court injunction and decide against doing fund-raising trips to earn bail money for other activists in prison. He asked for suggestions. His advisors said no, because raising money would become too difficult without him. King went off to meditate on his own. He decided that, even though he didn't know where the money would come from, he needed to take action. And so he and Ralph Abernathy went into Bull Connor's prison on Good Friday, 1963.

## "Letter From Birmingham Jail"

MARTIN LUTHER KING WROTE his most resonant document of the Civil Rights Movement during his eight-day incarceration in Jefferson County Courthouse in Birmingham, Alabama. He wrote the "Letter From Birmingham Jail" in the margins of a newspaper until he ran out of room. He finished it on toilet paper.

In early April 1963, King and the SCLC had commenced "Project C" (for "confrontation") to battle racial injustices in Birmingham, the South's most segregated city. After sit-ins and marches, city officials on April 10 secured a state court injunction against further demonstrations. In defiance, King led a protest two days later, on Good Friday. He had hoped other clergymen in the city would join him. However, most of the city's black ministers remained aloof, and eight leading white ministers and priests issued an open letter to Birmingham's black citizens not to support the demonstrations.

In jail, King began composing a response to the white clergymen in the margins of *The Birmingham News*, which had printed the open letter. Eventually, he wrote 6,500 words. In his letter, King responded to calls for negotiation rather than direct action and to the assertion that the Birmingham campaign was untimely. He wrote: "We know through painful experience that freedom is never voluntarily given by the oppressor; it must be demanded by the oppressed.... Frankly, I have yet to engage in a direct-action campaign that was 'well-timed' in view of those who had not suffered unduly from the disease of segregation." King wrote that in his experience, "wait" had almost always meant "never."

On a personal level, King wrote about the anguish an African-American felt when telling a daughter that she couldn't visit an amusement park: "[You] see tears welling up in her eyes when she is told that Funtown is closed to colored children, and see ominous clouds of inferiority beginning to form in her little mental sky...."

After associates outside the jail assembled it, King's letter was published in pamphlet form by the American Friends Service Committee, a Quaker group. It soon was reprinted in mediums throughout the country.

William L. Moore is one of the few white Movement martyrs. A Baltimore postal worker, Moore used his 1963 vacation time to march to Mississippi to deliver a special letter that he himself wrote—a plea for racial tolerance. Moore's letter, addressed to Mississippi Governor Ross Barnett, asked him to be gracious. It also stated that white Americans couldn't be free until all Americans had equal rights. As Moore walked, he wore signs reading "Equal Rights for All (Mississippi or Bust)" and "Eat at Joe's, Both Black and White." During his march, Moore was ambushed and shot to death, twice at close range. The body of the 35-year-old was found sprawled on a desolate stretch of highway near Gadsden, Alabama.

In 1963, one year before the Freedom Summer voter registration drive, a smaller group of activists attempted to lay the groundwork for black enfranchisement in Mississippi. Among them was comedian Dick Gregory, who is shown being removed from the County Courthouse in Greenwood after seeking to register a group of African-Americans on April 2. Gregory, who laced his humor with stringent racial commentary, served as a public voice of both the integrationist and militant phases of the Civil Rights Movement. He worked with leaders as diverse as Martin Luther King and Stokely Carmichael. In the late 1960s, Gregory ran for both mayor of Chicago and president of the United States.

James Bevel was a young activist who always walked his own path. A leader who cut his teeth in SNCC campaigns, Bevel was high-strung, charismatic, and eccentric (he liked to wear a yarmulke with his SNCC-signature coveralls). Martin Luther King's aides were uneasy about using children to fill the jails, but Bevel maintained that children did not have jobs to lose. He told King that if Baptists believed their children were old enough to decide to follow God, they were old enough to engage in struggle. King was convinced, and on May 2, 1963, more than 1,000 children assembled for a march from Birmingham's Sixteenth Street Baptist Church.

# 1960s

## 1963

**May 2:** More than 1,000 black schoolchildren leave the Sixteenth Street Baptist Church to march to downtown Birmingham. Hundreds are arrested and sent by school buses to various jails.

**May 3:** Hundreds of black children gather at the Sixteenth Street Baptist Church in Birmingham for another march. When the children leave the church, they're blasted by firefighters with high-pressure hoses, clubbed by police officers, and attacked by police dogs. The assault triggers outrage around the country and the world.

**May 4:** U.S. Justice Department official Burke Marshall helps mediate negotiations in Birmingham between the SCLC and city officials.

**May 4–7:** In Birmingham, protests continue with daily marches and hundreds of arrests.

**May 8:** The SCLC agrees to a cooling-off period to enable black leaders and Birmingham business owners to begin negotiations. *See* May 10, 1963.

**May 8:** Activists demonstrate against segregation in Nashville.

**May 10:** Birmingham city officials reach an agreement with the SCLC. The city promises to desegregate downtown stores and release from jail all those arrested during the protests. The SCLC agrees to end its boycotts and demonstrations.

**May 11:** The KKK denounces the Birmingham agreement while bombs explode at the home of Reverend A. D. King (Martin Luther King's brother) and at the Gaston Motel (where Martin Luther King recently had been staying). Angry black citizens begin to riot.

**May 20:** The U.S. Supreme Court finds Birmingham and other city segregation ordinances unconstitutional, thus making sit-ins legal. ➤

"All you gotta do is tell them you're going to bring the dogs. Look at 'em run. I want to see the dogs work. Look at those niggers run."

—BIRMINGHAM PUBLIC SAFETY COMMISSIONER BULL CONNOR

What group of people would allow their own children—some as young as six—to face white racist violence and jail in Birmingham? The answer wasn't pretty. Using children was the only way to get enough protesters to fill the jails—the key to the Movement's success. Moreover, as front-line warriors, children—as symbols of innocence—would expose once and for all the cruelty that was Birmingham, and elicit world sympathy. Of the more than 1,000 children who marched on May 2, 1963, hundreds were arrested and taken in paddy wagons and school buses to jail (*above*). The next day, Birmingham officials turned hoses and dogs on the children. Through May 6 more than 2,000 demonstrators were arrested in Birmingham, many of whom were sent to makeshift, outdoor jail yards (*right*).

After the massive arrest of children on May 2, Movement leaders assembled another 1,000 children to march the next day. Birmingham Public Safety Commissioner Bull Connor decided to deter the demonstrators with fire hoses and police dogs. "I want 'em to see the dogs work," Connor said. While watching the attack dogs snap at black children, Connor added, "Look at those niggers run!" African-American Walter Gadsden (*pictured*), who did not take part in the demonstration, was at the wrong place at the right time for one of the most famous photographs of the Civil Rights Movement.

Birmingham firefighters were proud of their fire hoses, which could strip bark from trees and knock bricks loose from their mortar. On May 3 they put their hoses on display, blasting young African-Americans who had gathered to demonstrate. The firefighters' water slammed kids against buildings, rolled them down the street, tore clothes off their bodies, and inflicted numerous injuries. The next day, images such as this made the front pages of newspapers across the country.

# Bull Connor

THEOPHILUS EUGENE CONNOR, who became a symbol of hard-line segregation in the South, entered politics after a career as a radio sportscaster in Birmingham, Alabama. He served in the Alabama House of Representatives from 1934 to 1937 before being elected public safety commissioner of Birmingham, a position that he held, except for one term, until 1963.

Born in 1897, Connor used his administrative authority over Birmingham's police and fire departments to fend off attempts to integrate the city's facilities. Aware that a Trailways bus carrying Freedom Riders was due to arrive in Birmingham on Mother's Day in 1961, he posted no officers there "because of the holiday." Unchecked by police, a mob assaulted the riders, beating them brutally. In December Connor and his two fellow city commissioners closed Birmingham's 68 parks, 38 playgrounds, and four golf courses rather than integrate.

In 1962 Birmingham voted to change from a city commission system to a mayor-council system. Bull Connor promptly announced his intention to run for mayor. Though defeated in the election, he was still in control of the police and fire departments in spring 1963 when he ordered the use of police dogs and fire hoses to disperse civil rights demonstrators in Birmingham. Televised images of snarling dogs lunging at black citizens and powerful blasts of water hammering black children dramatized the plight of African-Americans in Birmingham.

Reverend Fred Shuttlesworth, a leader of the Birmingham movement, was injured so badly by the punishing water that he had to be taken away in an ambulance. "I waited a week down here to see that," Connor said, "and then I missed it. I wish it had been a hearse."

Connor lost his bid for mayor, but in 1964 began the first of two terms as president of the Alabama Public Service Commission. He retired after losing the race for a third term in 1972, and he died the following year.

The abuse of African-American demonstrators in Birmingham sparked protests in other cities, including New York. On May 9 (*above*), members of African Nationals in America, Inc., carried a mock coffin of Jim Crow while a child protested against the arrest of youths in Birmingham.

An effigy of Martin Luther King hangs from the National States Rights Party headquarters in Birmingham on May 6, 1963. Both racist whites and conservative blacks in Birmingham viewed King as a troublemaker and outsider who would create more problems than he would solve. Racist whites did not want King to succeed because they did not want desegregation. Conservative blacks felt that King would force violently to the forefront issues that they had worked on quietly, privately, behind the scenes. But the forces of direct action in Birmingham were tired of the racist intimidation of whites and the conservatism of the black middle class. If it meant making sacrifices to get freedom *now,* then so be it.

Political cartoonist Bill Mauldin captured the hypocrisy of many northern whites with this "biting" commentary. The German shepherd represents the Birmingham police dogs and, in a figurative sense, aggressive segregation. Northern whites, represented by the seemingly benign white poodle, could be equally cruel to blacks, with subtle forms of discrimination and exclusion.

"Up North we sort of nibble 'em to death."

In early May 1963, U.S. Attorney General Robert F. Kennedy (*right*) sent Burke Marshall (*left*) to Birmingham to help solve the racial crisis. Marshall arrived to find animosity between white business leaders and white law enforcement officials as well as between Movement leaders and the city's conservative blacks. Of course, whites and blacks in general were on opposite sides. Despite such tension, Marshall convinced Martin Luther King to work out an agreement with Birmingham's business leaders. Due to the boycotts and turmoil in the downtown area, merchants had been losing money by the day—and were looking to stop the financial bleeding.

# Fred Shuttlesworth

ORN IN 1922 IN THE BACKWOODS of Alabama, Reverend Fred Lee Shuttlesworth became pastor of Sixteenth Street Baptist Church in Birmingham. He was an active member of the NAACP when the Montgomery bus boycott began, and in June 1956 he formed his own organization, Alabama Christian Movement for Human Rights (ACMHR). As a high-profile black activist in the heart of Dixie, Shuttlesworth became a prime target for southern hate mongers and police. "I was in jail so many times," he said, "I quit counting after 20."

In 1955 Shuttlesworth called for the hiring of black police officers in Birmingham. The demand was ignored. After he began to organize a bus boycott in the city, Ku Klux Klan members detonated a bomb outside his home on Christmas. Neither Shuttlesworth nor his wife and four children were injured.

In September 1957, when Shuttlesworth attempted to enroll his children at an all-white high school, a mob attacked and chain-whipped him. His wife was stabbed. White students boycotted classes to protest his desegregation efforts. In 1958 Shuttlesworth and others were arrested when they tried to sit in the front of a city bus. In 1959 the ACMHR called for the integration of public parks. The City Commission responded by closing down all of Birmingham's parks and playgrounds as well as its four golf courses.

Shuttlesworth kept up the fight. In March 1963 he conceived "Project C" (for "confrontation") and invited

Fred Shuttlesworth, Ralph Abernathy, Martin Luther King (*left to right*)

Martin Luther King and the SCLC to help him desegregate Birmingham. During the campaign, King's jailing and the specter of black children being attacked with fire hoses and police dogs began to turn public opinion. In May the SCLC and the ACMHR signed an agreement with the city to desegregate Birmingham's businesses (although the city repealed its desegregation ordinances in July).

Shuttlesworth left Birmingham in 1961. He moved to Cincinnati, where he served as pastor at two churches and became active in job programs.

# Photographing the Movement

PERHAPS MORE THAN with any previous movement in American history, the Civil Rights Movement was a media event. Both Movement leaders and segregationist leaders recognized the power of the graphic image to convey a message. Martin Luther King referred to the brutality in Birmingham in 1963 as being "imprisoned in a luminous glare revealing the naked truth to the whole world." Two years later, mindful of the power of those images in Birmingham, deputies of Sheriff Jim Clark in Selma, Alabama, beat up photographers, snatched their cameras, and covered camera lenses. Yet they could not prevent the "luminous glare."

SNCC was creative and aggressive in its use of photography, turning many photos into powerful poster images and publishing the first book of civil rights photography, *The Movement*. Photographers ranged from grizzled white photojournalists on established newspapers to young black camera buffs caught up in the spirit of the times. Black photographers captured some of the most arresting images. Moneta Sleet took photos for *Ebony*, and Gordon Parks and Frank Dandridge shot for *Life*, the most important magazine in America in the 1950s and 1960s.

At a May 10 press conference, Martin Luther King and Fred Shuttlesworth, joined by the other SCLC leaders, spelled out an agreement they had reached with Birmingham's Senior Citizens Committee, which represented the majority of the city's businesses. The terms: The city's lunch counters, fitting rooms, restrooms, and drinking fountains would be desegregated within 90 days; a process would begin that would ensure black employment in downtown stores; and all jailed demonstrators would be released. Bull Connor and Alabama Governor George Wallace soon denounced the settlement.

The six weeks of restraint showed by the Ku Klux Klan ended on May 11, 1963, the day after the Birmingham accords were signed. The home of Reverend A. D. King, Martin's brother, was bombed after Movement activists had their regular meeting at his First Baptist Church in Ensley, a Birmingham suburb. The same night, the Gaston Motel—the meeting place for Martin Luther King and other Movement activists—was bombed. Angry black citizens responded by throwing rocks at police, and some stores were set afire. A. D. King (*pictured*) attempted to calm rioters late that night. On May 12 President John F. Kennedy sent 3,000 troops to nearby Fort McClellan, but they would not be needed.

Former heavyweight boxing champion Floyd Patterson (*left*) and baseball legend Jackie Robinson inspect the bomb damage at the Gaston Motel in Birmingham on May 14, 1963. Both were in town to address a Movement rally. The bombing turned out to be the last noteworthy act of protest by segregationists during the Birmingham campaign. Moreover, new Mayor Albert Boutwell and the new City Council honored the May 10 agreement between Movement and local business leaders.

According to the Nation of Islam's Malcolm X, Movement leaders were foolishly allowing black blood to spill in order to prove their humanity to those who oppressed them. But Malcolm did see that direct confrontation with what he called "the white power structure" was stirring blacks to be braver and bolder than they had been. That's why it had disturbed him to follow the order of NOI leader Elijah Muhammad to avoid retaliation when Los Angeles police shot Nation of Islam followers in 1962. Here, Malcolm addresses a Harlem rally in May 1963 while showing a picture of the Los Angeles incident. Malcolm said at this rally that Los Angeles allowed a Ku Klux Klan-like police force to terrorize the black community.

# 1960s

## 1963

**June:** During a sit-in in Gadsden, Alabama, police use electric cattle prods to remove the protesters.

**June:** The U.S. Defense Department announces that the Armed Forces Reserves have been integrated.

**June 11:** Escorted by National Guardsmen, Vivian Malone and James Hood try to become the first African-American students to register at the University of Alabama in Tuscaloosa. Alabama Governor George Wallace stands defiantly in front of the schoolhouse door before eventually stepping aside. During a televised speech in the evening, President John F. Kennedy informs the nation that it is time for equality in America and that he will push Congress to enact strong civil rights legislation. *See June 19, 1963.*

**June 12:** In Jackson, Mississippi, NAACP Field Secretary Medgar Evers is shot and killed while getting out of his car at his home; his attacker is Byron de la Beckwith, a white racist. Mass demonstrations in Jackson follow, leading to more than 150 arrests. *See February 5, 1994.*

**June 18:** About 3,000 black students in Boston demonstrate for civil rights.

**June 19:** President Kennedy submits a civil rights bill to Congress. *See July 2, 1964.*

**June 22:** President Kennedy meets with civil rights leaders to try to dissuade them from holding the proposed March on Washington. Kennedy later will publicly support the march. *See August 28, 1963.*

**June 23:** In Detroit, 125,000 people march in protest of discrimination. Martin Luther King speaks to the assembled group.

**July 4–7:** Protestant, Catholic, and Jewish clergymen join black demonstrators at Gwynn Oak Amusement Park near Baltimore. More than 300 are arrested. ➤

In spring 1963 NAACP Field Secretary Medgar Evers began a full-scale, direct-action campaign to force downtown Jackson, Mississippi, to desegregate. In response, Mayor Allen C. Thompson went on television on May 12 and asked blacks not to participate with Evers and the "outside agitators" of the NAACP and other civil rights groups. Evers, with help from the Federal Communications Commission, got a chance to rebut Thompson on television a week later. Blacks in Mississippi, he said, wanted segregation abolished as well as the right to vote. He mentioned that a Congo native could become a locomotive engineer, but an African-American in Jackson couldn't even get a job driving a garbage truck. Many whites in Jackson were touched by the speech; in fact, some quietly removed segregation signs. Other whites, though, seethed with racist rage.

The Movement had come to Mississippi, whether Mississippians wanted it to or not. This sit-in at the Woolworth lunch counter on May 28, 1963, showed the type of resistance that activists would encounter in Mississippi. John Salter, Joan Trunpauer, and Anne Moody (*seated left to right*) were doused with sugar, mustard, and ketchup. The white counterprotesters sprayed them with paint and threw pepper in their eyes. The protest made the nightly news, and Mayor Allen C. Thompson publicly promised to desegregate some public facilities. But some members of the state legislature and the White Citizens' Council changed his mind before the sun finished setting.

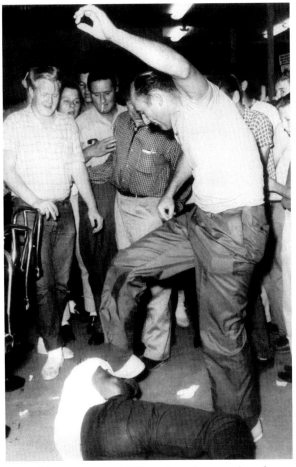

Memphis Norman, an African-American student from nearby Wiggins, Mississippi, attempted to be served at a Jackson lunch counter on May 28, 1963. This was his welcome, provided by former Jackson police officer Benny Oliver. By month's end, protests resulted in the desegregation of city facilities and other concessions.

Charlayne Hunter and Hamilton Holmes faced adversity as the first black students at the University of Georgia, but they made it to graduation day on June 1, 1963. "[T]he only sounds to be heard were the cheers and applause emanating from our family and close friends," recalled Hunter. "No one else seemed to notice, and I remembered thinking to myself, 'This is how it ought to be,' as I sat there in my place." Holmes, after becoming the first black student at Emory Medical School, went on to become an orthopedic surgeon. Hunter would become an award-winning correspondent and anchor for public television's *The McNeil/Lehrer NewsHour*. In 1999 she became CNN's bureau chief for Johannesburg, South Africa.

Vivian Malone and James Hood (*both pictured*) knew that an attempt to desegregate the University of Alabama in June 1963 was risky, but they persevered. Malone told the press that she was in no way afraid of Alabama Governor George Wallace. The governor, who symbolically stood in front of the "schoolhouse door" at the university, clearly was not in Malone and Hood's corner. Hood received reassurances from President Kennedy that he and Malone would be safe, but tension remained. The night after Hood settled in, signs around the campus gloated: "NAACP is for black buzzards. They shot a NAACP nigger in Jackson [Medgar Evers]. Do you think you are safe?"

# 1960s

## George Wallace

GEORGE WALLACE SERVED as governor of Alabama during the height of the Civil Rights Movement, 1963 to 1967, as well as from 1971 to 1975. When civil rights protestors swarmed to Birmingham in '63 and to Selma in '65, Wallace stood up to the "outside agitators" and vehemently defended his segregationist stance. In the eyes of the world, he himself symbolized segregation.

Wallace was actually a progressive on racial issues until his unsuccessful campaign for governor in 1958. He reinvented himself as an ardent segregationist by 1962. Although he claimed not to condone racial violence, his "stand up for segregation" attitudes effectively gave permission for racists to commit violent acts. During his first term as governor, a dozen slayings of civil rights activists occurred in Alabama, many of which went unprosecuted.

A savvy exploiter of media opportunities, Wallace's most electric moment came on June 11, 1963, when he kept a campaign pledge to stand in the schoolhouse door to block integration of Alabama public schools. At the entrance of the University of Alabama, he read a proclamation that called for "segregation now, segregation tomorrow, segregation forever." Since President John F. Kennedy had federalized the Alabama National Guard and ordered its units to the university campus, Wallace then stepped aside and allowed two black students to enter.

In later years, as the black vote became more influential in Alabama, Wallace softened his antiblack rhetoric and trumpeted conservatism and states' rights. In 1968 he made a run for the U.S. presidency as an independent, law-and-order candidate. Four years later, he was shot by Arthur H. Bremer, a white man, and became partially paralyzed for the rest of his life. Wallace taught at the University of Alabama from 1982 to 1987 and died at age 79 in 1998.

Alabama Governor George Wallace promised during his gubernatorial campaign of 1962 that he would "stand in the schoolhouse door" to prevent public school desegregation. He got his chance to keep his promise on June 11, 1963, when Vivian Malone and James Hood attempted to register at the University of Alabama. Wallace personally barred their admittance even though the National Guard was on hand to enforce the law. Wallace read aloud a proclamation to assorted reporters and National Guard Brigadier General Henry Graham (*pictured*): "I stand here today, as governor of this sovereign state, and refuse to willingly submit to illegal usurpation of power by the Central Government. . . . It is not defiance for defiance's sake, but for the purpose of raising basic and fundamental constitutional questions." After his speech Wallace stepped aside, and Hood and Malone were admitted.

George Wallace's schoolhouse stand on June 11 forced President John F. Kennedy to make a decisive statement on the status of black Americans. Kennedy addressed the nation on television that same day. "Now the time has come for this nation to fulfill its promise," Kennedy said. "The events in Birmingham and elsewhere have so increased the cries for equality that no city or state or legislative body can prudently choose to ignore them. The fires of frustration and discord are burning in every city, North and South, where legal remedies are not at hand. Redress is sought in the streets, in demonstrations, parades, and protests, which create tensions and threaten violence and threaten lives." Kennedy vowed to push Congress to enact strong civil rights legislation.

Attorney General Robert F. Kennedy played a more active role in civil rights issues than his brother John did. RFK met with author James Baldwin and other Movement activists in what turned out to be a fiery encounter in New York City. Here in Washington on June 14, 1963, he addresses civil rights demonstrators. Although Robert Kennedy started out as a racial pragmatist (he did sign FBI head J. Edgar Hoover's order authorizing wiretaps on Martin Luther King), he gradually established a powerful moral voice on the issues of race and class.

# Murder of Medgar Evers

**O**N THE NIGHT OF JUNE 12, 1963, Medgar Evers, Mississippi field secretary for the NAACP, drove home from yet another long day of civil rights work. As he crossed the front yard of his home in Jackson, he was shot in the back. Evers staggered toward his front door and then fell, dead.

Only 37 years old when he was killed, Evers had been one of the most effective and articulate activists against segregation. Not long after graduating from Alcorn College and moving with his wife, Myrlie, to Mound Bayou, Mississippi, he joined the NAACP. Evers helped establish chapters in other parts of the Mississippi Delta region, and he organized boycotts of gas stations that refused to allow blacks to use their restrooms. After the Supreme Court's 1954 *Brown* ruling, Evers attempted to enroll in University of Mississippi's law school. Although he was denied admission, his efforts attracted the attention of the NAACP, which hired him as the organization's first field secretary for Mississippi.

From his home base in Jackson, Evers drew national attention when he investigated violent crimes against blacks and organized a boycott of Jackson merchants. The national spotlight focused even more on Mississippi when Evers assisted James Meredith in his successful effort to gain admission to Ole Miss in 1962. But the glare

of that spotlight exposed Evers to resentful white Southerners.

After Evers made a televised speech against racism in Jackson on May 20, 1962, his days on earth were numbered. The assassin, a white supremacist named Byron de la Beckwith, was soon arrested. He was tried twice in the 1960s, but in both trials all-white juries failed to reach a verdict. Three decades later the state of Mississippi brought de la Beckwith to trial again, and in 1994 he was convicted and sentenced to life in prison. The trial was dramatized in the 1996 Hollywood film *Ghosts of Mississippi*.

African-Americans in Jackson, Mississippi, reacted with rage to the June 12, 1963, killing of NAACP activist Medgar Evers. Here, two black youths throw rocks and bottles at city police officers following a "March of Mourning" for Evers. About 3,000 people marched, but that number dwindled to 500 after police arrived. At least 27 people were arrested.

> ## "You can kill a man, but you can't kill an idea."
> —MEDGAR EVERS

Myrlie Evers had screamed so hard after watching her husband's assassination that it briefly affected her hearing. But now she had to hold onto her reserves of strength for her three children—Darrell, Rena, and Van. At the funeral, she saw Darrell, sitting between her and Rena, stare at his father's casket, "and I felt what he must be thinking," she wrote. "There would be no more telephone calls from his father, no more basketball and football with him, no riding bicycles with him in front of the house, no fishing. . . . Darrell sat there and stared at the casket, shoulders straight, one hand in the other, his head slightly bowed, and then suddenly he sobbed and sobbed until I guess no more tears would come."

The killing of NAACP activist Medgar Evers emboldened African-Americans in Mississippi. As the funeral procession passed a white restaurant, music blaring from the jukebox angered some of the marchers. They went inside the restaurant and unplugged the music machine—eliciting not a word from the white customers.

Byron de la Beckwith (*right*) was one of Mississippi's unrepentant racists. A fertilizer salesman by day and Ku Klux Klan member by night, he flew his Confederate flag proudly, and openly spoke out for white supremacy. On June 23, 1963, he was arrested in connection with the murder of NAACP activist Medgar Evers. However, two white policemen would claim they saw de la Beckwith 60 miles away in Greenwood on the night of the murder. Two all-white juries remained deadlocked the following year, allowing him to go free twice. Thirty years later, however, in 1994, de la Beckwith was convicted.

# Myrlie's Last Days with Medgar

WE CAME TO REALIZE in those last few days, last few months, that our time was short. It was simply in the air. You knew that something was going to happen, and the logical person for it to happen to was Medgar. It certainly brought us closer during that time. As a matter of fact, we didn't talk, we didn't have to. We communicated without words. It was a touch, it was a look, it was holding each other, it was music playing. And I used to try to reassure him and tell him, Nothing's going to happen to you, the FBI is here—laugh—everybody knows you, you're in the press, they wouldn't dare do anything to you.

—*Myrlie Evers, wife of Medgar Evers*

This Gib Crockett cartoon, dated June 21, 1963, was captioned, "Don't Push Too Hard—Let Him Work!" A delicate balance needed to be maintained to get the Civil Rights Bill passed by Congress. The administration of President Kennedy had to be seen as a racially moderate force guaranteeing constitutional rights for all Americans. Movement leaders had to be viewed as pushing hard for the legislation but not hard enough to be threatening, since both halls of Congress were filled with white men, including many southern segregationists. Yet 1963 was the centennial year of Lincoln's signing of the Emancipation Proclamation, and the *zeitgeist*—the spirit of the times—demanded real change in the status of blacks in America.

This demonstration in Detroit on June 23, 1963, known by civil rights activists as the Detroit Freedom March, was one of the largest—if not *the* largest—demonstrations in Michigan's history. Approximately 125,000 attended. This march was about jobs for blacks—in the auto plants, at construction sites, and in other industries. Such local civil rights leaders as Tony Brown organized the march, which was notable for remarks by Martin Luther King. King delivered a "rough draft" of the speech he would immortalize at the March on Washington two months later.

On July 3, 1963, black physicians marched in Chicago, the site of the 1963 national NAACP convention. Joined by NAACP members, the doctors picketed in front of the city headquarters of the American Medical Association, the nation's largest organization of doctors. The protesters demanded that the AMA help desegregate the profession. Specifically, they complained that black physicians were mostly excluded from the county medical societies. This meant that they could treat their patients (those in "colored" wards) only with the permission of white doctors.

Under Jim Crow, all public spaces were segregated, including amusement parks. Here, Baltimore police arrest protesters at Gwynn Oak Amusement Park on July 4, 1963. Four years earlier, five black visitors to Gwynn Oak were spat at by a group of angry whites, at least one of whom yelled, "Lynch them!" The park finally desegregated in August 1963. Amusement parks were a common target of Movement activists. A month after this protest, CORE members attempted to desegregate Fairyland in Kansas City—which came to fruition in 1964 after the passage of a public accommodations law.

Gloria Richardson was one of the few women in the Movement to lead an activist organization, the Cambridge (Maryland) Nonviolent Action Committee. Richardson was strong, independent, and dedicated to eradicating not just Jim Crow in Cambridge but all of the economic disparities that plagued African-Americans in the city. The committee's seven-week protests against all phases of city government in 1963 made national headlines and got Richardson and 79 other activists arrested, including her own daughter and mother. She created real change in Cambridge, as city leaders desegregated schools and public accommodations, and began to hire blacks for positions in government and business.

Dizzyland Restaurant owner Robert Fehsenfeldt (*left photo*) smashes an egg on a demonstrator's face during a sit-in outside his Cambridge, Maryland, eatery on July 9, 1963. The Cambridge Nonviolent Action Committee was involved in a go-for-broke campaign against segregation in the city. In the right photo, Gloria Richardson (*white blouse*), chair of the Cambridge Nonviolent Action Committee, watches as demonstrators who tried to get service at the Dizzyland Restaurant are arrested after they refuse to leave.

# 1960s

## 1963

**August 1-4:** After the family of Reginald Williams moves into the predominantly white Englewood section of Chicago, white protesters bombard the family's apartment building with bricks and bottles. More than 220 people are arrested.

**August 2:** After two months of protests and violence, business and civic leaders in Savannah, Georgia, agree to desegregate hotels, motels, bowling alleys, and some theaters.

**August 3:** In Gadsden, Alabama, 685 people are arrested for protesting segregation.

**August 18:** James Meredith graduates from the University of Mississippi.

**August 28:** In an event orchestrated by A. Philip Randolph and Bayard Rustin, 250,000 people, many of whom are white, march to the Lincoln Memorial in Washington, D.C. Various civil rights leaders speak, including Martin Luther King, who delivers his "I Have a Dream" speech.

**August 31:** Law officers in Plaquemine, Louisiana, use tear gas and electric prods to prevent 500 black demonstrators from marching to city hall.

**September:** Despite Governor George Wallace's efforts to block a desegregation order, schools are integrated in Alabama's major cities. The Alabama National Guard, federalized by President Kennedy, ensures integration.

**September 3:** Public schools in South Carolina begin desegregation.

**September 4:** A two-hour riot ensues in Birmingham after the house bombing of black civil rights lawyer Arthur D. Shores. Twenty-one people are injured in the riot, while police shoot and kill a 20-year-old African-American. ➤

Foes of the Movement tried repeatedly, but unsuccessfully, to make the charge of communism stick. This pamphlet shows Martin Luther King at what it calls a "Communist training school." The school actually was the Highlander Research and Training Center, a Tennessee-based institution that was a key gathering place for Movement activists. King opposed communism and was always fearful of the Movement being smeared with this charge. He was, however, a democratic socialist, and some of his close and trusted advisers were socialists. Among them were Stanley Levison (his lawyer and occasional ghostwriter) and Bayard Rustin (an organizer for the 1963 March on Washington). The Communist charge was used by white racists to divert attention away from Jim Crow.

All segregated public spaces—no matter how small—were targets of civil rights activists. In July 1963 members of CORE decided to sit in at a White Castle restaurant in the Bronx borough of New York City because of the restaurant's lack of black employees. A week's worth of tension culminated in an all-night demonstration on July 13–14. When one protester collapsed due to heat exhaustion and had to be brought to a local hospital, CORE accused restaurant officials of turning off the air conditioning and turning up the heat.

Jeering crowds of whites follow three black youths who tried to desegregate Savannah Beach on July 14, 1963. The three were arrested, initiating applause from the white onlookers. But times were about to change in Savannah. Several "night marches," organized by blacks who demanded the vote, took place in the city in 1963. A year later, Savannah would desegregate its public facilities.

These youngsters were happy to arrive safely in Ringwood, New Jersey, in July 1963 after a frightening experience at summer camp. Because they attended an integrated camp in Rosman, North Carolina, in the Smoky Mountains, their bus was fired upon by angry locals. A shotgun blast blew a hole in the windshield.

Police officers in Brooklyn surround demonstrators protesting the construction of Downstate Medical Center on August 5, 1963. Protesters were angry because African-Americans were racially excluded from trade unions. Demonstrators chained themselves together, making it more difficult for police to remove them from the site. The chaining practice also symbolized and crystalized the commitment of protesters, who would endure punishment as an indivisible group.

After African-Americans moved into a Chicago South Side community in late July 1963, whites responded by planting and burning this cross. As in many cities, Chicago's neighborhoods were strongly segregated. The *de facto* segregation enforced by local officials pitted working-class whites against working-class blacks. Major race battles would be waged in Chicago throughout the mid- and late 1960s.

James Meredith exemplified the courage and conviction of the Civil Rights Movement. In 1962 he risked his life by registering at the University of Mississippi, breaking Ole Miss's color barrier. In doing so, he stood up against Mississippi Governor Ross Barnett, the university administration, and those who rioted on campus. On August 18, 1963, Meredith graduated from Mississippi with a bachelor of arts degree while wearing an upside-down "Never" button on his graduation gown. "Never" had been a rallying cry of white Southerners who had resisted integration.

On August 3, 1963, Movement leaders in New York plot the route of the March on Washington for Jobs and Freedom. A spokesperson for the group said the march promised to be the largest civil rights demonstration in the nation's history. Seated (*left to right*) are A. Philip Randolph, president of the Brotherhood of Sleeping Car Porters; Roy Wilkins, executive secretary of the national NAACP; and Anna Arnold Hedgeman, the only female on the march's central organizing committee and the first black woman to serve in a New York mayoral cabinet. Hedgeman successfully pushed the men to include a tribute to black women at the march.

Black activists who stood up for themselves sometimes were treated like cattle. Here, a black protester grimaces in pain as a mounted Louisiana state trooper tags his back with an electric cattle prod on August 21, 1963. The man received this punishment for getting too close to Plaquemine's City Hall. Officers arrested more than 100 African-Americans during demonstrations there.

# March on Washington

IN LATE 1962, at a time of mass protests in the South, veteran civil rights and labor leader A. Philip Randolph called for a march on Washington, D.C. Having used the threat of such a march to wrest concessions from President Franklin D. Roosevelt in 1941, Randolph proposed using the same tactic to pressure President John F. Kennedy and to give discontented black people a nonviolent outlet for their frustrations.

On June 11 Kennedy proposed new civil rights legislation. In a nationally televised address, he announced that a "moral crisis" faced the nation and told viewers that African-American demands could not be "quieted by token moves or talk." He pleaded, "It is a time to act in the Congress, in your state and local legislative body, and above all, in all of our daily lives."

Soon after Kennedy's address, Randolph and a delegation of black leaders met with President Kennedy at the White House. While assuring Kennedy of their support for new civil rights legislation, the delegation also made clear that substantial changes would have to come quickly in order to prevent black discontent from exploding into violence nationwide. When President Kennedy initially objected to the march, Randolph told him that black Americans would hit the country's streets regardless of an organized march. Randolph insisted that it would be better if they were led by disciplined organizations dedicated to the civil rights cause than by militant black leaders who didn't subscribe to nonviolent methods. Although Kennedy remained skeptical about the march, he supported the efforts of moderate leaders such as Randolph and Martin Luther King to remain in control of planning the event.

The resulting March on Washington for Jobs and Freedom, held on August 28, 1963, was the largest civil rights

Despite hot and humid weather, more than 200,000 people participated in the March on Washington on August 28, 1963.

Martin Luther King delivers his "I Have a Dream" speech.

demonstration ever held. Randolph and other major civil rights leaders succeeded in drawing a crowd of more than 200,000 to the front of the Lincoln Memorial. The program for the day featured not only the leaders of major civil rights groups but also entertainers, such as gospel singer Mahalia Jackson and folk singers Joan Baez and Bob Dylan.

Former Freedom Rider and SNCC Chairman John Lewis provoked controversy at the march when he drafted a speech criticizing the lack of strong federal action on behalf of civil rights workers in the Deep South. In his prepared text, Lewis bluntly asked which side the federal government was on. Lewis was convinced to tone down his remarks through the intervention of Randolph and others. Even in its modified form, Lewis's speech was a powerful critique of American politicians. He said politicians built their careers on immoral compromise and allied themselves with forms of political, social, and economic exploitation.

Lewis's speech reflected resentments and frustrations that would soon become more evident in the African-American freedom struggle. The march, however, was mainly an expression of hope for the future.

Martin Luther King's concluding "I Have a Dream" speech carefully summed up the themes that had guided the black struggle, as well as previous efforts by African-Americans to "demand the riches of freedom and the security of justice."

Calling upon America to live up to the ideals expressed in the Constitution and the Declaration of Independence, King proclaimed: "Now is the time to make real the promises of democracy.... Now is the time to lift our nation from the quicksands of racial injustice to the solid rock of brotherhood. Now is the time to make justice a reality for all of God's children." Recounting the difficulties the black freedom struggle had faced, King pronounced, "I have a dream that one day this nation will rise up and live out the true meaning of its creed: We hold these truths to be self-evident, that all men are created equal."

The optimism conveyed by King's "I Have a Dream" speech began to falter after the march when a bomb planted in a Birmingham, Alabama, church killed four African-American children on September 15. Soon after the bombing, King joined a delegation of black leaders, who angrily confronted President Kennedy at the White House. He warned the president that "the Negro community is about to reach a breaking point" and that racial violence threatened to undermine nonviolent leadership of the black struggle.

"We have been consistent in standing up for nonviolence," King pleaded. "But more and more we are faced with the problem of our people saying, 'What's the use?' And we find it a little more difficult to get over nonviolence. And I am convinced that if something isn't done to give the Negro a new sense of hope and a sense of protection, there is a danger we will face the worst race riot we have ever seen in this country."

Seen from the vantage point of the Birmingham bombing, the Washington march would become the culminating event of the civil rights protests of the early 1960s. In the months and years that followed, the African-American freedom struggle would become increasingly militant and distrustful of the interracial alliances that had made the march possible.

# 1960s

Martin Luther King said that the day of the March on Washington belonged to A. Philip Randolph. The veteran activist had spent his entire adult life organizing black people to push for economic and civil rights. In 1941 he had called for a national march on Washington to protest Jim Crow in defense plants. The march was called off after President Franklin D. Roosevelt issued an executive order that banned Jim Crow in defense-plant hiring. Randolph's idea of a national Washington march still hung in the air. In 1962 he began talking about it again with civil rights leader Bayard Rustin. Those discussions evolved into the high point of the Movement.

## A Mighty Drama

AT THE DEMONSTRATION I saw Americans who were dedicated to the principles of individual liberty, political freedom, and the Constitution of the United States. I saw there an integrated audience. It has been said that one picture is worth a thousand words. Today, millions of the American people saw, by television, people of various races, creeds, and nationalities standing together, singing together, speaking together, walking together, playing together, and working together in the nations's capital. Let no one tell me it is necessary to have segregation. . . .

The participants were like actors in a mighty drama. Who was the audience, and where was the audience? Not here. The audience was back in every village, town, hamlet, city, and farm home in America—185 million people—because this great drama went out to the people this afternoon. I venture to say that there was more mass education on the issues of social justice and human rights in America than in all the history of our Republic.

—*Senator Hubert H. Humphrey (D–MN), addressing the Senate on August 28, 1963*

The time had come to make a stand, so they came from all directions to participate in the March on Washington. Ledger Smith, a 27-year-old Chicagoan, skated 698 miles to the nation's capital. Impassioned activists in Chicago, Birmingham, Newark, New Orleans, Philadelphia, and other cities chartered "Freedom Buses." Meanwhile, three teenagers from Gadsden, Alabama—Robert Avery, James F. Smith, and Robert Thomas—walked 692 miles . . . and arrived early. Support and assistance for the march came from various quarters. The National Council of Churches contributed 80,000 box lunches, while the U.S. Army advised on how to set up thousands of restroom facilities.

Celebrities who had strong political and social consciences were drawn to the Movement. Black notables such as novelist James Baldwin (*center foreground*) and entertainer Harry Belafonte (*behind Baldwin*) spent much of their free time raising funds and making personal appearances on behalf of the civil rights struggle. The March on Washington attracted other celebrities who wanted to lend their name to the cause of equal rights, such as actors Marlon Brando (*right foreground*) and Charlton Heston (*left background*).

"We are tired. We are tired of being beaten by policemen. We are tired of seeing our people locked up in jail over and over again, and then you holler to be patient. How long can we be patient? We want our freedom and we want it now."

—SNCC CHAIRMAN JOHN LEWIS, DURING HIS MARCH ON WASHINGTON SPEECH

The first draft of John Lewis's March on Washington speech reflected SNCC's militancy. It called some political leaders "cheap." It said Movement people would march "through the heart of Dixie, the way [destructive Union Army General] Sherman did." And it asked the question, "Which side is the government on?" Movement leaders, trying to keep the Kennedy Administration as a march ally, were upset and demanded that Lewis cut those references. SNCC folks got hot. As he recalled the standoff, Lewis was ready to put up a fight. But A. Philip Randolph, looking "beaten down and tired," spoke his piece: "I've waited all my life for this opportunity. Please don't ruin it." Lewis relented, saying there was no way he could say no to such a "dignified plea."

# Bayard Rustin

BAYARD RUSTIN, A QUAKER, a pacifist, a conscientious objector, a member of the Communist Party for a time, and a homosexual, could never have been a public leader in the civil rights cause. But he did not have the temperament for that kind of leadership anyway. Possessed of a powerful intellect, Rustin was responsible for much of the thinking behind the Civil Rights Movement and was one of the major architects of its nonviolent protest tactics.

Born in Chester, Pennsylvania, in 1912, Rustin spent his early career working with the Quaker group Fellowship of Reconciliation (FOR). While organizing for FOR, he helped found the Congress of Racial Equality (CORE) to fight racial discrimination by using the techniques of nonviolent protest. He participated in CORE's first Freedom Rides in 1947.

When the Montgomery bus boycott began, Rustin traveled to the city to make sure the movement adhered to the philosophy of nonviolence. He later helped Martin Luther King establish the Southern Christian Leadership Conference. Working largely behind the scenes, Rustin planned and implemented the 1963 March on Washing-

ton, a feat only a man with his organizational talent could have pulled off. In later years, he ran the A. Philip Randolph Institute, working largely in the economic sphere, especially with labor unions.

## "I Have a Dream"

THE SPEECH THAT REVEREND Martin Luther King, Jr., delivered on the steps of the Lincoln Memorial during the 1963 March on Washington firmly established him as an extraordinary American leader. Relatively few people ever had heard King give a complete speech before. This one was carried live on national television.

King had intended a formal delivery of his prepared speech. Although in church he was known to take off on the wings of words and soar to great heights, he was not a preacher on this occasion. He was acting the part of a major civil rights leader on an important day. When he spoke the following words, however, he allowed his voice to rise and fall in preacher fashion: "We will not be satisfied until justice rolls down like waters and righteousness like a mighty stream." The crowd responded with such emotion that he knew he could not continue with his prepared speech.

King had planned to say, "And so today, let us go back to our communities as members of the international association for the advancement of creative dissatisfaction." He realized, however, that he should build on the emotion of the crowd, and so he departed from his text and began to preach. "I have a dream," he said, "that one day on the red hills of Georgia, sons of former slaves and sons of former slaveowners will be able to sit down together at the table of brotherhood. I have a dream that one day, even the state of Mississippi, a state sweltering with the heat of injustice, sweltering with the heat of oppression, will be transformed into an oasis of freedom and justice."

When King finished, the huge crowd, which filled the Washington Mall, was utterly silent, so overcome were they by King's words. Then, in a great rush of emotion, they cheered and wept openly. It was a defining moment of the Civil Rights Movement.

The extemporaneous end to King's "I Have a Dream" speech, a more polished version of what he had said at the Detroit march weeks earlier, moved the crowd more than the critical first two-thirds of the speech had. The ovation was a roar that would remain burned in the memories of those in attendance. King knew he had succeeded in providing a highlight to a spectacular day. King's supporters praised him enthusiastically as he left the podium. King then joined the other Movement leaders in a meeting with President John F. Kennedy.

President John F. Kennedy (*fourth from right*) met with Movement leaders after the March on Washington. National Urban League head Whitney Young (*fourth from left in foreground*), Martin Luther King (*fifth from left*), labor leader A. Philip Randolph (*left of Kennedy*), and NAACP Executive Secretary Roy Wilkins (*far right*) were among the leaders. Wilkins asked the administration to strengthen the civil rights bill in Congress. Randolph, meanwhile, talked about the increasing number of black school dropouts, which he saw as one result of black youths' loss of faith in whites, black leadership, God, and government.

This is the welcome Horace Baker and his wife, Sara, a black couple, got when they moved into an all-white neighborhood in Folcroft, Pennsylvania, in August 1963, just days after the March on Washington. Gerald Early, a black youngster who grew up in the state, remembered: "They were driven from the home twice that day by whites throwing bricks and bottles. That night, the whites pulled out all the plumbing fixtures in the home and wrecked the furnace and hot-water heater. The family finally moved in on Friday, but a mob of 1,500 whites stoned the house after they moved inside. Every window in the house was broken. The doors were virtually torn off the hinges. One hundred state troopers were required to prevent the mob from murdering or maiming the family."

The Movement was not just a fight for voting rights and desegregation. It was very much a fight to participate in America's economic mainstream. In St. Louis on August 31, 1963, black activists protested against the Jefferson Bank and Trust's lack of black employees. The demonstrators later flooded into the bank and stopped business.

Many white Americans, such as these women marching outside Chicago City Hall in September 1963, felt that a gain for African-Americans would mean a blow to their rights. The women protested an ordinance that would have made discrimination in real estate illegal, asking instead for a referendum. They opposed the ordinance because they felt that the desegregation of their neighborhoods would lower their property values and their quality of life. Such opinions—later expressed by "white flight," when whites left desegregated neighborhoods—continue to be expressed in the 21st century.

While Martin Luther King talked hopefully about blacks and whites someday sitting down at the table of brotherhood, author James Baldwin expressed a different viewpoint in his essay *The Fire Next Time* (1963). Baldwin warned that if white America did not change its attitude and policies, blacks eventually would revolt: "The Negroes of this country may never be able to rise to power, but they are very well placed indeed to precipitate chaos and ring down the curtain on the American dream." The book was prophetic; from 1964 through 1968, race riots raged in cities all over America.

# Birmingham Church Bombing

ON SUNDAY, SEPTEMBER 15, 1963, four girls, ages 11 to 14, attended the Sixteenth Street Baptist Church in Birmingham, Alabama, preparing for the annual Youth Sunday service. At 10:22 A.M., a bomb exploded, killing the girls instantly and wounding 20 other people, many of them also children.

The bombing, the deadliest single act during the Civil Rights Movement, revealed the growing hostility of segregationists toward the campaign for equal rights in the South. The Sixteenth Street Church had been a center for civil rights organizing and was serving that function at the time, trying to desegregate Birmingham schools. The city had suffered seven other bombings in the previous six months, living up to the nickname "Bombingham" that it had earned in the 1950s.

The bombing galvanized world and national opinion against white racist violence as never before—although that was not the case among many white officials in Birmingham. While an eyewitness reported seeing four men plant the bomb, police made only one arrest: Ku Klux Klan member Robert "Dynamite Bob" Chambliss, who was released shortly after being taken into custody. No further arrests were made for 14 years.

In 1977 the Alabama attorney general reopened the case and charged Chambliss again. Convicted of first-degree murder, he died in prison at age 81 in 1985. A sec-

Chris and Maxine McNair with photo of daughter Denise

ond prime suspect, Frank Herman Cash, died in 1994 at the age of 75 without ever having been formally charged.

In 2000 U.S. Attorney Doug Jones prepared to try the two remaining suspects, Bobby Frank Cherry and Thomas Edwin Blanton, Jr., for the bombing. On May 1, 2001, a racially mixed jury took less than two hours to convict Blanton of first-degree murder. He was sentenced to life in prison. A year later Cherry, too, received a life sentence for murder. Nearly 40 years after the horrible crime, justice, though delayed, was done.

The fourth bombing in Birmingham in four weeks took place on Sunday, September 15, 1963, during Youth Day at Sixteenth Street Baptist Church. The blast was so strong that two cars were flattened and all the windows were blown out in the church and in nearby buildings. Four girls were killed and at least 20 were injured. Those who survived looked like they came out of World War II-era London. People dug in the ashes, looking for their loved ones. Family members of the four girls eventually saw their bodies in a makeshift morgue.

Denise McNair, 11, loved to play with dolls. Carole Robinson, 14, had just registered for junior high. She was an avid reader who played the clarinet. Addie Mae Collins, 14, was such a nature lover that she convinced family and friends to hold a funeral for a dead bird, complete with singing, a casket, and a burial. Cynthia Diane Wesley, 14, would have been a church-service usher for the first time that Sunday. She was adopted. Her father was the principal of a school. All four girls (*pictured left to right*) were victims of the racist bomb blast at Sixteenth Street Baptist Church.

"[The victims] weren't children. Children are little people, little human beings, and that means white people.... They're just little niggers, and if there's four less niggers tonight, then I say, 'Good for whoever planted the bomb.'"

—Reverend Connie Lynch, white supremacist

Connie Lynch toured the South in a coral-colored Cadillac to stir the cauldron of race and religious hatred. A Klansman, Lynch founded the National States Rights Party.

America was outraged by the bombing of the Sixteenth Street Baptist Church. Black children were not safe even in the house of God! Anyone who naively thought that the Birmingham campaign and the March on Washington somehow began to "solve" the problem of black rights now knew that nothing was out of bounds for the Movement's enemies. These protesters in New York City felt Alabama Governor George Wallace should be held responsible for the injustices in his state.

# 1960s

## 1963

**September 15:** Klansmen bomb the Sixteenth Street Baptist Church in Birmingham, killing four black girls and injuring 20 others. *See* November 18, 1977.

**September 18:** In St. Augustine, Florida, four NAACP members are dragged from their car and viciously beaten with chains, wrenches, and ax handles. Four KKK members will be acquitted by an all-white jury.

**September 29:** Following a desegregation order, every white student in Tuskegee (Alabama) High School withdraws, leaving only five black students. For the rest of the century, black students in Macon will attend Tuskegee and whites will attend a local private school, Macon Academy.

**September 28–October 1:** More than 1,000 protesters of segregation are arrested in Orangeburg, South Carolina.

**October 22:** In Chicago, 220,000 students boycott classes to protest *de facto* segregation in the city's public schools.

**November 7:** More than 70,000 disenfranchised black citizens cast "freedom ballots" in a mock election in Mississippi. The demonstration is staged to prove that black Mississippians want to vote.

**November 9–10:** In Detroit, the Northern Negro Grass Roots Leadership Conference is held. Malcolm X delivers his "A Message to the Grass Roots" speech.

**November 22:** President Kennedy is assassinated in Dallas. Vice President Lyndon B. Johnson becomes president.

Orangeburg, South Carolina, began its desegregation campaign in July 1963. By the time this water hose was readied at the Orangeburg County jail compound on September 30, hundreds of civil rights protesters had been arrested. As in Birmingham, large numbers of students and young people participated in the Orangeburg demonstrations. In one week, more than 1,000 students from a local college and high school were arrested for protesting.

In 1963 a federal court ordered several Alabama school systems, including Birmingham's, to desegregate by September of that year. Governor George Wallace mobilized state troopers—and later the Alabama National Guard—to prevent desegregation. He was joined in his beliefs by parents of Birmingham's Graymont School (*pictured*), many of whom took their kids out of school after two black students were registered on September 4. That same day near Graymont School, rioting broke out and a black attorney's home was bombed. After President John F. Kennedy federalized the Alabama National Guard on September 10, Wallace had no choice but to allow desegregation.

Sonnie Hereford IV is escorted by his father to his first day of class in the formerly all-white Fifth Avenue Elementary School in Huntsville, Alabama. Fifth Avenue was one of four Huntsville schools that desegregated in September 1963, the same month as the bombing of the Sixteenth Street Baptist Church.

Schools in Montgomery, Alabama, were going to be desegregated, but it didn't mean that everyone would like it. These teenage girls (*left photo*) screamed obscenities in front of their high school, which was desegregated in September 1963. For many in the city's white community, the federal court order to desegregate was paramount to a second siege of the South by northern carpetbaggers. One of the black girls who would desegregate the school (*right photo*) likely knew she would become the object of ridicule and hatred.

# 1960s

The whites in Montgomery, Alabama, who were against desegregation felt their world was crumbling right before their eyes. They felt that they were no longer in control of their own communities, their own culture. In the minds of the white racists, the federal government—and its "agents," Jews and Communists, they reasoned—was responsible for the South losing its sovereignty.

These four leaders of the National States Rights Party, a white group that encouraged southern resistance to desegregation, were indicted in September 1963 by a federal grand jury on charges of interfering with court-ordered school desegregation. Jack Cash (*far left*) was part of a KKK group that often hung out at his restaurant. The group included Thomas Blanton, Robert "Dynamite Bob" Chambliss, and Bobby Cherry, all of whom would be convicted years later for the 1963 bombing murders of the four girls at Sixteenth Street Baptist Church in Birmingham.

The state of South Carolina held on to segregation for as long as it could. Nine years of legal agitation after the 1954 *Brown v. Board of Education* ruling were needed to get black students into South Carolina's Jim Crowed high schools. Some whites retaliated against desegregation. When parents in Columbia and other areas of the state signed a petition asking for students to be admitted on a "nondiscriminatory basis," blacks in one town, Estill, discovered that their credit was no good and their rent money was no longer accepted.

The white racist idea that *black* meant *inferior* knew no geographic or ethnic bounds. White ethnics in America's working-class neighborhoods, such as Queens, New York, could be as virulently against racial integration as southern whites. These four women were arrested on October 1, 1963, after staging a three-week sit-in at P. S. (Public School) 137 in Queens's Laurelton section. Redistricting had led to the desegregation of Laurelton's all-white schools.

A sit-in protest (*left photo*) did not just mean sitting down somewhere. It was claiming a space for the Movement by not budging until the protest was over. These protests often would end when an officer physically removed a protester from the premises. Because Gandhian philosophy called for noncooperation with evil, the protester would refuse to move, meaning the officer would have to physically drag a protester to jail. Here, New Orleans police officers haul away Reverend Avery Alexander, who was protesting against the city's racial policies in the City Hall cafeteria on Halloween, 1963.

Dr. Joseph H. Jackson, pastor of Chicago's Olivet Baptist Church and president of the National Baptist Convention, did not believe in civil disobedience. Thus, he was not in favor of the school boycotts that Movement activists were organizing in 1964 in Boston, New York, and Chicago. The boycotts were designed to pressure  the school boards in those cities to desegregate the schools. Jackson knew that it was mandatory for children to attend school, so he could not in good conscience support them. Jackson said that the struggle needed to stay within the framework of law and order, or else "anarchy awaits us." These activists, protesting in Chicago in February 1964, felt that Jackson was behind the times.

# 1960s

## 1964

**1964:** The United Nations Subcommission on Prevention of Discrimination and Protection of Minorities selects Atlanta as the focus of its investigation of racism in the American South.

**1964:** *Nothing But a Man*, an honest film about prejudice in the South, is released.

**January 3:** Martin Luther King appears on the cover of *Time* as "Man of the Year."

**January 13:** A Louisiana law that requires the race of a political candidate to be printed on the ballots is invalidated by the U.S. Supreme Court.

**January 17 and 26:** Comedian Dick Gregory and SNCC lead demonstrators in Atlanta, protesting segregation in hotels, restaurants, and other public facilities.

**January 21:** Carl Rowan is named director of the U.S. Information Agency—the highest federal position ever held by a black American up to this time.

**January 23:** The United States Congress ratifies the 24th Amendment to the Constitution, prohibiting any poll tax in elections for federal officials.

**February 3:** Thousands demonstrate in New York City to protest racial imbalances in schools, while a half-million New York City students protest by staying home from classes.

**February 4:** Austin T. Walden becomes the first black judge in Georgia in the 20th century.

**February 11:** In Cincinnati, 19,000 students boycott school in a protest led by the NAACP and CORE. ➤

In 1964 the New York City public school system was more segregated than it had been at the time of the *Brown* decision 10 years earlier. In response, local civil rights leaders staged pro-integration boycotts and marches in February and March. Although the marches were well attended in black communities, they were countered by demonstrations staged by whites who advocated "neighborhood schools." The movement to desegregate the city's public school system stalled by mid-decade, replaced by a campaign for local control of schools in black communities.

*Muhammad Speaks* was more than just an organ of and a fundraising vehicle for the Nation of Islam. Founded by NOI Minister Malcolm X in 1960 in his basement, the newspaper spread the word of the Honorable Elijah Muhammad, the leader of the religious organization. Sold by NOI followers on major street corners in black America, it introduced many black Americans to the teachings of the Nation. The newspaper featured the section "What Muslims Believe," which clearly explained the organization's goals and beliefs. By 1964 the paper, run by the Nation's national office in Chicago, was defaming Malcolm after his split from the Nation.

In urban areas in the 1960s, black radio stations began to broadcast talk shows that took an active interest in the Civil Rights Movement. Black broadcasters such as Georgie Woods in Philadelphia, Martha Jean "The Queen" Steinberg in Detroit, and Nat Williams in Memphis educated their audiences about the Movement. Both Martin Luther King and Malcolm X (*left*) would befriend many of these radio hosts, allowing those leaders, for the first time, to reach thousands of black Americans simultaneously. George Schuyler (*right*), an iconoclastic columnist for *The Pittsburgh Courier,* broadcast on Harlem's WLIB.

One of the sad ironies of the Civil Rights Movement is that it often took the arrest, abuse, or death of white activists to call attention to the terrorism whites inflicted on blacks. The violence in St. Augustine, Florida, provoked a strong response by Mrs. Malcolm Peabody (*center*), the mother of Massachusetts Governor Endicott Peabody, as she staged a sit-in at St. Augustine's Ponce De Leon Hotel on March 31, 1964. Her arrest made national headlines and led to her interview on NBC's *Today* show. It shone the national spotlight on St. Augustine as a city burning with racism.

A new civil rights bill that would outlaw legalized segregation, the ardent goal of President Lyndon Johnson, was stalled in the Senate in spring 1964. The bill was sent from the House directly to the Senate calendar in an attempt by Senate leaders to move it past the Senate Judiciary Committee. Southern Democratic senators tried to sink the bill by organizing the longest filibuster—the process of delaying the vote of a bill by making long speeches on the floor—in Senate history. The filibuster began on March 9 and lasted for more than two months. Northern Democrats used the time to successfully find Republican votes for the bill. Pictured here are Democratic senators (*left to right*) Sam Ervin (North Carolina), James Eastland (Mississippi), Allen Ellender (Louisiana), Harry Byrd (Virginia), and Olin Johnston (South Carolina).

# 1960s

## 1964

**February 13:** Former Vice President Richard Nixon criticizes the "irresponsible tactics" of civil rights leaders. He says that civil disobedience, demonstrations, boycotts, and violations of property rights will hurt the cause in the long run.

**February 26:** Maryland State College students demonstrating for civil rights are dispersed by state troopers and police dogs, which inflict severe bite wounds on 14 people.

**March:** In Atlanta, militant black activist Jeremiah X and an integrated group of SNCC members invade and disrupt a KKK rally.

**March 5:** In Frankfort, Kentucky, Martin Luther King leads a 10,000-person march in support of the passage of a state public accommodations law.

**March 8:** Malcolm X leaves the Nation of Islam and establishes the Muslim Mosque, Inc.

**March 23–24:** After two weeks of unsuccessful sit-ins in Jacksonville, Florida, violence erupts after a black woman is shot and killed. About 400 people are arrested.

**March 24:** Amiri Baraka's groundbreaking play *Dutchman*, in which racial injustice is portrayed in the interaction between a black man and a white woman who share a subway car, opens in New York City.

**March 26:** In Washington, D.C., Martin Luther King and Malcolm X meet for the first and only time.

**April 3:** In Cleveland, Malcolm X delivers his famous "The Ballot or the Bullet" speech.  ➤

On January 29, 1964, protesters in Cleveland demanded integration of the city's public schools, which were overcrowded in the black neighborhoods. Whites attacked protesters that day, but a week later the Board of Education agreed to integrate the city's schools immediately. The decision was to bus black students to white schools but keep the black children completely separated from the white kids while in the schools. In April 1964 black students stayed home from school to protest what they felt was a racist decision. Civil rights activists created "Freedom Schools," such as the one seen here, as substitutes.

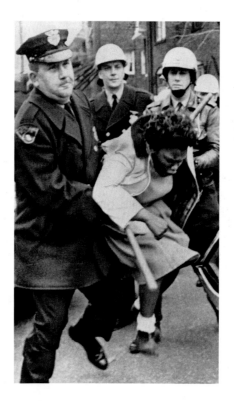

By 1964, relations were boiling between the blacks who had moved up north to Cleveland and the city's working-class ethnic whites. The city made it worse when it decided to deal with its overcrowded public schools by building a new school in one of the city's black neighborhoods. The local CORE chapter balked, saying the scenario would reinforce *de facto* school segregation. Soon, protests began at the site. One of the demonstrators was Reverend Bruce W. Klunder, a white man who was assistant pastor of the city's Church of the Covenant. He attempted to block a bulldozer on April 7 by lying down behind it. The driver didn't see him, and crushed Klunder to death. The reverend's noble sacrifice and violent death begat violence the next day (*pictured*). An interracial committee successfully quashed the tension.

Hundreds of activists, led by CORE, protested in and around the World's Fair in Queens, New York, in April 1964. Besides picketing on the grounds, protesters blocked traffic with "stall-ins" and clogged entrances to subways, leading to numerous arrests. The protests were strongly criticized, even by Movement leaders. In a speech, however, Martin Luther King said the nation's white power structure should be as vigorous in denouncing the Senate's stall-in of the civil rights bill as it was in criticizing CORE's efforts.

Pennsylvania state police use their nightsticks at this failed sit-in demonstration in Chester, Pennsylvania, in April 1964. The city, which was one of the many that witnessed race riots in 1918, ironically was the home of Crozer Theological Seminary, the school that Martin Luther King had attended as a graduate student.

# Robert Moses

BORN IN HARLEM IN 1935, Robert Parris Moses was teaching in New York City and working toward a Ph.D. at Harvard when he left it all to join the Civil Rights Movement. He eventually became the leading activist in Mississippi, the most dangerous of all civil rights playing fields.

Moses first worked as a recruiter for SNCC in 1960 and traveled on the organization's behalf to recruit more members. He participated in the Freedom Rides in May 1961 and started a voter-registration education project in Mississippi that summer. Concerned about competition between SNCC and other civil rights organizations in Mississippi, Moses helped establish the Council of Federated Organizations (COFO) to coordinate civil rights efforts in the state.

A founder of the Mississippi Freedom Democratic Party, Moses also continued his concentration on voter education and registration in the state. As one of the chief architects of Freedom Summer in 1964, Moses led the establishment of "freedom schools" and oversaw a network of more than a thousand volunteers. They persevered despite dozens of shootings, beatings, and bombings that summer.

In 1966, after Stokely Carmichael assumed the chairmanship of SNCC and issued a call for "Black Power," Moses resigned from the organization. He traveled to Africa, completed his Ph.D. at Harvard, and in 1982 created the Algebra Project, a new way to teach math to urban children that has been adopted by school systems in several states.

# 1960s

## 1964

**April 7:** African-American Louis Allen is murdered near Liberty, Mississippi. Allen reportedly was considering testifying against E. H. Hurst, who had shot and killed civil rights activist Herbert Lee on September 25, 1961. Hurst was acquitted.

**April 13:** For his work in *Lilies of the Field*, Sidney Poitier becomes the first African-American to win an Oscar for Best Actor.

**April 20:** About 86 percent of Cleveland's black students boycott school for a day in protest of discrimination.

**April 22:** The Brooklyn chapter of CORE attempts a "stall-in" on the first day of the World's Fair in New York. Inside, members of national CORE demonstrate.

**April 26:** SNCC members form the Mississippi Freedom Democratic Party (MFDP) as an alternative Democratic party in Mississippi. *See* August 22–27, 1964.

**April–September:** Multiple house bombings are reported in McComb, Mississippi.

**May 25:** In *Griffin v. Prince Edward County School Board*, the U.S. Supreme Court rules that it's unconstitutional for a city to close all of its public schools, which Prince Edward County, Virginia, had done to circumvent segregation.

**June:** Martin Luther King and the SCLC stage citywide demonstrations in St. Augustine, Florida, but repeatedly are met with hostilities from the Ku Klux Klan and other white racists.

**June:** AFL–CIO President George Meany urges union leaders to apply "economic pressure" on employees who refuse to provide fair employment opportunities for African-Americans. ➤

Nashville, Tennessee, was still a prominent site for civil rights protests in 1964. Activists such as 22-year-old Bertha Gilbert (*pictured*) still targeted lunch counters and restaurants for desegregation. Gilbert was arrested on May 6, 1964, on a disorderly conduct charge. Tensions in Nashville increased after a local movement leader was arrested and beaten by police.

In Nashville, authorities squeeze 36 demonstrators into one paddy wagon during a 1964 protest after local movement leaders vowed to fill the city's jails. As the 1960s progressed, jail packing took its toll on southern cities. Police departments found it difficult to process, house, and feed dozens and sometimes hundreds of civil rights activists.

# Malcolm X

A S A NATIONAL SPOKESMAN for the black separatist Nation of Islam, Malcolm X often contrasted his own advocacy of self-defense with the nonviolent tactics of Martin Luther King. Reacting to the Birmingham demonstrations of spring 1963, he remarked that if a four-legged dog or a "two-legged dog" attacked an African-American, he should be killed. Since becoming a follower of Elijah Muhammad during the early 1950s, Malcolm had denounced "white devils" and ridiculed efforts to achieve racial integration. "Respect as *human beings*! That's what America's black masses want," he explained.

Born in 1925, Malcolm Little had felt the sting of racism at an early age. He suspected his father's death in 1931 was the work of a white supremacist group angered by Earl Little's work on behalf of black nationalist Marcus Garvey. As a teenager, Malcolm quit school and moved from Lansing, Michigan, to Boston, where he engaged in criminal activities that eventually landed him in prison. There, Malcolm joined the Nation of Islam.

Malcolm in Birmingham, May 1963

Following his release from prison in 1952, Malcolm dropped his "slave name" of Little and became Malcolm X. The young minister quickly earned a reputation for his forceful, cogent calls for black pride and militancy. Even as he publicly challenged King's leadership, however, Malcolm also became increasingly discontented with the Nation of Islam's "nonengagement" policy that isolated the religious group from the increasingly massive black protest movement. He explained, "I felt that, wherever black people committed themselves, in the Little Rocks and the Birminghams and other places, militantly disciplined Muslims should also be there—for all the world to see, and respect, and discuss."

During 1963 Malcolm began to establish close ties with some of the "grassroots" local leaders of the black struggle. He lambasted the March on Washington as a "picnic"—a "Farce on Washington"—compromised by the participation of national civil rights leaders and their white allies. Malcolm's ties with his own organization deteriorated during 1963 after he learned of Elijah Muhammad's illegitimate children. However, the final break came after Malcolm referred to President John F. Kennedy's assassination as a case of "chickens coming home to roost."

After Muhammad suspended him and ordered him to refrain from public statements, Malcolm at first acquiesced and then in March 1964 announced that he was leaving the Nation of Islam. He formed the Muslim Mosque, Inc., before making a pilgrimage to Mecca that spring—an experience that pushed his racial perspective away from Muhammad's separatism and moderated his attitudes toward whites. Stating that he hoped to cooperate with non-Islamic political groups, Malcolm formed the Organization of Afro-American Unity (OAAU) in June 1964.

Malcolm established ties with members of SNCC. In February 1965 he journeyed to Selma, Alabama, where a voting rights campaign was underway. He stated that he supported the activists but did not believe in nonviolent protest.

Meanwhile, Malcolm's increasingly pointed criticisms of Elijah Muhammad further soured his relations with the Nation of Islam. On February 21, 1965, a few months after being labeled a traitor by his former protégé, Louis X (later Louis Farrakhan), members of the Nation of Islam assassinated Malcolm X. Malcolm's ideas lived on, however, in his published speeches and the best-selling *The Autobiography of Malcolm X*.

Although King's views differed from Malcolm's, he nonetheless offered a posthumous tribute: "He was an eloquent spokesman for his point of view, and no one can honestly doubt that Malcolm had a great concern for the problems that we face as a race."

# 1960s

In spring 1964 SCLC leaders targeted St. Augustine, Florida, in the campaign to kill and bury Jim Crow. The violence whites inflicted on blacks in St. Augustine had been discussed in Movement circles, and it came to public attention when prominent whites began to be arrested. Martin Luther King ventured to St. Augustine and rented a cottage, which was fired upon on May 28, 1964, while he was away at a meeting. King, who called the city lawless, was protected by armed guards during his stay in St. Augustine.

"OK, this is acid. Acid! If you don't get out, I'll pour it in the water."

—JAMES BROCK, MANAGER OF MONSON MOTOR LODGE IN ST. AUGUSTINE, FLORIDA

Martin Luther King and Ralph Abernathy were among those arrested for protesting segregation at the Monson Motor Lodge in St. Augustine, Florida. On June 18, 1964, Abernathy and other protesters returned to desegregate the pool. "You can't do that. Get out!" screamed motel manager James Brock. They didn't move. Brock came back with a container of hydrochloric acid. "OK," he said, "this is acid. Acid! If you don't get out, I'll pour it in the water." They didn't, so he did. (The next day, Brock deposited an alligator in the pool to discourage activists.) Brock was angry enough about the intrusion to also attack Movement-sympathetic rabbis who were holding a prayer service in the parking lot (*left photo*).

To many southern whites, sharing a swimming pool with African-Americans was as unthinkable as sharing the same bathrooms. As the protesters got ready to enter the Monson Motor Lodge pool, recalled SCLC leader Ralph Abernathy, the whites "stared at us with uncomprehending eyes, telling themselves we weren't going to do what it appeared we would do." The whites quickly climbed out of the pool when it was clear what was going to happen. The hydrochloric acid that manager James Brock poured into the water did not deter the protesters. The police were summoned. When they arrived, the swimmers huddled in the center of the pool until one man dove in to drag them out.

The controversy over the Monson Motor Lodge "wade-in" hadn't yet subsided when white beachgoers clashed with black Movement protesters on a "whites only" beach in St. Augustine on June 25. State troopers, called in to restore order, physically abused some of the whites. A furious Klan returned to town and attacked both the troopers and the black protesters. Wrote the SCLC's Ralph Abernathy: "St. Augustine . . . put us on notice that the violence we experienced during our marches in Birmingham was by no means the worst we could expect." The SCLC soon pulled out of St. Augustine to focus on other concerns.

# Freedom Summer

IN JUNE 1964, SNCC organizer Robert Moses spoke to volunteers at a Freedom Summer Project training session. Moses instructed them not to go south that summer to save the Mississippi Negro. He told them to go only if they truly understood that "his freedom and yours are one."

About three-quarters of the approximately 1,000 Freedom Summer volunteers were white, northern college students from middle- and upper-class backgrounds, most of whom were unprepared for what they found when they arrived in Mississippi.

The training sessions in Oxford, Ohio, were intended to prepare the volunteers to register black voters, teach at "Freedom Schools," and assist in other ways in the ongoing efforts of the Council of Federated Organizations (COFO), a coalition of Mississippi civil rights groups. Simply by being in the state, the volunteers working under Moses's leadership would, it was hoped, draw the nation's attention to the violent repression of voting rights activism and perhaps prod the federal government to intervene. The project also aimed to develop a grassroots freedom movement that could be sustained after student activists left Mississippi. Moses was realistic about his goals, saying that just getting through the summer alive would be an accomplishment.

The presence of the volunteers marked the greatest number of people to enter the southern struggle at one time, but many black civil rights workers, namely SNCC members, were ambivalent about working with the white volunteers. These tensions were intensified by the COFO staff's awareness that only violence perpetrated against the white students would prompt any meaningful federal intervention.

Children read in a Freedom Summer library.

The violence against both black and white volunteers was severe. More than 60 black churches, businesses, and homes were burned or bombed. Dozens of blacks and whites were beaten by white mobs or police, and more than 1,000 volunteers were arrested.

On June 21 three civil rights workers were reported missing. African-American James Chaney and whites Michael Schwerner and Andrew Goodman had disappeared while visiting a town near Philadelphia, Mississippi, to investigate the burning of a black church. The abduction of the three civil rights workers intensified the activists' fears, but staff and volunteers moved ahead with the summer campaign.

The Freedom Schools were developed to address the separate-but-unequal Mississippi school system. In 1964 state educational expenditures averaged $81.66 per white student and $21.77 per black student. Further, during the fall cotton harvest many of the black schools in the Delta were closed, since black children provided cheap labor. Classroom curriculum was carefully controlled, and state-selected textbooks ignored the significant achievements of black Americans.

The project established 41 Freedom Schools, and more than 3,000 young black students took classes that summer. In addition to math, reading, and other traditional courses, they were taught black history, the philosophy of the Civil Rights Movement, and leadership skills.

Freedom Summer teacher Pam Parker wrote of her experience. She stated that the atmosphere in her classroom was "unbelievable," as students expressed genuine enthusiasm and an unquenchable desire to learn. She wrote that she went home every night drained and exhausted, but in high spirits.

Voter registration served as the cornerstone of the Summer Project. The fact that approximately 17,000 black residents of Mississippi attempted to vote revealed the persistence of the volunteers and the extraordinary courage of those attempting to register. While only 1,600 of the completed applications were accepted by the registrars, the inequities uncovered throughout the course of the summer helped to highlight the need for legislation—and helped generate momentum for the Voting Rights Act of 1965.

SNCC leaders also set their sights on the Mississippi Freedom Democratic Party (MFDP), an alternative to the Mississippi "Jim Crow" Democratic Party. The goal of the MFDP was to challenge the seating of the all-white Mississippi delegation at the 1964 Democratic National Convention in Atlantic City. The MFDP planned to challenge the seats traditionally held by white Mississippians by arguing that the MFDP delegates belonged to the only freely chosen party in the state, as blacks had been systematically denied access to choosing delegates in the Mississippi Democratic Party.

On August 4 the MFDP challenge gained increased attention when the bodies of the three missing civil rights workers were found in Philadelphia, Mississippi. Goodman, Schwerner, and Chaney had been shot, and Chaney also had been brutally beaten. Media attention refocused on Mississippi just 18 days before the start of the Democratic National Convention.

In an effort to persuade members of the Credentials Committee to vote in their favor, the MFDP offered testimony regarding the difficulty blacks had voting in Mississippi. Fannie Lou Hamer, the daughter of Mississippi sharecroppers, gave an impassioned speech to the committee. President Lyndon Johnson, hoping to avoid dissension within the Democratic ranks, hastily called a press conference in an effort to shift attention away from Atlantic City. Nevertheless, the evening television news showed portions of Hamer's testimony that evening. Her emotional remarks moved people throughout the nation, prompting the president to arrange a compromise.

Johnson offered MFDP delegates the right to participate vocally in the convention proceedings but not vote;

Two youths in Hattiesburg contribute to Freedom Summer.

MFDP leaders quickly rejected the compromise. A new compromise was then offered: The MFDP would receive two at-large seats at the convention while the other delegates would be accepted as "guests." In addition, the convention in 1968 would bar any subsequent state delegation that discriminated against blacks. After hours of discussion, the compromise was overwhelmingly rejected. The offer split civil rights adherents. Martin Luther King supported the compromise; younger activists did not.

While the Mississippi Freedom Democratic Party members did not fully realize their goals, their efforts were not in vain. They showed African-Americans that they could exert some measure of political power and put a spotlight on the issue of voting rights, reminding Americans that the recently passed Civil Rights Act was not enough.

While certainly not without internal conflicts and setbacks, the 1964 Summer Project symbolized the southern freedom struggle's ideals of nonviolence and interracialism. Moreover, the volunteers (such as Students for a Democratic Society leader Tom Hayden) brought much of what they learned that summer into later social justice movements. The project also changed the lives of many black Mississippians. Reflecting on the summer, Robert Moses concluded, "What the project really accomplished was that it brought Mississippi, for better or worse, up to the level of the rest of the country."

## Triple Murder in Mississippi

On Sunday, June 21, 1964, three civil rights workers drove to Lawndale, Mississippi, to investigate the burning of a black church there. Andrew Goodman and Michael Schwerner were white and from New York. James Chaney was a black Mississippian. All were in their 20s and working as volunteers for the Mississippi Freedom Summer project. Each had just returned from Ohio, where they had attended a three-day training session sponsored by the National Council of Churches.

Around 3 P.M., as the three were returning to Meridian from Lawndale, their car was stopped by Cecil Price, deputy sheriff of Meridian. Charged with speeding, the men were taken to jail but released later that night. What happened next is not known. They failed to check in at Freedom Summer headquarters, whereupon the local police, the FBI, and the Justice Department were quickly notified and a mas-

**MISSING** CALL FBI

THE FBI IS SEEKING INFORMATION CONCERNING THE DISAPPEARANCE A PHILADELPHIA, MISSISSIPPI, OF THESE THREE INDIVIDUALS ON JUNE 21, 1964. EXTENSIVE INVESTIGATION IS BEING CONDUCTED TO LOCATE GOODMAN, CHANEY, AND SCHWERNE WHO ARE DESCRIBED AS FOLLOWS:

ANDREW GOODMAN · JAMES EARL CHANEY · MICHAEL HENRY SCHWERNE

SHOULD YOU HAVE OR IN THE FUTURE RECEIVE ANY INFORMATION CONCERNING THE WHEREABOUTS OF THESE INDIVIDUALS, YOU ARE REQUESTED TO NOTIFY ME OR THE NEAREST OFFICE OF THE FBI. TELEPHONE NUMBER IS LISTED BELOW.

DIRECTOR
FEDERAL BUREAU OF INVESTIGATION
UNITED STATES DEPARTMENT OF JUSTIC
WASHINGTON, D. C. 20535
TELEPHONE, NATIONAL 8-7117

June 29, 1964

sive search began. Finally, after six weeks and intense national media coverage, the three bodies were discovered in an earthen dam on a farm outside Philadelphia, Mississippi, on August 4. All three had been shot, and the skull of the sole black victim, Chaney, had been fractured in a savage beating.

Not until December did the FBI make any arrests in connection with the killings. Deputy Sheriff Price and Sheriff Lawrence Rainey were among the 21 Mississippians, most of whom were members of the Ku Klux Klan, taken into custody. All charges were subsequently dropped in state court. The Justice Department then brought charges against the men for violating federal civil rights laws. Sheriff Rainey was among those men acquitted. Price and six others were convicted and received prison sentences ranging from four to 10 years. The convictions in the case were the first in Mississippi for the killing of a civil rights worker.

Freedom Summer volunteers James Chaney, Andrew Goodman, and Michael Schwerner disappeared on June 21, 1964. Two days later, their station wagon was discovered in a swamp near Philadelphia, Mississippi. Their dead bodies were found on August 4. Dave Dennis, a Mississippi field secretary for CORE, was asked to give Chaney's eulogy but was told by the national office to keep it cool. He agreed. "Then when I got up there," he said, "and I looked out there and I saw little Ben Chaney [James's younger brother], things just sort of snapped and I was in a fantasy world, to be sitting up here talking about things gonna get better, and we should do it in a easy manner, and with nonviolence and stuff like that." At the pulpit, Dennis could not hold back his rage. The dying—the *killing*—of Movement people seemed as if it would never end, and he was sick of telling black people that someday they would overcome.

"Although you may be as white as a sheet, you will become as black as tar.... You're going to be classified into two groups in Mississippi: niggers and nigger-lovers. And they're tougher on nigger-lovers."

—AFRICAN-AMERICAN ATTORNEY R. JESS BROWN, IN A SPEECH TO FREEDOM SUMMER PROJECT VOLUNTEERS, JUNE 18, 1964

It was hard keeping the different Movement organizations coordinated. Sometimes, umbrella organizations had to be created, such as the Council of Federated Organizations, a Mississippi-based coalition of local SNCC, SCLC, CORE, and NAACP workers. In 1963 COFO hosted a mock election as a protest against the barring of the ballot to African-Americans. In 1964 the organization, comprised mostly of SNCC workers, coordinated Freedom Summer, the Movement's massive interracial student campaign.

During the Freedom Summer campaign in Mississippi in 1964, northern whites joined with local black SNCC members as volunteers. Here, two volunteers work at one of the local headquarters, Freedom House, in Vicksburg. Volunteers conducted literacy and voter education programs, and they set up Freedom Schools to provide politically engaged instruction to black children. Volunteers also established community service centers in black neighborhoods.

Relationships between northern white volunteers and local African-Americans during the Freedom Summer campaign were complex. Blacks feared reprisals from Mississippi whites if they cooperated with the volunteers, most of whom would be leaving the state when the summer ended. In addition, vast gulfs of class and culture separated rural, impoverished blacks and the middle-class, college-educated volunteers. Despite these barriers, whites were able to forge bonds with area children through Freedom Schools, which were notable for incorporating black history and culture into their curricula.

# Warm Memories of Freedom Summer

FOR BLACK PEOPLE in Mississippi, Freedom Summer was the beginning of a whole new era. People began to feel that they wasn't just helpless anymore, that they had come together. Black and white had come from the North...and we wasn't a closed society anymore. They came to talk about that we had a right to register to vote, we had a right to stand up for our rights. That's a whole new era for us. I mean, hadn't anybody said that to us, in that open way, like what happened in 1964.

There was interaction of blacks and whites. I remember cooking some pinto beans—that's all we had—and everybody just got around the pot...sitting on the floor, sitting anywhere...and they was talking and we was sitting there laughing, and I guess they became very real and very human, we each to one another. It was an experience that will last a lifetime.

—*Unita Blackwell, member of SNCC*

# 1960s

## 1964

**Summer:** SNCC's Bob Moses heads the Freedom Summer project in Mississippi. Thousands of people, many of whom are white college students from the North, help Mississippi's black citizens register to vote. Whites in the state react to the "threat" with shootings, bombings, beatings, and other acts of violence.

**June 21 and 23:** On their way back from investigating a burned-down church, Freedom Summer volunteers James Chaney, Andrew Goodman, and Michael Schwerner are arrested. After their release, they disappear. Two days later, their abandoned station wagon is found in a swamp near Philadelphia, Mississippi. *See* August 4, 1964.

**June 25:** Hundreds of whites attack an antisegregation march in St. Augustine, Florida. More than 50 African-Americans are injured.

**June 28:** Malcolm X cofounds the Organization of Afro-American Unity.

**July 2:** President Lyndon Johnson signs the Civil Rights Act of 1964. The act bans discrimination in places of public accommodations; bars unequal voter registration requirements; gives the U.S. attorney general more power to file lawsuits in order to protect citizens against discrimination; requires the elimination of discrimination in federally assisted programs; establishes the Equal Employment Opportunity Commission (EEOC); and authorizes the commissioner of education to help communities desegregate schools.

**July 10:** FBI director J. Edgar Hoover opens an FBI office in Jackson, Mississippi. While staff members will pursue the disappearance of civil rights activists, they will also keep tabs on activists. ➤

At the City College of New York on May 21, 1964, Ross Barnett (*pictured, right photo*), the segregationist former governor of Mississippi, argued against major civil rights legislation then pending in Congress. CORE demanded support from Senator Everett Dirksen (R–IL), a defender of civil rights who was justifiably irritated. In the House, the Rules Committee was controlled by Republicans who opposed the bill. Thanks largely to the efforts of President Johnson, Dirksen, and Senator Hubert Humphrey (D–MN), the bill, though compromised, got through Congress. LBJ signed it into law on July 2.

Clarence Mitchell, Jr., director of the NAACP's Washington bureau, became an effective lobbyist for civil rights bills, including the one that became the Civil Rights Act of 1964. He was so successful that some called him "The 101st Senator." Mitchell routinely walked the halls of the Senate, urging senators—pleasantly but emphatically—to push for civil rights legislation. He even had discussions with President Johnson. Joe Rauh, founder of Americans for Democratic Action, said that Mitchell didn't eat, drink, or rest because he was so committed to the cause.

On July 2, 1964, the barbers of the Hotel Muehlebach in Kansas City, Missouri, refused to cut the hair of 13-year-old Eugene Young (*pictured*). However, members of CORE, who were staying at the hotel while attending a local convention, protested firmly enough that the barbers reluctantly agreed to give Young a haircut. With more and more Americans supporting the Movement, activists by 1964 had more clout to handle such matters.

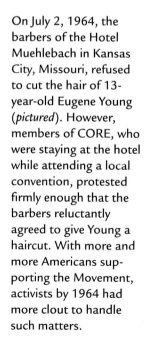

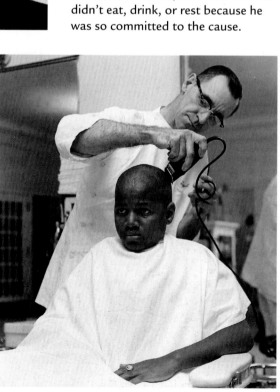

# Civil Rights Act of 1964

THE HEIGHTENED PACE OF civil rights protest in the early 1960s was met with a corresponding increase in violent response. After Birmingham firefighters blasted black children with fire hoses in spring 1963, President John F. Kennedy went on national television to urge Americans to guarantee equal treatment to every individual. Kennedy subsequently submitted a new civil rights bill to Congress.

One purpose of the March on Washington in August 1963 was to persuade members of Congress to support the civil rights bill. Major interest groups, including organized labor, lobbied on its behalf. Determined to thwart the passage of a strong bill, the southern bloc in Congress used every delaying tactic at its disposal to prevent the bill from reaching a vote. Passed by the House at last, the bill reached the Senate floor in March 1964 (four months after Kennedy's death), where it encountered a sustained filibuster on the part of southern senators. After three months, the Senate voted for cloture, a means by which to end a filibuster, and the bill passed the Senate.

On July 2, 1964, President Lyndon B. Johnson signed the Civil Rights Act of 1964. Its five major provisions were the result of tortured legislative bargaining and difficult compromises. It barred unequal application of voter registration rules but did not abolish literacy tests. It outlawed discrimination in public accommodations,

LBJ presenting a signing pen to Martin Luther King

exempting private clubs, which it failed to define. It encouraged the desegregation of public schools but did not authorize busing. It authorized, but did not require, the withdrawal of federal funds from programs that practiced discrimination. It outlawed discrimination in employment but contained no meaningful enforcement powers. Within a year, the Voting Rights Act of 1965 was passed to strengthen the voting provisions of the Civil Rights Act of 1964.

FBI Director J. Edgar Hoover (*left*) thought the Civil Rights Movement was a serious threat to the internal security of the United States. He cared little about slain civil rights workers Andrew Goodman, James Chaney, and Michael Schwerner, but the murders made national headlines and upset the Johnson Administration. So Hoover's agents were on the case, and Hoover himself made an appearance in Jackson, Mississippi, on July 10, 1964 (*pictured*). Ironically, by establishing a new office in Jackson that day, the FBI was able to keep better tabs on Movement members.

# 1960s

## 1964

**July 11:** Lemuel Penn, a black lieutenant colonel in the Army Reserve, is murdered by Klansmen in Colbert, Georgia.

**July 18–21:** One person is killed and more than a hundred are injured during rioting in Harlem and Brooklyn.

**July 24–26:** Four people are killed and more than 350 injured during rioting in Rochester, New York, where *de facto* segregation, unequal economic opportunities, and the large population growth of African-Americans had led to turbulent unrest.

**August:** CORE members, angry with the deadly violence levied against civil rights workers in Mississippi, send a coffin to President Johnson.

**August 2–4:** A race riot rages in Jersey City, New Jersey. At least 56 people, including 22 police officers, are arrested.

**August 4:** The bodies of civil rights workers James Chaney, Andrew Goodman, and Michael Schwerner are found under an earthen dam near Philadelphia, Mississippi. *See* December 4, 1964.

**August 11–13:** Rioting ensues for three days in Elizabeth and Paterson, New Jersey.

**August 15–16:** After a local black woman is arrested for stealing a bottle of liquor, African-Americans riot in the Chicago suburb of Dixmoor. Dozens of injuries are reported. ➤

On July 10, 1964, CORE activists protested inside this Cambridge, Massachusetts, restaurant because of its discriminatory hiring practices. The signs on the backs of those in the center read: "Don't Eat Here! Fight Job Discrimination. Boston CORE." Cambridge, home to Harvard University, was supposedly one of the most liberal cities in the country.

On July 11, 1964, Army Reserve Lieutenant Colonel Lemuel Penn (*right*) was driving in northern Georgia with two other reservist friends when the car's windows were shot up in Colbert, as indicated by Deputy Sheriff H. L. Pulleam (*above*). Penn, who had won a Bronze Star for his fighting in World War II, died from shotgun wounds to the head and neck. The sniper car's driver fingered two Klansmen—Cecil Myers and Howard Sims. They initially were acquitted of murder by an all-white jury, but they served six years in federal prison after being convicted of violating Penn's civil rights.

Barry Goldwater, the 1964 Republican candidate for president who actively fought against the Civil Rights Act, represented the far right. His platform, which emphasized limited government and the fight against communism, appealed to many southern whites, who used the concept of "states' rights" and the anti-Communist struggle as excuses to clamp down on the Civil Rights Movement. Goldwater's "extremism" remarks were used by many whites as a call to arms. They wanted to stop what they thought was the coming anarchy instigated by those seeking social change. Goldwater won just six states.

CORE made its presence known at the 1964 Republican convention in San Francisco. Here, protesters sit in front of a turnstile at the Cow Palace, preventing delegates from leaving at the end of the convention session. The demonstrators were protesting against the Republican Party platform adopted at the convention's end—one that did not endorse civil rights. The candidacy of ultraconservative Barry Goldwater meant that the New Left and civil rights activists had a common enemy, as indicated by this racially mixed group. Outside the Cow Palace, one white protester's sign read, "Be with Barry when they burn the crosses."

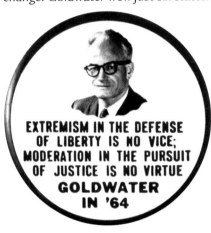

EXTREMISM IN THE DEFENSE OF LIBERTY IS NO VICE; MODERATION IN THE PURSUIT OF JUSTICE IS NO VIRTUE

GOLDWATER IN '64

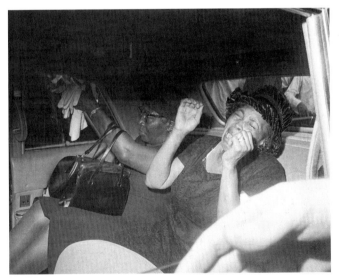

Civil insurrections, otherwise known as "riots" or "race riots," erupted for four straight summers throughout the United States beginning in 1964. Usually, police brutality against African-Americans triggered the violence. Harlem exploded after 15-year-old James Powell, the son of Anna Powell (*left photo*), was fatally shot by a white police lieutenant on July 16, 1964. The crowd gathered outside the station two days later, demanding the officer be arrested for murder. Police began to arrest members of the crowd, who turned on Harlem's store windows, buildings, and police. The insurrection spread to the Bedford-Stuyvesant section of Brooklyn (*right photo*), a predominately black section of the borough. All told in Harlem and Bed-Stuy, one person was killed and hundreds were arrested over three days.

# 1960s

## 1964

**August 20:** President Johnson signs the Economic Opportunity Act, a major part of Johnson's declared War on Poverty. The act devotes nearly $1 billion to programs designed to help the poor.

**August 22–27:** The Mississippi Freedom Democratic Party arrives at the Democratic National Convention in Atlantic City, New Jersey, and asks that its delegates be seated rather than the regular Mississippi Democratic Party delegates. In heartfelt testimony on national television, MFDP leader Fannie Lou Hamer pleads her case. The Democratic Party rules that only two seats at large will be given, a compromise that the MFDP rejects.

**August 28–30:** Hundreds are injured during rioting in Philadelphia. Some black leaders blame black nationalists for planning the riot.

**September 8:** Closed for five years, public schools in Prince Edward County, Virginia, finally reopen. More than 99 percent of registered students there are black.

**September 18:** Martin Luther King meets with Pope Paul VI despite efforts by the FBI to prevent the meeting.

**September 20 and 25:** African and Asian delegates to the United Nations meet to discuss the racial prejudice they have experienced in New York City.

**Fall:** Court-ordered school integration is carried out in Jackson, Biloxi, and Leake County, Mississippi.

**September 27:** About 450 white and black inmates at New York's state prison in Comstock clash in a racially motivated riot. Guards use tear gas and billy clubs to quell the disturbance. ➤

By 1964 increasing numbers of white students wanted to be involved in the Civil Rights Movement. John Lewis and Bob Moses decided that if the Movement was to succeed, it needed as many nonviolent soldiers as it could gather. Lewis wrote in his autobiography: "He [Moses] felt that the Movement should not be about black versus white, that it should be about black and white, united against something that was simply wrong." Massive white involvement meant that SNCC organizers had to deal with many issues: explaining local customs, redirecting whites away from trying to lead, soothing resentment from black activists, and emphasizing the danger associated with their work.

Jersey City, New Jersey, a multiracial city that is a short ferry ride away from Manhattan, joined Philadelphia and Dixmoor, Illinois, as cities that exploded in 1964, beginning four consecutive "long, hot summers" of insurrections in American cities. The Jersey City riot in early August left 30 people injured, 10 of whom were police officers. It began when police arrested 26-year-old Delores Shannon, a black woman, for causing a disturbance. Later that night, blacks angry with Shannon's arrest taunted police. Bricks, bottles, and garbage-can covers whistled in the air, as did the precinct's nightsticks.

Overcrowded living conditions, police brutality, and hot weather all contributed to a three-day riot in Paterson, New Jersey, a predominately white working-class city, in August 1964. No one was killed, but a black youth was thrown through a plate-glass window by police and more than a dozen store windows were shattered.

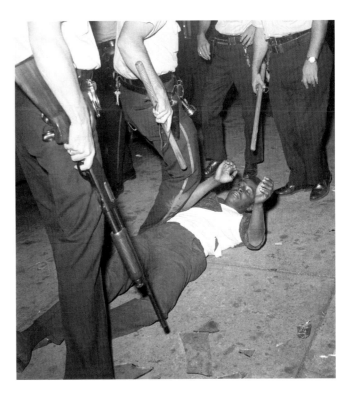

On August 12, 1964, Martin Luther King took Yolanda and Martin III on this Magic Skyway Ride at the World's Fair in New York City. Back in Atlanta, when Yolanda was six, she often asked her daddy to take her to Funtown, a local amusement park. King evaded the issue several times, but she persisted. Finally, Coretta and a tongue-tied Martin explained to their daughter that black children weren't allowed at Funtown. Yolanda cried. Eventually Funtown desegregated, and Martin and Yolanda attended together.

Many segregationist whites believed in militant tactics. Lester Maddox, the owner of a restaurant in Atlanta, was one such man. On July 3, 1964, he pulled a revolver to threaten three African-Americans (*left photo*) who had attempted to be served at his cafeteria-style Pickrick restaurant, which was their right under federal law. Maddox, who was known to give his patrons ax handles ("Pickrick Drumsticks") to intimidate blacks, closed his restaurant in August 1964 rather than racially integrate it. For a while, he sold his ax handles and other "patriotic" merchandise (such as his "Gold-water" soft drink) as souvenirs to local whites, who considered him a hero. With help from this constituency, he was elected Georgia's governor in 1966. But even Maddox could not stop desegregation from becoming a reality. He eventually pioneered the appointment of African-Americans to state government jobs.

# 1960s

Police in Dixmoor, Illinois, carry away a woman who refused to leave the scene of a riot on August 17, 1964. Two days earlier, a different black woman got into an argument with a white liquor store owner in Dixmoor, a mostly black Chicago suburb. The owner accused Rhondella Woods of stealing a bottle of liquor. Local blacks, who said the owner assaulted Woods, rallied—and then rioted—outside the store. Two people were shot and 50 were injured. Police said a sniper shot a black man and a white man shot himself in the hand.

Seven weeks after signing the Civil Rights Act of 1964, President Lyndon Johnson signed the $947.5 million Economic Opportunity Act, known as the "War on Poverty" legislation, on August 20, 1964. It created the Office of Economic Opportunity, which oversaw several programs, including Job Corps, welfare reform that assisted poor families with children, and educational programs for the disadvantaged. But American poverty would last well beyond 1964. Only two weeks before, Congress had approved the Gulf of Tonkin Resolution, which marked the beginning of serious U.S. involvement in the Vietnam War and, consequently, the derailment of Johnson's domestic policy. Moreover, by the late 1960s critics of the legislation talked about the "poverty pimps" who received large salaries to manage programs that were marginally helpful at best.

# Fannie Lou Hamer

ORN IN MONTGOMERY COUNTY, Mississippi, the granddaughter of a slave, Fannie Lou Hamer was a sharecropper most of her life and endured many hardships—among them, involuntary sterilization by a local doctor after she had borne two children. Like most black people in the South, Hamer had a strong sense of her own self-worth but no idea how to fight for her rights.

Thanks to the efforts of SNCC workers in Mississippi, Hamer registered to vote. Ordered off the plantation where she sharecropped, she joined SNCC's voter registration campaign. She said that the worst thing whites could do in retaliation would be to kill her, but she added that it seemed like they'd been trying to do that all of her life.

A key figure in the Mississippi Freedom Democratic Party, Hamer was a star witness at the televised Credentials Committee hearings at the Democratic National Convention in August 1964. Describing how blacks in

Mississippi were prevented from the most basic forms of participatory democracy, she related in detail a beating she had suffered in Winona, Mississippi, after attending a civil rights meeting. She then broke down and wept. It was one of the most searing moments of the convention.

Aaron Henry, chairman of the Mississippi Freedom Democratic Party (MFDP), was a druggist from Clarksdale, Mississippi, who courageously served as the NAACP's Mississippi State Chapter president. Henry, a diplomatic leader, wedged himself between SNCC's militancy and the NAACP's conservatism while becoming a target of the Ku Klux Klan. Here, Henry speaks to the national Democratic Party's credentials committee in Atlantic City, New Jersey, on August 22, 1964. The MFDP was trying to replace the all-white Mississippi delegation at the Democratic National Convention.

During the 1964 Democratic National Convention, black Democratic delegates met secretly to find a way to squash the protest of the Mississippi Freedom Democratic Party. William Dawson, a congressman from Chicago, and others argued that it was more important to reelect President Lyndon Johnson because he would be better for the cause of civil rights than Republican Barry Goldwater. The MFDP was not invited, but MFDP delegate Annie Devine (*left*) found out about it. She went to the meeting and spoke her mind. Devine said that white Mississippians had treated African-Americans like beasts and had shot them like animals. She said that politicians didn't care about African-Americans. She cried throughout her passionate speech, which prompted the black delegates to end their meeting.

Who was going to sit in the spots earmarked for members of the Mississippi delegation at the Democratic National Convention? Was it going to be the all-white delegation that excluded blacks from participating? A representative of the white delegation stated: "We submit, not by way of threat as by matter of cold facts, even though we suspect our opposition to accuse us of threats, that there can be no surer way of forever killing the Democratic Party in the state of Mississippi than to seat this rump group who represent practically no one." National Democratic Party leaders proposed to seat the all-white Mississippi delegation as well as two delegates of the MFDP—and accept the other MFDP representatives as "guests." Both groups initially rejected the compromise, leaving all of Mississippi's seats empty.

## Mississippi: Cauldron of Hate

W E'RE TIRED OF ALL this beatin', we're tired of takin' this. It's been a hundred years and we're still being beaten and shot at, crosses are still being burned, because we want to vote. But I'm goin' to stay in Mississippi and if they shoot me down, I'll be buried here.

But I don't want equal rights with the white man; if I did, I'd be a thief and a murderer. But the white man is the scardest person on earth. Out in the daylight he don't do nothin'. But at night he'll toss a bomb or pay someone to kill. The white man's afraid he'll be treated like he's been treatin' Negroes, but I couldn't carry that much hate. It wouldn't solve any problem for me to hate whites just because they hate me. Oh, there's so much hate. Only God has kept the Negro sane.

—*Fannie Lou Hamer, cofounder of the Mississippi Freedom Democratic Party*

# 1960s

## 1964

**October:** White homeowners of the Stony Island Heights Civic Association, near Chicago, protest block-busting real estate tactics with yard signs, such as "This Is Our House. It Is Not for Sale."

**October 4:** A black church in Vicksburg, Mississippi, which had been used as a center for voter registration, is bombed. Two people are killed.

**November 3:** California voters approve a constitutional amendment that bans antidiscrimination housing laws. The effect will be an end to federal funds earmarked for California urban-renewal projects.

**November 3:** Incumbent Lyndon Johnson defeats ultraconservative Republican Barry Goldwater in a landslide in the U.S. presidential election.

**November 18:** FBI Director J. Edgar Hoover publicly labels Martin Luther King "the most notorious liar in the country" after King criticizes the FBI for its failure to protect civil rights workers in the South.

**December 4:** President Johnson issues an executive order that bars discrimination in federal aid programs.

**December 4:** The FBI charges 19 men, including Neshoba County Sheriff Lawrence Rainey, with conspiring to violate the constitutional rights of James Chaney, Andrew Goodman, and Michael Schwerner. *See* October 20, 1967.

**December 10:** Martin Luther King accepts the Nobel Peace Prize in Oslo, Norway.

**December 14:** In *Heart of Atlanta Motel v. United States*, the U.S. Supreme Court upholds the power of Congress to prohibit discrimination in privately owned hotels.

The Philadelphia riot of 1964 was one of the rare urban uprisings in which white police officers were not initially involved. The riot started on August 28 after a scuffle between a black woman and a black police officer got out of control in North Philadelphia, a predominately black and poor area of the city. Simmering black anger easily boiled over onto Columbia Avenue, a main thoroughfare, as shops were looted and buildings were set afire. In three days of rioting, two people died and almost 340—including 100 police officers—were injured.

Jim Crow customs were so entrenched that even the most basic courtesy—the right to be addressed as "Mr." or "Miss"—had to be won by struggle. Mary Hamilton was a southern field worker for CORE. During a court case in Alabama, she was found in contempt of court because she had refused to answer questions from the prosecution, which had addressed her as "Mary" instead of "Miss Hamilton," a common sign of disrespect that whites had shown blacks since slavery. The U.S. Supreme Court ruled in Hamilton's favor in 1964.

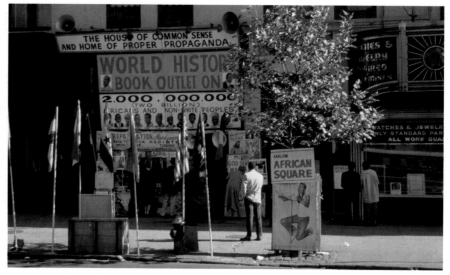

In Harlem, black bookstores were cultural centers in which black intellectuals met and debated each other. The House of Common Sense and Home of Proper Propaganda, located at the corner of Seventh Avenue and 125th Street in the heart of Harlem, was run by "Professor" Lewis Michaux. Michaux was a little man with a strong memory and a powerful Pan-African spirit. Malcolm X was a "regular" in the store's back room, where Michaux would hold court with the nationalist and Pan-African intellects of the day.

# Hoover vs. King

DURING THE COLD WAR, when anti-Communist paranoia was at its height, FBI Director J. Edgar Hoover was convinced that the Civil Rights Movement was infiltrated and directed by Communists. Because of this suspicion—as well as his general disdain for social agitation groups—Hoover targeted the leader of the Civil Rights Movement, Martin Luther King.

During the Freedom Rides in May 1961, as Montgomery, Alabama, came under martial law and King flew to the city to offer his support to the riders, Hoover ordered that King be investigated. In 1963 Hoover secured from U.S. Attorney General Robert Kennedy authorization to wiretap King and his associates. Hoover's suspicions of King were relatively subdued, however, until King criticized the FBI for its conduct during the SCLC-led campaigns for integration in Albany, Georgia.

In November 1964 King remarked to a *New York Times* reporter that FBI agents in Albany were Southerners and too close to local law enforcement to respond appropri-

ately to civil rights complaints. Stung by such public criticism, Hoover called King "the most notorious liar in the country." Hoover soon began a vengeful campaign against King that grew ugly and absurd. The FBI mailed a letter to King that urged him to commit suicide; if not, they would bare his "filthy, fraudulent self" to the nation on the eve of his acceptance of the Nobel Peace Prize.

The FBI's surveillance, infiltration, and intimidation against black activists was formalized in a system called COINTELPRO, an anacronym for counterintelligence programs. Begun in the middle 1950s, COINTELPRO was aimed at neutralizing enemy agents within the United States. The Black Panther Party was a special target. COINTELPRO activities finally ended in 1971 after several incidents: an unsolved break-in at the FBI's resident agency in Media, Pennsylvania; separate lawsuits by two COINTELPRO targets (NBC correspondent Carl Stern and the Socialist Workers' Party); and a U.S. Senate investigation.

Should a man who organizes protests designed to provoke whites into racist violence against blacks be given the Nobel Peace Prize? The award committee said yes. On December 10, 1964, at age 35, Martin Luther King became the youngest person ever to accept the Peace Prize. King won the award because of the success the SCLC had achieved in the Birmingham struggle the previous year. King, who lived in a rented house and accepted only $1 in annual SCLC salary, divided and distributed the $54,000 in award money to the major civil rights organizations. King now had become a world leader, with the responsibility to share his vision of peace with all mankind. He would do so regardless of unrelenting criticism.

Lawrence Rainey (*right*) and Cecil Price, the sheriff and deputy of Neshoba County, Mississippi, don't seem too concerned about their December 1964 arraignment for their alleged involvement in the murders of James Chaney, Andrew Goodman, and Michael Schwerner earlier that year. The two officers were joined as defendants by 19 others in connection with the slaying of the civil rights workers. All 21 were released on bond. Rainey, who would speak at a Ku Klux Klan rally in Meridian, Mississippi, in 1965, would be acquitted. Price was sentenced to prison for conspiring to deprive the slain men of their civil rights.

# The Selma Movement

"SELMA, ALABAMA, WAS TO 1965 what Birmingham was to 1963," Martin Luther King later wrote. "The right to vote was the issue, replacing public accommodation as the mass concern of a people hungry for a place in the sun and a voice in their destiny."

Although the Selma voting rights movement gained national attention during the mid-1960s, the Dallas County Voters League (DCVL) had been active as far back as the 1920s, registering black voters despite intense white opposition. DCVL leaders Samuel William Boynton and C. J. Adams were among the courageous black activists who had sustained the voting rights struggle during the 1930s and 1940s. After Boynton's death in 1963, his widow, Amelia Boynton, convinced SNCC workers Bernard and Colia Lafayette to assist DCVL in a major voter registration effort.

SNCC's initial efforts were met with hostility from city officials and a mixed response from local blacks. By late 1964 the increase in registered black voters in the Dallas County area was minimal, and only three people worked full-time at SNCC's headquarters in Selma. In January 1965 King announced the start of the Alabama Project, designed to eliminate black disfranchisement by organizing a campaign of mass marches centered in Selma.

On February 18, during a peaceful evening march in Marion, Alabama, participants were attacked by Alabama state troopers. During the fray, 26-year-old Jimmie Lee Jackson was shot in the stomach by a state trooper while attempting to protect his mother from the officer's billy club blows. Jackson died eight days later. Meanwhile, Marion and Selma activists organized a March 7 march, which would bring further national attention to their demand for a just federal voter registration law.

In the early morning of Sunday, March 7, roughly 600 people gathered at Selma's Brown Chapel. The group departed from the chapel late that morning, made its way down several blocks, and arrived at the edge of the Edmund Pettus Bridge. At that point, the fateful decision was made for the approximately 600 marchers, led by SNCC chairman John Lewis and SCLC organizer Hosea Williams, to proceed toward the armed state troopers awaiting across the bridge. The violence of "Bloody Sunday" was about to begin.

As they reached the end of the bridge, the marchers ignored Major John Cloud's final order to turn back or face the consequences. After a brief span of eerie silence, a brigade of gas-masked Alabama state troopers attacked the crowd with tear gas and billy clubs. Sheyann Webb,

Alabama state troopers overrun civil rights marchers on March 7, 1965, in what would become known as "Bloody Sunday."

who was eight years old at the time, recalls the horror: "[T]he people were turning and I saw this first part of the line running and stumbling back towards us … and somebody yelled, 'Oh, God, they're killing us!' I think I just froze then. There were people everywhere, jamming against me, pushing against me." When the mayhem finally ceased, more than 50 people had suffered various injuries.

Following the march, King talked with SCLC officials and decided to hold a second Selma-to-Montgomery march on March 9. King, though, had a difficult decision to make: Many protesters wanted the march to go on since they had traveled from great distances to participate, but Federal District Court Judge Frank M. Johnson issued a restraining order that prohibited a march to Montgomery. Though he had never disobeyed federal orders before, King decided to go ahead with the march.

As the marchers reached the bridge on March 9, they once again were confronted by state troopers. Rather than confront the force arrayed against the marchers, King knelt in prayer and then turned around and led the protesters back to Selma. "Everything went as planned," according to King assistant Andrew Young. Later that evening, several white men beat Reverend James Reeb, a white Unitarian minister from Boston, in front of Selma's Silver Moon Café. Reeb died two days later in a Birmingham hospital.

Facing widespread disappointment among the marchers, King and his associates sought court approval for a third march. The injunction was granted on Wednesday, March 17, two days after President Lyndon Johnson made a nationally televised address to a joint session of Congress. Johnson vowed to "strike down restrictions to voting in all elections  federal, state, and local—which have been used to deny Negroes the right to vote. This bill will establish a simple, uniform standard which cannot be used, however ingenious the effort, to flout our Constitution."

On Sunday, March 21, 1965, King led an attempted third march from Selma to Montgomery. This time the injunction provided the marchers with ample protection through various federal law enforcement agencies. During this final successful attempt, participants marched an average of 10 miles a day, sometimes in dismal weather, with simple tents serving as their only form of shelter. Upon arriving at the state capitol in Montgomery on

Martin Luther King leads the successful third march.

Thursday, March 25, approximately 25,000 protesters attended a victory rally.

In his address at the conclusion of the march, King proclaimed: "Selma, Alabama, became a shining moment in the conscience of man. There never was a moment in American history more honorable and more inspiring than the pilgrimage of clergymen and laymen of every race and faith pouring into Selma to face danger at the side of its embattled Negroes."

The efforts of civil rights organizations in Selma and throughout the United States achieved their desired effect. On August 6 President Johnson signed the Voting Rights Act of 1965. This act simultaneously protected the rights of voter registration workers and prohibited discriminatory election practices, which had included land ownership as a voting prerequisite, poll taxes, and "literacy" tests that were purposely designed to confuse and disenfranchise black voters. Within three weeks after the passage of the Voting Rights Act, federal registrars registered more than 27,000 African-Americans in Mississippi, Alabama, and Louisiana.

## 1965

**1965:** CORE and SNCC stage Freedom Rides in the North. They protest discrimination by such companies as Trailways Bus Co. and Niagara Mohawk Power Corp.

**1965:** Anti-integrationist school boards fire black teachers in southern states, particularly Florida, Georgia, Virginia, and Texas.

**1965:** *The Autobiography of Malcolm X*, cowritten by Alex Haley, is published after Malcolm X's death.

**1965:** Kenneth Clark's *Dark Ghetto: Dilemmas of Social Power* is published. It likens the white American establishment to imperialists who abuse colonists.

**1965:** Claude Brown's novel *Manchild in the Promised Land*, a realistic portrayal of street life in Harlem, is published.

**January:** Martin Luther King announces the SCLC's intention of leading a protest campaign in Selma, Alabama, where the city's strong-arm tactics have prevented African-Americans from registering to vote. *See* January 18–26, 1965.

**January:** Black players who arrive in New Orleans for the American Football League's All-Star Game are denied access to social clubs—once at gunpoint. When the black players say they will boycott the game, AFL Commissioner Joe Foss decides to move the contest to another city.

**January 4:** Taking advantage of its new powers bestowed by the 1964 Civil Rights Act, the U.S. Justice Department files school desegregation suits in Tennessee and Louisiana.

**January 15:** A federal grand jury indicts 18 men involved in the murders of civil rights workers Andrew Goodman, James Chaney, and Michael Schwerner. ➤

Regardless of what some SNCC leaders sometimes thought, Martin Luther King did more than lead marches and appear on television while leaving the dirty and dangerous work for the students. Oftentimes, he personally put his own life on the line for freedom. In January 1965 King and his associates, including Fred Shuttlesworth (*center*), registered at Selma's Hotel Albert, one of the city's most prominent all-white institutions. They became the first African-Americans to become guests there. But the act was not without consequence, as a white woman stood on a chair and shouted, "Get him! Get him!" James Robinson, a member of the National States Rights Party, punched King twice before SNCC's John Lewis grabbed him. Wilson Baker, Selma's new police director, subdued Robinson and arrested him.

On January 19 African-Americans in Selma marched to the county courthouse to dramatize black disenfranchisement. During one such march, Sheriff Jim Clark, wielding a club, confronted protester Amelia Boynton and forcibly shoved her along the sidewalk. About 60 demonstrators responded by storming into the courthouse, which led to their arrests. The next day, this photo made the front pages of newspapers nationwide.

Annie Lee Cooper tried twice to vote in Selma, Alabama. This time, on January 25, 1965, she was participating in a march led by Martin Luther King. Dallas County Sheriff Jim Clark had begun to crack down on those who gathered at the courthouse to register. Cooper decided to respond to Clark's physical restraint by punching him several times, knocking his hat to the ground. Officers swarmed around Cooper, pinning her down. King quickly reminded the marchers of their commitment to nonviolence. Meanwhile, Cooper was subdued and sent to jail in double handcuffs.

A police officer in Selma confiscates a demonstrator's sign on February 3, 1965. In that first week of February, police arrested hundreds of marchers in Selma, a large percentage of whom were children, and sent them to jails and makeshift jail yards. The incarcerated activists complained about abusive guards and having no toilets, only buckets. On February 4, President Lyndon Johnson addressed the Selma events at a press conference. "All Americans should be indignant when one American is denied the right to vote," he said. Also on that date, a federal judge ordered Selma's registrar to process at least 100 applications per day.

While Martin Luther King was in a Selma jail cell in early February 1965, Malcolm X traveled to the city in response to a call from SNCC. Speaking to students, Malcolm said he fully supported the black activists in Selma but didn't believe nonviolent protests would work. Instead, he endorsed militant actions against racism. Malcolm told Coretta Scott King to tell her husband that he came so that whites would understand "what the alternative is" if they refused to deal with Dr. King. The students were energized by Malcolm's speech. Coretta spent several minutes trying to calm the students, and SCLC leaders hastily postponed a planned march.

On February 5, 1965, SCLC leader C. T. Vivian exploded into the national spotlight as television cameras recorded his confrontation with Dallas County Sheriff Jim Clark. Vivian had led a group of blacks to the Selma courthouse to register to vote. They were refused registration, but Vivian launched a verbal tirade against Clark, comparing him to Hitler. His monologue was interrupted when one of Clark's deputies slugged Vivian, bloodying him and knocking him down the stairs. Vivian was placed under arrest. The encounter showed to the nation's television viewers the price of black citizenship.

# 1960s

## 1965

**January 18–26:** Sheriff Jim Clark's police force arrests more than 200 black demonstrators when they attempt to register to vote in Selma.

**January 22:** More than 100 black teachers march to the Selma courthouse to protest the discriminatory voter registration system. The march counters some whites' claims that blacks can't vote because they're uneducated.

**February 1:** More than 700 protesters, including Martin Luther King and many children, are arrested in Selma. The national TV networks showcase the drama.

**February 4:** A federal judge outlaws Selma's complicated voter registration test and orders the city's registration board to speed up its registration of black citizens. President Lyndon Johnson, speaking to a nationwide TV audience, promises to secure voting rights for all citizens. *See* February 9, 1965.

**February 5:** Vice President Hubert Humphrey is appointed to lead the Council on Equal Opportunity, which will coordinate federal civil rights activities.

**February 9:** Martin Luther King meets with President Johnson regarding voters' rights.

**February 10:** Sheriff Jim Clark and his officers impel more than 150 black teenage protesters on a forced march, making them run alongside cars for three miles while being spurred with electric cattle prods. *See* February 18, 1965.

**February 16:** Police and FBI arrest three male members of the Black Liberation Front and one French-Canadian woman for plotting to blow up the Statue of Liberty, the Liberty Bell, and the Washington Monument. ➤

Black militancy took many forms in 1965. The Black Liberation Front, a small group of black students radicalized by a recent trip to Cuba, decided to blow up the Statue of Liberty to expose America's hypocrisy. In February 1965 two of the group's members—Walter A. Bowe and Kahleel S. Sayyed—were arrested. The action was thwarted because one of the Front's members, Raymond Wood, was an undercover police officer who had infiltrated the group. Similar organizations—such as the Black Liberation Army, a spin-off of the Black Panther Party—considered violent attacks against symbols of white America. All of the groups would have to deal with police and FBI infiltrators.

On February 21, 1965, Malcolm X was shot and killed by at least two black men inside the Audubon Ballroom in New York City. Malcolm was shot more than a dozen times as he was about to speak at his Organization of Afro-American Unity rally. Two of five gunmen, in the crowd, pretended to be involved in a scuffle as a distraction. When Malcolm called for calm, at least two of the five ran to the front of the ballroom and fired at Malcolm through the podium. During the previous several months, Malcolm had sensed his days were numbered. In death, his life and autobiography would be used as models for black nationalists around the world.

Tensions were high in Harlem following Malcolm X's murder. The Nation of Islam's Harlem mosque was set afire shortly after the assassination. Several Harlem churches turned down the opportunity to host the funeral for its favorite son. Finally, the Unity Funeral Home agreed to host the viewing and the funeral (*pictured*). Thousands of people stood in line in frigid weather to say goodbye to the man whom actor Ossie Davis, in his eulogy, called black America's "shining black prince."

"They're killing my husband!" Betty Shabazz (*center*) screamed as she made it to the front of the Audubon Ballroom. Her life was thrown upside down with the assassination that took place in front of her eyes and her children's. She was on her own, with four children and two on the way. Percy Sutton (*behind Shabazz*), Malcolm's attorney, would quietly assist the family in the years to come. Malcolm's half-sister, Ella Collins (*left*), who had loaned Malcolm the money he needed to travel internationally, would attempt to lead the Organization of Afro-American Unity after Malcolm's death. But the torch of black nationalist activism, held in Malcolm's name, would be carried by others.

Nation of Islam leader Elijah Muhammad denied that his followers had anything to do with the murder of Malcolm X. Muhammad referred to Talmadge Hayer, one of the men arrested in Malcolm's murder, as a "stranger to us." At a NOI rally after the assassination, Muhammad said that the Nation did not want or try to kill Malcolm. He added that Malcolm's preachings and "foolishness" were the reasons for his death.

Norman 3X Butler (*pictured*) and two others were arrested for the assassination of Malcolm X. They were convicted and sentenced to life in prison. Only one, Talmadge Hayer, said he was guilty. The alleged killers, who were tied to a Nation of Islam mosque in nearby New Jersey, reportedly were angry about Malcolm's increasingly critical comments about NOI leader Elijah Muhammad. Many NOI members considered Malcolm X to be a "chief hypocrite" who deserved the swift, violent punishment of Allah. Hayer told Malcolm X biographer Peter Goldman: "The talk of retaliating and everything, or stopping hypocrites who were trying to tear down the Nation of Islam—I think they just got drunk and said, 'Well, let's stamp out all of them who disagree with us.'"

## 1965

**February 18:** Weeks of demonstrations in Selma finally turn deadly, as black protester Jimmie Lee Jackson is shot. He will die from his wound on February 26. *See* March 7, 1965.

**February 21:** Malcolm X is assassinated while speaking in New York City. *See* March 10, 1966.

**March 7:** To protest the denial of voting rights, more than 500 marchers begin a 54-mile trek from Selma to Montgomery. As soon as they cross the Edmund Pettus Bridge that leads out of Selma, they're attacked by state troopers and local police, who use tear gas, clubs, and electric cattle prods. Dozens require medical treatment. Numerous congressmen are among the many who express their outrage over "Bloody Sunday."

**March 9:** Martin Luther King leads a group of 2,000 people on a second march toward Montgomery. Instead of challenging the line of police that meets them as they cross Selma's Edmund Pettus Bridge, the group says a prayer and then retreats. Later in the day, three white ministers who participated, including James Reeb from Boston, are attacked by whites. *See* March 11, 1965.

**March 10:** In *Griffin v. State Board of Education*, a three-judge federal panel rules that Virginia tuition grants cannot be used to fund all or most of the costs incurred to operate segregated private schools.

**March 11:** Reverend James Reeb dies after being severely beaten on March 9.

**March 11:** Entering with tourists, 14 youths stage a sit-in in the White House, demanding federal intervention in Selma.

**March 13:** In a personal meeting with Alabama Governor George Wallace, and on national TV, President Johnson strongly denounces the injustices in Selma. ➤

Jimmie Lee Jackson died defending his mother, Viola, from white state troopers who were intent on beating her. In Marion, Alabama (outside of Selma), on February 18, 1965, the Jacksons protested for the right to vote. Viola was attacked for trying to push off troopers who were beating her father, 82-year-old Cager Lee. Jimmie Lee was beaten and shot when the authorities turned on Viola; Jimmie Lee died eight days later. Jackson, 26, had worked at a wood plant, had been the youngest deacon at his church, and had attempted unsuccessfully to vote five times. His shooting, though ignored by much of white America, increased tensions in Selma.

After the shooting of Jimmie Lee Jackson, the SCLC's James Bevel suggested in a sermon that Selma's black citizens take their grievances directly to Alabama Governor George Wallace. Thus, the idea of the 54-mile Selma to Montgomery march was born. Wallace prohibited the march, but—against some hesitancy by SCLC leaders—600 protesters took to the streets on Sunday, March 7, 1965. Led by the SCLC's Hosea Williams and SNCC's John Lewis, they crossed the Edmund Pettus Bridge that led out of Selma, waiting for the inevitable confrontation.

Alabama state troopers and Selma police lined up near the foot of the Edmund Pettus Bridge, ready to enforce the order laid down by Alabama Governor George Wallace. The authorities were hell-bent on preventing the marchers from fully traversing the bridge. March leader John Lewis looked down at the water a hundred feet below. Williams asked Lewis if he could swim. Lewis said no. Williams couldn't, either.

# Bloody Sunday

IN EARLY MARCH 1965, Martin Luther King chose to preach at his Atlanta church pulpit rather than lead the 54-mile march from Selma, Alabama, to the state capital in Montgomery. Hosea Williams "won" the coin toss to determine which SCLC leader would take his place. SNCC Chairman John Lewis walked beside him, participating as an individual, for SNCC did not officially support what it considered a dangerous demonstration.

On Sunday, March 7, 1965, 600 civil rights marchers walking two by two headed to the Edmund Pettus Bridge in east Selma. As they reached the midpoint of the span across the Alabama River, they saw a sea of blue-clad state troopers slapping billy clubs against their hands. Major John Cloud, the troops' commander, waited until the marchers were about 40 feet from him, then ordered them to disperse. The marchers knelt to the ground to pray. Mounted troopers then charged, flailing their billy clubs and lobbing tear gas canisters at the terrified marchers as they drove them back across the bridge. Troopers on horseback lashed out right and left with their clubs.

Sheyann Webb, eight years old, ran as hard as she could with mounted troops in pursuit. Hosea Williams picked her up, but she told him to put her down since he

wasn't running fast enough. Williams, Lewis, and many others were beaten bloody.

Television cameras recorded the brutal assault, and some networks interrupted their regular programming to broadcast it live. A wave of revulsion swept the nation, and the White House was inundated with calls and telegrams. As a direct consequence, President Lyndon Johnson introduced the legislation that would become the Voting Rights Act of 1965.

# 1960s

The civil rights marchers on the Edmund Pettus Bridge came within 50 feet of Major John Cloud of the Alabama State Troopers, who told them to stop marching. They complied. Cloud, through his bullhorn, said that the march was not conducive to public safety, that the protesters should disperse and go back home. Hosea Williams asked to talk to Cloud, who refused. Cloud announced that the marchers had two minutes to retreat. No one moved. A minute passed. Cloud then ordered the troopers to advance.

## Horrors of Bloody Sunday

THE TROOPERS RUSHED FORWARD, their blue uniforms and white helmets blurring into a flying wedge as they moved.

The wedge moved with such force that it seemed almost to pass over the waiting column instead of through it.

The first 10 or 20 Negroes were swept to the ground screaming, arms and legs flying, and packs and bags went skittering across the grassy divider strip and on to the pavement on both sides.

Those still on their feet retreated.

The troopers continued pushing, using both the force of their bodies and the prodding of their nightsticks.

A cheer went up from the white spectators lining the south side of the highway.

The mounted possemen spurred their horses and rode at a run into the retreating mass. The Negroes cried out as they crowded together for protection, and the whites on the sidelines whooped and cheered.

*—Roy Reed*, The New York Times, *covering "Bloody Sunday" in Selma, Alabama*

"[T]he people were turning and I saw the first part of the line running and stumbling back towards us . . . and somebody yelled, 'Oh, God, they're killing us.' I think I just froze then. There were people everywhere, jamming against me, pushing me."

—SHEYANN WEBB, AGE EIGHT AT THE TIME, RECALLING BLOODY SUNDAY

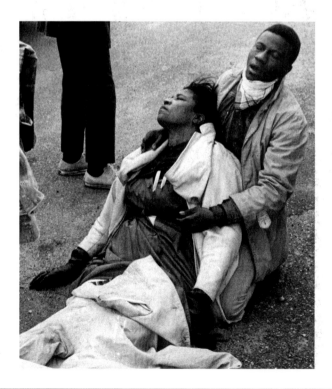

The police attacked the marchers in a variety of ways. Police on horseback chased protesters as if they were rounding up cattle. They pounded men and women with nightsticks. They tossed canisters of tear gas. Crying, children gasped for air. The protesters retreated as fast as they could. The Alabama state troopers had succeeded. And it was all captured on film.

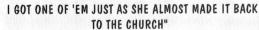

This editorial cartoon by Herbert Block (Herblock) reflected the anger many Americans felt about law enforcement officials in Selma, Alabama. The cartoon refers to Bloody Sunday on March 7, 1965, when state troopers used clubs to beat men and women on the Edmund Pettus Bridge. With the words "Special Storm Trooper," Herblock draws a clear parallel between the cartoon character and the notorious Storm Troopers of Nazi Germany.

After Bloody Sunday, the mood in Selma ranged from sorrow to shock to rage. Andrew Young of the SCLC had to calm down marchers who wanted to get their guns. The naked brutality of the troopers—on a Sunday, no less—intensified the anger in Selma. Civil rights leaders had to move immediately to channel this rage productively.

When Andrew Young and Hosea Williams told Martin Luther King on the phone about what happened in Selma hours before, King wasted no time. After some conference calls, two strategies were developed and executed. First, they sent messages to the White House and Congress denouncing the events of Bloody Sunday. Then, they set Tuesday, March 9 for a protest march. The Johnson Administration, however, wanted a halt to the violence, so officials pressed King for a compromise solution that would scuttle a second march. Administration officials offered to intervene in Selma, but it was too late. The people wanted to march.

# 1960s

On March 9, the date of the second march across Selma's Edmund Pettus Bridge, everyone was worried. The marchers thought they were going to face the police again, and not back down. The police wondered if they would have to battle the crowd again. But little did the marchers know that the Johnson Administration, trying to avoid a bloodbath at almost any cost, had already cut a deal with King and the lawmen: The marchers, who were under a court injunction not to proceed, would go over the bridge, conduct a public prayer, then turn around. And that's what happened on what subsequently would be called "Turnaround Tuesday." King kept his eyes open during the prayer.

Why did King agree to turn the marchers around? There were at least three reasons. The first was that King never strove to initiate nonviolent direct action when a legitimate compromise was on the table; he did not believe in confrontation for confrontation's sake. He saw that the Johnson Administration was on his side, actively working for a compromise. Second, he knew that the troopers would beat the marchers again without hesitation, and that would solve nothing. The third reason was that he had never defied a court injunction. From the beginning, King had considered the courts an ally to the Movement. SNCC leaders, who did not know of these last-minute negotiations, thought King had sold them out.

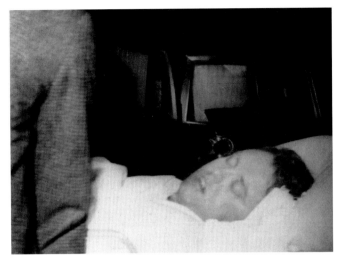

James Reeb was a white minister from the Unitarian Universalist Church in Boston who went to Selma to support the Movement. On March 9, just hours after King turned the Selma–Montgomery marchers around, Reeb was viciously attacked. He and two other men had been walking down a Selma sidewalk when a group of white men called them "niggers" and approached them. Reeb died two days after being clubbed in the head by one of the mob. The outrage spread nationwide. President Johnson even mentioned Reeb as he introduced the bill that would become the Voting Rights Act of 1965. King delivered Reeb's eulogy, calling his fellow clergyman a martyr. It became painfully clear that Reeb's death would awaken the conscience of more Americans than the recent murder of Jimmie Lee Jackson, a black man.

Selma Mayor Joe Smitherman, who had been in office only a few months, was unprepared for the turbulence in his city in early 1965. Still, he did not want Martin Luther King—whom he accidentally called "Martin Luther Coon" on national television—in his city, causing "trouble." Smitherman and Wilson Baker (*left*), Selma's public safety director, were afraid the city would be ripped apart by civil unrest.

The violence in Selma inspired many Americans to take some sort of action. This protest in Los Angeles on March 10, 1965, was in support of the protesters in Selma, Alabama. The demonstrators—who blocked a federal building's driveway, halting the progress of at least two mail trucks—demanded federal intervention for the Selma marchers. Their solidarity is symbolized by their grip on each other.

A white civil rights advocate burns the Confederate flag in Selma, Alabama, on March 10, 1965. City officials understood that any protests by civil rights workers would inflame racial tensions in the city. The release of racist white anger, thinly and unconvincingly masquerading as white southern pride, could easily turn to violence—and did, as evidenced by the death of white minister James Reeb.

Small demonstrations for the vote continued in Selma. Here, a policeman employs a billy club to hold back a group of demonstrators on March 13. Selma Mayor Joe Smitherman had attempted to avoid scenes like these, because he understood that the Movement needed villains to make its heroes look good. Smitherman said Movement leaders chose Selma the way a movie producer chose a set. With Sheriff Clark and his men, the Movement had the villains it needed: men who would not worry about how they looked to the world while upholding Jim Crow for their communities.

In the eyes of the world, the events in Selma shamed America. Once again, the self-proclaimed seat of modern democracy failed to live up to the ideals it proclaimed to other nations. All throughout America, civil rights demonstrators added to the pressure President Johnson put on himself to resolve the situation quickly and neatly. The White House was an irresistible target of activists. Here, on March 12, members of a racially integrated group of demonstrators throw themselves across Pennsylvania Avenue, blocking evening rush-hour traffic. Police cleared the street in 15 minutes, using their nightsticks. At least 32 people were arrested and charged with disorderly conduct.

**"How do we want to be remembered in history? Do we want to be remembered as petty little men, or do we want to be remembered as great figures that faced up to our moments of crisis?"**

President Johnson, a master of persuasion, practiced his craft on Alabama Governor George Wallace on March 13, 1965. In the meeting, Wallace attempted to defend himself, blaming Martin Luther King for his problems. Johnson, however, was on the side of the protesters. Burke Marshall, a staff member of the Justice Department, recalled the conversation: "Governor Wallace didn't quite grovel, but he was [very] pliant by the end of the two hours, with President Johnson putting his arm around him and squeezing him and telling him it's a moment of history, and 'How do we want to be remembered in history? Do we want to be remembered as petty little men, or do we want to be remembered as great figures that faced up to our moments of crisis?'"

Throughout America, persons of conscience continued to bear witness to the struggle in Selma. In Harlem on March 14, 1965, nuns of the New York Archdiocese took to Seventh Avenue, a main thoroughfare, to protest against injustices in the Alabama city. About 100,000 protesters joined them in their Sunday demonstration.

Even though Bloody Sunday had been a public relations nightmare for Alabama on March 7, law enforcement officials assaulted SNCC workers in Montgomery just nine days later. Mounted police, wielding clubs and cattle prods, injured eight people. Later that day, a thousand marchers conducted a second demonstration in Montgomery under police protection.

# 1960s

## 1965

**March 15:** President Johnson, addressing a joint session of Congress, requests the passage of a strict voting rights bill. Within the televised address, Johnson uses the civil rights maxim "We shall overcome."

**March 16:** Mounted police with clubs and whips attack demonstrators in Montgomery.

**March 17:** Federal Judge Frank M. Johnson rules that demonstrators are allowed to march from Selma to Montgomery.

**March 20:** President Johnson federalizes the Alabama National Guard, 2,000 members, to oversee the Selma to Montgomery march planned for the next day.

**March 21–25:** After two previous unsuccessful attempts, Martin Luther King leads a five-day march from Selma to Montgomery. Thousands participate in the 54-mile journey, singing freedom songs and sleeping in tents.

**Spring:** Organizations, companies, and individuals throughout the country boycott Alabama's goods and services.

**March 25:** About 25,000 marchers reach Montgomery, where Martin Luther King speaks at the state capitol building. Later in the day, Viola Liuzzo, a white woman from Detroit who participated in the march, is murdered by Klansmen.

**March 26:** In Alabama, SNCC's Stokely Carmichael helps found the Lowndes County Freedom Organization—a precursor to the Black Panther Party.

**April 25:** Segregationist Lester Maddox leads a march of 2,000 supporters through Atlanta.

**May 28:** School integration is achieved in Greenville, Mississippi, without a court order—a first for that state. ➤

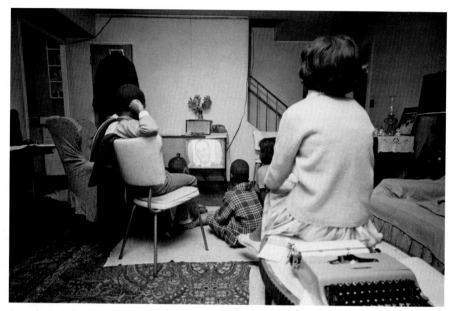

Promoting the Voting Rights Bill, President Lyndon Johnson addressed Congress on March 15, 1965. "It is wrong—dead wrong—to deny any of your fellow Americans the right to vote in this country," he said. Johnson openly allied himself with the civil rights protesters. "Their cause must be our cause, too," he said. "Because it's not just Negroes, but it's really all of us who must overcome the crippling legacy of bigotry and injustice. And we shall overcome." Those last three words—the slogan of the Movement—thrilled African-Americans. C. T. Vivian of the SCLC watched the speech with Martin Luther King and other staffers. While others cheered, Vivian recalled that King sat quietly in his chair, with a tear streaming down his cheek.

While the nation's eyes focused on Alabama in March 1965, Movement activists battled segregation in other parts of the South. On March 19, 1965, in Little Rock, Arkansas, demonstrators attempting to desegregate the state capitol's cafeteria scuffled with police officers. The protesters tried at least three times to integrate the cafeteria, but were unsuccessful. Once, they were attacked with mustard gas.

"We want the right to vote, and we want it now. You white brothers can join the ranks, too. Come, enter the ranks of humanity. Just fall in the rear. Come along with us. We're going to tell brother Wallace he'll have to go."

—BILL BRADLEY, CORE ACTIVIST AND SELMA TO MONTGOMERY MARCHER

By March 21, 1965, the court injunction against the Selma-Montgomery march had been rescinded. President Johnson, fresh from a historic speech defending the Civil Rights Movement, federalized the Alabama National Guard to protect the marchers. It was time to march from Selma to Montgomery, to write the voting rights bill in the streets of Selma using the blood of Jimmie Lee Jackson, James Reeb, and all those who had suffered and died for the right to vote across the South since Reconstruction. It was a festive occasion, racially integrated and filled with a sense of purpose. Freedom songs and American flags filled the air. Martin Luther King and his wife, Corretta Scott King, led a march of at least 4,000 people.

During the Selma to Montgomery march, one young man spat into a television news camera. Some lofted signs such as "Yankee Trash Go Home." Some held Confederate flags. The marchers, escorted by federalized Alabama troops, felt only somewhat protected. When SCLC leaders heard about a threat on Martin Luther King's life, they moved ministers of similar build with blue suits (as King wore) to the front of the line in an attempt to confuse a possible sniper. Despite the racist opposition, the march continued.

# Freedom Songs

AFRICAN-AMERICAN musical culture played a powerful role in the Civil Rights Movement. The songs of the Movement contributed to a feeling of cohesion and provided some sense of uplift and hope during times of terror and despair.

Interviewed for the 1987 PBS documentary *Eyes on the Prize*, folklorist Bernice Johnson Reagon recalled singers' effect on police officers during the civil rights campaign in Albany, Georgia. She said that police pleaded with them to stop singing, but they continued regardless, adding that their word was being heard, "and you felt joy."

The song "We Shall Overcome" was the most clearly recognizable expression of the battle against oppression. The song has been sung by demonstrators of many causes throughout the world.

*We shall overcome, we shall overcome,*
*We shall overcome someday.*
*Oh, deep in my heart, I do believe,*
*We shall overcome someday.*

By 1963 the song had become the anthem of the Civil Rights Movement. When President Lyndon Johnson urged passage of the Voting Rights Act of 1965 on national television, he concluded by saying, "And we shall overcome."

An element of sacrifice was always part of the Movement. The Selma–Montgomery marchers slept on blow-up mattresses in tents that looked like they belonged in a circus sideshow. (Martin Luther King slept in a mobile home.) Sympathizers on the sidelines offered food and drink, and a committee of volunteers delivered food each night. The Medical Committee for Human Rights provided foot care for the 54-mile walk. Under the federal order authorizing it, the march had to be completed in five days. Of those who walked 16 miles on the first day, many drove back to Selma to sleep in beds—including John Lewis, who was suffering from head injuries endured on Bloody Sunday. He described the marchers as "sunburned, wind-burned, [and] weary."

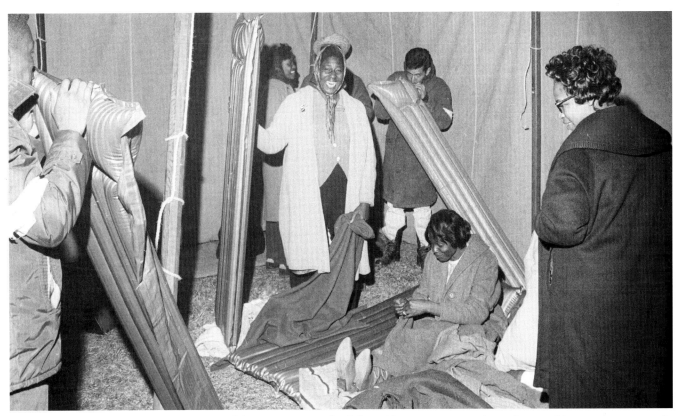

By the time the marchers had reached downtown Montgomery on March 25, 1965, their ranks had swelled to nearly 50,000. For the Kings, it was a joyous homecoming. They passed Dexter Avenue Baptist Church, where—half a lifetime ago, it seemed—King had rallied his parishioners to boycott the city's bus company. Ten years after the Montgomery Bus Boycott, black Americans believed that they could free themselves—as long as they understood that their blood might pay the price of the ticket.

Montgomery may have been the former home of the Kings, but it was Governor George Wallace's home as well. Here, a line of police officers guards the capitol building on March 25. The Confederate flag—the symbol of southern secession and, to black Americans, white supremacy and white racist violence—waved from its summit. Wallace was nowhere in sight; he watched the rally from behind his window blinds.

Ten years of marches, rallies, meetings, threats, murders, intimidation, and forbearance all climaxed in one shining moment in Montgomery on March 25, 1965. The marchers had made the 54-mile trek from Selma without incident. A bloody Sunday had been transformed into a transcendent Thursday. A voting rights bill—backed by a president who publicly declared his support for the Movement—had been introduced in Congress. Whites and blacks had marched together to expand democracy for all citizens, regardless of race, creed, or national origin. Martin Luther King spoke from the capitol steps. "I come to say to you this afternoon however difficult the moment, however frustrating the hour, it will not be long, because truth pressed to earth shall rise again. How long? Not long, because no lie can live forever."

The euphoria of the Selma rally was quickly dampered by a bullet that snatched the life of Viola Liuzzo, a white Detroit housewife who was driving marchers back to Selma in her Oldsmobile sedan. The murder happened on the night of March 25, when Liuzzo and Leroy Moten, a black teen-ager, were driving on the same road that the marchers had walked days before. Ku Klux Klansmen pulled their car beside Liuzzo's, and one of them shot her in the face twice. The Johnson Administration swooped into action, and the FBI quickly found several suspects. Governor Wallace said he regretted the incident but praised white Alabamans for their overall "restraint."

Immediately following Viola Liuzzo's murder, the Alabama Klan and the FBI (whose paid informant may have fired the shots that killed Liuzzo) circulated lies about Liuzzo's alleged promiscuity, drug use, and Communist sympathies. The smear campaign inspired racists to burn crosses at the Liuzzo home in Detroit (*cross shown*), as well as at the Detroit city council building and the local office of the NAACP. Three men who rode in the car with the FBI informant were acquitted of murder by a white jury, but were sentenced to 10 years in prison in 1966 for conspiring to violate Liuzzo's civil rights.

# Julian Bond

HORACE JULIAN BOND WAS BORN in 1940, the son of distinguished educator Horace Mann Bond. While a student at Morehouse College in Atlanta, Julian helped organize a sit-in movement at Atlanta University. Thus began his lifelong commitment to the pursuit of civil rights.

A founding member of SNCC in 1960, Bond served as the organization's communications director. In 1965 he ran for a seat in the Georgia House of Representatives in a special election following court-ordered reapportionment of the legislature. Initially, Bond was prevented from taking his seat because of his opposition to the Vietnam War. However, the U.S. Supreme Court voted unanimously in his favor.

In 1968 Bond co-chaired an alternate, biracial delegation from Georgia at the Democratic National Convention. The delegation even nominated him for vice president—a first for an African-American—although the nomination was later withdrawn. At 28, Bond was, by law, too young to be the nation's VP.

Bond served four terms in the Georgia House and six terms in the Georgia Senate. He hosted *America's Black Forum*, the longest running black-owned show in television syndication, from 1980 until 1997. In 1998 he was elected chairman of the board of the NAACP.

During the Civil Rights Movement, victory by one group in one area of a state encouraged others to try the same tactics. Here, police use smoke bombs to disperse a group of civil rights marchers in Camden, Alabama, on March 31, 1965. The protest was an outgrowth of what was happening in Selma. Camden, a city in neighboring Wilcox County, was 80 percent black, but civil rights leaders claimed that no blacks were on the voting rolls. The city's approximately 18,700 citizens included 3,000 whites who were registered to vote.

Robert Shelton was a working-class man who did not attend college. He was a line worker and, later, a salesman for B.F. Goodrich. He was fired from his job because the organization he was involved in, the Ku Klux Klan, took up too much of his time. Shelton remained loyal to the KKK and eventually became its imperial wizard, its equivalent of a national president. During a huge KKK rally on Easter 1965 in Halifax County, North Carolina, Shelton spoke out against numerous groups: African-Americans, the Civil Rights Movement, Native Americans, Jews, Communists, the federal government, foreign nations, the United Nations, and labor unions.

As in the United States, blacks in South Africa lived under laws and customs that denied their status as full human beings. In May 1965 this butcher shop in Johannesburg, South Africa, sold an inferior grade of meat for black servants. Apartheid in South Africa was even more extreme than segregation in the American South. In Johannesburg, blacks lived as servants in the homes of whites or in shacks on white property. Others lived in impoverished "dormitory towns." If the Peri-Urban police caught a black man without his passbook (official papers), he would be sent to work in a mine or a prison camp. Throughout the 1960s, black Americans became increasingly aware of the plight of South Africans, while the sufferers of Apartheid drew inspiration from the Civil Rights Movement.

Again and again, the Civil Rights Movement showed young people that they could stand up for their rights as citizens. In Jackson, Mississippi, in June 1965, about 500 demonstrators, approximately half of whom were teens, were arrested for protesting against the state legislature. Civil rights leaders reasoned that since black people were discouraged to register to vote, the state legislature was illegitimate. (Ironically, the legislature was in special session debating the question of abolishing its Jim Crow laws.) Police set up a temporary jail facility on the State Fairgrounds to accommodate the arrested demonstrators.

While a police officer confiscates a protester's sign that says "No More Police Brutality," a state highway patrolman rips a small American flag from five-year-old Anthony Quinn at the governor's mansion in Jackson, Mississippi, in June 1965. Quinn, his three siblings, and his mother, civil rights activist Aylene Quinn, waved their flags while they sat on the mansion's steps. They were protesting the seating of the state's congressional leadership—white men elected from districts in which African-Americans were denied the right to vote.

## 1965

**May 30:** Vivian Malone becomes the first African-American to graduate from the University of Alabama.

**June 4:** Patricia Roberts Harris is appointed U.S. ambassador to Luxembourg, becoming the first black female ambassador to a foreign nation.

**June 14:** In Jackson, Mississippi, nearly 500 civil rights demonstrators are arrested and held in livestock facilities at the state fairgrounds.

**June 16:** Chicago Mayor Richard Daley agrees to meet with civil rights leaders about *de facto* segregation after arrests of protesters exceeds 500.

**Summer:** The SCLC's SCOPE (Summer Community Organization and Political Education) attempts to register black voters in 50 counties throughout the South.

**July 10:** The Deacons for Defense and Justice, an armed, black self-defense group, is formed in Jonesboro, Louisiana. The group is created after attacks by Ku Klux Klan members on local black citizens. The Deacons will spread nationally in 1965.

**July 13:** Thurgood Marshall becomes the first African-American to be named U.S. solicitor general. *See* June 13, 1967.

**July 24–26:** Martin Luther King and the SCLC demonstrate against racial injustices in Chicago.

**August 6:** Already passed by Congress, the Voting Rights Act of 1965 is signed by President Johnson. The act bans biased literacy tests and other exclusionary screening devices used by registrars to keep blacks from registering. The act also allows federal workers to register black voters when necessary. ➤

African-Americans and other citizens correctly viewed the Ku Klux Klan as a terrorist organization. But Klan members saw themselves as part of a superior race who felt justified in maintaining segregation. Klan members brought their children to rallies, such as this one in Atlanta on June 5, 1965. The children were indoctrinated into a zealous, prideful culture filled with hatred of other races.

Not all African-Americans opposed the Vietnam War. Some, including those in this American Legion parade in Philadelphia in July 1965, remained loyal to the United States and its policies. Historically, blacks had fought in every war of the nation, from the Revolutionary War to the conflict in Korea. African-Americans had paid for their freedom over and over again, in blood. The war in Vietnam, reasoned some politically conservative blacks, was just another opportunity to prove their collective worth and loyalty abroad in hopes of better treatment at home.

The issues surrounding the Civil War, as well as its Confederate symbol, resurfaced as the Civil Rights Movement gained steam. The idea of "state's rights"—the right of a state to govern itself—resurfaced in many forms as southern states were forced by the federal government to desegregate and extend the right to vote to black Americans. One of the white organizations that seized and channeled white unhappiness was the National States Rights Party, led by Reverend Connie Lynch (*foreground, left of center*). Here, with Confederate flags flying proudly in the air, the party marches through Bogalusa, Louisiana, in July 1965.

Images such as this "Coon Bank" were still prevalent in the United States in the mid-1960s. America's racial stereotypes fed off themselves and were constantly updated. Films, music, and television shows created by whites followed the pattern. The television images of the Civil Rights Movement, however, began to shatter the myth of the happy, inarticulate "darkey."

It didn't take much for a predominately black section of a northern urban area to explode in the mid- to late 1960s. The conditions for insurrections in black communities were already present in too many American cities: bad housing, bad schools, police brutality, and lack of economic opportunity. In Chicago in 1965, for instance, African-Americans held only five percent of the city's "professional" jobs. So when a truck from the city's white fire department struck and killed a black woman on the West Side on August 12, 1965, war was declared, accident or not. The groups that gathered in front of the fire station quickly turned into a mob. Two nights of rioting resulted in 80 injuries and 140 arrests.

# 1960s

## The Watts Riot

THE LARGELY BLACK AND POOR neighborhood of Watts in south-central Los Angeles exploded in violence on August 11, 1965. Soon after a police officer stopped a 21-year-old black motorist he suspected of intoxication, a crowd gathered, a scuffle ensued, and rumors of police brutality spread. A heat wave and escalating racial tensions provided additional kindling for a firestorm of looting and burning.

For six days in Watts, entire blocks burned to the ground, buses and ambulances were stoned, and snipers fired at law enforcement officers, firefighters, and even airplanes. By the time the riots were put down by thousands of National Guardsmen and local law enforcement personnel, 34 people were dead (28 of them African-American), nearly 900 were injured, and more than 3,000 had been arrested. Destruction of mostly white-owned property was estimated in the tens of millions of dollars.

Responding to a plea from black churchmen in Los Angeles to visit and help restore peace, Martin Luther King flew to Watts in the midst of the crisis. Shocked at what he saw, King described the Watts riot as a revolt of the underprivileged against the privileged. He admitted that the gains of the movement in the South over the past decade had bypassed the millions of African-Americans trapped in urban ghettos. King's new awareness of high jobless rates, poor housing, and bad schools in the inner cities of the North spurred him to take the nonviolent crusade to Chicago in early 1966.

The Watts riot, and particularly the manner in which it was put down by law enforcement, provided ammunition for militant black leaders to dismiss the tactics of the nonviolent movement in favor of active self-defense. Further, it spurred the Johnson Administration's War on Poverty, which included plans for urban redevelopment that bore fruit in the 1970s.

In Los Angeles, black people lived in predominantly black communities. But the whites whose job it was to "protect and serve"—the police officers—did not. They were trained to restrain, not understand, the black communities they patrolled. Add the fear fueled by racism to the mix and it is easy to see how white police officers and black residents, particularly black youth, could easily come into conflict. By the time of the Watts insurrection in August 1965, the L.A. Police Department had become nationally known for its brutal treatment of African-Americans. Younger, more militant blacks began to stand up to the police in ways that threatened the officers. The officers responded harshly, whether news cameras were present or not.

An estimated 35,000 African-Americans participated in the Watts riot. Rioters lashed out against institutions of white authority, especially businesses. This drugstore was completely destroyed. About 16,000 law enforcement officials—National Guardsmen, city police, and county deputies—needed five days to restore order. On a national level, the Watts riot doused the flames of optimism that the victory at Selma had sparked.

The message on this sign, "Turn Left or Get Shot," symbolized how out of control the situation got in Watts. Riots happen because people in oppressed communities have no productive way of channeling their anger. ("A riot is at bottom the language of the unheard," Martin Luther King said.) Now that white-owned property had been destroyed, the attention Watts residents thought they should have received all along finally came. Studies on the "Watts Ghetto" would be conducted, social workers would arrive. Still, the living conditions in Watts would not improve, nor would its reputation. Watts would become synonymous with the word *riot* in Los Angeles until South Central, a new ghetto, took its place in 1992.

Against the counsel of several of his advisers, Martin Luther King traveled to Los Angeles on August 18, 1965, to talk with Police Chief William H. Parker and California Governor Edmund G. Brown. Parker angrily denied any racial prejudice in his department and bristled at King's suggestion of a civilian review board empowered to look at police brutality cases. King called for Parker's removal from office. Bayard Rustin (*smoking*) told King biographer David Garrow that, after the riot, King began to seriously incorporate the problems of class into his public analysis.

Concern about the National Guard's presence in Watts spurred this New York City demonstration by white leftists. While pedestrians filed by, about 50 members of "Youth Against War and Fascism" carried signs demanding the withdrawal of troops from the area. Complaints about the National Guard's presence and conduct in black communities would increase dramatically from 1965 through 1968, the last of the "long, hot summers." The conflicts reminded America that black communities were, in many ways, colonies separated from the rest of the nation.

# 1960s

## 1965

**August 7:** Empowered by the new Voting Rights Act, the U.S. Justice Department files suit against the use of the poll tax in Mississippi. *See* August 25, 1965.

**August 11–16:** Massive rioting, triggered by the arrest of a black man for drunk driving, spreads through south-central Los Angeles. Thirty-four people are killed and more than 3,000 are arrested.

**August 12–14:** In Chicago, violence erupts after a black woman is hit and killed by a fire truck. Eighty people are injured.

**August 25:** In just 19 days since the passage of the Voting Rights Act, federal registrars register 27,385 African-Americans in Alabama, Mississippi, and Louisiana.

**September:** In "Operation Exodus," hundreds of black parents in Boston pay to have their children bused from substandard schools to nicer white schools.

**October 22:** Thirty white men, shouting "Kill the niggers," attack more than 90 black marchers in Lincolnton, Georgia.

**November 15:** The U.S. Supreme Court states that "delays in desegregation of school systems are no longer tolerable."

**November 22:** The homes of four civil rights leaders are bombed in Charlotte, North Carolina.

**December:** In Anniston, Alabama, an all-white jury convicts a white man, Hubert Strange, for the murder of a black man, Willie Brewster.

**December 3:** After months of boycotts and race-related violence in Natchez, Mississippi, city officials agree to a list of African-American demands, including the hiring of black police officers and the integration of the local hospital.

This member of the American Nazi Party flaunts his racist opinion on the streets of Dallas on August 12, 1965. However, there was nowhere to "Ship Those Niggers Back" to, as his sign says. Whether whites liked it or not, African-Americans were slowly becoming first-class citizens in their own country. Houston, home of the nation's largest segregated school system, desegregated without violence. Dallas followed, also without major incidents.

In 1965 African-Americans protested for weeks in Natchez, Mississippi. Blacks boycotted downtown stores that were still segregated. The NAACP gave a list of demands to the city fathers. Demonstrations occurred all throughout the month of September—so many, in fact, that a judge issued an injunction at the end of the month barring them. Demonstrators ignored the judge; several hundred were arrested for violating the order. By 1965 in the South, white intimidation tactics were no longer working. Jack Seale (*foreground*), who identified himself as a "major" in the Security Guard of the Ku Klux Klan, watches as some 1,000 civil rights marchers pass by. Seale said that he and other security guards were on hand "to keep the peace" during the demonstration.

# Voting Rights Act of 1965

RESISTANCE TO BLACK enfranchisement in the Deep South continued unabated after passage of the Civil Rights Act of 1964. Three weeks after that act was signed into law, three voting rights activists were murdered in Mississippi. In the weeks that followed, scores of beatings, arrests, and other forms of intimidation attempted to thwart efforts by civil rights organizations to register black southern voters.

The final straw was the unprovoked attack by Alabama state troopers on peaceful marchers attempting to cross the Edmund Pettus Bridge in Selma, Alabama, en route to Montgomery on March 7, 1965. Eight days later, President Lyndon Johnson issued a call for a strong voting rights law, charging that, "Every device of which human ingenuity is capable has been used to deny this right ... [and] the fact is that the only way to pass these barriers is to show a white skin."

Testimony during hearings on the bill proved that as soon as one discriminatory voter registration practice had been banned, another one had taken its place. Although opposed by congressmen from the Deep South, the Voting Rights Act was approved by large majorities in the House of Representatives (333 to 48) and the Senate (77 to 19).

The act temporarily suspended literacy tests, since they had been used to unfairly deny blacks the right to register. It also provided for new voting practices and procedures to be cleared by the United States attorney general or the District Court for the District of Columbia. Section 2 of the law effectively repeated the language of the 15th Amendment to the Constitution, as it prohibited the denial of the right to vote on account of race or color.

The Voting Rights Act of 1965 finally provided for the enforcement of that language. On August 7, 1965, one day after President Johnson signed the bill into law, the U.S. Justice Department suspended literacy and similar tests in six southern states.

Annie Maude Williams of Selma, Alabama, proudly displays her voting eligibility certificate on August 10, 1965. She was registered by federal examiners dispatched to Dallas County as a result of the Voting Rights Act. The law changed voting in the South almost overnight. In Alabama, black registration grew from 66,000 in 1960 to 250,000 six years later. During the same time period in South Carolina, the number soared from 58,000 to 191,000. And in Mississippi, the black voting rolls jumped from 22,000 in 1960 to 175,000 in 1966. Nearly 60 percent of African-Americans in that state were registered to vote in 1968.

In Boston in 1965, African-Americans took responsibility for their children's education. Since the all-white school board refused to desegregate the city's schools, black parents, led by Ellen Swepson Jackson, started "Operation Exodus." Beginning in September 1965, the Exodus Bus transported 400 black students to the Faneuil School in the Back Bay section of the city. School busing would become a highly charged issue in Boston in the years ahead.

# 1960s

## *De Facto* Segregation

IN SPITE OF THE MAJOR civil rights bills passed in the 1960s, much of the United States remains segregated by race and ethnicity. This segregation is not by law (*de jure*) but by custom (*de facto*), which is much more difficult to combat.

Through the 1940s, practices by real estate companies effectively ensured continued residential segregation. "Restrictive covenants" were clauses in real estate title documents that restricted the sale of a property to people of the white race. "Red-lining" referred to a color-coding system used by the federal Home Owners Loan Corporation that classified black neighborhoods as the riskiest in which to make home loans. The U.S. Supreme Court banned restrictive covenants in 1948. In the 1970s, Congress began to require banks to maintain records on the ethnicity of home mortgage buyers; compliance, however, is uneven.

Similarly, real estate agents are legally constrained from engaging in racial "steering"—not showing houses in white neighborhoods to black prospective home buyers, but instead steering them to black neighborhoods. However, undercover "sting" operations routinely expose the continuation of the practice by some. In suburban areas, exclusionary zoning—for example, requiring each homeowner's lot to be at least one acre—assures that well-to-do (usually white) residents will be protected from unwanted neighbors.

Federal housing and urban renewal programs commonly have been manipulated by local authorities to maintain residential segregation. The placement of sewage-treatment plants and other potentially hazardous public works consistently affects nonwhite neighborhoods more than white residential areas. Conversely, highly prized improvement projects, such as new parks and public transportation routes, are more likely to be situated in white areas than in black.

A direct result of residential segregation is school segregation, which can be entrenched even more by such strategies as discriminatory pupil transfer policies, selection of locations for new schools, and gerrymandering of school district boundaries. Also, since in many localities property taxes pay for schools, another consequence of residential segregation is unequal funding for education. Combined together, residential and school segregation perpetuate the black underclass.

THE AUTOBIOGRAPHY OF **MALCOLM X**

*The Autobiography of Malcolm X*, written by Malcolm with journalist Alex Haley, is an aggressive odyssey of self-discovery. Malcolm relates his progression from Harlem stickup artist and convict to a self-taught scholar of the humanities, a fervent racial separatist, and a convert to the Muslim faith via Elijah Muhammad's New York-based Nation of Islam (NOI). Malcolm's expressed belief that all whites are irredeemable "devils"—a notion calculated to give every reader something spicy to chew on—is balanced later in the book by Malcolm's account of his joyous 1964 journey to Mecca, where he found fellowship with Muslims of many colors and nationalities. In a hopeful passage, Malcolm acknowledges that a brotherhood of races is possible. The book's final pages are dominated by Malcolm's disillusionment with Elijah Muhammad, and his acrimonious split from the NOI. As he expected, Malcolm did not live to see the book's publication.

From White House whispers to Klan rally shouts, the rumor was always the same: that Martin Luther King and others in the Civil Rights Movement were directly linked to communism. While civil rights activists took care not to allow their ranks to be infiltrated with Communists, King's detractors would maintain the charge even decades after his death. These right-wing protesters picketed outside Detroit's Cobo Hall, where King was speaking, on November 19, 1965.

The Negro—that humble, seemingly unassertive, comforting presence—was dying a quick death in 1965, and in his place stood the loud, bold black man. Boxer Muhammad Ali (*left*), the heavyweight champion who would not keep his mouth shut, personified black America's changing sensibility. Shunning his "slave" name of Cassius Clay after joining the Nation of Islam, Muhammad Ali (which he said meant "worthy of all praises" and "most high" in Arabic) was adamant about being accepted on his own terms. He fought former heavyweight champion Floyd Patterson (*right*) in November that year—Muslim vs. Catholic, brash vs. humble, "bad guy" vs. the "white man's champion" (as Ali called him). Ali won the fight by technical knockout in the 12th round.

Atlanta segregationist Lester Maddox (*center, in dark suit*) developed quite a following for his refusal to serve African-Americans in his Pickrick restaurant. His folk-hero status increased as he led this march through downtown Atlanta in April 1965. The city "too busy to hate" actually included visible racists who were not too busy to support their favorite segregationist.

The three defendants on trial for the murder of Reverend James Reeb—Stanley Hoggle, O'Neal Hoggle, and Elmer Cook—were acquitted by an all-white jury in Selma, Alabama, in December 1965. Although African-Americans made martyrs of heroes such as Jimmie Lee Jackson, whose murder by Alabama state troopers stirred the Selma to Montgomery marchers to action, his death received limited news coverage in the national press. However, the murders of Reeb and Viola Liuzzo, two white Northerners who volunteered to go to Selma to participate in the Civil Rights Movement, generated massive media coverage.

## 1966

**1966:** Black voters take advantage of their right to vote in Mississippi, Alabama, and other southern states.

**1966:** The National Welfare Rights Organization is formed to better the lives of mothers receiving welfare payments.

**1966:** Black soldier Milton Olive III is awarded a Congressional Medal of Honor for heroism in Vietnam. He saved the lives of others by leaping on an enemy grenade.

**1966:** Black nationalist Maulana Karenga creates the holiday Kwanzaa as a complement to Christmas.

**January 3:** Militant civil rights leader Floyd McKissick succeeds James Farmer as national director of CORE.

**January 7:** Martin Luther King, the SCLC, and local organizations launch the Chicago Freedom Movement. They aim to eliminate slums by challenging the many avenues of economic exploitation. *See* July 10, 1966.

**January 10:** In Atlanta, state legislators vote to not allow Julian Bond to take his oath of office in the Georgia House of Representatives because of his recent anti-Vietnam War remarks. *See* December 5, 1966.

**January 11:** Vernon Dahmer, a prominent civil rights leader in Hattiesburg, Mississippi, dies when his house is firebombed.

**January 18:** Robert C. Weaver becomes the first black Cabinet member when he's sworn in as secretary of the Department of Housing and Urban Development (HUD).

**January 25:** Constance Baker Motley becomes the first African-American and first woman to be appointed as a federal judge. ➤

SNCC veteran Julian Bond's election to the Georgia House of Representatives signaled an important political advance for black Americans. But his swearing-in on January 10, 1966, was engulfed in controversy. Bond had endorsed a statement by SNCC chairman John Lewis, who had supported draft dodging. Response to Bond's endorsement was swift and furious. Georgia Governor Lester Maddox, a segregationist, denounced Bond. While the oath was administered to the other House members that morning, Bond sat. A special House committee, in executive session, voted to deny him his seat. The next day, the full House affirmed Bond's dismissal in a 182–12 vote. The U.S. Supreme Court finally settled the issue, ruling that legislators were entitled to the same First Amendment rights as other citizens. On January 9, 1967, Bond took his seat.

White supremacy manifested itself in many forms, including music. "Nigger, Nigger," a song from a group called The Coon Hunters, was one of many white supremacist songs released by Reb-Time Records in the 1960s. (Its B side was "We Don't Want Niggers.") Another Reb-Time record was "Move Them Niggers North"/"Segregation Wagon" by Colonel Sharecropper. As with the Confederate flag, these blatant displays of racism regained popularity as an expression of white backlash against the Movement.

The novelist Chester Himes basked in his ironic fame in 1966. His most recent detective novels, *Cotton Comes to Harlem* and *The Heat's On*, explored themes of race and greed in the Harlem section of New York. Himes's detective thrillers—originally done only to pay the bills—go beyond the genre's self-imposed limitations. They deal with the ridiculousness of racism amid a complex black community filled with saints and sinners, gangsters and common folks, black policemen and winos. Himes moved to Spain in 1968 and died there in 1984.

High-rise public housing was built as temporary housing to allow the urban working poor to make a transition to middle-class life. But the high-rises were built in isolated areas—or places that became isolated when working-class blacks became the primary tenants. These housing "projects" were not part of neighborhoods with grocery stores and parks, so their densely cramped residents were effectively shut off from the cities in which they lived. Martin Luther King, in his 1966 Chicago campaign, attempted to combat the problems of "slum" housing in Chicago (*pictured*) by attempting to organize tenants. Such efforts ultimately failed, and the problems worsened with the proliferation of drugs in the late 1960s and early 1970s.

In 1966 white supremacists still considered murder the most effective way of showing the consequence of helping black people register to vote. NAACP worker Vernon Dahmer, a black man, was one such target. The Hattiesburg, Mississippi, store owner let blacks pay their $2 "poll tax"—used to hinder black voting registration—at his grocery store. On January 10, 1966, the Ku Klux Klan retaliated. Two carloads of Klansmen firebombed and shot up his home. Dahmer suffered serious injuries and died hours later. It took until 1998 to convict the known leader of the attack, Mississippi Klan Imperial Wizard Sam Bowers. After five trials in front of all-white juries had ended in deadlocks, a multiracial jury finally sentenced Bowers to life in prison.

# 1960s

## 1966

**February 26:** Andrew Brimmer becomes the first African-American to be appointed as governor of the Federal Reserve Board.

**March 7:** In *South Carolina v. Katzenbach*, the U.S. Supreme Court upholds the constitutionality of the 1965 Voting Rights Act, squelching a states' rights challenge.

**March 10:** Talmadge Hayer, Norman 3X Butler, and Thomas 15X Johnson, all members of the Nation of Islam, are convicted of first-degree murder for the February 1965 assassination of Malcolm X.

**March 15:** Rioting erupts again in the Watts section of Los Angeles, resulting in two deaths.

**April 30:** Black Mississippians build a "tent city" in view of President Johnson's White House window to protest housing conditions in their state.

**May 16:** Militant activist Stokely Carmichael replaces John Lewis as the chairman of SNCC.

**June 1–2:** President Lyndon Johnson holds a White House Conference on Civil Rights, which attracts 2,400 various leaders.

**June 5–6:** Wearing a pith helmet, James Meredith begins a one-man "March Against Fear" from Memphis, Tennessee, to Jackson, Mississippi. On the second day, he's shot and wounded in an ambush.

**June 7–26:** Martin Luther King, Stokely Carmichael, and others complete the March Against Fear.

**June 17:** In a speech in Greenwood, Mississippi, during the March Against Fear, Stokely Carmichael revs up the crowd with cries of "Black Power." ➤

In January 1966 Robert Weaver became the first African-American to head a Presidential Cabinet post, the new Department of Housing and Urban Development. Many years earlier, Weaver had been part of President Roosevelt's "Black Cabinet"— an unofficial group of "Negro affairs" advisers. In 1961 President Kennedy appointed him to lead the agency that preceded HUD, the Housing and Home Finance Agency. President Johnson promoted the agency to Cabinet status in 1966. Weaver held the HUD post until 1968, pushing Congress to pass the Fair Housing Act and fighting to increase the amount of affordable housing.

Martin Luther King and Elijah Muhammad, head of the Nation of Islam, are known to have met only once—in Chicago on February 24, 1966. King reportedly asked Muhammad if he really believed that *all* white people were devils. Muhammad reportedly smiled before responding. "Dr. King," he said, "you and me both grew up in Georgia, and we know there are many different kinds of snakes. The rattlesnake was poisonous and the king snake was friendly. But they were both snakes, Dr. King." The pair of Southerners, who grew up during different decades under the oppression of Jim Crow, shared a laugh.

# March Against Fear

AFTER INTEGRATING THE University of Mississippi, James Meredith continued his crusade against racism in his native state. In 1966 Meredith announced his intention to "walk against fear" from Memphis, Tennessee, to Jackson, Mississippi. By doing so, he hoped to encourage black turnout in Mississippi's June 7 primary election and to demonstrate that blacks could overcome the fear of white violence that inhibited them from voting. On June 5 Meredith set off on the 220-mile hike. The next day, he was shot in the back and hospitalized.

Martin Luther King of the SCLC, Floyd McKissick of CORE, Stokely Carmichael of SNCC, and others quickly flew to Memphis to continue the "Meredith March Against Fear." The civil rights leaders issued a manifesto outlining the purpose of their march. It called for federal voting examiners to be sent to 600 southern counties, proposed antipoverty measures to aid low-income African-Americans, and urged passage of pending civil rights legislation.

Eventually, the number of marchers reached several hundred. On June 14 marchers persuaded 650 African-American residents to vote in Grenada, Mississippi—and placed an American flag on a Confederate monument there. In Greenwood on June 17, Carmichael thrilled the

Coretta and Martin Luther King in the March Against Fear

marchers with his cries of "Black Power," which many historians consider a turning point in the Movement—the crossover from nonviolent to militancy.

On June 21, 300 whites in Philadelphia, Mississippi, attacked the marchers with stones, clubs, and bottles. Meredith demonstrated true courage by rejoining the march on June 24 and participating in the culminating rally in Jackson two days later.

On June 6, 1966, the second day of James Meredith's "March Against Fear," Meredith was shotgunned from ambush in Hernando, Mississippi. Aubrey James Norvell, a white man, was arrested and charged with the crime. Meredith recovered from the shooting and returned to finish the march.

# 1960s

**June 21:** In Philadelphia, Mississippi, 300 whites attack March Against Fear demonstrators with clubs, rocks, bottles, and firecrackers.

**June 23:** March Against Fear demonstrators are clubbed and tear-gassed by police in Canton, Mississippi.

**Early July:** At their national convention, CORE members express their support for "Black Power."

**July 9:** At its national convention, the NAACP refuses to support the concept of Black Power.

**July 10:** Martin Luther King leads at least 5,000 protesters from a rally at Soldier Field (which attracted 30,000 people) to Chicago's City Hall, where King tapes the movement's demands on the door.

**July 12–15:** In Chicago, police arrest black children because they used a fire hydrant's water for fun. The incident escalates into a riot in which two black citizens are killed and dozens are wounded. *See* August 5, 1966.

**July 18–23:** In Hough, a black section of Cleveland, tensions between white police officers and black citizens erupt into a riot after a black man was refused service at a bar. Two thousand members of the National Guard are needed to end the violence, which claims the lives of four people.

**August 5:** Hostile whites throw bricks, bottles, and stones at protesters as they march through Marquette Park, a white neighborhood in Chicago. Martin Luther King is hit in the head with a rock.

**August 26:** Martin Luther King and Chicago authorities agree on a 10-point housing accord.

**September 12:** Police in Grenada, Mississippi, allow a mob to attack black students at a newly integrated school.          ➤

The Meredith March Against Fear was an opportunity for militant black activists to express themselves. The sign on this marcher's back is the symbol of the Lowndes County Freedom Organization, SNCC's political party project in Alabama. The symbol would be appropriated by the Black Panther Party for Self-Defense, which was formed late in 1966. The Meredith march, which was led by proponents of both nonviolence (Martin Luther King) and militancy (SNCC), would become a fight over the soul of the Civil Rights Movement.

Neshoba County Sheriff Lawrence Rainey (*center, wearing tie*) watches a rally during the March Against Fear. Rainey was one of the Civil Rights Movement's many enemies. He had been suspected of being involved in the murder of civil rights organizers Andrew Goodman, James Earl Chaney, and Michael Schwerner in 1964. The FBI arrested him and several Ku Klux Klan leaders in connection with the murders, but he was acquitted. Rainey, who once spoke at a Klan rally in Meridian, Mississippi, was notorious for engaging in police brutality and harassment against blacks.

On June 23, 1966, during the March Against Fear, authorities in Canton, Mississippi, arrested an advance group of marchers for trying to pitch their tents at the McNeil Elementary School. Martin Luther King, stating that it was an all-black school, urged activists to pitch tents again. As the day wore on, King joined SNCC's Stokely Carmichael and CORE's Floyd McKissick on a flatbed truck used as a makeshift speaking podium. As state troopers brought out the tear gas, King instructed the activists to refrain from fighting back but to stand their ground. However, authorities, armed with gas and billy clubs, forced the marchers from the site in less than five minutes.

# Stokely Carmichael

STOKELY CARMICHAEL, in addition to his famous call for Black Power, trumpeted the phrase "Black Is Beautiful." Besides castigating the policies and actions of white America, Carmichael tried to instill pride in African-Americans. "Go home and tell your daughters that they're beautiful," he said.

Born in Trinidad and raised in New York City, Carmichael enrolled at Howard University in 1960 to be close to the Civil Rights Movement in the South. That same year, he joined SNCC. In 1961 Carmichael participated in the Freedom Rides and was arrested and jailed for 49 days in Jackson, Mississippi.

Three years later, Carmichael returned to Mississippi to contribute to SNCC's Freedom Summer project; he was arrested several times. The arrests, killings, beatings, and other forms of violent white reaction caused him great personal upset. Carmichael subsequently eschewed the philosophy of nonviolence and helped wrest control of SNCC from those who continued to pursue it. In June 1966, as the new chairman of SNCC, Carmichael issued his call for Black Power.

Carmichael formed a short-lived alliance with the Black Panther Party, serving as its honorary chairman. He spoke out against the war in Vietnam and traveled to North Vietnam, which led to the revocation of his passport. Shortly after it was returned to him, he left the country with his wife, South African singer Miriam Makeba, with the parting words that America did not belong to blacks.

Settling in Conakry, Guinea, in 1969, Carmichael devoted the rest of his life to pan-Africanism. He died of cancer in 1998 at the age of 57.

# 1960s

## Black Power

SNCC, THE MOST IDEALISTIC of the civil rights organizations, made a philosophical shift to greater militancy during the mid-1960s. Many in the organization did not feel that the physical, mental, and emotional toll of the Freedom Rides, Mississippi Freedom Summer, and other nonviolent direct-action campaigns had been worth the limited success. In June 1966, Stokely Carmichael, executive director of SNCC, issued a call for "Black Power" while speaking during the March Against Fear in Mississippi. In 1969 SNCC removed *Nonviolent* from its name, adopting the word *National* in its place.

In October 1966, four months after Carmichael's call for Black Power, Huey Newton and Bobby Seale formed the Black Panther Party for Self-Defense in Oakland, California. While the Panthers' major emphasis was armed resistance to police brutality, they also stressed economic self-determination. For a time, the BPP was formally allied with SNCC, but the alliance dissolved after Carmichael left the student organization.

RETALIATION TO CRIME: REVOLUTIONARY VIOLENCE
RÉPONSE AU CRIME: LA VIOLENCE RÉVOLUTIONNAIRE
RESPUESTA AL ASESINATO: VIOLENCIA REVOLUCIONARIA

Moderate civil rights leaders and elements within SNCC criticized the new militancy as counterproductive and threatening to the earlier gains. Martin Luther King asserted that the slogan was not a smart choice of words. He said it caused significant confusion and alarm and had proven dangerous and harmful to the Movement. Federal and local law enforcement deemed the Black Power movement especially dangerous and devoted considerable resources to infiltrating and neutralizing it.

As a program, Black Power was vague and ill-formed, leading to more backlash than progress. As a philosophy, however, it had considerable resonance among disaffected northern urban blacks whose lives had been largely untouched by the nonviolent Civil Rights Movement in the South. They were tired of turning the other cheek and waiting for white people to grant them equality. Young blacks, who had grown up in a society that made them feel inferior, began to take pride in their race as well as in themselves.

The March Against Fear was a turning point for the Movement. The civil rights leaders who participated in the march argued over the philosophy of the Movement itself. According to the cover of this September 1966 issue of *Sepia*, Martin Luther King insisted that he had not lost faith in nonviolence. But Stokely Carmichael

of SNCC argued for "Black Power." Floyd McKissick of CORE, a Carmichael ally, rejected nonviolence. The NAACP's Roy Wilkins supported King, saying his organization wanted nothing to do with Black Power. Internal disagreements over nonviolence and Black Power would plague the Civil Rights Movement for years to come.

Like James Baldwin, Claude Brown became an important literary voice for black Americans. Brown's classic semi-autobiographical novel, *Manchild in the Promised Land,* told the gritty story of black youngsters growing up in Harlem amid violence and poverty. Published at a high point of the Civil Rights Movement, it was not considered classic literature but produced great sales and a national discussion of the plight of blacks in urban areas. Brown became a sought-after speaker on these issues.

> "I am America. I am the part you won't recognize, but get used to me. Black, confident, cocky—my name, not yours. My religion, not yours. My goals, my own. Get used to me."
>
> —MUHAMMAD ALI

In 1966 Barbara Jordan was elected to the Texas Senate. It was a major feat, as she was the first woman ever and the first African-American since 1883 to win that post. As a state senator, Jordan introduced the first minimum wage bill in Texas, and worked to establish the state's Fair Employment Practices Commission. In 1972, the same year in which she became the first black southern woman to be sent to Congress, Jordan was named president pro tempore of the Texas body. It was the first time a black elected official presided over a state body. Jordan's oratory as a House Judiciary Committee member during the Watergate hearings in 1974 won her a deserved national spotlight.

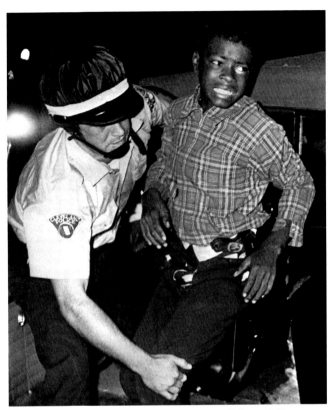

Henry Townes, a 22-year-old black man, did not follow police instructions to stop his car. Instead, according to Cleveland police, he drove the vehicle in front of a policeman. Townes's family was escaping a roller rink that had been set afire by young vandals. Police fired on his car and its occupants, which included Townes's wife, their son, a stepson, and her brother. Townes was the only one not hit. It was July 1966, and the predominately black Hough section of Cleveland burst into flames. The National Guard was called in, but one Guardsman was shot and four people died during the six-day riot. This 12-year-old boy, Ernest Williams, was shot. Black activists claimed the violence was caused by the substandard living conditions in Hough.

The Congress of Racial Equality had been an interracial organization committed to racial integration since its founding in 1942. CORE slowly evolved from a Gandhian activist group to an organization concerning itself with the problems of the black community. When Floyd McKissick replaced James Farmer in 1966 as CORE's national chairman, it was a reflection of the times. McKissick, shown here protesting in front of New York City's Apollo Theatre in July 1966, endorsed the "Black Power" slogan and opposed the war in Vietnam. Under McKissick's two-year tenure, CORE lost many of its white financial supporters and backers while becoming popular in more militant circles.

# Chicago Freedom Movement

IN ITS EFFORT to transport the tactics of the direct-action Civil Rights Movement to the North, the SCLC selected Chicago as its first target. Bayard Rustin warned Martin Luther King that he would fail in that most segregated of northern cities, but King would not be swayed. He had faith that, by staging an effective nonviolent movement in the nation's second largest city, they could arouse the conscience of America to deal with the problems of northern ghettos.

Meetings between the SCLC and a coalition of local civil rights groups in the fall of 1965 failed to produce a clear set of priorities for the campaign, although housing emerged as the major issue. Meanwhile, Chicago's economically and ideologically diverse black population was largely resistant to the activists' efforts. Only one-third to one-half of the expected number came out for a rally on July 10, 1966, at Soldier Field to kick off the "action phase" of the Chicago campaign. Nevertheless, King proceeded as planned with a march to City Hall. When Mayor Richard Daley closed City Hall in response, King taped a list of demands to the door.

While leading a march against racial discrimination in housing in Chicago, King was stoned by angry whites.

African-Americans marching proudly in suburban Chicago

It was the specter of violent confrontation over the housing issue that eventually led Daley to announce an open-housing agreement in August 1967. The creation of Operation Breadbasket, under the direction of King lieutenant Reverend Jesse Jackson, also came out of the Chicago campaign.

Martin Luther King was accustomed to taking important tactical gambles for the Civil Rights Movement. One of his greatest was attempting to bring the Movement north, to Chicago. In an attempt to make nonviolence work in the North, civil rights leaders held a massive nonviolence workshop for the thousands who gathered in Soldier Field on July 10, 1966. King said at the rally that the philosophy of nonviolence had been a major factor in the Movement's success. But less than a week later, rioting occurred in Chicago when police shut off a fire hydrant in a West Side black neighborhood.

On August 5, 1966, Martin Luther King was struck in the head by a rock-throwing protester in Marquette Park, a white neighborhood in Chicago. Civil rights leaders had called for the march to expose the sanctioned *de facto* housing discrimination that kept blacks in urban areas, regardless of their income. Local residents opposed the march, brandishing signs, epithets, rocks, bottles, firecrackers, and an anger fueled by fear. King ducked when he was hit, but he kept on walking. He told reporters that he had never seen such racial hatred, not even in such Klan strongholds as Mississippi.

Many residents of southwest Chicago, some of whom are shown here during an August 5, 1966, counterdemonstration to Martin Luther King's march, were white, working-class citizens. Many of them were the children and grandchildren of immigrants. Like other ethnic whites across the nation, they worked hard for generations in order to achieve middle-class status. For many, that meant living in residential areas that were all white by *de facto* community consensus. The idea of living next door to people of color, all too many believed, was a significant step back in terms of their hard-won class achievement.

The United States' history of white supremacy stigmatized people of color, particularly blacks, as subhuman. Although there were very few Ku Klux Klan-like public displays of racism in all-white northern suburbs, the residents' racial fears—*"Would you live near one? Would you allow one to date your daughter?"*—were shared by other ethnic working-class whites across the nation's northern cities. Unofficial policies denied blacks the right to buy homes or rent apartments in residential neighborhoods, including this one in Cicero, Illinois.

On August 21, 1966, the major Movement leaders appeared on national television together for the first and last time. A special 90-minute version of NBC's *Meet the Press* featured guests Roy Wilkins of the NAACP, Whitney Young of the National Urban League, Floyd McKissick of CORE, Stokely Carmichael of SNCC, James Meredith, and Martin Luther King, who left early and is not pictured. The leaders presented a united front, but they did not shy away from their ideological differences, particularly on the question of violence. King called the riots sweeping America "self-defeating," while McKissick called nonviolence "something of the past" and stated that CORE protesters would now defend themselves if attacked.

Black Power proponents likely had many more critics than admirers. Some people in the Movement, black and white alike, thought that Black Power would lead to violent white backlash. Cartoonist *Gib Crockett* of *The Washington Star* implied as much in this cartoon dated September 8, 1966. Martin Luther King also predicted backlash: "Anyone leading a violent rebellion must be willing to make an honest assessment regarding the possible casualties to a minority population confronting a well-armed, wealthy majority with a fanatical right wing that would delight in exterminating thousands of black men, women, and children."

Ron Karenga was a black nationalist leader in California. He developed a theory called *Kawaida* that encouraged black political and cultural development based on the best traditions and practices of classical African civilizations. In the aftermath of the Watts insurrection, Karenga was one of many leaders who created organizations and programs in Los Angeles to serve the black community and to prevent police brutality. Karenga's cultural nationalist organization was called US (United Slaves). In 1966 he created Kwanzaa, an annual holiday based on African harvest festivals.

Attempts at integration, even as late as 1966, continued to lead to violence. The SCLC's campaign to integrate schools in Grenada, Mississippi, infuriated the city's white residents, many of whom formed mobs that attacked demonstrators, black schoolchildren, and, as shown here on September 12, 1966, a Memphis news photographer. He was stomped on after being thrown to the ground by the crowd. The campaign began after government officials there had broken their word during the Meredith March Against Fear to integrate local schools. Black children attended classes on September 14, accompanied by state troopers and FBI agents.

Opposition to the Vietnam War was the common denominator of the American left in the late 1960s and early 1970s. SNCC, under the leadership of its new chairman, Stokely Carmichael, became actively involved in the nation's antiwar efforts. The top student organization opposing the war was the predominately white Students for a Democratic Society. Like SNCC, the SDS was a militant organization unafraid of radical, dramatic action to create substantial social change. The SDS, which defended SNCC's call for Black Power, praised SNCC for its antiwar stance and willingness to say— as Carmichael declared in this October 1966 rally—"to hell with the draft."

# 1960s

## 1966

**September 19:** Martin Luther King and folk singer Joan Baez lead a march in Grenada, Mississippi, protesting the beatings of African-American schoolchildren after schools were desegregated. *See* October 24, 1966.

**September 19:** A filibuster by southern senators leads to the withdrawal of the Civil Rights Bill of 1966, which includes a controversial section on housing discrimination.

**October:** In Oakland, Bobby Seale and Huey Newton create the Black Panther Party. The militant black organization seeks decent housing and a good educational system for African-Americans, an exemption of blacks from the military, the release of all blacks from jail, restitution for slave labor, and an end to police brutality.

**October 24:** In Grenada, Mississippi, police arrest 200 black citizens who are protesting the harassment of black students.

**November 8:** Edward Brooke (R–MA) is elected as the first African-American U.S. senator since Reconstruction.

**November 21:** Aubrey Norvell pleads guilty to shooting James Meredith during the March Against Fear.

**December 1:** SNCC rules to exclude all white activists from its membership.

**December 5:** The U.S. Supreme Court rules that the Georgia Legislature must allow Julian Bond to take his seat. The legislature originally refused to seat Bond because of his antiwar sentiments and opposition to the draft.

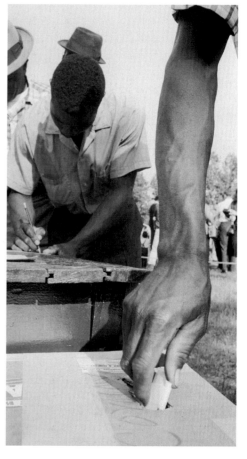

The voting line at the Greene County, Alabama, general store was long. But in contrast to the hundred-year wait that African-Americans had endured to exercise their franchise, it was one of the shortest lines in history. The number of African-Americans registered to vote in Alabama jumped from 66,000 in 1960 to more than 220,000 in 1966. Although whites still attempted to intimidate southern blacks from using the ballot, the newly passed Voting Rights Act, paid for in blood, allowed the majority of African-Americans to cast their votes. Blacks in Alabama's Lowndes County, with the help of SNCC organizers H. Rap Brown and Stokely Carmichael, became bold enough to organize their own political party with a slate of candidates. Even getting thrown off their share-cropped land by the white land-owners didn't discourage the members of the Lowndes County Freedom Organization.

Edward Brooke, a Republican, was the voice of black moderates during the 1960s and 1970s. The former Massachusetts attorney general became in 1966 both the first black U.S. senator since Reconstruction and the first African-American to be elected to the Senate by popular vote. Brooke's brand of low-key politics allowed him to win the white vote. In 12 years in office, Brooke became a member of the President's Commission on Civil Disorders, the Senate's Aeronautical and Space Sciences Committee, and the Banking and Currency Committee.

In 1967 Martin Luther King came out publicly against the Vietnam War. At this April 15 speech in New York City, he led 125,000 demonstrators in a chant to end the bombing. Public opinion sharply turned against King because he dared to add his voice to the rising chorus of dissent. The very idea of the merging of the civil rights and antiwar movements, was, according to a resolution of the NAACP's board of directors, a serious mistake. But for King, who held steadfast to the teachings of Jesus Christ and Mahatma Gandhi, the three great evils in the world were racism, militarism, and economic exploitation. He was killed believing all three had to be fought at the same time.

# Black Panther Party

JUST AS THE YOUTHFUL organizers of SNCC expressed the militancy of the southern civil rights protests of the early 1960s, the insurgents of the Black Panther Party (BPP) exhibited the militancy of the urban Black Power movement of the late 1960s. Indeed, Oakland-based activists Huey Newton and Bobby Seale, who founded the BPP in October 1966, borrowed the Black Panther symbol from SNCC's voter registration project in Lowndes County, Alabama. Newton respected SNCC "for having some of the most disciplined organizers in the country." In addition, during BPP's early years, some of SNCC's most prominent "Black Power" proponents, notably Stokely Carmichael, also worked closely with the Black Panthers.

The "Platform and Program of the Black Panther Party," drafted by Newton and Seale, listed 10 demands. They included basic needs—full employment and decent housing—as well as more radical objectives, such as

BPP founders Bobby Seale *(left)* and Huey Newton *(right)*

exemption of black men from military service and "freedom of all black men held in federal, state, county, and city prisons and jails."

The last item on the Panthers' list of demands summarized their goals: "We want land, bread, housing, education, clothing, justice, and peace. And as our major political objective, a United Nations-supervised plebiscite to be held throughout the black colony in which only black colonial subjects will be allowed to participate for the purpose of determining the will of black people as to their national destiny."

The Black Panther Party's considerable appeal among young African-Americans was based less on its program or its leaders' Marxist rhetoric than on its willingness to expose police brutality. Newton, who carried law books in his car, would often question police conduct by reading aloud the relevant portions of the California legal code. The Black Panthers' most publicized early action came when Seale led a group of well-armed Panthers to California's capitol in Sacramento to protest proposed gun-control legislation.

One of those attracted to the Black Panther Party was Eldridge Cleaver, a former convict and author whose autobiographical essays were later collected in the bestseller *Soul on Ice* (1968). Cleaver quickly became one of the Party's most effective and best-known spokespersons. His position as a writer for the New Left journal *Ramparts* brought the Party additional publicity and created a link between the Panthers and white leftist sympathizers. After Cleaver became editor of BPP's Black Community News Service and a public speaker on behalf of the group, his uniquely caustic, bombastic verbal attacks on white authorities became part of the Black Panther Party's public image.

Cleaver became more prominent after October 28, 1967, when Newton was arrested after an altercation ended in the death of an Oakland police officer. The Panthers immediately mobilized to free Newton, holding a "Free Huey" rally in Oakland on February 17, 1968. This well-attended event increased the national visibility of the Black Panther Party and broadened support for the effort to free Newton.

Eldridge Cleaver stands outside BPP headquarters, shot up by Oakland police in 1968.

intensified the sometimes vicious factionalism that occured within the Black Panther Party.

In 1970, when Newton was released on bail after his conviction on a voluntary manslaughter charge was reversed on appeal, he returned to the Party and found it in disarray. He sought to revive the Party and reestablish his control by deemphasizing police confrontations in favor of survival programs—programs that would meet the everyday needs of black communities while also educating black people. During the late 1960s and early 1970s, the Black Panther Party concentrated on developing four main programs: the petition campaign for community control of police, free breakfast for schoolchildren, free health clinics, and liberation schools. Such programs attracted new members, allowed Panthers to interact with diverse segments of black communities, and helped to counter the Party's negative image in the media.

Newton's efforts to shift the Black Panther Party's emphasis from revolutionary rhetoric and armed confrontations to survival programs did not prevent further external attacks and internal schisms from plaguing the group. By the mid-1970s the Panthers had been weakened by years of conflict. Nevertheless, some chapters maintained their activities during the period.

In 1973 Bobby Seale ran a strong but unsuccessful campaign for mayor of Oakland. Following Newton's departure for self-imposed exile in Cuba, Elaine Brown experienced some success in continuing Newton's emphasis on community service programs. Nevertheless, amid intense police repression and an increasingly hostile political climate, the group could not reverse its decline as a political force. The Panthers disbanded in 1982.

Despite the success of the February rally, the BPP was soon weakened by internal conflicts and external repression from government police agencies. Also, its alliance with SNCC broke up during the summer of 1968. The FBI's Counterintelligence Program (COINTELPRO) decimated the BPP's leadership and disrupted its relations with other militant organizations. The FBI's disinformation efforts precipitated a gun battle in January 1969 on the UCLA campus that left two Panthers dead. In March 1969 Seale was arrested for conspiracy to incite a riot at the 1968 Democratic National Convention in Chicago. In August Connecticut officials charged Seale and several other Panthers with the murder of Party member Alex Rackley, who was believed to be a police informant.

In New York in April 1969, 21 Panthers were charged with plotting to assassinate policemen and blow up buildings. Then in December 1969 police killed two Chicago Panthers, Fred Hampton and Mark Clark, while they were sleeping at Hampton's apartment. The police raid was planned with the help of a police informer. Other covert operations by the FBI and local police forces further

# 1960s

## 1967

**1967:** Jonathan Kozol's book *Death at an Early Age*, about Boston's substandard educational system for black children, is published.

**1967:** Harold Cruse's *The Crisis of the Negro Intellectual: A Historical Analysis of the Failure of Black Leadership* is published. Cruse attacks the notion of integration and encourages a sense of black nationalism.

**1967:** "US," an exhibit of civil rights photography, is displayed at Harlem's Countee Cullen Library.

**January 16:** In Macon County, Alabama, Lucius D. Amerson becomes the first black sheriff in the South since Reconstruction.

**March 22:** For the first time, a federal court orders a state (Alabama), not just an individual school board, to desegregate its public schools.

**April 4:** Martin Luther King condemns the U.S. government's Vietnam policy in a speech at Riverside Church in New York. *See* April 10, 1967.

**April 8–10:** Black students riot at Fisk University and Tennessee A&M following Stokely Carmichael's speech at Fisk.

**April 10:** In reaction to Martin Luther King's antiwar speech, the NAACP votes against merging the Peace Movement with the Civil Rights Movement.

**April–May:** The Black Panthers introduce two periodicals, *Black Panther Party: Black Community News Service* and *The Black Panther*.

**May 2:** More than two dozen armed Black Panthers march into the California state capitol to voice their opposition to an anti-gun bill.

**May 11:** At Jackson State, an all-black college in Mississippi, student protesters storm a police barricade. Police fire into the crowd, killing one student. ➤

"We had seen the Oakland police and California Highway Patrol begin to carry their shotguns in full view as another way of striking fear into the community. We had seen all this, and we recognized that the rising consciousness of Black people was almost at the point of explosion. Out of this sprang the Black Panther Party."

—HUEY NEWTON, *REVOLUTIONARY SUICIDE*

Black Panther Party Minister of Defense Huey Newton was not a great public speaker, to the disappointment of many of his admirers. He also had a fascination with the underworld that eventually would be his undoing. But Newton, a law student turned vanguard leader, was a revolutionary theorist who motivated the world from his jail cell. When he compared blacks to the Vietnamese and other "colonized" people, intellectuals and activists absorbed his words and took them—and his bravado—as their own.

## Understanding the Rebellion

AS I SUFFERED through Sambo and the Black Tar Baby story in *Brer Rabbit* in the early grades, a great weight began to settle on me. It was the weight of ignorance and inferiority imposed by the system. I found myself wanting to identify with the white heroes in the primers and in the movies I saw, and in time I cringed at the mention of Black. This created a gulf of hostility between the teachers and me, a lot of it repressed, but still there, like the strange mixture of hate and admiration we Blacks felt toward whites generally.

We simply did not feel capable of learning what the white kids could learn.... Our image of ourselves was defined for us by textbooks and teachers. We not only accepted ourselves as inferior; we accepted the inferiority as inevitable and inescapable.

...Predictably, this sense of despair and futility led us into rebellious attitudes. Rebellion was the only way we knew to cope with the suffocating, repressive atmosphere that undermined our confidence.

—*Huey P. Newton*, Revolutionary Suicide

As veterans of the urban streets, members of the Black Panther Party for Self-Defense knew when they were being targeted. So when the Oakland police pushed the California State Assembly to pass a bill that would have banned the showing of loaded guns in public places, the Panthers responded quickly and decisively. Guns fully displayed, Black Panther Party Chairman Bobby Seale marched 30 Panthers into the statehouse on May 2, 1967. Governor Ronald Reagan was on the Capitol lawn, speaking to a group of students, oblivious to what was occurring. Reagan, as governor, would later become one of the fiercest enemies of the BPP and its allies in struggle.

James Brown's music represented the guttural, black, southern-meets-urban experience that Motown softened up for white audiences. He began writing anthems in the late 1960s, the most famous being "Say It Loud, I'm Black and I'm Proud." The hit song struck the right spiritual chord among African-Americans who were inspired by the Civil Rights Movement and empowered by the Black Power movement.

One person was fatally wounded in this protest at Jackson State College in Mississippi on May 11, 1967. Protesters stormed a police barricade, and authorities responded with gunfire. The National Guard was called in to reestablish peace. This scene would play over and over again through the late 1960s and early 1970s on college campuses. The issues would be either Black Power and/or Vietnam, but the tensions would not subside.

# 1960s

## 1967

**May 12:** Black militant H. Rap Brown replaces Stokely Carmichael as national chairman of SNCC.

**May 16:** A policeman is killed as black students riot at Texas Southern University in Houston.

**June 12:** In *Loving v. Virginia*, the U.S. Supreme Court strikes down laws in 16 states that prohibit interracial marriage.

**June 13:** Thurgood Marshall becomes the first African-American nominated to the U.S. Supreme Court.

**June 19:** A U.S. District Court rules that the *de facto* segregation in Washington, D.C., schools is unconstitutional and that the city must desegregate its schools by fall.

**Summer:** Riots rage in many major northern cities, resulting in approximately a hundred deaths.

**June 22:** Stokely Carmichael is convicted of fomenting a riot in Atlanta four days earlier.

**June 23–28:** In Detroit, police raid an illegal black drinking establishment, angering blacks in the area. A riot ensues, resulting in 43 deaths.

**July 12–17:** Rioting sweeps through Newark, New Jersey, resulting in the deaths of 26 people.

**July 20:** The first Black Power conference is held in Newark, New Jersey.

**July 24:** In a speech in Cambridge, Maryland, black militant H. Rap Brown proclaims: "If America don't come around, we're going to burn it down." After the speech, rioting ensues throughout the city.

**July 26:** H. Rap Brown is arrested for inciting the Cambridge riot after Maryland Governor Spiro Agnew announces: "It shall now be the policy of this state to immediately arrest any person inciting to riot, and to not allow that person to finish his vicious speech." ➤

When the smoke cleared at Texas Southern University on May 16, 1967, nearly 500 students, many of whom are shown face down (*above photo*), were arrested. Three were wounded and a police officer was killed. The police claimed they had been fired upon from a dormitory window when a campus rally got out of hand. A student's arrest had ignited the nightlong insurrection. In the photo at right, a law enforcement official attempts to exert authority by firing his shotgun.

The police beating of Newark cab driver John Smith was the spark that ignited a riot in Newark, New Jersey, a working-class enclave next to New York City, on July 12, 1967. Over a span of five days, 26 people were killed. The insurrection occurred because of police brutality against the city's black citizens, the lack of black political representation in a city where half of the population was black, and the uprooting of a black neighborhood for the construction of a state teaching hospital center.

Longtime Newark residents still remember the police brutality before, during, and after the 1967 riots. When the police and the National Guard saw that stores with "Soul Brother" signs were left unmolested, they smashed their windows. Black Newarkers—including children—were shot by National Guard troops, who claimed they had been responding to sniper attacks. (Later it was discovered that the "sniper attacks" actually had been the Guardsmen's own bullets ricocheting off the walls of Newark's high-rise housing projects.) The three to four days of gunfire and rumors of gunfire stained the city's reputation for decades.

The date for Newark's Black Power Conference was set before the 1967 insurrection that almost tore the city asunder. It was the second of a series of meetings between 1966 and 1969. This meeting, occurring a week after the Newark riot, was attended by black nationalists as well as black mainstream reformists who sought a collective black agenda. The most significant accomplishment was Newark activist/poet Amiri Baraka's establishment of the United Brothers, a group that would evolve into the Committee for Unified Newark. United Brothers/CFUN would run a slate of black candidates for office, culminating in the 1970 election of Kenneth Gibson as the city's first black mayor.

# 1960s

## Summer Riots

IN THE SUMMER OF 1967, two years after the Watts section of Los Angeles exploded in violence, similar riots afflicted urban centers with large black populations. Riots erupted in such cities as Newark, Detroit, New York, Cleveland, Washington, Chicago, and Atlanta. Sparked usually by confrontations with the police, the uprisings were expressions of black rage and despair over continued economic and political powerlessness.

All told in 1967, 75 major riots occurred throughout the country, resulting in 83 deaths—43 in Detroit. On July 28, 1967, while rioting was still underway in the Motor City, President Lyndon Johnson formed the National Advisory Commission on Civil Disorders to study the root causes of the disturbances and to recommend action.

More commonly known as the Kerner Commission (after its chairman, Illinois Governor Otto Kerner), the commission presented its findings in February 1968. Concluding that the riots reflected the profound frustration of blacks over the deeply embedded racism in American society, the commission warned that the United States was "moving toward two societies, one black, one white—separate and unequal."

Johnson had little opportunity to act on the commission's findings, however. Hobbled politically by the war in Vietnam, he chose not to run for reelection in 1968. Republican Richard Nixon, who succeeded him as presi-

Rioting in Newark, New Jersey

dent, largely ignored the suggestions of the commission. The riot-scarred cities saw an exodus of white residents to the suburbs and the disintegration of liberal coalitions, which had begun to address the economic and social disparities between blacks and whites.

Though progressive laws emerged, such as the Michigan Fair Housing Act of 1968, inner-city blacks became more isolated from white society. Ghetto life worsened in the 1970s and '80s, with increased rates of unemployment, poverty, crime, and drug abuse.

The Detroit riot of 1967 was the most devastating uprising of America's "long, hot summer." All the elements for a racial explosion were present. Police raids of the city's black after-hours social clubs were causing community outrage. In previous weeks, a white gang had killed Danny Thomas, a black Army veteran, and got off scot-free. In addition, the weather was unbearably hot. When a police officer smashed the window of a social club with a sledgehammer on July 23, the riot began. The National Guard (*pictured*) was eventually called in.

Thomas Allen, age three, stands on the ruins of his home on Detroit's East Side on July 26, 1967. As with most urban riots, black citizens suffered the most during the Detroit uprising. Forty-three people were killed, 33 of whom were African-Americans. More than 7,200 people were arrested, 6,400 of them black. About 1,300 buildings were burned, and 5,000 people were left homeless by wind-swept fires. Thomas and his family stayed in one of several emergency housing centers.

The Detroit riot was yet another symbolic Molotov cocktail thrown at President Lyndon Johnson's presidency. Johnson created the National Advisory Commission on Civil Disorders so that the causes of the riots could be studied. When the commission, headed by Governor Otto Kerner of Illinois, finished its report the following year, Johnson, who had decided not to run for reelection, did little to acknowledge its findings—that white racism was the cause of the insurrections.

# 1960s

## Muhammad Ali

BORN IN SEGREGATED LOUISVILLE, Kentucky, in 1942, Cassius Clay started boxing after his bicycle was stolen and a white policeman taught him to defend himself. Boastful and charismatic, Clay won an Olympic gold medal in Rome in 1960. He "shocked the world" in 1964 by knocking out Sonny Liston to win the world heavyweight championship.

That same year, Clay announced his conversion to Islam, his membership in the Nation of Islam (then called Black Muslims), and his name change to Muhammad Ali. He maintained his world title until 1967, when he refused induction into the United States Army because of religious reasons. Ali said he did not support the Vietnam War and that he had "no quarrel" with the Vietcong.

Prosecuted for draft evasion, Ali was sentenced to five years in jail but allowed to remain free while he appealed the verdict. He was banned from boxing, however, and stripped of the world heavyweight championship title. At the time, he was 29–0 with 23 knockouts and nine successful title defenses.

In October 1970—43 months after his last fight—Ali returned to the ring, and in 1971 the U.S. Supreme Court overturned his conviction. Four years later, he regained the heavyweight title with a win against George Foreman. He retired with a 56–5 record and recognition as the greatest heavyweight boxer of all time—which he was fond of telling people.

While a hero to black militants and Vietnam War protesters, Ali also was beloved by much of white America for his convictions, courage, talent, and zest. Many historians consider Ali the most socially significant athlete of the 20th century. "What other athlete had such an impact on his times?" asked *Newsday* editor Greg Long. "His story serves to enrich all Americans."

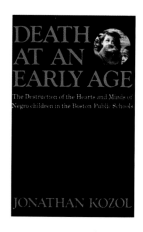

Jonathan Kozol began teaching at elementary schools in Boston's mainly black Roxbury district in 1963. A young, white graduate of Harvard who attended Oxford University as a Rhodes Scholar, Kozol struggled to overcome the effects of rotting school buildings; overcrowded classrooms; outdated, blatantly racist history books and readers; violent physical punishment of students; and other acts by teachers that inadvertently or purposely pummeled young children's self-regard. Racism was rampant among teachers and other staff members. Black students were assumed to be stupid, unsocialized, and unteachable. When Kozol proved in the classroom that this was false, he was fired. His 1967 book, *Death at an Early Age*, describes this nightmare with quiet anger, and with tenderness for the boys and girls Kozol hoped to see learn and thrive. The book was an immediate sensation, and established Kozol as a major voice in social and educational studies.

H. Rap Brown, national chairman of SNCC, was committed to revolution by whatever means necessary. He had no qualms, moral or otherwise, about calling for violence to achieve revolutionary goals. During a speech in Cambridge, Maryland, on July 24, 1966, Brown said that if black liberation was not quickly forthcoming, blacks would burn America down. After a fire broke out at a school following Brown's speech, Maryland Governor Spiro Agnew blamed him for inciting arson. FBI agents arrested Brown at Washington National Airport, charging him with flight to escape prosecution.

John Daniels (*pictured*) of Milwaukee, a pre-med student, was shot at twice because his summer job at the post office kept him out during the city's riot curfew hours in early August 1967. Tensions began with shootings and fires on July 30, just days after the Detroit riot ended. Fearing the worst, Mayor Henry Maier stated that no Milwaukee citizens were allowed to leave their homes on July 31 and August 1; he then established a 7 P.M. curfew over the next week. The turbulence inspired activists to make Milwaukee the "Selma of the North." Protesters pushed for strict open-housing legislation, which came to fruition the following year.

In 1967 President Lyndon Johnson named U.S. Solicitor General Thurgood Marshall (*top right*) to the U.S. Supreme Court. Marshall would become the first black person to serve on the nation's highest court. The former NAACP lawyer had come a long way from arguing the landmark *Brown v. Board of Education* case in 1954. That discussion pushed the first domino that eventually would topple Jim Crow. Now Marshall would defend and shape the law of the land according to the same Constitution that once regarded a person of his race as three-fifths of a man. Marshall, who strove to preserve equal protection under the law, served on the court until his retirement in 1991.

Congressman John Conyers (D-MI) was one of a generation of outspoken black leaders who became members of the House of Representatives. In August 1967 he introduced a $30 billion bill that would provide nondiscriminatory full employment, education, and housing. Conyers would go on to become one of the founders of the Congressional Black Caucus and the author of a bill studying reparations for the descendants of enslaved Africans.

# 1960s

## 1967

**July 29:** In the wake of the summer riots, President Lyndon Johnson appoints a National Advisory Commission on Civil Disorders to determine the specific causes for the violence. *See* February 29, 1968.

**July 31:** The National Urban Coalition is founded to improve the quality of life for the disadvantaged in urban areas.

**August 15:** At the SCLC's annual convention in Atlanta, Martin Luther King urges a massive civil disobedience campaign in northern cities and proclaims he will support only presidential candidates who oppose the Vietnam War.

**August 25:** FBI Director J. Edgar Hoover instructs his Counterintelligence Program to "expose, disrupt, misdirect, discredit, or otherwise neutralize the activities of black nationalist, hate-type organizations and groupings, their leadership, spokesmen, membership, and supporters, and to counter their propensity for violence and civil disorder."

**September 10:** About 250 black demonstrators are arrested at the University of Illinois.

**October 1:** *Wall of Respect*, a large mural at 43rd Street and Langley Avenue on Chicago's South Side, is dedicated. The wall depicts images of accomplished African-Americans.

**October 20:** Seven Ku Klux Klan members are convicted of conspiracy in the 1964 murders of three civil rights workers.

**October 28:** Black Panther Party cofounder Huey Newton is arrested on charges of killing an Oakland police officer and wounding another. *See* August 5, 1970.

**November 7:** Carl Stokes in Cleveland and Richard Hatcher in Gary, Indiana, become the first black mayors of large U.S. cities.

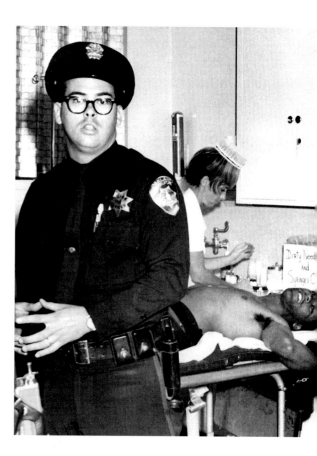

Huey Newton, the Black Panther Party's Minister of Defense, was shot in a confrontation with Oakland police officer John Frey on October 28, 1967. Frey had stopped Newton while Newton was driving by a city intersection. A citation was issued. Somehow the traffic stop became an altercation between Newton and Frey that led to Frey's death and Newton's injury. Newton was charged with and convicted of voluntary manslaughter, and he stayed in jail for two years. His case became a cause célèbre, with Panthers and others shouting "Free Huey!" at rallies. His conviction was overturned when evidence showed that another officer shot the bullets that killed Frey and injured Newton. By the time he was released, Newton had become a household name.

While Huey Newton was in jail, the Black Panther Party underwent significant changes. Chairman Bobby Seale (*pictured*) turned the BPP from a local organization into a national one, with chapters and branches in every major city in the United States as well as in Algiers. The power of the "Free Huey" campaign and the rage over the assassination of Martin Luther King in 1968 would increase BPP membership substantially. Seale was always proud of his organizing skills, and running the BPP's various and growing interests was a showcase for his talent and passion.

# Loving v. Virginia

A LEGACY OF SLAVERY TIMES, antimiscegenation laws barred interracial marriages well into the 20th century. In fact, these laws remained on the books of 16 states until 1967, when the U.S. Supreme Court declared them unconstitutional in the case of *Loving v. Virginia*.

In June 1958 two residents of Virginia, Mildred Jeter, a black woman, and Richard Loving, a white man (*both pictured*), went to the District of Columbia to get married because the laws of their state barred interracial unions. The Lovings then returned to Virginia. Four months later they were arrested and charged with violating Virginia's ban on interracial marriages. The Lovings pleaded guilty, and in January 1959 they received one-year jail sentences, which Judge Leon M. Basile said he would suspend if they left the state and did not return for 25 years. Basile stated in his opinion that "Almighty God created the races white, black, yellow, malay and red, and he placed them on separate continents.... The fact that he separated the races shows that he did not intend for the races to mix."

The Lovings moved to Washington, D.C., and in 1963 began efforts to fight their conviction. After two courts upheld the constitutionality of the Virginia antimiscegenation statutes, the case went all the way to the U.S. Supreme Court. Its decision, delivered by Chief Justice Warren Burger on June 12, 1967, held that the Virginia ban on interracial marriage constituted an abridgement

of the Equal Protection and Due Process Clauses of the 14th Amendment.

The Supreme Court's opinion stated: "The fact that Virginia prohibits only interracial marriages involving white persons demonstrates that the racial classifications must stand on their own justification, as measures designed to maintain White Supremacy. We have consistently denied the constitutionality of measures which restrict the rights of citizens on account of race. There can be no doubt that restricting the freedom to marry solely because of racial classifications violates the central meaning of the Equal Protection Clause."

Carl Stokes was elected mayor of Cleveland in November 1967, thus becoming the first black elected leader of one of America's 10 largest cities. He and Richard Hatcher, elected mayor of Gary, Indiana, that same year, showed that African-Americans could run for and win elected offices against white candidates. Stokes strived to be a good mediator in a racially polarized city, and he was credited with improving the city's water, streets, and welfare system. He served two two-year terms before voluntarily stepping down in 1971.

# Black Soldiers in Vietnam

URING THE VIETNAM WAR, the United States Army was better integrated racially than the rest of American society, at least among its enlisted ranks. However, the officer ranks remained predominantly white, and the poor and working classes, including African-Americans, were over-represented among noncommissioned personnel.

In part, this disparity was the result of many young blacks entering the military in order to escape from poverty. However, it also was due to the discriminating policies of the predominantly white draft boards. On the battlefields, blacks suffered casualty rates that were roughly twice those of whites. This glaring imbalance did not go unnoticed, and militant black leaders began to speak out against the war because of its disproportionate sacrifice of black life. By the late 1960s, black soldiers themselves became more militant, resulting in racial tension on military bases.

Eventually, moderate leaders, including Martin Luther King, also began to speak out against the war in Vietnam, not only because of the high black casualty rates but also because it had deflected attention from the Civil Rights Movement. President Lyndon Johnson could not wage both his War on Poverty and a war in Vietnam at the same time. Speaking at Riverside Church in New York City on April 4, 1967, King charged that Johnson's idea of a Great Society had been destroyed on the battlefields of Vietnam.

Like white Vietnam veterans, black vets received little public appreciation or support after the war. Many had to overcome physical and/or psychological damage, and most returned to economically depressed communities.

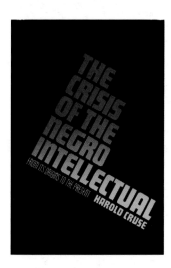

One of the most influential books to come out of the Civil Rights Movement was Harold Cruse's *The Crisis of the Negro Intellectual*, published in 1967. It argued for an independent black cultural reawakening. Cruse believed that African-Americans had been robbed of their cultural identity by their ostensible "friends" on the left, including Marxists and pro-integrationist liberals. He envisioned a self-sufficient black community, free from the dictates of even the most well-meaning whites. Cruse's work contributed to the creation of black studies departments at universities across the United States.

In November 1967 Richard Hatcher was elected mayor of Gary, Indiana, a working-class city with a large black population. Along with Cleveland's Carl Stokes, he became one of the first two African-Americans to be elected mayor of a major city. Hatcher served as Gary's leader for five terms before his defeat in a 1987 primary. In addition to his local duties, he hosted the National Black Power Convention in 1972 and became chairman of the National Board of Directors for Operation PUSH in the 1980s.

Stokely Carmichael (*above*) and others in SNCC led the black activist vanguard against the Vietnam War. Protests gained strength on college campuses, and leaders of SNCC and the Black Panther Party became popular speakers against a war they said used blacks as cannon fodder for U.S. imperialism. They felt that African-Americans had more than enough battles to fight in their own country. As this bitterly satirical leaflet states, "You can't die fast enough in the ghettos."

Muhammad Ali wasn't the only black man who refused to fight for America against the Viet Cong. Private Ronald Lockman, shown here embraced by his girlfriend, Lynette Polk, and his mother, Mrs. Vivian Williams, was court-martialed after he refused orders to go to Vietnam. Lockman said he couldn't subject himself to the "atrocities" being committed by American soldiers in Vietnam. The 23-year-old Philadelphia native was sentenced to a dishonorable discharge and 2½ years of hard labor.

This sign, posted somewhere in Vietnam, reads: "U.S. Negro armymen! You are committing the same ignominious crimes in South Vietnam that the KKK clique is perpetuating against your family at home." This was a cleverly worded piece of Communist propaganda, but the message undoubtedly struck a chord with black soldiers. Upon turning 18 in 1967, most black males faced the risk of dying or being forced to kill in a seemingly purposeless war, imprisonment for draft dodging, and/or discrimination and harassment at home.

In Milwaukee, police drag a female protester down the street after she was arrested in a demonstration for open housing on December 5, 1967. More than 800 protesters celebrated the 100th day of open-housing marches in that city. Protests, police crackdowns, and insurrections filled the national news throughout 1967. During the year, major riots erupted in Milwaukee; Detroit; Newark; Tampa; Atlanta; Buffalo; Memphis; Cambridge, Maryland; Durham, North Carolina; New Haven, Connecticut; and Cairo and East St. Louis, Illinois.

## 1968

**1968:** The documentary film *No Vietnamese Ever Called Me a Nigger* is released.

**1968:** Dorothy Lee Bolden organizes the National Domestic Workers Union.

**January 2:** Robert Clark becomes the first African-American to join the Mississippi legislature in the 20th century.

**January 18:** Invited to a White House luncheon, black entertainer Eartha Kitt criticizes America's involvement in the Vietnam War in front of hostess Lady Bird Johnson. Kitt subsequently will become the subject of a CIA investigation.

**February:** In Washington, D.C., Martin Luther King meets with militant black activists H. Rap Brown and Stokely Carmichael. King pleads with them to keep future campaigns nonviolent.

**February 8:** In Orangeburg, South Carolina, state and local police fire on a crowd of unarmed black students protesting a segregated bowling alley. Three students are killed and 27 are wounded.

**February 29:** The National Advisory Commission on Civil Disorders, chaired by Illinois Governor Otto Kerner, issues its report on the race riots that have plagued the country. The report focuses the blame on poverty, discrimination, unequal enforcement of the law, substandard education, and inferior housing and public services.

**March:** *Soul on Ice*, a collection of essays by Black Panther leader Eldridge Cleaver, is published.

**March 19:** Students at Howard University seize an administration building and demand more Afro-American studies courses. ➤

Congressman Adam Clayton Powell, a powerful civil rights activist since the 1930s, faced adversity throughout the '60s. He was sued by a woman in his Harlem district for libel, which led to a monetary settlement. Though Powell was reelected in 1966, the House refused to seat him because he had used House committee funds for his personal use. The U.S. Supreme Court supported Powell, ruling that Congress could not deny newly elected officials their seats. On January 9, 1968, Powell told UCLA students (*pictured*) that they should continue, like himself, to fight on against the odds. "You must not scorn the black revolution," he said. "You must not scorn Black Power." Controversial and confrontational, Powell served as a veteran role model to young, militant African-Americans.

The final report of the National Advisory Commission on Civil Disorders—nicknamed the "Kerner Commission" because it was headed by Illinois Governor Otto Kerner (*second from left*)—was blistering. "This is our basic conclusion," the report stated. "Our nation is moving toward two societies, one black, one white—separate and unequal." The commission's purpose had been to study the

cause of the 1967 summer riots. Commission members interviewed a wide range of people, from established civil rights leaders to black youth from the inner cities. They determined that white racism was the cause of the riots: "Discrimination and segregation have long permeated much of American life; they now threaten the future of every American." The report of the commission, created by President Johnson, fell on deaf ears in both the Johnson and the Nixon administrations. Nixon's response to the insurrections was a stronger police presence.

Singer/actress Eartha Kitt (*right*) caused a storm of controversy after this photo was taken at a White House luncheon on January 18, 1968. First Lady Lady Bird Johnson (*center*) asked the group about the causes of youth delinquency. "Vietnam is the main reason we are having trouble with the youth of America," Kitt responded. "It is a war without explanation or reason." Her candor startled Lady Bird Johnson and the nation. Instead of being respected for her opinions, Kitt would be investigated by the FBI and CIA and shunned by the American entertainment industry. She continued her career in Europe before returning to the States in the late 1970s.

On February 8, 1968, African-American students from South Carolina State and Clafin College demonstrated against the whites-only policy at an Orangeburg, South Carolina, bowling alley. White police officers opened fire, killing three and wounding 27 unarmed students as they ran. The killings sparked a week of more violent demonstrations, which were subdued forcibly by National Guardsmen and state highway patrolmen. Here, patrolmen stand over two wounded students. Unlike the killings at Kent State University two years later—which involved white students—the Orangeburg incident faded quickly from national public consciousness.

In the 1960s, young people—black and white—had learned that they could create dramatic change through the most dramatic action available: the sacrifice of their very bodies. Here, state troopers move in to arrest demonstrators who block the path of a school bus in Social Circle, California, on February 15, 1968. The students were protesting against bad school conditions. About 60 demonstrators, most of them minors, were hauled off to the Walton County Prison Farm in a bus.

The lively essays that comprise the 1968 best-seller *Soul on Ice* were written by Eldridge Cleaver while he was incarcerated at Folsom Prison in California following a marijuana conviction. Cleaver successfully skewered what he viewed as white society's tireless efforts to emasculate black men, even as it rewarded the "bootlickers." (One of Cleaver's recurring inventions, a victimized yet sexually potent black male he called the Supermasculine Menial, was probably misread by whites, who viewed this symbol as affirmation of their long-held prejudice.) Among the book's other subjects are Vietnam and nationalism; racial pride; and the New Left. White "parlor liberals" were eager to praise *Soul on Ice* in 1968, and much of that initial acclaim now seems overeager. But the book is tough, intelligent, and—in its final essay, "To All Black Women, from All Black Men"—heartbreakingly beautiful.

In March 1968 student activists took over Howard University, a black school in Washington, D.C. The students demanded that Howard's curriculum and its campus culture reflect the more militant mood among the nation's young African-Americans. Many of the students were tired of being fed what they considered a "white" reflection of academics and culture from an administration they considered behind the times. They demanded that the university, funded largely by money appropriated by Congress, show public solidarity with the struggling black masses. Although that didn't happen, several black studies conferences were held at Howard during the following years.

# The Memphis Crusade

ARTIN LUTHER KING'S LAST civil rights crusade was an effort to help garbage collectors in Memphis, Tennessee, secure fair wages and working conditions. King was asked to aid the Memphis workers while he was in the midst of planning the Poor People's March on Washington, and he really did not have time to interrupt his work to go to Memphis. But King found it hard to say no to such appeals, especially when they came from such friends as Reverend Billy Kyles of Memphis. So, King traveled to the city to support a protest scheduled for March 28.

The original issue in Memphis had been a strike by the predominantly black sanitation workers, who earned far less than their white counterparts. However, their cause grew into something more: a protest by the Memphis black community against the overall racial situation in the city. During the March 28 protest, about 150 young black militants (out of 6,000 demonstrators) instigated violence—smashing windows, looting, and attacking police—leading to at least 50 injuries and the death of a black youth. Deeply troubled by the rioting, and fearing that the nonviolent Civil Rights Movement would suffer unless the images of black violence were erased, King announced a peaceful protest march in Memphis within a week.

Sanitation workers marching in Memphis on April 8

King returned to Memphis on April 3 and attended a pre-march meeting at the Mason Street Temple. The next evening, he was shot to death on the balcony of the Lorraine Motel. On April 8 King's widow, Coretta Scott King, and dozens of national figures led a peaceful march in Memphis in tribute to Dr. King and in support of the strike. Eight days later, the city and the sanitation workers agreed on a new contract.

The Memphis march quickly turned into a riot on March 28, 1968. Rumors that a policeman had injured or killed a black child riled the angry crowd. The protesters, particularly the young people who formed the rear, were not trained in non-violence as thoroughly as others had been in previous SCLC campaigns. Youths threw the sticks that had held protest signs through store windows. Looting ensued. Martin Luther King's aides rushed him away. Protesters threw stones at the police, who, in turn, cracked down hard with billy clubs and tear gas. A curfew was imposed, and National Guardsmen were brought in to restore order. King grew despondent, wondering how he could galvanize the nation's poor if he couldn't lead one nonviolent march in Memphis.

Though troubled by the failure of the Memphis march and a Movement that had lost direction, Martin Luther King summoned the strength to speak at Mason Temple in Memphis on April 3, 1968. At one point King spoke about the never-ending threats on his life. "Like anybody, I'd like to live a long life," he said. "Longevity has its place. But I'm not concerned about that now. I just want to do God's will." With cheers ringing in his ears, King slumped to his chair at the end of what history would record as a self-delivered eulogy. He had reminded himself that God had never left him, and wouldn't now. Tragically, he wouldn't live to see the next night.

## Marching in Memphis for Martin Luther King

IN MEMPHIS [after the assassination of Martin Luther King], we continued the sanitation strike. There were no fires there. We were engaged in the *movement*; we effectively were able to continue the strike.

Anger and despair feed on nihilism when there's no plan of action.... *We had a goal in mind.* I spent the night of April 4 speaking over the radio, walking the streets. I hit *all* the radio stations, talked about Martin King and the strike... rather than the burning of our streets and all....

The police were worried. They wanted to stop us from marching on the 5th. We had about 900 people at Claiborne Temple, and I told [police chief Frank] Holloman we're marching, whether you like it or not, so if you want to arrest all of us, OK.

They had the National Guard there, so on that day... we marched under the glare of bayonets and tanks. We did not waver. That Friday, that Saturday, that Monday. That put a lot of energy in Memphis in the right place.... There were no burnings in Memphis.

—*Reverend James Lawson, former chairman of the Southern Christian Leadership Conference*

# The King Assassination

"WE'VE GOT SOME DIFFICULT days ahead," Martin Luther King, Jr., told a crowd in Memphis, Tennessee, where the city's sanitation workers were striking. "But it really doesn't matter with me now, because I've been to the mountaintop...and I've seen the promised land. I may not get there with you. But I want you to know tonight that we, as a people, will get to the promised land."

The next day, April 4, 1968, at approximately 6 P.M., a rifle shot hit King in the face as he stood on a balcony outside his second-floor room at the Lorraine Motel in Memphis. SCLC Secretary Treasurer Ralph Abernathy ran to King and cradled his friend's head until the paramedics arrived and rushed him to St. Joseph's Hospital. Doctors pronounced King dead at 7:05 P.M.

King had arrived in Memphis the previous day to prepare for a march on behalf of the striking workers. Just before King died, he was getting ready to leave for a dinner at a friend's home. Earlier in the afternoon, a district judge had agreed to lift his antiprotest restraining order, which had been prompted by violence that disrupted a march a week earlier. The new march offered hope for the Memphis workers and, more generally, for the nascent Poor People's Campaign—designed to prod the federal government to strengthen its antipoverty efforts. The violence in recent marches had led to extensive press criticism of King's antipoverty strategy.

News of the assassination swept the nation. Racial violence erupted in more than 120 cities, including Washington, D.C. President Lyndon Johnson sent 20,000 regular troops and more than 20,000 National Guardsmen to the cities, and many cities enforced curfews. By the end of the rioting, 46 people had died, approximately 3,000 had been injured, and more than 20,000 had been arrested, mostly for looting.

Many militant black leaders encouraged retaliation. Black Power proponent Stokely Carmichael advocated a violent struggle in which black men would stand up for their cause and fight till their death. If it was their only act of manhood, he said, "then goddamm it we're going to die." NAACP Executive Director Roy Wilkins countered that King would have been "outraged" by the disorders and that "millions of Negroes in this country" were opposed to the violence. Wilkins then announced a nationwide campaign against racial violence that would emphasize jobs for the unemployed and better community relations.

President Lyndon Johnson urged unity. "We can achieve nothing by lawlessness and divisiveness among the American people," he said. Johnson called for a national day of mourning. Memorials and rallies were held throughout the country. Public schools, businesses, and stock exchanges closed. Many sporting events and Hollywood's Academy Awards ceremony were postponed. In addition, Johnson requested that a joint session of Congress convene to discuss a positive response to the events.

On April 8 Abernathy, chosen to succeed King as SCLC president, led more than 20,000 silent marchers, including King's widow, to honor King and to support the Memphis sanitation workers. Eight days later, the city and the workers reached a settlement of the 65-day strike. The Poor People's Campaign, however, did not survive much longer. It slowly fizzled after an unsuccessful march

Coretta Scott King comforts her daughter Bernice.

on Washington, when Abernathy was arrested and the rest of the participants were dispersed with tear gas.

On April 9 King's funeral took place in Atlanta at Ebenezer Baptist Church, where King had served as co-pastor along with his father. Many of the nation's political and civil rights leaders attended, including Jacqueline Kennedy, Vice President Hubert Humphrey, U.S. Supreme Court Justice Thurgood Marshall, and numerous senators. Thousands of people blocked the streets outside, while millions more watched the nationally televised broadcast.

Later, two Georgia mules pulled King's coffin on a four-

More than 100,000 people joined the funeral procession through the streets of Atlanta.

mile course through the Atlanta streets. More than 100,000 mourners followed. King's body was interred at South-View Cemetery following a funeral at Morehouse College, where King had studied 20 years earlier.

Former Morehouse President Benjamin Mays gave a eulogy. In his closing remarks, he said that if death was the price King had to pay to eliminate prejudice and injustice in America, "nothing could be more redemptive."

Following an international manhunt, white racist James Earl Ray was arrested for King's murder on June 8 in London and later extradited to the United States. In a plea bargain, Tennessee prosecutors agreed in March 1969 to forgo seeking the death penalty if Ray pled guilty to murder charges. The circumstances surrounding this decision later were questioned because Ray recanted his confession soon after being sentenced to a 99-year prison term. He claimed that his attorney had provided inadequate representation because the attorney focused on lucrative arrangements to publish Ray's story. Ray fired him, but he was unsuccessful in his subsequent attempts to reverse his conviction and gain a trial.

In the following years, several factors prompted calls for a new investigation into King's murder. Factors included evidence of extensive surveillance of King by the FBI and other government agencies, new congressional investigations of illegal FBI activities following the Watergate scandal, and new books about the assassination. A new investigation, by the House Select Committee on Assassinations, suggested that Ray may have been motivated by a reward offered by two St. Louis businessmen and may have had coconspirators, possibly his brothers, John and Jerry Ray. Despite detailing the FBI's activities targeting King, the report nonetheless concluded that there was no convincing evidence of government complicity in the assassination. Nevertheless, the single report and 12 volumes of evidence provided a wealth of information that would continue to fuel speculation.

After recanting his guilty plea, Ray consistently maintained his innocence, claiming in his 1992 memoir that he was framed. In 1997 members of King's family publicly supported Ray's appeal for a new trial, and King's son, Dexter Scott King, proclaimed Ray's innocence. Tennessee authorities nonetheless refused to reopen the case, and Ray died while incarcerated on April 23, 1998. Even after Ray's death, conspiracy allegations continued.

**March 28:** Martin Luther King marches with sanitation workers on strike in Memphis, Tennessee. The protest turns violent, resulting in the death of a 16-year-old boy and the arrests of 280 people.

**March 31:** President Lyndon Johnson announces he will not seek reelection.

**April:** A group of priests forms the National Black Catholic Clergy Caucus in Detroit to discuss and respond to racism within the Catholic Church.

**April 3:** At Mason Temple Church in Memphis, Martin Luther King delivers his "I've Been to the Mountaintop" speech, in which he says he's not worried about dying.

**April 4:** While standing on the balcony outside his room at the Lorraine Motel in Memphis, Martin Luther King is shot dead by a sniper.

**April 4–mid-April:** News of Martin Luther King's murder triggers rioting in more than 120 American cities over several days. An estimated 46 people (most of them black) are killed, approximately 3,000 are injured, and more than 20,000 are arrested. In Chicago, Mayor Richard J. Daley issues a "shoot to kill" order to police. *See* April 7, 1968.

**April 6:** In Oakland, police ambush prominent members of the Black Panthers, killing Bobby Hutton and wounding Eldridge Cleaver and Warren Wells.

**April 7:** At Tuskegee Institute in Alabama, more than 200 students hold school trustees captive for 12 hours, demanding campus reforms.

**April 7:** A national day of mourning is held in honor of Martin Luther King.

**April 8:** In Memphis, Coretta Scott King leads a march of more than 20,000 people in honor of her late husband and to support the Memphis sanitation workers' strike. ➤

King's spirits were high on the morning of April 4, 1968, the day after he had delivered his "I've Been to the Mountaintop" speech. He and his aides—(*from left*) Hosea Williams, Jesse Jackson, and Ralph Abernathy—were with him at the Lorraine Motel, while Jim Lawson and Andrew Young were in federal court trying to get approval for another march. Young came back with good news: the march could go on as scheduled. King and his group changed for a dinner at the home of Billy Kyles, a Memphis pastor. At six o'clock King and Abernathy were standing on the motel's balcony when the crack of gunfire shook the neighborhood. King fell to the cement. Abernathy ran over to him and saw that he had been shot. King, the victim of a sniper's bullet, was pronounced dead at 7:05 P.M.

Martin Luther King was dead, and the nation steeled itself for the worst. President Lyndon Johnson (*seated*) canceled a trip to Hawaii regarding developments in the Vietnam War. He phoned Coretta Scott King to express his sorrow, then asked the nation to discard violence and to pray for "peace and understanding throughout this land." Johnson ordered his staff to set up meetings with Movement leaders, and he pressed Attorney General Ramsey Clark to push the FBI to find King's killer.

Enraged by the King assassination, black Chicagoans took to the streets. Thousands of high schoolers smashed windows in one of Chicago's business districts. Richard Daley, an old-school mayor, ordered his police force to "shoot to kill arsonists" and "shoot to maim looters." After two days of rioting, nine people had been killed, more than 1,000 were left homeless, and more than 2,500 had been arrested.

**NO YOUNG BLOOD on the PAVEMENTS**
*--Prevent Riots*
NAACP – 1790 BROADWAY, NEW YORK, N. Y. 10019

**HOT HEAD -- HOT LEAD -- COLD DEAD**
*--Prevent Riots*
NAACP – 1790 BROADWAY, NEW YORK, N. Y. 10019

**ALIVE, you can fight DEAD, you're dead**
*--Prevent Riots*
NAACP – 1790 BROADWAY, NEW YORK, N. Y. 10019

**OVER NO DEAD BODIES**
*--Prevent Riots*
NAACP – 1790 BROADWAY, NEW YORK, N. Y. 10019

America felt itself under siege in the wake of the King assassination. Many feared that a full-fledged national race war—black against white—was underway. Angry urban rioters felt that since nonviolent protests had done little for them, it was time to see what righteous black anger and directed violence could accomplish in America—a country created by the killing of the majority of its native population. Stickers such as these pleaded with those too angry to see anything but America's racial hypocrisy.

New York was one of the 120 cities that went up in flames after the assassination of Martin Luther King. Window smashing, looting, and fires turned the city into a battle zone. In this photo, New York City firefighters battle a blaze on Harlem's West 125th Street. The last riot in Harlem had occurred four years earlier.

Troops stand with machine guns on the steps of the U.S. Capitol in Washington, D.C., a day after Martin Luther King's assassination. President Johnson called in federal troops after a day of arson and looting. The flag was at half-staff in tribute to the civil rights leader, and Johnson declared Sunday, April 7, a day of national mourning. Such tributes rang hollow to Black Power advocates such as Stokely Carmichael, who reasoned that by killing King, white America had declared war on black America. Carmichael called for an open, armed insurrection in the nation's capital. His words were not ignored.

**WANTED** BY THE **FBI**

CIVIL RIGHTS - CONSPIRACY
INTERSTATE FLIGHT - ROBBERY
**JAMES EARL RAY**          FBI No. 405,942 G

Photographs taken 1960          Photograph taken 1968 (eyes drawn by artist)

Aliases: Eric Starvo Galt, W. C. Herron, Harvey Lowmyer, James McBride, James O'Conner, James Walton, James Walyon, John Willard, "Jim,"

**DESCRIPTION**

Age: 40, born March 10, 1928, at Quincy or Alton, Illinois (not supported by birth records)
Height: 5' 10"                    Eyes: Blue
Weight: 163 to 174 pounds         Complexion: Medium
Build: Medium                     Race: White
Hair: Brown, possibly cut short   Nationality: American

> "The day that Negro people and others in bondage are truly free, on the day 'want' is abolished, on the day wars are no more, on that day, I know my husband will rest in a long-deserved peace."
> —CORETTA SCOTT KING, DURING THE EULOGY FOR MARTIN LUTHER KING

With the death of Martin Luther King, the world and the nation lost a moral leader who had shown the power of combining the teachings of Jesus Christ with the methodology of Mahatma Gandhi. But on a personal level, Yolanda King (*center*) had lost her daddy. So did her brothers, Dexter and Martin III, and her little sister, Bernice. Her mother, Coretta Scott King, was without a husband. Her grandparents, "Daddy" King and Alberta, had to bury their child. King had shown people the greatness they could achieve in service of humanity. But that greatness would not replace the family birthdays and Christmases missed, the time and love lost. A flesh-and-blood man, not a television image, was now gone.

James Earl Ray, an unemployed, racist vagabond, joined the FBI's "10 Most Wanted" list in 1968 for the assassination of Martin Luther King. Somehow Ray, who had stalked King, acquired a bogus Canadian passport, four sets of phony identification, money, and tickets to Europe, which he used after King was fatally shot. Scotland Yard detectives arrested Ray at a London airport more than two months after King's death. Without expressing any motive, Ray pled guilty and accepted a 99-year jail sentence, all without a trial. Three days later he recanted and asked for a trial, claiming he had been framed.

Martin Luther King, the heart and soul of the Southern Christian Leadership Conference, was dead. But the SCLC's work had to continue. Wyatt T. Walker, the SCLC's executive director, was considered a skillful manager. His talents were needed as the SCLC grew in the 1960s into an organization prepared to fight serious, sustaining campaigns to end discrimination. In 1968 Walker's leadership was tested as the SCLC prepared to launch the Poor People's Campaign. After Walker left the SCLC in 1964, he became the pastor of Caanan Baptist Church in Harlem as well as a renowned scholar of gospel music.

Black Power advocates Stokely Carmichael (*left*) and H. Rap Brown speak outside Columbia University's Hamilton Hall, one of five Columbia buildings taken over by demonstrators in April 1968. "These students are resisting the university's racist policies," Brown said. "Hamilton Hall is a black fortress." Black students took over this hall while the predominately white Students for a Democratic Society occupied the remaining four buildings. The students were angry over two issues: the university's connection with the Institute for Defense Analysis, and its plan to take over some of Morningside Park in Harlem for a university gym. Over a week's time, approximately 700 demonstrators were arrested.

# The Movement as a Model

THE STRATEGIES AND TACTICS of the Civil Rights Movement proved useful to activists in other movements that arose in the 1960s and later. The antiwar movement, the women's rights movement, the gay rights movement, the movement for the rights of disabled Americans, and others all used such tools of protest as sit-ins, marches, and voluntary arrest.

Moreover, laws and policies instituted to bring about racial parity also benefited women and other minorities. The Civil Rights Act of 1964, for example, was created to combat racial discrimination. But as they debated the bill, legislators added a prohibition against sex discrimination in employment. In later years, affirmative action programs—pushed for by civil rights supporters—improved working conditions for women.

The efforts of civil rights activists have made Americans more sensitive to all historically oppressed groups. Big-city police departments have created community outreach divisions and required sensitivity training sessions. In some cities, police departments are answerable to civilian review boards for the actions of their officers. Though these reforms were instituted in response to charges of racism against blacks, they have benefited homosexuals and other minorities as well.

Activists abroad also have been influenced by the Civil Rights Movement. "We Shall Overcome," the unofficial anthem of the Movement, has been sung by protesters in Northern Ireland, South Korea, Lebanon, India, and South Africa—as well as at China's Tiananmen Square.

## 1968

**April 8:** A bill to establish a national holiday to honor Martin Luther King is introduced in the U.S. House of Representatives by John Conyers (D–MI). The bill will fail to reach the House floor for a vote. *See* November 2, 1983.

**April 9:** After funeral services at Ebenezer Baptist Church, Martin Luther King is buried. *See* June 8, 1968.

**April 11:** President Johnson signs the Civil Rights Act of 1968 (aka Fair Housing Act), which bans discrimination in the sale or rental of housing. The bill also gives federal protection to civil rights workers and makes it a federal crime to cross states lines for the purpose of inciting a riot.

**April 23–24:** At Columbia University in New York City, 300 students barricade the office of the dean, protesting the construction of a gymnasium. They feel it's a racist decision since it will deprive Harlem blacks of a recreation area.

**April 25:** Black students occupy the administration building at Boston University. They demand recruitment of black students, more black faculty and staff members, and better financial assistance for black students.

**April 25:** The U.S. Justice Department files a school segregation suit against School District 151 in Cook County, Illinois. It's the department's first such lawsuit in a northern city.

**April 28–June 24:** In Washington, D.C., the SCLC stages the Poor People's Campaign, which had been planned by Martin Luther King. Protesters demand federal legislation guaranteeing jobs, better wages, and low-income housing. Over 50,000 people attend Solidarity Day on June 19. "Resurrection City" is pitched near the Lincoln Memorial. ➤

The Fair Housing Act of 1968, signed into law by President Johnson, was an attempt to stop the housing market from segregating African-Americans into ghettos. It prohibited racial discrimination in the rental, sale, or financing of housing. Although the law had little teeth, it would be another arrow in the quiver of civil rights advocates who would sue those they believed were discriminating on the basis of race, gender, or handicap.

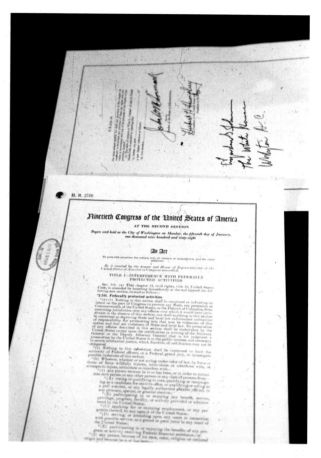

Black student rebellion surfaced at Northwestern University, just north of Chicago, on May 3, 1968. Black Northwestern students wanted black enrollment to reflect the nation's population. When their demands did not receive a response, students took over the bursar's office. The two-day nonviolent protest, supported by 30 white students, was called off when the university agreed to negotiate.

Andrew Young was not fiery, like Martin Luther King aide Hosea Williams. Nor did he exhibit the spiritual dynamism of King. But Young was one of the few people who could be relied on to continue the work of MLK. Shown here at a press conference concerning the Poor People's Campaign, Young would help organize the campaign, a go-for-broke protest in Washington, D.C. In the next decade, his political skills would take him to the Atlanta mayor's chair and to the United Nations.

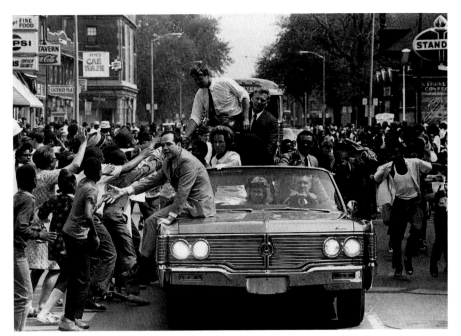

Many African-Americans considered New York Senator Robert F. Kennedy, pictured on the presidential campaign trail in Detroit on May 15, 1968, their last hope after Martin Luther King died. Kennedy had made allegiances with antiwar protesters, Cesar Chavez's migrant farm workers, and civil rights leaders. Had he become president, perhaps he would have pushed the nation into an era of true brotherhood. The night King died, Kennedy was brave enough to speak to a crowd of black supporters, asking them to turn their anger into resolve. "What we need in the United States," he said, "is not violence or lawlessness but love and wisdom and compassion toward one another, and a feeling of justice toward those who still suffer within our country, whether they be white or they be black." The black community's hopes suffered another tragic blow on June 5, 1968, when Kennedy fell to an assassin's bullet.

# The Battle for School Control

IN 1967, 13 YEARS AFTER the historic Supreme Court decision in *Brown v. Board of Education*, only 700 of the 30,000 New York City high school graduation diplomas awarded went to black students. The teachers union blamed the black children's environment for their failure to succeed in school. Black parents, on the other hand, accused teachers of being out of touch, of pursuing insensitive curricula, and generally of "educational imperialism."

New York City tried community management in 1968. However, the leaders of the first experimental district, Ocean Hill–Brownsville in Brooklyn, angered the powerful teachers union when they tried to transfer out some veteran white teachers in order to achieve a more integrated teaching staff. Racial strife between school administrators and classroom teachers continued not just in New York but throughout America.

Even in the 21st century, white children in general score higher on standardized tests. Many black activists have blamed the discrepancies on the educational system. Some activists have pushed for curricula that are multicultural instead of European-centered. Others have advocated the acceptance of "black English" as a medium for instruction in inner cities. Many have railed against the inferior funding of urban public schools compared to those in the suburbs. Since schools are funded by *local* tax dollars, affluent suburbanites—most of whom are white—can and do pour more money into their school systems.

To this day, American public schools remain a battleground for adults with opposing agendas for control. It likely will take decades or generations for the issues to be resolved.

Ralph Emerson McGill, publisher of *The Atlanta Constitution,* did not support integration in his newspaper columns. However, he did attempt to convince the "city too busy to hate" that changes were coming. The title of one of his books, *No Place to Hide: The South and Human Rights,* reflects his perspective. McGill, who was referred to as the "Conscience of the South," won the Pulitzer Prize for his editorial writing.

In May 1968 a local school board in the predominantly black Ocean Hill–Brownsville section of Brooklyn, New York, attempted to fire a group of white unionized teachers as a test of its power. The result was a series of three racially incendiary citywide teachers strikes, aimed at restoring the white educators to their jobs, in the fall of that year. The strikes, while successful, left permanent racial scars on the city, and many observers believe that race relations in New York haven't been good since. Here, a supporter of the Ocean Hill–Brownsville local board tells black students not to go to a "white power school."

# Poor People's Campaign

BY 1967 MARTIN LUTHER KING and the SCLC believed that although black people's basic rights had been taken care of by law, most blacks were prevented from enjoying equality because they were poor. Thus, the SCLC expanded its vision to include poor people of all races.

King believed the time was right for a national poor people's movement to alert the government and the rest of society to their plight. On December 4, 1967, King announced publicly that poor people would march for jobs, for a guaranteed income for everyone not able to work, and for some sort of economic Bill of Rights. Four months later, King was in the midst of final preparations for the march when he was assassinated in Memphis.

Reverend Ralph David Abernathy (King's chief aide), Reverend Jesse Jackson, and others in the SCLC continued the campaign without him. The protest, held from May 13 to June 24, 1968, attracted between 50,000 and 100,000 demonstrators to Washington, D.C., many of them determined to avenge King's death by keeping his dream alive.

The campaign included the first "live-in" of the Civil Rights Movement—an encampment of tents and A-frame shelters on the Mall next to the Lincoln Memorial. It was

Mule train, a symbol of the Poor People's Campaign

called Resurrection City, and Jackson served as city manager. Because of unusually heavy rain, Resurrection City was soon awash in mud.

Muddied as well was the message the live-in was intended to convey. Without its charismatic leader, the SCLC never successfully articulated the needs of the poor or their demands for remedies. After six weeks, police moved into Resurrection City with tear gas, and the hastily vacated encampment was torn down.

In May 1968 people traveled from all parts of the country, particularly from the Black Belt South, to the Poor People's Campaign in Washington, D.C. Some came from cosmopolitan cities such as Atlanta, as shown in this photo. Others traveled from the poorest areas of rural Mississippi and Alabama.

Coretta Scott King did not retreat into solitude after the death of her husband. Instead, she moved into a more prominent role in the struggle for peace and justice. Just a few days after MLK's death, Coretta led a march on behalf of sanitation workers in Memphis. Later in April, she kept his speaking engagement at an antiwar rally in New York. Coretta also spoke at the "Solidarity Day" rally of the Poor People's Campaign on June 19 (*pictured*), stating that poverty, racism, and war had combined to hurt all Americans, regardless of color.

Martin Luther King, Jr., saw no wisdom in a course of racial separatism, so when his idea of a Poor People's Campaign was brought to fruition about a month after his murder, organizers encouraged a certain inclusiveness. This illustrated button shows a black adult cradling a non-black baby, and is suggestive of King's desire to see justice done for *all* disadvantaged people.

**Late April:** Ralph Abernathy succeeds Martin Luther King as president of the SCLC.

**May 23:** Henry Dumas, a civil rights activist and a prominent poet, is shot to death at a Harlem train station by a transit police officer, who claims the killing was a case of "mistaken identity."

**May 27:** In *Green v. County School Board*, the U.S. Supreme Court rules that a school district cannot sidestep desegregation through a "freedom of choice" plan.

**June 5:** Senator Robert F. Kennedy (D–NY), a candidate in the 1968 presidential race and a strong proponent of civil rights, is assassinated in Los Angeles by Palestinian immigrant Sirhan Sirhan.

**June 8:** James Earl Ray is arrested in London and charged with murdering Martin Luther King. *See* March 10, 1969.

**June 17:** In *Jones v. Alfred H. Mayer Co.*, the U.S. Supreme Court states that Congress has the authority to prohibit racial discrimination in the sale of homes.

**June 24:** In Washington, D.C., police use tear gas to clear those still living in "Resurrection City."

**July 23:** In Cleveland, eight African-Americans and three police officers are killed and many are wounded as police battle black radicals who ambushed them.

**August 1:** President Johnson signs the Housing and Urban Development Act, which promises $5 billion for the construction and subsidizing of 1.7 million units of housing for low-income families.

**August 3:** Members of the Peace and Freedom Party nominate Eldridge Cleaver for president of the United States. ➤

Martin Luther King envisioned the Poor People's Campaign as a potent demonstration against the poverty that was a byproduct of the American economic system. Reverend Ralph Abernathy and the SCLC acted on the idea five weeks after King's death, attracting some 200,000 people to the nation's capital. Among that number were about 2,500 who, by late May, had settled in West Potomac Park, south of the Mall's reflecting pool. There, demonstrators erected makeshift tents of plywood and canvas. The community was called Resurrection City, and was the base for demonstrators who marched daily on federal agencies to demand poverty relief. Besides African-Americans, Resurrection City was inhabited by Hispanics, Native Americans, and Appalachian whites.

Ralph Abernathy (*right*) and other representatives of the Poor People's Campaign made daily visits to Cabinet members and other federal officials throughout May and June 1968. Interior Secretary Stewart Udall (*left*) was a committed, liberal conservationist who, during his 1961–69 tenure, oversaw the creation of four national parks and 56 wildlife refuges, the establishment of the Land and Water Conservation Fund,

and much more. Of more immediate concern to Abernathy was that, given the location of Resurrection City, law enforcement there was the responsibility not of the D.C. Metro Police, but the Park Police, who fell under Secretary Udall's purview. U.S. Attorney General Ramsey Clark had granted Resurrection City dwellers virtual immunity from arrest. But when Clark's patience ran out, Park Police acted on June 24, arresting demonstrators and razing the City.

Civil Rights leaders in Prichard, Alabama, stare at police officers' bayonets as authorities stop demonstrators from marching on City Hall in June 1968. Physical bravery was a profound element of the Movement. Blacks, particularly in the South, had been taught all their lives to fear whites, especially whites in authority. It was white authorities who physically abused African-Americans publicly and allowed lynchings to occur. But blacks had taken too much from whites over the years to continue to live as second-class citizens, regardless of the physical consequences.

In the late 1960s, Blank Panthers chapters held rallies across the nation, such as this one in Oakland, for Huey Newton, the group's minister of defense. Newton, who had been charged with killing a police officer in October 1967, went on trial in July 1968. Two months later he was found guilty and sentenced to two to 15 years imprisonment. At the rallies, Panthers marched in formation while chanting, "Free Huey! Off the pigs!"

Charles Kenyatta, formerly Charles 37X, attempted to carry out the goals of his murdered friend and mentor, Malcolm X. He organized a Harlem Mau Mau, named after the violent, anticolonialist revolutionaries in Kenya. Wrote Malcolm X biographer Peter Goldman: "He took (Kenyan President) Jomo Kenyatta's name, because Malcolm had met and liked him, and organized a Harlem Mau Mau, because Malcolm had said in a lot of speeches that that ought to be done. The Mau Mau was never much more than Kenyatta speaking from a stepladder at 125th and Seventh with a grown-out 'Fro and a Bible folded around a machete." Kenyatta was one of many of Malcolm's followers who kept his ideas alive.

## 1968

**August 5 and 25:** A total of five Black Panthers are killed by Los Angeles police in two separate encounters.

**August 8:** A race riot erupts in Miami, where the Republican Party is holding its national convention. The deaths of several African-Americans are connected to the uprising.

**September:** The Black Panthers enter the national media spotlight as members gather daily at an Oakland courthouse in support of party cofounder Huey Newton, who is on trial for manslaughter after a shootout with an Oakland police officer in 1967. On September 27, Newton is sentenced to two to 15 years imprisonment.

**October 16:** At the Summer Olympics in Mexico City, American sprinters Tommie Smith and John Carlos give a "Black Power" salute on the medal podium during the playing of the American national anthem. They'll be suspended from the U.S. team and banned from the Olympic Village.

**November:** Black Panthers Chairman Bobby Seale announces that the party will focus more on community service, such as providing free breakfasts to poor black children, creating free health clinics, and establishing "black liberation schools."

**November 5:** Richard Nixon, a conservative Republican, defeats Democrat Hubert Humphrey in the presidential election.

**November 5:** Shirley Chisholm (D–NY) becomes the first African-American woman elected to the U.S. Congress. *See* January 25, 1972.

**December:** Police and FBI agents raid Black Panther offices in Denver, Indianapolis, Des Moines, and San Francisco. Police bomb Panthers headquarters in Newark.

The National Welfare Rights Organization quickly became a powerful force for the nation's poor by 1968, two years after its founding. The organization grew out of the advocacy of women who sought employment opportunities and basic needs for their families. In Chicago on August 22, 1968, NWRO leader Beulah Sanders (*pictured*) told members of the Democratic Platform Committee that they should back a radical overhaul of the nation's welfare system. Partisans in the audience supported her with shouts of "Sock it to 'em!"

**PURPOSE:**

To recommend attached item be given news media source on confidential basis as counterintelligence measure to help neutralize extremist Black Panthers and foster split between them and Student Nonviolent Coordinating Committee (SNCC).

**BACKGROUND:**

There is a feud between the two most prominent black nationalist extremist groups, The Black Panthers and SNCC. Attached item notes that the feud is being continued by SNCC circulating the statement that:

"According to zoologists, the main difference between a panther and other large cats is that the panther has the smallest head."

This is biologically true. Publicity to this effect might help neutralize Black Panther recruiting efforts.

In 1956, frustrated by Supreme Court rulings that limited FBI power to investigate dissident groups, the bureau began secret "counterintelligence programs" (COINTELPRO). These targeted the Socialist Workers Party, the KKK and other white hate groups, the Black Panther Party and other black nationalist groups, and the New Left. Agents utilized informants placed within targeted groups; propaganda; IRS audits; and covert encouragement of street violence. The program's Racial Intelligence Section was particularly eager to destroy the Panthers. One way was to encourage friction between the Panthers and SNCC. This October 10, 1968, COINTELPRO internal memorandum, from G. C. Moore to W. C. Sullivan, describes a (purportedly) SNCC-generated news item emphasizing that panthers, of all the big cats, have the smallest heads. The memo notes that the attached item is captioned "Panther Pinheads."

> "People thought the victory stand was a hate message, but it wasn't. It was a cry for freedom."
>
> —OLYMPIC MEDALIST TOMMIE SMITH

In the late 1960s, the Congress of Racial Equality continued its work as a black nationalist civil rights organization. Roy Innis (*second from right*), a charismatic leader from Harlem, replaced Floyd McKissick as CORE's national chairman in 1968. In his early years with CORE, Innis was a proponent of black nationalism as a viable philosophy for black America. In later years, he disavowed black nationalism and pushed CORE to the right.

At the 1968 Olympic Games in Mexico City, black American activists Tommie Smith and John Carlos finished first and third, respectively, in the 200-meter sprint. At the medal ceremony, the two mounted the victory platform barefoot (to represent the slavery and discrimination that African-Americans had suffered) and wearing civil rights buttons. Their medals were placed around their necks. As the national anthem began, Smith and Carlos elected not to stand at attention as was customary. Instead, they raised black-gloved fists in the Black Power salute. The International Olympic Committee expressed outrage, and the U.S. Organizing Committee immediately ordered Smith and Carlos to leave the Olympic Village for violating a basic principle of the Olympic Games—that politics plays no part in them.

Gordon Parks fought his way up from poverty to become *Life* magazine's first black photographer. With passion and sophistication, he became one of the most revered photo journalists of the civil rights era. Along the way, Parks honed other talents, including writing and music composition. He penned several books, including an autobiographical novel, *The Learning Tree*. Parks directed the film version of the book, thus becoming the first black director of a major Hollywood movie. Gordon Jr. (*left*) became a successful filmmaker himself, directing the 1973 hit *Superfly*.

# Black Is Beautiful

MILDRED McCAIN, WHO eventually would earn her doctorate in education from Harvard, never forgot the words of her black first-grade teacher in Savannah, Georgia, in 1956: "Mildred, you are ugly, you have nappy hair and big lips, and you are black." As she matured, McClain realized that the only thing "ugly" was America's perception of beauty.

The slogan and movement known as Black Is Beautiful, an outgrowth of the Black Power movement, aimed to create a new aesthetic for African-Americans. Arising in the late 1960s, it emphasized a return to the "natural" look and an effort to debunk the European-centered standards of beauty that had been imposed on black Americans for generations.

Physically, this philosophy was best expressed in hairstyles. Both men and women forswore hot irons, pomades, and other hair-straightening methods and adopted "natural" hairstyles, which eventually morphed into large Afros, followed by braids and cornrows. For some, hairstyle became a political statement rather than simply a personal choice. In reaction to the movement, the hair and beauty products industry began to manufacture cosmetics for black skin tones and a range of hair products aimed at "natural" care.

In clothing, the movement emphasized African styles of dress. A loose, patterned shirt called a dashiki became a veritable uniform for many men. Long, patterned skirts and head cloths were the outfits of choice for many women. Interior design for African-Americans featured African fabrics, such as Kente cloth, as well as baskets, sculptures, and rattan furniture. Many blacks felt that, for the first time, they truly could be themselves.

Shirley Chisholm learned politics the traditional way: She joined a Democratic club in her New York City borough of Brooklyn. In addition to working in child care and education, Chisholm licked envelopes and went door to door for the party's candidates. In 1964 it was her turn, running for and winning a state assembly seat. In 1968 she went after a newly created congressional seat from Brooklyn. Her opponent was James Farmer, the celebrated former head of the Congress of Racial Equality. He had the national name, but he didn't do enough of the grassroots political work or the debate preparation. Chisholm did—and won. She thus became the first African-American woman ever elected to Congress.

Vice President and presidential candidate Hubert H. Humphrey was considered a longtime friend of civil rights. On June 19, 1968, he participated in the Solidarity March, the culmination of the Poor People's Campaign. With Robert Kennedy dead, Humphrey was the last hope to prevent law-and-order Republican Richard Nixon from becoming president. On election day in November, 90 percent of African-Americans voted for Humphrey. Nixon, however, prevailed, amassing 301 electoral votes to Humphrey's 191.

Alabama Governor George Wallace ran for president in 1968 as part of the American Independent Party. The man who became famous for standing in the schoolhouse door to prevent the University of Alabama from being integrated in 1963 now portrayed himself as a champion of the white working class. Wallace railed against forced busing, the U.S. Supreme Court, big government, and hippies. With virtually zero support from black voters, he amassed 46 electoral votes.

President Lyndon Johnson presents the Medal of Honor to Mrs. Wula Pitts, the widow of Army Captain Riley Leroy Pitts, who was killed near Ap Dong, Vietnam, in 1967. Pitts, a 30-year-old ROTC graduate of Wichita State University, became the first black officer to receive the nation's highest military honor. He was killed while leading an assault that overran Viet Cong positions. Pitts had been respected as a courageous solider who was unfazed by enemy fire.

Black U.S. Marines greet each other with the Black Power salute in Con Thien, Vietnam, in December 1968. Martin Luther King's assassination earlier that year fueled an increasing black militancy, especially among those of draft age. Partly to pull militant blacks off the streets, the U.S. Defense Department in 1966 had launched "Project 100,000." The department lowered the standards for draft requirements, making an estimated 100,000 former "rejects" acceptable for induction. The project resulted in a disproportionate number of black soldiers being sent to the front lines "to guarantee liberties in Southeast Asia which they had not found in southwest Georgia and East Harlem," as King himself had said on April 4, 1967.

# 1960s

## 1969

**1969:** Sam Greenlee's satiric novel *The Spook Who Sat by the Door* is published.

**January 20:** In *Hunter v. Erickson*, the U.S. Supreme Court rules that cities cannot pass discriminatory housing ordinances or charter amendments.

**February 27:** Demanding an increase in black enrollment and the establishment of an Afro-American Studies program, 3,000 students rampage through nine buildings at the University of Wisconsin in Madison.

**March 10:** James Earl Ray pleads guilty to murdering Martin Luther King and is sentenced to 99 years in prison.

**March 20–June 27:** In Charleston, South Carolina, Coretta Scott King and SCLC President Ralph Abernathy support several hundred striking hospital workers, who protest against racial discrimination.

**April 19:** About 80 armed black students take over the student union at Cornell University in Ithaca, New York, to protest racism on campus. They will cut a deal with intimidated administrators for total amnesty.

**April 22:** City College of New York is closed while black and Puerto Rican students strike to demand higher minority enrollment.

**April 22:** Harvard University puts together a plan to establish an Afro-American study center.

**April 26:** Civil rights leader James Forman issues the "Black Manifesto," demanding that U.S. churches and synagogues pay $500 million for slave reparations. About $500,000 will be collected and used primarily to fund Black Star Publications, a black publishing house.

**May 5:** Photojournalist Moneta Sleet, Jr., becomes the first African-American man to win a Pulitzer Prize—ironically for a photo of Martin Luther King's funeral. ➤

Black college students attempted to seize control of their own educations in the late 1960s. At the University of California at Berkeley, by this time a nationally known center of student radicalism, students of color formed a Third World Liberation Front. This ad-hoc coalition demanded, among other things, a "Third World College" and for people of color to control all programs designed for them. Several faculty members and many white student radicals supported their demands. Their general strike early in 1969 resulted in arrests. Students of color all over the country, even at historically black Howard University, would use this pattern of confrontation to demand programs that were relevant to their experiences.

During his two terms as president, Richard Nixon (*right*) showed an outward concern for black development: He met with civil rights leaders, such as NAACP Executive Secretary Roy Wilkins (*left*); his "black capitalism" programs created economic opportunities for black businesspeople; and affirmative action was constructed under his watch. However, Nixon also gave support to FBI Director J. Edgar Hoover's and Attorney General John Mitchell's crackdown on the Black Panther Party and other black militant groups. Moreover, the U.S. Commission on Civil Rights criticized Nixon for his approval of delays for school desegregation.

The assassination of Martin Luther King and the rise of the Black Power movement did little to change the mind-set of Reverend Joseph H. Jackson, the president of the National Baptist Convention, U.S.A. Inc., the nation's largest black organization. Jackson, who led the NBC from 1953 to 1982, was one of many Baptist ministers who opposed the Civil Rights Movement and its most prominent leader. In a time of black "revolution," Jackson still believed in economic development over civil disobedience.

## "Oh, my God, look at those goddamned guns!"
—ASSOCIATED PRESS PHOTOGRAPHER, AS ARMED BLACK STUDENTS EXITED CORNELL'S STUDENT UNION

Black students at Cornell University in Ithaca, New York, wanted a degree-granting black studies program. So they did what many black students decided to do in 1969: take over a building and list demands. Here, a contingent of students led by Ed Whitfield (*right*) leaves Straight Hall on April 20. After 36 hours, university officials relented to the students' demands. The students believed that education about the condition of black people was an essential part of the struggle for black liberation. Their boldness showed that the days of the passive, nonconfrontational "Negro" were gone.

# Coretta Scott King

BORN IN RURAL AND racist Marion, Alabama, in 1927, Coretta Scott was studying piano at the New England Conservatory of Music in 1951 when she met young theological student Martin Luther King, Jr. Corretta married Martin in June 1953, and she reluctantly returned to the South with him in September 1954 when he assumed the pastorship of the Dexter Avenue Baptist Church in Montgomery, Alabama.

While her husband became embroiled in civil rights work, Corretta bore four children and tried to maintain a normal family life amidst bomb threats, frightening telephone calls, and the constant glare of the media spotlight. When her husband was assassinated on April 4, 1968, she was just shy of her 41st birthday with four children under the age of 14.

Determined to carry on her husband's work, King served as a steady and eloquent keeper of the flame. In spring 1968 she marched on behalf of sanitation workers in Memphis and spoke at the rally of the Poor People's Campaign in Washington, D.C. In 1969 she founded the Martin Luther King, Jr. Center for Social Change in Atlanta, where she still remains actively involved. In 1983 King organized the 20th anniversary March on Washington, an event that attracted a half-million demonstrators.

# Black Studies Movement

THE BLACK STUDIES MOVEMENT, largely restricted to black college students and faculty, was a logical outgrowth of the Black Power movement that had emerged in 1966. At several universities, angry, determined African-Americans went to extreme measures to demand the formation of black studies programs.

On March 19, 1968, students at Howard University seized an administration building, insisting on more Afro-American studies courses. On February 27, 1969, 3,000 students at the University of Wisconsin in Madison protested for a black studies program. At City College of New York on April 22, 1969, black and Puerto Rican students chained the gates of the south campus, forcing the school to close for the rest of the week. They demanded a school of black and Puerto Rican studies.

Motivations for and even definitions of "black studies" differed greatly, and continue to do so today. While some campaigners for black studies sought to bring a new, African-American perspective to traditional disciplines, others had less lofty goals. Psychologist Nathan Hare, one of the organizers of the first black studies department in the country, at San Francisco State College in 1969, asserted that black studies programs were important because they encouraged black students to become more involved in the educational process.

The best known proponent of black studies, Ron Karenga, also had the black community in mind. He believed that the 1965 Watts riots had resulted partly from a lack of dignity and pride in their heritage among poor, urban blacks due to the paucity of instruction of African and African-American history and culture. To Karenga, the newly independent nations of Africa (21 achieved independence from their former colonial rulers from 1960 through 1964) could be a source of both pride and the development of traditions. Karenga founded an organization called US (United Slaves) and created the trappings of a distinct culture, the best known of which is the African-American holiday Kwanzaa.

In 1968 US and the Black Panther Party, a newly formed community-based black power organization, clashed over control of the new black studies program at the University of California at Los Angeles. On January 23, 1969, just before a meeting of black faculty in the UCLA student cafeteria, two Panthers were shot dead. That fall, three members of US were tried and convicted of the killings.

On other campuses around the United States, black students and faculty created and oversaw black studies departments without bloodshed, often employing tactics borrowed from the direct-action Civil Rights Movement. Such tactics included boycotts, sit-ins, and teach-ins. Unlike other academic disciplines, black studies has been characterized by a tension between the needs of the school and those of the black community.

The best black studies departments, however, have brought fresh interpretations, innovative methodologies, and a stronger awareness of diversity to students throughout the schools. Moreover, movements for women's studies, minority studies, and lesbian and gay studies took cues from the black studies movement. Leaders of those movements made their own demands for revised curricula as well as diversified faculties.

Brandeis University students demanded a black studies program in 1969.

Reparations for African-Americans was an issue in the 1960s. James Forman, a former organizer for SNCC, demanded that white churches and synagogues pay $500 million in reparations for their roles in perpetrating slavery. He read his "Black Manifesto" in front of Riverside Church in New York City on May 11, 1969. "Our patience is thin," he stated. "Time is running out. We have been slaves too long. The Church is racist. The Church has profited from our labor. We are men and women, proud black men and women. Our demands shall be met. Reparation or no Church! Victory or death!" Although Forman's demand was rejected, the idea of reparations would continue to be articulated by others, including Harlem activist Queen Mother Moore.

Charles Evers (*grasping pole*) replaced his brother Medgar, who had been assassinated in 1963, as Mississippi field secretary for the NAACP. Charles possessed his brother's fighting spirit, leading a group of delegates that unseated the all-white Mississippi delegation at the 1968 Democratic National Convention. The following year Evers did something that no black person had done since Reconstruction: He became mayor of a biracial Mississippi town. Evers would serve as mayor of Fayette until 1981, then again from 1985 to 1987.

A hospital workers' strike in Charleston, South Carolina, was the time to shine for Reverend Ralph Abernathy (*right*). Charleston County's attempts to stop the city's hospital workers from unionizing brought the SCLC to that city in 1969. Abernathy, who became SCLC president after Martin Luther King's assassination, led marches and stayed in jail for two weeks. Union officials, such as Walter Reuther (*left*), lent support to SCLC's efforts. Abernathy wrote in his autobiography that the victory established him as a credible SCLC leader: "For the first time people were beginning to believe that the SCLC would have a life and a purpose beyond completing the projects already begun by Martin."

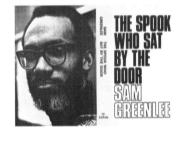

Novelist Sam Greenlee struck a nerve when he wrote *The Spook Who Sat by the Door*, a satirical novel that was published in 1969. The novel's hero, Dan Freeman, the first African-American allowed to graduate from the CIA training corps, pretends to be an apple-polishing social worker to hide his true existence as a ghetto guerrilla leader. Freeman uses his CIA training to convert members of a Chicago street gang into black revolutionaries willing to die in the fight against white supremacy and capitalism. The idea that black militants were hiding in plain sight, ready to violently sacrifice their lives to take down "The Man," resonated with reality at the time: In the late 1960s, H. Rap Brown and others were calling for an open rebellion against white America. *Spook*, which became an instant classic for those with clenched fists, was adapted into a film in 1973.

# 1960s

**June 26:** Coretta Scott King establishes the Martin Luther King, Jr. Center for Nonviolent Social Change in Atlanta.

**June 27:** The U.S. Department of Labor issues the "Philadelphia Plan." It requires contractors on federally assisted construction projects that exceed $500,000 to hire a specific number of minorities.

**July 7:** Charles Evers, brother of Medgar Evers, becomes mayor of Fayette, Mississippi. He is thus the first African-American mayor of a racially mixed Mississippi town since Reconstruction.

**August 6:** Gordon Parks's *The Learning Tree* premieres. It's the first major Hollywood film directed by an African-American.

**October 29:** In *Alexander v. Holmes County Board of Education*, the U.S. Supreme Court rules that school districts must end racial segregation "at once."

**October 29:** Black Panthers cofounder Bobby Seale is one of eight activists on trial for involvement in the Vietnam War protest at the 1968 Democratic National Convention in Chicago. After Seale repeatedly challenges District Court Judge Julius Hoffman, the judge has him handcuffed to a chair and gagged.

**December 4:** Chicago Black Panthers leader Fred Hampton and Black Panthers member Mark Clark are killed in a violent police raid. Of the dozens of shots fired, only one is from the Panthers. *See* November 1982.

In its founding document, the 1966 "Ten-Point Platform," the Black Panther Party demanded "education that teaches us our true history and our role in the present-day society." The liberation schools the Party operated in the San Francisco Bay Area in the late 1960s represented a short-lived effort to realize that goal. The schools featured what would later become known as the Afrocentric approach to education, emphasizing black resistance to white authority. In this liberation school lunchroom, images of Malcolm X and Black Panthers leader Bobby Seale adorn the walls as students display Black Power salutes.

Black Panther Party leaders, like many in the Black Power movement, used art as a way to communicate political messages to African-Americans. The BPP published a newspaper, pamphlets, and, for children, the *Black Panthers Coloring Book*. This controversial image is captioned: "THE PIG IS AFRAID OF BLACK CHILDREN BECAUSE THEY ARE BRAVE WARRIORS." For the Party's critics, this image provided more evidence that the Black Panthers were a group of armed thugs trying to indoctrinate children. Conversely, the Party's supporters saw such cartoons as ways to liberate the mind of the black child.

Urged on by the FBI, police began to crack down on the Black Panther Party in 1969. Police raids of party headquarters and homes of Panther leaders occurred in Los Angeles, Des Moines, Indianapolis, Detroit, San Diego, and Philadelphia. Four raids took place in Chicago alone that year. As shown in this August 1969 photo of party headquarters in Chicago, the raids often provoked exchanges of gunfire. After such raids, the police typically said they were looking for evidence of illegal activity. The Panthers said the authorities were looking to intimidate party members.

Nina Simone represented the anger of the Civil Rights Movement in song and the black consciousness movement in look. Her music seared as well as soared. The song "Mississippi Goddamn" was a fiery denunciation of Jim Crow and the violence Civil Rights Movement protesters endured in that state during the 1960s. Her song "The King of Love Is Dead" reflected the shock and sorrow that followed the assassination of Martin Luther King. With her regal African appearance, politically charged lyrics, and ability to sing a variety of black musical styles, she was dubbed the "High Priestess of Soul" by music critics and fans.

# The Killing of Fred Hampton

FRED HAMPTON BECAME chairman of the Black Panther Party's Illinois chapter at age 18. He died at 21, pumped with 44 bullets in a raid of the party's headquarters in Chicago on December 4, 1969. Mark Clark, the 22-year-old leader of the Panther Party's Peoria chapter, also was killed, and several others were wounded in a fusillade of bullets fired by more than a dozen Chicago police officers.

The police later charged that those in the apartment had shot first. However, evidence indicated that the victims had been asleep at the time of the 4:30 A.M. raid and that Hampton actually had been drugged by an FBI informant who had infiltrated his inner circle. The raid had been carried out with the knowledge of FBI Director J. Edgar Hoover. Hoover's counterintelligence program (COINTELPRO) had identified Hampton as a danger due to his connections to a Chicago street gang named the Blackstone Rangers, whom he was trying to persuade to focus on community work.

After the raid, the FBI and Chicago police orchestrated a cover-up of the events. Cook County State's Attorney Edward V. Hanrahan said, "We wholeheartedly commend the police officers' bravery, their remarkable restraint and discipline in the face of this vicious Black Panther attack."

No one ever was prosecuted for the killings, but suspicions remained. In 1982 the survivors of the raid and the families of the deceased settled with the city, county, and federal governments for $1.85 million.

# THE 1970s

Court-ordered busing of children to achieve integrated classrooms roused passions across the nation, particularly in heavily Irish Boston. Here, in September 1974, black students are returned under police guard to their homes in the city's Roxbury section at the end of Day Three of Boston's busing plan.

IN ESSENCE, THE 1960s ended and the 1970s began on that Lorraine Motel balcony on April 4, 1968. The winding path that the Martin Luther King funeral cortege took through the streets of Atlanta quickly became a metaphor for a rudderless movement that lost direction by decade's end. The abortive 1968 Poor People's Campaign in Washington, D.C., was as mired in leadership squabbles as its participants were in the mud of the poorly moored Resurrection City. King's dream was rapidly going up in flames, as had Watts and Detroit and the West Side of Chicago. The busing of schoolchildren to achieve racial integration, which began in the late 1960s, was met with fierce opposition, such as the bombing of school buses in Denver in February 1970.

The 1970s began with Angela Davis's Afro as the best known icon of African-American identity. Davis, an intellectual activist, was the subject of the nation's most publicized "manhunt" since the kidnapping of the Lindbergh baby. Any black woman, of virtually any age, was subject to being stopped and interrogated if she wore an Afro that was large (or, as folks said back then, if it was "leapin'").

The hunt for Davis, the FBI's assault on the Black Panther Party, and the emergent issue of black imprisonment were all part of a new era of threat and containment. George Wallace, the Alabama governor who stood in the schoolhouse door, rode the law-and-order bandwagon to a third-party presidential candidacy in 1968 and '72. But it was a Republican, the once discredited Richard Nixon, who won each of those elections while spouting law-and-order clichés.

In the late 1960s and early '70s, urban riots and the incendiary rhetoric of the "Black Power" movement created a backlash. White Americans, who began to open their arms to black and liberal causes in the early to mid-1960s, were now fleeing for the suburbs and voting for get-tough Republicans to crack down on agitators. Nixon, having promised swift and harsh prosecution of lawbreakers, took a page

Action films featuring aggressive black antiheroes found enthusiastic, usually male audiences, but were often criticized for their generally negative portrayals of black life. *Superfly*, the adventures of a stylish drug dealer, was a hit in 1972.

Cleveland Mayor Carl Stokes *(right)* and activist Jesse Jackson attended the 1971 Black Expo in Chicago, where Stokes unveiled a national strategy for black political action.

out of the Wallace playbook. He lumped black militants, civil rights protesters, and antiwar demonstrators together as enemies of the state.

Yet, at the same time, Nixon sought to attract some black leaders to the Republican cause. The Nixon Administration pursued affirmative action policies with remarkable vigor. Nixon promoted black capitalism. A civil society, he felt, could be assured only when more blacks felt that they had an economic stake in the future of their country. Throughout the 1970s, the administration and many of its supporters in the business community worked with former officials from CORE to help finance the construction of an all-black planned community in North Carolina called "Soul City." As President Lyndon Johnson had done with the War on Poverty, Nixon used federal patronage to secure black support. Several prominent former activists, including James Farmer of CORE, were recruited by the administration.

Despite these efforts, it was difficult to determine Nixon's views regarding African-Americans and civil rights. He welcomed ultraconservative white politicians Strom Thurmond and Jesse Helms with open arms, and he played on white fears and resentments. Yet he *still* pressed for resources for minority businesses, promoted minority hiring, and associated himself with the cause of black empowerment. Ultimately, black Americans rejected Nixon. In the 1972 presidential election, despite coasting to a landslide victory over George McGovern, Nixon garnered only 18 percent of the black vote.

In the 1970s the Democratic Party was greatly divided, largely because of the legacy of the Civil Rights Movement (as well as President Lyndon Johnson's handling of the Vietnam War). Scarred by the racial divisions of the 1960s, white urban political machines—such as Mayor Richard Daley's network in Chicago—were under siege. Demographic changes were creating large black minorities, and in some cases black majorities, in American cities. In 1972 black leaders met in one of these "chocolate cities," Gary, Indiana, at the National Black Political Convention, to discuss important political, social, and economic issues.

Gary Mayor Richard Hatcher, elected in 1967, was emblematic of an important era of black political empowerment. Hatcher, Cleveland's Carl Stokes, Los Angeles's Tom Bradley, Atlanta's Maynard Jackson, and Detroit's Coleman Young all represented the consolidation of urban political power. Shirley Chisholm's 1972 candidacy for the

Democratic presidential nomination was also a cause of optimism. Chisholm was the first black woman to run for president in either major political party. All the while, Jesse Jackson, leader of Operation PUSH and protégé of Martin Luther King, was emerging as a voice for black America and minorities in general.

In 1971 the Kerner Commission determined that America was splintering into two nations, one white and one black, where each side viewed the other with apprehension. That was certainly true in the 1970s. Boston and other northern communities were divided over court-ordered busing. On one hand, busing was the price the nation was being forced to pay for centuries of *de facto* segregation. On the other hand, it was a disastrous public policy that was despised by most whites, unsatisfying to many blacks, and often unfair to affected schoolchildren, who were yanked by both arms in a political tug-of-war.

In general, black America lost much of its hope during the 1970s. Though most discriminatory laws had been toppled, it was still difficult for African-Americans to make ends meet, let alone move ahead. Financially stagnant, many black Americans grew accustomed to life in the ghettos. In fact, the ghetto-based situation comedy *Good Times* seemed to suggest to African-Americans that *this is your life; make the best of it*. Culturally, "blaxploitation" antiheroes drew bigger raves than the real people of genuine accomplishment, such as baseball record-setter Hank Aaron or author Toni Morrison.

Yet, despite dispiriting conditions, the 1970s was an extraordinary era of progress for black education. Black enrollment in colleges and universities more than tripled from 1964 to 1976 (225,000 to 810,000), giving hope for an eventual black middle class. Moreover, in the aftermath of Vietnam and Watergate, a new wave of liberalism swept over America, as evidenced by the election of kindly Democrat Jimmy Carter as president in 1976. Meanwhile, Alex Haley's *Roots* became a phenomenally successful book and TV miniseries. Despite some inaccuracies, *Roots* awakened the nation to the horrors of slavery and helped all understand the roots of black Americans.

Though sensitive to the black cause, President Carter and his administration were unable to effectively handle the nation's economic problems. As the decade drew to a close, it seemed inevitable that Carter's days were numbered—and that conservative Republicans would rise to power in the 1980 elections.

Democratic presidential hopefuls in 1972 encompassed a lot of philosophical territory, from the right-wing populism of George Wallace (*bottom row, center*) to the progressive politics of New York Congresswoman Shirley Chisholm (*bottom row, right*). She was the first black woman to mount a credible bid for the Oval Office.

## 1970

**1970:** *Soledad Brother,* a collection of letters by Soledad (California) Prison inmate George Jackson, is published.

**January 20:** The Pasadena, California, school district is ordered by a Los Angeles judge to submit a desegregation plan. The Pasadena desegregation lawsuit is the first filed by the federal government against a non-southern school district.

**January 24:** A report out of South Vietnam states that racial tension on military bases is high and that black soldiers appear to have lost faith in the Army system.

**January 30:** Seven Black Panthers are charged with instigating a shootout with Chicago police. The charges will be dropped due to lack of evidence.

**February 1:** Only six of 41 southern school districts comply with the U.S. Supreme Court's orders to desegregate. Fifteen of the 41 school districts are granted delays, while 20 defy the orders.

**February 6:** Opponents of Denver's busing plan bomb some of the city's school buses.

**February 18:** The U.S. Senate passes an amendment that pledges to deny federal funds to school districts whose racial imbalances result from residential segregation.

**March 3:** After two buses of black children arrive at a formerly all-white high school in Lamar, South Carolina, they're stormed and over-turned by a large mob of whites.

**April:** According to an ABC-TV poll, 62 percent of urban African-Americans say they admire the Black Panthers and their "revolutionary" platform. ➤

A South Carolina National Guardsman eyes a school bus after it arrives with black students at the Lamar High School in Lamar, South Carolina, in March 1970. A girl watches the guard with understandable uncertainty. Earlier that month, U.S. Representative Albert Watson (R–SC) made a speech in Lamar saying how much he sympathized with whites who didn't want their schools desegregated. The speech forever would be linked with what happened next: On March 3 whites turned over two buses carrying black children to the school. Many of the children were injured. Police charged 28 white men with rioting.

Eleanor Holmes Norton (*center*), shown at a New York press conference in 1970 as a member of a sex discrimination suit against *Newsweek* magazine, was one of a new generation of black women who came out of the Civil Rights Movement. A veteran of SNCC, Norton became an outspoken civil rights advocate organizer. She would later continue her fight for equal rights as a congressional delegate for the District of Columbia.

During the early 1970s, members of the SCLC spoke out against the Vietnam War, organized marches for striking workers, and led marches against repression. In May 1970 the SCLC organized a five-day, 100-mile march that culminated in a rally in downtown Atlanta. Coretta Scott King, Ralph Abernathy, South Dakota Senator George McGovern, and others spoke at the rally on such topics as Vietnam, racism, and police brutality.

Race riots continued in the 1970s, including a conflict in Augusta, Georgia, in May 1970. The murder of a black teenager in his jail cell brought smoldering racial tensions to the surface. Protesters, stymied in their attempts to get an explanation for the murder, torched the state flag after ripping it from a pole. Hundreds were arrested without bail. Georgia Governor Lester Maddox, a staunch segregationist, called in the National Guard. He also asked singer James Brown, an Augusta native, to walk the streets calling for calm. Brown did. However, when the smoke cleared, six African-American men were dead.

# The Jackson State Tragedy

ON MAY 14, 1970, just 11 days after National Guardsmen opened fire on student protesters at Kent State University in Ohio, a similar tragedy occurred at Jackson State College in Jackson, Mississippi.

Preceding the violence at historically black Jackson State, the students had protested against harassment against blacks by the local white community and local police. When a false rumor spread that Mayor Charles Evers of nearby Fayette had been killed, a group of Jackson State students grew unruly on the evening of May 14. They started several fires, luring the fire department, local and state police, and the National Guard to the area.

Around midnight, some students—among a crowd estimated at 75 to 100—taunted police and threw bricks at the officers. After an unidentified popping sound was heard, police opened fire on the unarmed students for 28 seconds—15 seconds longer than at Kent State. Phillip Gibbs, the father of a baby boy, and James Earl Green, 17, were killed. Twelve others were struck by gunfire. The windows of a nearby women's dormitory were riddled with bullets and buckshot pellets—an estimated 460 rounds in all.

On June 13, 1970, President Richard Nixon established the President's Commission on Campus Unrest. However, no arrests ever were made for the Jackson State violence. Demetrius Gibbs, son of Phillip Gibbs, said that when he brings up the tragedy with people, "they don't know about it." Many have argued that the Kent State story received far more media coverage than the Jackson State debacle because the Kent State victims were white, not black.

Jackson State students displaying solidarity after the shooting

# 1970s

## 1970

**April 8:** After lobbying by the NAACP, the U.S. Senate blocks the nomination of segregationist Judge G. Harrold Carswell to the Supreme Court.

**May:** *Essence,* a magazine for middle-class black women, premieres.

**May 11:** A riot begins in Augusta, Georgia, in reaction to the fatal beating of a 16-year-old black boy while in jail. Six African-Americans are killed.

**May 14:** At an antiwar demonstration at Jackson State College in Jackson, Mississippi, police open fire on the black demonstrators for 28 seconds, killing two. No one will be indicted.

**June 14:** Cheryl Brown is crowned Miss Iowa, thus becoming the first black woman to earn a spot in the Miss America pageant.

**June 16:** In Newark, New Jersey, Kenneth Gibson becomes the first African-American to be elected mayor of a major eastern city.

**June 22:** President Richard Nixon signs a bill that extends the Voting Rights Act of 1965 to 1975.

**July 4–7:** In Asbury Park, New Jersey, more than 40 people are shot during four days of violence.

**August 5:** Black Panther Party cofounder Huey Newton, convicted for involuntary manslaughter of an Oakland police officer, is released because of procedural errors during his trial.

**September 5:** At the Revolutionary People's Constitutional Convention, Black Panthers leader Huey Newton promises a revised U.S. Constitution based on socialist ideals.

**September 14:** In New Orleans, police battle militant African-Americans in a day-long gun battle, leaving one black youth dead and 21 people injured. ➤

New Jersey state police take a black youth into custody in Asbury Park, a seashore community, in July 1970. Burning and looting, which began at the edge of the downtown area, spread into the main part of the city. In four days of violence, 43 people were shot. The rioting didn't stop until local authorities agreed to consider a list of demands from a coalition of black organizations, which included more drug enforcement and better jobs and housing. Like other cities across the country, Asbury Park would take decades to recover from the riot.

Martin Luther King's body rests in a tomb at the Martin Luther King, Jr. Center for Nonviolent Social Change in Atlanta. Coretta Scott King, his widow, created the center in 1969. Visitors can read the words inscribed on the crypt: "Free At Last, Free At Last, Thank God, Almighty, I'm Free At Last." The memorial includes an eternal flame.

> "Jails and prisons are designed to break human beings, to convert the population into specimens in a zoo—obedient to our keepers, but dangerous to each other."
>
> —ANGELA DAVIS

# Angela Davis

EMERGING FROM A MIDDLE-CLASS family in Birmingham, Alabama, Angela Davis found herself on the FBI's Most Wanted list at age 26. Before and since her days as a fugitive, Davis has challenged the white male establishment. "Racism," she said, "cannot be separated from capitalism."

Raised in the segregated South of the 1940s and 1950s, Davis knew girls who were killed in the bombing of the Sixteenth Street Baptist Church in 1963. Atypically, she was sent north for her high school years to a liberal-minded private school. After graduating from Brandeis University, Davis studied in Germany before starting work on a Ph.D. at the University of California at San Diego. Along the way, her activism began to incorporate the philosophies of socialism, Marxism, decolonization, and feminism.

After securing a teaching position at UCLA, Davis was eventually dismissed at the urging of Governor Ronald Reagan because of her membership in the Communist Party. Her dismissal set off a storm of protest in liberal and civil rights circles. Davis had been fired for her political beliefs.

As a university professor, Davis championed a number of liberal, left-wing, and civil rights causes. She came to the attention of the nation in 1970 after inmate/activist George Jackson was killed in Soledad Prison in California. When Jackson's brother, Jonathan, attempted to free another prisoner from a Marin County courthouse, four people were killed in a shootout. Davis was placed on the FBI's Most Wanted list because guns used in the raid belonged to her. Apprehended, she spent 16 months in jail but was ultimately acquitted by an all-white jury. Still active politically and academically, Davis champions the cause of individuals wrongly imprisoned for crimes they may not have committed.

## WANTED BY THE FBI

### INTERSTATE FLIGHT - MURDER, KIDNAPING
### ANGELA YVONNE DAVIS

FBI No. 867,615 G

Photograph taken 1969

Photograph taken 1970

Alias: "Tamu"

### DESCRIPTION

| | | | |
|---|---|---|---|
| Age: | 26, born January 26, 1944, Birmingham, Alabama | | |
| Height: | 5'8" | Eyes: | Brown |
| Weight: | 145 pounds | Complexion: | Light brown |
| Build: | Slender | Race: | Negro |
| Hair: | Black | Nationality: | American |
| Occupation: | Teacher | | |
| Scars and Marks: | Small scars on both knees | | |

Fingerprint Classification:  4 M  5 Ua 6
                              I 17 U

### CAUTION

ANGELA DAVIS IS WANTED ON KIDNAPING AND MURDER CHARGES GROWING OUT OF AN ABDUCTION AND SHOOTING IN MARIN COUNTY, CALIFORNIA, ON AUGUST 7, 1970. SHE ALLEGEDLY HAS PURCHASED SEVERAL GUNS IN THE PAST. CONSIDER POSSIBLY ARMED

Angela Davis was on the run from authorities after police discovered that weapons registered to her were used in a shootout at a San Rafael, California, courthouse on August 7, 1970. That day, Soledad Prison inmates George Jackson (a radical political leader while imprisoned), John Clutchette, and Fleeta Drumgo were on trial for killing a white prison guard. When Jackson's brother, Jonathan, attempted to overtake the courthouse and free the accused, a shootout ensued; Jonathan, the judge, and two prisoners (who had been tossed guns by Jonathan) were killed. Davis, who had campaigned to acquit the "Soledad Brothers," stayed underground for approximately two months before she was captured. She was later acquitted on murder and kidnapping charges.

# 1970s

The television show *Julia* starred Diahann Carroll as a widowed mother raising her son alone while working as a nurse. The sitcom was groundbreaking since it featured a black woman in a lead role. However, her role fit into the mold that television still had not entirely abandoned. As far as many executives were concerned, blacks could have starring roles as long as they were "colorless." Such characters made little or no mention of race or social conditions, and did not display any cultural characteristics.

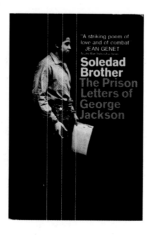

George Jackson is one of the best-remembered martyrs of the Black Power movement. Sentenced to one year to life for robbing a Los Angeles gas station while on parole in 1960, Jackson became a political activist while in Soledad Prison. In 1970 he and two other black inmates, John Clutchette and Fleeta Drumgo, were charged with the killing of a white prison guard at Soledad. A year later, Jackson was fatally shot by a guard at San Quentin Prison, but not before writing his masterpiece collection of prison letters, *Soledad Brother,* as well as a sequel, *Blood in My Eye.* An insightful, poignant writer, Jackson made readers acutely aware of the injustices of the judicial system.

When Kenneth Gibson became mayor of Newark, New Jersey, in 1970, black people in that city literally danced in the streets. The election was the outgrowth of the political organizing achieved by Amiri Baraka and other black activists. They attempted to practically implement the goals and objectives of the Black Power movement after a violent insurrection in 1967 threatened to tear the city apart. Gibson's advances in healthcare and constructing affordable housing were slow, but he made the city's working-class black residents—many of whom received good jobs for the first time—believe that the power they demanded was indeed in their hands.

Although no longer lynching and openly terrorizing African Americans, the Ku Klux Klan was still a powerful presence in the South as the new decade dawned. Open Klan membership, though, would fall to about 5,000 by the mid-1970s, prompting its leaders to re-create its public image as a group fighting for white political rights. By 1980 membership had begun to increase.

By 1970 the philosophy of Black Power pervaded many American cities, including New Orleans (*pictured*). The assassinations of Martin Luther King and Robert F. Kennedy had drained the hope of civil rights activists, while the presence of "law and order" President Richard Nixon led to anger and resentment among the less fortunate. By '70, the Black Panther Party had grown dramatically, with chapters or branches in every major American city. Although many black Americans still believed in America and its ideals, the ideas of Malcolm X—the black nationalist American martyr—had begun to take hold.

Around 1970 African-Americans began to study their history and culture not from traditional school textbooks but from the viewpoint of themselves as a colonized African people. Activists in some cities began to hold Kwanzaa celebrations. Community schools focusing on African history and culture began to be built and staffed. Swahili and African dance classes were prevalent in many urban cities. Some blacks welcomed the embrace of an African-based cultural nationalism—a black "consciousness"—while others felt their time was better spent preparing for the new, post-segregated nation.

Members of the Black Panther Party did more than just march in black jackets and berets, carry rifles, and chant "Off the Pigs!" The Panthers established what they called "survival programs." The day-to-day activities of many branches included the operation of free breakfast programs (such as this one in Oakland), along with free health clinics, food giveaways, and, in North Carolina, a free ambulance program. The FBI was especially concerned about the donation-funded breakfast program, feeling it was a way of indoctrinating kids into the Panther philosophy. (Film footage shows the Panthers teaching a "Free Huey" song to black kids while serving breakfast.) The Panthers fed thousands of black children every day, showing the world that African-Americans would take care of themselves.

# 1970s

## 1970–1971

**October 1970:** School desegregation in Pontiac, Michigan, results in two days of rioting.

**October 12, 1970:** The U.S. Commission on Civil Rights labels President Nixon's desegregation policy as "inadequate, overcautious, and indicative of possible retreat."

**October 13, 1970:** After spending two months in hiding, activist Angela Davis is discovered and jailed. She is charged with kidnapping, conspiracy, and murder for her connection to the failed attempt to free a prisoner from a courthouse in San Rafael, California. *See* June 4, 1972.

**1971:** Aileen Hernandez becomes the first black president of the National Organization for Women.

**1971:** *Shaft* and *Sweet Sweetback's Baadasssss Song*, two films that epitomize the "blaxploitation" genre, hit theaters.

**January 5, 1971:** African-Americans accuse Bethlehem Steel of discrimination, stating that its seniority system effectively excludes minorities. Bethlehem will agree to establish new hiring and promotion procedures for blacks.

**January 16, 1971:** An Oregon court rules that racial prejudice can cause mental anguish and can be compensated for with cash awards.

**January 22, 1971:** The newly formed Congressional Black Caucus boycotts President Nixon's State of the Union Address after Nixon refuses to meet with them.

**March 1971:** President Nixon creates the Office of Minority Business Enterprise to help black citizens excel in business ventures.

**April 20, 1971:** In *Swann v. Charlotte–Mecklenburg*, the U.S. Supreme Court rules that busing schoolchildren to achieve racial integration is constitutional. *See* July 25, 1974. ➤

After boycotting Richard Nixon's 1970 State of the Union address, the Congressional Black Caucus finally caught the President's attention. The caucus had been asking for a meeting for more than a year. At this meeting, on March 25, 1971, the caucus gave Nixon a list of 61 policy recommendations, ranging from civil rights to foreign policy. It was a sign that blacks were not going to be ignored in the national political arena. Nixon, who constructed affirmative action, later was heard on White House audiotapes, released during the 1990s, referring to black people as "niggers" during his private meetings.

The Black Panthers were constant targets of police and federal law enforcement harassment. In 1969 virtually the entire leadership of the New York City chapter was arrested and charged with multiple counts of conspiracy, arson, and attempted murder. Authorities charged the "Panther 21" with planning to blow up department stores and subway and police stations. Bail was set at $100,000 each. At the trial, the prosecution failed to prove that such a plot existed; even the testimony of Eugene Roberts, a Panther exposed as a government informant, didn't help. On May 13, 1971, the jury took less than an hour to acquit those who eventually stood trial.

Amiri Baraka, the former Greenwich Village beatnik playwright and poet who was born LeRoi Jones, had become a full-fledged, black nationalist artist and intellectual by the early 1970s. His work in organizing black people to elect Kenneth Gibson as mayor of Newark, New Jersey, in 1970 and his fiery black nationalist poetry had catapulted him to national attention. In 1972 he helped organize and moderate the National Black Political Convention in Gary, Indiana, an event that would shape black politics for the decade.

*Sweet Sweetback's Baadasssss Song*, the low-budget 1971 film that started the "blaxploitation" film era, was a triumph for multitalented artist Melvin Van Peebles. He wrote, produced, directed, and starred in the film about a black man who witnesses white police brutality and goes on the run as a result. The film is a tribute to black militancy, nerve, and trickery utilized against the white power structure. Van Peebles, who worked as a journalist in France in the 1960s, wrote novels and starred in plays that he wrote and directed as a result of his *Sweetback* success.

# Uprising at Attica

IN SEPTEMBER 1971, the eyes of America focused on Attica State Prison in upstate New York. On September 9, Attica's prisoners—politically aware and long resentful of their harsh treatment—overpowered their guards and seized control of the prison. Inmates captured the exercise yard and took several guards hostage. Prisoners selected a negotiating team to address grievances, and for four tense days they negotiated with authorities.

For months prior to the uprising, Attica's prisoners had filed various grievances, complaining about overcrowding, poor food, substandard medical care, and racist brutality by guards. The prisoners also read as much as they could from Black Power advocates, who considered black prison inmates as "political prisoners" in the black liberation struggle. In this view, the high number of black inmates was attributed to racism that had created depressed black ghettos. Racism, according to the theory, further manifested itself in the criminal justice system, with African-Americans arrested, convicted, and sentenced in greater numbers than whites. At Attica, 54 percent of the inmates were black while nearly all of the guards were white. Prisoners argued that the poor treatment was racially motivated.

Attica inmates during uprising

Preceding the Attica uprising, black prisoners had worn black armbands to protest the killing of African-American activist George Jackson by prison guards in California. When calls for improvements fell on deaf ears, Attica's prisoners revolted. After four days of negotiations, New York Governor Nelson Rockefeller ordered the state police to storm the prison yard by force. The battle to recapture the prison left 43 dead, including 10 hostages.

A subsequent investigation concluded that all 43 casualties were the result of police gunfire. The inmates had no firearms. The Attica ordeal sparked public debates about prison reform, although only token improvements would be made.

## 1971

**May 21–26:** Racial tensions escalate in Chattanooga, Tennessee, leading to more than 400 arrests.

**June 7:** The U.S. Supreme Court rules that individuals who are denied their civil rights can sue in civil court.

**June 14:** In *Palmer v. Thompson*, the U.S. Supreme Court upholds the constitutionality of Jackson, Mississippi's decision to close its public pools rather than integrate them.

**June 28:** The U.S. Supreme Court overturns the 1967 draft evasion conviction of boxer Muhammad Ali.

**July 10:** Congresswoman Shirley Chisholm (D–NY) helps found the National Women's Political Caucus.

**August 11:** The White House announces that President Nixon has warned administrative officials that they risk losing their jobs if they continue to push for busing.

**August 18:** Police and the FBI raid the Jackson, Mississippi, headquarters of the Republic of New Africa, a group devoted to establishing an autonomous black country within the South. One police officer is killed; 11 RNA members are arrested for murder.

**September 9:** Six KKK members are arrested for bombing 10 school buses in Pontiac, Michigan.

**September 9–13:** Prisoners, mostly black and Hispanic, revolt at the Attica Correctional Facility in New York. They hold 39 guards and civilians hostage in the "D yard." The inmates demand prison reform, including higher wages, religious freedom, more educational programs, and an alleviation of overcrowding—plus amnesty for their actions during the uprising. Acting on orders from Governor Nelson Rockefeller, state troopers open fire on the D yard, killing 43 people, including 10 hostages. ➤

A clock at the Attica State Correctional Facility stopped at the time the Attica prison riot began, 9:30 A.M. on September 9, 1971. Above the clock, police in heavy gear watch over the prison during the second day of the inmate takeover. The authorities are standing and waiting because of the inmate threat that the 30-plus hostages would be killed if police used force to take back the prison.

Amnesty—a pardon prohibiting any legal or other retaliation for a particular action—was the main issue that prolonged the inmate takeover at Attica. New York State Corrections Commissioner Russell Oswald refused to guarantee amnesty for the inmates. Moreover, Governor Nelson Rockefeller refused the inmates' request to visit Attica to negotiate.

William Moses Kunstler often took up the fight for civil rights. He served as an attorney for groups such as SNCC, the SCLC, and the Mississippi Freedom Democratic Party. His clients included Adam Clayton Powell, H. Rap Brown, Stokely Carmichael, and the "Chicago 7." Here, he tells Attica inmates that he stands in their defense.

# Attica Prisoners: "We Are Men!"

To the people of America

THE INCIDENT that has erupted here at Attica is not a result of the dastardly bushwacking of the two prisoners Sept. 8, 1971 but of the unmitigated oppression wrought by the racist administration network of the prison, throughout the year.

WE are MEN! We are not beasts and do not intend to be beaten or driven as such. The entire prison populace has set forth to change forever the ruthless brutalization and disregard for the lives of the prisoners here and throughout the United States. What has happened here is but the sound before the fury of those who are oppressed.

We will not compromise on any terms except those that are agreeable to us. We call upon all the conscientious citizens of America to assist us in putting an end to this situation that threatens the lives of not only us, but each and everyone [sic] of us as well.

—*Preface to statement of demands by prisoners at Attica State Prison, New York State, September 9, 1971*

New York Governor Nelson Rockefeller and Corrections Commissioner Russell Oswald (*pictured*) were under increased pressure to end the uprising at the Attica State Prison. State authorities made their move on September 13, four days after the inmates had taken over. A task force of state troopers and police rushed in, shooting rifles and throwing tear gas canisters. Forty-three people, including 10 hostages, were shot to death, all by authorities. When control of the prison was restored, guards rounded up the inmate organizers, stripped them naked, and checked them for weapons. Inmates were beaten and burned with cigarettes. They were abused by guards for months after the uprising.

# 1970s

## 1971–1972

**December 25, 1971:** In Chicago, Jesse Jackson founds People United to Save Humanity. PUSH will focus on economic advancement and education for African-Americans.

**December 28, 1971:** The U.S. Justice Department sues Mississippi officials for ignoring the ballots of black voters.

**January 10, 1972:** A U.S. district court orders the merger of the mostly black school districts of Richmond, Virginia, with the predominately white school districts in the suburbs in order to eliminate segregation.

**January 25, 1972:** Congresswoman Shirley Chisholm (D–NY) launches her run for the U.S. presidency, becoming the first African-American to do so.

**March 10–12, 1972:** Gary, Indiana, hosts the National Black Political Convention. About 8,000 delegates and observers attend to discuss such issues as capital punishment, health care, education, crime, and a guaranteed minimum income. The convention passes a resolution against school integration.

**March 24, 1972:** The Equal Employment Opportunity Act is passed. It prohibits discrimination against federal employees based on race, sex, or religion.

**June 4, 1972:** After 16 months in jail, black activist Angela Davis is acquitted by a white jury.

**July 3, 1972:** The NAACP passes an emergency resolution condemning President Richard Nixon's stance against school busing.

**July 10–13, 1972:** African-American Yvonne Brathwaite Burke serves as vice-chair of the 1972 Democratic National Convention. ➤

**The mob wanted Harlem back. They got Shaft... up to here.**

**SHAFT**

SHAFT's his name. SHAFT's his game.

METRO-GOLDWYN-MAYER Presents RICHARD ROUNDTREE Co-Starring MOSES GUNN Screenplay by ERNEST TIDYMAN Based on a novel by ERNEST TIDYMAN Music by ISAAC HAYES Produced by JOEL FREEMAN Directed by GORDON PARKS METROCOLOR MGM

*Shaft* is perhaps the most famous "blaxploitation" film, a genre in which black characters and their lifestyles are depicted in a manner that reinforces negative stereotypes. The 1971 movie, directed by black filmmaker Gordon Parks, is at heart a typical detective drama. The plot: a black private eye (Richard Roundtree as Shaft) gets caught between a rock and a hard place. The rock is black mobsters. The hard place is white mobsters and black revolutionaries. The fact that *Shaft* fit the model of crime movies and television shows of the day made it popular with whites as well. Two sequels, a television show, and many similar films would follow.

Maya Angelou became one of the most prominent voices for African-Americans in the arts. By the early 1970s, she had been a dancer, a poet, a journalist, and an aide in Martin Luther King's and Malcolm X's organizations. She also raised autobiography to the level of literature with the publication of her first memoir, the 1970 classic *I Know Why the Caged Bird Sings*. In 1971 Angelou was hired to direct a film version of *Bird,* becoming the first black woman to direct a major Hollywood movie.

Jesse Jackson permanently stepped out of the shadow of the late Martin Luther King by creating Operation PUSH (People United to Save Humanity) in 1971. PUSH would continue the work Jackson had done with Operation Breadbasket, an SCLC self-help program that pressured corporations to provide jobs for blacks in black communities. Jackson would establish himself as the nation's top civil rights leader by the end of the 1970s. He met with world leaders, led civil rights protests, and toured high schools with his powerful "I Am Somebody" speech. Jackson combined PUSH with his Rainbow Coalition, the grassroots political organization that supported his two presidential runs.

The National Black Political Convention, held in March 1972 in Gary, Indiana, was a triumph for many black nationalists and progressives. The mixture of men in dashikis (the visual symbol of Black Power) mingling with business suits (such as that worn by CORE National Director Roy Innis, *pictured*) was "an incredible sight to behold," said Gary Mayor Richard Hatcher. The mayor co-convened the meeting with black nationalist Amiri Baraka and Congressman Charles Diggs of Michigan. Queen Mother Moore, a nationalist representing Harlem, canvassed the halls, handing out pamphlets calling for reparations. Meanwhile, Jesse Jackson of Operation PUSH called for a Black Liberation Party. Without a black political party, he declared, African-Americans were destined to remain in the "rumble seat" of the Republican Party and the "hip pocket" of the Democratic Party.

# National Black Political Convention

"IT'S NATION TIME! It's nation time!" That was the repeated refrain of the delegates attending the National Black Political Convention at Gary (Indiana) Westside High School in March 1972. About 8,000 delegates, including black elected officials, civil rights and Black Power leaders, and representatives from organized labor, gathered to craft a national black political agenda.

This historic event mirrored the National Negro Convention movement in the 1800s, when black leaders strove to abolish slavery and achieve full citizenship rights. In 1972 the convention attendees also were concerned about securing full and equal citizenship rights for black people.

Though the delegates—who ranged from Jesse Jackson and Julian Bond to Louis Farrakhan and actor Richard Roundtree—had different viewpoints, most embraced black nationalism. This was illustrated by one of the major planks in the convention platform, which called for an end to forced busing of black schoolchildren to white schools in white neighborhoods. Instead, convention members called for the empowerment of the black community (Black Community Control) so that majority-black schools would be equal to their white counterparts.

Some of the other issues on the delegates' agenda included: the establishment of a national network of community health centers; a system of national health insurance; elimination of capital punishment; a government guarantee of a minimum annual income of $5,200 for a family of four; and the establishment of a black United Fund. Though most of their goals would be out of reach, delegates at least created a plan, a basis from which to move forward.

# Black Feminism

"**A**IN'T I A WOMAN?" thundered former slave Sojourner Truth in 1851. Black feminism is as old as the black liberation struggle in America. From Harriet Tubman to Zora Neale Hurston to Bell Hooks, black women have struggled for their rights. But unlike their white female counterparts, black feminists have been fighting against sexism *and* racism.

The white feminist movement of the 1970s was led largely by middle-class, highly educated women fighting against white male domination. Black feminists of the era, from Fannie Lou Hamer to Angela Davis, fought white domination and black male "patriarchy." The Civil Rights and Black Power movements of the 1960s and '70s were criticized for their patriarchal tendencies. Ella Baker of the SCLC constantly railed against the patriarchy exhibited in the hierarchy of the organization. Black Power advocate Stokely Carmichael opined in jest that the "position" of women in SNCC was prone.

Some black feminists were accused of abandoning the struggle for racial freedom to join the Women's Movement. Black feminists felt pressured to choose between supporting their race and their gender. Some black men rejected the claim of female oppression, insisting that they didn't have the necessary power to oppress anyone and that white men were oppressing both black sexes. Still, most black women saw no contradiction in supporting the liberation of both African-Americans and women.

While the debate in the black community still resonates, some definite strides have been made in the past 30 years. More black women have entered the professions in higher education, politics, business, and commerce. This empowering development has strengthened the push for black liberation within the black community.

"There was a time when I was a picketer across the street. Then I decided I didn't want to be there outside of policy-making. I wanted to be inside, fighting right there on their turf."

—YVONNE BRATHWAITE BURKE, FORMER CONGRESSWOMAN

When Yvonne Brathwaite Burke graduated from law school at the University of Southern California in 1956, not one law firm in Los Angeles granted her an interview. Persevering, she started her own law practice, and a decade later she began a groundbreaking political career. The highlights came in 1972, when she became the first black woman elected to Congress from California and also served as vice-chair of the Democratic National Convention. A year later Burke became the first congresswoman to give birth while in office. The high-profile politician was hailed as a great role model for young African-American women.

The Pan-African Liberation Committee took over Harvard University's presidential offices in April 1972, demanding that the university sell its stock in Gulf Oil Corp., which was aiding the Portuguese colonial regime in the African nation of Angola. The students stayed in the building for six days. An investment committee was set up to monitor future investments. This pattern would be repeated in the 1980s when students demanded that their universities stop investing in companies that did business with South Africa's white-minority regime.

In 1972 Shirley Chisholm became the first black candidate to make a credible run for the White House. The woman who rose from directing nursery centers in Brooklyn to winning a congressional seat from that borough campaigned for women's rights, abortion rights, and an end to the Vietnam War. In the Democratic primaries, her share of the vote never exceeded seven percent. However, her campaign served as an example of the power of black candidates to place issues on the national agenda—a power Jesse Jackson tested in his 1984 and 1988 Democratic nomination runs.

The Black Arts movement was sometimes referred to as the "artistic sister" of the Black Power movement. Black dance companies, including the Harlem-based Dance Theatre of Harlem (*pictured*) formed by Arthur Mitchell (*center*), helped to integrate as well as culturally redefine the overwhelmingly white world of dance. Other troupes, including those led by Katherine Dunham and Alvin Ailey, toured the world for decades, introducing a new generation of African-American dancers. Dunham's work in particular incorporated African and Caribbean movements into the European ballet form.

Tennis powerhouse Arthur Ashe (*right*) fought racism his own dignified way. In 1973, three years after winning the Australian Open and two years before prevailing at Wimbledon, he competed in a tournament in South Africa. His decision angered some South African blacks, who called him an Uncle Tom for giving legitimacy, they thought, to the apartheid regime. Ashe, however, felt it was good for black South Africans to see him, a successful black American athlete. He also thought that his presence would open the door for others to follow. In America in the 1960s and 1970s, Ashe was viewed as a racial moderate, a "good Negro" in a time of black militancy. In later years, however, he helped lead the anti-apartheid movement.

# 1970s

## 1972–1973

**November 7, 1972:** Incumbent Richard Nixon wins 49 states as he defeats Democrat George McGovern in the presidential election.

**November 16, 1972:** Southern University in Baton Rouge, Louisiana, is closed after local police officers kill two students. The students had protested against the school president, who they claimed weeded out professors whom he deemed too militant.

**1973:** The U.S. Supreme Court rules that the Denver school system is guilty of school segregation and must remedy the situation.

**1973:** Bobby Seale of the Black Panthers makes a strong but unsuccessful run for the mayoralty of Oakland.

**May 1973:** Marian Edelman forms the Children's Defense Fund, which will become an influential advocacy group for underprivileged kids in the United States.

**May 29, 1973:** Tom Bradley, an African-American, is elected mayor of Los Angeles.

**August 15, 1973:** Eleanor Holmes Norton helps found the National Black Feminist Organization.

**October 16, 1973:** African-American Maynard Jackson is elected mayor of Atlanta, the largest city in the Deep South.

**November 6, 1973:** Coleman Young becomes the first black mayor of Detroit. ➤

In 1973 New Jersey Assemblyman Anthony Imperiale (*foreground*) fought against the development of Kawaida Towers, a predominately black housing project in the predominately white North Ward of Newark, New Jersey. Imperiale and poet/playwright Amiri Baraka (*right, hand on barrier*), then a black nationalist political organizer who had helped shape or inspire Black Power movements locally and nationally, were considered racially polarizing opposing forces in Newark. Imperiale, a leader of the city's Italian communities in the North Ward, allegedly had called Martin Luther King "Martin Luther Coon" during a ward rally in the late 1960s. That and other antics led him to be tarred as a racist vigilante—a charge that sometimes, rightly or wrongly, was hurled against Baraka as well.

New York's Co-Op City, the nation's largest housing complex, was one of the many attempts at social engineering orchestrated by white liberals who wanted whites and blacks of all incomes to live together. In Co-Op City, whites and people of color created a balance in their 55,000-member "neighborhood" that other government-funded housing complexes have been unable to match.

Stanford University professor William Shockley (*left photo*), winner of the 1956 Nobel Prize for Physics, caused a national uproar when he theorized that black people were inherently less intelligent that whites. He argued that this inferiority made welfare and other social programs a waste of time, and that the government should pay "undesirables" (those with IQs less than 100) to be sterilized. It was an old argument in a new form. Earlier in the century, eugenics—a greatly disputed branch of science that studied genetic "superiority" and "inferiority"—had been used by the Nazis to justify the murder of six million Jews. And black Americans had heard about their genetic "inferiority" from whites for centuries. Shockley's lectures at major universities during the 1970s were always the target of protests, including one at Princeton (*right photo*) in 1973.

Coleman Young was elected mayor of Detroit, then the nation's fifth largest city, in 1973. Young, a civil rights activist in the 1960s, was very outspoken. During his first campaign, he called the city's virtually all-white police department "an army of occupation." As mayor of a predominately black city, he said in the 1980s that the city's banks "ain't shit when it comes to issuing mortgages to Detroiters." Young was often blamed for the deterioration of his city, which many of its residents (black and white) abandoned for the suburbs. Nevertheless, Young won the loyalty of the city's working-class blacks and remained mayor for 20 years.

The hard-won right to vote did not improve the economic condition of many black Southerners in the 1970s. Blacks there, particularly those in many rural areas, still were dependent on factory labor, farming, and small business opportunities. Affirmative action in urban areas such as Atlanta, however, created a black middle class that would draw professional blacks to the South in the 1980s and 1990s.

# Black Elected Officials

N NOVEMBER 1967, just over two years after President Lyndon Johnson signed the Voting Rights Act into law, Carl B. Stokes was elected mayor of Cleveland, becoming the first black mayor of a major American city. That same month, Richard G. Hatcher, also an African-American, won the mayoralty of Gary, the second largest city in Indiana.

Farther south, in Fayette, Mississippi, black citizens voted into office a black constable, two justices of the peace, a supervisor, and a school board member. Charles Evers, who had taken over the job of NAACP Mississippi field secretary after his brother, Medgar, was slain in 1963, was elected mayor of Fayette in 1969. Evers said that the black citizens of his town had the electoral power to vote in African-Americans for every office.

In 1968 Evers was among some 40 black Mississippians who participated in the state Democratic convention—the first time African-Americans were represented at the convention since 1876. The following year, he became the first African-American elected mayor of an integrated southern town.

As those who had campaigned for black voting rights understood, the ballot is one of the most important rights of citizenship. The ability to exercise that right means power, and indeed not until African-Americans were able to register and vote without intimidation did the famous 1960s slogan "Black Power!" come to have substantive meaning.

By the 1970s, 102 counties in 11 southern states were at least 50 percent black. The southern cities of Bessemer and Prichard, Alabama; Greenville, Mississippi; Petersburg, Virginia; and Atlanta, Georgia, were more than 50 percent black. As more and more African-Americans won public office in those localities, only die-hard racists refused to admit that blacks were equally as qualified to govern as whites—and only die-hard racialists could maintain that blacks were better at governing than white leaders were.

Former police officer Tom Bradley served as mayor of multiracial Los Angeles from 1973 to 1993.

African-Americans had no premium on fairness, competence, morality, or any other qualities possessed by the ideal politician. As officeholders, they covered the character spectrum, just as whites did. And like whites, some could be both competent and unethical at the same time.

African-American elected officials were more common in large cities, whose populations had become increasingly black by the 1970s. The corresponding "white flight," eroding tax base, and increase in crime rates occurred at the same time as a nationwide period of high inflation and economic stress. Moreover, following passage of the 1965 Hart–Cellar Act, which lifted restrictions on immigration from Asia, South Asia, and the Caribbean, most cities experienced a large influx of new immigrants, new strains on the social programs and services of the large cities, and new tensions among ethnic groups.

In 1967, the same year in which the first black mayors were elected in two major northern cities, several other large northern urban areas exploded in riots, among them Carl Stokes's Cleveland, Newark, Detroit, New York, and Chicago. The charge often has been made, in fact, that by the time African-Americans got a chance to govern the big cities, those population centers had become virtually ungovernable.

Looking back, it is clear that African-American mayors performed as well as their white counterparts in coping with social and economic conditions stemming from circumstances largely beyond their control. Coleman Young, mayor of Detroit from 1973 to 1993, worked successfully to get more blacks on the police force and in government positions. However, he also witnessed the economic decline of his city, as white flight and auto industry hardships took their toll. Other mayors elected in the 1970s included Kenneth Gibson in Newark (elected in 1970), Maynard Jackson in Atlanta (1973), Tom Bradley in Los Angeles (1973), Walter E. Washington in Washington (1974), and Richard Arrington, Jr., in Birmingham (1979).

Birmingham Mayor Richard Arrington

In a nation in which African-Americans constitute a minority of the population, not just demographics but myths and customs as well continue to govern the behavior of American voters. For this reason, even women—who constitute a slight majority of the population—are still underrepresented in elective office. African-Americans have been successful in achieving elective office in localities where blacks constitute a significant voting bloc, such as in congressional districts or big cities. They have not been as successful at winning the right to represent a larger population spectrum.

The U.S. Senate remains largely white. In fact, in the entire history of the United States just four African-Americans have served in the Senate, and two of them did so during Reconstruction. The two black senators who have served in modern times were Edward Brooke, Republican of Massachusetts (who served in the Senate from 1967 to 1979), and Carol Moseley–Braun, Democrat of Illinois (1992 to 1998), the first black woman to serve in that government body.

In the 20th century, one African-American, Democrat Douglas Wilder, served as governor of a state. Wilder had been the only African-American in the Virginia Senate and had served as lieutenant governor before his election to the state's highest office in 1989. He served as governor from 1990 to 1994 (Virginia governors are not permitted to serve consecutive terms). Wilder then challenged Charles Robb for his seat in the U.S. Senate. Running as an independent, Wilder was unable to garner sufficient support in the polls to continue his campaign, and thus withdrew. He has not entered another political race.

Two African-Americans, both Democrats, campaigned for a major political party's presidential nomination in the 20th century: Congresswoman Shirley Chisholm in 1972 and Jesse Jackson in 1984 and 1988. Jackson won two primaries in 1984 and seven in 1988, giving hope that an African-American might one day lead the nation.

# 1970s

## 1974

**April 8:** After receiving death threats from racist whites, Atlanta Braves slugger Hank Aaron belts his 715th home run, breaking the major-league record held by icon Babe Ruth.

**April 15:** Nine steel manufacturers agree to pay more than $30 million in back pay to victims of job discrimination (women and minorities).

**May 16:** The U.S. Senate passes a bill to limit court-ordered busing to achieve school desegregation, although it states that the limitations are not intended to inhibit courts from ordering busing if necessary to enforce the equal rights provisions of the United States Constitution.

**June 21:** In response to unconstitutional segregation in Boston's public schools, U.S. District Court Judge W. Arthur Garrity orders massive forced busing to integrate the city's schools. The decision sparks an uproar among the city's white population. *See* September 12, 1974.

**July 25:** In *Milliken v. Bradley,* the U.S. Supreme Court rules that busing children between different school districts is not allowable as a solution to an area's *de facto* segregated schooling.

**August 9:** President Richard Nixon resigns. Vice President Gerald Ford assumes office.

**September 12:** In response to the unpopular busing decree in Boston, many students boycott the first day of classes. White students harass black students who are bused to their schools, shouting racial profanities and throwing things at them.

**October 3:** Frank Robinson is named manager of the Cleveland Indians, becoming the first black skipper in major-league history.

**November 5:** African-American Walter E. Washington becomes the first elected mayor of Washington, D.C. ➤

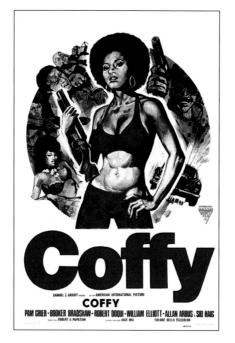

SAMUEL Z. ARKOFF presents an AMERICAN INTERNATIONAL PICTURE

**COFFY**

PAM GRIER · BOOKER BRADSHAW · ROBERT DOQUI · WILLIAM ELLIOTT · ALLAN ARBUS · SID HAIG

PRODUCED BY ROBERT A. PAPAZIAN    WRITTEN AND DIRECTED BY JACK HILL    COLORE DELLA TELECOLOR

Not all baseball fans rejoiced when Hank Aaron of the Atlanta Braves surpassed Babe Ruth's major league home run record of 714 on April 8, 1974. Aaron received piles of hate mail and even death threats from bigoted whites, who resented that a black man would usurp the fabled Ruth. Unfortunately, Aaron, the last player from the Negro Leagues to play in the majors, was accustomed to blatant racism. As a teenager playing with an all-black club, he remembered how Washington, D.C., restaurant workers broke all the plates off which he and his teammates had eaten. "If dogs had eaten off those plates, they would have washed them," he wrote.

Pam Grier exploded onto the big screen in the 1970s with such "blaxploitation" films as *Coffy, Sheba Baby,* and *Foxy Brown.* Her popular films combined sexuality with gritty violence and a smattering of racial tension. They also established the buxom, Afro-wearing "soul sister" as the first black female action hero. The majority of her 1970s movies showcase Grier as a strong, independent woman who fights and wins her own battles. This image appealed to white feminist women: In 1975 Grier became the first African-American to grace the cover of *Ms.* magazine, a major feminist forum.

The old South was shaken in 1974 when Maynard Jackson became the first African-American to be elected mayor of a major southern city, Atlanta. Jackson's eight-year tenure included the growth of Hartsfield Atlanta International Airport, which by century's end would be the busiest in the world. Moreover, Jackson pushed the city's corporations to hire African-Americans, and he standardized affirmative action policies for city employees and the city's public works projects. Jackson would serve as mayor again from 1990 to 1994.

Elaine Brown (*left*) joined the Black Panther Party in 1968 and became deputy minister of information in the early '70s. When Panther leader Huey Newton (seen here, center, at a 1971 news conference) exiled himself to Cuba in 1974, Brown assumed Panthers leadership as chairperson and minister of defense—posts she held until 1977. Brown viewed the BPP as a "servant of the people," and under her stewardship the party expanded the slate of community service programs forged by party cofounders Newton and Bobby Seale. Today Brown is an author, lecturer, and president of the nonprofit Fields of Flowers education corporation. Her papers are held by Emory University.

In April 1975 Lee Elder became the first black golfer to play at the prestigious Masters Tournament. Eight years earlier he had become the second African-American to join the Professional Golfers' Association, following Charlie Sifford. Golf long has been a racially exclusive sport, with many country clubs barring, and then quietly refusing to admit, members of color. In 1990, contoversy shrouded Shoal Creek Country Club in Birmingham, Alabama, after its founder admitted that they didn't accept African-Americans. Under threat of losing the PGA Championship, scheduled to be played there that summer, they quickly admitted a black member.

# Busing in Boston

IN 1974 THE FOCUS of school desegregation shifted to the North. The city of Boston, renowned for its liberal tradition, became the site of a bitter struggle for equal education for African-Americans.

By order of U.S. District Judge W. Arthur Garrity in June 1974, black students from the Roxbury district of Boston would be bused to the majority-white South Boston community. White students from South Boston would be bused to Roxbury.

Proponents of busing applauded the decision. They felt that since most blacks were confined to urban ghettoes, the only method to integrate schools was by cross-district busing. White parents argued that they worked hard to live in a "nice" area, and their children shouldn't be penalized by being shipped to subpar (i.e., "black") schools. Many Boston residents, black and white, detested that children were being used as "pawns." The order shook the city as greatly as the *Brown v. Board of Education* decision had affected the South 20 years earlier.

Many white students boycotted the first day of school in September 1974, while some whites hurled insults, rocks, and bottles at the African-Americans who were bused to white schools. In fall 1975, 400 white mothers marched while clutching rosary beads and reciting the "Hail Mary"—then scuffled with Boston police officers. "Eighty percent of the people in Boston are against busing," said Boston Mayor Kevin White. "If Boston were a sovereign state, busing would be cause for a revolution." Marches, boycotts, violence, firings, and temporary school closings plagued the city for two years.

Other northern cities implemented busing plans, but in general the practice fell out of favor. In Boston, busing continued but with disturbing consequences. White enrollment in the city's schools dropped dramatically, as parents moved to the suburbs or put their children in private schools. Today, Boston's public schools are more than 80 percent black, and the level of education is markedly inferior to that in Boston's suburbs and private institutions.

# 1970s

## 1975–1976

**1975:** Gary Thomas Rowe, Jr., a former undercover FBI agent who posed as a Ku Klux Klan member, states that the FBI knew the KKK was going to attack Freedom Riders in Birmingham, Alabama, in 1961 but did nothing to prevent the violence. The FBI will deny the charge.

**1975:** PBS television debuts the children's show *Vegetable Soup*, which strives to broaden racial attitudes.

**January 1975:** Margaret Bush Wilson becomes the first chairwoman of the board of the NAACP.

**May 1975:** The national unemployment rate for African-Americans is 12.8 percent, compared to 7.8 percent for whites.

**July 27, 1975:** With racial tensions high in Boston, dozens of whites attack several black salesmen.

**August 6, 1975:** The 1965 Voting Rights Act is expanded and extended for seven more years. *See* June 29, 1982.

**August 6, 1975:** *The New York Times* reports that conditions in the Watts ghetto in Los Angeles are worse than they were before the 1965 riot there.

**September 29, 1975:** WGPR-TV, the first TV station owned by African-Americans, debuts in Detroit.

**Early 1976:** After black high school students in Pensacola, Florida, protest the flying of the Confederate flag at sporting events, racial tensions flare throughout the city for weeks, leading to shootings, cross burnings, and house burnings.

**February 15, 1976:** Near South Boston High School in Massachusetts, numerous police officers are injured during a melee over busing.

**April 18, 1976:** Jesse Jackson urges African-Americans to take more responsibility for their lives and not resign themselves to a "welfare mentality." ➤

Black students board a school bus outside South Boston High School on September 12, 1974, the first day of court-ordered busing. The students had been taunted and abused by angry whites in South Boston. Ellen Jackson, who worked at Freedom House—a community center in Roxbury, Boston's black community—remembered when black elementary students returned from their first day of school in September. When they came off the bus that afternoon, she said, their eyes were filled with tears. They were shivering, had glass in their hair, and said they wanted to go home. Jackson and other adults tried to comfort the students. They cleaned them up and picked the glass out of their hair.

Opponents of busing throw rocks at pro-busing marchers in Boston on May 3, 1975. Most of the white working-class residents of the south end of Boston, known as "Southie," did not care that they were being called the "Little Rock of the North" during the city's busing crisis. They didn't care that they were called racists by media around the world. What they *believed* was what mattered to them. Southie's white adults believed that black activists and white "limousine liberals" were destroying the only chance their children had to achieve the American Dream. Their hard-won autonomy as a white ethnic community had been violated, and they were clear as to who was threatening their way of life.

# Busing in Boston: Kids Feel Used

IN MY SOPHOMORE CLASS there were only three students—two white boys... and Janice, a black girl, who had to sneak out to school because her mother didn't want her to go. Earlier in the year Janice had talked about her belief in the ideals of Martin Luther King, that there would be integration one day, and her own dream of the world as one community with everyone owning a piece of it. Now she was bitter. Now, she said, she realized that whites didn't want blacks to have a chance at jobs, and wanted to keep them down. The blacks were ruining their own community. They were frustrated. Their leaders told them to go to school, then to stay home.... They're tired of talking and getting nowhere, so they're stoning and beating up whites when they drive through their neighborhoods—"even my friends." Some kids are depressed and don't want to go to school anymore. They feel they have been used as political pawns, and when... ordered... back to school today, only a few would come, she said. But she was going to get an education and a college degree.

—*Ione Malloy, a white teacher,* Southie Won't Go: A Teacher's Diary of the Desegregation of South Boston High School

Frank Robinson became the first black manager in Major League Baseball when he led, as well as played for, the Cleveland Indians in 1975. The long struggle to desegregate baseball that Jackie Robinson began in 1947 continued decades afterward. On ABC's *Nightline* in 1987, Los Angeles Dodgers Vice President Al Campanis said that blacks lacked "the necessities" for baseball management jobs. Campanis was promptly fired, but the percentage of minorities in management—in baseball and all other major sports—remained low even in the 21st century.

Racial tensions in Pensacola, Florida, reached full boil on February 5, 1976. A riot involving 1,500 people erupted after black students at Escambia High School protested the flying of the Confederate flag. Four white students were injured by gunfire, and a riot squad employed tear gas and attack dogs to disperse the brick- and rock-throwing mob. Here, police take a black teenager into custody after chasing him in the woods. He was questioned about one of the shootings.

# 1970s

## 1976–1977

**June 25, 1976:** The U.S. Supreme Court rules that private schools can not exclude applicants due to race.

**July 12, 1976:** Black Congresswoman Barbara Jordan (D–TX) gives the keynote address at the Democratic National Convention.

**Fall 1976:** Alex Haley's book *Roots,* in which he traces his family history back to an 18th century slave, is published. *See* January 23, 1977.

**October 25, 1976:** Willie Norris, a "Scottsboro Boy" wrongly convicted of rape in 1931, is granted a full pardon by Alabama Governor George Wallace. Norris has been a fugitive since fleeing parole in 1946.

**November 2, 1976:** In the presidential election, former Georgia Governor Jimmy Carter wins more than 90 percent of the black vote and defeats Republican incumbent Gerald Ford.

**December 16, 1976:** Andrew Young is appointed ambassador to the United Nations.

**January 20, 1977:** Patricia Roberts Harris is nominated by President Jimmy Carter to be secretary of the Department of Housing and Urban Development. She thus becomes the first black woman to serve in a president's Cabinet.

**January 23, 1977:** The television miniseries *Roots* premieres on ABC. It will attract 130 million viewers.

**January 26, 1977:** The U.S. Supreme Court nullifies a forced-busing plan in Indianapolis—a major defeat for proponents of busing.

**November 6, 1977:** Benjamin Hooks succeeds Roy Wilkins as executive director of the NAACP.

**November 18, 1977:** Robert Chambliss is found guilty of first-degree murder for the 1963 bombing of the Sixteenth Street Baptist Church in Birmingham, which killed four girls. *See* May 1, 2001. ➤

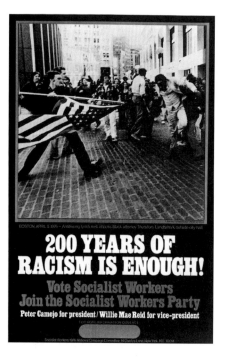

BOSTON, APRIL 5, 1976 – Antibusing fanatic meets attacks Black attorney Theodore Landsmark outside city hall.

## 200 YEARS OF RACISM IS ENOUGH!
### Vote Socialist Workers
### Join the Socialist Workers Party
Peter Camejo for president / Willie Mae Reid for vice-president

Socialist Workers 1976 National Campaign Committee, 14 Charles Lane, New York, N.Y. 10014

Larry Lester's baptism (*pictured*) and confirmation into the Mormon Church in 1976 was considered "null and void" by the church's officials. The man who performed the ceremony, Douglas A. Wallace, was excommunicated. The church's official policy would bar blacks from its priesthood until 1978. Mormon theology followed many other Christian denominations in referring to blacks as the cursed sons and daughters of Ham. According to Mormon beliefs, blacks were given the mark of Cain's murder of his brother. The church's historic prophet, Brigham Young, preached against interracial marriage.

Radical white groups, such as the Socialist Workers Party, targeted their causes to blacks and Hispanics during the 1970s. This 1976 SWP poster features the Pulitzer Prize-winning photograph of Theodore Landsmark, in which a white anti-busing protester in Boston uses an American flag to attack a black lawyer. The image's symbolism shocked white Americans and burned into the consciousness of black Americans. The SWP hoped that its association with Malcolm X and its recent involvement in the movement to acquit Angela Davis would help win black adherents. However, the days of black radicalism occupying the mainstream of black life came to a close in the early 1970s, leaving left-of-center groups stuck in America's political margins.

Patricia Roberts Harris was a symbol of black female achievement. In 1977 President Jimmy Carter appointed her secretary of the Department of Housing and Urban Development. Years earlier, she had become the first African-American woman to serve as a U.S. ambassador (Luxembourg, beginning in 1965) and also the first woman to head Howard University's law school (starting in 1969).

Alex Haley, the coauthor of Malcolm X's classic autobiography, labored for 12 years on his historical novel *Roots: The Saga of an American Family* (1976). Haley pored through documents at the National Archives in Washington, D.C., made speeches about his work-in-progress, and even stripped to his underwear in the cargo hold of a freighter traveling from Africa to the United States. He stayed there for numerous nights in order to "experience" the Middle Passage. *Roots* put the story of slavery in the forefront of the American psyche. The book sold more than 8.5 million copies and won more than 270 awards, including the Pulitzer Prize.

The 1977 ABC television miniseries *Roots,* starring LeVar Burton (*pictured*) as Kunta Kinte, was based on Alex Haley's novel published just one year earlier. The power of seeing the tragedy of slavery portrayed in human, individual terms riveted Americans to their sets. Stores closed. Movie theaters were empty. Even bar patrons forced their owners to air it. During a time when network television programs dominated American cultural life, *Roots* brought slavery and its impact into American public discussion. It taught a generation of blacks about their ancestry and whites about the horrors of slavery. And it did so without alienating the white audience.

As the 1970s progressed, students began to enroll in the black studies classes that had emerged in colleges and universities earlier in the decade. Research facilities such as the Schomburg Center for Research in Black Culture (*pictured*) in New York City, which had for decades tailored itself to the needs of those researching African-American and African history and culture, welcomed a new generation of patrons. Today, the Schomburg Center houses more than five million items related to black history.

Robert "Dynamite Bob" Chambliss (*foreground*) was sentenced to life in prison in 1977 for the murder of four young girls at the Sixteenth Street Baptist Church in Birmingham in 1963. The bombing of the church, which also injured more than 20 people, had galvanized the Civil Rights Movement in the months after the March on Washington. Eyewitnesses had identified Chambliss near the black church that morning. One witness at the trial said she saw explosives at Chambliss's home and heard him talk about the bombing after it occurred. In the 2000s, two more men were convicted for their involvement in the bombing.

# 1970s

## 1978–1979

**June 9, 1978:** The U.S. Census Bureau reveals that black enrollment in colleges and universities rose 275 percent from 1966 to 1976, with women comprising the majority of black college/university students.

**June 28, 1978:** In *University of California Regents v. Bakke,* the U.S. Supreme Court rules that it is reverse discrimination for a school to set aside a set number of places for black students.

**April 4, 1979:** In Birmingham, 21 Ku Klux Klan members are indicted on charges that include firing into homes of interracial couples.

**May 26, 1979:** Violence erupts in Decatur, Alabama, when a hundred Ku Klux Klan members try to block an SCLC march.

**June 9, 1979:** Police in Decatur, Alabama, blockade the streets as hundreds of African-Americans march past more than a hundred armed Ku Klux Klan members.

**June 27, 1979:** In *United Steelworkers v. Weber,* the U.S. Supreme Court rules that employers can give special preference to black workers to counteract racial imbalances.

**September 20, 1979:** A Southern Regional Council study reveals that about 60 percent of judges in 11 southern and border states belong to all-white social organizations.

**October 30, 1979:** Richard Arrington, Jr., becomes the first black mayor of Birmingham.

**November 3, 1979:** At an anti-Klan rally in Greensboro, North Carolina, a group of KKK members drives up and opens fire. Five anti-Klan protesters are killed.

**December 17, 1979:** Arthur McDuffie, a black insurance agent, is clubbed to death in Miami by four white Dade County police officers, who will be charged with manslaughter but acquitted.

As whites in major northern cities flocked to the suburbs in the 1960s and '70s, poor blacks and other people of color were left behind. Without good jobs or access to resources, most could not reasonably expect to achieve the American Dream. Moreover, the tax bases in the abandoned communities became too low to support quality schools. So while white, suburban children thrived with the best public education tax money could buy, inner cities struggled to provide basic instruction—as cartoonist Herbert Block illustrates in this 1977 drawing.

The United Negro College Fund, founded in 1944, was a coalition of the nation's historically black colleges and universities. During the late 1970s, the UNCF benefited from the increasing affluence of African-Americans. Its membership grew from 27 institutions to 39. Singer Lou Rawls (*second from left*) hosted a national telethon for the fund. The *Lou Rawls Parade of Stars* became an annual fixture on television. By the close of the century, the UNCF had provided financial assistance to more than 300,000 black students, including the four brothers pictured. Raymond, Adrian, Roland, and Vernon Dobard (*from left, foreground*), all orphans, graduated from Xavier University.

Allan Bakke attends his first day of medical school at the University of California at Davis on September 25, 1978. Bakke had previously sued UC–Davis over "reverse discrimination," claiming the school had rejected his application in 1973 and 1974 while letting in less-qualified black students. In 1978 the U.S. Supreme Court ruled in his favor. In a five-to-four decision, the high court ruled that the medical school's racial quota system discriminated against Bakke because of his race. The decision set the stage for decades of legal battles over affirmative action and the use of racial quotas.

Whites in Birmingham display the Stars and Bars in front of Jerry's Convenience Shop in July 1979. Racial tensions in Birmingham had swelled in June after Bonita Carter, an African-American woman, was fatally shot by a white policeman. The city's mayor, David Vann, refused to fire the officers involved in Carter's death, outraging black residents. On July 6 a group of whites, including Ku Klux Klan members, were arrested for fomenting racial violence. On July 20 about 2,000 African-Americans marched in protest of Vann's inaction. Just a few months later, the city elected its first black mayor, Richard Arrington, Jr.

In 1979 Roland Wayne Wood (*pictured*) was arrested for his connection to a group of Ku Klux Klan/American Nazi members who allegedly killed five leftist workers. The activists, many of whom were Communists, had organized an anti-Klan rally at a predominately black housing project in Greensboro, North Carolina. Five of the anti-Klan protesters were shot to death. The rally was one of many actions taken against the Klan's resurgence in the South in the late 1970s. Two all-white juries acquitted the Klan members, but a wrongful death suit, which ended in 1985, held police, an informant, and several of the alleged gunmen liable.

# THE 1980s

> "Any time there is a self-loving, self-respecting, and self-determining black man or woman, he or she is one of the most dangerous folks in America. Because it means you are free enough to speak your mind, you're free enough to speak the truth."
>
> —CORNEL WEST, PHILOSOPHER AND ACTIVIST

HOW IS IT POSSIBLE, a quarter century after the Supreme Court decided *Brown v. Board of Education,* and almost a generation after the passage of historic civil rights legislation, that nearly half of all minority students still attended "racially isolated" schools? How had a nation moved so precipitously from the liberalism of the "New Frontier" and the "Great Society" to the "Make My Day" pugnacity of the Ronald Reagan Era?

The 1980s were, for good or ill, the "Age of Reagan," and the Reagan presidency serves as an appropriate prism through which to view the transformed struggle for black empowerment. Much has been made of two important sources of Reagan's political appeal. One group was the "Reagan Democrats," white, blue-collar workers and union members who crossed party lines to vote for Reagan in 1980 and 1984. They felt that the bootstrapping Reagan had a better chance of revitalizing an economy that had sagged under President Jimmy Carter. Other Reagan fans were "angry white males." They supported Reagan's policies because they thought Democrats were "soft" on national defense and felt a generalized discomfort with the threats posed by feminists, civil libertarians, and various rights groups.

A different but compatible analysis focuses on a changed electoral map. More and more, white urbanites were fleeing the central cities for the shelter of virtually all-white suburbs. Some were escaping declining public school systems. Others followed the migration of jobs and the disappearance of heavy industrial employment in the inner cities. Still others were fleeing racially changing neighborhoods. Major American cities, predictable sources of Democratic votes, lost population and clout. Many Americans moved to the Sunbelt, where the air was fresher, the employment more white-collar, and minorities rare. Most significantly, the South, for almost a century the most loyal Democratic region of the country, had moved firmly and perhaps irretrievably into the Republican camp. In 1965, after the passage of the

During the Reagan and Bush administrations, many black urbanites were displaced from their homes by political maneuvering designed to placate corporate interests and conservative white voters. In this image from the early 1980s, a weary Detroit resident contemplates the razing of her neighborhood.

# 1980s

The fervor and optimism of the Movement as it existed in the 1960s seemed to have turned to ashes—often literally—by the 1980s. This bleak "playtime" tableau was snapped in the Poletown area of Detroit around 1982.

During the 1980 presidential campaign, GOP candidate Ronald Reagan paid a courtesy call to Jesse Jackson at Operation PUSH headquarters in Chicago. For Reagan, the meeting was a useful "photo op," a painless acknowledgment of the existence of America's black voters.

historic Voting Rights Act, President Lyndon Johnson predicted that the Democratic Party's support for civil rights would cost them the South for a generation. He was right.

After a landslide victory in the 1980 election, Reagan and his administration focused much of their attention on what they characterized as "reverse discrimination," instances where the enforcement of civil rights laws negatively affected whites. In 1983 the administration announced it would no longer let the IRS deny tax-exempt status to private schools that discriminated on the basis of race. A year later Reagan actively opposed new civil rights legislation.

At first, Reagan even seemed reluctant to sign an extension of the 1965 Voting Rights Act. And, if his private correspondence is any indication, he was not entirely enthusiastic about a national holiday commemorating the life and accomplishments of Dr. Martin Luther King. One of the politicians leading the charge for an extension of voting rights legislation, and one of Reagan's harshest critics, was Harold Washington, a U.S. congressman from Chicago.

Washington was a born legislator who loved public speaking and who represented a safe Democratic district. African-Americans in Chicago constituted nearly 40 percent of the city's population and chafed under the policies of the city's white mayor, Jane Byrne. With the help of a massive voter registration campaign and a financial commitment from leaders in the African-American business community, Washington was elected mayor in 1983. His victory not only changed racial politics in Chicago, but it contributed to the presidential candidacy, a year later, of Reverend Jesse Jackson (black and liberal disenchantment with American fiscal and foreign policies was another factor). Jackson's 1984 and 1988 runs for the Democratic nomination reflect the transition from protest to politics in the 1980s.

In 1984 Jackson carried Louisiana and the District of Columbia. Four years later he won 1,218 out of 2,082 delegate votes needed to win the Democratic nomination. Jackson had become a major force within the ranks of the Democratic Party, emblematic of continued black political successes that would culminate with the elections of David Dinkins as New York City mayor and L. Douglas Wilder as governor of Virginia, both in 1989. Wilder became the first African-American governor since Reconstruction.

David Dinkins was elected mayor of New York in 1989. He inherited a $500 million deficit and a city in which one resident in four was classified as "poor."

Washington, Jackson, and to a lesser extent Dinkins and Wilder all were able to mount sustained candidacies because they were supported by a larger, wealthier, and more self-confident black middle class. A significant gap still remained between the income of blacks and whites. But the African-American middle class, aided in part by affirmative action policies of the 1960s and 1970s, provided the resources, manpower, and skills necessary for the trailblazing political candidacies of the era.

Not until the 1980s, moreover, did America begin to see substantial suburbanization of the black middle-class. Although open-housing legislation had been passed in 1968, years passed before blacks felt comfortable enough to flee declining inner-city neighborhoods. Two black Americas were beginning to emerge. One was white-collar and college educated, able to take advantage of the new opportunities afforded by civil rights legislation. The other group was increasingly marginalized, serially unemployed, and prey to the violence, addiction, and social anomie that increasingly characterized America's inner cities.

In the South, African-Americans made great strides against the once potent forces of "white supremacy." By decade's end, the United Klans of America was bankrupt and Forsyth County, Georgia, a Klan haven that once expelled its black population, squirmed uneasily under a national spotlight. Congress passed a Civil Rights Restoration Act over President Reagan's veto in 1988, and African-American Colin Powell was confirmed as chairman of the Joint Chiefs of Staff in 1989. Beneath the surface, however, flowed swelling tides of backward-looking reaction.

In *City of Richmond v. J. A. Croson Co.,* in 1989, the U.S. Supreme Court struck down a set-aside program that gave a set number of city contracts to women- and minority-owned companies—a major blow to the civil rights cause. Beleaguered after eight years of Reagan, black leaders were anxious to work with President George Bush, who took office three days before the *Croson* decision.

Unemployed African-Americans shout "We want jobs!" at a Madison Avenue construction site in New York City in July 1981. In the 1980s and beyond, many labor unions resisted integration.

# 1980s

## 1980–1981

**January 16, 1980:** The U.S. Civil Rights Commission reports that nearly half of all minority-group children attend "racially isolated" schools.

**January 25, 1980:** Black Entertainment Television (BET) airs its first broadcast.

**April 9, 1980:** In Wrightsville, Georgia, 75 black demonstrators are attacked by a hundred whites outside the county sheriff's office.

**May 17–18, 1980:** Riots rage in Miami, resulting in 18 deaths and more than 800 arrests. The violence began after five police officers were acquitted of charges of beating a black man to death.

**May 29, 1980:** A white racist shoots and seriously wounds African-American Vernon Jordan, president of the National Urban League.

**November 4, 1980:** Conservative Republican Ronald Reagan defeats incumbent Jimmy Carter in the presidential election.

**February 19, 1981:** President Reagan releases his proposed budget, which calls for a $16 billion reduction in spending on social programs.

**May 23, 1981:** U.S. Attorney General William French Smith announces that the Justice Department will no longer pursue mandatory busing or advocate affirmative action plans. The department will consider amendments that would make "reverse discrimination" illegal.

**September 19, 1981:** In a Solidarity Day march in Washington, D.C., 300,000 demonstrators from civil rights and labor organizations protest the domestic policies of the Reagan administration.

**October 29, 1981:** Andrew Young is elected mayor of Atlanta. ➤

The inner-city tensions that dominated the summers of the late 1960s flared again in 1980 in Miami. Arthur McDuffie, a black insurance executive, was beaten to death with flashlights by city police officers after a chase. The police officers, who had tried to cover up the beating death, were acquitted by an all-white, all-male jury in May (Janet Reno was the prosecuting attorney). Three days of rioting resulted in multiple deaths, more than 800 arrests, and $80 million in damage.

African-Americans, including this Detroit auto worker, were hit hard by the 1980 recession. The unemployment rate among American blacks was 14 percent that year and rose even higher over the next several years. Because African-Americans remained unemployed longer than whites, black working-class families often were stuck at the bottom of the socioeconomic ladder.

The death of Michael Donald in 1981 at the hands of white racists in Mobile, Alabama, showed that the Old South would not die a quick death. Henry Hayes, the son of a Ku Klux Klan leader, and his friend, James Knowles, killed the 19-year-old Donald to avenge the hung jury of another black man who had been charged with a white policeman's murder. Police had attempted to link Donald with drug-dealing in order to cover up the incident. Jesse Jackson protested, and the FBI investigated. The subsequent civil lawsuit by Beulah Mae Donald, the victim's mother, bankrupted the Mobile Klan. History was made when Hayes was executed for the crime in 1997—the first time since 1913 that a white man received the death penalty for victimizing a black man.

The administration of President Ronald Reagan slammed the door on 1970s liberal optimism. The Republican administration decreased federal support for affirmative action, cut social programs that provided more than a decade's worth of job training for the working poor, and took a stance against union organizing. The NAACP, the Congressional Black Caucus, labor officials, and other liberals would march and organize throughout the decade. This Solidarity Day contingent, which marched through Washington, D.C., on September 19, 1981, was 300,000 strong. Throughout the decade, protesters aimed to preserve civil rights gains, fight for economic sanctions against South Africa, and preserve the coalition between blacks, labor, and the women's movement.

# 1980s

## 1982–1983

**January 8, 1982:** The Reagan Administration announces it will no longer allow the Internal Revenue Service to deny tax-exempt status to private schools that discriminate against minorities. The NAACP will counteract by filing a lawsuit in the U.S. Supreme Court a week later.

**June 29, 1982:** Congress approves the extension of the Voting Rights Act of 1965 for 25 years.

**July 1, 1982:** The U.S. Supreme Court rules to allow federal judges to order major restructuring of racially discriminatory electoral systems, even if evidence of intentional bias is not found.

**July 19, 1982:** The U.S. Census Bureau reports that the poverty rate for African-Americans has reached 36 percent.

**October 1982:** The unemployment rate in October for African-Americans is 19.9 percent, compared to 8.6 percent for whites.

**November 1982:** The U.S. government awards $1.85 million to the survivors of Black Panthers Fred Hampton and Mark Clark. The two were killed in an aggressive raid by Chicago police in 1969.

**April 12, 1983:** Harold Washington becomes the first black mayor of Chicago.

**May 24, 1983:** In *Bob Jones University v. the United States,* the U.S. Supreme Court upholds the IRS rule denying tax exemption to private schools that participate in racial discrimination.

**August 27, 1983:** On the 20th anniversary of the March on Washington, more than 250,000 demonstrators march in the nation's capital for jobs, peace, and freedom.

**November 2, 1983:** President Reagan signs a bill proclaiming Martin Luther King, Jr., Day a national holiday. *See* January 20, 1986. ➤

Civil Rights Movement veterans such as Marian Wright Edelman found much to fight for during the Reagan years. Edelman's Children's Defense Fund battled against administration cuts affecting children and working families. Through an enormous advertising campaign, the CDF also made the public aware of teen pregnancy, which had reached crisis levels within black communities. Edelman's and the CDF's campaigning on Capitol Hill would lead to an increase in Medicaid funding for children as well as increased funding for Head Start.

Harold Washington's election to the mayor's office in Chicago in 1983 represented the hope that a progressive, interracial coalition was possible in the Reagan era. Washington was a veteran politician who had worked his way up the political ladder of the Democratic Party. He had been a state representative and congressional representative from Illinois before running for mayor. As mayor, he stopped the city's famous patronage system, in which jobs were doled out for party loyalty. Like other black mayors of his era, he desegregated powerful city offices. Washington was reelected in 1987 but his death by heart attack that year was a major setback for black political power.

# Honoring Martin Luther King, Jr.

I T TOOK AMERICA 207 years to create a holiday honoring a person of African descent—and even that was a bitter struggle. From 1968 to 1983, the Congressional Black Caucus introduced legislation to create a holiday honoring Martin Luther King, Jr., only to see it defeated in every congressional session.

Five days before Ronald Reagan's first presidential election in 1980, more than 100,000 people staged a march on Washington calling for the creation of a day honoring Dr. King. Finally, on November 2, 1983, President Reagan signed a bill creating a federal holiday, to fall on the third Monday of every January, on behalf of the civil rights martyr.

During his first term, Reagan had seemed disinterested if not hostile to the idea of a King holiday. And during the holiday celebration in January 1986, many felt that the President insulted the fallen leader when he said that his personal disdain for quotas was in line with King's hope of a color-blind society.

In the 1980s, some states and cities refused to honor the holiday, with some whites hitting the streets in

Coretta Scott King (*left*), President Reagan (*signing bill*)

protest. When the state of Arizona refused to honor the holiday as late as 1990, the National Football League reneged on its plan to hold the Super Bowl in Phoenix in January 1993. Arizona voters approved the holiday in 1992 after a threatened tourist boycott.

For years, Philadelphia police butted heads with the MOVE Organization, a black militant back-to-nature group. In 1981 MOVE illegally created a compound on a city block on Osage Avenue in one of the city's black communities. Neighbors, tired of being victims of MOVE's intimidation tactics and unorthodox living habits, complained loudly. Philadelphia's police commissioner decided to end the conflict decisively on May 13, 1985. After firing thousands of bullets at the compound, city authorities—under the authority of black Philly Mayor W. Wilson Goode—dropped a bomb on MOVE. Smoke and flames rose into the night sky. Two blocks were engulfed, with more than 60 homes damaged or destroyed. Eleven MOVE members, including five children, perished in the fire.

# 1980s

**February 1, 1984:** A circuit court judge in Mobile County, Alabama, sentences a Ku Klux Klan member to death—overruling the jury's recommendation for life imprisonment—for the brutal murder of African-American Michael Donald in 1981.

**February 28, 1984:** In *Grove City College v. Bell,* the U.S. Supreme Court rules that federal laws prohibiting discrimination by schools and colleges extend only to the affected programs, not to the entire institutions.

**March 7, 1984:** The U.S. Census Bureau announces that the black voter turnout in the South has increased while white turnout in the region has decreased.

**April 1984:** KKK Imperial Wizard Bill Wilkinson endorses President Reagan for reelection, saying his platform is "pure Klan." Reagan will denounce Wilkinson's action.

**May 2 and 7, 1984:** In his run for president, Jesse Jackson wins the Democratic primaries in the District of Columbia and Louisiana.

**June 13, 1984:** The U.S. Supreme Court rules that when cutbacks become necessary, white workers with seniority may not be laid off to preserve the jobs of recently hired blacks or women.

**November 6, 1984:** President Ronald Reagan wins reelection.

**January 7, 1985:** The U.S. Supreme Court upholds the use of affirmative action plans to increase the number of minorities employed by state agencies.

**May 13, 1985:** In Philadelphia, police drop a bomb on the home of John Africa and members of MOVE, a black countercultural organization. The bomb kills 11 MOVE members, including Africa and five children, while burning more than 60 nearby homes. ➤

The 1985 bombing of the MOVE Organization headquarters brought up disturbing questions in Philadelphia and across the nation. A predominately white police department and a black mayor had decided to bomb a working-class, black Philadelphia neighborhood. This never would have been considered, argued the group's sympathizers and mourners, if MOVE's members were white or if Osage Avenue was a street on which white people lived. The idea was even articulated in the city commission's final report on the bombing. Criminal charges were never filed against any of the officials involved. To many, the assault on MOVE became a symbol of how a police force would destroy black militancy regardless of the color of the mayor.

Philadelphia Mayor W. Wilson Goode, the son of southern sharecroppers, won the mayor's chair in 1983. He defeated Frank Rizzo, the racially polarizing former Philadelphia police chief who had made his name by cracking down on the city's Black Power movement. Goode promised to racially unify the city and fight for the city's economic development. He did so, winning reelection in 1987. However, the lingering shadow of the 1985 MOVE bombing forever obscured Goode's accomplishments.

# Jackson Runs for President

DURING 1984 THE CRY "Run, Jesse, Run" was heard throughout the United States. A dozen years earlier, New York Congresswoman Shirley Chisholm had become the first black presidential candidate, but Jesse Jackson's campaigns during the 1980s broke new ground in African-American political history. Demonstrating his ability to attract the votes of whites as well as the majority of black voters, Jackson forced Democratic Party leaders to take his campaign seriously.

Jackson's campaign marked the culmination of his rise from humble beginnings to national prominence. Born in 1941 to an unwed mother in Greenville, South Carolina, Jackson spent much of his life as an ambitious outsider. Attending North Carolina A&T College during the heyday of civil rights protests, he emerged as a leader. After graduation, he decided to study at a Chicago seminary to become a minister. In spring 1965 he left his classes to participate in the Selma voting rights drive. His oratorical abilities soon attracted the attention of Martin Luther King, who encouraged him to work for the SCLC.

Jackson represented a "Rainbow Coalition."

As a protégé of King, Jackson directed SCLC's Operation Breadbasket effort in Chicago and was at the Lorraine Motel in Memphis at the time of King's assassination in 1968. Highly ambitious, Jackson soon left the SCLC to form his own group, Operation PUSH (People United to Serve Humanity). His "Nation Time" rhetoric at the 1972 National Black Political Convention in Gary, Indiana, evolved into an enduring, if uneasy, relationship with the Democratic Party.

Jackson's 1984 campaign strategy was based on the belief that President Ronald Reagan's victory in 1980 had resulted from the Democratic Party's failure to mobilize its core strength in black communities. The number of black registered voters had almost doubled since 1965, but seven million potential black voters remained unregistered. Jackson was convinced that those voters, and millions of dissatisfied voters of other races, could be mobilized into a powerful "Rainbow Coalition" that could at least get the attention of Democratic Party leaders and perhaps even win the party's nomination. Jackson's "I am somebody" refrain had unexpected appeal among disadvantaged and discontented people of all races. In January 1984 his campaign received an unexpected boost when he used contacts with Syrian leaders to secure the release of a black Navy pilot, Robert O. Goodman, Jr., whose plane had been shot down over Syrian positions in eastern Lebanon.

A month later, however, Jackson's campaign experienced a major setback when a black reporter quoted him using the term "Hymietown" in reference to New York. Although Jackson apologized, his campaign lost momentum as he struggled to defend himself. Jackson received about three and a half million votes and arrived at the Democratic National Convention with 300 delegates committed to him. His speech at the convention stirred the emotions of delegates, but he lost the nomination to former Vice President Walter Mondale, who in turn lost to Reagan in the general election.

Jackson continued to mobilize Rainbow Coalition voters in a second, even more successful run for the Democratic nomination in 1988. He won several primaries and for a while was considered the front-runner before eventually losing the nomination to Michael Dukakis. Several of the issues Jackson brought to the forefront remained crucial issues during the 1990s, including nationwide healthcare and taxing the rich.

Despite his defeat in 1988, Jackson inspired millions of minorities with his speech at that year's Democratic National Convention: "I was born in the slum, but the slum was not born in me. And it wasn't born in you, but you can make it. Wherever you are tonight, you can make it.... It gets dark sometimes, but the morning comes. Don't you surrender."

# 1980s

**January 20, 1986:** Martin Luther King, Jr., Day is officially observed nationally for the first time.

**May 19, 1986:** In *Wygant v. Jackson Board of Education,* the U.S. Supreme Court supports teacher seniority over affirmative action.

**July 30, 1986:** The U.S. General Accounting Office agrees to pay $3.5 million to 300 employees who were denied promotions because of racial discrimination.

**December 20, 1986:** Several African-Americans are attacked by a white mob in Queens, New York, resulting in the death of Michael Griffith, 23. The incident exacerbates race relations in the city.

**1987:** The United Klans of America goes bankrupt after a court orders the group to pay $7 million to the family of Michael Donald, who was lynched by UKA members in 1981.

**January 24, 1987:** Seven days after a smaller march was disrupted by the KKK, 20,000 civil rights demonstrators march in Forsyth County, Georgia. They're protected by National Guardsmen. *See* October 25, 1988.

**March 25, 1987:** The U.S. Supreme Court rules that private employers can give special consideration to minorities and women in hiring and promotion decisions if their intention is to correct "a conspicuous imbalance in traditionally segregated job categories."

**March 22, 1988:** Congress passes the Civil Rights Restoration Act over President Reagan's veto. The Act expands the reach of nondiscrimination laws to include entire institutions that receive federal funds rather than just the department that received the money.

**July 20, 1988:** Presidential candidate Jesse Jackson garners 1,218.5 of the 2,082 delegate votes needed to win the Democratic nomination. ➤

As late as the 1980s, some white neighborhoods in the urban North were as racially volatile as any in the South. On December 21, 1986, three young African-American men were attacked by whites in the Howard Beach section of Queens, New York. One of the black men, Michael Griffith, was struck and killed by a car as he attempted to flee. Murder charges against the white attackers were initially dismissed. Here, C. Vernon Mason, a leader in the crusade to obtain justice in the Griffith case, addresses the media after that ruling. Eventually, prosecutors obtained homicide convictions against three members of the white mob.

Although blacks in urban areas experienced erratic economic growth during the 1970s, for southern rural blacks, poverty remained an unchanging reality. This photo was snapped in Tunica, Mississippi (known as "Sugarditch"), in 1988. The town was by no means unique, and the message was clear: African-Americans living in the rural South were a forgotten people, and were falling ever farther behind their brothers and sisters. By the mid-1980s, 34 percent of southern blacks lived below the poverty line.

# Affirmative Action

THE CIVIL RIGHTS ACT OF 1964 effectively ended *de jure* (legalized) segregation. Beyond that, civil rights leaders pushed for measures that would close the educational and economic gaps between the black and white communities. To that end, affirmative action programs were initiated to bolster minority representation in schools, job hiring and promotion, and contracts awarded to companies doing business with government agencies.

Rarely has a public policy been so misunderstood, distorted, and vilified as the concept of affirmative action. The stereotypical view contends that it allows unqualified minorities to secure jobs, university admissions, and promotions over "more qualified" whites. In the 1980s, terms such as "racial quotas" and "set-asides" became buzz words for what critics labeled "reverse discrimination." In response, a group of white New Yorkers founded SPONGE—Society for the Prevention of Niggers Getting Everything.

Yet the facts are in stark contrast to public perception: The group most aided by affirmative action has been white women, not blacks. Many universities use quotas/goals in admission polices to ensure balance in gender, a fair ratio of students from all regions of the home state, and a certain number of out-of-state and foreign students.

Politically, affirmative action has been a black/white issue. In 1981 the Reagan Administration announced it would not pursue affirmative action programs. In fact, it was concerned about reverse discrimination. Several affirmative action cases went to the U.S. Supreme Court, which usually ruled against the practice. On August 26, 1989, 30,000 civil rights advocates marched in Washington, D.C., protesting the Supreme Court's decisions. And in 2003, President George W. Bush created a storm of controversy when he supported a legal challenge to University of Michigan's affirmative action program.

Mourners pay their respects to African-American Yusuf Hawkins, 16, who was shot to death on August 23, 1989, in Bensonhurst, a predominantly Italian section of Brooklyn, New York. Hawkins and three friends had been approached by whites after they ventured into the neighborhood to inspect a used car. The murder inspired a "Day of Outrage," as some 8,000 protesting blacks marched through Bensonhurst, led by local activist Al Sharpton. Some white onlookers held up watermelons in derision. New Yorkers' reactions to the Hawkins murder contributed to the election of the city's first black mayor, David Dinkins, later that year.

Benjamin Hooks was the public face of the NAACP during the Reagan Administration. A former head of the Federal Communications Commission under President Richard Nixon, Hooks rose to prominence in the 1950s and 1960s as a civil rights leader and lawyer in his hometown of Memphis. A Republican, he spoke at his party's 1980 national convention. As the decade progressed, Hooks criticized the administration's policies, mobilized the NAACP to fight for economic sanctions against South Africa, and pushed for economic opportunities. He remained NAACP executive director until 1993.

## 1988–1989

**October 25, 1988:** A federal court orders two KKK organizations and 11 Klan members to pay nearly $1 million to those black citizens who were attacked in Forsyth County, Georgia, on January 17, 1987.

**1989:** The American Council of Education reports that while national enrollment in colleges and universities grew by a million from 1976 to 1986, black male enrollment dropped by 34,000.

**January 23, 1989:** In *City of Richmond v. J. A. Croson Co.,* the U.S. Supreme Court states that a city cannot create a "set-aside program" to give a certain number of public contracts to minority contractors.

**June 5, 1989:** In *Wards Cove Packing Company v. Antonio,* the U.S. Supreme Court rules that, in instances of alleged discrimination, proof falls on the employees.

**August 21, 1989:** A package explodes in an NAACP office in Atlanta, injuring 15 people. *See* December 16–19, 1989.

**August 23, 1989:** African-American Yusuf Hawkins, 16, is killed by a mob of whites in the predominantly white Bensonhurst section of Brooklyn. Reverend Al Sharpton and others will lead angry protest marches.

**October 1, 1989:** African-American Colin Powell becomes chairman of the Joint Chiefs of Staff.

**November 7, 1989:** L. Douglas Wilder is elected governor of Virginia, becoming the first elected black governor in U.S. history.

**November 7, 1989:** David Dinkins, an African-American, is elected mayor of New York.

**December 16–19, 1989:** Mail bombs kill Robert Vance, a federal judge in Birmingham, and Robert E. Robinson, a black civil rights lawyer in Savannah, Georgia.

"Sometimes I wonder if they really want what they say they want.... Because some of those leaders are doing very well leading organizations based on keeping alive the feeling that they're victims of prejudice."

—PRESIDENT RONALD REAGAN ON CIVIL RIGHTS LEADERS, *60 MINUTES*, JANUARY 14, 1989

THE FACE ON THE BARROOM FLOOR.

Hugh Antoine D'Arcy's famed 1887 poem, "The Face on the Barroom Floor," is in the form of a dramatic monologue given by a former artist, now a hopeless drunk, who falls dead after sketching on a tavern floor the face of his beloved, who betrayed him. This 1984 *Los Angeles Times* cartoon by Paul Conrad is about betrayal of another sort: Despite President Ronald Reagan's high-sounding rhetoric about a just and generous America, his conservative administration encouraged a backward-looking judicial system that took pains to slow or reverse the progress of civil rights for African-Americans. Opportunities for higher education, funding of social welfare programs, minority employment and economic growth, services for public school children of color—all of these were hobbled during the Reagan years.

# Jesse Prepares to Take a Bullet

ONE EXPERIENCE I'll never forget from '88, when [Jesse Jackson] was going to give a speech...in the Capitol building where a bunch of Democratic senators were waiting for him.... He takes off his coat while he's talking to them about the campaign, and starts strapping on a bulletproof vest...to go out and give a speech from the steps of the Capitol of my country. And Fritz Hollings and Alan Cranston too—both of these guys had run for president in 1984, and never incited any enthusiasm or rancor or any other feeling to ever have to do what this guy who'd beaten them both was now having to do in front of them—and I could see on their faces the same feeling I had: What the hell are we watching? This man putting on a bulletproof vest to speak at the Capitol of the United States? But Jesse never said a word about what he was doing, just went on talking about his hopes for the country and the campaign while he was strapping the thing on absolutely matter of course.

—*Journalist Ken Bode*

Spike Lee emerged during the 1980s as a bold, creative filmmaker unafraid to present an uncompromising black aesthetic and the controversy it would generate. Unlike the post-blaxploitation black filmmakers of late 1970s, who made and distributed their works independently, Lee chose to make movies for commercial audiences. His first three films—*She's Gotta Have It, School Daze,* and *Do the Right Thing*—won over the growing black middle class, especially black college students. *Do the Right Thing,* which premiered in 1989, depicts racial and class divisions among blacks and between blacks and whites in Brooklyn. In almost journalistic fashion, Lee shows how a race riot can easily occur because of America's complex racial history and cultural misunderstandings. Calling himself "a black nationalist with a camera," Lee made political statements in his films that enraged some whites. He also angered some African-Americans by putting black community contradictions on the screen.

The NAACP, the United Auto Workers, and other civil rights and labor groups demonstrate in Washington, D.C., on August 26, 1989, against the Republicans' racial policies. The Ronald Reagan years had been lean ones for the Civil Rights Movement. The Republican administration cut social services for the poor while lowering taxes for businesses; opposed affirmative action and busing; slashed the number of lawyers in the Department of Justice's Civil Rights Division; emasculated the Equal Employment Opportunity Commission; and even attempted to dissolve the United States Commission on Civil Rights. African-Americans responded by supporting the Democratic Party and its candidates in greater numbers than ever before.

In December 1989 it appeared that radical white racists had unveiled a new weapon of terror. Mail bombings, suspected by the FBI to be the work of white supremacists, began appearing to deadly effect. Here, in downtown Atlanta in December 1989, a bomb squad specialist handles a package thought to be a pipe bomb outside the 11th U.S. Circuit Court of Appeals, which was known to be pro-civil rights. Earlier that month, package bombs had killed Robert S. Vance, a U.S. Appeals Court judge in Birmingham, and Robert E. Robinson, a black civil rights attorney in Savannah, Georgia. Another bomb, detected before being opened, was mailed to the NAACP's Jacksonville, Florida, headquarters.

# 1990 TO TODAY

"It is ironic that virtually every Martin Luther King Jr. Boulevard in America is a street of abandoned buildings, abandoned businesses, abandoned people, abandoned dreams. Those who honor King's name need to think about fulfilling the promise of his dream to those who have been forsaken in our inner cities."

—JAMES P. DANKY, STATE HISTORICAL SOCIETY OF WISCONSIN/UNIVERSITY OF WISCONSIN–MADISON

A Los Angeles resident pleads for peace in the aftermath of the 1992 L.A. riot. Racial tensions between blacks, whites, and Korean-Americans in Los Angeles sparked one of the worst riots in American history.

IN FEBRUARY 1990 the Sentencing Project reported that one-quarter of black males in their 20s were in jail, on parole, or under some form of legal supervision. The lives of African-Americans in inner cities had become, to borrow the words of 17th century philosopher Thomas Hobbes, "solitary, poor, nasty, brutish, and short."

Conservatives viewed inner-city blacks as uncontrollable criminals, while African-Americans and white liberals blamed the hardball politics of Presidents Ronald Reagan and George Bush for the plight of poor blacks. In Los Angeles in April 1992, the battle lines were drawn in blood. Following the acquital of four L.A. police officers who had beaten black motorist Rodney King, a race riot raged for three days, resulting in more than 50 deaths and 17,000 arrests.

President Bush, fresh from his 1991 triumph in the Gulf War and with approval numbers sky-high, seemed poised to ride a patriotic wave to victory in the 1992 presidential election. However, choppy waters lay ahead. Bush's nomination of conservative black jurist Clarence Thomas to the U.S. Supreme Court was met with bitter resentment by many white liberals as well as by blacks who favored activism rather than Thomas's history of conciliation. Many blacks perceived Thomas as worse than simply self-serving. He was viewed as a traitor to the legacy of his predecessor, Thurgood Marshall.

Bush's successful challenger in the 1992 election was Arkansas Governor Bill Clinton, a former chairman of the centrist Democratic Leadership Conference. The man whom Toni Morrison would later dub the "first black President" began his presidency with a crime bill that included mandatory sentencing provisions and tougher penalties for drug possession. He ended his first term as president with what many in the Civil Rights Movement viewed as draconian welfare reform legislation.

Yet Clinton also appointed a record number of African-American Cabinet officers and department heads, and he solicited the support of

civil rights leaders who had been pointedly ignored during the Reagan-Bush years, their concerns dismissed as "quota" issues. But neither Clinton's center-left political agenda nor his coterie of black "insiders" properly explains African-Americans' sustained and genuine affection for him. How did Bill Clinton become "black"? More importantly, what did "being black" mean in a post-civil rights age?

Initially, Clinton reshaped the period with his very basic and striking political and personal contrasts to his recent predecessors. Affable, casual, and of humble beginnings, he also was honestly concerned about racial injustice and was anxious to redress wrongs. Then, too, the Clinton economy was the best in a quarter century. The black

After L.A. motorist Rodney King was pulled over for speeding in March 1991, he was savagely beaten by four white police officers. The assault, which was captured on amateur video, shocked the nation.

middle-class grew. The gap between black and white incomes for males shrunk, and for females it almost disappeared. Black unemployment was the lowest it had been in half a century. Even former welfare recipients could find jobs.

Moreover, Clinton's mainstream social policies seemed to work. When he made a special point to criticize New York rapper-activist Sistah Souljah in 1992 for rhetorically asking why not have a week and kill white people, some civil rights activists felt momentarily betrayed. But Clinton's black supporters stuck with him, arguing that a tactical shift to the right was necessary in a more conservative political atmosphere. And middle-age African-Americans may themselves have grown more conservative, as many were unhappy with the anger and posturing that passed for "authenticity" in the black pop music of the '90s.

Of particular concern to black voters was that the U.S. Supreme Court, once their most reliable ally, seemed determined to roll back the victories of the 1960s. Further, University of California Regent Ward Connerly, a black man, led that state's crusade to ban state affirmative action programs. In this climate, Clinton offered more than

Nation of Islam leader Louis Farrakhan (*center*) had seemed a relatively marginal political figure until October 1995, when his notion of an organized Million Man March on Washington, D.C., came to fruition. Most of the gathering's participants were visibly moved and inspired.

hope to African-Americans. He seemed to be one of the few people in their corner who actually knew how to win.

By the early 1990s, the civil rights groups of the 1960s had taken wildly different paths. SNCC had disbanded. CORE had been side-tracked by the Libertarian and pro-gun activities of its longtime head, Roy Innis. And the SCLC had struggled for years to overcome inadequate funding.

The National Urban League and the NAACP carried on, but in mid-decade the NAACP was awash in controversy. NAACP Executive Director Benjamin Chavis tried to establish close ties between his organization and the separatist Nation of Islam, causing concern among members of the historically integrationist NAACP. Chavis resigned his post in 1994 after misappropriating funds during a time when the NAACP already was facing financial hardship. Myrlie Evers–Williams, widow of slain civil rights hero Medgar Evers, emerged as the rallying point for a coalition of groups determined to rescue the NAACP from factionalism and financial ruin. With the naming of a new executive secretary, Kweisi Mfume, and the subsequent involvement of civil rights icon Julian Bond, the NAACP emerged, at century's end, as the most respected African-American institution outside of the black church.

Black politicians made gains during the Clinton years, and worked the system effectively. Here, four U.S. representatives gather for the September 2001 opening of the annual legislative conference of the Congressional Black Caucus. They are, from left, William Jefferson (*D–LA*); Eddie Bernice Johnson (*D–TX*); Bennie Thompson (*D–MS*); and Sheila Jackson Lee (*D–TX*).

Still, the organization was not embraced by all. Some suggested that a generational shift in black leadership was needed, and many proclaimed Reverend Al Sharpton as Jesse Jackson's heir apparent in the civil rights crusade. Others claimed that the success of the 1995 Million Man March legitimized the leadership of controversial Nation of Islam Minister Louis Farrakhan.

In the end, it is simple decency and commitment that may have the last word. As the new millennium dawned, it was Rosa Parks who served as a symbol of a people's journey. Her life has four acts. First and foremost, the unassuming woman of transcendent grace became a symbol of struggle and resolve, shattering the color line and changing a nation. There is also the Detroit Rosa Parks, a congressman's secretary, who was the victim of a beating by a young, black substance abuser who neither knew nor cared that he was battering a secular saint. Then there is the Rosa Parks invoked by the rap group Outkast, whose vulgar lyrics reveal profound generational alienation.

Finally, at the dawning of the 21st century there is the revered Rosa Parks, who accepted the Presidential Medal of Freedom from President Clinton, not on behalf of her people, not as a symbol of a movement, but on behalf of a grateful nation.

# 1990 TO TODAY

## 1990–1991

**January 1990:** Under pressure, R. J. Reynolds Tobacco, Co., cancels its plans to market Uptown, a brand of cigarettes designed for blacks, who—critics pointed out—suffer from especially high rates of lung cancer, heart disease, and stroke.

**February 1990:** The U.S. General Accounting office reports that the death penalty is more likely to be given when a white person is killed than when a black person is killed.

**February 11, 1990:** In South Africa, anti-apartheid leader Nelson Mandela is released from prison after nearly 28 years of imprisonment.

**November 7, 1990:** The National Football League abandons its plan to hold the 1993 Super Bowl in Phoenix because Arizona refuses to honor Martin Luther King, Jr., Day.

**December 10, 1990:** A report by the Joint Center for Political and Economic Studies states that nearly half of black children live in poverty.

**February 1991:** The Detroit Board of Education approves a plan for an all-male academy to combat the high male dropout rate and lack of strong black male role models in high schools.

**March 20, 1991:** Education Secretary Lamar Alexander lifts the ban on federally funded minority scholarships (established three months earlier).

**April 15, 1991:** A national poll reveals that only 15 percent of white men and 16 percent of white women feel the government is obligated to help improve the living standards of African-Americans.

**July 1, 1991:** President George H. Bush nominates U.S. Court of Appeals Judge Clarence Thomas for the Supreme Court. The NAACP will oppose the nomination because of Thomas's conservative leanings. ➤

Black politicians continued to advance in the 1990s, but on different terms than their counterparts of decades past. For example, Lawrence Douglas Wilder of Virginia became the nation's first elected black governor in 1990, but he ran and governed as a centrist healer. As governor, he tightened the belt on state spending and was accused of pandering to whites when he decided in favor of capital punishment. Although Civil Rights Movement veterans continued to win elected office, the need to change with more conservative times meant that moderation, not confrontation, would better win the day.

Nelson Mandela's release from a South African prison in February 1990 was the first major event of the decade. Mandela had served nearly 28 years in prison for opposing apartheid—the oppressive, violent system of segregation created by South Africa's white minority government. He became an international symbol of the struggle for black liberation and universal human rights. His freedom was a day of celebration for most African-Americans, many of whom had marched during the 1980s, demanding that the U.S. government place economic sanctions on the South Africa regime. Mandela's release, and subsequent international fundraising tour, was the first time many African-American youngsters had the opportunity to see and hear a living, breathing internationally respected black leader.

Clarence Thomas took the oath of office as an associate justice of the U.S. Supreme Court on October 23, 1991. Sexual misconduct allegations brought earlier in the year by a former coworker, Anita Hill, led to a halfhearted Senate confirmation (the vote was 52–48), and nearly obscured the fierce conservatism that has informed Thomas's career. An appointee of President George H. Bush, Thomas has been willing to roll back affirmative action guidelines and allow harsh treatment of prison inmates. He has taken conservative stances on the death penalty, abortion, gun control, and school prayer. Although a significant proportion of African-Americans share some of Thomas's conservative views, Thomas is, and will likely remain, a paradox.

## A Letter to Justice Thomas

DURING THE TIME when civil rights organizations were challenging the Reagan Administration, I was frankly dismayed by some of your responses to and denigrations of these organizations.... You ... criticized traditional civil rights leaders because, instead of trying to reshape the Administration's policies, they had gone to the news media to "bitch, bitch, bitch, moan and moan, whine and whine.".... I suggest, Justice Thomas, that you should ask yourself every day what would have happened to you if there had never been a Charles Hamilton Houston, a William Henry Hastie, a Thurgood Marshall, and that small cadre of other lawyers associated with them, who laid the groundwork for success in the twentieth-century racial civil rights cases? Couldn't they have been similarly charged with, as you phrased it, bitching and moaning and whining when they challenged the racism in the administrations of prior presidents, governors, and public officials? If there had never been an effective NAACP, isn't it highly probable that you might still be in Pin Point, Georgia, working as a laborer as some of your relatives did for decades?

*—A. Leon Higginbotham, Jr.,* An Open Letter to Justice Clarence Thomas from a Federal Judicial Colleague

*Boyz N the Hood,* released in 1991, epitomized a new genre of African-American filmmaking. During the 1990s, filmmakers such as *Boyz* writer and director John Singleton, Matty Rich, and brothers Allen and Albert Hughes told stories of gritty, violent street life in Los Angeles and other urban areas. Some of the films were more sophisticated than others, but all showed the contradictions of post-Civil Rights Movement life in urban black America. Audiences saw how the criminal justice system, street crime, and lack of economic and educational opportunities contributed to social problems among young blacks, particularly black males.

Oprah Winfrey, the most popular woman in television, was one of the most powerful opinion leaders in the United States from the late 1980s through the early 2000s. Her television talk show lured 20 million viewers every day for years. Winfrey, the first black woman to have such a nationally televised forum, has evolved her program into a forum for self-improvement. Her Oprah's Book Club selections in the late 1990s generated millions in sales, virtually guaranteeing their placement on the nation's bestseller lists.

# 1990 TO TODAY

## 1991–1993

**September 1991:** The National Civil Rights Museum opens in Memphis. The museum is a conversion of the Lorraine Motel, where Martin Luther King was assassinated.

**November 21, 1991:** President George H. Bush signs the Civil Rights Act of 1991, which strengthens the previous civil rights law and increases the monetary awards available to people who have been intentionally discriminated against.

**April 29–May 1, 1992:** Four Los Angeles police officers are acquitted of assault against African-American motorist Rodney King, who they pummeled with clubs, kicks, and shots from a stun-gun on March 3, 1991. The ruling incites L.A.'s black community, which had seen a videotape of the beating. Rioting ensues, resulting in more than 50 deaths and 17,000 arrests. *See* August 4, 1993.

**June 26, 1992:** In *United States v. Fordice,* the U.S. Supreme Court rules that the state of Mississippi still needs to address segregation issues at its public colleges and universities.

**November 3, 1992:** Arkansas Governor Bill Clinton, a Democrat, defeats incumbent George H. Bush in the presidential election.

**November 3, 1992:** Carol Moseley-Braun (D–IL) becomes the first black woman to be elected to the U.S. Senate.

**November 15, 1992:** The Birmingham Civil Rights Institute, a museum with interactive exhibits, opens.

**November 18, 1992:** *Malcolm X,* an epic film directed and produced by Spike Lee, opens nationwide.

**January 4, 1993:** Three white men douse an African-American with gasoline and set him on fire in Valrico, Florida. ➤

This "Black Power" salute in Los Angeles reflected a time in which riots were believed by some militant activists (such as H. Rap Brown) to be "dress rehearsals" for the overthrow of a racist, capitalist America. But in the early 1990s, the Black Power movement was a memory, while the bad conditions—poverty, police brutality, lack of adequate health care, subpar schools—still remained for blacks in urban areas. Staging a riot was a way for the black disenfranchised to remind the world, including some of the now-affluent blacks who shouted "Black Power" decades before, that they were still here.

A child in Beaumont, Texas, walks past the crime scene where African-American Bill Simpson and another black person had been fatally gunned down on September 2, 1993. Earlier in the year, Simpson, 36, and African-American John DecQuir moved to Vidor, Texas, after a federal court ordered the town desegregated. For six months, Simpson endured unrelenting taunts, obscene gestures, and threats of lynching. Fed up, he left the town—only to be murdered 11 hours later.

414

# Los Angeles Riot

TO THE REST OF THE WORLD in 1991, Los Angeles portrayed an image of fun and cheer—year-round beaches, swaying palm trees, and Hollywood glitz. In reality, much of Los Angeles consisted of economically depressed black ghettoes and Hispanic *barrios*, where drug use ran rampant and drive-by shootings were commonplace.

Moreover, many minorities despised the predominately white police force, and the feeling from at least some of the officers was mutual. A public commission reviewing the Los Angeles Police Department reported that hundreds of racist, homophobic, and sexist remarks were made by police officers on the department's car-communication system. "I would love to drive down Slauson [a street in a black neighborhood] with a flamethrower...," one officer said. "We could have a barbecue."

On March 3, 1991, white police officers pulled over Rodney King, a black man with a criminal record, for speeding. A group of officers repeatedly hit, clubbed, and kicked King more than 50 times and shot him with a stun gun. It was all videotaped by a local resident, and when it aired on television the black community was outraged. For more than a year, they waited for justice.

On February 3, 1992, a trial began for the four white policemen who had beaten King. Even though the trial was held in mostly white Simi Valley in Ventura County, experts predicted a guilty verdict. However, when a jury of 11 whites and one Asian returned a verdict of "not guilty" on all counts, South Central Los Angeles exploded into violent chaos.

From April 29 through May 1, 1992, at least 50 people were killed, more than 2,000 injured, and about 17,000 arrested in the worst American riot in generations. Enraged African-Americans burned not only hundreds of white businesses but many Korean and black stores, too. Interviewed by reporters, a shaken Rodney King asked, "Can't we all just get along?"

In the aftermath, L.A. Police Chief Daryl Gates resigned and two of the officers who beat King were convicted in a subsequent trial. City officials, who promised a reconstruction effort after the riots, came through. Since 1992, businesses have invested more than $1.4 billion in south Los Angeles. Reverend Cecil Murray, pastor of a South Central church, said in 2002 that the emotional wounds had not healed, but "you can note progress here on this hill."

Reverend Al Sharpton was one of America's most visible and controversial civil rights leaders during the modern era. He was a child preacher, an event promoter with Don King, and an aide to musical artist James Brown, whose hairstyle Sharpton adopted in tribute. He came to national prominence in the 1980s defending people of color in several high-profile New York City police brutality cases. One of those cases, in which teenager Tawana Brawley claimed she was raped by a group of white men in upstate New York, was later found to be a hoax. In recent years Sharpton has established political credentials by running for the U.S. Senate, and for President. He has established his own national organization, the National Action Network, and uses some of the same tactics as his mentor, Reverend Jesse Jackson.

## 1993–1995

**June 28, 1993:** In *Shaw v. Reno,* the U.S. Supreme Court rules that districts drawn in "bizarre" shapes for no other plausible reason except to exclude or contain certain racial groups are unconstitutional.

**August 4, 1993:** Laurence Powell and Stacey Koon, white Los Angeles police officers charged with beating motorist Rodney King, are each sentenced to two years in prison.

**February 5, 1994:** Byron de la Beckwith is convicted for the 1963 murder of Mississippi NAACP field secretary Medgar Evers.

**February 28, 1994:** The American Council on Education reports that 30 percent of black male high school graduates in 1992 moved on to college that year.

**April 1994:** Apartheid ends in South Africa, as free elections are held and the constitution is rewritten. Nelson Mandela is elected president.

**May 23, 1994:** The State of Florida agrees to pay $2.1 million in reparations to black survivors and descendants of Rosewood, a town razed by a mob of white citizens in 1923.

**May 24, 1994:** Flagstar Co., the parent company of Denny's restaurants, agrees to pay more than $54 million to settle discrimination lawsuits filed by black customers.

**May 14, 1995:** Myrlie Evers–Williams, widow of slain civil rights leader Medgar Evers, becomes chairwoman of the NAACP.

**June 12, 1995:** The U.S. Supreme Court rules that preferential treatment based on race is almost always unconstitutional—a blow against advocates of affirmative action.

**October 16, 1995:** Hundreds of thousands of black men gather in Washington, D.C., in a Million Man March organized by Nation of Islam leader Louis Farrakhan. ➤

The Civil Rights Movement of the 1950s and 1960s had become old enough to be publicly honored in the 1990s. In Alabama, the Birmingham Civil Rights Institute, a multimedia museum, was created in 1992. Its exhibit items include "white" and "colored" drinking fountains, the pews from the Sixteenth Street Baptist Church (where four black girls were killed by a bomb in 1963), and this statue of two children in jail. It was one of many institutions built in the South to preserve Movement history.

For all its controversy, the Million Man March in October 1995 was historic in many ways. It was the largest demonstration in Washington's history. It attracted all types of black men—working class, professionals, students, even gang members. Its spiritual focus drew criticism from many in the black activist community, who thought it was a waste of time to gather so many men who would personally "atone" in front of a government that owed black people so much. But it was the event's spiritual focus that unified hundreds of thousands to take a public pledge to do as much as they could in their communities—and to return home without one violent incident.

# Million Man March

"SAY IT LOUD, I'm black and I'm proud," singer James Brown declared in the 1960s. Those words could have described the sentiment of every man present at the Washington Mall on October 16, 1995. An estimated 900,000 people, predominantly black men, converged on the nation's capital for the Million Man March, which Nation of Islam leader Louis Farrakhan, the event's organizer, called "a day of atonement."

Black men from 34 states gathered to show their commitment to their families and the black community, and to counteract the negative image of black men portrayed in the media. Farrakhan, Jesse Jackson, Rosa Parks, and Maya Angelou all spoke to the masses. The demonstration brimmed with positive energy. Attendee Ayene Baptiste asserted that black youths would no longer seek drugs as an escape because there would be outlets for them to develop themselves.

Many people opposed various aspects of the march. Jews pointed to Farrakhan's history of antisemitic rhetoric. Others claimed that blacks shouldn't bear the full responsibility for the troubles that plagued African-American society; that the "system" was largely to blame. Also, black women wondered why they were excluded from the march. "I encourage black men to stand up and take care of their families," said NAACP Chairwoman Myrlie Evers–

Participants in the Million Man March in Washington

Williams. "But in all honesty, to eliminate women completely from this march does bother me a great deal."

The march clearly had an uplifting, if unmeasurable, effect on the black men in attendance. It also bolstered the Nation of Islam's influence within the black community, and inspired additional grassroots activism among African-Americans. In 1997, 1.5 million black women participated in the Million Woman March in Philadelphia.

This Cabrini Green building in Chicago fell to a wrecking ball in November 1995. The 1990s saw the beginning of the end of high-rise public housing buildings, which had proved to be failures. The concentration of the working poor in economically segregated areas had resulted in public housing projects that devolved into havens for crime, prostitution, gang-related violence, and drug dealing. In the 1990s, cities began to create new, low-rise housing for their residents. However, the destruction of the projects left many working-class people scrambling for decent places to live in areas that had begun to attract upper middle-class professionals.

# The Criminal Justice System

WHEN PEOPLE FILLED Flatbush Avenue in front of Brooklyn's Club Rendez-Vous at about 4:00 A.M. on August 9, 1997, police officers from the 70th Precinct arrived to disperse the crowd. A white officer named Justin Volpe was struck in the head by an assailant Volpe did not see. The officer chased down another man, a young, black Haitian immigrant named Abner Louima, and arrested him.

In the patrol car on the way to the precinct house, Volpe and another white officer beat and kicked Louima, whose hands had been cuffed behind his back. At the station, officers marched the still-cuffed Louima to a men's room, where Volpe shoved the wooden handle of a bathroom plunger deep into Louima's rectum, puncturing the victim's bladder and severely damaging his colon. Volpe then forced the handle through Louima's teeth and into his mouth. Besides the physical pain and degradation, Louima was subjected to a nonstop litany of racial epithets and curses.

A subsequent police coverup, which encompassed an officer's perjured testimony, stonewalled the official investigation of the brutality. Later, at trial, defense attorneys claimed that Louima's terrible injuries had come while he engaged in homosexual intercourse. Ultimately, Officer Volpe pled guilty and was sentenced to 30 years in prison.

By the 1990s police forces had become more integrated, but the level of mistrust and dissatisfaction with police among black citizens remained much higher than among whites. This dissatisfaction related not only to actions on the part of the police but also to inactions. For example, calls for help from African-Americans, who are far more likely to be victims of crime than whites, were more likely to go unheeded or be answered after lengthy delays than calls for help from whites.

State law enforcement officers are also distrusted by a high percentage of African-Americans, largely because of the practice of racial profiling: stopping and searching people and/or their vehicles based on a statistical profile of the detainee's race or ethnicity. Racial profiling inten-

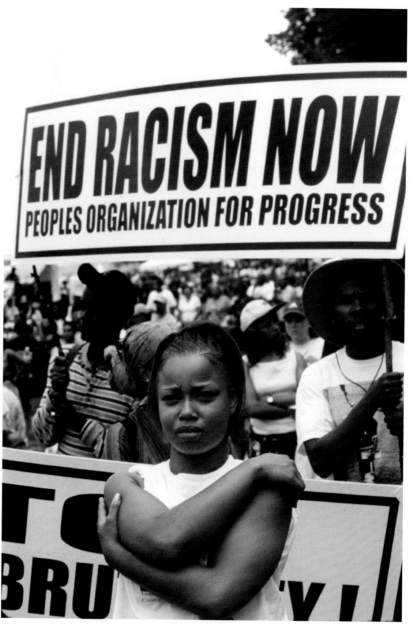

Activists rally against police racism in Washington, D.C., in August 2000.

sified in the 1990s, some observers suggest, as a result of the War on Drugs that had begun in the 1980s.

Racial profiling has made headlines in New Jersey. In 1999 Governor Christine Todd Whitman fired State Police Superintendent Carl A. Williams after he had justified racial profiling and linked minority groups to drug trafficking. In Illinois, racial profiling was the subject of a federal lawsuit brought by the American Civil Liberties Union on behalf of three black high school students. The youths had been subjected to unlawful detention and a racial slur after a routine traffic stop by a state trooper in Peoria in November 2000. In 2002 Eleanor Holmes Norton, the District of Columbia's nonvoting member of Congress, introduced the Racial Profiling Prohibition Act. The act would withhold federal highway dollars from states that have not explicitly banned racial profiling.

Historically, the criminal justice system has not worked for African-Americans on any level, from police to courts to prisons. In the 1990s, blacks comprised about 12 percent of the national population and almost half of the prison population. Black men went to prison at six times the rate of white men. A 1990 report by the Sentencing Project stated that one out of every four young black males was in prison or jail, on probation, or on parole.

A computer analysis of nearly 700,000 criminal cases in California from 1981 to 1990 revealed that whites were more successful at avoiding punishment than minorities. Whites were more likely to get cases dismissed and charges dropped, to avoid harsher punishment, and to have their criminal records wiped clean.

The logical outcome of such racial disparities is the inequitable application of the death penalty. After the U.S. Supreme Court upheld capital punishment as a legitimate punishment for certain crimes in 1976, the number of executions nationwide rose, peaking in 1999, a year in which 98 people were executed in 20 states. By that year, the American Civil Liberties Union, which had established a separate Capital Punishment Project in 1976, and many other individuals and organizations had made significant inroads in their campaign against the death penalty.

Startling facts about the death penalty have reduced the popularity of capital punishment. For instance, about 90 percent of those executed had been unable to afford a lawyer and had been represented by court-appointed

Los Angeles Police Chief Daryl Gates took heat in the early 1990s for running a racist police department.

attorneys. Also, more than 40 percent of those on death row have been African-American. While some 80 percent of Americans approved of the death penalty in the 1980s, only about 70 percent did by 2000. Moreover, between 40 and 50 percent agreed that the death penalty was not administered fairly.

In 1999, after DNA tests revealed that 13 men on death row in Illinois had been wrongly convicted since the state resumed capital punishment in 1977, Illinois Governor George Ryan halted executions in the state. In January 2003, as he prepared to leave office, Ryan commuted the sentences of 167 death row inmates to life in prison—emptying death row in one sweep—rather than see them put to death by a system that was, in his words, "fraught with error."

Whether riddled with error, racism, or a combination of both, the American criminal justice system remains for African-Americans one of the last bastions of systemic inequality.

## 1995–1997

**1995–97:** Several dozen black churches throughout the South are set ablaze.

**June 13, 1996:** In two landmark cases, *Bush v. Vera* and *Shaw v. Hunt,* the U.S. Supreme Court rules that using race as a factor in the creation of congressional districts is unconstitutional. The decision dissolves two majority black and Hispanic districts—one in Texas and the other in North Carolina.

**August 22, 1996:** President Clinton signs a major welfare reform bill, as welfare funds will now be given to the states. Most states will put certain recipients on five-year timetables and require them to work to receive their benefits.

**December 18, 1996:** A heated national debate begins when the Oakland, California, school district announces a controversial plan to use "ebonics" ("black English") in Oakland's classrooms.

**May 16, 1997:** President Clinton formally apologizes for the infamous Tuskegee syphilis experiments, in which treatment was withheld from nearly 400 black, male syphilis victims from 1932 to 1972 in order to conduct research on the devastating long-term effects of the disease. Public Health Service doctors knew the men had syphilis but never told them.

**June 12, 1997:** President Clinton forms the President's Commission on Race Relations.

**October 25, 1997:** Approximately 1.5 million African-American women demonstrate their solidarity in the Million Woman March in Philadelphia.

**November 1, 1997:** Martin Luther King III is elected to succeed Reverend Joseph Lowery as president of the SCLC. ➤

A New Beginning
*Welfare to Work*

President Bill Clinton's signing of two congressional bills in 1996 that reformed welfare ended an era that had started during the New Deal of the 1930s. Welfare had been a series of federal programs that allowed unemployed poor people with children a monthly minimum of financial aid and services for an indefinite period of time. Under welfare reform, the funds went to the states, which set up their own programs with specific criteria. Most states gave welfare recipients a five-year timetable and required that recipients work in order to receive their benefits. Although the welfare rolls dropped lower than before the reform, advocates for the poor argued that the new system robbed poor people of the chance to gain the skills they needed to permanently join the professional workforce.

Urban public schools, such as this one in Chicago, remained danger zones in the 1990s. Violence and drug-dealing were constant threats to schoolchildren. Inside, students read out-of-date textbooks in crowded classrooms. The tax revenues in urban areas weren't high enough to fund the schools properly.

Affluent blacks moved to the suburbs or put their children in parochial or private schools. The National Urban League and other organizations attempted after-school programs and other services, but troubles still continued. In some major cities, minority males were more likely to drop out of high school than graduate.

Kwanzaa, an African-American holiday begun in 1966, surged in popularity in the 1990s. Dr. Maulana Karenga, former leader of United Slaves (a Los Angeles-based cultural nationalist group during the Black Power movement), created Kwanzaa as a way for African-American families to spiritually and culturally reclaim the best traditions of African culture without commercialization. The seven-day holiday observes a set of principles called the *Nguzo Saba*. These principles include unity, self-determination, collective work and responsibility, cooperative economics, purpose, creativity, and faith. A principle is assigned to each day, from December 26 to January 1.

From 1995 to 1997, black churches throughout the South and border states were set afire. Here, Sunder Henry, a trustee for St. John's United Methodist Church in Berlin, Maryland, shows the destruction of the sanctuary on June 19, 1996. Investigations by the media, the National Council of Churches, and others indicated that the fires were racially motivated. "We do not now have evidence of a national conspiracy," said President Bill Clinton on June 8, 1996, "but it is clear that racial hostility is the driving force behind a number of these incidents." At the time of Clinton's statement, an estimated 30 churches had been burned.

The Million Woman March brought 1.5 million African-American women to the streets of a rainy Philadelphia on October 25, 1997. For publicity, the march organizers had relied on community-based networks, not mainstream black institutions. The Million Woman March focused on issues such as healthcare, education, homelessness, and human rights. Despite its numerical success, the march did not translate into an ongoing, organized mass political movement of black women.

The Million Man March of 1995 spawned imitators. During September 1998, a pair of "Million" gatherings were sponsored for black youth. In New York, the nationalist-oriented Million Youth March attracted only a few thousand, with some clashing with New York City police officers. In Atlanta on the same day, the NAACP and other groups held a national youth rally called the Million Youth March, which attracted about 4,000 people. Both were calls for black youngsters to regain the reform spirit of young 1960s activists.

## 1998–2001

**April 23, 1998:** James Earl Ray, convicted of assassinating Martin Luther King, Jr., dies in prison.

**June 7, 1998:** In Jasper, Texas, African-American James Byrd, Jr., is beaten by three white men, chained to a pickup truck, and dragged three miles until decapitated.

**July 24, 1998:** The Christian Knights of the Ku Klux Klan is ordered to pay $37.8 million to the Macedonia Baptist Church in Bloomville, South Carolina. The church had been burned by Klan members in 1995.

**December 2, 1999:** The National Capital Planning Commission approves the location for a monument to Martin Luther King, Jr., on the National Mall in Washington, D.C.

**February 2000:** The Oklahoma state legislature receives a recommendation from the Tulsa Race Riot Commission that reparations be paid to the survivors of the Tulsa Race Riots of 1921.

**July 1, 2000:** Months after a January rally of nearly 50,000 protesters, the Confederate flag is lowered from the South Carolina state capitol dome.

**December 2000:** President-Elect George W. Bush names General Colin Powell as his secretary of state and Stanford Provost Condoleezza Rice as his national security adviser.

**January 20, 2001:** George W. Bush is inaugurated as U.S. president following a contentious election in which Florida's archaic voting infrastructure raised concerns of disenfranchisement of black voters.

**April 2001:** The police shooting of an unarmed black man in Cincinnati ignites several days of rioting.

**May 1, 2001:** Thomas Blanton, Jr., is sentenced to life in prison for his involvement in the 1963 bombing of the Sixteenth Street Baptist Church in Birmingham that killed four girls. ➤

Jesse Jackson leads a march in Palm Beach County, Florida, on December 13, 2000, protesting the state's handling of the recent presidential election. Republican George W. Bush would eventually be named by the U.S. Supreme Court the winner over Democrat Al Gore after a weeks-long recount of ballots in Florida. Civil rights leaders claimed that officials in Florida, governed by Bush's brother Jeb, intentionally tried to squelch the votes of African-Americans, most of whom were Gore supporters. Jackson and Florida Black Caucus members filed a civil rights lawsuit claiming that 16,000 votes were not counted in black inner-city neighborhoods in Duval County. Meanwhile, the NAACP compiled 300 pages of testimony that included accusations of voter intimidation in Florida and polling sites in black neighborhoods being closed without notice.

Violence became a daily part of life in many of the public housing projects in American cities. Here, Donna Wilson, a resident of the Robert Taylor Homes in Chicago, plugs up a bullet hole with a rag in December 2000. Journalist Sylvester Monroe wrote about the Chicago projects in the book *Brothers*. He called them "a city of lost hope—of dudes . . . with no money, no home, and no prospects hustling the few dollars left on the street; of barely adolescent girls with babies, living starved lives on welfare and the impermanent affections of their men; of little kids growing up vicious."

Urban areas became popular places to live in again during the 1980s and '90s. Tired of the suburban commute, a new generation of working professionals, including some affluent black Americans, moved into new or rehabbed condominiums near downtown. Yuppie restaurants, stores, and shops arose nearby. This gentrification process turned rundown neighborhoods into trendy hot spots—but not without negative ramifications. After landlords sold their old buildings to developers, or jacked up rents to the new market value, longstanding residents needed to scramble for new homes. Such was the case on March 1, 2001, when the resident of this Harlem building held a street auction to raise some needed cash.

Gangsta rap, a subgenre of hip-hop music that documented and mythologized urban life, was flying off the music shelves in the 1990s. Label heads such as Suge Knight (*pictured*) of Death Row Records provided a platform for many hip-hop artists to spin tales about street life and its components—drug dealing, prostitution, police brutality, and drive-by shootings. Critics such as C. Delores Tucker of the National Political Congress of Black Women waged war on gangsta rap. Tucker stated that the lyrics glorified violence and degraded women. Defenders claimed the music was the legitimate expression of the conditions of young working-class urban blacks that the Civil Rights Movement left behind. Ironically, hip-hop music had tremendous crossover appeal, as most records were sold to young suburban whites.

Racial insurrections moved into the 21st century when Cincinnati erupted over the fatal shooting of Timothy Thomas, an unarmed black teenager, by a white police officer. The shooting took place in April 2001 in the city's predominately black neighborhood. Police chased Thomas, 19, because he was wanted on traffic offenses and other misdemeanors. Thomas became the 15th black man to be fatally shot by Cincinnati police since 1995. His case became another symbol of excessive police force, which was rarely seen when white men were crime suspects.

In the 1990s and 2000s, African-Americans were just one racial/ethnic group vying for political power. The nation's Hispanic population, for example, increased 58 percent during the 1990s. In Los Angeles, where Antonio Villaraigosa (*above*) ran for mayor in 2001, Latinos totaled 46.5 percent of the population while black citizens comprised only 11.2 percent. Latinos and Asians were amassing political clout through grassroots organizing. This caused concern among many African-Americans, who felt that the added competition would cost them much of their own political power.

## 2001–2003

**June 6, 2001:** Congress introduces the End Racial Profiling Act of 2001.

**July 2001:** Hispanics replace African-Americans as the nation's largest minority group, according to the U.S. Census Bureau.

**March 24, 2002:** African-Americans take top honors at the Oscars. Halle Berry wins Best Actress for her role in *Monster's Ball,* Denzel Washington wins Best Actor for *Training Day,* and Sidney Poitier accepts a lifetime achievement award.

**March 26, 2002:** A federal lawsuit is filed that may seek billions of dollars in reparations for the descendants of slaves in America from corporations that historically benefited from the trade. The lawsuit names Fleet–Boston Financial and the Aetna insurance company, among others.

**May 22, 2002:** Bobby Frank Cherry is found guilty of first-degree murder for his involvement in the 1963 bombing of the Sixteenth Street Baptist Church in Birmingham.

**December 20, 2002:** Senator Trent Lott (R–TN) resigns as Senate majority leader after enduring widespread criticism of his remarks at Senator Strom Thurmond's 100th birthday party. Lott had said America would have been better off if Thurmond, who ran for president on a segregation-based platform in 1948, had won the election.

**January 23, 2003:** ABC news reports that eight in 10 whites think African-Americans in their communities have equal opportunities, while fewer than half of blacks agree.

**June 23, 2003:** In two split decisions related to affirmative action, the U.S. Supreme Court strikes down a University of Michigan point system that favors minority applicants for undergraduate admission, but upholds the same university's less-structured program that encourages minority law school applicants.

Antoinette Harrell of New Orleans demonstrates in front of the U.S. Capitol on August 17, 2002, demanding reparations for slavery. The issue had gained momentum in the 1990s when survivors of the Japanese internment camps and the Holocaust successfully sued, respectively, the United States government and European corporate collaborators with the Nazi regime. Black attorneys have attempted to sue American companies who insured slaves. Those who opposed reparations for African-Americans argued that the idea was not practical because there are no living victims of the centuries-old slave trade.

Early in 2003, Michigan Senator Carl Levin (*pictured*) and former University of Michigan President Lee Bollinger defended the school's affirmative action policies. A "point system" that awarded 20 points to minority applicants for undergraduate study helped ensure diversity of the student population, though white applicants with higher test scores were sometimes turned away. Another, less-structured program encouraged minority applicants to Michigan's law school. White litigants, supported by President George W. Bush, challenged these admissions practices. Bush supported California's system, which considered income but not race. On June 23, 2003, the U.S. Supreme Court struck down Michigan's undergraduate system, but upheld the law school program.

In the new millennium, states continued to look at lotteries as a way to fund their education budgets. The states, viewing sanctioned gaming as a legal and legitimate way to raise funds, characterize lotteries as painless, exciting ways to pay for state programs. Antigambling organizations and advocates for the poor claim that states have created gambling addicts out of poor and working-class people, many of whom are blacks and other people of color.

**"Violence is black children going to school for 12 years and receiving six years' worth of education."**

—CIVIL RIGHTS ACTIVIST JULIAN BOND

Lisa Stanley of Decatur, Illinois, expresses deep concern for the future of her son. In Stanley's city in the early 2000s, more than half of minority males weren't graduating from high school. Discussion of the "endangered black male" dominated newspaper and magazine articles in the 1990s and 2000s. Statistics showed that more black men between the ages of 20 and 40 were in jail than in college. The top killer of young black males in the 1990s was death by gun violence, usually perpetrated by other young black men. Males of color became half of the nation's prison inmate population, a rate that rose after the federal government passed laws requiring mandatory sentencing for certain drug-related crimes.

# Late Justice

IN 1963 TWO TRAGIC EVENTS—the slaying of Medgar Evers and the bombing of the Sixteenth Street Baptist Church that killed four girls—brought Americans to tears. Yet because of the climate of the times, with white Southerners unwilling to prosecute whites for crimes against blacks, the killers escaped justice... or so it seemed.

In 1965 Birmingham FBI agents recommended that at least four suspects be charged with the Sixteenth Street Baptist Church bombing in Birmingham. However, FBI Director J. Edgar Hoover blocked the prosecution, claiming they had a "remote" chance of winning a conviction. In 1971 Alabama Attorney General Bill Baxley, a white progressive, reopened the case. Despite receiving hate mail, Baxley pursued suspects for six years before nailing down a conviction against Robert "Dynamite Bob" Chambliss. Twelve jurors—male and female, three black and nine white—sent Chambliss away for life. In 2002, Bobby Frank Cherry was also sentenced to life imprisonment for his role in the bombing.

In 1964 Byron de la Beckwith, who had shot Evers in the back in Jackson, Mississippi, walked free after two all-white juries remained deadlocked. In 1989 Evers's widow, Myrlie Evers–Williams, asked the Hinds County assistant district attorney to reopen the case. Armed with new evidence and testimony against Beckwith, the prosecutors presented the case to a 12-person jury, eight of whom were black. Beckwith, whom even his attorney said was "consumed by racial hatred," was sentenced to life in prison.

In the more sympathetic modern climate, Chambliss and Beckwith made for compelling villains. Films about each event, the Spike Lee documentary *4 Little Girls* (1997) and Rob Reiner's *Ghosts of Mississippi* (1996), mesmerized both black and white audiences.

Convicted murderer Byron de la Beckwith (*center*)

# Index

# Acknowledgments

**Special thanks** to Myrlie Evers-Williams and the Medgar Evers Institute for granting permission for her image to appear on the cover of this book.

**We also wish to thank the following individuals and collections who have so graciously shared their civil rights images for this volume:** Ward Churchill, Jonathan Eubanks, Georgia Division of Archives and History/Office of Secretary of State, Howard Greenberg Gallery, Bruce Hartford in association with the Veterans of the Civil Rights Movement website/www.crmvet.org, Matt Herron/Take Stock Photos, Highlander Research and Education Center, James and Esther Jackson, Jim Crow Museum of Racist Memorabilia/Ferris State University, Library of Congress, The Estate of Bill Mauldin, Nebraska State Historical Society Photograph Collection, Herbert Randall, Ernest Ritchie, Schomburg Center for Research in Black Culture Photographs and Prints Division/The New York Public Library, Flip Schulke, The Tennessean, University of Alabama Press, University of North Carolina at Chapel Hill Libraries/Documenting the American South, University of Southern Mississippi/McCain Library and Archives, University of Tulsa/McFarlin Library Special Collections, Wayne State University/Walter P. Reuther Library.

**Publications International, Ltd., and Legacy Publishing** have made every effort to locate the owners of all copyrighted material to obtain permission to use the selections that appear in this book. Any errors or omissions are unintentional; corrections, if necessary, will be made in future editions.

All included material by Dr. Martin Luther King, Jr., and Mrs. Coretta Scott King, copyright © The Estate of Dr. Martin Luther King, Jr. All copyrights renewed, The Estate of Dr. Martin Luther King, Jr. Reprinted by permission of Writers House, LLC, New York City.

Page 53: Passage from *Proud Shoes: The Story of an American Family*, by Pauli Murray, © 1956, 1999, Beacon Press, Boston.

Page 62: Quote by Leroy Boyd from *Remembering Jim Crow: African Americans Tell About Life in the Segregated South*, William H. Chafe, Raymond Gavins and Robert Korstad (eds.), © 2001 The New Press. Reprinted by permission of The New Press.

Page 72: Quote by Charles Hamilton Houston from *Groundwork: Charles Hamilton Houston and the Struggle for Civil Rights*, by Genna Rae McNeil, © 1983 University of Pennsylvania Press. Reprinted by permission of University of Pennsylvania Press.

Page 79: Lyrics for "Strange Fruit," words and music by Lewis Allen, © 1939 (renewed) by Music Sales Corporation (ASCAP). Reprinted by permission of Music Sales Corporation and the Edward B. Marks Music Company/Carlin America, Inc. International copyright secured. All rights reserved.

Page 92: Passage by Sergeant Lester Duance Simons from *The Invisible Soldier: The Experience of the Black Soldier, World War II*, by Mary Penick Motley (ed.), © 1975 Wayne State University Press.

Page 94: ©1946 Bill Mauldin; page 191: © 1960 Bill Mauldin; page 230: ©1963 Bill Mauldin. Reprinted by permission of the Estate of Bill Mauldin.

Page 95: Southern Negro Youth Congress fliers. Courtesy of James and Esther Jackson.

Page 102: Passage from the January 4, 1941, article "Democracy and the Negro People Today," by Metz T. P. Lochard, in *The Nation*. Reprinted by permission of *The Nation*.

Pages 106, 167: Passages from the May 18, 1954, *Jackson Daily News* editorial "Bloodstains on White Marble Steps." Reprinted by permission of *The Clarion Ledger*.

Page 111: Verse from "Montage of a Dream Deferred," by Langston Hughes, from *The Collected Poems of Langston Hughes* by Langston Hughes, © 1994 the Estate of Langston Hughes. Reprinted by permission of Alfred A. Knopf, a division of Random House, Inc.

Pages 124, 239, 269: Passages by Bayard Rustin, Myrlie Evers-Williams, and Unita Blackwell from *Voices of Freedom: An Oral History of the Civil Rights Movement from the 1950s through the 1980s*, by Henry Hampton (ed.), © 1990 Bantam Doubleday Dell. Reprinted by permission of Bantam Books, a division of Random House, Inc.

Page 129: Quote by Mamie Bradley Mobley from a September 17, 1955, *Pittsburgh Courier* article. Reprinted by permission of GRM Associates, in association with the *Pittsburgh Courier*.

Page 139: Passage from *Rosa Parks, My Story*, by Rosa Parks with Jim Haskins, © 1992 by Rosa Parks. Reprinted by permission of Dial Books for Young Readers, a division of Penguin Young Readers Group, a member of Penguin Group (USA) Inc., 345 Hudson Street, New York, NY 10014. All rights reserved.

Page 156: Quotes from a September 23, 1957, Associated Press article by Relman Morin, describing the scene outside Central High School in Little Rock. Reprinted by permission of the Associated Press.

Page 156: Passage by Elizabeth Eckford from *The Long Shadow of Little Rock*, by Daisy Bates, © 1986 by Daisy Bates. Reprinted by permission of the University of Arkansas Press.

Page 159: Quotes by Ernest Green, recalling his experiences as one of the nine African-American students to desegregate Central High School in Little Rock. Reprinted by permission of Ernest G. Green.

Page 173: Passage from a 1964 Los Angeles *Herald–Dispatch* column written by Malcolm X. Reprinted by permission of Herald-Dispatch Publications, Inc.

Page 182: Quote by Diane Nash, a Civil Rights Movement leader. Reprinted by permission of Diane Nash.

Page 198: Quote by Freedom Rider Henry Thomas in a May 18, 1961, article in *The New York Post*; Page 355: Quote by Olympic medalist Tommie Smith as it appeared in *The New York Post*. Reprinted by permission of *The New York Post*.

Page 199: Passage by Ralph David Fertig recalling his experiences on June 2–3, 1961. Courtesy of Ralph David Fertig.

Page 206: Passage from article "The Mammy Caricature," by Dr. David Pilgrim, © 2000 the Jim Crow Museum of Racist Memorabilia, Ferris State University. Reprinted by permission of Dr. David Pilgrim.

Page 217: Passage from *Three Years in Mississippi*, by James H. Meredith, © 1966 James H. Meredith. Reprinted by permission of James H. Meredith.

Page 219: Passage from "My Dungeon Shook: Letter to My Nephew on the One Hundredth Anniversary of the Emancipation," © 1963 by James Baldwin. Copyright renewed. Collected in *The Fire Next Time*, published by Vintage Books. Reprinted by permission of the James Baldwin Estate.

Page 251: Passage from essay "The Lights Are Much Brighter There," by Dr. Gerald Early, from *Three Essays: Reflections on the American Century*, published by Washington University and Missouri Historical Society Press. Reprinted by permission of Dr. Gerald Early.

Page 277: Passage by Fannie Lou Hamer, cofounder of the Mississippi Freedom Democratic Party, from a June 1, 1964, article in *The Nation*, by Jerry DeMuth. Reprinted by permission of Jerry DeMuth.

Page 288: Passage from the March 8, 1961, article "Alabama Police Use Gas and Clubs to Rout Negroes," by Roy Reed, covering "Bloody Sunday" in Selma, Alabama, in *The New York Times*, © 1965. Reprinted by permission of the New York Times Company.

Page 341: Passage from Reverend James Lawson, former chairman of the Southern Christian Leadership Conference. Courtesy of Ralph David Fertig.

Page 354: FBI Counterintelligence Program (COINTELPRO) document dated October 10, 1968. Courtesy of Ward Churchill, coauthor of *The Cointelpro Papers: Documents from the FBI's Secret Wars Against Dissent in the United States*, by Ward Churchill, Jim Vander Wall, and John Trudell.

Page 377: Preamble to "The Five Demands to the People of America" by inmates of Attica Prison, as it appeared in *A Time to Die*, by Tom Wicker, © 1975 by Tom Wicker, published by Quadrangle/The New York Times Book Company. Reprinted by permission of Tom Wicker.

Page 380: Quote by Yvonne Brathwaite Burke, former congresswoman. Reprinted by permission of the Honorable Yvonne Brathwaite Burke.

Page 389: Passage from *Southie Won't Go, A Teacher's Diary of the Desegregation of a South Boston High School*, by Ione Malloy, © 1986 The University of Illinois Press. Reprinted by permission of Ione Malloy.

Page 394: Quote by Cornel West, philosopher, historian, and activist. Reprinted by permission of Cornel West.

Page 406: Passage by journalist Ken Bode on Jesse Jackson, from *Jesse: The Life and Pilgrimage of Jesse Jackson*, by Marshall Frady, © 1996 Random House, Inc.

Page 408: Quote by James P. Danky. Reprinted by permission of James P. Danky, of the State Historical Society of Wisconsin and the University of Wisconsin-Madison.

# Photo Credits

REV. JAMES REEB · MARCH...
BEATEN TO DEATH · SELMA AL...

STATE TROOPERS BEAT BACK MARC...
EDMUND PETTUS BRIDGE · SELMA...

1965    JIMMIE LEE JACKSON · CIVIL RIGH...
KILLED BY STATE TROOPER · MAR...

LT. COL. LEMUEL PENN · KILLED
WHILE DRIVING NORTH · COLB...

1964

PRESIDENT JOHNSON SIGNS...
ACT OF 1964

1964

JAMES CHANEY · ANDR...
MICHAEL SCHWERN...
WORKERS ABDUCT...
KLAN · PHILADELP...

UN · 1964

FREEDOM S...
CIVIL RIG...

1964